BLUEPRINT for a GREEN SCHOOL

BLUEPRINT
for a
GREEN
SCHOOL

JAYNI CHASE
Founder, Center for Environmental Education

Foreword by
THOMAS E. LOVEJOY
Smithsonian Institution
Center for Teaching
The Westminster Schools

SCHOLASTIC

LEADERSHIP
POLICY
RESEARCH ™

New York • Toronto • London • Auckland • Sydney

This book is dedicated to finding realistic solutions to human-made and naturally occurring threats to the health of all life on Earth and, of course, to my amazingly supportive family.

Library of Congress Cataloging-in-Publication Data

Chase, Jayni
　　　Blueprint for a Green School.
　　　　　　p.　cm.—(Scholastic Leadership Policy Research)
　　　Includes bibliographical references and index.
　　　ISBN 0-590-49830-4
　　　1. Environmental education—Handbooks, manuals, etc.
　　　2. Environmental sciences—Study and Teaching—Handbooks, manuals, etc.
　　　I Title,　II Series.
　　　GE70.C48　1995
　　　363.7'007' 1—dc20　　　　　　　　　　　　　　　　94-36126
　　　　　　　　　　　　　　　　　　　　　　　　　　　　CIP

Art Direction by Vincent Ceci
Design by Drew Hires
Cover and Interior Illustrations by Drew Hires

Center for Environmental Education
Advisory Board

Contents

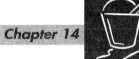

Resources

Foreword

By Thomas E. Lovejoy

No plant, animal, or microbe can exist without affecting its environment. Even green plants, which depend on energy provided by the sun and which in turn make that energy available to herbivorous animals, affect their environment. They depend on it for nutrients, and they release wastes into it. By casting shade, a tree denies the opportunity for sun-dependent plants to live beneath it.

So for us the issue is not whether we affect our environment but in what ways and by how much. This has always been complicated, but it is very much more so given the overwhelming size of the human population today and what our powerful technology, for both good and usually unintended ill, brings to the picture. No longer can we afford to have our children grow up in blissful ignorance about the environment.

Blueprint for a Green School is intended to remedy that. Covering a wide range of environmental topics, it endeavors to provide an initial background summary with information about where one can find more. Inevitably, some will disagree about some of the information in this book. Inevitably, scientific understanding of some of these topics will change. That is the nature of science: constantly self-testing and both upfront and precise about uncertainty.

Some people use this to criticize concern about the environment, saying there wasn't that much to worry about after all. The right attitude is to respect science for its fundamental honesty, to remember that although one problem may be overestimated, another will be underestimated. So in applying the information herein, it is important to understand the scientific process. The truth is that uncertainty abounds; indeed, it is pervasive in our lives, and science is often unfairly pilloried, because it is so candid.

I hope that this blueprint will lead to a generation that automatically questions and makes learning about the environment a lifelong process. That consciousness is what sets us apart among living things. Our consequent responsibility is to use it.

Acknowledgments

Blueprint for a Green School is a collaborative work that has taken 5 years to complete. Besides those who did the research and the writing, many have helped to make my dream of environmental education a reality.

At the top of the list is my husband, Chevy Chase, whose faith in me and my beliefs has kept this project alive. His insights, wisdom and support have contributed immeasurably to this book.

Then there is Natasha Garland, who came into my life at a time when I needed to take action. Natasha's belief in the importance of environmental education was all I needed to move forward. With her support and strong convictions, we became an energetic, unwavering team.

In 1989 Mary Edie and Leslie Crawford began coming to my office and developing materials to use in their own children's schools. They shared my vision and passion for environmental education. Today Mary is the Outreach Director for the Center for Environmental Education. Her contagious enthusiasm has kept all of us at the center focused and stimulated. Her daily contact with students and educators has added important perspectives to this book and to our daily work. Leslie Crawford nurtured this book through its infancy. Her viewpoints and observations contributed substantially to its development.

In the summer of 1990 Bruce Harlan was the first teacher to walk through our doors and dig through our materials. Although his quest for information to design his own curriculum gave me hope for environmental education, it also gave me pause. I couldn't help thinking that there had to be an easier way to obtain similar information for other teachers.

Over the past 5 years, many other teachers have come into our library and carefully reviewed all our environmental education curricula—Pamela Ahearn, Erin Barnhill, Linda Breen, Bob Brigham, Jane Crawford, Amy E. Holm, Ula Pendleton, Meredith Smith, Ann Stalcup, Elizabeth Teicher, Carolyn Tokunaga, Juanita Walker, Erik Warren and Sharon Wetzel— to name a few. I would like to thank them all for their exceptional awareness and for their wholehearted involvement in their students' lives and the world around them.

Lloyd Chilton and Claudia Cohl at Scholastic, Inc., immediately recognized the importance and potential of this book. Vincent Ceci and Drew Hires, our Art Directors, were always a calming influence. Drew managed to take our words and drawings and give them a life of their own.

The dedicated staff members at the Center for Environmental Education, Cory Walsh, Bonnie Slagel, Libby Huff and Amy Goldberg, have not only contributed to this book in many and varied ways, but have also been an incredible support team. Their hard work and shared beliefs in this project have been invaluable.

Researching, discovering and acquiring all the curricula, books, videos, brochures, periodicals, catalogs and reports was only half the battle. At the next step, we enlisted the help of Howard Colburn as our computer consultant. Today, the center's databases are organized, thorough and user-friendly, all thanks to Howard.

Special thanks must also be given to Hecht & Company, most notably Michael Hecht and Steven Stern, for the generous donation of accounting services to the Center for Environmental

Education, and to Gipson, Hoffman & Pancione, Ken Sidle, Ray Gross and Rita Silverman in particular, for the pro bono legal advice. Both of these firms have graciously shared their invaluable expertise at every step in establishing and running the center.

Finally, I would like to thank my parents, Beverly and Frank Luke, and my three daughters for all their love and support. Cydney, Caley and Emily, this book is for you and all children of the world who serve as the beacon for our commitment and dedication.

List of Contributors

The research, energy and talents of many people were brought together to create this thought-provoking, user-friendly resource.

This book represents 5 years of work done with deep passion by many caring individuals. Each chapter had a life of its own. Each chapter experienced birth, childhood, adolescence, a few teenage years and then matured into adulthood (not necessarily in that order). One conversation would change the outline and goals of a paragraph, a section or even an entire chapter.

One of the most difficult things for me to do was to acknowledge that a chapter was finished. It often seemed we could include more information or more stories to better illustrate the possibilities or simplicity of a message. I sifted through some complex concepts and tried to make them understandable and relevant. Sometimes the words fell into place—sometimes they didn't.

It has been a great pleasure to see this vision develop from a simple idea into a complete work, touched by many hands. This could not have happened without the contributions of the following people:

Researchers/Writers Suzanne Armet-Burkhofer, Mari Clemments, Leslie Crawford, Mary Edie, Chris Garbacz, Natasha Garland, Gerald Garner, Woody Hastings, Eric Ingersol, Maurine O'Rourke, Dean Paschall, Becky Riley, Neal Shapiro, Elizabeth Van Ness, Tim Varney

Reviewers Annie Berthold-Bond, Linda Blackstock-Hayes, Amy Cabaniss, Sally Clinton, Bonnie Cornwall, Debra Dadd-Redalia, Lynne Edgerton, Joan Edwards, Sandra Jerabek, Craig Johnson, Terry Kennedy, Hunter Lovins, Karina Lutz, Ann Reed Mangals, Bill McDorman, Dorothy McCormick, Vingina Messina, Deborah Moore, Cynthia Murphy, Maureen O'Rourke, Gary Peterson, Linda Phillips, Gary Prosch, Lisa Rath, Joel Ray, John Robbins, Bill Roley, Monona Rossol, April Smith

Consultants Pearl Chen, Howard Colburn, Brittany Kesselman, Nili Moghaddam, Eva Perkins, Lisa Sisso, Sean Smith, Mandiee Tatum, Brett Wellington

Staff Mary Edie, Amy Golberg, Libby Huff, Bonnie Slagel, Cory Walsh

Preface

Everything in our lives has a natural origin: the air, water and minerals of our planet have provided us with all things, from flowers and vegetables to television sets and airplanes. Although the power of natural resources abounds, the resources themselves do not. We all need to learn how to manage our natural resources. Until recently it was not necessary for schools to have formal methods for teaching children about the complexities and delicacies of nature. Surprisingly, many current textbooks still would have students believe that our resources are unlimited and available for endless exploitation.

Recent scientific findings and global events have made it clear that it has become necessary for our schools to address the health of our air, soil and water. The Center for Environmental Education has responded to these needs by creating a resource that not only contains vital and accurate information, but also presents it in a manner that lends itself to classroom use. *Blueprint for a Green School* is that resource.

Blueprint draws on more than 7,500 sources of information covering 40 environmental topics that we have accumulated over the past 5 years. In addition, we have compiled 3 chapters of curricular applications and additional resources, such as videos; books; state resource lists; student/teacher activities, grants and awards; and environmental organizations. These chapters seek both to educate and to empower Pre-K through Grade 12 administrators, teachers, students, parents and maintenance crews. We encourage careful investigation of the school and its grounds and give pragmatic solutions for problems, whether they are poor air quality, contaminated water or lunches lacking in nutritional value.

Written in simple and clear language, *Blueprint for a Green School* aims to ensure good health, safety and conservation in our classrooms and communities. Once decision makers understand the consequences of their policies and we all learn to think about how we live and how our actions affect our world, we will be able to make the environmentally sensitive and sound decisions our planet deserves.

This has been a collaborative work that I have overseen and nurtured. I hope the effort proves beneficial.

Jayni Chase
Founder
Center for Environmental Education
Pacific Palisades, CA

How to Use This Book

Blueprint for a Green School focuses on creating environmentally safe and healthy school buildings and grounds and on what we as school administrators, teachers, maintenance staff, students, community leaders and parents can do to meet this goal.

This book functions as an introduction to environmental problems and issues relevant to schools, provides a wealth of resources for further investigation and suggests ways to incorporate the information into daily instruction. Outlines at the beginning of each chapter ensure easy, accessible reference.

Organization

Chapters 1 through 17 present basic facts so that environmentally educated decisions can be made in the operation of school buildings and classrooms. These facts will assist school leaders in deciding what to encourage in their lessons and activities, and how everyone's actions can affect the environment.

Chapter 18 contains suggested activities for students and teachers including examples of what others are doing. We hope the reader will use this information and find inspiration in what others have done to advance environmental awareness.

Chapters 19 and 20 list curricula, books for children and general use, videos and state-by-state agency resources. These carefully compiled lists will make it easier to obtain the necessary information and educational materials to transform a school into an environmentally sound and safe place to learn.

Illustrations

To enhance the clearly written text, there are more than 360 charts, graphs, tables and pictograms, each designed so that you can easily grasp the significance of the topic at hand.

Conclusion

We believe you will find this comprehensive, valuable resource essential in planning for the health and safety of children and youth everywhere. We wish success to our readers in their efforts to make schools across the country environmentally safe and healthy.

Environmental and Health Issues

Chapter 1

CONTENTS

INTRODUCTION

Campus Audit

An audit is a formal examination. This means looking carefully at your school's buildings and yards. We will outline what you need to look for, how to find it, and what to do about your findings. You may need professional, licensed people both to find environmental problems and to help solve them for your school.

Why Audit?

Radon, asbestos, indoor air quality, lead and formaldehyde may pose serious health risks. Individually, and at low-level exposures these may not be of great danger to a person's health. However, scientists and health experts are learning that the cumulative effect of the many toxins and contaminants that we encounter every day may be taking a great toll on our health.

This chapter defines each of the above substances, tells some ways to discover if it is a problem on your campus and then tells what to do.

Although **some** legislation governs a **few** of these health hazards, there is still much reason for concern and action, especially since most school campus grounds have not been audited.

There are many ways that safe exposure levels are determined. Unfortunately, most of these exposure levels have been set for adults with industrial or work related exposures. Some factors that have been considered for establishing adult exposure standards are toxic reactions, cancer and birth defects.

Few standards are based on long-term exposure of children to compounds in indoor air at low levels, like those that may be encountered in schools. Some low level exposures may cause sensitivities, allergies, immune disorders and neurotoxicity (reactions affecting moods, behavior, perception and the ability to concentrate or learn).

Children's lungs are more efficient at trapping particles than adults'. Therefore, the cumulative effect is heightened in small bodies, as illustrated in the graph at right.

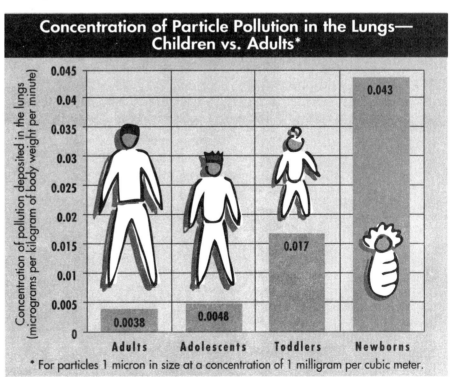

Concentration of Particle Pollution in the Lungs— Children vs. Adults*

Concentration of pollution deposited in the lungs (micrograms per kilogram of body weight per minute)

- Adults: 0.0038
- Adolescents: 0.0048
- Toddlers: 0.017
- Newborns: 0.043

* For particles 1 micron in size at a concentration of 1 milligram per cubic meter.

Source: University of California, Irvine, Air Pollution Laboratory.

The health and safety of everyone at your school should come first regarding all maintenance, renovation and building design decisions. Before you begin your campus audit, find out how your school, school board and school district are addressing these problems. Chances are no one has taken the time and trouble to find out how to do a campus audit. Using the information in this book, you will be able to go to those who are making decisions for your school and show them how to make your campus healthy. The following is an overview of all the related facts. We do not intend to create a feeling of panic; rather, we will provide basic information for awareness and resources for those who want to do a campus audit.

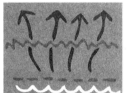

RADON

Definition

Radon is a naturally occurring, odorless, tasteless, invisible radioactive gas formed from decaying uranium and radium. It comes primarily from granite, shale and phosphate rocks and soil containing these radioactive elements. It may also be emitted by industrial wastes such as uranium and phosphate mining by-products.

Where It Is Found

Radon has been found throughout the country in homes and in schools. It enters buildings through cracks in concrete floors and walls, dirt floors, floor drains, sumps, joints, tiny openings in hollow block walls and water from private wells. Radon is also found in soil and, because it is soluble in water, in the underground water supply. "All groundwater has radon, and some has very high concentrations. Radon that enters the home

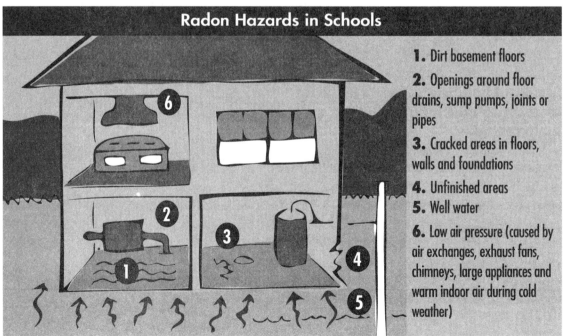

Radon Hazards in Schools

1. Dirt basement floors
2. Openings around floor drains, sump pumps, joints or pipes
3. Cracked areas in floors, walls and foundations
4. Unfinished areas
5. Well water
6. Low air pressure (caused by air exchanges, exhaust fans, chimneys, large appliances and warm indoor air during cold weather)

Source: U.S. Environmental Protection Agency, *A Citizen's Guide to Radon: What It Is and What to Do About It*, Washington, DC, 1986.

through the water supply escapes from the water when flushed, heated or sprayed in showers, dishwashers and clothes washers. Radon concentrations are typically much higher in water than in air."[1]

Testing is the only way to know if your school is at risk from radon. Radon has been found at unacceptable levels in every state. The EPA now recommends testing be performed in every school to asses the risks to students and faculty. Testing should be performed at all levels of the building below the third floor.

The EPA Recommends

✔ Test your school for radon—it's easy and inexpensive

✔ Fix your school if your radon level is 4 picocuries (pCi)

✔ Radon levels less that 4 pCi/L still pose a risk, and in many cases may be reduced.

Radon is estimated to cause about 14,000 deaths per year–however, this number could range from 7,000 to 30,000 deaths per year. The numbers of deaths from other causes are taken from 1990 National Saftey Council reports.

Source: U.S. Environmental Protection Agency, *A Citizen's Guide to Radon*, Washington, DC, 1992.

Risks

Radon is considered the second leading cause of lung cancer after smoking. The U.S. Environmental Protection Agency (EPA), American Medical Association, surgeon general, American Lung Association and World Health Organization consider indoor radon one of the most serious environmental health problems.

Radon gas releases decay products called radon daughters that attach themselves to dust particles in the air. When these particles are inhaled, they decay inside the lungs, giving off radioactivity that damages the lungs. Smoking makes the lungs more vulnerable to the dangers of radon. The health risks increase with length and level of exposure to radon. Therefore, it is highly recommended that both schools and homes be checked because children spend so much of their time in these buildings. In fact, the EPA recommends that all schools be checked for radon.

Related Diseases

Lung cancer is the only disease that is known to be associated with elevated levels of radon. In fact, radon gas is the nation's second leading cause of lung cancer.

Radon and Your Lungs

1. Radon gas causes decay products called radon daughters.

2. The radon daughters become part of airborne dust particles and are inhaled into the lungs.

3. Once in the lungs, radon daughters decay and emit radioactivity, which can be harmful.

4. Over a period of time (10 to 30 years) this exposure to radioactivity can result in lung cancer.

Radon Risk Comparison for Smokers and Nonsmokers

Radon Level	If 1,000 people who smoked were exposed to this level over a lifetime...	If 1,000 people who never smoked were exposed to this level over a lifetime...
20 pCi/L (740 Bq/m3)*	About 135 people could get lung cancer	About 8 people could get lung cancer
10 pCi/L (370 Bq/M3)	About 71 people could get lung cancer	About 4 people could get lung cancer
8 pCi/L (296 Bq/M3)	About 57 people could get lung cancer	About 3 people could get lung cancer
4 pCi/L (148 Bq/M3)	About 29 people could get lung cancer	About 2 people could get lung cancer
2 pCi/L (74 Bq/M3)	About 15 people could get lung cancer	About 1 people could get lung cancer
1.3 pCi/L (48.1 Bq/M3)	About 9 people could get lung cancer	Less than 1 person could get lung cancer
0.4 pCi/L (14.8 Bq/M3)	About 3 people could get lung cancer	Less than 1 person could get lung cancer

*Bq/M3 = Bequerel/meter3

Source: Radon: *The Health Treat with a Simple Solution*, EPA, 1993.

The National Academy of Sciences estimates that radon-caused lung cancer accounts for 16,000 annual deaths nationwide. Unfortunately, there are no known immediate symptoms to warn a person of exposure to radon.

Solutions

Your campus radon level must be tested. If it is elevated, radon-reducing measures must be taken. Radon test kits are available through local and state health departments. (For state health department listings, see the state resource list in Chapter 20.) Some states offer free testing. Hardware stores now carry easy-to-use kits. The results must be mailed to the manufacturer for analysis. The manufacturer will then mail you its findings.

The EPA sponsors a 24-hour hotline providing information on how to test radon in the home. Dial **800-SOS-RADON.**

EPA grants are available to schools and local governments to address radon in the schools. Contact your regional EPA office or your state health or radiation control department for further information. (See the state resource list in Chapter 20.)

Along with providing a hotline and offering grants, the EPA has compiled three very useful lists to assist your efforts in testing for high radon levels and reducing them if they are found:

◆ The RMP (Radon Measurement Proficiency) list identifies companies that meet minimum proficiency standards and measure radon or sell test kits.

◆ The RCP (Radon Contractor Proficiency) list evaluates contractors' ability to fix radon problems in the home.

◆ Lists of local contractors experienced in radon reduction in schools are also available. You can obtain them by contacting your state radiation office. (See the state resource list in Chapter 20.)

The EPA has recently completed a national assessment of radon in schools. The results indicate that approximately 15,000 public schools in the United States, or almost one in five schools have at least one room with an elevated screening level above the EPA's action level of 4 picocuries per liter. For most school children and staff, the home is likely to be the largest radon exposure source with the school being the second highest. The results of this study reaffirm the EPA's recommendation that all schools be tested.

The good news is that the steps necessary to reduce unhealthy levels of radon can be easy to implement. Correction may involve nothing more than sealing cracks (point of entry) or changing/increasing the flow of ventilated air. The best way to deal with radon may be to open windows, doors and vents to dilute the gas or allow it to escape.

ASBESTOS

Definition

The term *asbestos* includes a group of minerals (chrysotile, amosite, crocidolite, anthophyllite, actinolite and tremolite) that occur naturally in certain types of rock formations. When mined, they take on the form of very fine, small, silky fibers. Once bound together the asbestos fibers are strong, fire resistant, corrosion resistant and good heat insulators. Because of these properties asbestos was once considered a miracle fiber and thus widely used in many manufacturing applications.

◆ The EPA estimates annual releases into the air of about 700 tons of asbestos during mining and milling operations, 100 tons during product manufacture and 18 tons from landfills.

◆ The National Academy of Sciences (NAS) estimates that a person with a typical exposure in an urban area faces a lifetime risk of between 1 in 100,000 and 29 in 100,000 of developing cancer from the asbestos in the air both indoors and outdoors. Women are at less risk than men.

◆ It may require 15 to 40 years for the health effects of asbestos exposure to become apparent.

◆ Over the past two decades, some uses of asbestos have been banned. Contrary to popular belief, some

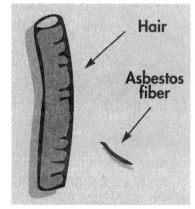

asbestos use may still legally continue; however, reputable manufacturers have voluntarily phased out asbestos from their new school products.

◆ Often labels of products with asbestos do not reveal their asbestos content. To find out if asbestos is present, the product should be tested. The manufacturer or the U.S. Consumer Product Safety Commission at **800-638-8326** may have helpful information.

Where It Is Found

In July 1989 the EPA issued an "Asbestos Ban and Phaseout" proposal, an almost complete ban on the use of asbestos in the United States, scheduled to take effect in the mid 1990's. The Fifth Circuit Court of Appeals weakened the ban by allowing asbestos to be used in some products. A qualified laboratory with a special microscope can determine the presence of asbestos in existing materials.

If you are ever unsure if a new material contains asbestos, you can contact the manufacturer and ask for a MSDS (Materials Safety Data Sheet). (See chapter 17 for more information on this.)

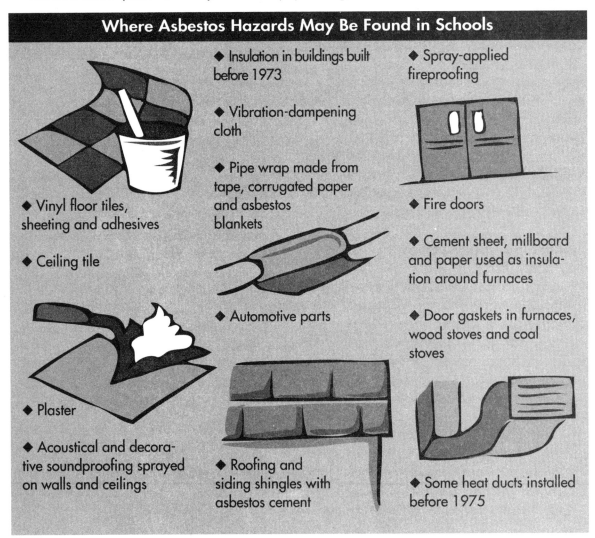

Where Asbestos Hazards May Be Found in Schools

◆ Vinyl floor tiles, sheeting and adhesives

◆ Ceiling tile

◆ Plaster

◆ Acoustical and decorative soundproofing sprayed on walls and ceilings

◆ Insulation in buildings built before 1973

◆ Vibration-dampening cloth

◆ Pipe wrap made from tape, corrugated paper and asbestos blankets

◆ Automotive parts

◆ Roofing and siding shingles with asbestos cement

◆ Spray-applied fireproofing

◆ Fire doors

◆ Cement sheet, millboard and paper used as insulation around furnaces

◆ Door gaskets in furnaces, wood stoves and coal stoves

◆ Some heat ducts installed before 1975

The EPA estimates that most of the nation's primary and secondary school buildings (about 107,000) contain asbestos. It is usually present in the building materials or insulation.[2]

Some older, asbestos-containing items that may still be around your school are:
◆ Fireproof gloves
◆ Bunsen burner pads
◆ Ironing board covers
◆ Kilns or ceramic ovens

Risks

In the 1970s we began to act on the health risks associated with breathing asbestos fibers. It is only when they are disturbed, deteriorated or damaged and become airborne—and therefore can be inhaled—that they become a hazard.

> **Asbestos has the following known effects on human health:**
>
> **1. Lung cancer.**
>
> **2. Mesothelioma** (cancer of the membrane lining of the chest or abdominal cavity).
>
> **3. Asbestosis** (occurs when fibers build up in the lungs. Side effects include shortness of breath and higher risk of lung infections).
>
> **4. Other cancers** (for example, those of the esophagus, stomach, colon and rectum).

When asbestos fibers are damaged or disturbed, the very small and light fibers that are released into the air can remain there for some time. **Having these small, sharp asbestos fibers in the air is dangerous because, once inhaled, they may forever be trapped in the lungs and digestive system, posing serious health risks.** Thus far, serious health problems have been identified mostly in people who handle asbestos professionally. But the EPA is still concerned about schoolchildren and school custodial workers who are exposed to any level of asbestos.[3]

Related Diseases

Effects may not be noticeable for as many as 15 to 40 years after exposure. But two early-warning signs of upcoming disease are shortness of breath and tightening of the chest.

Solutions

Asbestos-containing material will pose little health risk if it is properly handled, managed and maintained. If your campus has not already been inspected, the law requires school buildings be checked by an accredited inspector. Qualified persons can be found by checking your yellow pages for an AHERA certified inspector. Your local health department may also be able to help.

This initial inspection should identify the location(s) and condition(s) of all asbestos. Identifying locations is essential so that problems relating to everyday school and maintenance activities do not occur unknowingly. The school custodial staff should then be trained in proper work practices, both to avoid disturbances and to clean up minor ones.

Asbestos Caution

Do not dust, sweep or vacuum materials suspected of containing asbestos fibers, as this may make them airborne. Asbestos dust should be removed with a wet mop or a specially designed "HEPA" (high-efficiency particulate air) vacuum cleaner. Because asbestos fibers are so tiny, they can pass through normal vacuum cleaner bags and be rereleased into the air.

Under the Asbestos Hazard Emergency Act (AHERA), all public and private non-profit elementary and secondary schools are required to inspect for asbestos-containing building materials (ACBM), develop asbestos management plans that address asbestos hazards in each school building and implement response actions in a timely fashion. Schools must also conduct a periodic inspection every six months in each school building containing ACBM. This can be conducted by a non-accredited but trained employee. Once every three years, a reinspection of the school buildings must be conducted by an accredited inspector.

Certain asbestos-related work in schools must be done by an accredited person. The AHERA Model Accreditation Plan specifies training, examination and other requirements for inspectors, management planners, workers, contractor, supervisors and project designers. (See the resource section of this chapter for help finding accredited AHERA training.) **Any renovation work that takes place on the campus needs to be closely monitored to avoid accidental disturbance of asbestos fiber.**

There are several proper methods of response to asbestos:
- ◆ Develop a special maintenance plan to ensure that the asbestos remains in good condition.
- ◆ Repair any damaged asbestos-containing materials.
- ◆ Encapsulate, using a sealant to spray the material to prevent the release of fibers.
- ◆ Enclose the materials with airtight barriers.
- ◆ Remove the asbestos using trained abatement professionals. **Do not try to save money by doing it yourself.** A poorly handled removal can make the health hazards much worse than they were before. Always remember that once asbestos has been disturbed and released into the air, it remains there for a long time.

INDOOR AIR QUALITY

Definition

A school's Indoor Air Quality (IAQ) is defined by the particles, gases, temperature and humidity affecting the occupants safety, comfort and health. Indoor air is frequently more polluted that outdoor air. School children spend more of their time indoors and breathe a greater volume of air relative to their body weight than do adults, so they are probably at a greater risk of accumulating higher concentrations of pollutants in their bodies.

Causes of Indoor Air Pollution

There are many different factors that may contribute to IAQ problems. Indoor-related health problems can be caused by both natural and man-made sources. Some include chemicals, smoke, dust and biological contaminates like molds and dust mites.

Some of these pollutants may be released into the air only intermittently, others may be emitted continuously. Poor maintenance is frequently a cause. By determining the source(s) of pollutants it may be possible to minimize their hazardous effect. A 1984 World Health Organization Committee report suggested that up to 30 percent of new and remodeled buildings worldwide may be the subject of excessive complaints related to indoor air quality.[4]

An EPA panel report concluded in December 1992 that passive smoke, the smoke that one smells when a smoker is around, can be a health hazard, especially for children. The panel designated passive smoke as a group A carcinogen, based on studies that indicate an increase of lung cancer in nonsmoking spouses of smokers and respiratory problems in children of smoking parents. The report was unable to pinpoint the amount of exposure to passive smoke necessary to trigger the cancer or respiratory problem. It did estimate that passive smoke is responsible for 3,300 lung cancer deaths annually in nonsmokers and former smokers and 8,000 to 26,000 new asthma cases in children each year.

A burning cigarette emits:

- ◆ Benzene
- ◆ Carbon monoxide
- ◆ Formaldehyde
- ◆ Ammonia
- ◆ Hydrogen cyanide

Plus more than 4,000 different chemicals, 43 of which are known to cause cancer.

Tobacco smoke is a major cause of indoor air pollution. Secondhand smoke has been linked to the following in nonsmoking adults:

- ◆ Lung cancer
- ◆ Heart and lung disease
- ◆ Aggravation of allergies and asthma
- ◆ Headaches, nausea, nose and eye irritation

Where Indoor Air Pollution Sources May Be Found in Your School

1. Radon. (Addressed separately in this chapter.)

2. Asbestos. (Addressed separately in this chapter.)

3. Cleaning solutions. (See Chapter 14.)

4. Pesticides. (See Chapter 3.)

5. Formaldehyde. (Addressed separately in this chapter.)

6. Printing and copying machines. These may emit a wide range of volatile organic compounds and ozone. All of these machines will have some type of emissions, but machines with liquid toner emit higher levels.

7. Synthetic materials. Acetate, nylon and polyester may outgas harmful vapors when they are new.

8. Combustion appliances. These burn oil, gas, coal or wood and may release carbon monoxide (NO2) particulates .

9. Furniture and building materials. Most glues, adhesives and finishes emit vapors particularly when new. (See the "Formaldehyde" section of this chapter.)

10. Heating, cooling and humidification systems. These can provide a breeding ground for microbials like mold and bacteria. Air flow in air handling systems can spread the microbes and other pollutants throughout the building. When properly designed and maintained these systems can help reduce air quality problems by diluting indoor contaminants with fresh air.

11. Tobacco products. Just read the labels!

12. Paint and paint strippers. "A study done at Johns Hopkins University revealed that more than 300 toxic chemicals and 150 carcinogens may be present in paint."[5] Even water-based latex paints often contain volatile organic compounds including mold retardants, preser-

vatives and biocides. Biocides destroy or retard the growth of molds, slime, bacteria and fungi. Many are poisonous to humans.

Oil-based paints usually contain petroleum solvents that emit toxic fumes for a long time. Many U.S. manufacturers have voluntarily agreed to stop using mercury in interior paints. Exterior and industrial paints may still contain mercury.

> **NOTE: Nontoxic paints are available that do not contain petrochemicals, mercury, formaldehyde and other toxic or hazardous chemicals.**
> (See the resource section at the end of this chapter.)

13. Solvents. These are used in art, industrial arts and vocational shop classes. (See Chapter 10 for more in-depth information.)

14. Lab materials and chemicals. (See Chapters 2 and 9 for more in-depth information.)

15. Art and craft materials and chemicals. (See Chapter 10 for more in-depth information.)

16. Carpeting. This is often treated with fungicides, pesticides and other chemicals for fire retardation plus stain resistance. Although many volatile organic compounds (VOCs) are added during the manufacture of carpet, there are VOCs that are accidentally produced as by-products of the production process. Another problem, is carpet that becomes wet and is not quickly dried. It will become moldy. Also, elevated humidity may support growth of fungus and dust mites in carpet.

17. Adhesives, spackling and joint compounds. These may all contain mercury.

18. Scents (e.g., from perfumes, aftershave and air freshener). Many people have allergic reactions to the chemicals used in these products.

Many synthetic chemicals commonly found in fragrances (perfume) and cosmetics (hair and skin products) can result in varying health complaints depending upon the amount of offending odors being emitted. Some of these chemicals include methylene chloride, toluene, methyl ethyl ketone, methyl isobutyl ketone, ethanol and benzyl chloride.

In her article "Perfume or Pollutant" (Green Alternatives, November/December 1992, page 34), Irene Wilkenfeld indicated that complaints from these and other chemicals found in perfumes have included headaches, spaciness, inability to concentrate, mood changes, dizziness, nausea, short-term memory loss, restlessness, agitation, depression, sleepiness, lethargy and sinus pain in sensitive individuals.

Since a formal ban on the use of perfumes in schools is likely to create enforcement problems, an informal approach is more likely to succeed. Teachers should set a good example and be aware of the problems that can be associated with synthetic fragrances. Students with noted sensitivities should be allowed to sit closer to fresh air supplies or windows. Natural perfumes made from plant extracts tend to be milder and better tolerated by people sensitive.

Risks

Studies by the EPA have determined indoor air pollution is an important risk to the health of people living in the United States. The EPA's 1987 report, "A Comparative Assessment of Environmental Problems" identifies indoor air pollutants, other than radon as the fourth highest risk in a field of almost 30 different environmental problems. In many cases indoor air pollution levels exceed outdoor levels. If more than 20 percent of the occupants of a building are complaining about air quality, a thorough investigation should be conducted. When an unknown cause is resulting in air quality complaints, the structure is referred to as a "sick building". If illness in a building is related to a specific cause (such as Legionnaire's disease), it is called a "building related illness".

Often poor indoor air quality is not even considered to be a cause of decreased comfort, health and productivity because very few are aware of it or understand it.

Related Diseases

Multiple chemical sensitivity (MCS) is attributed to chemical exposures. MCS may be triggered by the following:
◆ New carpets
◆ Vehicle exhaust

◆ New clothing
◆ Cleaning products
◆ Mold and dust mites
◆ Laser printers
◆ Mothballs
◆ New particle board and plywood
◆ Pesticides
◆ Paper
◆ Perfumes and cosmetics
◆ Gas stove emissions

One or more of the following symptoms may be reported: respiratory problems, headache, fatigue, flu-like symptoms, mental confusion and short-term memory loss, gastrointestinal tract difficulties, cardiovascular irregularities, skin disorders, muscle and joint pain, irritability and depression.

Airborne Contaminants and Their Possible Symptoms

Contaminants	Symptoms
Dust mites	Headaches, asthma
Bacteria	Sore throat
Mold	Runny nose, asthma
Insect fragments	Flu-like symptoms
Viruses	Cold-like symptoms
Radon	Lung cancer
Gasses	Fatigue

Source: Rodale's *Allergy Relief.*

People with MCS can be divided into four categories:

1. **Industrial workers** (exposure to industrial chemicals).
2. **Tight-building occupants** (off-gassing from construction materials, office equipment or supplies, tobacco smoke and inadequate ventilation).
3. **Contaminated communities** (toxic waste sites, aerial pesticide spraying, groundwater contamination, air contamination by nearby industry and other community exposures).
4. **Individuals** (indoor air pollution and emission of toxic vapors from consumer products and indoor pesticides).

Solutions

If you suspect that your school buildings suffer from poor indoor air quality, you must identify and reduce or eliminate any known sources. It is also important to switch to less toxic cleaning and maintenance materials. (See Chapters 3 and 14—"Pesticides" and "Cleaning Products"—for suggestions of alternative cleaning and maintenance materials. The resource list at the end of this chapter also lists companies that sell nontoxic or low-toxic building materials.)

Proper design and maintenance of the ventilation systems are essential for avoiding indoor air quality problems. Ventilation systems should have the following:

◆ Adequate air flow of outdoor air into the building and indoor air out of the building
◆ Good air distribution
◆ Proper cleaning/maintenance
◆ Temperature/humidity controls maintained at appropriate levels

◆ Adequate ventilation of the specific sources of contaminants listed earlier

◆ Air-intake vents and open windows located where there is no obvious outdoor pollution, such as near trash areas, plumbing vents, boiler emissions and traffic areas (e.g., bus loading zones and parking lots).

The EPA is developing an IAQ (indoor air quality) management plan for school districts to provide specific actions for the operation and maintenance of school facilities. This document, entitled "Improve Your School's IAQ," will target schools K–12 and will tentatively be available in early 1995 from the Government Printing Office for a nominal fee. Training to supplement the documents will also be offered. Contact the Environmental Engineer at the EPA, **202-233-9056**, with any questions concerning these projects.

Any questions about these programs or indoor air quality can be answered by the EPA's Indoor Air Quality Information Clearinghouse at **800-438-4318** (9—5 eastern time, Monday through Friday). The Clearinghouse can also direct you to your regional EPA Indoor Air Coordinator.

Can House Plants Remove Toxins?

Wolverton Environmental Services studied indoor plants for NASA and found the following percentages of toxins are removed by one plant in a 24-hour period in a 12-cubic-foot area:

Common Name	Toxins Removed
Aloe vera	Formaldehyde: 90%
Elephant ear philodendron	Formaldehyde: 86%
English ivy	Benzene: 90%
Ficus (weeping fig)	Formaldehyde: 47%
Golden pothos	Carbon monoxide: 75%; benzene: 67%; formaldehyde: 67%
Janet Craig (corn plant)	Benzene: 79%
Peace lily	Benzene: 80%; trichloroethylene: 50%
Spider plant	Carbon monoxide: 96%

Although much attention has been given to this study, proof that plants effectively clean air in real-life building settings is not available. Plants abilities to improve indoor air quality is limited when compared with adequate ventilation. Also, fungal growth in soil can trigger allergies and asthma in susceptible people.

Source: Wolverton Environmental Services.

LEAD

Definition

Lead a heavy, blue-gray metal is classified as a toxic substance that is know to cause adverse effects in humans and the environment. In the body lead acts like calcium and accumulates in bone.

Children are more at risk to the dangers of lead-poisoning than adults. Young children's digestive systems absorb lead up to four times more readily than do adults' plus their developing nervous systems are especially vulnerable to the toxic effects of lead, even at low levels.

Where It Is Found

Major sources of lead exposure are from lead-based paint, contaminated drinking water, contaminated soil, certain home remedies (such as Greta and Azarcon), lead-glazed pottery and certain industrial related sources.

Lead enters water when it comes into direct contact anywhere along the water's path to the

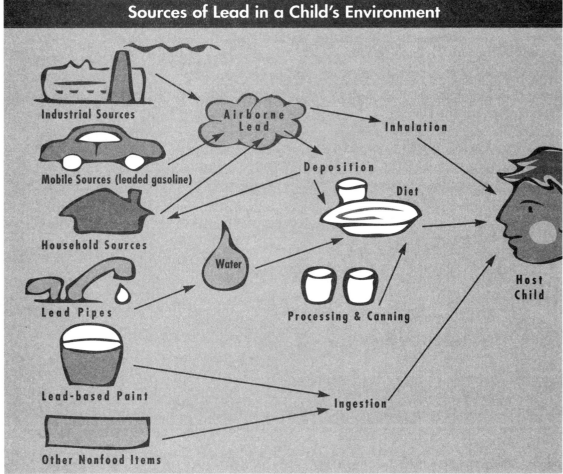

Sources of Lead in a Child's Environment

Industrial Sources
Mobile Sources (leaded gasoline)
Household Sources
Lead Pipes
Lead-based Paint
Other Nonfood Items
Airborne Lead
Water
Processing & Canning
Deposition
Inhalation
Diet
Ingestion
Host Child

Source: Center for Disease Control.

17

tap. **Many water pipes made of lead have been installed in this country as recently as 1986. Also, copper pipes are often joined together with solder containing lead.**

Lead enters water when it comes into direct contact anywhere along the water's path to the tap. **Water pipes containing lead have been installed in this country as recently as 1986. Also, copper pipes are often joined together with solder containing lead. Which is one of the leading causes of lead contamination in water.**

Lead also enters drinking water through water coolers that have a lead-lined storage tank or lead parts.

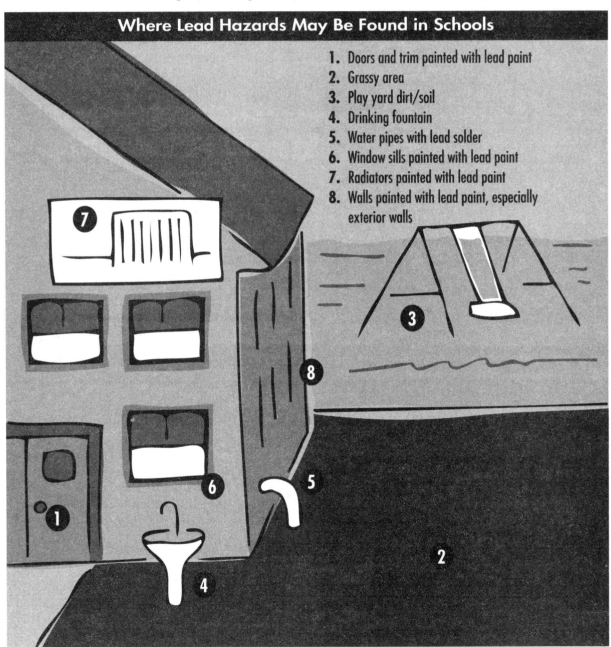

Where Lead Hazards May Be Found in Schools

1. Doors and trim painted with lead paint
2. Grassy area
3. Play yard dirt/soil
4. Drinking fountain
5. Water pipes with lead solder
6. Window sills painted with lead paint
7. Radiators painted with lead paint
8. Walls painted with lead paint, especially exterior walls

Lead-based paint is the most common source of exposure for children. The use of lead in paint was banned for residential structures in 1978. Any housing built before that time may contain lead-based paint and houses built before 1950 very likely do contain lead-based paint. There are several main pathways for exposure from lead-based painting sources. Common hazard sources are

◆ Paint particles or chips. Children may ingest these through normal hand-to-mouth activity.

◆ Lead dust. When painted surfaces regularly rub together, such as door frames, window sills or cabinet doors, the friction creates lead dust, which in turn is readily ingested by children and others.

◆ Contaminated soil. Paint particles from deteriorating paint, friction surfaces or renovation actives can contaminate nearby soil, creating another exposure pathway.

Aside from water and food, children may also be exposed during play and from air, dust, dirt and paint, creating a greater risk from cumulative exposure. If a window frame has been painted with lead-containing paint, every time that window is opened and closed lead dust is released into the air. If the classroom was painted with lead-containing paint, the children are at risk from any paint chips or flakes.

Risks and Effects of Exposure

There are no safe levels for lead exposure. It is especially dangerous for young children because their bodies absorb more of the lead they consume (through inhalation or ingestion) than do those of adults. The early stages of lead poisoning cannot be easily detected. The only way to know for sure is through a blood test.

"**A**lthough all children are at risk for lead toxicity, poor and minority children are disproportionately affected. Lead exposure is at once a by-product of poverty and a contributor to the cycle that perpetuates and deepens the state of being poor."

"Preventing Lead Poisoning in Young Children: A Statement by the Center for Disease Control," Dept. of Health and Human Services, Oct. 1991.

A child's health care provider can screen a child for lead poisoning as part of regular well-child care. Most health plans and Medical Assistance will pay for a blood test. Call your local health department or pediatrician if you need help getting your child tested.

U.S. federal agencies are now calling lead poisoning the No. 1 environmental health hazard to children.

Solutions

Schools with lead-based paint should consider exposure control a priority. This does not mean removal of all lead-based paint, but rather the controlling of the risk of exposure. It is always best to use a certified contractor because preparation

Effects of Lead Exposure

With time, even low levels of lead can cause:

♦ *Damage to the kidneys, nervous system and red blood cells*
♦ *Learning and behavior problems*
♦ *Interference with growth*
♦ *Hearing problems*
♦ *High blood pressure*
♦ *Decreased intelligence and learning disabilities*
♦ *Impaired visual motor function*
♦ *Short-term memory loss*
♦ *Loss of motor control*
♦ *Anemia*

Serious cases may even result in coma or death.

for repainting can generate large amounts of dust which is extremely hazardous to kids.

Controlling exposure to lead involves identifying and eliminating causes of paint deterioration and treating friction and impact surfaces such as window sills, cabinet doors and door frames. Contact the National Lead Information Clearinghouse at 1-800-424-LEAD or 1-800-LEAD-FYI for more detailed information.

Because we cannot see, smell or taste the lead in water, the water must be tested by an EPA or state approved laboratory.

To find a qualified laboratory, you can
    1. Call your local water utility.
    2. Call your state health department. (See state resource list in Chapter 20.)
    3. Check your yellow pages for "Laboratories."

Federal standards limit the acceptable amount of lead in water to 50 parts per billion (50 ppb); however, the EPA has proposed that standards be tightened in light of new health data to a limit of 15 ppb.

If you find that there is lead in your water supply, you should follow these guidelines:

1. **Never drink water that has been in the pipe for more than 6 hours, such as overnight or over the weekend.**
   a. Flush the water (let it run) until the it is as cold as it normally gets from the tap. This needs to be done at each faucet.
   b. If your building was built before 1930, it may have lead service connectors, which will be flushed by letting the water run an extra 15 seconds after it has cooled.
   c. If you are concerned with waste, flushed water can be used for nonconsumable purposes. Once the water is flushed, bottles can be filled and refrigerated for later use.

2. **Do not consume or cook with water from the hot-water tap.** Lead dissolves more easily and quickly in hot water. Use the cold water and heat it on a stove. Cafeteria workers and those in cooking classes must be educated about these facts.

3. **Accessible screens in faucets should be cleaned frequently, perhaps once every 3 or 4 weeks.**

4. **Use bottled water for drinking. Bottled water must have a lead level below 5 ppb for consumption.**

5. **If the test results indicate levels of lead above 15 ppb:**
   a. Work with a qualified technician so that the sources of contamination are pinpointed.
   b. Contact your water supplier to find out plans for treating the water supply. Although usually the contamination occurs as a by-product of corrosion within the plumbing system, the supplier may need to check the pH (acidity/corrosivity) level of the water leaving the treatment plant.
   c. Consider installing corrosion reduction devices. Your water supplier can tell you where to find these devices.
   d. Work with your state Department of Health or Department of the Environment if the problem continues at unacceptable levels. (See the state resource list in Chapter 20.)

The EPA recommends that all schools flush drinking water outlets after weekends and vacations, unless the testing included additional tests to determine lead levels for these periods.

In 1974 the Safe Drinking Water Act (SDWA) was passed, requiring the EPA to set drinking water standards. In November 1988, as an amendment to the SDWA, the Lead Contamination Control Act of 1988 became law. This amendment specifically requires the EPA to give states and localities guidance on testing for and lowering lead contamination in schools and day care centers. It also sets guidelines for water coolers with any lead parts.

FORMALDEHYDE

Definition

Formaldehyde is a water-soluble, colorless, toxic gas with a very noticeable odor. Students who have dissected frogs will remember well the smell of the preservative. It is a primary ingredient in products with the trade names Formalin, Methylaldehyde, Lysoform, Morbicid and Paraform.

Where It Is Found

Because it is inexpensive and has a great variety of uses, formaldehyde appears to show up just about everywhere in our lives. Some is naturally occurring (a product of living cells), and much of it is manmade. In fact, the United States makes about **6 billion pounds** a year.

Formaldehyde is used in disinfectants, preservatives, fumigants and embalming fluids; it can also make a fabric wrinkle- or fireproof. Formaldehyde can result as a by-product of some chemical processes. In some cases the greater the purity of ingredients, the less chance there is of formaldehyde forming accidentally.

Formaldehyde has been used in wood products as a binder/glue. It may form an incomplete chemical bond and thus can outgas for years—long after there is a noticeable odor. Formaldehyde containing products may be used in counters, cabinets, furniture, paneling and even stereo speakers. Manufacturers of plywoods and particle board have voluntarily reduced their products emission levels, but they may still affect some individuals.

In textiles formaldehyde has been used to help bond important substances, such as dyes, stiffeners and crush-resistant agents. Repeated washings help remove formaldehyde from clothing and linens.

In the United States alone, production of formaldehyde-containing products has accounted for 8 percent of the gross national product. Formaldehyde is essential to plant operations in 17 major industries and is an important basic raw material in 70 other industries. Formaldehyde was first used as a biological preservative in 1868.

Risks

Formaldehyde may not bind completely; therefore, it continues to slowly outgas invisible vapors for years. These vapors can cause problems even in the absence of an odor. After the "new" smells associated with new carpeting, cars, furniture, paint and so on, have dissipated, the outgassing of the formaldehyde may continue.

The following materials may contribute to formaldehyde pollution:

- ◆ Urea formaldehyde foam insulation
- ◆ Household waxes, oils
- ◆ Particle board, chip board and interior plywood
- ◆ Shampoo, mouthwash, toothpaste
- ◆ Beverages, beer, wine
- ◆ Carpets, carpet pads
- ◆ Exterior plywood
- ◆ Upholstery fabrics
- ◆ Wallpaper
- ◆ Upholstery foam
- ◆ Glass fiber insulation
- ◆ Construction adhesive
- ◆ Plaster, stucco, concrete
- ◆ Furniture, cabinets
- ◆ Fabric dyes
- ◆ Paints
- ◆ Fabric treatments
- ◆ Burning of gas, oil, wood
- ◆ Wallboard
- ◆ Tobacco smoke
- ◆ Car interiors
- ◆ Milk cartons and paper products

Source: *Your Home, Your Health and Well-Being* by David Rousseau, W. V. Rea and J. Enwright. Copyright 1988 by David Rousseau, W. V. Rea and J. Enwright. Used by permission of Ten Speed Press, P.O. Box 7132, Berkeley, CA 94707.

"It is estimated that every day as many as 20 million people in the United States experience symptoms from formaldehyde outgassing and don't know it."[6]

Two main contributors to this are mobile homes and portable classrooms; both are constructed with a high level of inexpensive pressed-wood products and very little ventilation.

Related Diseases

Symptoms of low exposure to formaldehyde mostly involve irritations to the eyes, nose and respiratory system. Formaldehdye exposure can trigger acute chemical sensitivity and is a suspected carcinogen.

Commonly heard complaints from exposure in sensitive individuals include the following:

- ◆ Breathing difficulties
- ◆ Runny nose
- ◆ Sore throat
- ◆ Fatigue
- ◆ Chest pain
- ◆ Menstrual/gynecological problems

- ◆ Bronchitis
- ◆ Irritations of the sinus and eyes
- ◆ Headaches
- ◆ Sleeping difficulties
- ◆ Nausea

Symptoms may be more noticeable when the weather is colder and when buildings and homes are more airtight.

People can become sensitized to formaldehyde. This means that after an initial exposure, future exposures at even lower concentrations may trigger symptoms.

Solutions

Formaldehyde levels can vary at different times of the day and year, depending in large pare on the level of ventilation. There are many ways that formaldehyde levels can be reduced or limited in schools.

Source Control

One of the best ways to limit formaldehyde levels in buildings is to avoid using materials that contain formaldehyde. This is easier than it used to be. Many manufacturers of particle board and plywood have voluntarily joined a program to limit formaldehyde emissions from their products. These products will be stamped to show they meet emission standards established by the Department of Housing and Urban Development (HUD). If a product is not stamped, the manufacturer should be able to supply information about the emissions from their product.

New furnishings should be allowed to outgas the largest amount of their volatiles outside in the sun for a few days. Some product distributors, if asked, will remove furnishings, drapes and other items from their wrappings to air them out for a few days before delivering them.

Increase Ventilation

Increasing the ventilation to an area can help reduce the buildup of vapors from new materials. A fan may help, but it is vital to have fresh air coming into the room because the fan can create depressurization which may cause pollutants to be pulled from walls, attics and crawlspaces.

Reduce Humidity

As the humidity level increases, so does the emission of formaldehyde from products. By keeping humidity levels around 30 percent, the emission of formaldehyde vapors will be limited without the room becoming uncomfortably dry. If your school is located in an extremely damp or humid area, a dehumidifier may be necessary. Dehumidifiers regular maintenance to avoid the growth of molds and biological contaminants.

Air Purifiers

Air purification may be helpful, but is probably the last option since it is more expensive, less effective and requires more on-going maintenance than the techniques of sources control and increased ventilation.

RESOURCES

Government Agencies

The following lists what government agencies offer:

Local and state health departments
◆ Free environmental testing offered by some
◆ Grant information

State radiation offices
◆ RMP list—evaluation of test kits
◆ Experienced contractors list
◆ Grant information

Regional EPA Offices
◆ Test kits
◆ Grants (to schools and local governments) and information
◆ RMP list
◆ RCP list—evaluation of experienced contractors

General Information Sources

The following publications contain information covering more than one environmental health issue:

Brochures/Papers/Reports

Environmental Hazards in Your School: A Resource Handbook
Publication 2DT-2001
U.S. Environmental Protection Agency
Washington, DC 20460
202-260-7751

Environmental Testing?
Stephen U. Lester and Lois Marie Gibbs
Citizen's Clearinghouse for Hazardous Wastes, Inc.
P.O. Box 6806
Falls Church, VA 22040
703-237-2249

Books

Healthy Homes, Healthy Kids
Joyce Schoemaker and Charity Vitale
Island Press, 1991
1718 Connecticut Avenue NW, Suite 300
Washington, DC 20009

Poisoning Our Children: Surviving in a Toxic World
Nancy Sokol Green
The Nobel Press, Inc. 1991
213 W. Institute Place, Suite 508
Chicago, IL 60610

Your Home, Your Health and Well-being
David Rousseau et al.
Ten Speed Press, 1988
P.O. Box 7123
Berkeley, CA 94707

Radon Resources

Hotlines

EPA 24-Hour Radon Hotline
800-SOS-RADON

Brochures/Papers/Reports

About Radon
Virginia Department of Air Pollution
P.O. Box 10089
Richmond, VA 23240
804-786-2378

Radon Measurement in School, Revised Edition
U.S. Environmental Protection Agency
401 M Street SW (PM 211B)
Washington, DC 20460
202-260-7751

Radon Prevention in Design and Construction of Schools and Other Large Buildings
U.S. Environmental Protection Agency
ORD Publications (G72)
26 Martin Luther King Drive
Cincinnati, OH 54268
513-569-7562

Radon: The Citizens' Guide
Environmental Defense Fund
257 Park Avenue South
New York, NY 10010
212-505-2100

Reducing Radon in Schools-A Team Approach
U.S. Environmental Protection Agency
401 M Street SW (PM 211B)
Washington, DC 20460
202-260-7751

Books

Radon: The Invisible Threat
Michael LaFavore
Rodale Press, 1987
33 East Minor Street
Emmaus, PA 18098

Asbestos Resources

Hotlines

The EPA Ombudsman for Asbestos in Schools
800-368-5888

The EPA Toxic Substances Control Act Hotline
202-554-1404

Brochures/Papers/Reports

The ABCs of Asbestos in Schools
U.S. Environmental Protection Agency
Washington, DC 20460
202-260-7751

Asbestos: Recent Developments in Abatement, Management and Waste Disposal
Legislative Commission on Solid Waste Management
Senator Nicholas A. Spano, Vice Chairman
New York State Senate
Albany, NY 12247
518-474-2121

Asbestos in Schools: Evaluation of the Asbestos Hazard Emergency Response Act (AHERA): A Fact Sheet
U.S. Environmental Protection Agency
Office of Toxic Substances
Washington, DC 20460
202-260-7751

Asbestos in Schools: Evaluation of the Asbestos Hazard Emergency Response Act (AHERA): A Summary Report
U.S. Environmental Protection Agency
Office of Toxic Substances
Washington, DC 20460
202-260-7751

Guidance for Controlling Asbestos-Containing Materials in Buildings
U.S. Environmental Protection Agency
Office of Toxic Substances
Washington, DC 20460
202-260-7751

A Guide to Performing Reinspections Under the Asbestos Hazard Emergency Response Act (AHERA)
U.S. Environmental Protection Agency
Office of Toxic Substances
Washington, DC 20460
202-260-7751

State Asbestos Programs: Related to the Asbestos Hazard Emergency Response Act
National Conference of State Legislatures
1560 Broadway, Suite 700
Denver, CO 80202
303-830-2200

Indoor Air Quality Resources

Hotlines

Indoor Air Quality Hotline
800-438-4318

Brochures/Papers/Reports

If You Think the Danger's Out There, You'd Better Look Inside
American Formulating and Manufacturing
350 West Ash Street, Suite 700
San Diego, CA 92101-3404
619-239-0321

Indoor Air Quality: Selected References
U.S. Department of Health and Human Services
4676 Columbia Parkway
Cincinnati, OH 45226
513-533-8236

The Inside Story: A Guide to Indoor Air Quality
U.S. Environmental Protection Agency
Consumer Product Safety Commission
Washington, DC 20207
800-438-4318

Report to Congress on Indoor Air Quality: Executive Summary and Recommendations
U.S. Environmental Protection Agency
Washington DC 20460
202-260-7751

Tobacco's Toll on America
American Lung Association
1740 Broadway
New York, NY 10019-4374
212-315-8700

Books

Healing Environments: Your Guide to Indoor Well-being
Carol Venolia
Celestial Arts, 1988
P.O. Box 7327
Berkeley, CA 94707

Legal Responses to Indoor Air Pollution
Frank B. Cross
Quorum Books, 1990
88 Post Road West
Westport, CT 06881

Residential Indoor Air Quality and Energy Effiency

Peter DuPont and John Morrill
American Council for an Enery-Efficient
Economy, 1989
1001 Connecticut Avenue NW, Suite 535
Washington, DC 20036

Individuals/Companies/Organizations

AFM Enterprises, Inc.

1960 Chicago Avenue, E7
Riverside, CA 92507
909-781-6860 or 909-781-6861
Suppliers of paints, enamels, stains, mildew control, cleaners, carpet guard, sealers and shampoos for home and industrial use for the chemically sensitive and environmentally aware. Catalog available.

Allergy Resources

P.O. Box 888 (mail)
263 Brookridge (UPS)
Palmer Lake, CO 80133
303-488-3630
A mail-order resource with a wide range of products designed to meet the needs of allergenic patients and chemically sensitive individuals.

The American Academy of Environmental Medicine

The Discipline of Clinical Ecology
P.O. Box 16106
Denver, CO 80216
303-622-9755
Over 400 physicians have grouped together to form the academy in the United States, Canada, Australia and England to study and treat people with illnesses or health problems caused by adverse, allergic or toxic reactions to a wide variety of environmental substances.

BAU, Inc. (Biofa Naturprodukte)

P.O. Box 190
Alton, NH 03809
603-364-2400
This company sells natural wall paints, thinner, cleaners, wood and floor finishes.

Chemical Injury Information Network

P.O. Box 301
White Sulphur Springs, MT 59645
406-547-2255
A nonprofit charitable support, advocacy organization run by the chemically injured for the benefit of the chemically injured. They provide research assistance to doctors, lawyers and victims in the form of medical and governmental studies, reports, articles and computer on-line services that deal with chemical usages and injuries. They also sell a pamphlet of resource material.

Environmental Education and Health Services, Inc.

Mary Oetzel
3202 W. Anderson Lane, #208-249
Austin, TX 78757
512-288-2369
Mary Oetzel provides for individuals, businesses, schools and community group consultations on building materials used in the indoor environment and makes recommendations for alternatives. Consultations are done by phone, on the site or by review of plans.

Human Ecology Action League (HEAL)

P.O. Box 49126
Atlanta, GA 30359
404-248-1898
Incorporated in 1977, HEAL serves those whose health has been adversely affected by environmental exposures providing information to those who are concerned about the

health effects of chemicals and has launched campaigns to alert the general public about the potential dangers of chemicals.

I & J Construction
33 Thorton
Venice, CA 90291
310-395-7533
I & J is working toward a sustainable architecture program for children. Curing Sick Building Syndrome, increasing resource conservation and making the site as sustainable as possible are some of their goals.

The Living Source for a Healthy Environment
7005 Woodway Drive, #214
Waco, TX 76712
817-776-4878
This group offers cleaning and household products for the chemically sensitive and environmentally aware.

Masters Corporation
Paul Bierman-Lytle
P.O. Box 514
New Canaan, CT 06840
203-966-3541
An environmental architect both inside and out, Paul Bierman-Lytle designs homes that are suitable for the chemically sensitive and are energy efficient. Environmental Outfitters is his resource sales center. It carries natural building products such as petrochemical-free paints, insulation from seawater minerals, natural carpets, untreated wood and wallpaper.

Norma Miller
P.O. Box 16147
Ft. Worth, TX 76162
817-292-2022
Norma Miller suffered from indoor air pollution and now she's a consultant who visits schools and homes, explaining what to fix. It's $60 an hour to talk by phone. The first five minutes of a phone consultation are free. She did one thesis on the subject of indoor air pollution titled "Ecological Perspective on a Healthful School Environment: A Delphi Study." The soft-cover version of this is $34.50 and available through University Microfilms at 800-521-0600.

National Center for Environmental Health Strategies
Mary Lamielle, President
1100 Rural Avenue
Voorhees, NJ 08043
609-429-5358
Active in the fight against indoor air pollution, the center fights for political protection of the chemically sensitive in Congress and other government offices. Those who call can receive a free information packet and newsletter. The center is a clearinghouse for indoor air pollution issues and is listed with the EPA. It is also beginning to get more involved with other issues, such as asbestos and pesticides.

National Ecological and Environmental Delivery System (NEEDS)
527 Charles Avenue, 12A
Syracuse, NY 13209
800-634-1380
NEEDS publishes a catalog of products for the chemically sensitive and environmentally aware. Included are cosmetics, household products, appliances, water purifiers, products for the home (could be used in schools), supplements and publications.

Natural Building Network
Jennifer Badde-Graves
P.O. Box 1110
Sebastopal, CA 95473
707-823-2569

The Natural Building Network is a nonprofit organization that promotes awareness of life-enhancing building practices and natural, nontoxic building materials and construction. It also provides a directory of members (not an endorsement) to be used as a resource. The group publishes the "Building with Nature" newsletter 6 times per year. Contributors to the newsletter are among the "continent's finest fanatics for eco-healthy design and construction."

The Natural Choice Eco Design Co.

1365 Rufina Circle
Santa Fe, NM 87501
505-438-3448
Publishes a catalog with a wide selection of healthy home products, such as nontoxic paints, finishes, cleaning products, gardening items and clothes.

Irene Wilkenfeld

52145 Farmington Square Road
Granger, IL 46530
219-271-8990
Irene Wilkenfeld runs a workshop entitled "How Environmentally Safe Are Our Schools? Detoxifying Contaminated Classrooms." Contact her if you would like to have her bring her workshop to your school district.

Lead Resources

Hotlines

National Lead Information Center Hotline

800-LEAD-FYI (532-3391)
The hotline is run by the National Safety Council for the United States. Environmental Protection Agency and provides information on lead to the general public.

Brochures/Papers/Papers

Childhood Lead Poisoning: Blueprint for Prevention

Alliance to End Childhood Lead Poisoning
227 Massachusetts Avenue NE, Suite 200
Washington, DC 20002
202-543-1147

Get the Lead Out

New York Public Interest Research Group Fund, Inc.
9 Murray Street
3rd Floor
New York, NY 10007
212-349-6460

Lead and Your Drinking Water

United States Environmental Protection Agency
Office of Water
Washington, DC 20460
202-260-7751

The Lead Contamination Control Act: A Study in Noncompliance

Natural Resources Defense Council
40 West 20th Street
New York, NY 10011
212-727-2700

Lead in School Drinking Water

U.S. Environmental Protection Agency
Office of Water
Washington, DC 20460
202-260-7751

Lead Prevention Information Guide

Lead Free Kids, Inc.
110 E. 31st Street, Box 8595
Minneapolis, MN 55408-0595
612-377-4304

Preventing Lead Poisoning in Young Children
Department of Health and Human Services
Public Health Services
Centers for Disease Control
Lead Poisoning Prevention Branch
4770 Buford Highway NE
Building 101, MS:S42
Atlanta, GA 30341-3724
404-488-7330

What Everyone Should Know About Lead Poisoning
Scriptographic Booklet
Channing L. Bete Co., Inc.
200 State Road
South Deerfield, MA 01373
800-628-7733

What You Should Know About Lead In Your Water
Scriptographic Booklet
Channing L. Bete Co., Inc.
200 State Road
South Deerfield, MA 01373
800-628-7733

What You Should Know About Lead Safety
Scriptographic Booklet
Channing L. Bete Co., Inc.
200 State Road
South Deerfield, MA 01373
800-628-7733

Books

Lead Poisoning Prevention: Directory of State Contacts
Doug Farquhar
National Conference of State Legislatures,
1993

1560 Broadway, Suite 700
Denver, CO 80202

Individuals/Companies/ Organizations

Alliance to End Childhood Lead Poisoning
600 Pennsylvania Avenue SE, Suite 100
Washington, DC 20003
202-543-1147
This is a nonprofit organization, formed in 1990, working to raise awareness and change perceptions about childhood lead poisoning and to develop and implement effective national prevention programs.

Frandon
Pace Environs
120 West Beaver Creek Road, Unit 16
Richmond Hill, Ontario, Canada L4B 1L2
800-359-9000
This test kit is best for testing the whole house/building as opposed to individual items.

LeadCheck
P.O. Box 1210
Farmingtham, MA 01701
1-800-262-LEAD
A test kit that detects lead on any surface, instantly.

Lead Free Kids, Inc.
110 E. 31 Street, Box 8595
Minneapolis, MN 5508
612-641-1959
Lead abatement contractor that publishes books and brochures.

The Lead Institute
P.O. Box 591244
San Francisco, CA 94118
800-532-3837
A lead hazard information clearinghouse.
This group provides information and sells
books and different types of lead testing kits.
They help the consumer pick the right lead
kit and guarantees every kit they sell. The
institute tries to be a one-stop place for lead
information and kits as well as an unbiased
resource for testing kits.

National Lead Watch
P.O. Box 2236
Fairfield, IA 52556
800-531-6886 for test kit orders
515-472-8476 for information
This organization offers information on how
to prevent and test for lead poisoning.

Formaldehyde Resources

Individuals/Companies/Organizations

Brochures/Papers/Reports
Designing Healthy Buildings: Paper
Presentations
The American Institute of Architects
1735 New York Avenue NW
Washington, DC 20006

Individuals/Companies/Organizations
Consumer Products Safety Commission
4330 East West Parkway
Bethesda, MD 20207
301-504-0580 (7:30 am to 6:00 pm,
Monday - Friday)

The Formaldehyde Institute
1330 Connecticut Avenue NW, Suite 300
Washington, DC 20036-1072
202-659-0060
The Formaldehyde Institute answers questions and has information on formaldehyde.
Their phone hours are 8:30 am to 5:00 pm.

Chapter 2

Toxics

Chapter 2
CONTENTS

INTRODUCTION

Schools do not usually spring to mind when one thinks about toxics and toxic exposure, but many of the common items used directly by students in normal, everyday activities may contain toxic compounds. In addition, toxics may be present in the school environment that relate not to items directly handled by students, but to the general background environment created by nearby industrial facilities. These may include the use of pesticides, building materials that emit toxics, and toxic cleaning products.

Schools may provide the setting for unnecessary exposure to some potentially dangerous toxic substances. Synthetic compounds have become quite common in our everyday lives over the last few decades. Synthetics are compounds which are man-made, they are often present in automotive products, cleaning agents, cosmetics, hobby products, prepared foods and pesticides. When technological advances enabled scientists to synthesize new compounds, the chemical industry embarked on an aggressive marketing campaign to sell them, whether needed or not. Unfortunately, many of these compounds have proven to have unexpected and detrimental effects on human health and the environment.

What Is a Toxic Substance?

In simplest terms, a toxic is a poison. In this chapter we discuss the many substances created by people that may be harmful to people, other animals and plants. **Toxics** are human-made compounds, and **toxins**, are poisonous substances produced naturally by plants and animals. The differences are important. Most toxins are easily avoidable, are limited or stable in quantity and are biodegradable, whereas most toxics are less easily avoided, are increasing in quantity and saturation in the environment and, worst of all, tend to persist in the environment and in many cases to accumulate in living systems.

How Do We Absorb Toxics?

There are three principal ways we take toxics into our bodies: through the air we breathe, the water and food we ingest and the things that touch our skin.

Routes of Exposure

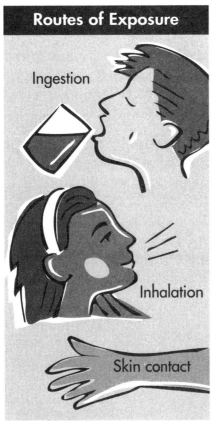

Ingestion

Inhalation

Skin contact

Your Rights

All people have an inalienable **right** to breathe clean air, drink pure water and eat safe food. When someone is responsible, either inadvertently or deliberately, for contaminating these, that person should be held accountable for their action.

Two Types of Exposure

There are two main ways of being affected by toxics. One is by getting a lot of poison in a very short time, known as **acute** exposure. This is what happens when a train carrying dangerous chemicals derails or an oil refinery explodes and people living nearby are exposed to enormous amounts of poison instantly. The other is by being exposed to small amounts of poison over a longer period of time, or **chronic** exposure. This is what occurs when small amounts of chemicals are present in the water we drink, the food we eat and the air we breathe every day. In this chapter we primarily address the problems associated with chronic exposure to toxics and the means of reducing that exposure.

Types of Reactions to Toxics

The compounds mentioned in this chapter have been linked to cancer, birth defects, reproductive disorders, immune system dysfunction, breathing impairment, headache, nausea, allergies and other deleterious health effects. It is beyond the scope of this chapter to list the many common toxics and their health impact. But we highly recommend *Toxics A to Z: A Guide to Everyday Pollution Hazards* for more indepth information. (See the resource section at the end of this chapter.)

Toxics and Risks

We all take risks every day. Some of these risks are directly in our control (assumed risk), and we have the power to decide whether or not to take them. Some people choose nutritious foods and balanced diets to reduce the risk of health problems from a poor diet. Other risks are imposed upon us by the activities of others, over which we may have far less control. For instance if all farmers use pesticides and these pesticide residues end up on the food we think is safe, we are exposed to a risk unknowinglyr. Many have begun to recognize the injustice of these imposed risks and have begun to address them. This is the reason laws are being passed to limit smokers' rights, because secondary smoke has been confirmed as a cause of cancer among nonsmokers.

The goal of this chapter is to promote the notion that it is appropriate for everyone to try to reduce exposure to both assumed and imposed toxic risks.

New information regarding the relative risks associated with certain chemicals emerges every day as the results of continuing studies become available. Quite often, as you research toxics you will inevitably encounter conflicting information. When in doubt, it is usually best to consult knowledgable sources (e.g. poison control center or the EPA).

Toxic Signal Words

If the label has this signal word...   **you know that this is how toxic the product is.**

Category	Signal word required on label	Approximate amount needed to kill an average person
I Highly toxic	**DANGER POISON**	A few drops to one teaspoon
II Moderately toxic	**WARNING**	1 teaspoon to one ounce
III Slightly toxic	**CAUTION**	over one ounce
IV Not toxic	not required	

Source: *Guide to Hazardous Products Around the Home*, Household Hazardous Waste Project, Springfield, MO.

THE SCHOOL SURVEY

The first step in assessing the nature and extent of toxics on your campus is to conduct a thorough audit of every department, with the elimination of toxics in mind. It is important that everyone, from students to faculty and administrators, be involved. For many purposes, such as asbestos abatement and radon testing, it will be necessary to get outside expert help to assist in knowing what to look for and how to best handle the problems that are discovered. For elements of the audit that can be carried out by nonexperts, please see Chapter 1 of this book. Also, the Citizen's Clearinghouse for Hazardous Waste publishes a guide—"Environmental Testing: Where to Look, What to Look For, How to Do It, and What It Means"—that will be very useful in this endeavor. (See the resource section at the end of this chapter.)

By ridding the school environment of toxics and therefore becoming a safer place for everyone, the school becomes a model of healthy living and provides a powerful lesson.

Are Any of These Products Used at Your School?

- ◆ Batteries
- ◆ Gasoline
- ◆ Motor oils
- ◆ Antifreeze
- ◆ Car waxes/polishes
- ◆ Rust removers
- ◆ Metal polishes
- ◆ Weed killers
- ◆ Pest strips
- ◆ Insect/roach spray
- ◆ Synthetic fiber carpet
- ◆ Nail polish remover

- ◆ Particle board
- ◆ Plywood
- ◆ Lead pipes
- ◆ Glues/adhesives
- ◆ Paint thinners
- ◆ Ink pens/markers
- ◆ Ceramic glazes
- ◆ Floor/ceiling tiles
- ◆ Photography chemicals
- ◆ Corrugated paper pipe wrap
- ◆ Paint stripper

- ◆ Bleaches
- ◆ Deodorizer
- ◆ Drain cleaners
- ◆ Rug cleaners
- ◆ Pool cleaners
- ◆ Toner
- ◆ Insulation
- ◆ Paint
- ◆ Cement pipe
- ◆ Spray-applied fireproofing

School Buildings

The school buildings can be a source of toxics. Most of these problems must be addressed by school administrators, along with environmental experts.

◆ **Asbestos** can be found in older buildings in insulation, floor and ceiling tile, cement pipe, corrugated paper pipe wrap and spray-applied fireproofing. State-certified asbestos abatement firms will be required to analyze materials for asbestos content and to remove any friable asbestos discovered. Asbestos is addressed in further detail in Chapter 1.

◆ **Indoor air pollution** is caused by design characteristics, construction materials used and conventional maintenance practices. For example, formaldehyde, a colorless toxic gas that causes upper-respiratory-tract irritation, can be emitted by synthetic fiber carpet, particle board and plywood. If any remodeling of the school is planned, consideration of construction materials that do not present this danger should be included in plans. This is discussed in greater detail in Chapter 1.

◆ **Radon** is the second leading cause of lung cancer after cigarettes. Radon is a radioactive gas produced naturally in the ground in some areas of the country. As the gas migrates upward, it can be trapped in buildings that do not have adequate ventilation. This is particularly a problem in areas with cold winters, when windows are kept shut. Ironically, construction practices that developed in the 1970s to increase energy conservation by making structures nearly airtight, have served to exacerbate the radon problem. Again, this is covered in greater detail in Chapter 1.

◆ **Lead** from the pipes and connectors that carry water to school washrooms and fountains can leach into drinking water. It can also be present in paint, especially in older structures. Lead has long been known to cause severe health problems, including irreversible brain damage and retardation. Health effects of lead are covered in greater depth in Chapter 1.

The School Grounds

The school grounds must also be carefully evaluated:

◆ **Chemical cleaners**. School custodial maintenance crews use toxic disinfectants, bleaches and abrasive cleaners that may pollute the school environment. Chapter 14 and "The Best Solution: Reduction and Elimination" section in this chapter discuss this in greater depth.

◆ **Outdoor air pollution**. Bus and car exhaust, pesticides and particulate matter (dust) are common outdoor school ground air pollutants. Diesel exhaust from buses should be avoided. School administrations need to explore the phasing in of vehicles that use cleaner fuels, such as methanol, compressed natural gas and electricity. Dust may seem at most to be merely a nuisance, but fine particulate matter that can lodge deep in the lungs is increasingly being acknowledged by experts as a significant source of respiratory problems. Children are especially susceptible to the dangers of fine particulate matter because they spend a lot of time

Dose of Pollutant Delivered As a Function of Age in ug/ (min. ppm)

OZONE	(Rest)	Exercise	Exercise	Exercise
Infants (0-1 yr)	7.34	—	—	—
Children (1-5 yr)	7.26	17.24	46.07	74.80
Children and Adolescents (6-17 yr)	6.37	15.14	40.46	65.69
Adults (18 and older)	6.46	15.35	41.04	66.62
NITROGEN DIOXIDE				
Infants (0-1 yr)	3.61	—	—	—
Children (1-5 yr)	3.51	9.89	37.21	60.36
Children and Adolescents 96-17 yr)	3.12	8.79	33.10	53.70
Adults (18 and older)	3.07	8.64	28.57	52.76
SULFUR DIOXIDE				
Infants (0-1 yr)	0.60	—	—	—
Children (1-5 yr)	0.54	1.14	12.83	26.30
Children and Adolescents (6-17 yr)	0.49	1.82	11.42	23.40
Adults (18 and older)	0.48	2.23	11.21	22.96

* Normalized to the equivalent effective dose in a 70 kg adult.

Source: California State University, Fullerton; Fullerton Foundation.

outdoors and tend to inhale more deeply when at play in dusty areas. Dusts are especially hazardous in areas with higher pollutant levels, especially where diesel exhaust is present.

◆ **Playground/recreation areas**. Many schools are located in areas near factories, farms, urban congestion and other sources of potential pollution. Some schools have even been built directly adjacent to or on top of toxic waste dumps! The school setting should be taken into account in a thorough audit, and any serious risks discovered must be addressed. Historical records should be obtained to determine the past uses of the property to discover if children could be exposed to hidden hazards. Relocating the school or petitioning for the closure or relocation of a source of pollution should not be excluded from consideration.

◆ **Pools**. If your school has a pool, many chemicals are present and used for maintenance. The primary chemical used in pool maintenance is chlorine. Chlorine is a toxic gas, but in the diluted quantities used in swimming pools it is relatively safe. However, improperly maintained pools can pose significant health risks. If organic materials, such as leaves and dead insects, are permitted to decompose in a pool, chloroform and choramines are produced. Chronic exposure to chloroform has been associated with cancer and the EPA has designated it a probable human carcinogen. Chloramines are both irritating and odorous. Pools should be maintained by professional pool maintenance service personnel.

Companies employing new alternative maintenance methods have emerged in the past few years. One of the best alternative maintenance methods is the German "DIN" standard, according to which (1) a very large amount of ozone is used to treat the water in the filter system, (2) all ozone is removed before it returns to the pool and (3) a small amount of chlorine is added just before the water returns to the pool. If this system is done correctly, ozone should have the following advantages over chlorine:
- ◆ Is odorless.
- ◆ Does not discolor hair or fade bathing suits.
- ◆ Does not irritate eyes or skin.
- ◆ Makes your water sparkle.
- ◆ Does not harm pool equipment.
- ◆ Eliminates cloudy water.
- ◆ Reduces odor and emissions due to chloramines
- ◆ Makes swimming more enjoyable because the water is more like freshwater.
- ◆ Is more environmentally friendly.

For more information about the DIN standard contact the International Ozone Association 203-348-3542.

AROUND THE CAMPUS

Materials found in auto shops and in art, photography, and science rooms are the most direct and reducible school toxics.

The Science Room

If your school has a chemistry and/or biology lab, it is highly probable that many hazardous and toxic chemicals are stored and used there. Unfortunately, for many of these chemicals there are no known alternatives. Science teachers and students can get the best available information on specific toxic substances, safe-use measures and possible alternatives from the Schools Health and Safety Alliance, listed in the resource section of this chapter. Please turn to Chapter 9, The Science Room, for more information.

All dangerous substances on campus should be minimized and students taught safe and responsible handling procedures A complete audit of chemicals stored on campus should be undertaken with the goal of eliminating as many as possible. For

To the teacher:
When any toxic compounds are deemed necessary for instruction the students should be taught safe handling procedures. It is always better to err on the side of safety; so read labels and follow instructions carefully.

those toxics that cannot be substituted, proper storage, use and disposal are essential. Ask where your school's toxic waste is going. Of course, it is best to recycle any and all toxic chemical compounds whenever possible. It is illegal to dispose of many toxic materials in a municipal landfill. Therefore, it is necessary to verify that all toxic materials leaving the campus for disposal are taken to a licensed toxic waste dump.

The Photography Lab

A photography lab uses a number of hazardous chemicals. Among them are acetic acid, hydroquinone and sodium sulfite. These chemicals are corrosive, toxic and may cause irritation if they come in contact with the skin. No alternatives are known for film developing. Proper care in use, minimization of waste and proper disposal should be practiced.

Because of the possible dangers involved, this may not be an activity for elementary school students.

Teachers in public schools and universities should not find disposal difficult. School districts should have instituted regular waste disposal services. Photography teachers need to coordinate their waste disposal with that of the art, science, maintenance and any other waste-generating departments.

Disposing of small quantities of photography waste down drains is not advised, though it is permissible in some areas, provided local regulations are followed. Never discharge any chemical down a drain that leads to a septic tank; it may leach into groundwater, and then into drinking water. When disposing of small quantities of photographic chemicals down the drain, they should be flushed with a lot of water. It is always best to use all of any unavoidable toxic substance for its intended purpose and in accordance with the instructions on the label.

Chemicals that should be handled by waste disposal companies or household waste programs include selenium toners, bleaches containing sodium or potassium dichromate, ferricyanide or ferrocyanide, zinc-containing chemicals and large amounts of silver-contaminated fixers. Never mix different waste chemicals!

Consult your local environmental protection regulations for disposal of large quantities of photographic chemicals. For black-and-white waste chemicals, contact the manufacturer of your photochemicals for technical information on disposal. For more information see *Overexposure: Health Hazards in Photography*, *Health Hazards for Photographers* and *Artist Beware* in the resource section of this chapter.

The Auto Shop

If your school has an auto shop, it stores, uses and disposes of a wide variety of toxic materials. For many of these substances there are no known alternatives. Therefore, three courses of action must be considered: responsible usage, minimal usage and proper disposal.

Motor Oil

The most common substance used in the auto shop is motor oil. Motor oil is toxic, is flammable and contains heavy metals and hydrocarbons such as benzene. Fortunately, the re-refining of used motor oil has become common. If your school is not recycling motor oil you should first locate recycling centers or service stations in your area that do. Next, make it school policy to buy re-refined or recycled motor oil. Recycled products must be demanded for recycling to thrive. Otherwise you contribute to the tragic waste of our limited natural resources! There is only a finite amount of oil on our planet. Once it is gone, it is gone.

Here are two manufacturers of re-refined motor oil:

> **SOAR** (Save Our American Resources)
> Re-Refined Motor Oil
> Christianson Oil Company
> P.O. Box 17339
> Portland, OR 97217
> 503-286-1673

> **Lyondell Lubricants**
> P.O. Box 4454
> Houston, TX 72710-4454
> 800-447-4572

Although some cities also conduct hazardous waste round-ups in which used oil can be disposed of in a reletively safe manner, we do not recommend disposing of this useful resource. Motor oil never wears out; it just gets dirty. Acids accumulate and eat metal in the engine. That's why we get our oil changed every 3,000 miles. As far as its lubricating properties go it is stable, but it must be cleaned/re-refined. There's no good reason to throw out used motor oil because there's always a use for it. Ninety percent of used motor oil goes into fuel blending, which is then generated into electricity.

Alternatives: Currently, there are no practical alternatives to petroleum-based oil. However, research is being conducted to develop jojoba and other vegetable-based motor oils. In addition, the development of alternative-fuel vehicles that do not utilize internal combustion engines, such as electric vehicles, will eventually reduce the need for motor oil.

If you pour hazardous waste in a storm drain, a ditch or a hole in the ground, there is a good chance the waste will end up in a nearby stream, river, lake or ocean.

"In the U.S. alone, over 1 million gallons of used motor oil are released into the environment every day, not including commercial and industrial sources. This amount is equivalent to over 41 Exxon Valdez spills per year."

Mark Adams, Chairman, Conservation, Recycling and Disposal Committee, the Society of Tribologists and Lubrication Engineers, Birch Run, MI, personal communication, September 1, 1989.

Antifreeze/Coolant

Antifreeze/coolant is ethylene glycol, which is a dangerous poison. Because of its sweet taste, this substance can be particularly hazardous to young children and pets. Consequently, both should not be in areas where ethylene glycol is stored and used. Limited recycling of antifreeze is being established in some areas. Check with local service stations for information. Also, check with your city, county or state agencies for information on community hazardous waste round-ups.

Alternatives: Plain water can be used, but rust in the cooling system can develop over time. Currently, there are no practical alternatives for antifreeze. However, substitutes containing less toxic propylene glycol are being developed. Once again, ask your supplier.

Transmission Fluid

Transmission fluid is an oil that is flammable, is toxic and contains hydrocarbons. It can be recycled. It is not recommended that this be recycled along with used motor oil because of its chlorine content, which poses air pollution problems. Transmission fluid can be recycled separately and reused. Once again, check with local service stations for information.

Alternatives: There are no known alternatives for transmission fluid.

Brake Fluids

Brake fluid contains ethylene glycol and heavy metals; it is flammable and toxic. However, brake fluid is not changed very frequently. When there's a line failure it is changed; otherwise mechanics don't usually drain whole systems and replace the fluid. Brake fluids are recyclable, although this recycling is not practiced on a large scale. Check with your local service stations.

Alternatives: There are no known alternatives for brake fluid.

Batteries
Batteries contain lead and highly corrosive, toxic sulfuric acid. Batteries should never be disposed of in a dumpster. They should be properly maintained to extend their useful life for as long as possible. It is quite common to exchange old batteries for new ones, but it is not always easy to find reconditioned batteries. If your school purchases batteries, every effort should be made to buy reconditioned ones.

Many auto parts stores, service stations, large recycling centers and auto repair shops accept old car batteries for reconditioning or proper disposal, and in some cases they give discounts for new batteries in exchange. Check in your local area.

To complete the cycle it is important to demand reconditioned batteries from your local suppliers.

Alternatives: There are no alternatives for batteries.

The Art Room
Many easily substituted toxics can be found in the art room, where the potential for acute poisoning is considerable. It is imperative that alternatives be used. This subject is addressed in more detail in Chapter 10.

Battery Recycling: Better Lead Than Dead

"Car owners currently dump about 20 million dead batteries a year, each containing about 18 pounds of lead. About 60 percent of all the lead that ends up in landfills or incinerators comes from car batteries."

"About 85 percent of car batteries are now recycled, according to Jonathan Kimmelman of the Natural Resources Defense Council. In about three dozen states the law mandates this practice, though there is still no federal statute forcing anyone to recycle auto batteries. In New York, for example, car owners pay a deposit on batteries, which they collect when they turn them in. The lead in the plates is then salvaged and reused."

Steve Nadis and James J. MacKenzie, *Car Trouble* (Boston, MA: Beacon Press, 1993), p. 77.

Paints
Many paints contain volatile organic compounds (VOCs), oils and toxic pigmentation ingredients. Nontoxic water-based paints are available for most purposes and should be used whenever possible.

Inks, Pens and Markers

Many ink pens and markers contain volatile and toxic substances. Among them are acetone, cresol, ethanol, phenol, toluene and xylene. It is unhealthy to breathe these substances; this is especially true for small children. Some children are attracted by the scent of markers and increase their exposure by unnecessarily inhaling the fumes.

> *Ink use may seem insignificant, but the quantities add up. U.S. daily newspapers alone use 326 million pounds of ink every year.*
>
> Scott McClinton, American Newspaper Publishers Association, Reston, VA, personal communication, January 23, 1989.

Fortunately, it is easy to substitute readily available water-based ink pens and markers for the potentially hazardous ones. Demand them from your suppliers.

Correction Fluids

Correction fluids may contain cresol, ethanol, trichloroethylene and naphthalene, all of which are toxic chemicals that can be fatal in high enough doses. As a result of public demand in the late 1980s, the maker of one of the most popular brands of correction fluid reformulated its product to eliminate these harmful substances.

Make sure that the correction fluid you buy is the reformulated, nontoxic product. It should be labeled as such. If you only have old correction fluid, it should be used carefully in a well-ventilated area. Avoid inhaling its vapors or coming into contact with it. Correction fluids should be disposed of at a toxics round-up dropoff.

Glues and Adhesives

Adhesives and glues may contain volatile chemicals, such as naphthalene, phenol, ethanol, vinyl chloride, formaldehyde, acrylonitrile and epoxy. Immediately after they are opened and as they dry, toxic vapors are released. The most likely glues to contain harmful substances are the fast-drying glues, model glues and "superglues."

Hand Protection

The hand and fingers are most exposed to hazardous products. To protect your hands, wear the appropriate glove for the product you are using.

Nontoxic pastes and glues are readily available; there is no need to expose students unnecessarily to the risks of toxic adhesives. Generally, the safest are the white and yellow wood glues, which are very versatile and are effective on virtually any porous or semiporous surface. Use paper clips, staples or string, if possible, as an alternative.

Ceramic Glazes

The function of a glaze in ceramics may be to waterproof, change color or texture, or generally enhance the appearance of the ware. Whether glazes are low fire, middle range or high fire determines the type, quantity and strength of toxic ingredients exposure. These ingredients include the following toxic elements:

- Lead
- Cadmium
- Antimony
- Arsenic
- Barium
- Lithium

Toxic colorants include:

- Uranium
- Chromium
- Cobalt
- Manganese
- Nickel
- Vanadium

Some luster glazes also contain highly toxic mercury and arsenic and such highly toxic solvents as chloroform and aromatic hydrocarbons.

Sprays

Though aerosol sprays have not contained ozone-layer-damaging CFCs for more than 10 years, they do contain VOCs as propellants. VOCs can be an irritant at ground level and are precursors of photochemical smog. In addition, chronic exposure to some VOCs can increase the risk of cancer. VOC levels should always be labeled. If they are not don't purchase the product. When they are available, pump-type sprays are the responsible choice. If they are unavailable, the supplier needs to hear your concern/demand.

The Cafeteria

Many aspects of the food service industry are toxics intensive. Detergents, degreasers and abrasive or caustic chemicals are used in large quantities in cleaning. Pesticides and poisons are used frequently to control ants, roaches, rodents and other sources of infectious diseases. Herbicide and pesticide residues can be found on many nonorganically grown fruits and vegetables, which should be washed before being eaten. Hormones and other drugs can be found in meat, cheese and  other animal products. The USDA and FDA do not test for many of the potentially detrimental chemicals that have been found in commercially provided foods. Chapters 3, 4 and 14 offer further insight into these problems and their solutions. It is up to each school administration to review current practices and make changes.

Miscellaneous

Toxic materials are stored or used elsewhere around the school. It is up to you to be alert and thorough in your school environmental audit. This is of urgent concern when pertaining to toxics, which in many cases can be hidden.

Center for Teaching
The Westminster Schools

Photocopying Machines

Photocopying machines usually use a dry toner that must be regularly replenished. Some also require a liquid dispersant. Both are toxic and should be handled only by adults. See the list of resources at the end of this chapter for recycling toner cartridges.

Soy Ink

Nontoxic soy ink should be demanded as an alternative to the petroleum-based conventional inks for all school printing needs. Soy ink does not smudge as badly as petroleum ink and is safer for the people who run the presses. When paper printed with soy ink is recycled, the deinking process creates nontoxic sludge, unlike the toxic sludge that is created when deinking paper printed with conventional petroleum-based inks.

SCHOOL MAINTENANCE

School maintenance is discussed in greater detail in Chapter 14. Refer to that chapter for more information and resources for consumer products.

Regular Custodial Care

Industrial cleaning products used by the janitorial staff may be among the most hazardous materials used in the school and may cause toxic and allergic reactions.

In the past few years many companies have emerged that are manufacturing cleaning products that are safer for both the environment and the person using the product. Urge your supplier to carry them.

Abrasive Cleaners

Abrasive cleaners may contain trisodium phosphate, ammonia and ethanol. Baking soda can be used as an alternative.

Disinfectants

Disinfectants may contain diethylene or methylene glycol, sodium hypochlorite (bleach) and phenol. Diluted borax can be used as a safer alternative. A borax cleaner can be made with one-half cup of borax, one-quarter cup of vinegar and 2 gallons of hot water. Use this to mop or wipe surfaces. Also, a borax spray can be made with 1 teaspoon of borax, 3 tablespoons of vinegar and 2 cups of very hot tapwater in a spray bottle.

Polishes

Polishes may contain diethylene glycol, petroleum distillates and nitrobenzene. Vegetable oils may be used as a substitute. Gymnasium floors do require special attention.

A wood floor wax can be made with a beeswax/carnauba wax/linseed oil combination. (See *Clean & Green: The Complete Guide to Nontoxic and Environmentally Safe Housekeeping* by Annie Berthold-Bond.) Washing the floor with club soda or seltzer and then polishing with a dry, clean cloth also works.

Bleach

Bleach is corrosive and toxic. Fortunately, there are many substitutes for its use in school cleaning. To make a Fantastik type of cleaner for a 16-oz. spray bottle combine:

> 1 tsp. borax
> 1/2 tsp. washing soda
> 2 tbsp. vinegar or lemon juice
> 1/4 to 1/2 tsp. vegetable-oil-based liquid soap
> 2 cups very hot tapwater

Never mix bleach with ammonia. This releases toxic chloramine gas.

Ammonia

Ammonia is corrosive and toxic. A vinegar, water and salt solution can be used for many applications where ammonia-based cleaners are used. Borax with a squeeze of lemon or splash of vinegar is great for cutting grease.

Pesticide and Herbicide Use

All pesticides are poisons, formulated to kill. They interfere with biological systems, posing a threat to all, especially the young. In some cases schools have schedules for routine spraying, whether or not an inspection has confirmed the need for it. The result is unnecessary exposure of students and teachers to dangerous chemicals.

Schools need to provide examples to both the students and the rest of the community on the safest ways possible to control pest problems. Health reasons alone should be compelling enough for all schools to commit to eliminating pesticides by providing safer alternatives.

During the 1980s approximately 100 million pounds of pesticides were applied in urban areas of California each year, according to the Department of Food and Agriculture. Schools use significant amounts of pesticides in urban areas. Many continue to use hazardous pesticides and herbicides to control insect and weed problems on school grounds and in classrooms and cafeterias to control pests and limit exposure to infectious diseases.

An enlightened solution to the "pest" problem is to adopt the concept of "Integrated Pest Management" (IPM). IPM is a comprehensive strategy for dealing with a problem organism by knowing its ecology. Some of the basic concepts include:

◆ Knowing what an organism needs to survive and removing those essentials.

◆ Encouraging or introducing natural enemies.

◆ Introducing sterilized populations of the pest so that they breed themselves out of existence.

◆ Using careful and selective chemical controls sparingly and at a critical point in the pest's breeding cycle to maximize effectiveness.

This is discussed in further detail in Chapter 3. In addition, see the resources section in this chapter.

We will discuss next some common pests and toxic pesticides.

Termites

Methyl bromide and Dursban are two chemicals commonly used on termites. Methyl bromide is highly acutely toxic and should only be used by trained applicators. Dursban is an organophosphate compound. Organophosphates attack the nervous systems of animals, including humans.

Three companies that kill termites with nontoxic methods are:

Tallon Termite and Pest Control
1949 E. Market Street
Long Beach, CA 90805
800-779-2653

Ecola Services
1209 Isabel Street
Burbank, CA 91506
818-842-0242

N.E.E.D.S.
527 Charles Avenue, Suite 12A
Syracuse, NY 13209
800-634-1380

Ants and Roaches

No amount of chemical spraying will solve a chronic ant/roach infestation permanently. The only complete solution is to deprive these pests of what has attracted them to the location. Stepping up efforts to keep problem areas clean and free of even the tiniest food particles is essential.

The next step, sealing cracks and small holes that serve as entryways, can be effective. With ants, another preventative solution is to wipe down counters and their trails with a water/vinegar solution.

A win/win method that works with ants when outdoor space is sufficient so that their presence does not pose a problem is to take the first three steps just mentioned and then to sprinkle something enticing (e.g., stale cookie or cake crumbs) where you don't mind ants. They will then have a free feast and far less incentive to enter your structure.

A natural alternative to synthetic petrochemical insecticides is pyrethrum powder (made from 100 percent natural chrysanthemum flowers). Once the infested area is clean, sprinkling the powder around places of entry and heavily traveled areas is an effective nontoxic method. The ants get the powder on them and die or carry it back to their nest.

The best prevention for roaches and ants is to caulk cracks and crevices, clean out storage areas, eliminate food sources and fix water leaks. Besides food, roaches like nonfood items such as soap and glue. They also like warm, dark, enclosed places.

Least toxic control for roaches is boric acid (in nonfood areas). Least toxic control for ants is to mop them up and drown them. Silica aerogel or diatomaceous earth are desiccating dusts that kill insects on contact. Boric acid also works, as do sticky barriers.

Peppermint oil, cayenne pepper/water solutions and other strong herbs and spices can kill ants instantly or discourage them from infesting a treated area.

When spraying cannot be avoided, it should be done by professionals only on a day when no students or faculty are present and when they will not return for at least 48 hours.

Weeds

The best way to deal with weeds is to prevent them. Start with healthy plants. Selecting plants suited to the local climate and soil makes them better able to compete with weeds. Least toxic weed control is manual removal methods, such as hoeing, hand pulling and cultivating, when the soil is moist and easy to work with. Remove weeds before they flower and reseed for another season.

Herbicides do not provide a permanent solution to weed problems. Roundup and 2,4-D are two chemicals commonly used for weed control. 2,4-D, also known as Weed-B Gone and Lawn-Keep, has been linked to cancer and birth defects, but research results have remained inconclusive. Roundup is a trade name for the chemical glyphosate. It is generally considered safe when used according to instructions and is effective against a wide variety of weeds. The most commonly available herbicide on the market, Roundup is linked to more skin, eye and internal injuries than result from any of the 200 pesticides used in California. These injuries, however, all result from improper handling.

More good ideas for nontoxic prevention methods and solutions are discussed in Chapters 3 and 5.

THE BEST SOLUTION: REDUCTION AND ELIMINATION

The long-practiced strategy of pollution *control* and *management* has not resolved the health and environmental risks posed by toxic materials. Our research and common sense tell us that we must shift away from toxic compounds in our daily lives. When industrial leaders are questioned as to why they manufacture and sell potentially harmful products, they often insist that they are only providing what the public is demanding. It is up to each individual—student, teacher, school administrator and custodian—to demand that environmentally benign and nonhazardous materials be substituted for the harmful ones we've been using.

Toxic Chemicals and the Food Chain

Today traces of toxics are found in even the most remote corners of the world. These chemicals get into the water, soil and air and contaminate our food sources. Toxics used on school grounds pollute the local environment. We eat, breathe and drink these pollutants.

RESOURCES

Art Hazards Information Center

For questions relating to hazards in the arts, crafts and theater programs.
Center for Occupational Hazards
212-777-0062

National Pesticides Telecommunications Network

Provides information about pesticides safety procedures and health effects.
Texas Tech University Health Sciences Center
800-858-7378

Toxics Information Hotline

For information from computer databases on toxics. Can also assist in responding to hazardous materials emergencies.
Tox-Center, Northridge, CA
800-682-9000 (in California)
800-227-6476 (outside California)

Toxic Substance Control, Assistance Information Service

Provides information on federal toxics regulations and can refer questions to the appropriate EPA department.
202-554-1404

U.S. Consumer Product Safety Commission Hotline

Information on health effects and safety of consumer products.
800-638-2772

U.S. EPA Community Right to Know Hotline

For information regarding emissions from industrial facilities near a school.
800-535-0202

U.S. EPA Headquarters

EPA Headquarters
401 M Street SW
Washington, DC 20460
Public Information Center: 202-260-7751

U.S. EPA Safe Drinking Water Hotline

Information on drinking water safety.
800-426-4791

Brochures/Papers/Reports

Creating a Healthy World: 101 Practical Tips for Home and Work, Everyday Chemicals

Beth Richman and Susan Hassol
Windstar Earth Pulse Handbook
2317 Snowmass Creek Road
Snowmass, CO 81654
800-669-4777

Environmental Testing: Where to Look, What to Look for, How to Do It, What it Means

Citizens Clearinghouse for Hazardous Waste
P.O. Box 6806
Falls Church, VA 22040
703-237-2249

Glossary of Environmental Health Terms and Guide to Reference Materials

New York State Department of Health
2 University Place
Albany, NY 12203-3399
518-474-2121

Household Hazardous Waste Wheel
A handy at-a-glance reference to many common chemicals, their properties and possible alternatives.
Chemical Waste Management, Inc.
Technical Services Division
4227 Technology Drive
Fremont, CA 94538
510-651-2964

How Green Is My Home?
Household Tips for Saving the Planet
Michael Belliveau, Citizens for a Better Environment
Published by Mother Jones Magazine
1663 Mission Street
San Francisco, CA 94103
415-357-0509

An Introduction to Toxic
Substances
New York State Department of Health
2 University Place
Albany, NY 12203
518-474-2121

Think Before You Spray!
Citizens for a Better Environment
501 Second Street, Suite 305
San Francisco, CA 94701
415-543-8591

The Toxics Directory:
References and Resources
on the Health Effects of Toxic
Substances
Hazard Identification and Risk Assessment Branch
CA Department of Health Services
2151 Berkeley Way
Berkeley, CA 94704
510-540-3063

Who to Contact for Help and
Information About Environmental
Health
New York State Department of Health
2 University Place
Albany, NY 12203
518-474-2121

Books

Art Hardware
Steven L. Saitzyk
Watson-Guptill, 1987
1515 Broadway
New York, NY 10036

Art Terms and Techniques
Ralph Mayer
HarperCollins, 1969
10 East 53rd Street
New York, NY 10022

Artist Beware
Michael McCann
Lyons and Burford Publishers, 1992
31 West 21 Street
New York, NY 10010

Artist's Complete Health and Safety
Guide
Monona Rossol
Allworth Press, 1990
10 East 23rd Street
New York, NY 10010

Basic Guide to Pesticides
Shirley Briggs
Taylor and Francis, 1992
1101 Vermont Avenue NW, Suite. 200
Washington, DC 20005

The Bhopal Syndrome: Where Will It Happen Next?
David Weir
Earthscan Publications Limited, 1988
3 Endsleigh Street
London, England WC1H 0DD

A Bitter Fog
Carol Van Strum
Sierra Club Books, 1983
730 Polk Street
San Francisco, CA 94109

The Bug Book
Helen and John Philbrick
Storey Communications, 1974
Schoolhouse Road
Pownal, VT 05261

Chemical Deception
Marc Lappe
Sierra Club Books, 1991
730 Polk Street
San Francisco, CA 94109

Chemical Exposure and Human Health
Cynthia Wilson
McFarland and Company, Inc. 1993
P.O. Box 611
Jefferson, NC 28640

Circle of Poison
David Weir and Mark Schapiro
Institute for Food and Development Policy, 1981
1885 Mission Street
San Francisco, CA 94188

Clean & Green: The Complete Guide to Nontoxic and Environmentally Safe Housekeeping
Annie Berthold-Bond
Ceres Press, 1990
P.O. Box 87
Woodstock, NY 12498

Common-Sense Pest Control
William Olkowski et al.
Taunton Press, 1991
63 South Main Street, Box 5506
Newtown, CT 06740-5506

Consumer's Dictionary of Household, Yard and Office Chemicals
Ruth Winter
Crown, 1992
201 East 50th Street
New York, NY 10022

Environmental Hazards: Toxic Waste and Hazardous Material
E. Willard Miller
National Conference of State Legislatures, 1991
1560 Broadway, Suite 700
Denver, CO 80202

A Growing Problem: Pesticides in the Third World
David Bull
Institute for Food and Development Policy, 1982
1885 Mission Street
San Francisco, CA 94188

Guide to Hazardous Products Around the Home
Sondra Goodman et al.
Household Hazardous Waste Project, 1989
1031 E. Battlefield, Suite 214
Springfield, MO 65807

Hazardous Substances Resource Guide
Richard Pohanish
Gale Research, 1992
835 Penobscot Building
Detroit, MI 48226-4094

Health Hazards for Photographers
Siegfried and Wolfgang Rempel
Lyons & Burford, 1992
31 West 21 Street
New York, NY 10010

Health Hazards Manual for Artists
Michael Mccann
Lyons and Burford, 1985
31 West 21 Street
New York, NY 10010

High Tech Holocaust
James Bellini
Sierra Club, 1986
730 Polk Street
San Francisco, CA 94109

**In Our Backyard:
A Guide to Understanding
Pollution and Its Effects**
Travis Wagner
Van Nostrand Reinhold, 1994
115 Fifth Avenue
New York, NY 10003

In the Wake of the Exxon Valdez
Art Davidson
Sierra Club, 1990
730 Polk Street
San Francisco, CA 94109 ·

Least Toxic Home Pest Control
Dan Stein
Hulogosi Communications, 1991
P.O. Box 1188
Eugene, OR 97440

The Nontoxic Home
Debra Lynn Dadd
Tarcher, 1986
5858 Wilshire Boulevard, Suite 200
Los Angeles, CA 90036

The Nontoxic Home and Office
Debra Lynn Dadd
Tarcher, 1992
5858 Wilshire Boulevard, Suite 200
Los Angeles, CA 90036

Nontoxic and Natural
Debra Lynn Dadd
Tarcher, 1984
5858 Wilshire Boulevard, Suite 200
Los Angeles, CA 90036

Nontoxic, Natural and Earthwise
Debra Lynn Dadd
Tarcher, 1986
5858 Wilshire Boulevard, Suite 200
Los Angeles, CA 90036

**Overexposure: Health Hazards in
Photography**
Susan D. Shaw and Monona Rossol
Allworth Press, 1991
10 East 23rd Street
New York, NY 10010

Pesticide Alert
Lawrie Mott and Karen Snyder
Sierra Club, 1987
730 Polk Street
San Francisco, CA 94109

Poisoning Our Children
Nancy Sokol Green
Noble Press, 1991
213 West Insititute Place, Suite 508
Chicago, IL 60610

Prosperity Without Pollution
Joel Hirschhorn and Kristen Oldenburg
Van Nostrand Reinhold, 1992
115 Fifth Avenue
New York, NY 10003

Radiation and Human Health
John W. Gofman
Sierra Club Books, 1981
730 Polk Street
San Francisco, CA 94109

Radon: The Invisible Threat
Michael Lafavore
Rodale, 1987
33 East Minor Street
Emmaus, PA 18098

Recognition and Management of Pesticide Poisonings
Donald P. Morgan, M.D., Ph.D.
Superintendent of Documents, 1989
U.S. Government Printing Office
Washington, DC 20402

Tackling Toxics in Everyday Products: A Directory of Organizations
Nancy Lilienthal et al.
Inform, Inc., 1992
381 Park Avenue South
New York, NY 10016

Toxics A to Z: A Guide to Everyday Pollution Hazards
John Harte et. al.
University of California Press, 1991
Berkeley, CA 94720

Your Home, Your Health and Well-being
David Rousseau et. al.
Ten Speed Press, 1988
P.O. Box 7123
Berkeley, CA 94707

Individuals/Companies/ Organizations

Bio-Integral Resource Center (B.I.R.C.)
P.O. Box 7414
Berkeley, CA 94707
510-524-2567
Membership organization that provides practical, up-to-date information on the least toxic methods of pest control.

International Ozone Association
31 Strawberry Hill Avenue
Stamford, CT 06902
203-348-3542
Information on the German "DIN" standards of using ozone in pools.

The Office of Health Hazard Assessment
2151 Berkeley Way
Berkeley, CA 94704
510-540-3063
They will connect you with a toxicologist who can answer questions about the health hazards of chemicals

Schools Health and Safety Alliance
Gayle Essary
P.O. Box 750471
Forest Hills, NY 11375-0471
718-997-7387
Information on toxic substances, safe-use measures and possible alternatives.

Chapter 3

Pesticides

Chapter 3
CONTENTS

INTRODUCTION

Pesticides are chemicals intended to kill plant, fungal and animal pests. **It is estimated that each year in the United States more than 1 billion pounds of pesticides are used, not including wood preservatives and disinfectants.** Pesticides are used in the production of our food, animal feed and fibers, such as cotton. In addition, they are used in homes and schools; on lawns; in pools; in forests; along roadsides; in restaurants, grocery stores and hospitals; on our pets; and more.[1]

Wherever we sleep, work or play, pesticides are in the air we breathe, the food we eat and the water we drink. It may surprise you to know that pesticide residues are found in the body tissues of nearly every living creature, even those in the remotest corners of the earth. Pesticides have been known to travel hundreds of miles by air and water. Scientists have tracked "toxic winds" that carried the pesticide toxaphene 900 miles from Mississippi cotton fields to Lake Superior, where it still persists in sediments on the bottom of the lake.[2] One 1991 study found pesticides in rain samples in all 23 Midwestern states monitored.[3] Researchers have also learned that toxic fogs containing surprisingly high concentrations of pesticides form over some parts of the country.[4] Although very little monitoring has been

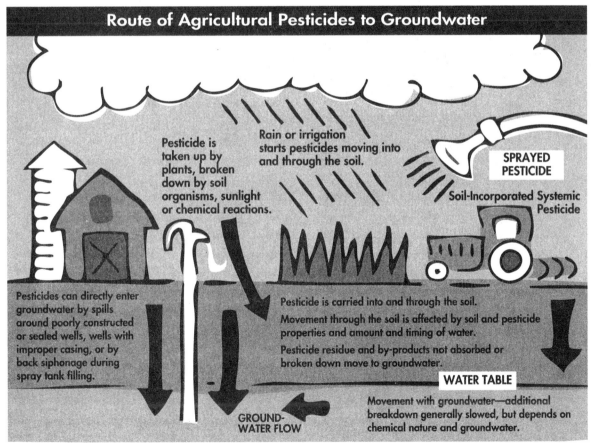

Route of Agricultural Pesticides to Groundwater

Pesticide is taken up by plants, broken down by soil organisms, sunlight or chemical reactions.

Rain or irrigation starts pesticides moving into and through the soil.

SPRAYED PESTICIDE

Soil-Incorporated Systemic Pesticide

Pesticides can directly enter groundwater by spills around poorly constructed or sealed wells, wells with improper casing, or by back siphonage during spray tank filling.

Pesticide is carried into and through the soil.

Movement through the soil is affected by soil and pesticide properties and amount and timing of water.

Pesticide residue and by-products not absorbed or broken down move to groundwater.

WATER TABLE

GROUND-WATER FLOW

Movement with groundwater—additional breakdown generally slowed, but depends on chemical nature and groundwater.

Source: Minnesota Department of Health/Minnesota Department of Agriculture, *Pesticides and Groundwater: A Health Concern for the Midwest*, Minneapolis, 1986.

done, the Environmental Protection Agency (EPA) reported that as of 1988, 74 different pesticides had been found contaminating the groundwater of 38 states. Over 15 million Americans drink water from pesticide-contaminated wells.[5]

Pesticides cause a range of acute and chronic health effects. An estimated 138,000 pesticide-related poisonings were reported to the nation's Poison Control Centers in 1992, 65 percent of those involved children.[6] According to the EPA, 8 of the 18 most commonly used pesticides cause cancer in laboratory animals. About 375 million pounds of just those 8 cancer-causing pesticides are estimated to be used annually in the United States.[7] In the "Are Pesticides Safe?" section of this chapter we give some general background information about the health risks of pesticides, with emphasis on the particular risks to children. This is followed by more specific information about some selected pesticides commonly used in schools.

The use of dangerous pesticides and the environmental, health and safety factors that affect the well-being of our children must be addressed. In Chapter 4, which deals with nutrition, we discuss the use of pesticides on food crops and the steps each person can take to minimize exposure. Chapter 1 provides suggestions for avoiding building materials that are heavily treated with toxic preservatives. Wood preservatives are regulated as pesticides and represent the largest single class of pesticides by volume used. In Chapter 14 we address toxic and nontoxic cleaning products, including disinfectants, which are also registered pesticides. Chapter 5 provides a plan for growing food, on campus, that is free of poisonous chemicals.

In this chapter we will address other pesticides and their risks, as well as ways to avoid using them to control unwanted plants and insects. By using least-toxic alternatives, we can all participate in stemming the tide of pesticide destruction to human life, animal life, wildlife, our water and air supply and the environment.

While reading this chapter it is important to keep in mind that children are particularly sensitive to the harmful effects of pesticides. They consume more food, more water and more oxygen per pound than adults. Also, their immune and nervous systems are still developing and are therefore more vulnerable than those of adults.

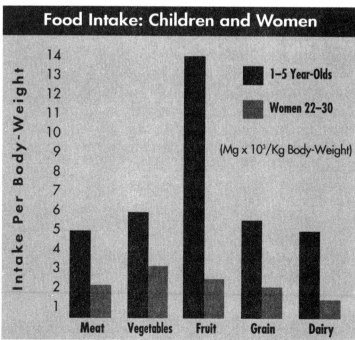

Source: Mothers and Others for a Livable Planet, *For Our Kid's Sake*, New York, NY, 1989.

CATEGORIES OF PESTICIDES

Pesticides fall into roughly five categories.

1. **Insecticides:** Preparations used for killing insects.
2. **Herbicides:** Preparations used for killing plants, especially weeds.
3. **Fungicides:** Preparations for destroying fungi, such as molds and mildew.
4. **Termiticides**: Preparations for killing termites.
5. **Rodenticides:** Preparations for killing rodents.

WHY SHOULD WE BE CONCERNED ABOUT PESTICIDES?

Toxic chemicals are being used on school grounds, parking lots, tracks and play areas and in cafeterias, classrooms, gymnasiums and restrooms. Pesticides are sometimes applied by untrained personnel or applied as a matter of routine, regardless of whether pests are present. Their use on school grounds is of grave concern because pesticides are:

1. **Often incompletely tested for health effects.** Required health effects studies had been completed for only 59 of 612 eligible groups of active chemical ingredients in pesticides, as of April 1994.[8] These figures continue to change as new tests are submitted or reviewed by the EPA. According to a study done by the Consumers Union in 1987, of 50 active ingredients in pesticides used around the home

   ◆ 66 percent had been inadequately tested to determine whether they would cause cancer.
   ◆ 72 percent had been inadequately tested for their ability to cause genetic mutations.
   ◆ 62 percent had been inadequately tested for their ability to cause birth defects.
   ◆ 64 percent had been inadequately tested for their adverse effects on reproduction.
   ◆ 98 percent had been inadequately tested for their neurobehavioral effects. It will probably be long after the year 2000 before currently required testing is completed for the health and environmental effects of pesticides now in use.[9]

2. **Not adequately tested for their effects on children.** According to a 1993 National Academy of Sciences report, current testing does not adequately address the toxicity and metabolism of pesticides in young animals or the effects of exposure during early developmental stages.

In light of this information, the following chart demonstrates why there are serious concerns about children's safety.

Pesticide Residues Detected on Fruits and Vegetables Heavily Consumed by Young Children

FDA 1990 — 1992

Food	Number of Samples	Number with One or More Pesticides Detected	Percent with One or More Pesticides Detected	Number of Different Pesticides Detected
Apples	1,044	673	64	34
Bananas	478	210	44	14
Blackberries	136	79	58	19
Blueberries	252	89	35	18
Broccoli	641	118	18	26
Cantaloupes	781	414	53	33
Carrots	345	143	41	24
Cauliflower	419	29	7	11
Celery	393	290	74	16
Cherries	455	291	64	23
Grapes	970	361	37	30
Green Beans	389	185	48	26
Lettuce	2,402	1,204	50	29
Oranges	502	354	71	20
Peaches	513	389	76	28
Pears	550	311	57	26
Peas	752	249	33	29
Potatoes	765	307	40	31
Raspberries	302	189	63	26
Spinach	388	218	56	24
Strawberries	988	720	73	38
Tomatoes	1,164	543	47	42
Total	**14,629**	**7,366**	**50**	**108**

Source: Environmental Working Group, *Pesticides in Children's Food*, Washington, DC, 1992.

3. Not tested for synergistic or immune system effects. Synergism occurs when different substances in combination have a greater total effect than the sum of their individual effects. Very little is known about the effects of pesticides in combination with other pesticides or in combination with other substances such as prescription drugs. EPA testing also does not require that pesticides be tested for potential effects on the immune system.

4. Often made up of unknown, yet toxic, "inert" ingredients, in addition to the active ingredients. Active ingredients are the ones designed to kill the target pest. Inerts are any other ingredients used in the pesticide, including solvents, preservatives, emulsifiers and surfactants, usually to aid with solubility or penetration. Most chronic toxicity testing required for EPA registration is done on the active ingredients only.

In addition to the human health risks of pesticide use, there are other problems. First of all, pesticides don't just kill pests; they also kill beneficial insects needed for pollinating flowers and for preying on harmful insects. Second, insect populations may develop a resistance to pesticides after repeated exposure, resulting in the need for more frequent use of pesticides and for use of more toxic compounds. Cornell University researchers cite a near doubling of crop losses due to insects during the last 40 years, despite a more than ten-fold increase in the amount and toxicity of synthetic insecticides used.

Beneficial Insects and the Pests They Control

Damsel Bugs control aphids, leaf hoppers, mites, psyllids

Ladybug controls aphids, aphid larvae, rootworms, weevils

Stingless Parasitic Wasp controls aphids, gypsy moths, caterpillars, cutworms

Green Lacewing controls aphids, white flies

Spiders control fleas, treehoppers, flies, carrot weevils

Toads/Frogs control flying insects, snails, slugs

Big-eyed Bugs control insect eggs, leaf hoppers, small caterpillars, Mexican bean beetles

Assassin Bugs control Colorado potato beetle, leaf hoppers, mites, psyllids

Syrphid Fly controls plant lice (aphids)

Birds/Bats control grubs, caterpillars, mosquitoes, flying insects

Source: *Handle with Care*, 1994 Copyright Terrene Institute, Washington, DC.

Other factors must be taken into account when discussing our dependence on pesticides. Only recently have environmental and social costs been considered.

The Pesticide Price Tag

It is impossible to put an exact dollar value on human life lost or wildlife destroyed because of pesticide poisoning. But for the past several years David Pimentel, a Cornell University entomologist, has taken on the monumental task of calculating the indirect or hidden costs of pesticide use — costs that don't get taken into account in the usual cost/benefit analyses conducted by industry or government regulators. In 1992 Pimentel estimated that the environmental and social costs from pesticides in the U.S. total more than $8 billion each year:

Public health impacts	$ 787,000,000
Domestic animal deaths and contamination	30,000,000
Loss of natural enemies	520,000,000
Cost of pesticide resistance	1,400,000,000
Honeybee and pollination losses	320,000,000
Crop losses	942,000,000
Fishery losses	24,000,000
Bird losses	2,100,000,000
Groundwater contamination	1,800,000,000
Government regulations to prevent damage	200,000,000
Total	**$8,123,000,000**

Source: Anne Witt Garland with Mothers & Others for a Livable Planet, *The Way We Grow: Good Sense Souloutions for Protecting Our Families from Pesticides in Food* (New York: Berkley Publishing Group, 1993), p. 2.

PESTICIDES SAFETY

According to the EPA, registered pesticides should not be characterized as safe even when applied according to the product label. EPA regulations prohibit pesticide manufacturers and distributors from making claims that their products are "safe," "nontoxic to humans and pets," "EPA-approved" or "environmentally friendly." The EPA considers these claims to be false or misleading to consumers. As the agency has stated, no pesticide is safe, because pesticides are by their very nature designed to be biologically active and kill various kinds of organisms.

Pesticides are registered on a risk/benefit basis. This means that even if there is evidence that a pesticide poses risks to human or animal health, it will still be registered if the EPA determines that the economic, social or environmental benefits of its use outweigh that risk. EPA registration definitely does not mean that a pesticide is safe. In addition, some pesticides may remain in stores (or on school warehouse shelves) long after they have been found by the EPA to pose unacceptable risks to health and safety or the environment.

Health Risks of Pesticides

We know that children make up a disproportionately large share of the acute poisonings reported annually to the nation's Poison Control Centers. We also know that by virtue of their life-styles and playing habits, children often face greater pesticide exposure risks than adults. They roll on the grass, hide or play in shrubbery and sometimes even put dirt in their mouths. Thus, they may absorb pesticides through inhalation, ingestion or contact with the skin. Children consume more food, more water and more oxygen per pound than adults, and thus receive a higher dose of pesticide residues per unit of body weight.

As pointed out earlier in this chapter, there are many unknowns about the effects of pesticides generally and about the special risks to children in particular. According to the National Academy of Sciences in a 1993 pesticide study, little work has been done to identify or to investigate the effects of pesticide exposure on neurotoxic, immunotoxic or endocrine responses in infants and children.

Organophosphate and carbamate insecticides are designed to kill insects by disrupting their normal nerve transmission. Unfortunately, insect nervous systems work in surprisingly similar ways to those of humans. Thus, humans are also susceptible to the neurotoxic effects of these poisons. This disruption may affect the brain and the nervous system. Children are thought to be more susceptible to neu-

Pounds of Selected Fruits and Vegetables Eaten by the Average Two-Year-Old per Year*

Food	Pounds Consumed per Year
Potatoes	23.5
Apples	16.4
Bananas	13.4
Tomatoes	9.5
Oranges	7.2
Grapes	6.1
Carrots	3.9
Peaches	3.8
Peas	3.5
Green Beans	3.4
Broccoli	1.9
Strawberries	1.9
Cherries	1.7
Pears	1.7
Lettuce	1.3
Cantaloupes	0.9
Celery	0.7
Blueberries	0.5
Spinach	0.4
Cauliflower	0.2
Blackberries	0.1
Raspberries	0.1

*Consumption based on a 30-lb two-year old.

Source: USDA Nationwide Food Consumption Survey, Continuing Survey of Food Intakes by Individuals, Children 1–5, 1985–86.

rotoxins than adults because of their incompletely developed blood/brain barrier and myelination of nerves, as well as other factors.

Many of the pesticides used in schools are neurotoxins. Neurotoxicity may manifest itself as:
◆ Learning problems
◆ Dizziness
◆ Poor memory
◆ Loss of coordination
◆ Headaches
◆ Nausea
◆ Muscular aches and other flulike symptoms

Other symptoms of low-level pesticide exposure may include appetite loss, exhaustion, nervousness, fatigue, breathing difficulties and irritability. Some pesticides also cause immune system damage. This immunotoxicity can lead to intensified problems with asthma or allergies and diminished capabilities to fight cancer.

Many of these symptoms can be easily mistaken for the flu. For this reason, pesticide illness is often misdiagnosed. In some cases the symptoms are abrupt; at other times they are gradual, so relating the cause and effect can be difficult.

Pesticide exposure has been linked to various types of cancer in animal and human epidemiological studies. Cancer results from a proliferation of genetically mutated cells. During early childhood cells divide very rapidly, making it more likely that a mutation of cellular genetic material will be reproduced and thus initiate cancer. Cancer is thought to be a multistage disease that may take many years from initiation to promotion and progression. Because they are younger, children have a longer lifespan in which cancer can progress to full-blown malignancy. Scientists have speculated that these factors may make children more susceptible to some cancers.

Some recent studies are finding correlations between pesticide use at home and cancers in children. A 1987 National Cancer Institute study found a statistically significant, nearly sevenfold increased risk of leukemia in children whose parents used pesticides in the home or garden. A January 1993 study found that the risk of childhood brain cancer increased more than fivefold in families that used no-pest strips, pesticide bombs, or flea collars in or around the home.[10] Childhood brain cancer was also significantly more common in families that used pesticides to control garden insects, head lice, termites and yard weeds.

Thus, pesticides may cause acute, immediate poisoning symptoms, subtle behavioral and learning difficulties, or chronic diseases with long latency periods, such as cancer. Pesticides have also been found to cause reproductive harm and birth defects.

Examples of Pesticide Illness in Schools

The risks posed to children by school use of pesticides are not purely hypothetical. We do not know the number of illnesses, diseases and cancers caused by exposure to pesticides used in the schools, but we do know of many exposure and poisoning incidents that raise serious concerns. We also know that some children are more sensitive than others to the effects of pesticide exposures. For example:

◆ On February 27, 1989, first-grader Michael Storey ingested granules of the pesticide disulfoton that had been carelessly applied on the school ground at Roosevelt Elementary School in Yakima, Washington. He spent 2 days in intensive care fighting for his life and another week in the hospital following the incident.

◆ Children, teachers and other staff of New York's Eastchester High School experienced headaches, eye and respiratory irritation and nausea immediately following their return to school Monday, October 26, 1992. The school had been sprayed over the weekend for roach control with the pesticides chlorpyrifos, diazinon and resmethrin. The school was closed for almost 3 weeks as crews worked to clean up the pesticide residues. Some children developed rashes, sore throats and other symptoms, and one child was hospitalized. Several lawsuits have resulted. Parents noted that the roaches returned to the school even before the students did.

◆ Chemically sensitive kindergartner Kenny Tye began having headaches, stomach problems and frequent urination and was generally tired and sick all the time after starting school at Mitchell Elementary School in Canyon Country, California. His mother noticed that his symptoms worsened toward the end of each month. Upon investigating, she learned that this was the time that the school applied pesticides. The Tye family had become chemically sensitive (see Chapter 1) following a pesticide misapplication in their own home.

The examples discussed here are just a few of the many school-related pesticide exposure incidents that occur annually. Some known exposure incidents are clearly the result of misapplications of pesticide chemicals. Others involve applications made according to directions on the pesticide label. Still others involve children who may be more sensitive than others to chemical exposures.

All these incidents raise legal and public policy questions about schools' rights and responsibilities relative to using poisons on school grounds. They also point out the special needs of some students and highlight the school's responsibility to take precautions to protect the health and safety of all the children in its care.

Schools actively counsel students to "just say no" to drugs. There are excellent reasons for schools themselves to just say no to pesticide "drugs." Fortunately, as we will see in the next section, preventive and least-toxic pest control alternatives are available and are being used successfully in large and small school districts around the country.

Some communities and 23 states require that chemical lawn care companies notify customers and neighbors of intent to spray. Some of these states require that warning signs are posted in the areas sprayed, and some states have established a registry of those chemically sensitive people who must be notified before spraying occurs.

Peter Guerrero Testimony before the U.S. Senate Committee on Environment and Public Works, Subcommittee on Toxic Substances, Environmental Oversight, Research and Development, "Pesticides: EPA and State Efforts to Ensure Safe Use of Lawn Care Pesticides," GAO/T-RECD-91-50 (Washington, DC: EPA, January 1992).

Pesticides Commonly Used by Schools

In addition to the presence of wood preservatives and use of disinfectants, the following active ingredients in pesticides are commonly used on school campuses:

- ◆ Diazinon
- ◆ Chlorpyrifos
- ◆ Glyphosate
- ◆ 2,4-D

We highlight next some information about the health hazards of each of these chemicals.

Diazinon (trade names Spectracide or Knox Out 2FM). Diazinon belongs to the class of insecticides known as organophosphates. Organophosphates interfere with the activity of the enzyme cholinesterase, which is involved in the transmission of nerve signals. Signs of poisoning include headache, dizziness, muscle weakness and lack of coordination, intestinal cramps, pinpoint pupils, vision problems, excessive secretions and spasms of the bronchial tubes.

As a result of Diazinon's frequent use in homes, yards and gardens, it is commonly involved in accidental poisonings. Two EPA surveys found diazinon to be the sixth most frequent cause of accidental death caused by pesticides and the sixth most frequent cause of pesticide-related hospitalizations.[11] Diazinon is also synergistic with a variety of other chemicals. For example, a person taking the ulcer medication Tagamet was poisoned when he treated his lawn with Diazinon.

As with most other pesticides, the public does not have complete information about all the ingredients in any diazinon formulation. It is known that some agricultural formulations of Diazinon contain ethylbenzene, trimethyl benzene and xylenes as "inert" ingredients. Exposure to these chemicals in humans or laboratory animals can cause both mild reactions, such as dizziness and serious illnesses, such as liver and kidney damage. Birth defects and fetal death can also be caused by exposure to these inert ingredients.

> **At Waianae Elementary School in Hawaii, a Dursban 4E application was made to the outside perimeter of the school building. The application was found by state investigators to have been made in accordance with the product label, yet the following day an unusually large number of students became ill, with difficulty breathing, stomachache, headache and nausea. The symptoms were thought to be related to exposure to the "inert" ingredients of Dursban 4E, not to chlorpyrifos itself.**

Chlorpyrifos (trade name Dursban). Chlorpyrifos is another organophosphate insecticide. Like other organophosphates, it is efficiently absorbed by inhalation, ingestion and skin penetration. Chlorpyrifos residues are very prevalent in our food supply. According to the EPA, U.S. children between the ages of 1 and 6 are already exposed to 78 percent of their maximum permissible intake just from food sources alone.[12]

Typically, people are told that they may reenter rooms within 1 to 2 hours after broadcast applications of chlorpyrifos. However, a 1991 study in a carpeted residence revealed the surprising result that the highest air concentrations occurred 3 to 7 hours after a broadcast application was done according to label instructions. These levels were higher in the infant breathing zone (near the floor) than in the adult breathing zone. The study found that in the first 2 days after application, infants would receive a dose 10 to 50 times higher than federal regulators consider acceptable.[13]

Glyphosate (trade name Roundup). Glyphosate is the active ingredient of several herbicides. Symptoms of acute Roundup poisoning include gastrointestinal pain, vomiting, swelling of lungs, pneumonia, clouding of consciousness and destruction of red blood cells. The California Pesticide Illness Surveillance Program reported 30 to 56 incidents related to glyphosate exposure each year from 1982 to 1988. Until 1986 glyphosate was one of the top 5 pesticide chemicals in the number of incidents reported; it was ninth and twelfth in 1987 and 1988.[14]

Roundup contains an "inert" ingredient, POEA, that is 3 times more acutely toxic than glyphosate itself. Despite this, POEA is not listed on the Roundup label. Furthermore, chronic toxicity studies required for the registration of glyphosate are done on glyphosate alone, not on the formulated product Roundup.[15]

2,4-D (trade names Weed B-Gone, Lawn Keep and others). 2,4-D is a widely used member of the class of phenoxy herbicides. It remains at the center of an ongoing scientific and regulatory controversy. A special advisory committee to the EPA recently concluded that there is "weakly suggestive" evidence that 2,4-D causes cancer in humans. However, parents and school administrators will want to consider the evidence for themselves.

A striking number of studies have now shown that 2,4-D use, or use of phenoxy herbicides in general, is associated with increased human cancer risks. These include four studies of soft-tissue sarcoma, three studies of non-Hodgkin's lymphoma and a study of prostate cancer among farmers or workers who apply the pesticide(s). Increased risks of both non-Hodgkin's lymphoma and soft-tissue sarcoma have also been found in workers manufacturing phenoxy herbicides. In addition, a recent National Cancer Institute study has shown that dogs living in houses with lawns that are treated with 2,4-D have up to twice the risk of developing lymphoma as dogs without 2,4-D exposure. Other studies have been unable to measure increased risk associated with 2,4-D exposure.

In March 1993 the EPA revealed that tests performed by 2,4-D manufacturers had found highly toxic dioxins. The most toxic dioxin, 2,3,7,8-TCDD, was found in 2 of the 8 samples analyzed. Dioxins are stored in fatty tissues and therefore can accumulate in the body. Tiny amounts of 2,3,7,8-TCDD have been shown to cause cancer in humans, as well as cancer, fetal death, birth defects, reduced fertility and miscarriages in laboratory animals.

It seems unconscionable that we would even entertain using such compounds where any life is present, let alone where growing and developing children spend a good amount of time.

THE IPM METHOD

In addition to its educational mission, the goal of a school is to maintain an environment that is attractive, usable and sustainable. A sustainable environment is one where the health of the people using the space has been safeguarded in all decision processes. In addition, green schools stress conservation of resources, preservation of the environment and economic good sense. In fact, the modeling of these concepts should be seen as an integral part of the educational mission!

Integrated Pest Management (IPM) is a problem-solving approach to pest control that employs least-toxic methods. IPM emphasizes preventing and reducing the source of pest problems rather than treating the symptoms (e.g., spraying). Though not a strictly non-chemical approach, an IPM program generally results in a dramatic reduction in the use of toxic chemicals.

The Bio-Integral Resource Center in Berkeley, CA (see the resource section at the end of this chapter for further information) describes IPM in this manner:

"The objective of an IPM program is to suppress the pest population below the level that causes economic, aesthetic or medical injury. Strategies are designed to require a minimum reliance on pesticides."

IPM can briefly be described as a five-step process:
1. **Inspect.** Gather information about the pest's life cycle and habits. This will indicate the appropriate course of action.
2. **Monitor.** Determine the seriousness of the problem.
3. **Establish the threshold or tolerance level.** Decide the point at which the number of pests is intolerable.
4. **Determine treatment.** Begin with the least toxic methods first. Select and time treatments to be most effective and least disruptive to human health, the environment and natural controls.
5. **Evaluate.** How successful was the IPM program?[16]

The IPM strategy will inhibit pest problems with:
◆ Minimum impact on human health.
◆ Minimum impact on the environment.
◆ Minimum impact on the school budget.
◆ Minimum impact on beneficial pests.
(Refer to page 67 for beneficial pest information.)

It should be noted that (as with any new technology) instituting an IPM program does have some start-up costs associated with information gathering and retraining the maintenance staff. In the long run, this pest prevention approach of addressing the causes of infestations has proven more cost effective than chemical-based pest control programs.

According to William Forbes, pest control operator with the Montgomery County Public Schools in Maryland, the district experienced a savings of $30,000 over 3 years in infested food products and $6,000 in labor and pesticide costs just in food services alone under its IPM program. Other costs are harder to compare, because the new program involves approximately 50 more buildings than the former program, as well as new pest control responsibilities. (The conventional program dealt only with crawling insects and rodents, whereas the new IPM program deals with all pests.) Dramatic savings have been realized in the (few) buildings that were formerly treated by outside pest control services.

Where School IPM Is Working: Eugene, Oregon

Since 1984, the Eugene 4J School District has been developing an IPM-based landscape management program. The 4J district manages just over 600 acres of developed grounds. Prior to 1983, 180 acres (or 30 percent) were sprayed annually, including herbicide or soil sterilant application to approximately 40 acres of tracks, softball diamonds and shrub beds. The district now uses no herbicides at all. Weeds (and gophers) are kept in good control in

high school fields using irrigation, aeration, fertilization, top-dressing and overseeding to keep the turf healthy. Concrete mowing strips are being put in behind backstops and elsewhere to control grass and weeds where mowing is difficult.

If yellowjackets are present, the district first attempts to remove the nest physically. Dumpsters and areas around them are kept clean and outdoor eating is prohibited. Children are educated not to swat at yellowjackets. If despite these measures the population exceeds a tolerable threshold and the insects are coming from a nest that cannot be located for removal, then pesticide bait stations may be used.

Pesticide applications are permitted only in response to concerns of safety and site preservation, or if initial use of pesticides allows a landscape to be changed, so that it can, on a sustainable basis, be managed by chemical-free means. Purely aesthetic concerns are not among the criteria for consideration of pesticide use.

IMPLEMENTING AN IPM PROGRAM AT YOUR SCHOOL

Implementing a grounds design and nonchemical (or least-toxic) school and grounds maintenance policy can be rewarding for students, teachers and parents as well as for grounds staff and school administrators. The process offers a firsthand, hands-on learning opportunity for everyone in the school community. Students can learn about insects and natural predators, the toxic effects of chemicals, and environmentally sound ways of managing natural resources. Teachers can gain a new "laboratory" for teaching these concepts and can enjoy a less toxic workplace. Most parents will feel greater peace of mind knowing that their children are being exposed to fewer pesticides at school. Grounds and building maintenance personnel will be happy to reduce their own exposure to toxic chemicals. By publicizing the new program, the district will benefit from improved public relations and will reduce the risk, and its own liability, from pesticide exposure incidents.

Find incentives for all of these groups to participate and feel good about a new IPM program. The greater the number of students, teachers and staff who get involved, the better. Involvement breeds empowerment. All who do get involved will feel that they have part ownership. And when someone owns something, that person always take care of it.

To begin:

1. From the preceding sections and by using the resources listed at the end of the chapter, collect information on the hazards of pesticides and on IPM alternatives.

2. Meet with your school officials to find out about current pesticide use, policies and practices. Share your concerns. The Northwest Coalition for Alternatives to Pesticides (NCAP) suggests the following list of questions to ask as a starting point:

◆ Which weed and insect pests are present (if any)?

◆ What chemicals or other means are used to control them? What are the active ingredients? What are the "inert" ingredients? Does the school have Material Safety Data Sheets (MSDS) for any chemicals it uses on file and available for public inspection?

◆ When and how often are pesticide applications done (on a schedule, or only when a pest problem is present)?

◆ Who makes the decision about whether to use pesticides?

◆ Who does the application (school personnel or outside contractors)? Are all applicators licensed?

◆ Is there a written record of reasons and justification for pesticide use?

◆ Are alternatives considered?

◆ What is their notification policy to parents? To teachers?

◆ Is there an appeals process if parents wish to challenge proposed use of a pesticide?

◆ Are treated areas posted?

◆ What kinds of records are kept of pesticide applications?

◆ Is the school nurse trained to recognize pesticide poisonings?

◆ Are any children known to be especially sensitive to chemical exposures? Are adequate measures taken to identify, notify and protect these children if pesticides are used at school?

◆ Does the school's emergency management plan address possible pesticide accidents or exposures?[17]

3. If the current policy and practices are not satisfactory, tell the school superintendent, school board and school district management of your concerns. Bring them also to the attention of the parent-teacher association, teachers' union, maintenance and food service workers' unions and others.

Petitions are a very effective way to raise everyone's awareness and focus their attention. Presenting a long list of supporters will surely get the school board's attention. The Environmental Health Coalition in San Diego, CA, created the **School Pesticide Use Reduction Petition** (see next page), which you can copy and use at your school.

4. From the research suggested by the preceding material, be prepared to suggest an IPM policy alternative.

5. Work with school grounds and building maintenance staff as early and often as possible to anticipate their concerns and build their input into the proposal. Their enthusiasm and support will be critical to the success of any school IPM program. They will work harder for the success of the program if they have a sense of control over it. Otherwise, they may feel that the new policy is unnecessary, impractical or forced on them by others. (Students can also be involved in doing research and recommending policy options.)

6. Form a committee to oversee the development and implementation of the new policy. Continue to involve as many interested parties as possible. This might include parents, students, teachers, school staff (including the school nurse), IPM and pest control specialists, architects, pesticide experts, neighbors, or other interested citizens. Be sure that the committee meets regularly to review the progress and setbacks as the new policy is carried out.

7. It may be desirable to consult (or even hire) an integrated pest management specialist when developing the policy. Such a specialist can tailor a grounds or interior maintenance plan to the specific needs and conditions in your area while helping you avoid start-up pitfalls. If your district is small, consider getting several districts or your local parks department to sponsor the visit of such an expert jointly to help defray costs. Also consider asking the school district's insurance company to help

School Pesticide Use Reduction Petition

"The incidence of pesticide-related illness among children and educators across the country is on the rise.

Many pesticides used in schools cause cancer, reproductive harm and nervous system damage with effects ranging from headaches and flu-like symptoms to behavior and learning disabilities and permanent brain damage.

THEREFORE, we, the undersigned, support school pesticides use reduction. We urge the school board to adopt a school Integrated Pest Management (IPM) Policy which will provide for the management of pest populations with the least possible hazard to people, property and the environment. Toxic pest control chemicals may be used only as a last resort."

Print Nane

Address

City, State, Zip Code

Phone Number

Signature

Print Nane

Address

City, State, Zip Code

Phone Number

Signature

Print Nane

Address

City, State, Zip Code

Phone Number

Signature

Print Nane

Address

City, State, Zip Code

Phone Number

Signature

Source: Sharon Taylor, "S.P.U.R. Guide: School Pesticide Use Reduction," Environmental Health Coalition, 1991.

pay the costs of hiring consultants or training district personnel. These companies have an interest in reducing risks (and thus liability) of the school district and may be very interested in supporting an IPM program.

8. After the policy is developed, be sure that all existing and new staff are trained in its principles. Information should be presented in the clearest way possible. If members of the maintenance crew do not speak English as their first language, have someone translate! You may be surprised how appreciative they will be that you went to the extra trouble. If their language is taught on campus, approach the teacher and ask if the students can work with you for extra credit.

9. Take regular opportunities to celebrate program accomplishments and to reward grounds and building staff for successes and innovative new approaches they might come up with to reduce pesticide use!

Two critical steps for continued success: (1) training of the maintenance staff and (2) follow-through and support.

LEAST-TOXIC PEST CONTROL STRATEGIES FOR SCHOOLS

Prevent insect problems in the first place by removing the sources of food, water and shelter that are an attraction for them. Students can work on these activities in teams. They include the following:

◆ Clean up all sources of food. Keep crumbs to a minimum and store all food in airtight containers.
◆ Check for and seal all leaks.
◆ Remove debris that serves as a home or breeding ground for unwanted pests. Keep all areas cleared of piles of unused paper, boxes, cardboard, lawn debris, old sacks, decaying matter and general waste that will harbor insects and disease.
◆ Use screens and caulk all possible insect entrances.

For weed problems install concrete mowing strips to prevent grass or weed growth in areas where mowing is impractical. Seal pavement cracks and crevices to prevent weed regrowth. Plant hardy and resistant varieties of turf grass that will be able to subdue weeds. Use manual weed pulling or weed eaters for spot treatments. Realize that eliminating every last weed is an unrealistic (and unnecessary) goal.

Weeds generally do not grow in well-drained, fertile soil. Plantings that are best suited for the local growing conditions also allow weeds less chance to get a foothold. Ground covers and mulches make good barriers to weeds.

When new structures or modifications to the school building or grounds are planned, evaluate plans to ensure that pest control problems are not created.

Why Planning and Prevention Are Important!

At one elementary school, parents donated their time to build a bark mulch track. When the winter rains came, the mulch absorbed and held water. By spring the track was overrun with a thriving crop of weeds. The district then wanted to spray herbicides regularly to control the weeds. With proper planning and design this pest problem could have been prevented. Proper site preparation, use of a weed mat or other weed barrier beneath the mulch, a thicker layer of mulch and use of gravel are all techniques that could have helped save the district from this pest control headache. Suitability of a track at this school could also have been considered more carefully. Weeds in a bark mulch track can be kept in check by pounding feet when the track gets lots of use. This track was only lightly used.

When Pests Do Get Out of Hand

Pest	Least-Toxic Control Measures
Weeds	Aerate, fertilize, top-dress, overseed with resistant grass varieties and irrigate playing fields to restore healthy turf. Use weed eaters or manual pulling. Infrared or hot-water technologies for spot treating weeds are currently being tested in this country. Look for more information to be available on them if they prove successful.
Cockroaches	Use good sanitation. Clean up all food and water sources. Caulk all cracks in kitchen and bathrooms. Use sticky traps to find problem areas or to trap small populations. Use boric acid, silica aerogel or diatomaceous earth dusts in wall voids and cracks. If necessary, consider cockroach growth regulators. Handle dusts or growth regulators as you would any chemical. Follow all label directions and avoid exposing children or others.
Yellowjackets	Physically remove the nest or use nontoxic bait stations available from local hardware stores. Place the stations as far from play areas as possible. Keep dumpsters and areas around them clean and eliminate outdoor eating. Educate children not to swat at yellowjackets.

(Continued on next page)

Pest	Least-Toxic Control Measures

Head Lice

Since head lice cannot live for long away from a warm human body, spraying at home or at school is never necessary. Successful lice control requires commitment on the part of parents and enforcement of a "no-nit" policy before children are allowed to return to school.

Some important steps to follow: Avoid contact with infested individuals. Don't allow students to share bedding, clothing, towels, or combs. Wash pillows or head wear in hot water during treatment. Use a coconut- or olive-oil-based shampoo with hot water and a head lice comb. Most soaps will kill all lice stages except eggs. Comb until all nits and lice are removed.

Avoid lindane-based shampoos. The EPA is currently reviewing lindane for its tendency to affect the development of the nervous system in laboratory rats.[18] An excellent fact sheet of the detailed steps needed for a successful lice control program is available through BIRC. (See the resources at the end of the chapter.)

Fleas

Determine where the fleas are breeding and eliminate flea-bearing mammals such as rodents. Vacuum and steam-clean carpeted areas. Flea growth regulators are available that effectively sterilize juvenile fleas, but not adult fleas. Pyrethrum powder or food-grade diatomaceous earth and silica gel products are available that smother and dry out fleas and their eggs. These products should be used with caution and only according to product labels.

Sugar Ants

Good sanitation is key. Empty trash daily, wipe the outside of jars clean, rinse out bottles and cans before recycling. Caulk all points of possible entry. Try to locate the ant nests. If outside, pour boiling water in the nest. Otherwise, nests can be spot treated with least-toxic materials. Boric acid dusts or sprays can be used in wall voids. Sticky barriers and bait traps are also available. Handle boric acid or bait stations as you would any pesticide. Follow all label directions and avoid exposing children or others.

Pest	Least-Toxic Control Measures
Carpenter Ants and Dampwood Termites	Locate and replace moisture-damaged wood. Remove stumps, bark mulch and wood debris from the area adjacent to buildings. Eliminate earth/wood contact around foundations of buildings and trim back any tree branches that touch the building. Caulk around pipes or electrical line entry points. Accessible ant nests can be removed with a vacuum cleaner. Other ant or indoor termite nests can be spot treated with least-toxic materials, such as boric acid or diatomaceous earth. Indoor termite nests in wood structures can also be destroyed with heat, cold or electricity; specialized equipment and professional assistance will be necessary.
Subterranean Termites	Build sand barriers around new construction. If underground nests can be located, dig out smaller ones or apply nematodes (a tiny soil-dwelling predator). Just exposing underground termite nests makes them vulnerable to ants, as they are a natural enemy. Heat or cold techniques are also available, and there is currently much active research into more effective subterranean termite control techniques. Seek professional assistance to determine all the treatment options. See the resource section of this chapter for names of contractors that apply freezing and/or heating methods.

For more information on least-toxic pest control see the resources list at the end of this chapter. The preceding information is derived from *Dan's Practical Guide to Least-Toxic Home Pest Control*, and *Common Sense Pest Control*. Please refer to these sources for more detailed information on these strategies. For these or any new alternative methods to work properly you must understand what you are doing.

RESOURCES

Hotlines

National Pesticide Telecommunications Network
800-858-7378
Provides information about pesticides to anyone in the United States., Puerto Rico and the Virgin Islands over the phone or by mail. Referrals are given for labs that perform analysis. Hours are 8 A.M. to 6 P.M. central standard time.

Brochures/Papers/Reports

After Silent Spring: The Unsolved Problems of Pesticide Use in the United States
Natural Resources Defense Council Publications
40 West 20th Street
New York, NY 10011
212-727-4474

America's Growing Dilema: Pesticides in Food and Water
The League of Women Voters Education Fund
1730 M Street NW
Washington, DC 20036
202-429-1965

Citizen's Guide to Pesticides
U.S. Environmental Protection Agency
Pesticides and Toxic Substances
401 M Street SW
Washington, DC 20460
202-260-7751

EPA's Pesticide Programs
U.S. Environmental Protection Agency
Pesticides and Toxic Substances
401 M Street SW
Washington, DC 20460
202-260-7751

Establishing Integrated Pest Management Policies and Programs: A Guide for Public Agencies
IPM Education and Publications
University of California
Davis, CA 95616-8620
916-752-4162

Exporting Banned Pesticides: Fueling the Circle of Poison
Greenpeace
1436 U Street NW, Suite 201A
Washington, DC 20009
201-319-2472

The Federal Insecticide, Fungicide and Rodenticide Act
U.S. Environmental Protection Agency
Office of Pesticide Programs
PMSD Information Services Branch
401 M Street SW
Washington, DC 20460
202-260-7751

For Our Kids' Sake: How to Protect Your Child Against Pesticides in Food
Mothers and Others for a Livable Planet
Natural Resources Defense Council
40 West 20th Street
New York, NY 10011
212-727-4474

Pest Control in the School Environment: Adopting Integrated Pest Management

U.S. Environmental Protection Agency
Public Information Center
401 M Street SW
Washington, DC 20460
202-260-7751

Pesticides in Children's Food

Environmental Working Group
1718 Connecticut Avenue NW, Suite 600
Washington, DC 20009
202-667-6982

Pesticides in Our Communities: Choices for Change

Concern, Inc.
1794 Columbia Road NW
Washington, DC 20009
202-328-8160

Pesticides and Lawns

Rachel Carson Council, Inc.
8940 Jones Mill Road
Chevy Chase, MD 20815
301-652-1877

Planning for Non-Chemical School Ground Maintenance

Northwest Coalition for Alternatives to
Pesticides (NCAP)
P.O. Box 1393
Eugene, OR 97440
503-344-5044

Recognition and Management of Pesticide Poisonings

U.S. Environmental Protection Agency
Office of Pesticide Programs
401 M Street SW
Washington, DC 20460
202-260-7751

School Pesticide Use Reduction (S.P.U.R.) Guide

Environmental Health Coalition
1717 Kettner Blvd.
San Diego, CA 92101
619-235-0281

Suppliers of Beneficial Organisms in North America

Department of Pesticide Regulation
Environmental Monitoring and Pest
Management Branch
Beneficial Organisms Booklet Request
PO Box 942871
Sacramento CA 94271-0001
916-654-1141

Taking the Pesticide Test: A Look at the Los Angeles Unified School District's Pest Control Program

Pesticide Watch
116 New Montgomery Street, Suite 530
San Francisco, CA 94105
415-546-2627

Books

Basic Guide to Pesticides

Shirley Briggs
Taylor and Francis 1992
1101 Vermont Avenue NW, Suite 200
Washington, DC 20005

Bhopal Syndrome: Where Will It Happen Next?

David Weir
Kogan Page Ltd.,1987
120 Pentonville Road
London N1 9JN, England

Breaking the Pesticide Habit:
Alternatives to 12 Hazardous Pesticides
Terry Gips
agAccess, 1987
P.O. Box 2008
Davis, CA 95616

Bug Book
Helen and John Philbrick
Storey Communications, 1974
Schoolhouse Road
Pownal, VT 05261

Bug Busters
Bernice Lifton
Avery Publishing Group, 1991
120 Old Broadway
Garden City Park, NY 11040

Circle of Poison
David Weir and Mark Schapiro
Institute for Food and Development Policy, 1981
1885 Mission Street
San Francisco, CA 94188

Common-Sense Pest Control
William Olkowski, et al.
The Taunton Press, 1991
63 South Main Street, Box 5506
Newtown, CT 06740-5506

Controlling Vegetable Pests
Cynthia Putman
Ortho Books, 1991
Chevron Chemical Company
San Ramon, CA 94583

A Growing Problem: Pesticides in the
Third World
David Bull
Institute for Food and Development Policy, 1982
1885 Mission Street
San Francisco, CA 94188

Least Toxic Home Pest Control
Dan Stein
Hulogosi Communications, 1991
P.O. Box 1188
Eugene, OR 97440

Natural Insect Repellants
Janette Grainger and Connie Moore
The Herb Bar, 1991
200 East Mary
Austin, TX 78704

Oganic Gardener's Handbook of Natural
Insect and Disease Control
Barbara W. Ellis
Rodale Press, 1992
33 East Minor Street
Emmaus, PA 18098

Pesticide Alert
Lawrie Mott and Karen Snyder
Sierra Club, 1987
730 Polk Street
San Francisco, CA 94109

Pesticide Conspiracy
Robert Van Den Bosch
University of California Press, 1978
Berkeley, CA 94720

Pesticide Hazard
Barbara Dinham
Zed Books, 1993
165 First Avenue
Atlantic Highlands, NJ 07716

The Pesticide Question: Environment,
Economics and Ethics
David Pimentel and Hugh Lehman (editors)
Routledge, Chapman and Hall, Inc., 1993
29 West 35th Street
New York, NY 10001-2291

Pesticides in the Diet of Infants and Children

National Research Council
National Academy Press, 1993
2101 Constitution Avenue
Washington, DC 20418

Pests of the Garden and Small Farm: A Grower's Guide to Using Less Pesticide

Mary Louise Flint
agAccess, 1990
P.O. Box 2008
Davis, CA 95616

Pests of the West: Prevention and Control for Today's Garden and Small Farm

Whitney Cranshaw
Fulcrum, 1992
350 Indiana Street, Suite 350
Golden, CO 80401

Regulating Pesticides in Food

Committee on Scientific and Regulatory
Issues Underlying Pesticide Use Patterns and
Agricultural Innovation
The National Academy Press, 1987
2101 Constitution Avenue NW
Washington, DC 20418

Silent Spring

Rachel Carson
Houghton Mifflin Company, 1962
1 Beacon Street
Boston, MA 02108

Tiny Game Hunting

Hilary Dole Klein and Adrian M. Wenner
Bantam Doubleday Dell, 1991
666 Fifth Avenue
New York, NY 10103

The Way We Grow

Anne Witte Garland with Mothers & Others
for a Livable Planet
Berkley Publishing Group, 1993
200 Madison Avenue
New York, NY 10016

Individuals/Companies/Organizations

Bio-Integral Resource Center (B.I.R.C.)

P.O. Box 7414
Berkeley, CA 94707
415-524-2567
The BIRC staff has been consulted by local
governments and businesses in developing
and implementing IPM programs. BIRC also
offers in-depth consultations, program
design and troubleshooting, community
workshops and in-service training programs.

Environmental Health Coalition (EHC)

1717 Kettner, Suite 100
San Diego, CA 92101
619-235-0281
EHC is dedicated to the prevention of illness
resulting from exposure to toxics in the community. Always looking to address the underlying causes of toxic pollution, EHC has created
community-based programs and policies that
have served as models throughout the country.
The coalition was also a driving force behind
recent adoption by the San Diego Unified
School District of a school-wide IPM policy.

Fleabusters

800-759-3532
As an alternative to liquid pesticides and
foggers, they use sodium polyborate, an
odorless, pH neutral powder. Also, they have
partnered with Sterling Home and Office Care
so that the fleabuster process can be immedi-

ately reapplied to carpets, thus keeping the 1-year flea guarantee in effect.

Gardens Alive

5100 Schenley Place
Laurenceburg, IN 47025
812-537-8650
Catalog of environmentally responsible organic products for a healthy garden. A quarterly newsletter available for Organic Garden Club members.

Great Lakes IPM

10220 Church Road NE
Vestaburg, MI 48891
517-268-5693, 517-268-5911
Catalog of insect monitoring systems for the professional grower. Includes kits, pheromones and bait attractants, colored visual traps, field equipment, books, and so on.

IPM Laboratories, Inc.

P.O. Box 300
Locke, NY 13092-0300
315-497-3129
Catalog of biological controls as well as free consultations.

National Coalition Against the Misuses of Pesticides(NCAMP)

701 E Street SE
Washington, DC 20003
202-543-5450
NCAMP was formed in 1981 to focus public attention on the serious public health, environmental and economic problems associated with the use and misuse of pesticides. The colition is available to assist community groups in advocating/instituting changes in public policy regarding pesticide control systems in their area.

National Pediculosis Association

P.O. Box 149
Newton, MA 02161
617-449-NITS
A nonprofit health agency established to build awareness about head lice and to help standardize head lice control policies nationwide.

Northwest Coalition for Alternatives to Pesticides (NCAP)

P.O. Box 1393
Eugene, OR 97440
503-344-5044
NCAP answers information requests on pesticide hazards and alternatives for particular pest problems. They also have an information packet that details the steps Eugene, Oregon's 4J School District took in implementing an IPM program for its grounds. They publish the *Journal of Pesticide Reform*.

Tallon Termite and Pest Control

30089 Ahern Street
Union City, CA 94587
800-300-COLD, 510-429-7200
They use nitrogen instead of harmful chemicals for debugging structures. The nitrogen is cooled, liquefied and inserted into the walls. Within an hour termites freeze to death; the nitrogen then warms, evaporates and returns to the air. This method is quick and clean. For subterranean termites they release natural predators, microscopic nematodes, into the soil to kill the termites at the source. The company also controls wood-destroying pests and fungi.

Nutrition: You and the Environment

Chapter 4

CONTENTS

INTRODUCTION

As responsible citizens of the earth we need to recognize the effects that our food choices have upon this planet. We share the same water and air with earth, with the animals and with all the people in the world. The water and air nourish the plants and animals that feed us. We are all affected by the agricultural use of chemicals and land to support our food choices.

We need to maintain a balanced environment within our own bodies in order to preserve our health. A diet that contains too much fat, salt or sugar and not enough vitamins, minerals or fiber can create an imbalance in our bodies. Chemicals such as pesticides, herbicides, drug residues, food additives and preservatives can also have negative effects on health. A "sustainable diet" (the phrase coined by Joan Gussow, Nutrition Professor at Teacher's College in New York) will sustain not only our own health but that of the earth as well.

The following are issues to consider in achieving a diet that is environmentally sustainable:
- ◆ Conserving land, water and energy
- ◆ Reducing Third World poverty
- ◆ Slowing global warming
- ◆ Keeping rivers clean
- ◆ Producing less garbage
- ◆ Saving trees
- ◆ Supporting local agriculture
- ◆ Supporting organic agriculture

ENVIRONMENTAL CONSIDERATIONS

The food choices we make have a direct effect on the environment. The foods we choose to eat determine the agricultural decisions made and food-processing methods around the world. The world's soil, water, air and energy sources are being polluted and depleted in an effort to provide the human race with the foods we demand.

Animal Farming

Meat eating is on the rise around the world. This has far-reaching environmental, economic and ethical implications as more and more resources are used to support the livestock industry:

1. Land is used for grazing the animals and raising crops for feed.

2. Water, fuel and **agricultural chemicals** are used to grow these crops.

3. Manure has become a large contributor to pollution problems.

4. People are **starving** while livestock are being fed.

Land Usage

One hundred and seventeen acres of the world's tropical rainforests are destroyed every minute. A primary reason for this destruction is the need to produce rangeland for cattle, a direct result of the increased demand for beef. Loss of rainforests cause more carbon dioxide, the major gas responsible for global warming, to be released into the atmosphere.

Forest Growth Slows Global Warming

A growing tree absorbs and stores carbon from carbon dioxide in the atmosphere. One acre of tropical trees will soak up 4 tons of carbon each year.

Carbon From CO_2

Source: National Wildlife Federation, *Wildlife Week Teacher's Education Kit*, New York, NY, 1993.

Many of the world's rangelands, covering one-third of the earth's land surface, bear the scars of improper livestock management, such as proliferating weeds, depleted soils and eroded landscapes.[1] These eroded landscapes are a part of global "desertification"—land that has lost its topsoil and hence its minerals and its ability to hold water and vegetation. As these lands lose their grazing and growing capacities, more forestland is cleared, accelerating the destruction of precious resources that took thousands of years to produce. Tropical rainforests store their nutrients in their trees and plants, not in the soil, as other forests do. Once cleared of its natural vegetation, this land can sustain grazing for only about 1 year.

Meat production involves inefficient land use. Farmland is used to produce the large amounts of grain and soy that must be fed to animals to produce small amounts of meat. Livestock consume 10 times the amount of grain that Americans eat directly. The following numbers might surprise you:

◆ 16 pounds of grain and soy produce 1 pound of beef.

◆ 6 pounds of grain and soy produce 1 pound of pork.

◆ 3 pounds of grain and soy produce 1 pound of chicken.[2]

In her classic book *Diet for a Small Planet*, Frances Moore Lappé called this system a "protein factory in reverse." More protein is actually fed to an animal than is produced from the animal! This waste means that large amounts of land, water and energy are used to produce small amounts of food that only the world's richest people can afford to eat. Considering that 40,000 children starve to death on this planet every day, this is an extremely inefficient use of protein food resources.[3] By eating the beans and grains directly, we can produce enough affordable food for everyone while using less land, water and fuel.

Water and Energy Consumption

Water is used to grow the grains that feed the livestock, to provide livestock with drinking water and to maintain livestock facilities. More than half of all the water used in the United States is consumed by livestock production. It's shocking to learn that 5,000 gallons of water are used to produce 1 pound of beef in the state of California. The USDA reports a national average of 2,500 gallons. Most of the water is used to produce the food that the cattle eat.[4]

Almost half of the energy used in American agriculture goes into the livestock industry. Fuel is used to
- ◆ Plant, harvest, process and ship livestock feed.
- ◆ Ship the livestock to the slaughtering houses.
- ◆ Ship the meat to markets across the nation.
- ◆ Transport the meat to your house.
- ◆ Ship around the world if the feed or livestock are not raised locally.

This is an amazing number of energy-consuming steps from farm to dinner table!

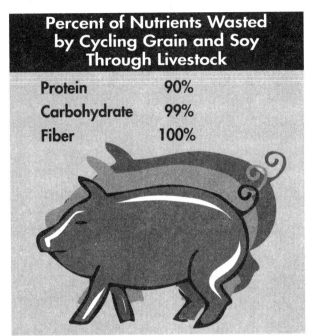

Percent of Nutrients Wasted by Cycling Grain and Soy Through Livestock

Protein	90%
Carbohydrate	99%
Fiber	100%

Source: Alan B. Durning and Holly B. Brough, "Taking Stock: Animal Farming and the Environment, Worldwatch Paper 103," Worldwatch Institute, Washington, DC, 1991.

How Much Water Is Used to Produce Your Food?

Food Item (One Serving)	Gallons of Water Needed
Steak	2,607
Hamburger	1,303
Chicken	408
Pork	408
Eggs	136
Margarine	92
Milk	65
Corn	61
Oranges	22
Apples	16
Wheat bread	15
Lettuce	6

Source: Drought Busters, "How Much Water Is Used to Produce Your Food?" Living Planet Press.

Pollution

The escalation of livestock farming has produced an overabundance of **manure,** which contributes to global warming through the release of methane formed during decomposition. This manure, with its high nitrogen and phosphorus content, also pollutes rivers and groundwater, suffocates aquatic ecosystems and contributes to acid rain. The intensive use of **fertilizers** for feed crops also contributes to these pollution problems.

One of the primary sources of the emission of **methane gas** into the atmosphere today is cattle feedlots. It is estimated that livestock produce 15 percent of all atmospheric methane (approximately 30 to 100 million tons per year).[5] "Cattle release so much gas because the microorganisms in their guts that digest cellulose are virtual factories for the production of methane. In fact, an average cow will belch 400 liters of gas a day."[6] Because cattle release 5 to 9 percent of what they eat as methane and monopolize land that could otherwise support forests capable of soaking up carbon dioxide, it is believed that they constitute the greatest "manmade" source of methane.[7]

Political Perspective

Governments in Third World countries, overburdened by debt, have increasingly turned to livestock farming for export. Problems that arise from this trend include the following:

- ◆ Livestock production in these countries benefits the wealthy, who consume the beef, and is often subsidized by the World Bank.
- ◆ The financial support that these farmers receive goes toward the purchase of farm machinery, which eliminates more jobs for the poor.
- ◆ The money is also used to purchase more pesticides and fertilizers; this causes more pollution.
- ◆ Common land is often taken from the poor and given to private industry.
- ◆ Food staples for the poor are neglected and such farm animals as goats and donkeys (poor people's farm animals) are not raised in these breeding programs.
- ◆ As available farming land diminishes, the poor are pushed onto marginal land, where they raze plots in the rainforest, plow steep slopes and overgraze fragile rangeland.[8]

In this way economic deprivation has added to the ecological deterioration of precious resources. The Third World poor are being forced to abuse their countries' limited natural resources.

Animal Suffering

Consumers are increasingly concerned over the large-scale animal suffering that takes place in factory farms. These are farms where the traditional methods of raising livestock in open grazing pastures have been replaced with factory-style stockyards and cages. In these new conditions animals are imprisoned in small, cramped and sometimes unhealthy quarters until ready for slaughter. These cruel methods are used because they are more efficient; factory farming is a direct result of the increased consumer demand for meat.

Chemical Farming
Pesticides and Fertilizers

Modern agriculture has come to rely on the use of chemical **pesticides and synthetic fertilizers** to prevent crop damage and promote growth. Such pesticides as DDT have been found to persist almost indefinitely in the environment, moving up through the food chain from plants to animals to humans. More than 2.5 billion pounds of pesticides are now used each year.[9] Moreover, crop pests become resistant to pesticides, making it necessary to produce new chemical alternatives.

Fertilizers come in two varieties, organic and chemical. Organic fertilizers feed both the soil and the plant. They are made from natural plant and animal materials or from mined rock minerals. Chemical fertilizers, on the other hand, contain mineral salts that feed the plant but not the soil. Over time, soils treated with only these chemicals will be deficient in organic matter and will show signs of altered biological activity. As the soil structure declines and its capacity for holding water decreases, more of the chemicals will leach through the soil and ever-increasing amounts of chemicals will be needed to feed the plants. Finally, most chemical fertilizers are synthesized from nonrenewable resources, such as coal, which are being depleted at a dangerous rate.[10]

Pesticide Proliferation

"Every year, more than 800 million pounds of pesticides are dusted on crops, poured into the soil, coated on seeds and sprayed onto fields from planes or helicopters."

Pesticides do the following:
◆ Decrease farm labor costs and help increase crop yields by reducing losses to some (though not all) insects, disease or weeds.
◆ Increase the storage life of some food.
◆ Can improve the appearance of food so that it can meet marketing standards and command a higher price on the market.

"But all of this pesticide use comes with an enormous price tag. Farmers spend about $6 billion a year directly. Other hidden costs, such as environmental damage and health problems, add up to an additional $8 billion."

"Since 1945, pesticide use on farms has increased more than 30-fold, but at the same time the portion of total harvest loss to pests has still increased by 20 percent."

It is a vicious cycle. Pests develop a resistance to the chemicals, and so new chemicals need to be developed. The poisons are losing, the pests are winning; it is time to try a different approach. The alternative, organic farming, is experiencing success on many levels!

Anne Witte Garland with Mothers & Others for a Livable Planet, *The Way We Grow: Good-Sense Solutions for Protecting Our Families from Pesticides in Food* (New York: Berkley Books, 1993), pp. 1 and 7.

Crop rotation is the practice of planting different crops (i.e., corn one year, wheat the next) in a specified order on the same field. Crop rotation has been practiced for thousands of years to protect soil and improve production. The different effects that various crops have on the soil, on each other and on insects require carefully planned sequences.

Monocropping is the practice of farming the same crop on the same field year after year. This method does not take into consideration soil protection and therefore leads to the need for chemical pesticides and synthetic fertilizers. Farmers usually choose to monocrop for economic reasons. (A certain crop may bring in more money because of a contractual agreement with a food company.)

Circle of Poison

Although it is illegal for American farmers to use pesticides that have been proven to be carcinogenic on domestically grown produce, a loophole in the law allows the exportation of these pesticides to countries where food is grown that is later imported into the United

Pesticides Used in Foreign Countries on Food Exported to the United States

Commodity	Countries Surveyed	Number of Pesticides		
		Allowed, Recommended or Used in the U.S.	Any Residue Prohibited (No U.S. Tolerance)	Not Detectable with FDA Tests
Bananas	Colombia, Costa Rica, Ecuador, Guatamala, Mexico	45	25	37
Coffee	Brazil, Colombia, Costa Rica, Ecuador, Guatemala, Mexico	94	76	64
Sugar	Brazil, Colombia, Costa Rica, Ecuador, Guatemala, India, Thailand	61	34	33
Tomatoes	Mexico, Spain	53	21	28
Tea	India, Sri Lanka	24	20	11
Cacao	Costa Rica, Ecuador	14	7	7
Tapioca	Thailand	4	4	1
Strawberries	Mexico	13	-	5
Peppers	Mexico	12	-	4
Olives	Italy, Spain	20	14	8
Totals		**340**	**201 (59%)**	**198 (58%)**

Source: David Weir and Mark Shapiro, *Circle of Poison* (Oakland, CA: Food First Books, 1981), p. 82.

States. U.S. chemical companies knowingly ship cancer-causing chemicals to Third World countries, telling them these chemicals will help produce more food! U.S. consumers are no more safe than they were before these pesticides were made illegal.

In addition, farmers in Third World countries often don't have the knowledge or the equipment needed to protect themselves and the environment from unsafe exposure to these toxic chemicals. They may be unable to read the directions and warning labels, which are printed only in English. **These farmers then export their produce grown with the banned pesticides to the United States, creating what is referred to as a "circle of poison."** Many of these exporting countries cannot afford the food safety and quality systems necessary for monitoring these foods.

Approximately 25 percent of the produce sold in the United States is imported. According to the FDA, about 5 percent is contaminated; however, these estimates may be low, since the FDA samples only 1 percent of the food that is imported.[11]

Pesticides whose use is illegal in the United States were exported by U.S. companies at a rate of 15 tons per day in 1991. Included in this total were more than 96 tons of the insecticide DDT, banned in the U.S. more than 20 years ago. The researchers identified shipments of an additional 41 million pounds of pesticides considered so hazardous that only government-certified specialists are allowed to use them. The majority of these pesticides were shipped to developing countries, where unsafe storage and application practices are common.

Educational Communications, "Pesticide Trafficking Documented," *The Compendium Newsletter* (Nov./Dec. 1993), p. 7.

Comparison of Pesticide Contamination in Domestic and Imported Foods (in Percent)

Commodity	Percent of FDA's Imported Samples with Residues	Percent of FDA's Domestic Samples with Residues
Apples	53	48
Bananas	2	0
Bell Peppers	81	30
Broccoli	33	14
Cabbage	53	20
Cantaloupes	78	11
Carrots	58	46
Cauliflower	16	2
Celery	75	72
Cherries	65	62
Corn	5	1
Cucumbers	80	30
Grapefruit	52	63
Grapes	44	28
Green Beans	46	27
Lettuce	57	52
Onions	18	28
Oranges	49	36
Peaches	58	53
Pears	35	45
Potatoes	24	39
Spinach	23	42
Strawberries	86	70
Sweet Potatoes	11	30
Tomatoes	70	23
Watermelon	25	2

Source: Lawrie Mott and Karen Snyder, *Pesticide Alert* (San Francisco, CA: Sierra Club, 1987), p. 23.

Convenience Foods

Convenience foods are produced by a system that is **energy wasting, polluting and expensive**. Each American throws away 4 pounds of trash each day, one-third of which can be traced to food products.[12] These food products include packaged, canned, jarred and fast foods. Disposal of this garbage requires polluting and energy-consuming transportation and has added to landfills that are an ever-increasing problem. Recycling helps, but it also consumes more energy. Manufacturing convenience foods requires food-processing methods that consume fuel and energy resources.

Only 24 cents of every dollar you spend on food goes toward farming costs. The other 76 cents pays for such expenses as processing, packaging, advertising, supermarket retailing and transportation.[13]

HEALTH RISKS

Environmental hazards brought about by our nutritional choices are only half of the story; of equal or perhaps greater importance are the health risks to humans, particularly children. We are now finding that many illnesses previously attributed to old age have more to do with the food choices that we make throughout our lives.

Animal Foods

Fat Factor

Early nutritional studies established the importance of protein as a component of our cellular structure. This led to the assumption that, since animal foods are the most concentrated form of protein, our diets should be based on meat and dairy. Modern nutritionists now recognize that diets based on animal foods increase the risk of cancer, heart disease, osteoporosis, diabetes, hypertension and obesity. Meat and dairy-based diets are excessive in fat, cholesterol and animal protein and are deficient in fiber.

The Dangers of Excessive Protein

Most people know that too much fat and cholesterol in the diet are dangerous. But too much protein can be a problem too. Repeated studies have shown that **eating large amounts of animal protein causes calcium loss through the urine**. Osteoporosis (a process in which the bones weaken and break easily) is more prevalent in Western countries than in less developed nations, even though calcium intake in the West is high. However, in countries where people eat a grain-based diet, which is lower in protein, but ingest less calcium, osteoporosis is less prevalent. Animal protein has also been shown to raise blood cholesterol levels and therefore may increase the risk of heart disease.

By-products of Animal Foods

Animal foods often contain undesirable by-products, such as **antibiotics, hormones, pesticides and bacterial contaminants** (e.g., salmonella).

Antibiotics are routinely used in the dairy and livestock industry to prevent disease and stunted growth. Because of overcrowding and other conditions, rampant disease and stunted growth are common in factory farms. Two separate studies done in 1989 by *The Wall Street Journal* and the Center for Science in the Public Interest found antibiotic drug residues in 38 percent of the milk samples tested. As the use of antibiotics continues, the targeted bacteria become resistant to the drugs.

Antibiotic-resistant salmonella provide an example of bacteria in our food supply that have been increasing. Salmonella have been found in the interior of eggs and can survive in the liquid yolks even when boiled for 8 minutes. In 1991 the state of New Jersey reported 1,800 cases of salmonella contamination, two-thirds of which were egg-borne. Reports of contamination of chicken, beef, milk and cheese are on the increase. Factory farms that confine the animals to small spaces foster the spread of diseases from animal to animal. Each year at least 1 to 2 percent of the American population suffers from salmonella poisoning.[14] Most cases go unreported as unsuspecting persons improperly identify their illness as a "24-hour virus." Infants, young children, the elderly and immune-deficient individuals are particularly vulnerable. For them salmonella can cause severe illness and even death.

The U.S. government has approved the use of 750 drug products in the livestock industry. The FDA also allows the over-the-counter sale of thousands of unapproved animal drugs. Of these drugs, **hormones are used to promote faster growth** and **leaner meat** in cattle as well as **increased milk production** in dairy cows. Hormones are given to between 65 and 99 percent of the cattle raised for slaughter.[15] Administration of these hormones on the farm is very poorly regulated. Exposure to even minute quantities of such a powerful drug poses a potential risk.

Animals consume large quantities of grain and soy that contain pesticides (see the Chemical Farming section of this chapter). These **oil-based toxins accumulate in animal fat** in concentrated amounts. When people consume pesticide-contaminated animal foods, the toxins become stored in human fat. These toxin levels do not decline for at least 6 or 7 years.

Fresh Produce

Fresh fruits and vegetables, recently harvested, are generally low in pesticides as compared to animal foods and contain many essential nutrients necessary for good health. Early harvesting of produce, time spent in long-distance shipping and extended periods in cold storage will lower nutrient contents.

Pesticides and Waxes

Children are at greater risk from exposure to low levels of pesticides because of their immature physiology and rapid growth rates. Relative to their size, children also consume more of these foods than adults. Certain fruits and vegetables contain more pesticides than others (see the "Solutions" section of this chapter). Some baby food companies, in response to public outcry, have begun using chemical-free produce. **Two foods that contain the most pesticides are raisins and peanuts.**[16]

> "Of about 300 pesticides approved by the federal government for use on food crops, 73 are probable or possible carcinogens (cancer-causing substances), including some of the most frequently used pesticides. The 4 most commonly used pesticides in the United States (atrazine, alachlor, metalochlor, and 1,3 -dichloropropene) are all classified as either probable or possible carcinogens, and of the 20 most frequently used pesticides, seven are potential carcinogens."

Anne Witte Garland with Mothers & Others for a Livable Planet, *The Way We Grow: Good Sense Solutions for Protecting Our Families for Pesticides in Food* (New York: Berkely Books, 1993), p. 8.

Waxes are applied to preserve some foods and enhance their color. Waxes can entrap fungicides and pesticides already present. Removal of waxes through careful washing or peeling eliminates many of the toxins. Imported produce generally has more pesticide residues than domestic produce. (See "Circle of Poison," earlier in this chapter.)

The list of fruits and vegetables that are commonly waxed includes apples, cucumbers, bananas, beets, cantaloupe, coconuts, garlic, grapefruit, oranges, lemons, limes, mangoes, pumpkins, eggplants, papayas, onions, potatoes, rutabagas, squash, tomatoes, turnips, watermelons, nuts, tangerines, plantains, peppers, avocados and pineapples. In addition to its role as a coating for fruits and vegetables, wax is used as a glaze for hard candies, as a coating for jelly beans and as a component of chewing gum.

Food Irradiation

Food irradiation exposes food to high doses of gamma radiation to kill pests and to extend shelf life. Extending shelf life has important applications for countries where refrigeration is not available, but it is not without cost. When produce is stored for an extended period of time, precious vitamins are lost, whether or not the item is refrigerated.

Very little food irradiation is being done at the moment because of the controversy surrounding the safety of this procedure. Many scientific communities, the World Health Organization included, agree that irradiated food is safe. Yet there are also studies that point to increased cancer risk and cell mutations in animals fed a diet of irradiated foods. Around the world different countries have banned irradiation, and some states in the United States have enacted laws banning the sale of irradiated foods. The FDA requires that foods irradiated in their entirety must bear the "radura" symbol. This means foods that have one or more ingredient irradiated do not need labeling.

Convenience Foods

Recent surveys show that **Americans have become cooking illiterates** and rely more and more upon convenience foods. In 1987 alone, the food industry presented the public with 7,900 new food products. Eating these pre-prepared foods is not without cost to those who eat them and to the environment. The excess packaging adds to the landfills and the **excess salt, fat, sugar and preservatives** compromise our health. Frozen meals often contain a lot of salt and are frequently high in fat. Canned foods are typically high in sodium too.

The refining and processing of the foods remove a lot of the natural nutrients, which the food industry attempts to replace with vitamin and mineral supplements. Unfortunately, the complex structure of plants makes replacing every removed component nearly impossible. Chemicals are also added for flavor and color. These chemicals change from year to year as research shows certain ones to be carcinogenic and the food industry devises new ones as replacements. Preservatives are also added to prolong the shelf life of these foods as they travel from the manufacturer to the store and into your kitchen.

Environmental Hazards of Irradiated Food Include:

1. Increased transport and handling of highly radioactive materials and wastes on America's highways, threatening numerous communities with contamination in the event of accident.

2. Increased sources of worker exposure to radioactive materials resulting in higher carcinogenic and/or mutagenic risk.

3. Potential for the contamination of the immediate environment and/or of groundwater supplies.

4. Continued generation of radioactive wastes for which a secure storage technology has yet to be developed.

Source: *Food Irradiation*, Food & Water, Inc., New York.

SOLUTIONS: THINK GLOBALLY AND EAT LOCALLY

Eat Less Animal Foods

Animal products—meat, poultry, dairy and seafood—all contain saturated fat and cholesterol in varying amounts. As a matter of fact, **animal products are the only source of cholesterol in our diet**. Greatly reducing consumption of animal products and limiting foods prepared with animal fats reduces the risk of heart disease, cancer and obesity. **Animal foods do not contain any fiber**. Fiber helps to prevent colon cancer, helps control blood sugar and aids in regular elimination.

The vegetarian diet is a viable option that is supported by the American Dietetic Association and the surgeon general. People choose to be vegetarian for a variety of reasons:
- ◆ To prevent cruelty to animals
- ◆ To maintain a sustainable environment
- ◆ To follow religious beliefs
- ◆ To improve the healthfulness of their diet

There are 3 types of vegetarian diets. The first 2 contain varying degrees of animal products:
- ◆ The **lacto-ovo** vegetarian diet includes dairy products and eggs.
- ◆ The **lacto** vegetarian diet includes dairy products.
- ◆ The **vegan** diet does not include any animal products.

All 3 vegetarian diets can supply adequate nutrition.

A vegetarian diet should include a variety of **grains, beans, fruits and vegetables** (the basic four of the vegetarian diet) to meet daily nutritional requirements. (People often need to be reminded that even though chips and soda are vegetarian foods, they do not constitute a healthy diet.)

According to the World Health Organization (WHO), the **protein** needs of children and adults can be adequately met by eating a varied diet based mostly on grains, beans, seeds and nuts. The 1988 American Dietetic Association's Position Paper on the vegetarian diet states that it is not necessary to combine these plant proteins at each meal, as was once thought. Eating a variety of grains, beans, seeds and nuts will meet the body's protein needs.

Percentage of Calories As Protein

Vegetables		Legumes		Nuts and Seeds	
Spinach	49	Tofu	43	Peanuts	18
Broccoli	47	Lentils	29	Sunflower	17
Cauliflower	40	Split peas	28	Walnuts	13
Mushrooms	38	Kidney beans	26	Almonds	12
Parsley	34	Navy beans	26		
Lettuce	34	Chick peas	23	**Fruits**	
Green peas	30			Lemon	16
Zucchini	28	**Grains**		Cantaloupe	9
Green beans	26	Rye	20	Orange	8
Cucumbers	24	Wheat	17	Grape	8
Celery	21	Oatmeal	16	Peach	6
Tomatoes	18	Buckwheat	15	Pear	5
Onions	16	Barley	11	Banana	5
Potatoes	11	Brown Rice	8		

Source: U.S. Department of Agriculture.

It is important to consider the following in maintaining a well-balanced vegetarian diet:

◆ **Iron** is found in many plant foods, such as cooked dried beans and peas, leafy dark greens, dried fruit, blackstrap molasses and fortified grains. Cooking in a cast iron skillet will provide some extra iron. Including a good source of vitamin C with your meal will enhance absorption of the iron in the food.

◆ **Calcium** needs can be met by eating dark leafy greens, tofu prepared with calcium sulfate, cooked dried beans, broccoli, sesame seeds and sunflower seeds. Calcium is also found in other fruits, vegetables and grains, but in lesser amounts. Vegetarians may need less calcium, since they consume little or no animal protein.

◆ Supplementation of **vitamin B-12** is necessary for young vegan children, pregnant women or anyone who adheres to the vegan diet for a long time.

◆ We manufacture **vitamin D** in our own bodies when our skin is exposed to sunlight. Exposing face and arms to sunlight for about 30 minutes, 3 times a week, will produce adequate vitamin D in most light-skinned people. Darker-skinned individuals or those who live in polluted or cloudy areas may need more exposure. (This is important information because the dietary sources for vitamin D are in animal products only.)

Eat More Plant Foods

Remember that despite the risk of pesticides, your diet should be made up predominantly of plant foods. Plants provide us with protein, carbohydrate, fiber, minimal fat and maximum vitamins and minerals.

To reduce your risk of exposure to pesticides follow these guidelines:

◆ Buy certified organically grown produce. If unavailable at your market or from your school food supplier, start requesting it as part of the food service contract. Encourage others to make similar requests. Public demand is all that is needed to turn the tide on rampant pesticide use.

◆ Purchase local, in-season produce.

◆ Avoid the purchase of imported foods.

◆ Be accepting of blemished, imperfect-looking produce because it may have fewer pesticides.

◆ Eat a variety of fruits and vegetables. This will minimize your exposure to any one pesticide.

Food Safety Tips

To reduce the amount of pesticide residues in your diet, follow these simple tips:

✔ Wash and scrub all fresh fruits and vegetables (such as pears, strawberries, tomatoes and potatoes) thoroughly under running water.

✔ Peel fruits and vegetables (such as apples, carrots and cucumbers) when possible. Throw away the outer leaves of leafy vegetables (such as lettuce and cabbage).

✔ Cooking and baking usually help to break down the pesticide residues in food, although cooking may concentrate residues in imported tomatoes.

✔ Trim fat from meat, chicken and fish. Some pesticides collect in animal fat.

✔ Don't pick and eat berries and other wild foods that grow on the edges of roads and fields where pesticides may have been sprayed.

✔ Grow your own fruits and vegetables without using pesticides.

Terms to Understand

"More and more signs are going up over produce shelves in the supermarket, but what do they mean?

Certified organically grown: No pesticides, fungicides, ripening agents or chemical fertilizers have been used. The farm has been inspected by a state-authorized certifying agency.

Transitional organic or transorganic: Grown on a farm which has not completed its certification process (in most states 3 years are required). No pesticides, ripening agents or other chemicals used, but residues may persist in the soil."

H. Patricia Hynes, *EarthRight* (Rocklin, CA: Prima Publishing, 1990), p. 26.

Source: Jennifer Zicht, "Pesticides and Food Safety: A Feature for Young Readers," *EPA Journal* (May-June 1990), p.50.

Eating produce that is in season will reduce your chance of ingesting wax added as a preservative and because of the shorter storage time, will improve the vitamin content of the food. Most seasonal produce is grown locally, which allows for lower transportation and packaging costs. Support your local farmers and encourage them to become organically certified.

It is best to eat foods that are grown organically, but if this is not possible, try the methods suggested in "Food Safty Tips," on the previous page.

The term *organic* refers to a system of food production that largely excludes the use of synthetically compounded materials at any point along the path from production, processing, handling and distribution.[17]

The Food Pyramid Guide

From 1956 until 1992 the basic 4 food groups—milk, meat, fruits/vegetables and grains—provided the standard guidelines recommended by the USDA for planning a healthy diet. Over the years nutrition experts have found that these guidelines are inadequate because they encourage a diet based on foods high in fat and cholesterol and low in fiber. As you can see, half of the recommended foods are from animal sources. Since then we have learned a lot more about good nutrition.

The USDA has issued new guidelines to replace the basic 4 food groups. The **Food Guide Pyramid** presents daily food choices, reflecting 7 dietary guidelines that provide a foundation for a healthy diet (see next page). It emphasizes eating a variety of natural foods, such as grains, vegetables and fruits. It de-emphasizes the importance of animal products, such as beef, poultry and dairy. The pinnacle of the pyramid recommends a limited intake of fats, oils and sweeteners; the second level recommends moderate intake of animal or high-protein foods; the third level recommends a larger intake of fruit and vegetables; and the base recommends an intake of mostly grains and cereals.

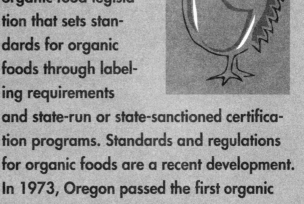

A number of states have enacted organic food legislation that sets standards for organic foods through labeling requirements and state-run or state-sanctioned certification programs. Standards and regulations for organic foods are a recent development. In 1973, Oregon passed the first organic food labeling laws. States without organic labeling laws or state-sanctioned certification programs, often have independent certification organizations that may certify foods to be organic.

Roy Popkin "What Is Organic Produce?" *EPA Journal* (May-June 1990), p. 33.

Food Guide Pyramid

A Guide to Daily Food Choices

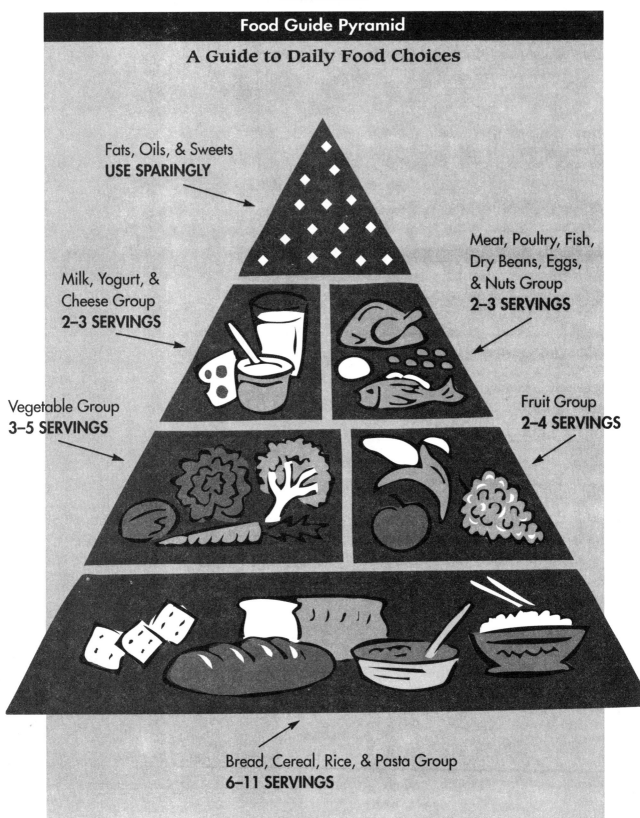

Fats, Oils, & Sweets
USE SPARINGLY

Meat, Poultry, Fish,
Dry Beans, Eggs,
& Nuts Group
2–3 SERVINGS

Milk, Yogurt, &
Cheese Group
2–3 SERVINGS

Vegetable Group
3–5 SERVINGS

Fruit Group
2–4 SERVINGS

Bread, Cereal, Rice, & Pasta Group
6–11 SERVINGS

USDA dietary guidelines include:

1. Eat a variety of plant foods.
2. Avoid too much fat, saturated fat and cholesterol (animal foods).
3. Eat foods with adequate starch and fiber (plant foods).
4. Avoid too much sugar (convenience foods).
5. Avoid too much sodium (convenience foods).
6. If you drink alcohol, do so in moderation.
7. Maintain desirable weight (not hard if you remain active and eat according to the guidelines).

Following these guidelines will provide a good foundation for a healthy diet. *Limiting* our intake of animal products and convenience foods can decrease the pollution of both the planet and our bodies. By *avoiding* animal products one can still eat healthfully and significantly decrease stress on the planet and their body.

Where Children Eat Lunch

Source	National Average
Home	41.2 %
School lunch program	39.7 %
At someone else's home	2.5 %
Fast food/restaurants	5.5 %
Bag lunches	10.5 %
Other	2.3 %

Source: Public Voice for Food and Health Policy, *Heading for a Health Crisis: Eating Patterns of America's School Children,* Washington, DC.

There are many who feel that the Food Pyramid is still misleading (i.e., it implies that dairy products are essential) and therefore does not provide the best guidelines for planning a diet for optimal health. When the original Food Pyramid was developed, there was a delay in introducing it to the public. There was much speculation that the dairy and meat industries were asserting political/economic pressure to influence the guidelines. During this controversial period changes were made that could be interpreted as supporting this viewpoint before it was unveiled to the public.

Physician's Committee for Responsible Medicine (PCRM) is a nonprofit group working for effective medical practice, research and health promotion. On April 8, 1991, PCRM introduced a proposal to replace the old 4 food groups with a nutritional plan based on fiber-rich plant foods. The new 4 basic food groups are whole grains, legumes, vegetables and fruits. PCRM feels these food groups provide the basis for an optimal diet and that animal products should only be consumed as condiments or in small amounts, not as the center or majority of the meal.[18]

Harvard's Dr. Dimitrios Trichopoulos sums up the consensus among nutrition researchers: "**I don't think anyone in public health likes meat very much anymore.**"

Harriet Washington, "Old Diets, New Wisdom," *Harvard Medical School Health Letter* (June 1994), p. 7.

IMPLEMENTATION OF NUTRITION EDUCATION

Learning to eat for the health of our planet as well as our bodies needs to take place in both our schools and homes. **Establishing good eating habits at an early age so they become part of a permanent life-style is an especially important goal**. Becoming more familiar with the impact that our eating habits have on ourselves as well as the environment is a good first step. The two major vehicles for bringing this information to students are education and school food.

Education

There is unlimited potential for educating members of your school community about food issues through both the classroom and through other opportunities provided in the school setting. Information on food and healthy eating is most typically covered in health and home economics classes but can easily be incorporated into a variety of subject areas, such as social studies/world cultures (different ethnic diets that are more healthful or sustainable than the standard American diet), science (examining the environmental consequences of animal agriculture), classes discussing ethics (animal rights), current issues (biotechnology) or even literature. Creating room for discussion on these issues is an important way of raising awareness and encouraging people to examine their food choices. This process of creating awareness can start during the beginning years in school.

Home economics emphasizes the importance of learning how to cook as a way to maintain good health. With so many families having little time to prepare meals these days, students need to be encouraged to participate in this activity. Through these classes students can learn to prepare healthful dishes and learn about natural foods. Experimenting with a variety of ethnic foods is an easy way to introduce meatless meals and can encourage cultural exchanges between students. Learning about the different vegetables, fruits, grains and beans that are available can be an enlightening experience that offers lifelong benefits!

Health classes or lectures typically offer a limited representation of diet and often fail to present information about the vegetarian option. It is important that students learn about this option. This can be done by arranging for a presentation by a registered dietitian or nutritionist knowledgeable about the vegetarian diet. (See the resource section at the end of this chapter for organizations that can provide resources, information and instructional materials.)

Nurses and doctors provide much of the nutrition education, although they are often poorly schooled in that area. Educators generally have outdated information because researchers are continually coming up with new findings. The Dairy Council and National Livestock and Meat Board are very aggressive in providing educational materials for schools and hospitals. In fact, they have been the main source for nutrition education materials since the 1950s.

The following are some of the many ways you can educate people at your school about food issues and healthy eating:

◆ Donate books (or ask others in the community) to the school library that cover all the issues of sustainable eating.

◆ Request a library display case and do a display on sustainable eating or a related topic. (This chapter raises many issues that can be developed for this.) Along with this, work with the librarian on displaying all the books available for circulation that address food choice issues. If such information is unavailable, create an informative bulletin board for display elsewhere on campus.

◆ Encourage reports on plant-based diets or another aspect of sustainable eating for one or several classes.

◆ Ask students in your class or club to bring in their favorite vegetarian recipes. Then put them together and sell the cookbook as a fund-raiser.

◆ Work with parents or other students and arrange for a presentation about food issues to the PTA or PTO at the school.

◆ Start a vegetarian club so that students, teachers and parents can explore vegetarian foods together.

◆ Create posters that address food issues or obtain them from the groups listed in the resource section and donate them to the school for hanging.

◆ At school events, festivals, or local fairs arrange to have an information table with literature on the health and environmental benefits of a plant-based diet. Handouts are available from some of the groups listed in the resource section.

◆ Start a column in the school paper on food

choice issues. This could include a survey of students regarding their knowledge or interest about food issues and contests (cooking/recipe, art, essay, etc.).

◆ Organize a Food (or Vegetarian) Education Day or Week at your school.

◆ Obtain, from the groups listed in the resource section, video tapes that explore the issue of dietary choices and the effects they have on health and the environment.

◆ Invite someone from a local health food store or co-op to visit a classroom or assembly and talk about natural and organic foods.

School Food

The cafeteria provides many opportunities for raising awareness about food and its effects on our health and the environment. It also offers many challenges. Since school cafeterias typically have a very restricted budget, they must rely on free surplus foods from the government, called *commodity foods*, which are processed and unhealthy. Cafeterias cater to a wide range of finicky eaters or others who only want "junk food." The foods that are served usually involve little or no preparation. These challenges limit the quality of the food that school cafeterias serve. Private schools, of course, have more freedom and resources at their disposal.

Making changes in school cafeterias can be a challenge, and in some ways government policies make this difficult for schools. Each year the government creates a list of surplus foods that it offers free to public schools as part of the National School Lunch Program. From this list food service directors in each state choose what they want for their schools. A few of the foods offered are canned meats, cheese, butter, milk, processed chicken, canned fruit and vegetables, canned beans, white bread and white sugar. Schools must rely on these foods because their budgets are so limited. It is a paradox that although the USDA's Food Pyramid emphasizes whole grains, fruits or vegetables, the foods it makes available to schools are often animal foods that are both highly processed and unhealthy.

How, then, can we implement the emphasis for more grains, fruits and vegetables in our school cafeterias? This is why the education part is so important. If more students demand healthy, earth-friendly foods, the cafeterias will respond. There are many examples of the influence students can exert over what is offered in the cafeteria. For example, many schools now use only dolphin-safe tuna because of student boycotts against the tuna caught in a way that endangers dolphins. Other schools have stopped using Styrofoam and disposable materials because of student demand. By making people at your school aware of the many effects their food choices have, they can see the benefits and reasons for choosing health- and earth-conscious options.

There are always ways to work around the obstacles, and improvements can be made. The following are some ways to improve the food choices in your cafeteria:

◆ Establish an organic school garden, as outlined in Chapter 5. Produce from this garden can be served in your cafeteria.

◆ Begin student-directed campaigns, as outlined in Chapter 13.

◆ Review the school recipe file to see how many meatless meals are included.

◆ Expand the school recipe file with more vegetarian recipes and have the students evaluate them. Provide the food service director with the tools to serve healthier options. Quantity vegetarian recipes are available from groups listed in the resource section. A class project may include doing a nutritional analysis of recipes to help the students make an informed choice.

◆ Arrange for a taste testing for some healthy options. Natural food companies or local markets are sometimes willing to donate foods for testing.

◆ Market healthy meals by featuring meatless options for special events, such as World Hunger Day, Earth Day, the Great American Meat-Out, even Valentine's Day. (Do your heart a favor!)

◆ Special food bars (e.g., a pasta bar, potato bar and salad bar) or food bars that feature different ethnic foods (e.g., Mexican, Chinese or Indian) are an excellent way to present a larger offering of grains and vegetables. Food bars can also be cost effective.

◆ Encourage the home economics teacher (or any teacher for that matter!) to include a lesson on growing sprouts. These sprouts can be an inexpensive and nutritious addition to salad bars and sandwiches.

◆ Request permission to set up an information table in the cafeteria any time new healthy options are served. Local environmental and vegetarian groups can help you out.

◆ Work with the school foods service director to see that plant-based food options are made available daily.

These are just a few ideas of what you can do. The possibilities are endless! Food is an intricate part of our lives, and the many issues it involves demand much more consideration than it typically receives in our schools. We have seen that healthy eating for ourselves and the planet is an essential component of sustainable living. Be creative in the ways you inform others; make it fun and be well organized. You'll undoubtedly make a significant contribution toward a healthy future!

RESOURCES

The following resources include not only reference books and magazines but also organizations that have nutrition education materials and knowledgeable speakers.

Hotlines

Consumer Nutrition Hotline
800-366-1655
Hotline offers registered dietitians that speak Spanish and English.

Nutrition Activist Hotline
202-332-9110
Dial the phone number. When the recorded message starts press 5; the hotline operates 24 hours a day. Callers will get a brief recorded message describing **why** it's important to tell **what** to **whom**. Addresses and phone numbers of people to contact will be given.

Brochures/Papers/Reports

30% Fat—What's That? A Simple Answer to a Complex Question
Vitaerobics, Inc.
41-905 Boardwalk, Suite B
Palm Desert, CA 92260-5141
619-779-5576

Agriculture First: Nutrition, Commodities and the National School Lunch Program
Public Voice for Food and Health Policy, 1992
1001 Connecticut Avenue NW, Suite 522
Washington, DC 20036
202-659-5930

Choice U.S.A
Vegetarian Education Network
P.O. Box 3347
West Chester, PA 19380
215-696-VNET (8638)

Environmental Nutrition
2112 Broadway, Suite 200
New York, NY 10023
212-362-0424
A professional newsletter for updated diet, nutrition and health information.

Heading for a Health Crisis: Eating Patterns of America's School Children
Public Voice for Food and Health Policy, 1991
1001 Connecticut Avenue NW, Suite 522
Washington, DC 20036
202-659-5930

Our Food Our World: The Realities of an Animal-Based Diet
EarthSave Foundation, 1992
706 Frederick Street
Santa Cruz, CA 95062
800-362-3648

Vegetarian Quanity Recipies
The Vegetarian Resource
P.O. Box 1463
Baltimore, MD 21203
410-366-VEGE

Vegetarian Times
P.O. Box 570
Oak Park, IL 60303
708-848-8100
A monthly magazine that contains recipes, dietary information, research news and general life-style advice.

Books

A to Z Guide to Toxic Foods and How to Avoid Them
Lynn Sonberg
Pocket Books,1992
1230 Avenue of the Americas
New York, NY 10020

Beyond Beef
Jeremy Rifkin
Dutton Press, 1992
375 Hudson Street
New York, NY 10014

Campus Favorites: Vegetarian Recipe Collection
Dietitians in College and University Food Services(DICUFS)
Grantlands Graphics, Inc., 1991
1110 Beetown Road.
Lancaster, WI 53813

Cooking for Consiousness
Joy McClure
Nucleus Publications, 1993
3223 County Road 1670
Willow Springs, MO 65793

Demanding Clean Food and Water: The Fight for a Basic Human Right
Joan Goldstein
Plenum Publishing Corporation, 1990
233 Spring Street
New York, NY 10012

Diet for the Atomic Age: How to Protect Yourself from Low Level Radiation
Sarah Shannon
Avery Publishing Group, 1987
120 Old Broadway
Garden City Park, NY 11040

Diet for a New America
John Robbins
Stillpoint, 1987
P.O. Box 640
Walpole, NH 03608-0640

Diet for a Poisoned Planet: How to Choose Safe Foods for You and Your Family
David Steinman
Ballantine Books, 1990
201 East 50th Street
New York, NY 10022

Diet for a Small Planet
Frances Moore Lappé
Ballantine Books, 1982
201 East 50th Street
New York, NY 10022

Dr. Dean Ornish's Program for Reversing Heart Disease
Dean Ornish
Random House, 1990
201 E. 50th Street
New York, NY 10022

Earl Mindell's Safe Eating
Earl Mindell
Warner Books, 1987
1271 Avenue of the Americas
New York, NY 10020

Earth and You: Eating for Two
April Moore
Potomac Valley Press, 1993
1424 16th Street NW, Suite 105
Washington, DC 20036

Ecological Cooking
Joanne Stepaniak and Kathy Hecke
Earthsave Foundation, 1991
706 Frederick Street
Santa Cruz, CA 95062-2205

Food for Thought
Amanda Mitra
Nucleus Publications, 1991
Route 2
Willow Springs, MO 65793-9802

Friendly Foods
Brother Ron Pickarski
Earthsave Foundation, 1991
706 Frederick Street
Santa Cruz, CA 95062-2205

Healing with Whole Foods
Paul Pitchford
North Atlantic Books, 1993
P.O. Box 1237
Berkely, CA 94701

Healthy School Lunch Action Guide
Susan Campbell and Tod Winant
EarthSave's Healthy School Lunch Program,
1994
706 Frederick Street
Santa Cruz, CA 95060-2205

**Heinerman's Encyclopedia of Fruits,
Vegetables and Herbs**
John Heinerman
Parker Publishing Company, 1988
P.O. Box 11071
Des Moines, IA 50380

**Keeping Food Fresh: How to Choose and
Store Everything You Eat**
Janet Bailey
Harper Perennial, 1985
10 East 53rd Street
New York, NY 10022

Kitchen Science
Howard Hillman
Houghton Mifflin, 1981
2 Park Street
Boston, MA 02108

Living Kitchen
Sharon Cadwallader
Sierra Club, 1983
730 Polk Street
San Francisco, CA 94109

May All Be Fed: Diet for a New World
John Robbins
William Morrow and Company, 1992
1350 Avenue of the Americas
New York, NY 10019

The McDougall Plan
John McDougall
New Win Publishing,1990
P.O. Box 5159
Clinton, NY 08809

**National Organic Wholesalers Directory
and Yearbook**
California Action Network, 1993
P.O. Box 464
Davis, CA 95617

Old MacDonald's Factory Farm
C. David Coats
Continuum Publishing Company, 1991
370 Lexington Avenue
New York, NY 10017

**Pesticides in the Diet of Infants and
Children**
National Research Council
National Academy of Sciences, 1993
2101 Constitution Avenue NW, Box 285
Washington, DC 20055

The Politics of Food
Joel Solkoff
Sierra Club, 1985
730 Polk Street
San Francisco, CA 94109

The Power of Your Plate
Neal D. Barnard
Book Publishing Company, 1990
P.O. Box 99
Summertown, TN 38483

Problems with Meat
John A. Scharffenberg
Woodbridge Press, 1982
P.O. Box 6189
Santa Barbara, CA 93160

Recipies from an Ecological Kitchen
Lorna J. Sass
William Morrow and Company, 1992
1350 Avenue of the Americas
New York, NY 10019

Safe Food
Michael F. Jacobson et al.
Living Planet Press, 1991
558 Rose Avenue
Venice, CA 90291

Shattering Food, Politics and the Loss of Genetic Diversity
Cary Fowler
The University of Arizona Press, 1990
1230 N. Park Avenue South, Suite 102
Tucson, AZ 85719

Simply Vegetarian!
Asha Praver and Sheila Rush
Dawn Publications, 1985
14618 Tyler Foote Road
Nevada City, CA 95959

Trading the Future
James Wessel and Mort Hantman
Institute for Food and Development Policy, 1983
1885 Mission Street
San Francisco, CA 94188

Vegan Cookbook
Alan Wakeman and Gordon Baskerville
Earthsave Foundation, 1986
706 Frederick Street
Santa Cruz, CA 95062-2205

Vegan Nutrition Pure and Simple
Michael Klaper
Earthsave Foundation, 1987
706 Frederick Street
Santa Cruz, CA 95062-2205

Vegetarian Journal's Guide to Natural Foods Restaurants in the United States and Canada
Vegetarian Resource Group
Avery Publishing Group, 1993
120 Old Broadway
Garden City Park, NY 11040

The Way We Grow
Anne Witte Garland with Mothers & Others for a Livable Planet
Berkeley Books, 1993
200 Madison Ave.
New York, NY 10016

What's Left to Eat?
Sue Gebo
McGraw-Hill, 1992
1221 Avenue of the Americas
New York, NY 10020

World Food and You
Nan Unklesbay
Haworth Press, Inc., 1992
10 Alice Street
Binghamton, NY 13904-1580

Books for Youth

Eating the Alphabet: Fruits and Vegetables from A to Z
Lois Ehlert
Harcourt Brace Jovanovich, 1989
1250 Sixth Avenue
San Diego, CA 92101

Food Resources
Robin Kerrod
Thomson Learning, 1993
115 Fifth Avenue
New York, NY 10003

Gregory, The Terrible Eater
Mitchell Sharmat
Scholastic, 1980
730 Broadway
New York, NY 10003

Growing Vegetable Soup
Lois Ehlert
HBJ Big Books, 1987
1250 Sixth Avenue
San Diego, CA 92101

Kids Ending Hunger
Tracy Apple Howard
Earthsave Foundation, 1992
706 Frederick Street
Santa Cruz, CA 95062-2205

Kitchen Fun for Kids
Michael Jacobson
Henry Holt and Company, 1991
115 West 18th Street
New York, NY 10011

Teaching Children About Food
Christine Berman and Jacki Fromer
Bull Publishing Company, 1991

P.O. Box 208
Palo Alto, CA 94302-0208

What's on My Plate
Ruth Belov Gross
Macmillan, 1990
866 Third Avenue
New York, NY 10022

Individuals/Companies/Organizations

American Dietetic Association
Vegetarian Nutrition Practice Group
216 West Jackson Boulevard
Chicago, IL 60606-6995
800-877-1600 ext. 4815

American Vegan Society (AVS)
501 Old Harding Highway
Malaga, NJ 08328
609-694-2887
Offers vegetarian videos and publications.

Cedarlane Natural Foods Company
1864 East 22nd Street
Los Angeles, CA 90058
213-745-4255
Distributor of frozen and refrigerated natural vegetarian foods for southern and northern California. Cedarlane has worked with several schools to help start vegetarian and vegan programs.

Center for Science in the Public Interest
1875 Connecticut Avenue NW, Suite 300
Washington, DC 20009
202-332-9110
Publishes the "Nutrition Action Healthletter" and "Healthwise Quantity Cookbook." CSPI also has a **Nutrition Activist Hotline.**

Earthsave Foundation

706 Frederick Street
Santa Cruz, CA 95062-2205
408-423-4069
The foundation is dedicated to educating people about the dietary link to environmental degradation and human health. It publishes a newsletter and a catalog of materials, including books and other publications.

Farm Animal Reform Movement

10101 Ashburton Lane
Bethesda, MD 20817
301-530-1737
A national organization that conducts annual campaigns (Great American Meat-Out, National Veal Ban Action, Downed Animals Project, and Compassion Campaign) to open the eyes, the minds, and the hearts of the American people to the tragedy of animal agriculture.

Farm Sanctuary

P.O. Box 150
Watkins Glen, NY 14891
607-583-2225
Slides and posters on the ethical treatment of farm animals.

Imagine Foods

350 Cambridge Ave., Suite 350
Palo Alto, CA 94306
415-327-1444
Suppliers of vegetarian burgers, veggie pockets, nondairy beverages and frozen desserts.

Kate Schumann Productions

537 Tyler Street
Port Townsend, WA 93868
206-385-4896
A speaker and educator who offers a course entitled "Going Vegetarian" and speaks on "No Cholesterol Way—A Health-Supporting Diet." She has several slide presentations designed for high school students, parents and school employees.

North American Vegetarian Society (NAVS)

53 West Jackson Boulevard, Suite 1552
Chicago, IL 60604
800-888-6287
A nonprofit educational organization that provides information to members, the public and interested organizations. It has introductory booklets and videos on the vegetarian diet.

People for the Ethical Treatment of Animals

P.O. Box 42516
Washington, DC 20015
301-770-PETA
For information on factory farming.

Physicians Committee for Responsible Medicine

P.O. Box 6322
Washington, DC 20015
202-686-2210
Doctors and laypersons working together for compassionate and effective medical practice, research and health promotion. Publishes a quarterly magazine–*Good Medicine*. Proposed the New Four Food Groups (grains, vegetables, legumes, and fruit) should replace the Food Guide Pyramid and Basic Four Food Groups.

Public Voice for Food and Health Policy

1001 Connecticut Avenue NW, Suite 522
Washington, DC 20036
202-659-5930
Provides various publications on food policy issues.

Pure Food Campaign

1130 17th Street NW, Suite 300
Washington, DC 20036
202-775-1132 or 800-451-7670
Under the auspices of the Foundation on
Economic Trends this public interest organization works in opposition to the development and introduction of genetically engineered foods.

Real Food Services

1155 Juniper Avenue
Boulder, CO 80304
303-938-1735
Supplies vegetarian, organic and whole food
products to the food service industry.

Society for Food Nutrition

2001 Killebrew Drive, Suite 340
Minneapolis, MN 55425-1882
612-854-0035
An association committed to linking nutrition, food and education. Its mission is to
enhance the ability of its members to help
the public make informed food choices.

USDA Human Nutrition Information Services

6505 Belcrest Road
Hyattsville, MD 20782
202-720-2791
Contact for more information on the Food
Guide Pyramid.

Vegetarian Education Network (VE-NET)

Sally Clinton, Director
P.O. Box 3347
West Chester, PA 19381
215-696-VNET
A nonprofit research and education organization dedicated to promoting the vegetarian
perspective in schools through education and
school lunches and to supporting young vegetarians. It publishes a vegetarian newsletter
for and by teenagers called "How on Earth!"
a quarterly publication that covers various
environmental, animal and global issues. It
provides lesson plans and a CHOICE! USA
action packet to help people work with their
schools in providing vegetarian meals. The
organization sells and loans videos, sells
books, offers other teaching aids, and refers
speakers. The group is compiling a vegetarian curriculum guide.

Vegetarian Resource Group

P.O. Box 1463
Baltimore, MD 21203
410-366-VEGE
Offers various publications, including *The
Vegetarian Journal*, a bimonthly publication
that contains current information on health,
environmental and ethical issues;
Foodservice Update, a magazine of healthy
tips and recipes for institutions; brochures on
vegetarian children and teens, and vegetarianism and the environment; and a packet
providing quantity recipes. The group has an
active outreach center that offers videos for
loan, brochures on the vegetarian diet and
quantity discounts.

Wholesome and Hearty Foods, Inc.

2422 SE Hawthorne
Portland, OR 97214
503-238-0109
Creators of a variety of gourmet meatless
burgers.

Chapter 5

The School Garden

Chapter 5

CONTENTS

INTRODUCTION

This chapter will outline how you can turn part of your school grounds into a wonderful garden. With the collaboration of students, teachers and maintenance workers, your school can become a special place where young people can learn about their connection with nature.

From this opportunity to interact within a "living classroom," respect for all living organisms is sure to grow. Students will develop the skills to make life decisions that are in harmony with the natural world rather than ones that are a manipulation of nature. This will be accomplished in three phases:

1. Work with the maintenance staff to develop an understanding of the current landscape management plan and develop a plan for the future.

2. Establish an organic garden, composting and vermicomposting on your school campus.

3. Develop a seed bank for the school and to assist the students in becoming seed savers.

THE LANDSCAPING

Increasing concerns about environmental issues are causing many people to rethink the way we use our natural resources. Unfortunately, when we are told that we must change our wasteful and polluting ways, most people envision images of hardship, sacrifice and a lower quality of life. However, this need not be the case.

Developing a Landscape Management Plan

The following are steps to take in developing a successful landscape plan:

◆ Examine and evaluate the current plan and existing resources of the school.

◆ Become familiar with the environmental issues and terms listed in this chapter and decide what you want to incorporate in your plan.

◆ Research alternatives and develop, in cooperation with the maintenance staff, a plan for the school.

◆ Take an active role in the implementation of the plan.

What Do We Want?

The first step is to evaluate the landscape management plan presently in use and the current state of the landscaping on your campus. With the instructions and questions that follow, the class should take a walk around the campus:

◆ Examine the current landscape plan and consider its environmental impact on the surrounding ecosystem. Most landscape plans were developed before the environmental concerns of today. It is time to try to demonstrate a concern for the environment.

◆ Find an area to set aside for an organic garden.

◆ Determine a location for establishing a compost pile.

◆ Imagine how you would like your school to look. What changes would you suggest?

◆ Could you create a stream, a pond, a walk lined with flowers and shrubs? Would a hedge be an acceptable replacement for that chain link fence? Why not? Don't let your imagination be limited; believe you can make it happen.

When you return to the classroom the students should be encouraged to discuss what changes they would like to see on campus. Discuss recent concerns about the environment and the importance of water conservation. Watch for articles on local gardens, landscaping and environmental issues.

Discuss with the students the subjects explored on the following pages. Ask them which ones they would like to introduce to your school.

Issues to Consider

The following are some issues and concerns that you will want to consider before developing your own plan:

Organic gardening uses natural methods for pest control and fertilizing. Everything you put in your system affects how you grow and live, so remember that you will be eating everything you put on your plants. For good health we want to eat food that is as pure as possible and not poison ourselves or the earth with chemicals. After all, "We are what we eat." Growing organically has also been proven to be cheaper than growing with pesticides, herbicides and artificial fertilizers.

Xeriscaping [pronounced ZIR-I-SCAPING (**xeri** means "dry")] is the practice of using plants that are adapted to the local environment. If you live in a wet climate, use plants that thrive in an abundance of water. If you live in a hot and dry climate, select those that can handle lots of sunlight and don't require much supplemental water.

Learning about water conservation can be fun and exciting. Xeriscape designs offer a way to reduce our environmental impact while actually improving our quality of life. For instance, we should question whether it is wise to invest so much of our time planting, fertilizing, watering and mowing our lawns only to send the cuttings off to an overcrowded landfill when so many more practical alternatives exist.

Be aware of "microclimates" within your landscaping area. For example, the north side of a building often differs from the south side in the amount of direct sunlight and precipitation that it receives.

Bioregions designate biological regions. Every plant and animal has different requirements for sunlight, water, soil type, altitude and other environmental factors. These life factors differ from region to region. To have a successful garden or landscape project it is critical that you know and understand the conditions of your "bioregion" so you can select the proper plants to grow in your area.

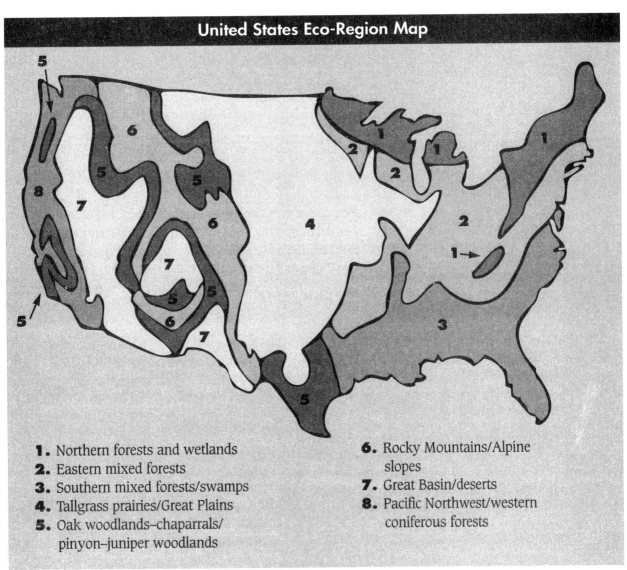

United States Eco-Region Map

1. Northern forests and wetlands
2. Eastern mixed forests
3. Southern mixed forests/swamps
4. Tallgrass prairies/Great Plains
5. Oak woodlands–chaparrals/
   pinyon–juniper woodlands
6. Rocky Mountains/Alpine
   slopes
7. Great Basin/deserts
8. Pacific Northwest/western
   coniferous forests

Adapted from *Landscaping with Nature*, ©1991 by Jeff Cox. Permission granted by Rodale Press, Inc., Emmaus, PA 18098.

Make a chart of all the conditions of your bioregion and then consult plant and garden books for what grows well in those conditions.

Native plants are suited for the climate and conditions of the area and therefore are easier to maintain and grow. Consider whether your campus was covered with vegetation before the school was built. Research the plants that grew in your region naturally before the soil was disturbed and buildings were erected. What are the native plants that would be good to use in your xeriscaping efforts?

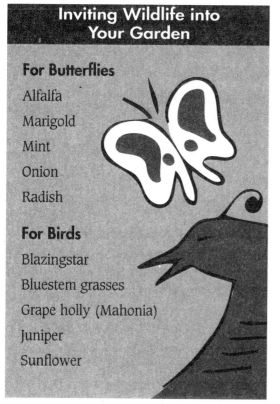

Inviting Wildlife into Your Garden

For Butterflies

Alfalfa

Marigold

Mint

Onion

Radish

For Birds

Blazingstar

Bluestem grasses

Grape holly (Mahonia)

Juniper

Sunflower

Consult your local library or neighborhood nursery for books on native plants for your area. California has a Native Plant Society. Check to see if your state has one. If not, many garden clubs will have information on this topic.

Studying the differences (e.g., demands for water, type of soil needs, temperature ranges) between native plants and the other cultivated species can be an interesting science project.

Permaculture (permanent agriculture) is a complex concept that may be too encompassing to introduce here, but since it will come up in your readings, we will try to present it in a simplified fashion.

Permaculture is a term coined by Bill Mollison of the Permaculture Institute in Australia. It refers to the design and maintenance of a productive agricultural ecosystem. It is a harmonious integration of people and landscape that provides food, energy, shelter and other needs in a sustainable way. Permaculture embraces a set of ethics and values that encourage the following:

◆ Caring for the earth by providing for the continued existence of all life systems.

◆ Caring for people by seeing that others have access to resources, such as healthy food and clean air, necessary for their existence.

◆ Setting limits on population and consumption so that resources can be used to meet these principles.

At the individual home or school level there is a way of taking personal responsibility and giving relevance to this philosophy. The school garden achieves this ethical approach to living by putting the school campus in better environmental balance, first by caring for the land (providing habitats for the return of flora and fauna) and then by taking it one step further and providing some of the food needs of the school.

Edible plants don't have to grow just in a garden. Many are very attractive and make a wonderful contribution to landscaping. When you cultivate a row of plants along the front of your school, why not make them broccoli, cauliflower, cabbage, carrots or include them all? They make a very attractive border and a great salad. When choosing trees to plant, why not choose an apple or pear? Both take the same amount of care as an ornamental elm but taste much better.

Open pollination occurs in a variety of ways:
   ◆ Insect pollination (honeybees usually)
   ◆ Self pollination
   ◆ Wind pollination

These plants are set apart from hybrids because they have a history of performing well, often under less than ideal conditions. They possess a reservoir of disease resistance, they have strong nutritional and flavor qualities, and the seeds can be saved. They have a strong set of genes but are not uniform, a trait that makes them unpopular with agribusiness.

F1 hybrid seeds are used by modern farmers to grow perfectly consistent produce that is plump, is easy to ship and store and has a long shelf life (especially when treated with the correct chemicals). F1 hybrid seeds are created when reproductive information from two different plant strains is artificially combined with the intent of getting the best characteristics of each plant.

Self-pollinating Seeds
   ◆ Endive
   ◆ Lettuce
   ◆ Oats
   ◆ Pea
   ◆ Soybean
   ◆ Tomato
   ◆ Wheat

The concern with this type of produce is that the seeds produced through this process are nonviable (unable to reproduce). If you plant the seeds produced from the plants grown from F1 hybrid seeds, either they won't produce a plant or the characteristics of that plant will be unpredictable.

Dangers arise from this system because
   ◆ They must be purchased new each year, since they do not necessarily reproduce true to form.
   ◆ They can be more fragile. (Most are bred to be grown with exact amounts of chemical inputs artificial fertilizers and pesticides.)
   ◆ It is seriously diminishing the gene pool. Without diversity there is always the long-term risk of greater exposure to threats posed by pests and diseases.

Heirloom seeds are nonhybrid varieties introduced before 1940. After that time, many traditional varieties were replaced by hybrids and many became scarce or lost. Heirloom seeds are old varieties that have adapted because of cross pollination, environmental forces and natural selection, and have been saved because they are naturally pest resistant or drought tolerant! Often heirloom seeds will be classified further as "family heirloom varieties," since they have been passed down within families. The resource section of this chapter provides sources for obtaining such seeds.

A **cover crop**, like composting and mulching, stems from a basic organic gardening tradition of feeding the soil. Green manure grains or legumes are planted for the purpose of being worked back into the soil or cut down for compost. They increase the soil's organic matter by introducing beneficial microorganisms, providing habitat for beneficial insects and stabilizing the soil's nitrogen levels. These are conditions that prepare the garden for the next planting and that aid in weed reduction.

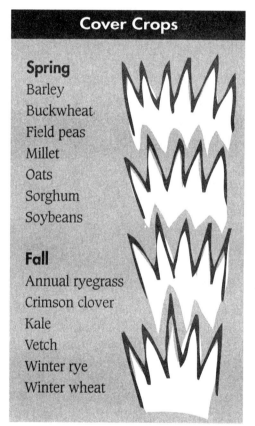

Cover Crops

Spring
Barley
Buckwheat
Field peas
Millet
Oats
Sorghum
Soybeans

Fall
Annual ryegrass
Crimson clover
Kale
Vetch
Winter rye
Winter wheat

The more popular cover crops include alfalfa, clovers, beans and vetches, in the legume family; and winter rye, barley, oats and rye grass, in the grain family. These are quick-growing plants, so gardeners in the north won't lose planting time. In the resource section of this chapter many books are listed that provide more in-depth explanation and lists of these plants. Also listed are supply catalogs that sell the seeds.

Organic fertilizers and soil supplements provide a way of gardening in cooperation with nature. Artificial fertilizers represent a human control and a chemical approach to gardening.

Animal manure is a good source of organic fertilizer. This can include cattle, rabbit, poultry, horse or goat. A source for these may be a local egg farmer, dairy or stable. These manures can be added to your compost or directly to the garden as a top dressing. If you do this be sure to let it compost for about 6 months before adding. Organic fertilizers are slow-acting, so they provide a long-term residual improvement to the soil.

The two most important soil supplements to provide are a *natural* form of *nitrogen* (green manure or compost) and *rock phosphorus*. Both of these are sold at garden centers.

Foliar-feeding is the feeding of plants by spraying nutrients onto the leaf surface, especially the underside, where the stomata function in the same way as the pores of our skin. Although this spraying is very beneficial to plants in full vegetative growth, it is really only necessary for plants that are undernourished from poor soil, suffering from insect damage or in stress from different conditions, such as a prolonged dry season. Some gardeners will use foliars when plants are just starting to bud, blossom, fruit or seed; or they may use them to extend the fruiting season. See the supply catalogs listed in the resource section; they all carry a number of different foliar feeders that serve in slightly different conditions.

Mulch materials—such as bark, wood chips, straw, hay or manure—are used to cover the soil where plants are or will be growing. The benefits are many:

- ◆ Moisture retention
- ◆ Weed suppression
- ◆ Soil erosion prevention
- ◆ Addition of organic matter
- ◆ Protection of the soil to create more bacteria and earthworm activity
- ◆ Enhancement of root development
- ◆ Improved drainage
- ◆ Soil that is cooler in the summer and warmer in the winter
- ◆ And more!

The following mulching materials can be found for free close to home or for a minimal cost nearby:

- ◆ Leaves
- ◆ Leaf mold
- ◆ Pine needles
- ◆ Sawdust
- ◆ Wood chips or shavings
- ◆ Spoiled hay
- ◆ Straw
- ◆ Seaweed
- ◆ Rotten wood
- ◆ Shells or hulls
- ◆ Corn cobs or stalks
- ◆ Newspaper
- ◆ Scrap material

Composting is quite simple. Organic waste is given the space to do what it will naturally do—break down and form an ideal soil conditioner. It is much better to work the grass clippings, leaves and left-over food products back into the soil, thereby returning to the earth what the earth has given us. This is a very basic form of recycling.

This concept is the foundation for any organic garden. Although it is important to learn how to grow your own food, it is equally important to know how to care for the soil. By composting you will be creating a very healthy soil amendment, avoiding the cost and inadequacies of synthetic fertilizers, and you will be sending less refuse to the landfill. The beneficial fungi and earthworms that live in the compost aid in the fight of soil pests as well.

Composting is an ancient art form that has been practiced since the beginning of time. It is only in the latter part of the last century that we have found it necessary to bag up the left-over food and yard waste and bury it in a land fill. (It is estimated that about 20 percent of the solid waste in the United States is yard and garden waste!)

(Please see "A Composting Plan for Your School" later in this chapter for a discussion of how to set up your compost pile.)

Vermicomposting is the practice of composting using worms to decompose organic material. This is an efficient method of making wonderful soil, and a great way to **utilize** and **reduce** your waste.

Vermicomposting can be done inside with great success. Schools that have instituted vermicomposting have found it to be a well-received class project. Classes can make some money through the sale of the worms and compost material. This exercise will take a little work to get started (building your box and ordering some red worms), but once you are up and running it takes very little effort to maintain. (Please see page 147, "Vermicomposting at School.") The resource section at the end of the chapter lists some sources for buying the boxes if you don't want to make your own.

Transplanting will be an important part of getting your school garden started. Germination of seeds can be done indoors in 4-inch pots with a mixture of potting soil, perlite and peat moss. The procedure for planting the seedlings in the garden is to

1. Dig a hole several inches wider than the root mass.
2. Rough up the edges of the hole and the root mass, being careful not to break too many roots.
3. Fill in around the plant with half the existing soil and half compost. (Don't add any fertilizer at this point; it might "burn" the roots.)

Cold frames are wooden boxes that sit on the ground with a secondhand storm window on top. Their design is one of simplicity with great usefulness. They are easy and cheap to make. (See the resource section for a guidebook on how to make your own.) Planting in the box makes it possible to extend the growing season (quite desirable for northern gardeners) and to increase the types of produce that can be grown.

Integrated pest management (IPM) is a method of controlling weeds and pests with little or no harmful chemicals. IPM consists of researching and understanding the characteristics and life-style of the weed or pest you want to control and then implementing appropriate natural or biological controls. It can also require a determination of an acceptable "pest tolerance level." See Chapter 3 for a more detailed explanation of IPM.

Pesticides are designed to control unwanted insects and other organisms. Unfortunately, pesticides also kill the beneficial insects as well. When pesticides are applied on school grounds, students are exposed to the toxic chemicals for a good part of their day both indoors and outdoors. Cafeteria and maintenance workers may use pesticides as a short-term method of killing unwanted pests. Also, agricultural pesticides used on our foods often contain toxic chemicals that we end up eating. It is best to try controlling "pests" through natural methods. See Chapter 3 for more information.

Herbicides are designed to control the invasion of unwanted plants or what we commonly call weeds. There are several nonchemical methods for controlling plants we don't want in our garden. You can plant a ground cover such as white clover that is good for the soil because it replaces lost nitrogen and it will "crowd out" the unwanted plants. You can also try the age-old practice of hand weeding, which has worked for centuries and is cost effective and good for the earth and us.

Generally, with well-balanced, healthy soil the weeds will grow at a minimum. See Chapter 3 for more suggestions on controlling weeds. If you have been careful in your planting practices, you should have very few weeds.

Taking a Look at What Is Here

Teachers can make it fun to look at what exists nearby. The way to begin is to take a walk around your campus. Ask the questions that appear in this section. Encourage everyone to look at the world as if through new eyes. For the moment, remove the limitations of time and money. If you could create a school, how would you like it to look? What changes would you suggest? Think about how water and plants are being used and what positive or negative effects your school is having on the environment.

All-Purpose Insect Spray

You Will Need:
- ✔ 1 garlic bulb
- ✔ 1 small onion
- ✔ 1 tablespoon cayenne pepper
- ✔ 1 quart water
- ✔ 1 tablespoon liquid soap (hand soap only)

Chop or grind garlic and onion, add cayenne and mix with water. Let steep 1 hour, then add liquid soap. Store in a covered jar in the refrigerator up to 1 week. Use as a spray wherever insects are causing a problem.

How close have you looked at your school in the past? Every square inch may be covered by lawn, asphalt or concrete, but it doesn't *need* to be that way. Are there places where you can put planter boxes or create a garden?

Stop at a nice, comfortable place to sit. Relax and try to visualize your campus as it was before the construction of the school. Consider that a natural, undisturbed environment is intended to be covered with life and living things. Imagine the environment, the plants and animals as they were before the school was built. Did deer or other wildlife come to graze on the grasses around the campus? Were there birds flying from branch to branch on the trees and bushes? Was there water on or near your campus?

In an attempt to "tame nature" and bend her to our will, we have destroyed natural ecosystems and re-created a world to fit our needs. We force plants to grow where they are not well suited. As a result, we have altered the environment to accommodate *their* special out-of-context needs. How can you work to restore some of the natural ecosystem?

As a class project, research which plants are adapted to grow in the local environment, given the temperature ranges and the amount of sun and water you receive. Are there areas where you can increase the number of living organisms and diversity without increasing your water demands?

The following are some more questions to pose in the class discussion of landscaping and gardening possibilities:
- ◆ What kinds of plants are being used in landscaping on your campus and where are they located?
- ◆ How much of the campus is covered with concrete and how much with turf?
- ◆ How are the borders around walks and play areas of your school defined? Could they be planted with flowers, plants and shrubs.
- ◆ Are the plants on your campus adapted to the local environment? Consider the landscaping in terms of the amount of rainfall and the amount of sun your school receives.
- ◆ How many different kinds of plants are on the campus?

Now that you have an idea of where you are going and what you are doing, let's get started. The library, local nurseries, garden clubs and your state's association of nurserymen are some of the resources to call or visit for your research.

Including the Maintenance Staff

Ask the maintenance supervisor to come and talk to your class. Before the visit have the students organize their ideas for a landscape plan and questions they would like to ask the staff. After the maintenance supervisor explains the landscape policy for the school, help your students present their ideas to the supervisor. This should incite a lively discussion on possibilities. An important aspect of this program is having the students assume an active role in the implementation of agreeable changes.

Keep a written record of the agreed changes and determine which activities your students can take on. The following are some suggestions:

◆ Clear a border around the perimeter of your school and use native plants with descriptive plaques of the plants. Because these plants are naturally suited to your area, they should do well. This will become a living classroom and a lesson for the entire school and community.

◆ Put in planter boxes around your school. This will add life and color and attract pollinating insects to your campus. Providing a source of nectar will also encourage birds to return. Having students make the planter boxes can provides another valuable project.

◆ As a long-term component of the project, consider planting fruit trees adapted to your area. This will provide students with a sweet natural treat during different seasons. For some it will be their first experience tasting fruit fresh from the tree. If you plant these trees on the south side of buildings, they will grow faster, provide cooling shade in the summer and allow light and sun through in the winter when they lose their leaves.

◆ Use edible plants for landscaping. Students can then harvest, prepare and eat what has been grown. Decorative cabbage makes a very attractive supplement to the planter boxes. Books on edible plants are available (see the resources section at the end of this chapter).

The main objective is to turn your entire school into a garden place and to offer your students a connection with the living earth. You may find that your school has an extensive landscape plan and that your grounds maintenance staff is doing an extraordinary job. However, you should allow your students to look at your school with fresh eyes. The lack of limiting beliefs may lead to new ideas!

How to Implement Your Suggestions

In every community many groups are available to lend assistance and expertise, such as garden clubs, neighborhood organizations and urban forestry groups. See the resource section of this chapter for some nationally based organizations.

To find funding for plant donations and supplies, there are many avenues to follow:
- ◆ The PTA
- ◆ Local retailers
- ◆ Local banks
- ◆ Hardware stores or garden centers
- ◆ A student-written notice about the school greening/gardening project in the local newspaper/media. (This often elicits a great response.)

It has been proven that property values increase near green spaces and that schools where students have actively participated in "naturescaping" have experienced significant drops in vandalism. It is more likely that students will feel proud of something they have had a part in creating that looks good and creates habitats for wildlife!

Terry Keller, director of the Bronx Green-Up project (aimed at restoring green spaces in urban environments), was quoted in the *Audubon Activist* (November 1992) as saying, "There simply are no drugs where there is a good, growing garden. The community bands together there and they are not about to let drug dealers ruin it."

THE ORGANIC GARDEN

Why have an organic garden? Because it will
- ◆ Teach students how to grow their own chemically free food and plants.
- ◆ Give students an opportunity to experience how untreated "fresh-from-the-vine" food can taste.
- ◆ Educate students how they can provide food for themselves and the world population through a hands-on method.
- ◆ Provide food for the school lunch program.
- ◆ Offer the students a chance to grow, nurture and take responsibility for a living organism.
- ◆ Allow the students a chance to get their hands dirty and work with the earth.
- ◆ Develop in students an understanding of the seasons and how all things are connected.

Developing a Plan

A key to successful gardening is first to develop a plan. Spending a few extra minutes with the plan can save you from wasting time later and may be the difference between success and failure. The plan should include the following information.

Location

Where are you going to put the garden? If you choose the right location, much of the work will be done for you and it will be easier to maintain. What is the sun exposure like throughout the year? Are there trees that will block the sun for significant portions of the day or in different seasons? How close is the water source for ease of access to maintain the garden? Is the soil good and what is the drainage like? Is the area protected from harsh elements? Finally, do not place the garden where it will get little attention!

Space Requirements Chart		
Plant	Average Height Allowed for Mature Plant*	Average Diameter Allowed for Mature Plant **
Asparagus	M	48"
Broccoli	M	18"
Corn	H	12"
Cucumber	L	18" (plus vines)
Lettuce		
(head)	L	12"
(leaf)	L	8"
Onion		
(bulb)	L	3"
(green)	L	—
Peas		
(bush)	M	3"
(pole)	H	4"
Pumpkin	L	36" (plus vines)
Tomato	M-H	18" (stalks)

*L = up to 24 inches, M = 24 inches, H = 48" and up.

**The "average diameter allowed" is intended as an approximate guide for intensive planting.

Source: Elizabeth Bremner and John Pusey, *Children's Gardens: A Field for Teachers, Parents and Volunteers,* University of California Cooperative Extension, Common Ground Garden Program, 1990.

Size

How big is your garden to be? The type of garden we will describe is called *French Intensive*. This is a design for growing a lot of produce in a relatively small area by creating deep, or "double-dug," beds. Although there are a few rules to follow, most of the design work is up to the gardener and depends on the available space.

If possible, you may want to allow enough space so that each student or group of students can grow what they choose. Ideally, you should allow about 3 square feet per student, but it is possible to get by with less.

Students planning their gardens should be aware of how much space plants require. The Space Requirements chart on page 133 will give an idea of how much area some plants need.

Water

Without exception, water is the most important aspect of your garden. Consider the source and type of watering system to be used. It is best to have a water source near the site you have selected. Watering your garden has both a practical and a philosophical purpose. When you plant the garden it is important to start with moist soil (although you should never dig in wet soil) and to keep the soil moist while the seeds are germinating. The soil must also be moist when transplanting seedlings.

An important point to keep in mind is that roots will go where the water is. If you water often and for short periods, the water primarily stays on the surface, as will the roots. The longer but less frequently you water, the deeper the roots will extend. Carrots, radishes and potatoes require deep watering, whereas lettuce and spinach use only water in the shallower soil horizons.

When students water the garden they will naturally observe how their young seedlings are doing and should take a few minutes to hand-pull any weeds that may have sprouted. Moreover, an exchange of energy takes place between living things that is difficult to describe but that appears to promote healthy, happy growth, whether in humans or plants!

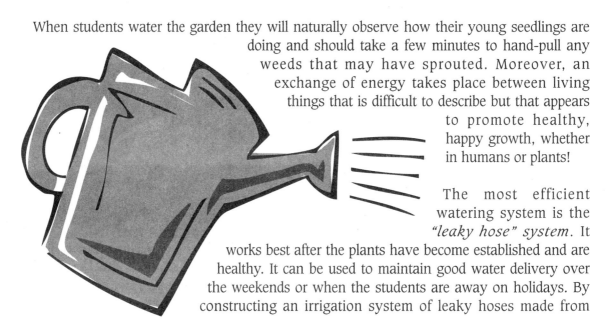

The most efficient watering system is the *"leaky hose" system*. It works best after the plants have become established and are healthy. It can be used to maintain good water delivery over the weekends or when the students are away on holidays. By constructing an irrigation system of leaky hoses made from recycled rubber and set on timers, you will be helping the recycling industry while using the most efficient waterwise system that is also the best for the plants. This system really shows its merit in the summer, when the students are away from school for extended periods. The leaky hose and timers can be found at local gardening centers. See the resource section at the end of the chapter for other sources.

Soil Condition

The condition of the soil you will be working with may spell success or disaster for your garden. However, you can have a successful garden in virtually any soil if you take the time to give it a little conditioning. Here are a few simple suggestions:

◆ If you have *sandy* soil that will not hold together when you squeeze a ball of it in your hand and that drains well but does not hold moisture very long, add some *organic material,* such as peat moss, compost, steer manure or clay.

◆ If your soil *"cakes"* on the surface, packs into tight balls when moist and does not drain well, add some *organic material* and some *sand* to it.

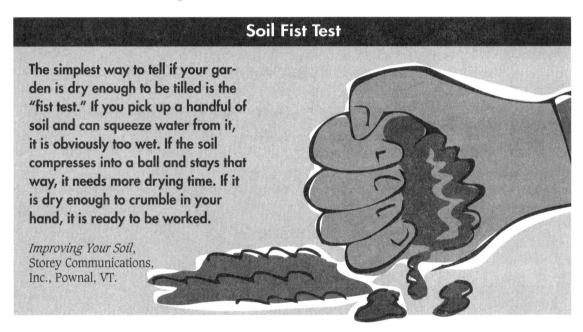

Soil Fist Test

The simplest way to tell if your garden is dry enough to be tilled is the "fist test." If you pick up a handful of soil and can squeeze water from it, it is obviously too wet. If the soil compresses into a ball and stays that way, it needs more drying time. If it is dry enough to crumble in your hand, it is ready to be worked.

Improving Your Soil,
Storey Communications,
Inc., Pownal, VT.

Regardless of the soil type, any time you are practicing intensive gardening you will need to feed your soil. Do this with any *natural* soil amendment (e.g., organic compost material) that contains phosphorus, potassium and nitrogen. You may find many commercial sources of processed chemical nutrients that will grow large, attractive plants, but overall the plants will be nutrient poor. Naturally occurring nutrient complexes provide a whole host of useful and necessary plant foods.

Organic material is also very important to any garden. You can provide a free natural source of this by starting and maintaining your own composting system on your campus.

What Do You Want to Plant?

Do you want to grow something you can eat or something to look at? Both are fun to grow, bring enjoyment and are good for the earth. When you are making your plant selections for your garden, consider the following:

◆ **What is the climate of your region and what will grow best there?** Do some research about the plants you are interested in growing and about your bioregion to determine if one is adapted to the other. You may save a lot of time and have better results by asking the owner of your local garden center to come to your class and discuss the plants that grow well in your area. He or she may also want to donate some plants and materials and work with you to get the garden going.

What to Plant, When to Plant*

For a fall garden, plant:

Artichokes	Celery	Mustard
Beets	Chard	Onions
Broccoli	Collards	Peas
Brussel Sprouts	Garlic	Parsnips
Cabbage	Kale	Radishes
Carrots	Kohlrabi	Spinach
Cauliflower	Lettuce	Turnips

For a winter garden, plant:

Artichokes	Celery	Onions
Asparagus	Chives	Parsley
Beets	Collards	Peas
Broccoli	Garlic	Potatoes (white)
Brussels Sprouts	Kale	Radishes
Cabbage	Leeks	Rhubarb
Carrots	Lettuce (Leaf)	Turnips
Cauliflower	Mustard	Spinach
Chard		

For a spring garden, plant:

Beans	Cucumbers	Okra
Beets	Eggplant	Pepper
Cantaloupe	Kohlrabi	Pumpkins
Carrots	Leeks	Radishes
Cauliflower	Lettuce (leaf)	Rutabaga
Celery	Melons	Squash
Chard	New Zealand	Tomatoes
Chayote	Spinach	Turnips
Corn		Watermelon

*Please keep in mind this is for climates similar to Southern California. In cooler parts of the country, fall and winter gardens may not be possible.

Source: *Children's Gardens: A Field Guide for Teachers, Parents and Volunteers*, University of California Cooperative Extension, Common Ground Garden Program.

◆ **During what season do you intend to start planting?** It is best to plant certain species in the fall and others in the spring. By working with the seasons you can have a garden that will produce food all year long. Determine what you want to harvest and when. This will help you decide what you should plant and when.

◆ **What sort of plants do you like?** If you don't like a plant you will be less likely to take care of it. This is your garden space to grow with and care for as you like. Grow what makes you happy!

◆ **What should you do with your harvest?** If you are going to grow food to contribute to the school cafeteria, meet with the food service staff to determine what their needs are. A food bank, soup kitchen or shelter providing meals for local people in need may be able to use the donation of free fresh food. You can check with your city council to find such organizations. Selling organically grown fruit and vegetables could also provide a good fund-raiser for the classes tending to the garden.

◆ **What should you do about pests?** A major consideration for gardeners is pests. These come in the form of unwanted plants and insects. Because this is to be a chemical-free garden, a need exists to explore nontoxic means of dealing with these problems.

For unwanted plants (weeds), the best method is to visit your garden often and to remove by hand the plants you don't want there. Weeds generally do not grow in soil that is fertile and well drained. Weeds have less of a chance to compete when plants that are best suited for the area are grown. Keep in mind that many plants, such as white clover, can help crowd out weeds and add valuable nutrients to the soil. Mulch (wood chips) and lawn cuttings not only act as a good barrier to weeds, but retain moisture in the soil as well.

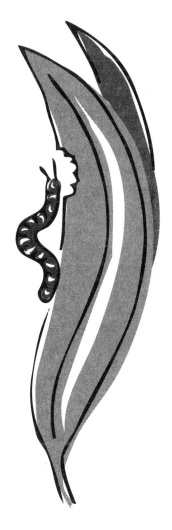

Insects pose a more difficult problem. They can move quickly from plant to plant, are difficult to treat and can damage a garden if left unchecked. Chapter 3 provides information on the IPM program, which describes methods for controlling insect pests without the need to use harmful chemicals. You should also investigate local sources for information on IPM that suits your area. You can try many biological and nontoxic chemical treatments. Check with your local garden center for these products. Refer to the resource section of Chapter 3 for further information.

One method of preventing destructive pests is to grow insect-deterrent plants. The chart, "Insect-deterrent Plants" on the next page suggests plants that accomplish this.

Insect-Deterrent Plants

Plant	Effect
Basil	Repels flies and mosquitoes
Celery	White cabbage butterfly
Chrysanthemum	Deters most insects
Eggplant	Deters Colorado potato beetle
Garlic	Deters Japanese beetle, other insects and blight
Geranium	Most insects
Horseradish	Plant at corners of potato patch to deter potato bug
Marigold	The workhorse of pest deterrents. Plant throughout garden to discourage Mexican bean beetles, nematodes and other insects
Mint	Deters white cabbage moth and ants
Mole Plant	Deters moles and mice if planted here and there.
Nasturtium	Deters aphids, squash bugs, striped pumpkin beetles
Onion family	Deters most pests
Pot Marigold	Deters asparagus beetles, tomato worms and general garden pests
Peppermint	Planted among cabbages, it repels the white cabbage butterfly
Radish	Deters cucumber beetle
Rosemary	Deters cabbage moth, bean beetle and carrot fly
Sage	Deters cabbage moth, carrot fly
Salsify	Repels carrot fly
Summer Savory	Deters bean beetles
Tansy	Deters flying insects, Japanese beetles, striped cucumber beetles, squash bugs, ants
Tomato	Deters asparagus beetle
Thyme	Deters cabbage worm

Source: *Gardening Answers*, Storey Communications, Inc., Pownal, VT.

The issues we have just discussed are important to address when planning your garden. You will undoubtedly have several more questions and answers that are specific to your area and your special challenges. It will save time and may prevent disappointment if these issues are addressed before you start your garden.

Companion Planting

It is well known that plants compete among each other for light, water, and nutrients. More surprising might be the discovery that certain plants actually work together for survival. There are plants that help each other repel insects and disease and that provide their neighbors with essential nutrients. Take carrots and leeks, for example. A major enemy of the carrot is the carrot fly, whereas the leek suffers from the leek moth and the onion fly. Yet when they live in companionship, the strong and strangely different smell of the partner plant repels the insects so well that they do not even attempt to lay their eggs on the neighbor plant.

The following chart shows some of those plants that get along well together and those that do not. Investigate the relationship between these plants.

Companion Planting		
Plant (Genus Species)	**Companion Plants**	**Not With**
Asparagus (Asparagus officinalis)	Parsley, basil, tomatoes	
Broccoli (Brassica oeraceae)	Aromatic plants, (dill, celery, chamomile, sage, peppermint, rosemary), potatoes, beets, onions	Tomatoes, pole beans, strawberries
Corn (Zea mays)	Potatoes, peas, beans, cucumbers, squash, pumpkin, melons	Tomatoes
Cucumber (Cucumis Sativus)	Corn, beans, peas, radishes, sunflowers, young orchards, lettuce, kohlrabi, two or three radishes and let them go to seed	Potatoes, aromatic herbs
Lettuce (Lactuca sativa)	Green onions, strawberries, cucumbers, carrots, radishes, beets	
Onion (Allium cepa)	Cabbage family, beets, tomatoes, strawberries, lettuce, summer savory, chamomile (sparsely)	Peas, beans
Pea (Pisum sativum)	Carrots, turnips, radishes, corn cucumbers, beans, potatoes, aromatic herbs	Onions, garlic, gladiolus
Pumpkin (Cucurbita pepo)	Jimson weed, thorn apple, corn	Potatoes
Tomato (Lycopersicon esculentum)	Asparagus, gooseberries, chives, onion, parsley, marigold, carrot, nasturtium, garlic, roses, celery	Cabbage family, apricot trees, corn, potatoes

Adapted from: Louise Riotte, *Carrots Love Tomatoes*, Storey Communications, Inc., Pownal, VT, 1975.

The French Intensive Method

Now that you have drafted a garden plan, let's get busy!

First gather the tools required to begin:
- A sharp square-nosed spade
- A strong 4-tine hay or pitch fork
- Small garden trowels
- Irrigation hoses
- Soil conditioner
- A few feet of chicken-wire (used for seed spacing)
- A ball of string or twine

The French intensive method was developed to get the most production from the least amount of soil under cultivation. To achieve this, follow these step-by-step instructions.

1. **Design a planting scheme and order your open-pollinated plant seeds.** If you can, it is a great idea to germinate your seeds in your classroom in small pots with holes. One place to find such pots is on the bottom of the large plastic PETE soda bottles! Or this may be an item that your local garden center will consider donating.

2. Go to your selected site and **determine the outer boundaries of your garden**. Use the twine to define where individual beds will be constructed. If the area is presently covered with sod, remove the sod and set it aside. It can be used elsewhere on campus or composted, so don't just throw it away!

   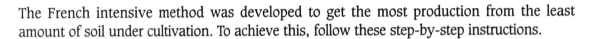

   Some people like to define their bed boundaries by building wooden-slat frames around them. But the wood will give insects (such as snails) a place to hide and breed and make it difficult to work the edges of the bed. Instead put gravel or wood bark chips between the beds to define the edge of each working area.

3. **Do a structure test on a soil sample.** See the soil structure discussion in "Developing a Plan" earlier in this chapter.

4. **Dig a 6-inch-deep trench** at the edge of the garden and running side to side. Carefully place the soil removed to the side. This soil will be used later in topping off the last trench at the opposite end of the garden plot.

5. **Use the pitch fork to loosen the exposed soil.** Do this by driving the tines in their full length and then wrenching toward the surface. By inserting the tines of your fork to

their entire depth and then lifting them to the surface, you will loosen or "fluff" the soil 10-12 inches deep and expose rocks, roots or weeds that need to be removed. By loosening the soil you have created some air space for the plants roots to grow and breathe. Plant roots, like any living organism, need air to be healthy. **It is important not to walk on the raised beds after the soil has been "fluffed."**

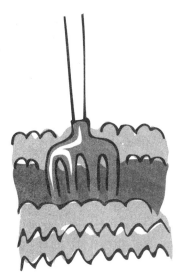

6. **Create another trench next to the first.** Use the topsoil removed from this trench to cover the row you just finished fluffing. When you create your planter beds within the garden plot, make them just wide enough for the students to reach halfway across. This will allow for weeding and harvesting from both sides of the bed. Be sure to allow for walkways between the beds.

7. **Repeat fluff with the pitch fork.** Apply removed topsoil to the last fluffed area. Use this procedure for the entire garden bed. When you get to the end, you will notice that the final row is slightly lower than the rest, so go back to the first row, bring the topsoil from the initial trench and place it on the last row.

8. **With your bare hands kneed the soil** (break apart any chunks) and take out all the old root stock, weeds and rocks. You now have a nice raised-bed garden. This is where the fun really begins—your hands are going to get really dirty!

9. **Add about 3 inches of compost or soil-structuring material** and sprinkle the soil nutrients in a thin layer across the top.

10. **Water them for a few days and let them sit.** Your beds are now healthy and ready for planting, but it is best to give them some time to mature.

11. **After a week or so you will notice some weeds popping up.** Now you know for sure that your garden is ripe for planting! But quick, go through and pull those weeds now, while they are young upstarts.

12. Your beds are now ready to plant. If you have already germinated your seeds, you can transplant the seedlings. *Remember to keep the garden moist while seeds are germinating and until the new plants have sprouted at least 4 sets of leaves. Then go to a routine watering pattern based on the need of your bioregion.*

13. Lay the chicken wire frame on the bed and put one seed in the center of each wire cell. Do this for the entire bed. Using the chicken wire will ensure even spacing between your plants. This will give you a solid ground cover rather than rows.

14. Now you get to wait, watch, assist and enjoy the process of growing plants. Because every garden is an experiment and an opportunity for learning through the process of trial and error, it is important to **keep careful notes** and record every observation and action you take in your garden. Things to note would include when plants get their first leaves, when you water, how many of your seeds sprout, and so on. Your notes will undoubtedly become vital to the success of future school gardens. **Keep in mind that the crop that has been planted by this year's class may be harvested by next year's students.**

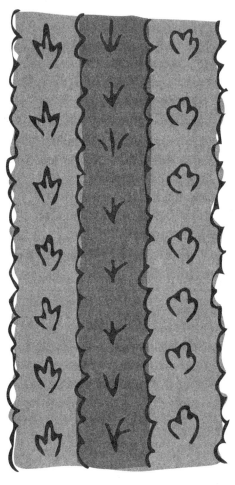

The intensive planting method explained here should require very little maintenance and weeding. It is still important, however, to remove the weeds and deal with pests when you see them. An important point to remember is that not all insects are harmful; some are very beneficial and should be encouraged to stay. Learn the difference. This will vary in different parts of the country and can easily be researched for your area.

With the help of some good gardening books (many are listed at the end of this chapter in the resource section) and the human resources of your community, you can have a happy and healthy garden.

Much of your garden's growth will occur during summer, while your students are away from school. You should try to make arrangements for the students who will be around to set up a schedule for regularly visiting the school and caring for the garden. If you have set up a leaky hose irrigation system with timers, you will not have to worry about watering throughout the summer. If you have any questions, your garden center can help you.

A COMPOSTING PLAN FOR YOUR SCHOOL

All of this section has been excerpted from the book, *Backyard Composting*, Harmonious Technologies, Ojai, CA, 1992. We felt that Harmonious Technologies did such a wonderful job explaining composting clearly, carefully and thoroughly, that we asked them if we could reproduce the following from *Backyard Composting*.

◆

Composting is a natural process that converts organic waste into an ideal soil conditioner. Heat, water, oxygen and tiny organisms all work together to break down organic matter. Composting saves landfill space and enriches the soil. And composting is fun!

What Materials Go Into a Compost?

Compost materials can be classified into 2 categories: greens and browns. Greens are high in nitrogen and browns are high in carbon. Greens include fresh weeds, fresh leaves, fresh grass clippings, food scraps and manure. Browns include dry leaves, dry grass clippings, straw and wood shavings.

The best mix is usually 1/4 to 1/2 green material and 3/4 to 1/2 brown materials. A compost pile containing high-nitrogen materials (greens) will heat up faster and become compost faster. Just remember this: *nitrogen = heat.*

◆ *Shredded* cardboard, paper, newspaper and paper towels can also be added to your compost pile.

◆ Flies are often attracted to food scraps placed on the very top of a pile. Bury your food scraps 6 to 12 inches below or cover them with leaves, straw and so on.

◆ Avoid rats and other animals by leaving out meat scraps, fats and cooking oils.

◆ Manure is high in nitrogen and perfect for getting a compost pile cooking. However, avoid feces from meat-eating animals (including dogs and cats) due to possible disease pathogens.

◆ Materials such as brush and tree branches with a diameter greater than 1/4 inch will break down very slowly. Shred branches when possible.

◆ If plants start growing in your compost, pull them out, solar-dry them for a few days and reload them onto the pile.

◆ Poisonous plants, such as oleander, hemlock and castor bean, can harm soil life and should be left out of your compost.

◆ Plants that have acids toxic to other plants and microbial life should be left out of your compost (e.g., eucalyptus, California bay laurel, juniper acacia, cypress and pine needles).

◆ Pesticides can kill earthworms and other organisms that help the compost process. Avoid using materials that have been treated with toxic chemicals.

How It Works

Nature does the work for you. Tiny microorganisms and macroorganisms break down the organic matter. Only 3 things are needed to keep these organisms alive in your compost: food, air and water.

Oxygen flow aids the decomposition rate. Turn your compost every so often or poke deep holes into the heart of the pile. Another method is to knock down the pile completely and then build it up again, mixing contents and adding water as you do so. Also, if you build your compost pile on top of something, such as wood slats, airflow can come up from underneath the center of the pile. By creating a chimney effect up through the pile, organic matter decomposes more quickly and odors are reduced.

Maintaining an adequate moisture level will create a friendly home for the microorganisms, earthworms and insects. The pile should be about as wet as a squeezed-out sponge. In a hot climate, a cover or tarp will help retain moisture. If your compost pile does get dry, sprinkle water on it and the composting process will resume. In a colder climate, a cover is also helpful to deflect rain and snow. Remember that a pile that is too wet will not compost properly either.

Composting Methods

The following are some composting methods:

1. **Dump and Run.** Simply dump materials onto the pile. It is better to always blend fresh materials into the warm interior of the composting mass. Then cover it with leaves, wood chips, straw or garden soil. This composting process will be a little slower.

2. **Layer.** Gather and store organic materials over a period of time (weeks or months). When enough have been gathered, the pile is started by placing brown materials on the base, 3 to 6 inches thick. The next layer should be green. Continue with another layer of brown, then green materials, and so on, until the pile is a minimum of 3 feet tall and preferably 4 to 6 feet tall. Add water with each layer.

Compost Containers

A compost pile works effectively if you have the time and patience to build it carefully, shape it properly and tend it as you add more materials. By using a compost bin you do not need to spend much time maintaining the compost, as bins keep the piles neat, efficient and manageable.

The **Three-bin System** is the most successful method we know of for treating organic debris because of the enclosed and efficient design. It is possible with this unit to have three piles at varying degrees of decomposition going at the same time.

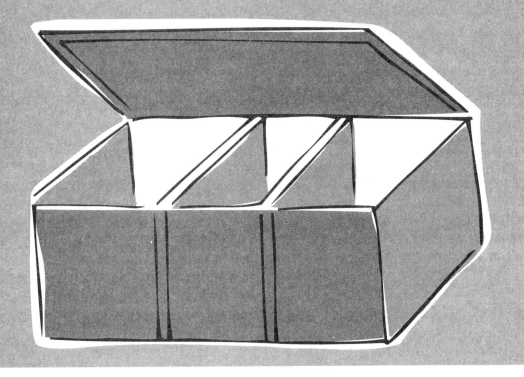

3. **Mixing.** Start by layering materials outside of the pile or bin. Dig into the pile with a pitchfork and throw forkfuls of layered material into the compost bin. The goal is to blend dry with wet materials and brown with green materials. Once the pile has started to simmer, fresh materials may be added by incorporating them into the center of the composting material.

When It's Ready

Your compost is ready when the materials you place in your pile have been transformed and blended into a crumbly soil texture. You can also test the center of the compost with your hand. It should not feel hot or wet; slightly warm is fine. Often the bottom of the compost will be ready before the top.

Have fun deciding what to do with your compost. Use it in your school garden or landscaping, make it available to your community (possible fund-raiser), or take it home. You could also start projects where you use your compost to recondition degraded and eroded landscapes in your community.

Keep Your Compost Happy

The following chart will help you avoid some of the common problems with composts.

Concern	Possible Causes	Solutions
Rotten odor	Excess moisture	Turn pile; add dry, porous materials such as leaves, sawdust, wood chips or straw
	Compaction	Turn pile or make smaller
Ammonia odor	Too much green material (nitrogen)	Add brown materials (carbon) such as dry leaves, wood chips or straw
Low pile temperature (below 100° F)	Pile too small	Make pile larger or insulate sides
	Insufficient moisture	Add water while turning pile or cover
	Poor aeration	Turn pile
	Lack of greens (nitrogen)	Mix in green sources, such as grass clippings, manure or food scraps
	Cold weather	Increase pile size or insulate pile with an extra layer of material such as straw
High pile temperature (+140° F)	Insufficient ventilation	Turn pile
	Pile too large	Reduce pile size or divide into 2
Pests (rats, raccoons, insects)	Presence of meat scraps	Remove meat and or fatty food scraps and fatty foods from pile or cover with a layer of soil, leaves or sawdust; or use an animal-proof compost bin or turn pile to increase temperature

Key Points to Remember

The following are some key points to remember:

- ◆ Vary the materials to create a balanced food supply for microorganisms.
- ◆ Mix all materials for optimum composting.
- ◆ Turn for aeration.
- ◆ Maintain ample moisture.

VERMICOMPOSTING AT SCHOOL

As with the preceding section, this section has been excerpted. We simply could not improve upon the article "As the Worm Turns" by Robert Kourik, which appeared in the Jan./Feb. 1992 issue of *Garbage* magazine on pages 48–51. Mr. Kourik did a wonderful job of explaining vermicomposting, and now we can all benefit from his work.

Sizing a Worm Bin

To determine your worm bin's optimum size, survey the amount of food scraps you actually generate. Collect your daily scraps, weigh them and calculate an average for the total number of pounds produced per week. Each square foot of the surface area of a worm bin, assuming a healthy population of worms, will digest one pound of kitchen scraps per week. To ensure sufficient oxygen, all bins should be between 12 and 18 inches deep.

Building a Worm Bin

The requirements for a good worm house are moist but not wet bedding; plenty of air, but not so much that the worms dry out; a cool but not cold temperature; and an insect-and-critter-resistant lid. Avid wormologists use everything from old metal drums to wooden boxes and plastic buckets.

When choosing a worm house, remember that the combination of darkness, wet food scraps and condensation can generate more moisture than you'd ever imagine. Metal or plastic containers with a closed bottom will often accumulate so much moisture that you may find drowned worms, not a pretty picture. To drain surplus liquid, punch holes into the bottom of the container (of course, a bin with drain holes is appropriate only for the outdoors). Wooden worm boxes avoid moisture overload because the wood soaks up the moisture and whisks it away from the bedding.

Two things to remember: If the container is deeper than 18 inches, worms will simply colonize the upper layer, where they find the best mix of oxygen, moisture and food. Also, a shady cool spot in the summer and a warm place in the winter are essential if you want to prevent mass wormicide.

Bedding Your Worms

Choice material for bedding includes peat moss or shredded cardboard and newspaper. Vermicomposting expert Mary Appelhof recommends ten pounds of shredded paper for a bin with 6 square feet of surface area. When in doubt, just fill the bin with snugly packed bedding. The worms will naturally colonize the amount of bedding they need. Worms are 75 to 90 percent moisture, so their bedding should be about 75 percent moist. Add 3 pounds of water for every pound of paper.

Most kitchen wastes are very moist. The gradual decomposition of the waste adds moisture to your bin. So keep adding bedding to maintain a moist but not wet environment. If the bin starts to develop too much condensation, you'll whiff a few strange odors. Snuff them by adding shredded newspaper.

Now it's move-in day and time to add a pound of hungry worms for every 3.5 pounds of kitchen scraps every week.

Variety of Food Waste Fed to Worms	
Apple peels	Lemon
Baked beans	Lettuce
Banana peels	Malto-Meal
Biscuits	Molasses
Cabbage	Oatmeal
Cake	Onion peel
Celery	Orange pee
Cereal	Pancakes
Cheese	Pears
Corn Bread	Pineapple
Cream Cheese	Pineapple rind
Cream of Wheat	Pizza crust
Cucumber	Potatoes
Deviled Eggs	Potato salad
Egg shells	Ralston
Farina	Tea leaves
Grapefruit peels	Tomatoes
Grits	Turnip leaves

Source: *Worms Eat My Garbage*, Flower Press, 1982.

Feeding Mr. and Ms. Worm

Worms eat organic food scraps. Many recommend against adding meat and fish scraps to worm bins. Actually, worms love the high nitrogen content of meat and fish scraps, which they can rapidly digest. While worms don't eat the hard bone itself, all leftover flesh quickly disappears. Carnivorous critters can be kept out of your worm bin if it's tightly sealed with a proper latch. Well-ventilated bedding eliminates odors.

Regardless of what you're feeding your worms, there are 2 ways to add the waste. The easiest is to simply apply the scraps in a thin layer on top of the bedding. This means the worms have to crawl up onto the new scraps, which is no problem if the bin is kept dark with a solid lid. To make the worms work even faster, use a garden trowel to open up a small cavity and bury the day's kitchen waste. Be sure to add each day's scraps to a different part of the bin.

Using Your Black Gold

After about 4 months, your industrious worms will have digested much of their bedding, leaving behind a deposit of rich castings. Worm feces are full of phosphorus, nitrogen and other minerals and nutrients. In a worm bin, the castings are mixed with the compost of decomposed kitchen wastes, bedding and dead worms. Any self-respecting gardener realizes this as horticultural black gold—virtually unsurpassed as a natural fertilizer. To harvest your black gold, simply push all the decomposed material (it looks, feels and smells like soil) over to one side of the bin. Add fresh, moist bedding to the remaining space, plus kitchen waste. Then wait. After a few days, the hungry little worms will migrate over to the new feeding grounds—and you've got a worm-free pile of vermicompost.

Note: The worm who thrives in worm bins is Eisenia fetida, commonly called redworm. Redworms eat kitchen scraps whereas earthworms eat dirt. Redworms can die from lack of oxygen and they're also afraid of carnivorous centipedes, which sometimes colonize worm bins. Redworms quickly burrow downwards at the first glint of sunlight and temperatures above 84 degrees Fahrenheit are fatal.

ESTABLISHING A SCHOOL SEED BANK

There is a growing interest in seed saving because for the past several decades we have seen a dramatic loss of genetic diversity. We are learning that this results in long-lasting and even permanent environmental damage. By incorporating a seed-banking program, students will be saving the seeds from this year's plants and setting them aside for the years to come. This system offers an opportunity to teach an important lesson with global perspectives!

A seed-banking process will guarantee open polli-nated indigenous plant diversity. The bigger picture revolves around the issue of **biodiversity** and what happens to life when there is species loss. We will define biodiversity and take a look at the ramifications of lost biodiversity in an effort to understand better the significance of this endeavor and the lessons we all can learn.

"Gardeners are emerging as principal biological heroes in the struggle ... to maintain the biological diversity that sustains life on the planet."

The Kingdom: The Fabric of Life, Seeds of Change, 1994 Catalog, Santa Fe, NM.

Biodiversity is being lost at an alarming rate and nowhere is this more critical than in the plant world. More than 80 percent of the plants that were here when Columbus landed are now extinct. These will *never be recovered*. Where once more than 1,000 varieties of corn were grown in the United States, only 4 main varieties are now commercially grown. There was a time when the agricultural community recognized that several genetically distinct crops planted together helped prevent crop failure. Unfortunately, this is no longer the case.

Two very important examples of what can happen to crops when genetic diversity has been eliminated are the Irish potato famine, which occurred in the 1840s, and the 1970 U.S. corn blight. In both cases, the cause of the crop losses can be directly linked to breeding and planting genetically uniform seeds.

In Ireland, farmers depended on a single strain of potato called Lumper, imported from the Caribbean. Because of the lack of genetic diversity when the blight appeared, none of the plants had the genes needed for resistance and the entire crop was wiped out.

In the United States a very similar problem occurred when corn breeders began using the Texas (T) cytoplasm. They incorporated the new genes into all their corn varieties, never realizing that they were also breeding in susceptibility to disease. Because of the proliferation of variety names, it was little known that a large proportion of the crop was based on the same genetic combination. As a result, the blight of 1970 wiped out 15 percent of the U.S. corn crop; in some states the figure reached 50 percent.

It is obvious that during the 130 years between the potato famine in Ireland and the corn blight in the United States, breeders and farmers had not taken the issue of biodiversity in seeds seriously. The fact that thousands of varieties of seeds, for hundreds of existing plants and crops, are becoming extinct must become a major concern not just for those in the industry but for all of us.

The United States government has taken some steps toward correcting the problem. Today there exists a National Plant Germplasm System, which was established by the Department of Agriculture shortly after the 1970 blight. The goal of the NPGS was to create a coordinated system that would clarify and oversee germplasm preservation in this country. We also have the National Seed Storage Library in Colorado, whose vaults are filled with 180,000 different types of seeds. Breeders and farmers must stop looking at the bottom line when it comes to seed and food production and look to the preservation of natural gene pools created over thousands of years. We could face a future in which many of the fruits, vegetables and grains that have been on earth for centuries will no longer exist.

Because our needs and very survival depend on biodiversity, many scientists and lay people argue strongly that the conservation of biodiversity should be a matter of national security. Concern is piqued when more than 90 percent of the companies that produce and sell seeds are owned by petrochemical corporations. These corporations also produce the pesticides and herbicides that are used in modern agricultural practices. The genetically engineered hybrid plants are chemically dependent and nonviable (i.e., cannot reproduce). A very compelling story to have older students read is "The Gift of Commitment" in *Shattering Food, Politics and the Loss of Genetic Diversity.*

Plants have taken millions and millions of years to develop resistances to various pest and environmental challenges, such as drought. But when we alter the genetic characteristics of the plants we breed by favoring the ones we desire (such as consistency in size to assist in mechanical harvesting), we also breed out such characteristics as resistance to a pest, developed over millions of years. Then we are forced to use pesticides!

When students use open pollinated plants of heirloom seed strains, which they collect and save, they will be preserving a crucial natural heritage. Use some of these seeds for next year's garden and put the remaining into a permanent seed bank maintained by the students. Students will learn an important lesson about ensuring the availability of seeds for their garden. They will also be saving the genetic diversity that may determine their future quality of life.

Thus, a school seed bank is a hands-on lesson that shares a common denominator with some of the toughest issues facing the global community today.

Conserving Biodiversity

"Conserving biodiversity is not just a matter of protecting wildlife in nature preserves. It is also about safeguarding the natural systems of the Earth that are our life-support systems; purifying the waters; recycling oxygen, carbon and other essential elements; maintaining the fertility of the soil; providing food from the land, fresh water and seas; yielding medicines; and safeguarding the genetic richness on which we depend in the ceaseless struggle to improve our crops and livestock."

Walter Reid, Charles Barber and Kenton Miller, *Global Biodiversity Strategy* (Baltimore, MD: WRI Publications, 1992), p. v.

The following are some basic guidelines for saving seeds:

1. **When harvesting, leave some of the fruit or flowering part of the plant** (from several different plants) **in the ground to develop seeds.** Seeds are formed after the flowering part of the plant has died back (bloomed and withered). Leave the plants with good flavor and/or other qualities worth preserving.

2. **Collect seeds from plants that had the best overall performance in your garden.** Save enough for planting next year and put some away in the seed bank. It may be helpful when you buy your heirloom seeds to ask about the schedule for harvesting seeds.

3. **Allow seeds to dry after harvesting.**

4. **Store seeds destined for next year's planting in a paper bag that is dry and airy.**

5. **Give seeds that are going into your bank a bit more care.** Once dry place seeds in glass jars that seal with a rubber gasket lid. The seal must be tight.

6. **Place jars in a cool (40°F, 4°C), dark and dry location.** A basement, cellar or refrigerator will do. The temperature needs to be relatively constant. Heat and humidity must be minimized.

7. **Develop an easy and accurate file system** for your seed bank so that future classes can follow your work.

8. **Keep records of your methods and activities.**

For the most part, dry vegetable seeds will stay viable for 3 to 5 years if stored in this manner. For those students or classes that take this project on, silica gels, which dry the seed, and vials or barrier pouches for storage are available. Also, there are methods for storing seeds longer. Students interested in such a project should refer to the catalogs we have listed in the resource section.

Average Seed Storage Times		
Dependable 1 Year	**2 or 3 Years**	**4 or 5 Years**
Onion	Asparagus	Beets
Sweet corn	Peas	Cabbage
Parsley	Beans	Cauliflower
Parsnips	Carrots	Cucumber
	Peppers	Eggplant
		Lettuce
		Muskmelon
		Pumpkin
		Spinach
		Squash
		Turnip
		Tomato
		Watermelon

Reprinted with permission from Storey Communications, Inc., Pownal, VT.

RESOURCES

Brochures/Papers/Reports

This list of publications on gardening could be very extensive, but we have had to focus on general topics. (One good source for specific topics is Storey Communications, 800-827-8673.)

The Art of Composting
Metropolitan Service District
2000 SW First Ave.
Portland, OR 97201-5398
503-221-1646

Creating Community Gardens
Minnesota State Horticultural Society
1970 Folwell Avenue, #161
St. Paul, MN 55108
612-645-7066

Drip Watering Made Easy
Raindrip, Inc.
21305 Itasca Street
Chatsworth, CA 91311
818-718-8004

Drought Gardening
Storey Communications, Inc.
Department 9000, Schoolhouse Road
Pownal, VT 05261
802-823-5811

Ecology of Compost
State University of New York
College of Environmental Science and
Forestry
Syracuse, NY 13210
315-472-0130

Gardening Answers
Storey Communications, Inc.
Department 9000, Schoolhouse Road
Pownal, VT 05261
802-823-5811

Grow 15 Herbs for the Kitchen
Storey Communications, Inc.
Department 9000, Schoolhouse Road
Pownal, VT 05261
802-823-5811

Grow a Butterfly Garden
Storey Communications, Inc.
Department 9000, Schoolhouse Road
Pownal, VT 05261
802-823-5811

Grow Super Salad Greens
Storey Communications, Inc.
Department 9000, Schoolhouse Road
Pownal, VT 05261
802-823-5811

Harvest of Hope: The Potential of Alternative Agriculture to Reduce Pesticide Use
Natural Resources Defense Council
40 West 20th Street
New York, NY 10011
212-727-2700

How to Have a Green Garden in a Dry State
Metropolitan Water District of Southern
California
P.O. Box 54153
Los Angeles, CA 90054
213-250-6485

Improving Your Soil
Storey Communications, Inc.
Department 9000, Schoolhouse Road
Pownal, VT 05261
802-823-5811

Increasing Organic Agriculture at the Local Level
Santa Barbara County Safe Food Project
730 Ayala Lane
Santa Barbara, CA 93108
805-969-1512

Starting Seeds Indoors
Storey Communications, Inc.
Department 9000, Schoolhouse Road
Pownal, VT 05261
802-823-5811

Suppliers of Beneficial Organisms in North America
California EPA
Department of Pesticides Regulation
Environmental Monitoring and Pest Management
1220 N Street
P.O. Box 942871
Sacramento, CA 94271-0001
916-654-1144

300 Expert Tips and Techniques
Rodale Press
33 East Minor Street
Emmaus, PA 18098
215-967-5771

Using Beneficial Insects: Garden Soil Builders, Pollinators and Predators
Storey Communications, Inc.
Department 9000, Schoolhouse Road
Pownal, VT 05261
802-823-5811

Waterwise Gardening
Sunset
Lane Publishing Company
Menlo Park, CA 94025
415-321-3600

What Every Gardener Should Know About Earthworms
Storey Communications, Inc.
Department 9000, Schoolhouse Road
Pownal, VT 05261
802-823-5811

Wildflowers for You
Pennsylvania Resources Council
PO Box 88
Media, PA 19063
610-565-9131

Books

Volumes have been written about gardening, the joys of gardening and how to cope in an environmentally responsible way with garden problems. The local library and bookstores have more available to read on the subject than one could ever use. Any of the following books will give you all the information you need and more.

Refer to the resource section of Chapter 3 for books that pertain solely to pest management.

The Art of Natural Farming and Gardening
Ralph and Rita Engelken
agAccess,1985
P.O. Box 2008
Davis, CA 95616

Backyard Cash Crops: The Source Book for Growing and Marketing Specialty Plants
Craig Wallin
agAccess,1992
P.O. Box 2008
Davis, CA 95616

Butterfly Gardening: Creating Summer Magic in Your Garden
Xerces Society/Smithsonian Institute, 1990
National Wildflower Research Center
2600 FM 973 North
North Austin, TX 78725-4201

Carrots Love Tomatoes
Louise Riotte
Storey Communications, 1975
Schoolhouse Road
Pownal, VT 05261

Color Handbook of Garden Insects
Anna Carr
Rodale Press, 1979
33 East Minor Street
Emmaus, PA 18098

Cornucopia: A Source Book of Edible Plants
Noel Vietmeyer
agAccess, 1990
P.O. Box 2008
Davis, CA 95616

Designing and Maintaining Your Edible Landscape Naturally
Robert Kourik
Metamorphic Press, 1986
P.O. Box 1841
Santa Rosa, CA 95402

Down-to-Earth Gardening: Know-how for the '90s
Dick Raymond
Storey Communications, 1991
Schoolhouse Road
Pownal, VT 05261

Eco Garden
Nigel Dudley and Sue Stickland
Avon Books, 1991

1350 Avenue of the Americas
New York, NY 10019

Feeding Plants the Organic Way
Jim Hay
Ward Lock, Ltd., 1991
Villiers House, 41/47 Strand
London, England WC2N 5JE

Fertile Soil: A Grower's Guide to Organic and Inorganic Fertilizers
Robert Parnes, Ph.D.
agAccess, 1990
P.O. Box 2008
Davis, CA 95616

Four-Season Harvest
Eliot Coleman
Chelsea Green Publishing Company 1992
P.O. Box 130, Route 113
Post Mills, VT 05058

Gardening at a Glance: The Organic Gardener's Handbook on Vegetables, Fruits, Nuts and Herbs
Tanya Denckla
agAccess, 1991
P.O. Box 2008
Davis, CA 95616

Global Biodiversity Strategy
Walter Reid, Charles Barber and Kenton Miller
WRI Publications, 1992
P.O. Box 4852, Hampden Station
Baltimore, MD 21211

Good Neighbors: Companion Planting for Gardeners
Anna Carr
Rodale Press, 1985
33 East Minor Street
Emmaus, PA 18098

Greening the Garden
Dan Jason
New Society Publishers, 1991
4527 Springfield Avenue
Philadelphia, PA 19143

Heirloom Gardener
Jo Ann Gardner
Storey Communications, 1992
Schoolhouse Road
Pownal, VT 05261

Introduction to Permaculture
Reny Mia Slay
agAccess, 1991
P.O. Box 2008
Davis, CA 95616

Low-Water Flower Gardener
Eric A. Johnson
Ironwood Press, 1993
2968 West Ina Road, #285
Tucson, AZ 85741

The Mulch Book
Stu Campbell
Storey Communications, Inc., 1991
Schoolhouse Road
Pownal, VT 05261

National Gardening Association Guide to Kids' Gardening: A Complete Guide for Teachers, Parents and Youth Leaders
Lynn Ocone
John Wiley & Sons, 1990
605 Third Avenue
New York, NY 10158-0012

The New Organic Grower: A Master's Manual of Tools and Techniques for the Home and Market Gardener
Eliot Coleman
agAccess, 1993

P.O. Box 2008
Davis, CA 95616

Plants for Dry Climates: How to Select, Grow and Enjoy
Mary Rose Duffield and Warren D. Jones
HP Books, 1992
11150 Olympic Boulevard, Sixth Floor
Los Angeles, CA 90064

Profits from Your Backyard Herb Garden
Lee Sturdivant
San Juan Naturals, 1988
Box 642
Friday Harbor, WA 98250

Rodale's All-New Encyclopedia of Organic Gardening
Rodale Press, 1992
33 East Minor Street
Emmaus, PA 18098

Rodale's Chemical-free Yard and Garden: The Ultimate Authority on Successful Organic Gardening
Anna Carr et al.
Rodale Press, 1991
33 East Minor Street
Emmaus, PA 18098

Rodale's Illustrated Encyclopedia of Gardening and Landscaping Techniques
Barbara W. Ellis
Rodale Press, 1990
33 East Minor Street
Emmaus, PA 18098

Rodale's Illustrated Encyclopedia of Herbs
Claire Kowalchick
Rodale Press, 1987
33 East Minor Street
Emmaus, PA 18098

Roses Love Garlic: Secrets of Companion Planting with Flowers
Louise Riotte
Storey Communications, 1983
Schoolhouse Road
Pownal, VT 05261

Saving Seeds: The Gardener's Guide to Growing and Storing Vegetable and Flower Seeds
Marc Rogers
Storey Communications, 1990
Schoolhouse Road
Pownal, VT 05261

Shattering Food, Politics and the Loss of Genetic Diversity
Carol Fowler
University of Arizona Press, 1990
1230 North Park Avenue South, Suite 102
Tucson, AZ 85719

Square Foot Gardening
Mel Bartholomew
Rodale Press, 1981
33 East Minor Street
Emmaus, PA 18098

The Wildflower Handbook
Elizabeth S. Anderson
National Wildflower Research Center, 1992
2600 FM 973 North
Austin, TX 78725

Worms Eat My Garbage
Mary Appelhof
Flower Press, 1982
10332 Shaver Road
Kalamazoo, MI 49002

Xeriscape Gardening: Water Conservation for the American Landscape
Connie Ellefson, Tom Stephens and Doug Welsh
Macmillan Publishing, 1992
866 Third Avenue
New York, NY 10022

Books for Youth

The Amazing Dirt Book
Paulette Bourgeois
Addison-Wesley, 1986
2725 Sand Hill Road
Menlo Park, CA 94025

A Child's Book of Wildflowers
M. A. Kelly
Four Winds Press/Macmillian Publishing Company, 1992
866 Third Avenue
New York, NY 10022

The Garden Book
Wes Porter
Workman Publishing, 1989
708 Broadway
New York, NY 10003

The Garden in the City
Gerda Muller
Dutton, 1988
375 Hudson Street
New York, NY 10014

The Great Seed Mystery for Kids
Peggy Henry
BMR, 1992
21 Tamal Vista Boulevard.
Corte Madera, CA 94925

Growing Things
Angela Wilkes
EDC Publishing, 1984
10302 East 55th Place
Tulsa, OK 74146

Grow It! An Indoor/Outdoor Gardening Guide for Kids
Erika Markmann
agAccess, 1991
P.O. Box 2008
Davis, CA 95616

In a Pumpkin Shell
Jennifer Storey Gillis
Storey Communications, 1992
Schoolhouse Road
Pownal, VT 05261

Kids Gardening
Kevin and Kim Raftery
Klutz Press, 1989
2121 Staunton Court
Palo Alto, CA 94306

My First Garden Book
Albie Celfe
BMR, 1991
21 Tamal Vista Boulevard
Corte Madera, CA 94925

My First Garden Book
Angela Wilkes
Alfred A. Knopf, 1992
201 E. 50th Street
New York, NY 10022

My Garden Companion
Jamie Jobb
Sierra Club, 1977
730 Polk Street
San Francisco, CA 94109

This Year's Garden
Cynthia Rylant
Macmillan Publishing, 1987
866 Third Avenue
New York, NY 10022

Individuals/Companies/Organizations

Seed Companies and Exchanges

This is by no means a complete list. It will provide all that you need to get started. The companies listed here are fairly broad based (a variety of seeds adaptable for most of the United States).

Abundant Life
P.O. Box 772
Port Townsend, WA 98368
206-385-5660
Catalog includes a large selection of open-pollinated vegetable and plant seeds as well as a number of helpful books.

High Altitude Gardens/Seeds Trust, Inc.
P.O. Box 1048
Hailey, ID 83333
208-788-4363
Their catalog includes quick-maturing, open-pollinated varieties for short seasons as well as seeds that will thrive at lower elevations.

Native Seeds/Search
2509 N. Campbell Avenue, #325
Tucson, AZ 85719
602-327-9123
This catalog of seeds focuses on the traditional native crops of the Southwest and northwest Mexico.

Seeds Blum

Idaho City Stage
Boise, ID 83706
208-338-5658
A catalog of heirloom seeds and other garden gems that are applicable for gardens around the country.

Seeds of Change

1364 Rufina Circle, #5
Santa Fe, NM 87501
505-438-8080
Sells certified organic seeds, hence their motto—"The First Link in a Safe Food Chain." Their seeds are suitable for growing just about anywhere in the United States. The Seeds of Change catalog has variety, from nutritious food plants to medicinals to botanical life, and provides some informative reading.

Southern Exposure Seed Exchange (SESE)

P.O. Box 158
North Garden, VA 22959
804-973-4703
A source for modern, high-performance non-hybrid varieties of seeds. They emphasize varieties adapted for the Mid-Atlantic region but successfully serve gardeners throughout the United States and some foreign countries. Nearly all the seeds are open-pollinated (nonhybrid). Also they provide the information and supplies for saving your own seeds. The seeds are free of chemical treatment; many are organically grown and have been germination tested.

Seed Savers Exchange

Rural Route 3, Box 239
Decorah, IA 52101
319-382-5990
This is a nonprofit, tax-exempt organization that exists to save old-time food crops from extinction. SSE does provide information on easy seed-saving techniques.

Shepherd's Garden Seeds

30 Irene Street
Torrington, CT 06790
203-482-3638
Collection of vegetable and herb seeds bred for flavor, tenderness and the best fresh-eating qualities, and flower seeds from original breeders for old-fashioned flowers as well as new variety introductions.

General Gardening

American Community Gardening Association

325 Walnut Street
Philadelphia, PA 19106
215-625-8280
ACGA is a nonprofit organization of gardening and open-space volunteers and professionals. ACGA promotes the growth of community gardening and greening in urban, suburban and rural America.

FAUNA (Friends and Advocates of Urban Natural Areas)

P.O. Box 1815
Portland, OR 97207
503-255-5769

Flowerfield Enterprises

10332 Shaver Road
Kalamazoo, MI 49002
616-327-0108
Supplies indoor vermicomposting containers (the bin is made of recycled plastic), redworms, the book *Worms Eat My Garbage*, a video on leaf composting and recycling labels.

Gardener's Supply Company
128 Intervale Road
Burlington, VT 05401
800-444-6417 and 802-863-1700
Wide assortment of garden supplies.

Garden's Alive
Highway 48, P.O. Box 149
Sunman, IN 47041
812-537-8650
Environmentally responsible, organic products for a healthy garden. This booklet is full of organic gardening tips, biological controls, pest traps for indoors and out and more. It is published 6 times a year and is free!

Harmony Farm Supply
3244 Gravenstein Highway
North Sebastopol, CA 95472
707-823-9125
Harmony supplies all the help and tools to garden without the use of synthetic pesticides or fertilizers. Their product line ranges from irrigation systems, fertilizers, ecological pest controls, tools, books and seeds, to services such as lab testing of your soil and general advice.

Let's Get Growing
1900-B Commercial Way
Santa Cruz, CA 95065
408-464-1868
This catalog will simplify your first step with some basic supplies. Contains projects, kits and supplies for indoor and outdoor garden science programs for any place and any season. Curriculum and books on weather/climate, gardening and nutrition.

Metropolitan Green Spaces Program
2000 SW First Ave.
Portland, OR 97201
503-224-7336
Working within the cities, this organization hopes to turn natural areas into green spaces, preserving wildlife habitat and creating greenway corridors for animals, plants and people. The program encompasses the Portland, Oregon/Vancouver, Washington region.

The Natural Gardening Company
217 San Anselmo Avenue
San Anselmo, CA 94960
415-456-5060
This catalog features a wide variety of tools and supplies for gardening. The company also sells red earthworms for composting and vermicomposting.

Natural Solutions for Organic Growing
One Nature's Way
New Castle, VA 24127-0305
703-884-5103
Catalogue of biopest controls, fertilizers, tools and books.

The National Arbor Day Foundation
100 Arbor Avenue
Nebraska City, NE 68410
402-474-5655
They sponsor a program called "Grow Your Own Tree" that encourages Americans to plant, manage and preserve trees to conserve soil, energy, water, wildlife and the atmosphere.

Ringer Natural Lawn and Garden Products
9959 Valley View Road
Eden Prairie, MN 55344-3585
800-654-1047
Natural lawn and garden care products, drip irrigation, tree care, composting, tools and more.

The Worm Concern
580 Erbes Road
Thousand Oaks, CA 91362
805-496-2872
A source for worm composting kits (several sizes), harvested worms, worm compost, worm castings, fertilizers and a number of related books.

Worm's Way
3151 South Highway 446
Bloomington, IN 47401
800-274-9676
Hydroponic and organic garden supplies.

Zoo Doo Compost Company
5851 Ridge Bend Road
Memphis, TN 38120
800-458-8366
From antelope to zebra, a wide assortment of fertilizers that are dry, odorless and ready for your garden. Fifty-one percent of the proceeds from the sale of Zoo Doo benefits the Memphis Zoo.

Chapter 6

Water

Chapter 6

CONTENTS

INTRODUCTION

We all require water to stay alive. When water is used wisely, the benefits to the environment are clear. Less waste means more supplies for future needs and less wastewater in need of treatment. The advantage for the school is lower water and energy bills. This chapter provides information on sustainable water practices and strategies so that you will know where to look, what to look for and what to do with your findings.

Information must be shared with family, friends, teachers, employers, campus suppliers and the administration. Decision makers should be approached in a cooperative manner, and facts should be presented. When the evidence is clear and convincing, people make rational decisions.

Students can bring about changes when they form groups with common goals. At the end of this chapter is a list of school organizations that have done this. For further assistance and advice, contact them to find out what strategies have worked for them. A list of appropriate literature also appears at the end of this chapter. And be sure to check the Kids Groups list in Chapter 18. You will find some wonderful ideas and inspirational stories there!

It is important to remember that one person can make a difference. Use the contacts in this book to find others who, like yourself, want to help our environment.

WATER ON THE PLANET EARTH

How Much Is There?

Images taken from space have given us a unique glimpse of our planet, the water planet. The earth's surface is approximately 70 percent water, equaling some 1.36 billion cubic kilometers, with 97 percent of this being saltwater.[1]

Even though this resource is large, it is not infinite. Consider the complex distribution systems necessary to get water from its source into our homes and schools. (In California the aqueduct system stretches for more than 444 miles!) Fresh water is contaminated daily. Every community across the country faces problems associated with storm drains, pesticide and fertilizer runoff, power plants, sewage treatment, industrial waste and more. Every community has experienced the problems resulting from such dramatic changes as droughts and floods. Consider the increasing demand that our growing population is making on our limited water resources.

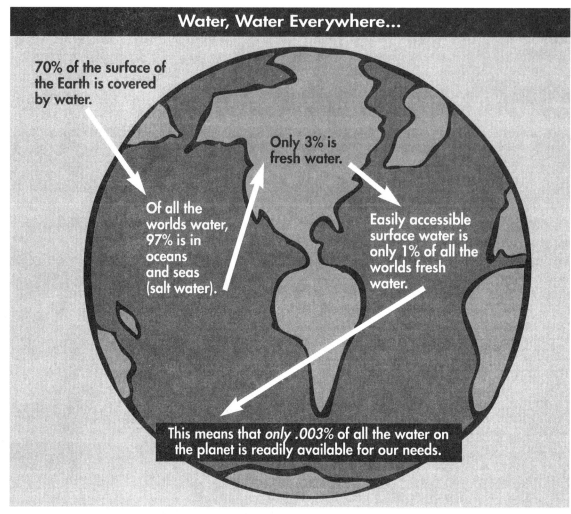

Water, Water Everywhere...

70% of the surface of the Earth is covered by water.

Only 3% is fresh water.

Of all the worlds water, 97% is in oceans and seas (salt water).

Easily accessible surface water is only 1% of all the worlds fresh water.

This means that *only .003%* of all the water on the planet is readily available for our needs.

Very little fresh water is accessible on a daily basis. Most of our fresh water comes from lakes, rivers and groundwater. In fact, groundwater makes up about 95 percent of the global fresh water supply.[2] In some areas, such as Israel, shallow groundwater resources are vital.

Of all global water, 3 percent is fresh; it breaks down as follows:
- ◆ Groundwater is about 20 percent
- ◆ Ice/glaciers make up about 79 percent
- ◆ Air, soil, lakes, rivers and life forms constitute 1 percent.[3]

Of the last 1 percent, only 1 percent is in rivers and streams, which provides people with 80 percent of their freshwater needs, a very small fraction of all water.

On average, **global freshwater use** percentages are as follows:
- ◆ Irrigation, 69 percent
- ◆ Industry, 23 percent
- ◆ Domestic, 8 percent.[4]

Water is renewable and finite. A fixed amount is cycled annually. However, demands for water are growing. Human mismanagement, climatic events (such as drought and floods) and population growth can dramatically alter supplies. It is vital that each person use fresh water wisely, so that we can make what we have last. The more water people use, the less is available for other species, such as birds and fish.

Most of us have seen dripping faucets, showers, tubs or water fountains. It may not seem like much, but **a slow drip from a leaky faucet can waste 15 to 20 gallons of water a day!**[5] A leak of 1 drop every second can waste up to 2,400 gallons of water a year.[6]

Properties of Water

Water is vital to life. Survival without food is possible for weeks or even a month, but life ends after a few days without water!

Water is found in three forms:
- ◆ Solid (snow, ice)
- ◆ Liquid (rain, rivers, lakes, oceans)
- ◆ Gas (water vapor, clouds).

Water's special role comes from its unusual physical properties:

◆ **It has a high boiling point.** This allows it to be a liquid at normal temperatures on earth instead of a gas. If it were a gas it would be unusable to most life forms.

◆ **It takes a lot of heat (i.e., energy) to evaporate it**. This is an important factor in distributing the sun's energy throughout the planet.

◆ **It has enormous capacity to store heat**. Water heats and cools more slowly than other substances. This characteristic moderates global climate.

◆ **It is less dense as a solid than as a liquid** (i.e., ice floats). This is a crucial property because water freezes from the top down. Generally, the surface water freezes, and life below the ice can survive. If the reverse occurred, all aquatic life in bodies of water that could freeze would perish. As water freezes, it expands. This results in the degradation of rock and releases nutrients.

◆ **It dissolves a wide variety of substances**, which is critical for carrying nutrients and wastes throughout animal and plant bodies.

Because of all these properties, the availability of clean fresh water is the primary limiting factor for civilization, ecosystems and quality of life.

The human body is made up mostly of water (approximately 70 percent depending upon age and size).[7] If we were to remove the water from our bodies, all that would remain would be a few pounds of minerals. We must have water to survive. Unwise water use is threatening our future water supplies. Therefore, we must be informed about unwise water strategies and improve them.

The Water Cycle

Water moves around earth via clouds, air, rain, hail, snow, waterways (surface and underground) and pipes. It cycles from land to sea to air to land, and back, over and over again. This cycle is called the hydrologic cycle.

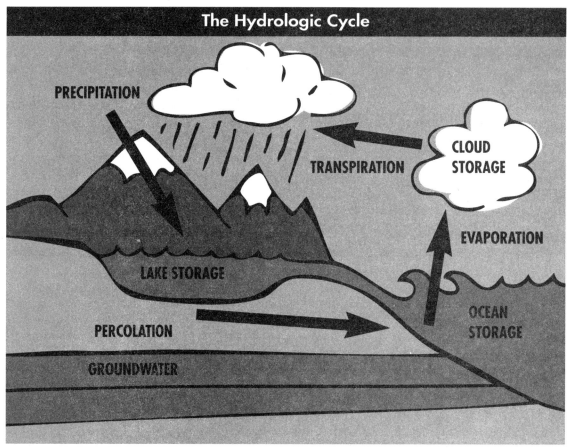

The Hydrologic Cycle

PRECIPITATION

CLOUD STORAGE

TRANSPIRATION

EVAPORATION

LAKE STORAGE

PERCOLATION

OCEAN STORAGE

GROUNDWATER

Source: *The Story of Drinking Water,* © 1990, American Water Works Association.

Fresh water, as shown on page 166, is a small percentage of all planetary water. Freshwater sources for people include

◆ Precipitation, such as rain or snow collected in lakes, rivers and aquifers (groundwater).
◆ Waste water, such as gray water, which can be reused immediately.
◆ Reclaimed water after it has been treated adequately. In Los Angeles some city sanitation districts are saving 60 million gallons per day for reuse in irrigation, industrial cooling and other purposes.[8] In 1991 Israel was reusing about 60 percent of its total wastewater, primarily for agriculture.[9]
◆ Desalinized seawater.

To reduce the impact of overwithdrawal from a local or distant ecosystem, as much water as possible should come from nearby sources. (Later in this chapter the discussion of overconsumption and destruction looks further at the impact of overwithdrawal.)

This strategy reduces
- ◆ Transportation costs and waste via evaporation, seepage and leaks
- ◆ Disruption of services and replacement
- ◆ Impacts on the environment and people.

In many areas local supplies from groundwater, lakes, rivers and sometimes oceans are adequate. Where they are inadequate, outside sources become necessary.

The ocean is a close and plentiful water supply. Through desalinization, fresh water is readily available, but it is more expensive than traditional supplies. The expense comes from the high amount of energy required, which is another limited resource. Drought conditions have convinced some California communities to invest in desalinization. The cities of Santa Barbara and Avalon (on Catalina Island) have new systems operating or nearing completion.

Alaska has more than 40 percent of the nation's fresh water and has a surplus to sell. There is talk of bringing water from Alaska in giant nylon bags towed by ships. Does it sound crazy to move water 2,000 miles? In the Middle East, there have been proposals to transport water in ocean-going bags or through a pipeline from Turkey to Syria and the Persian Gulf. And what about the discussion years ago of towing icebergs from Antarctica to the Middle East? Crazier than these projects is the insanity of wasting so much of a precious resource.

On average, almost half the water used in irrigation, which is the biggest user of water, never reaches a plant.[10]

Rather than build new projects or transport water over long distances, it is clear that proper conservation of the supplies we have is cheaper and better for the planet. Studies have shown that it is cheaper to treat wastewater for nondrinking uses than to pump fresh water from distant mountains, lakes or deep aquifers.

Life-Cycle Approach
We tend to view water use linearly or a straight line:
- ◆ A city provides water for its residents.
- ◆ People use the water.
- ◆ Used water is dumped as a useless material into the sewer system.

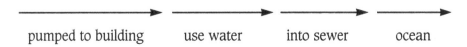

pumped to building   use water   into sewer   ocean

People expect that when they turn on the shower or faucet, clean, fresh water will come out. No thought is given to the monetary and environmental costs of supplying this water. When people are done using water, it goes down the drain, out of sight and out of mind. The waste becomes someone else's problem. Water is cheap because we don't pay for the real costs of supplying and treating it. Services such as water treatment and flood control are not evaluated and factored into the cost of water. Also, water projects have been subsidized to provide services to special interests, such as farmers. The polluter is not required to pay clean-up costs. All these factors lead to inefficient use.

"It is estimated that a ton of toxic waste is produced each year for every man, woman, and child in the United States. About 135 billion pounds of discharge into the nation's waterways."

Water: The Source of Life, America's Clean Water Foundation, Washington, DC, 1992.

The problem with this conventional thinking is that production and disposal are not connected. This promotes inefficiency and contamination. A circular approach that joins the beginning and end is preferable.

It is crucial to ask, "Is this the best way to use water, or is there a more efficient, less costly way that will save water and protect our environment in the long run?" A life-cycle analysis can examine each stage of resource use and determine improvements. "The Hydrologic Cycle," illustration on page 168 demonstrates this circular approach.

We need a new definition of waste. Most "waste" should not be thrown away! What is perceived as waste needs to become a raw material for reuse. A new ethic needs to be taught that emphasizes the realities of finite resource supplies. We in the United States are accustomed to the fallacy that resources are infinite and equally distributed.

Reusing wastewater drastically lowers the need for imported water and allows areas to recover their original levels. This is important for wildlife, which also depends on fresh water.

It is imperative that we be aware of the need not to squander water. The natural balance of our global water cycle has been disrupted by human intervention. This is evidenced by desertification, droughts, dried-up rivers, flooding, decimation of fisheries and waterfowl habitat, and so on.

We must promote the most efficient use of water in the least costly way to meet demands. Providers of public water should be rewarded for lowering consumers' bills and improving services and not solely for increasing sales. We do not need to change our quality of life to implement efficient techniques and policies for water use, but we must change our approach.

Technologies are now available that reduce the amount of water used to do the same or more work. By using less water, water bills are kept lower; less water is released downstream and into rivers, lakes and the ocean as sewage; and more of the resource is saved upstream for use during droughts, for aquatic life and for future use.

Just remember, dinosaurs once drank the water we drink today! And our grandchildren and great-grandchildren will drink the water we waste and contaminate today and tomorrow. Thus, we must maintain a long-term perspective on our use of this precious resource.

HUMAN IMPACT ON WATER

Pollution

Pollution has compounded the water supply problem by contaminating freshwater supplies. Now we either spend large sums to clean up the problem or we dump polluting substances into other bodies of water. Since pollution does not stop at political borders, local problems become regional, national and international. Some laws have been developed to help control, prevent, and clean up pollution of waterways.

The inefficient use, pollution and overconsumption of fresh water are causing us to plan and/or construct unsustainable water projects, such as dams, diversions and groundwater extraction. Although individuals have a great responsibility in protecting and conserving resources, it is important to be aware that farmers use and waste more water than any other group and that many corporations create pollution. Neither group has been held accountable for these problems.

Stormwater runoff from our nation's lands, both rural and urban, is a major source of pollution for both ground and surface water. This is called *nonpoint source pollution*. Runoff pollutants come from
◆ Golf courses, homes and businesses using pesticides on their landscaping
◆ Toxic substances spilled on parking lots and highways
◆ Soil disturbed by construction, logging and agricultural activities
◆ Sediments from vacant lots, poorly managed farms and grazing lands
◆ Leakage from septic systems, mines, landfills and animal waste feedlots.

"Americans are highly aware and concerned about protecting our clean water. An overwhelming percentage of the population considers these dangers to clean water to be serious environmental problems."

93%	Pollution of lakes and rivers
92%	Hazardous waste disposal
86%	Drinking water contamination
79%	Acid rain
79%	Radioactive waste disposal

Clean Water: A Bargain at Any Cost, Water Pollution Control Federation, Alexandria, VA, 1987.

Nonpoint source pollution accounts for more than half of the pollution in U.S. bodies of waterways. This is ranked as a major problem in 24 states and as a problem impairing surface water quality in 21 states.[11]

Industrial and Domestic Waste

The traditional disposal of wastewater at home or at work has been to dump it into waterways, fresh or salt, after minimal, if any, treatment. We must consider ways to reuse and reclaim wastewater before it is discharged. Minimizing the amount of waste saves money and protects water ecosystems. Reusing water and wastewater leaves more fresh water in lakes, rivers and reservoirs for future needs.

In large urban areas, water systems can be overwhelmed. Geographic characteristics can increase pollution problems if water is not adequately flushed and replaced. Heavy rains often produce additional problems, such as sewage treatment facilities overflow, allowing raw sewage into waterways.

Aquifers become contaminated when pollutants on land or in water seep through the ground and into the water table. Atmospheric pollutants mix with rain and fall to the ground as acid rain. This produces additional pollution problems.

Logging

When the trees are removed from an area and new trees are inadequately replanted, there is no ground cover to protect soil from erosion. Soil is washed into creeks, streams and rivers, reducing clarity and choking aquatic life. Breeding and feeding are disrupted. But if new trees are quickly replanted, this can be a short-term problem.

In some areas of Alaska and the Pacific Northwest, unwise logging practices have caused salmon spawning streams to become clogged with sediment. This has made them unsuitable for breeding, so that salmon do not spawn and their numbers decline. In 38 states logging has been blamed for nonpoint source pollution.[12]

In the Amazon River Basin, in Central America and in Southeast Asia large tracts of rainforests have been clear-cut. Heavy seasonal rains erode exposed unprotected soil, washing large amounts of sediment into waterways.

Erosion carves gullies and holes in the land. Deserts result. In tropical regions, topsoil is shallow and lacks nutrients. When it is washed away, nothing will grow back.

Rain patterns can be disrupted when large tracts of trees are removed. This occurs because trees take up water from the surface and release excess moisture into the atmosphere through pores in leaves, a process called evapotranspiration. This water vapor eventually returns as rain, completing the water cycle.

Surface Contamination

Ground and surface waters become contaminated by chemicals we use or dump onto land (e.g., in our backyards and school playgrounds). Pesticides and fertilizers soak into the ground or run off into waterways and eventually end up in the groundwater or in local bodies of water.

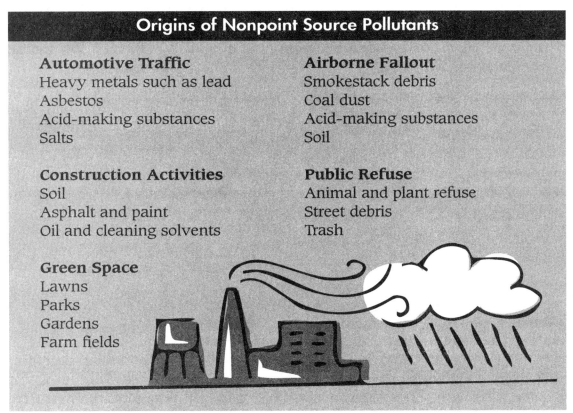

Origins of Nonpoint Source Pollutants

Automotive Traffic
Heavy metals such as lead
Asbestos
Acid-making substances
Salts

Airborne Fallout
Smokestack debris
Coal dust
Acid-making substances
Soil

Construction Activities
Soil
Asphalt and paint
Oil and cleaning solvents

Public Refuse
Animal and plant refuse
Street debris
Trash

Green Space
Lawns
Parks
Gardens
Farm fields

Source: Wisconsin Department of Natural Resources, Lake Management Program.

A common and serious problem results from dumping used motor oil. Unlike pollution cleanup on the surface, where there is access, groundwater is below the surface in aquifers and much harder to reach. Once it is contaminated, it will remain so for the foreseeable future. The costs of cleaning this water are prohibitive for most communities. We must all avoid spilling or dumping any chemicals onto the ground.

Chemicals used in agriculture and fed to livestock enter surface waters and aquifers. Because of the large amounts of agricultural and animal waste runoff, local water systems cannot neutralize dangerous materials fast enough.

173

What Practices Reduce Runoff?

In rural areas:
- ✔ Contour farming
- ✔ Conservation tillage
- ✔ Delaying tillage and fertilizing until spring
- ✔ Rotating crops
- ✔ Strip-cropping
- ✔ Terracing
- ✔ Diversion "channels"
- ✔ Grassed waterways
- ✔ Filtered strips for runoff from animal lots
- ✔ Retiring highly erodible cropland
- ✔ Practicing sound pesticide and fertilizer use

In urban and suburban areas:
- ✔ Maintain plant cover or a tree canopy to reduce erosion
- ✔ Mulch gardens and exposed soil
- ✔ Terrace land to slow runoff
- ✔ Direct runoff from rooftop downspouts to areas where it can soak into the soil
- ✔ Minimize paved and impermeable surfaces
- ✔ Avoid overloading banks or steep slopes
- ✔ Minimize soil disturbance during construction
- ✔ Maintain natural vegetation or plant vegetation to form a buffer zone along the water's edge
- ✔ Maintain septic systems
- ✔ Use low- or no-phosphate soaps and detergents

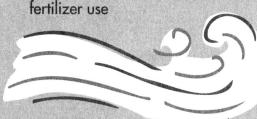

Source: Wisconsin Department of Natural Resources, Lake Management Program.

Storm Drains

Our storm drains can cause serious water pollution if we litter and pollute our streets. It is important to realize that any contamination and litter (such as, spilled oil, pesticides, chemical fertilizers and plastics) will be picked up by rainwater and flow, untreated, into surface bodies of water (i.e., rivers, lakes and oceans). When it rains and storm drains flow into the regular sewer system, treatment facilities can be overwhelmed, causing raw (untreated) sewage to overflow into surface bodies of water.

Oil Spills

Ocean-going tankers transport over half of the world's oil. Every day approximately 4.6 million tons of oil is afloat on our oceans.[13] According to Shell Oil, 20 percent of the world's tankers do not meet international safety standards. Some of the most notable spills have occurred from offshore oil drilling.

Oil drilling, extraction, refining and transporting do tremendous environmental damage. Oil leaks pollute at every stage—at the drilling site, along pipelines, at transfer points, to and from tankers, at refineries and at the underground storage tanks in our neighborhood gas stations. The EPA estimates that approximately one-third of the 5 million underground storage tanks are leaking.[14]

Oil spills happen everywhere. Boats of all sizes spill oil in our wetlands, lakes and oceans. Oil from trucks and cars leak onto our highways and streets. Over 1 million gallons of used oil enter the environment every day in the United States.[15]

Overconsumption and Destruction

In the United States each of us uses, on average, 150 gallons of water per day.[16] This excludes water used to manufacture and produce the variety of goods and food we need each day. Because of the large amounts of water used, even small changes in our use will save huge amounts.

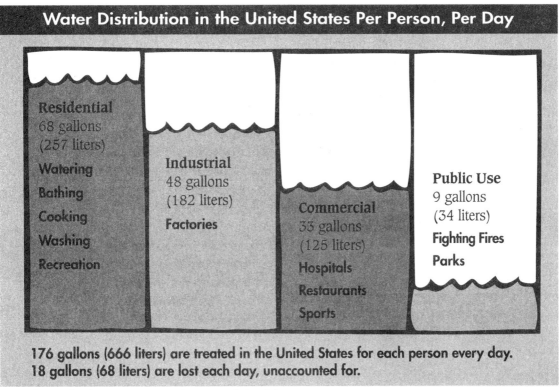

Water Distribution in the United States Per Person, Per Day

Residential
68 gallons
(257 liters)

Watering

Bathing

Cooking

Washing

Recreation

Industrial
48 gallons
(182 liters)

Factories

Commercial
33 gallons
(125 liters)

Hospitals

Restaurants

Sports

Public Use
9 gallons
(34 liters)

Fighting Fires

Parks

176 gallons (666 liters) are treated in the United States for each person every day.
18 gallons (68 liters) are lost each day, unaccounted for.

Source: *The Story of Drinking Water*, © 1990, American Water Works Association.

About 75 percent of water used in American homes is consumed in the bathroom. Toilets are responsible for 50 percent of the water used in bathrooms and 35 percent of the total water used in homes.[17]

Dams and Diversions

Many dams have been built to provide electricity and control flooding without regard for the long-term impact on people and the environment. Large areas are flooded behind a dam,

displacing people and wildlife. Moreover, the flooded vegetation decays and releases a sulfur compound that forms an acid and causes the electricity-producing turbines to decay. In addition, silt that rushes down a river becomes trapped behind a dam and causes the storage capacity to decline over time.

Silt and water that normally flow freely to the ocean are stopped by dams. This affects the ecology along the way, because the flow of nutrients needed to replenish the soil and to feed aquatic plants and organisms is stopped.

In addition, dams affect fish. In the Pacific Northwest, for example, those along the Columbia River have significantly endangered salmon stock.

Diversions of rivers to supply water are important in improving the quality of life. But like dams, if they are planned with short-term goals (e.g., to grow crops now) and without regard for future generations of people and wildlife, the result is long-term destruction.

In the former Soviet Union, 2 major rivers entering the Aral Sea, Amu-Dar'ya and Syr-Dar'ya, have been diverted for irrigation. Over the last 30 years, the sea volume has declined more than 60 percent and surface area has decreased over 40 percent.[18] The costs have been very high: changes in local climate, tremendous loss of habitats, changes in regional hydrology and grave socioeconomic difficulties, such as unemployment and deteriorating human health.

The Ogallala Aquifer

Aquifer Depletion

A major U.S. groundwater source is the Ogallala Aquifer, which lies under 8 Central states. Half of the nation's grain-fed beef is produced here. The enormous amount of water used for livestock comes from this aquifer. It took millions of years for it to form. By the year 2020 the Ogallala Aquifer should be 80 percent depleted if current rates of pumping continue.[19] But with more efficient water use (i.e., less meat production and better irrigation methods), it could sustain established ways of life for those living in these 8 states.

Groundwater can also become polluted by seawater, because overpumping reduces the pressure applied by groundwater to keep saltwater back.

Desalinization

In the Middle East, where water is much scarcer than in the United States, if one nation withdraws water rapidly, a shortage can result in a neighboring country. Thus, many coastal nations rely on desalinization of ocean water to supply fresh water. This has its drawbacks. Marine oil spills, such as those that occurred during the Persian Gulf War, can disrupt service. Desalinization is also energy-intensive. Because of the prolonged drought and overuse of water, a number of cities in California have built and are considering plans for desalinization plants.

Wetlands

Wetlands are unique ecosystems that occur wherever water covers land for various lengths of time. These ecosystems can be freshwater, saltwater or both as in an estuary where both meet. Many species of flora and fauna depend on wetlands for their life cycles. In addition, wetlands provide numerous benefits for society, such as

- ◆ Waste water purification
- ◆ Flood damage control
- ◆ Storm and wave protection
- ◆ Aquifer recharge
- ◆ Food
- ◆ Recreation
- ◆ Science experiment sites
- ◆ Aesthetics.

Originally, the continental United States had 200 million acres of wetland. Today less than 50 percent remain, largely because of draining and filling for agricultural development, building construction, and oil and gas development.[20]

During the late 1980s and early 1990s, land developers sought to weaken the federal guidelines that protect wetlands. The debate has centered around the amount of time land must be submerged to qualify as a wetland. Developers want federal guidelines to allow some wetlands that are not submerged throughout the year to be filled in for development. If they have their way, U.S. wetlands could be reduced by another 50 percent. The scientific and environmental communities agree that this is dangerous to flora and fauna, endangered species,

Major Causes of Wetland Loss and Degradation

Human Impacts
Drainage
Dredging and stream channelization
Deposition of fill material
Diking and damming
Tilling for crop production
Grazing by domesticated animal
Discharge of pollutants
Mining
Alteration of hydrology

Natural Threats
Erosion
Subsistence
Sea level
Droughts
Hurricanes and other storms
Overgrazing by wildlife

Source: *America's Wetlands: Our Vital Link Between Land and Water*, U.S. Environmental Protection Agency, Office of Water, Office of Wetlands Protection, Washington, DC, 1988.

*"**W**etlands are the home of 1/3 of the nation's endangered species and serve as a critical habitat for thousands of fish and wildlife. About 66 percent of the commercial fish catch taken along the United States Atlantic and Gulf coasts depend on wetlands for survival."*

Water: The Source of Life, America's Clean Water Foundation, Washington, DC, 1992.

people who live near major wetlands and those who do not live near wetlands but benefit from them.

When wetlands are destroyed, their environmental benefits—especially flood control, water treatment and breeding habitats for commercial shellfish and fish—are lost. The problem has been that the values assigned by developers and real estate interests to wetlands are underestimated. The value assigned to a mall or oil and gas extraction in place of a wetland is believed to be higher because the value of lost wetland services is not factored into cost–benefit analyses. Also, developers are subsidized by providing roads, flood control and water to new subdivisions, which makes the cost of development cheaper.

Fortunately, new research has begun to assign dollar values. In 1991, the Department of Commerce Wetlands Document estimated that the value of coastal wetlands to commercial and recreational fisheries ranges from about $2,200 to almost $10,000 per acre, depending upon location.

SOLUTIONS: WHAT YOU CAN DO

So, What's the Problem?

Here in the United States, the early settlers who came from the Old World were amazed by the vast supplies of water, forests, arable land and other resources. Because water was abundant and the populations relatively low, wise use didn't become ingrained in the American people. But now that our national population has grown and water is in short supply, efficiency has become paramount.

There was little, if any, limit on expansion of cities. If water was lacking for growth, new sources were found or developed. Generally, this was done at government (public) expense; individuals were not paying the real cost. Long-term needs or drought conditions were not considered in the planning. Decisions made by national, state and city officials have been concerned with growth. Those in Congress have pushed water supply projects, such as dams, in their own states. There has been a rush to obtain water at the expense of those downstream and future generations.

As cities expand, sewer systems carry more and more quantity with lower and lower quality, which requires more treatment. This means more money is needed for treatment. If funds are lacking, treatment systems are not expanded or improved. People may not notice the damage, but waterways suffer.

In the 1960s the Cuyahoga River (an offshoot of Lake Erie) in Ohio caught fire because of combustible chemicals in the water! Just think about how many flammable chemicals were dumped for this to happen. Some of the Great Lakes have been terribly contaminated.

Boston Harbor and Santa Monica Bay (Los Angeles) are so polluted that aquatic life has died and people are warned against swimming in the water or eating any fish that survive in it. The good news is that today some of these areas have been cleaned up or are being cleaned and indigenous species are returning. Much of the turnaround has come about because ordinary people became vocal and put pressure on government officials to act.

We must use water efficiently so that we can reduce pollution and the need for new, expensive reservoirs. This will leave more water in streams, lakes and oceans to maintain natural ecosystems. This is the circular approach illustrated on page 168. As droughts become common, groundwater supplies shrink and reservoir levels decline, unconventional strategies become necessary. The following methods offer suggestions on how to improve water use without reducing the quality of life.

As individuals, we need to change our water use habits. Young people need to show their parents that a new and improved approach works. Parents need to set an example of wise water use, reinforcing our children's behaviors. Finally, we all need to influence decision makers on campuses, in government and in corporations to promote and implement better water use practices.

Can You Drink It?
It is surprising to see bottled water available in the teacher's lounge in schools while students drink from the tap. All schools should test their tap water. It may contain radon and lead, which are both serious health threats. Radon will evaporate rapidly from water, enter the air and be inhaled. If the tap water comes from a surface source or an aerated underground source, you do not need to test for radon. Lead can show up anywhere. According to the EPA, more than 40 million Americans drink tap water containing dangerous levels of lead.[21]

Because **volatile organic chemicals (VOC's)** are absorbed through the skin when it comes in contact with water, schools with showers and baths should test their water for these substances. When the water is heated, these chemicals evaporate rapidly and, as with radon, are harmful if inhaled.

It is best to use a state-certified lab to test your school water. But, be sure you understand the results. For instance, although government standards allow 50 parts per billion of lead in drinking water, you still need to take action if your water tests postive at lower levels—especially if students with young, developing minds will be drinking it. For further information, read *The Drinking Water Book* by Colin Ingram. It is a wonderful resource, full of useful information and ideas. See also Chapter 1 of this book for more information on lead.

The following are some tips from *The Drinking Water Book* for reducing the pollutants in your tap water:
- ◆ Turn the tap on gradually and then let it run for about 10 seconds before filling your container.
- ◆ Because tap water contains chlorine, allow it to stand in a wide-mouth, open container for 2 or 3 days. This gives the chlorine time to evaporate.
- ◆ Boil water for 10 minutes. This will disinfect it and remove chlorine. Do not use an aluminum pot because drinking water with traces of this metal has been linked to Alzheimer's disease.

Here are some interesting facts that will put in perspective why you should be concerned about your drinking water:
- ◆ The United States has nearly 60,000 community water supply systems. Only 20 percent of these systems use surface water; most rely on groundwater.[22]
- ◆ An estimated 90 billion gallons of liquid from landfills and 100 billion gallons from liquid impoundments annually lead into groundwater in the United States.[23]

Indoor Water Use

Thousands of gallons a year can be saved by using water-efficient showerheads, faucet aerators and low-flow toilets, which use cionsiderably less water. The chart on page 181 shows how each person can reduce the amount of water he or she uses. These are all savings techniques that can be applied with positive results at schools as well.

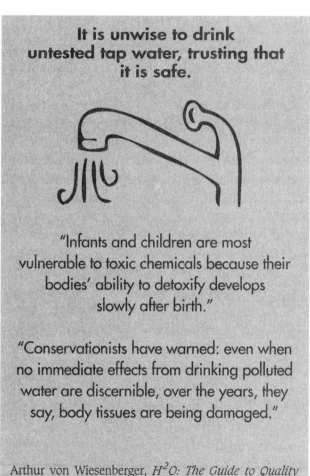

It is unwise to drink untested tap water, trusting that it is safe.

"Infants and children are most vulnerable to toxic chemicals because their bodies' ability to detoxify develops slowly after birth."

"Conservationists have warned: even when no immediate effects from drinking polluted water are discernible, over the years, they say, body tissues are being damaged."

Arthur von Wiesenberger, *H²O: The Guide to Quality Bottled Water* (Santa Barbara, CA: Woodbridge Press, 1988), p. 29.

Water Is Life...Don't Waste It!		
	Normal Use	**Conservation Use**
Shower (5 minutes)	Conventional showerhead: **30 gallons**	Water-saving showerhead: **10 gallons**
Brushing teeth	Tap running: **5 gallons**	Wet brush, rinse briefly: **1/4 gal or less**
Tub bath	Full **36 gallons**	Minimum water level **10-12 gallons**
Toilet flushing	Conventional toilet: **5 to 7 gallons**	Using tank displacement bags: **4 to 6 gallons**
Dish washing	Tap running: **30 gallons**	Wash and rinse in dishpans or sink: **5 gallons**
Automatic dishwasher	Full cycle: **16 gallons**	Short cycle: **7 gallons**
Shaving	Tap running: **20 gallons**	Fill basin: **1 gallon**
Washing hands	Tap running: **2 gallons**	Fill basin: **1 gallon**
Washing machine	Full cycle, top water level: **60 gallons**	Short cycle, minimal water level: **27 gallons**

Source: *Water Is Life...Don't Waste It!* East Bay Municipal Utility District, Oakland, CA, 1987.

New, efficient devices can reduce water use 20 to 80 percent, depending upon how far one wants to improve efficiency. This section discusses in detail the following water-flow devices:

1. Showerheads
2. Kitchen and bathroom faucet aerators
3. Low-flush and composting toilets
4. Other tips

Showerheads

New models of showerheads use less water per minute and come with a valve to turn off or reduce the flow while lathering. Taking shorter showers will also save water.

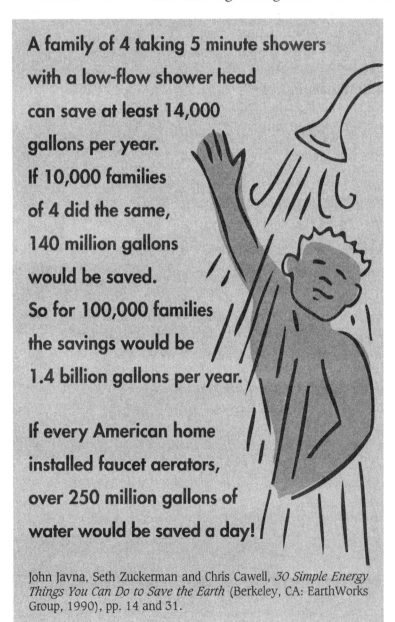

A family of 4 taking 5 minute showers with a low-flow shower head can save at least 14,000 gallons per year.

If 10,000 families of 4 did the same, 140 million gallons would be saved.

So for 100,000 families the savings would be 1.4 billion gallons per year.

If every American home installed faucet aerators, over 250 million gallons of water would be saved a day!

John Javna, Seth Zuckerman and Chris Cawell, *30 Simple Energy Things You Can Do to Save the Earth* (Berkeley, CA: EarthWorks Group, 1990), pp. 14 and 31.

Here is a simple test to see if you should replace your showerhead: **"The Milk Carton Test:** Hold an empty half-gallon milk carton under the showerhead. Turn the water on fairly forcefully. If it fills in less than 10 seconds (or 24 seconds for a gallon jug), you should get a more efficient (low-flow) model."[24]

Kitchen and Bathroom Faucet Aerators

New faucets include aerators that restrict flow and still provide power. Older models with inefficient aerators should be changed to efficient ones for bathrooms and kitchens. The savings in water will more than cover the initial costs. This also saves energy by saving hot water. The amount of time it will take to make back one's investment depends on the inefficiency of the replaced aerator, on the cost of water and the new aerator and on whether behavioral practices are modified to reduce waste. This time can range from a couple of months to more than a year.

Low-Flush and Composting Toilets

Most toilets on campuses are the wall-mounted, quick-flush types that use very little water. Any school with old tank toilets (3 to 7 gallons per flush) should replace them with new models that use 1 to 1.6 gallons per flush. As mentioned earlier, the amount of time to cover the cost of a new, efficient toilet depends upon a number of factors. If a city has a rebate program (e.g., Los Angeles and Denver) to encourage people to replace inefficient toilets, it is actually possible to make money.

A few schools may be unable to accommodate low-flush toilets because of the slope of the sewer line. Sewer lines need a minimum descent to allow passage of a certain volume of wastewater. Some older structures were built for large flushes only. Check with a local builder or plumber. Studies done on low-flow toilets have shown that they work in almost all cases.

For areas not hooked into a sewer system (distant from the main lines) or on a septic tank system, such as parks, a composting toilet might be the answer. These devices require no water. Human wastes are broken down by microorganisms into basic materials, such as water, carbon dioxide and other elements. There are a number of models. Using low-flush or composting toilets reduces the demand for fresh water and puts less stress on community sewage treatment facilities.

If older toilets cannot be replaced, reduction devices that are placed in toilet water tanks can be used. The following is a list of these devices:

1. Bottles filled with sand or water placed in the tank
2. Water dams placed on either side of the toilet drain
3. Adjustable floats and balls that regulate the amount of water that fills the tank.

Manufacturers of many of the preceding items are listed in the resource section of this chapter.

Other Tips

◆ Repair leaking faucets, showerheads and toilets as soon as a leak is observed. Encourage students and staff to report any leaks so that they can be repaired immediately.

◆ Reduce the number of times you flush the toilet. There is a humorous but perhaps applicable saying: "If it's yellow, let it mellow; if it's brown, flush it down." (This is not always appropriate in all places, so do try to use good judgment.)

◆ Do not use your toilet as an ashtray or wastebasket.

◆ Turn off running water while shaving, lathering, washing dishes and washing cars.

Exterior Water Use

Many cities have ordinances restricting and prohibiting certain uses of water. Offenses include hosing down sidewalks, street gutters and driveways or watering inefficiently (e.g., during the hottest and windiest part of the day). For severe situations of drought, some cities have a program where residents can call a special number to report wasters. Callers are advised to include the following information:

◆ Date
◆ Time
◆ Address of violation
◆ Type of action.

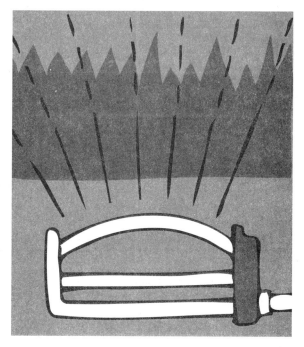

Though usually invoked because of drought conditions, this strategy should be adopted throughout the nation for efficient use of water, in times of both surplus and shortage.

During severe drought conditions in California, cities such as Santa Barbara and Los Angeles employed "water officers" (also called "drought busters"). These people reported wasteful water practices and provided residents with information about efficient strategies.

Gray Water

Gray water is water that has been used once for showers, baths, dishwashing, laundry or cooking. Though school campuses do produce this type of wastewater, it is not generally a sufficient enough volume to warrant the change of plumbing for reuse. But for schools that have laundry facilities or that wash a lot of dishes, there are systems (mentioned later) that can be integrated to divert water from the sewer and onto grassy areas or individual plants. Using gray water reduces the need for fresh water.

Caution: The reader is advised that many states prohibit individuals from using gray water systems because of possible public health hazards (when not done properly). Check with a local building inspector and plumber about the necessary permits and designs.

For those who want to start saving gray water at home and school for reuse, all you need are buckets of various sizes. You can start a simple water reclamation program just by saving water while warming the shower, saving used bath water and reclaiming water from bathroom faucets that are running.

Irrigation

Because campuses have large areas of lawn, trees, low bushes and flowers, a number of gardening strategies can help your school use water more wisely. Exterior water demand can use more than 50 percent of total (interior-exterior) water. Thus, any steps to reduce fresh-water demand will translate into significant savings in community water resources and school water bills. For example, when planting grass, flowers, shrubs and trees, choose those that are native (indigenous) to your area or that require the least watering. Xeriscaping or dry gardening favors hardier vegetation that requires little or no supplementary watering. (See Chapter 5 for resources.)

Lawn Watering. Many lawns are overwatered. If grass bounces back when stepped on, there is no need to water it. When a lawn is mowed less often and cut higher (2 to 3 inches), this encourages grass to grow deeper roots, which will need less watering. In most cases you will not harm a lawn by letting it get to the point of dryness, though it may not be the striking green to which we are accustomed. Some species of grass (Bermuda, St. Augustine, Zoysia) tolerate dry conditions better and require less maintenance. Check with a local nursery.

Lawn watering uses nearly half the water used around the home. Most of us tend to water too often and leave the sprinklers on too long. Turf studies have shown that most lawns only need to be watered once every 3 days to stay healthy and green. A simple way to determine your lawn-watering needs is to conduct the following experiment.

1. Set 3 flat-bottom cans or coffee mugs at various places on your lawn.
2. Turn on your sprinklers for 15 minutes.
3. Measure the depth of water in each can with a ruler and determine the average depth.
4. Read the number of minutes you should water every third day and record the time for future reference.

The watering times for three seasons follows:

Average depth in inches in the can:

	3/16	1/4	5/16	3/8	1/2	5/8	3/4	1	1-1/4	1-1/2
Watering time in minutes:										
Spring	30	22	18	15	11	9	7	5	4	3
Summer	45	34	27	22	17	13	11	8	6	5
Fall	24	18	14	12	9	7	6	4	3	3
Winter	Water only during warm or dry periods.									

Source: *Lawn Watering Guide*, Los Angeles Department of Water and Power.

Many campuses may put in a winter lawn. But this requires water that would not normally be used during the cold months, when plant growth slows or stops until spring. In temperate areas, winter is a time when plants rest between growing seasons. There is nothing wrong with having an ungreen lawn, it is natural, and it saves precious water and money.

> *In summer months, outdoor water use accounts for up to 30 percent of total household water consumption. In winter months outdoor water use drops to 5 percent.*
>
> Jonathan Erickson, *Saving Water in the Home & Garden* (Blue Ridge Summit, PA: TAB Books, 1993), pp. 75-76.

Watering You Garden

Knowing the plants in your garden will enable you to water them efficiently. Most established plants can survive with watering once a month.

Ground cover and mulch can prevent water loss. Rain falling on bare soil is lost to evaporation and runoff. Ground cover and mulch will contribute significantly to water conservation. They help soil retain moisture by reducing evaporation, moderate soil temperature, discourage weed growth and prevent soil compaction.

Sprinkler Systems. Many campuses use sprinkler systems to water lawns. Unfortunately, this system is wasteful. To minimize water loss due to its inherent inefficiency, observe the following:

◆ Make sure water-efficient sprinkler heads are used.

◆ Make sure any leaky sprinkler heads, pipes or valves are reported and repaired immediately.

◆ Water in the late afternoon, in evening or in early morning.

◆ If it might rain, delay watering. If it rains, there is no need to water for a few more days (see "Nature's Freebie" later in this chapter).

◆ Make sure water lands on grass and not on paved surfaces.

◆ Plant drought-resistant trees and plants.

◆ Deep-soak your lawn. A light, frequent sprinkling does not penetrate into the soil; much of the water evaporates.

Drip Irrigation. Drip irrigation and soaker systems use tubing with small holes that direct water to the roots of plants. These systems eliminate evaporation and runoff, and reduce the amount of water required. Very little water is wasted with these methods. The amount of water saved from using drip irragation can be as much as 95 percent. [25]

Drip Irrigation systems are ideal for vegetable gardens, ornamental gardens and hillsides. These systems can be purchased from nurseries, hardware stores or garden catatlogs. One homemade drip system is to turn a soaker hose face down and let water run at a trickle.

It is important to note that drip irrigation is not practical for large lawns and some ground covers because they have numerous individual root systems. Also, Children may trip over and dislodge the tubes.

Water Retention. To increase the water-holding capacity of soil, polymers can be mixed in. When a soil -polymer mixture is watered, individual polymers absorb water and can swell up to 100 times their original size. Then, over the next few days or weeks, the water is slowly released into the soil, where vegetation can absorb it. Water use can be reduced by as much as 75 percent.[26] This technique is appropriate and has been used for golf courses, private yards, country clubs and schools. Through this strategy, significant quantities of water are saved because water is used more efficiently. Also, labor costs are reduced because watering systems are used less often.

Car Washing

Try to wash your car on the lawn when possible, not in a driveway or street. This way you will wash not only your car, but also water the lawn. Cut back on the number of times you wash your car. Use non-toxic car-cleaning soap. Turn off the water during soaping. Going to a car wash can also be efficient if the building recycles its water. If it does not recycle its water, find one that does.

"The average car wash uses 40 gallons of water for each car. Each year in the United States about 160 million gallons of water are used to wash cars."

Water: The Source of Life, America's Clean Water Foundation, Washington, DC, 1992.

Sweep, Not Wash

Use a broom to clean sidewalks and driveways, not water. When you see someone using water to wash these areas, you might politely suggest using a broom. Gardeners and building maintenance personnel should be advised not to use water to wash sidewalks and driveways.

Nature's Freebie

When it rains, often people do not remember to adjust (turn off) their automatic sprinkler timers. This is obviously very wasteful and silly. If it is going to rain or has rained, there is no reason to water a lawn for at least a couple of days.

There are a couple of ways to capture rainwater. First, you can leave any unused garbage cans uncovered during a rainstorm. Or, if your campus roof has a rain gutter system that directs water runoff to a hard surface, consider adjusting the downspouts to allow the placement of a large garbage can to capture rainwater.

What We Eat Can Save or Waste Water

Meat is the least water-efficient element of a diet. Just consider these facts:

◆ 50 percent of the total amount of water consumed in the United States is used for livestock production.[27]

◆ Approximately 1,400 gallons of water is needed to make a meal of hamburger, french fries and a soft drink. That's enough to fill a small swimming pool.[28]

◆ A day's food for one meat eater takes more than 4,000 gallons of water; for a lacto-ovo vegetarian, 1,200 gallons; for a pure vegetarian, only 300 gallons.[29]

Students might try eating just 10 percent less meat or one less meat meal per week. Even this minimal action can help alleviate waste and promote positive change.

For more information, see Chapter 4.

Storm Drains

The amount of rainwater that runs off hard surfaces and enters storm drains can be reduced in 2 ways:

◆ We can reduce paved areas and increase areas covered with vegetation. These green areas or belts will absorb the rainwater, recharging groundwater for future use.

◆ We can collect rainwater and keep it from landing on hard surfaces and becoming runoff (see "Nature's Freebie" earlier).

As mentioned earlier, storm drains can be responsible for considerable pollution of water systems. We must protect local and global water resources by keeping harmful chemicals out of storm drains. The illegal dumping of motor oil, paints and solvents into storm drains occurs constantly in an attempt to avoid disposal fees. We can each help by making sure we do not spill chemicals onto hard surfaces and use little, if any, toxic chemicals on our yards and planted areas. Remember, rainwater washes all this into storm drains and waterways.

Look for a paved or compacted hard ground surface (lacking vegetation) on campus that water flows over before entering a storm drain. Submit a proposal to the administration to convert this hard surface to a green belt, better able to absorb runoff. See Chapter 5 for ways of maintaining this area in a safe, organic way.

Xeriscaping

As mentioned earlier under "Irrigation," the amount of water used on ground cover can be reduced if drought-tolerant species are planted. Every area of the country needs to orient its landscaping to native species. These plants are adapted to survival within the local climate. School or home grounds do not have to be totally green or totally in bloom. Landscaping should be suited to the amount of local rainfall, not to how much water can be imported from distant reservoirs or rivers where rainfall is higher. See Chapter 5 for more information on this topic and for how to find such plants.

Drinking Fountains

On most campuses drinking fountains give much relief. Unfortunately, they become sites of waste. Often the water will not turn off completely. Drinking fountains are notorious for developing leaks. If the problem is not repaired quickly, it will only become worse and more expensive.

THE BUDGET

Generally speaking, school administrators will not make changes unless they result in economic benefits. You may find that it is a challenge to convince them that any higher initial (short-term) costs for purchases will be made up quickly and that utility costs will be reduced in the near future, resulting in long-term savings.

Managers of resources and services often do not look beyond a couple of years. If the benefits will not be realized within this short time, they cannot see any advantage. Thus, a major challenge will be to show that the amount of water saved will result directly in lower water bills and quickly pay back the initial costs. This is also an opportunity to educate people about the need to think long term. Not everything is a quick fix, and this needs to be recognized and accepted.

RESOURCES

Hotlines

EPA's Safe Drinking Water Hotline
800-426-4791

Massachusetts Water Resources Authority
Water Works Division, Conservation Program
100 First Avenue, Building 39
Charlestown, MA 02129
617-242-SAVE

National Appropriate Technology Assistance Service
U.S. Department of Energy
P.O. Box 2525
Butte, MT 59702
800-428-2525 or in
Montana 800-428-1718

Brochures/Papers/Reports

Buyer's Guide to Ultra-Low-Flush Toilets
Garbage Magazine, March/April 1990 Issue
P.O. Box 5619
Boulder, CO 80322-6519
503-283-3200

A Citizen's Guide to Community Water Conservation
National Wildlife Federation
1400 16th Street NW
Washington, DC 20036-2266
202-797-6800

Conserving America: The Challenge on the Coast Resource Guide
National Wildlife Federation
1400 Sixteenth Street NW
Washington, DC 20036-2266
202-797-6800

Conserving America: Rivers Resource Guide
National Wildlife Federation
1400 Sixteenth Street NW
Washington, DC 20036-2266
202-797-6800

Conserving America: Wetlands Resource Guide
National Wildlife Federation
1400 Sixteenth Street NW
Washington, DC 20036-2266
202-797-6800

From the Mountains to the Sea
Environment Canada
Ottawa, Ontario K1A 0H3
306-780-5332

Gray Water Use in the Landscape
Edible Publications
P.O. Box 1841
Santa Rosa, CA 95402
707-874-2606

The Great Lakes Primer
Pollution Probe
12 Madison Avenue
Toronto, Ontario M5R 2S1
416-926-1907

Green Gardens: The Water-wise Way
National Wildflower Research Center
2600 FM 973 North
Austin, TX 78725
512-929-3600

Layperson's Guide to Groundwater
Water Education Foundation
717 K Street, Suite 517
Sacramento, CA 95814
916-444-6240

Layperson's Guide to Flood Management
Water Education Foundation
717 K Street, Suite 517
Sacramento, CA 95814
916-444-6240

Layperson's Guide to Water Conservation
Water Education Foundation
717 K Street, Suite 517
Sacramento, CA 95814
916-444-6240

Layperson's Guide to Water Quality
Water Education Foundation
717 K Street, Suite 517
Sacramento, CA 95814
916-444-6240

Layperson's Guide to Water Recycling and Reuse
Water Education Foundation
717 K Street, Suite 517
Sacramento, CA 95814
916-444-6240

Los Angeles Department of Water and Power
P.O. Box 111
Los Angeles, CA 90051-0100
213-481-4211
Has many lists of things you can do to reduce water use.

Needed: Clean Water
Channing L. Bete Co., Inc.
200 State Road
South Deerfield, MA 01373
800-628-7733

Nonpoint Source Pollution: Where to Go With the Flow
Groundwater Management Section
Box 7921
Madison, WI 53707
608-266-2621

Population and Water Resources
National Audubon Society's Population Program
801 Pennsylvania Avenue SE
Suite 301
Washington, DC 20003
202-547-9009

Sewage Treatment: America's Pipe Dream
Center for Marine Conservation
1725 DeSales Street NW
Washington, DC 20036
202-429-5609

Storm Water Runoff Guide
Isco Environmental Division
531 Westgate Boulevard
Lincoln, NE 65828-1586
800-228-4373 or 402-474-2233

Toxic Trick or Treatment: An Investment of Toxic Discharges to Our Nation's Sewers
U.S. Public Interest Research Group
215 Pennsylvania Avenue SE
Washington, DC 20003
202-546-9707

Water Conservation: Every Drop Counts
Environment Canada
Ottawa, Ontario, Canada K1A 0H3
306-780-5332

Water Reclamation Information
Tellurian Press
1102 N. Brand Boulevard, No. 64
Glendale, CA 9120
818-353-3767

Waterwise: The Catalog of Innovative Water Solutions
Gardener's Supply Company
128 Intervale Road
Burlington, VT 05401
802-660-3500

Books

A Citizen's Guide to Plastics in the Ocean
Katheryn J. O'Hara et al.
Center for Marine Conservation, 1988
1725 Desales Street NW
Washington, DC 20066

Coastal Alert
Dwight Holing
Island Press, 1990
1718 Connecticut Avenue NW, Suite 300
Washington , DC 20009

Coastal Marshes
Robert A. Chabreck
University of Minnesota Press, 1988
2037 University Avenue SE
Minneapolis, MN 55455

Down by the River
Constance Elizabeth Hunt
Island Press, 1988
1718 Connecticut Avenue NW, Suite 300
Washington, DC 20009

The Drinking Water Book
Colin Ingram
Ten Speed Press, 1991
P.O. Box 7123
Berkeley, CA 94707

Drinking Water Hazards
John Cary Stewart
Envirographics, 1990
P.O. Box 334
Hiram, CA 44234

Drought Busters
William Slater and Peter Orzechowski
Living Planet Press, 1991
558 Rose Avenue
Venice, CA 90291

Freshwater Marshes: Ecology and Wildlife Management
Milton W. Weller
University of Minnesota Press, 1987
2037 University Avenue SE
Minneapolis, MN 55455

Fresh Water Seas: Saving the Great Lakes
Phil Weller
Between the Lines, 1990
394 Euclid Avenue, #203
Toronto, Ontario, Canada M6G 2S9

H_2O: The Guide to Quality Bottled Water
Arthur von Wiesenberger
Woodbridge Press Publishing Company, 1988
P.O. Box 6189
Santa Barbara, CA 93160

How to Get Water Smart
Buzz Buzzelli et al.
Terra Firma, 1991
P.O. Box 91315
Santa Barbara, CA 93190-1315

Last Oasis: Facing Water Scarcity
Sandra Postel
Worldwatch Institute, 1992
1776 Massachusetts Avenue NW
Washington, DC 20036

A Life of Its Own
Robert Gottlieb
HBJ Big Books, 1988
1250 Sixth Avenue
San Diego, CA 92101

Our Common Seas: Coasts in Crisis
Don Hinrichsen
Kogan Page Ltd., 1990
120 Pentonville Road
London, England N1 9JN

Overtapped Oasis
Marc Reisner and Sarah Bates
Island Press, 1990
1718 Connecticut Avenue NW, Suite 300
Washington, DC 20009

Poison Runoff
Paul Thompson
Natural Resources Defense Council, 1989
40 West 20th Street
New York, NY 10011

The Poisoned Well
Eric P. Jorgensen
Island Press, 1989
1718 Connecticut Avenue NW, Suite 300
Washington, DC 20009

Rivers at Risk
John D. Echeverria et al.
Island Press, 1989
1718 Connecticut Avenue NW, Suite 300
Washington, DC 20009

Spill: The Story of the Exxon Valdez
Terry Carr
Franklin Watts, 1991
95 Madison Avenue
New York, NY 10016

Water: The Elements of Life
Theodor Schwenk and Wolfram Schwenk
Anthroposophic Press, 1989
Bell's Pond, Star Route
Hudson, NY 12534

The Water Encyclopedia
Frits Van Der Leeden et al.
Lewis Publishers, 1990
121 South Main Street
Chelsea, MI 48118

Water: The International Crisis
Robin Clarke
The MIT Press, 1993
Massachusetts Institute of Technology
Cambridge, MA 0214

Water: Its Global Nature
Michael Allaby
Facts on File, 1992
460 Park Avenue South
New York, NY 10016

Waterwise Gardening
Editors of Sunset Books and Sunset Magazine
Sunset Publishing Group, 1991
80 Willow Road
Menlo Park, CA 94025

Western Water Made Simple
Editors of High Country News
Island Press, 1987
1718 Connecticut Avenue NW, Suite 300
Washington, DC 20009

Books for Youth

Coastal Rescue: Preserving Our Seashores
Christina G. Miller and Louise A. Berry
Macmillan Publishing Company, 1989
866 Third Avenue
New York, NY 10022

Exploring Water and the Ocean
Gayle Bittinger
Warren Publishing House, 1993
P.O. Box 2250
Everett, WA 98203

Four Elements/Water
Carme Sole Vendrell and J. M. Parramon
Barron's, 1984
250 Wireless Boulevard
Hauppauge, NY 11788

The Magic School Bus at the Water Works
Joanna Cole
Scholastic, Inc., 1986
730 Broadway
New York, NY 10003

Oil Spills
Madelyn Klein Anderson
Franklin Watts, Inc. 1990
387 Park Avenue South
New York, NY 10016

Oliver and the Oil Spill
Aruna Chandrasekhar
Landmark Editions, Inc., 1991
Box 4469, 1402 Kansas Avenue
Kansas City, MO 64127

One World
Michael Foreman
Arcade - Little, Brown and Company, 1990
32 Beacon Street
Boston, MA 02108

Our Endangered Planet: Groundwater
Mary Hoff and Mary Rodgers
Lerner Publications, 1991
241 First Avenue North
Minneapolis, MN 55401

Our Endangered Planet: Oceans
Mary Hoff and Mary Rodgers
Lerner Publications, 1991
241 First Avenue North
Minneapolis, MN 55401

Our Endangered Planet: Rivers and Lakes
Mary Hoff and Mary Rodgers
Lerner Publications, 1991
241 First Avenue North
Minneapolis, MN 55401

Prince William
Gloria and Ted Rand
Henry Holt, 1991
115 West 18th Street
New York, NY 10011

Protecting Rivers and Seas
Kamini Khanduri
EDC Publishing
10302 East 55th Place
Tulsa, OK 74146

The River
David Bellamy
Potter, 1988
201 East 50th Street
New York, NY 10022

A River Ran Wild
Lynne Cherry
Gulliver Green/HBJ, 1992
1250 6th Avenue
San Diego, CA 92101

Tidepools: The Bright World of the Rocky Shoreline
Diana Barnhart
Blake Publishing, 1989
2222 Beebee Street
San Luis Obispo, CA 93401

Water Pollution
Darlene R. Stille
Children's Press, 1990
5440 N. Cumberland Avenue
Chicago, IL 60656

Individuals/Companies/Organizations

The following is a contact list for further information. If you are looking for faucet aerators, showerheads, efficient toilets, washing machines or information on water-efficient gardening products, you can contact any of the following or the Center for Environmental Education.

Bi-Cep, Inc.
20 Indian Valley Lane
Telford, PA 18969
215-723-3178
They sell plans for a graywater recycling system.

Bonar Plastics
19705 SW Teton Avenue, P.O. Box 487
Tualatin, OR 97062
503-692-0560
Bonar Plastics sells 40-gallon plastic containers called "rain banks" that easily connect to a downspout.

Environmental Test Systems
P.O. Box 4569
Elkhart, IN 46514
800-548-4381
They sell water testing kits.

Gardener's Supply
128 Intervale Road
Burlington, VT 05401
802-863-4535
Sells a variety of rainwater catchment devices.

Hach Company
P.O. Box 608
Loveland, CO 80539
800-227-4224
Sells water-testing kits.

LaMotte Chemical Products
P.O. Box 329
Chestertown, MD 21620
800-344-3100
They sell water testing kits.

Renew America
1400 16th Street NW, Suite 710
Washington, DC 20036
202-232-2252

Resources Conservation, Inc.
95 Commerce Road
Stanford, CT 06902
203-964-0600
Distributors of different showerheads, faucet aerators and toilet dams.

Rocky Mountain Institute
1739 Snowmass Creek Road
Snowmass, CO 81654
303-927-3851

Seventh Generation
49 Hercules Drive
Colchester, VT 05446-1672
800-456-1177
Many types of showerheads, faucet aerators and toilet dams.

Sun-Mar Corporation
900 Hertel Avenue
Buffalo, NY 14216
716-874-1825
Composting toilets are especially useful for remote campus sites where water is not easily accessible. Some models actually use no water, but compost wastes.

Water Conservation Systems, Inc.
Damonmill Square
Concord, MA 01742
508-369-3951

Water Control International, Inc.
2820-224 W. Maple Road
Troy, MI 48084
810-643-0030
Patented Flushmate, a flushometer water-conserving tank operating system.

Whedon Products
21 A Andover Drive
West Hartford, CT 06110
800-541-2184 or 203-953-7606
Affordable showerheads.

Worldwatch Institute
1776 Massachusetts Avenue NW
Washington, DC 20036
202-452-1999
They publish the Worldwatch Papers which deal with environmental issues. The two papers they did on water are: *Water: Rethinking Management in an Age of Scarcity,* #62, and *Conserving Water: The Untapped Alternative,* #67, both by Sandra Postel.

Drip and soaker systems can be purchased at home improvement centers, at nurseries or through the following:

Harmony Farm Supply
P.O. Box 460
Garton, CA 95444
707-823-9125

The Natural Gardening Company
217 San Anselmo Avenue
San Anselmo, CA 94960
415-456-5060

The Urban Farmer Store
2833 Vicente Avenue
San Francisco, CA 94116
415-661-2204
Catalog $1

Polymer Companies (Water Retention)

Amereq
50 N. Harrison Avenue
Congers, NY 10920
914-268-2122 or 800-832-8788

American Colloid Company
1500 W. Shure Drive
Arlington Heights, IL 60004-1434
708-392-4600

Arlan and Sons, Inc.
118811 Arroyo Avenue
Santa Ana, CA 92705
714-838-8539

Broadleaf Industries
3802 Main Street, Suite 3
Chula Vista, CA 91911
619-585-0500

Industrial Services International, Inc.
P.O. Box 10834
Bradenton, FL 34282-0834
800-227-6728, in Florida 800-227-6727

International Absorbent Marketing, Inc.
W. 1000 Silver Road, P.O. Box 219
Smelterville, ID 83868
208-783-1149

Rainsaver, Inc.
1009 N. 9th Street
Wala Wala, WA 99362
509-522-2400

Chapter 7

Energy

Chapter 7
CONTENTS

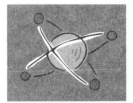

INTRODUCTION

Energy is the force that holds together atoms and molecules, gives us warmth, puts things in motion and lights our way. When environmentalists refer to saving energy, they are talking about the forms that humans find useful, such as the fuels that heat our school buildings and the electricity that lights them. Energy is a valuable resource that can be used wisely or destructively or that can be wasted. The most commonly used sources of energy can be very harmful to human health and to that of the planet. Wise use of energy doesn't pollute the earth.

This chapter explores the environmental impacts of nonrenewable energy sources and ways schools can save energy through efficient buildings, transportation systems and changed behavior. Wasting energy is also a waste of money, something no school can afford. This chapter will discuss the potential for renewable energy use on campuses and activity ideas for student energy conservation teams. A list of organizations, publications and product sources to help you get started can be found at the end of the chapter.

People have always used energy to survive and to make life more comfortable. Energy exists in many forms (light, heat, electricity, motion and nuclear and chemical reactions), most of which result from the sun. Energy from wind, wood and water results from an interaction of the sun and the earth. Solar energy is also stored in such organic matter as natural gas, oil and coal, which took millions of years to form but which is being consumed rapidly.

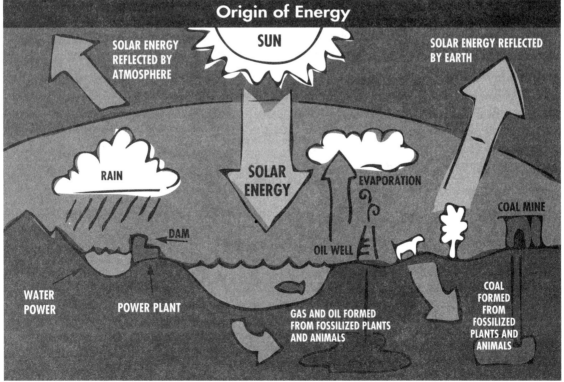

Source: "Energy: Powering Our Nation," *Cobblestone: The History Magazine for Young People*, Vol. 11, No. 10, Peterborough, NH, October 1990.

THE PROBLEMS

We must find more sustainable alternatives for 3 very important reasons.

1. We must find a way to provide energy that will **pollute less**. Whenever we burn coal, oil, gasoline or natural gas, we are polluting the air, soil and water of our planet. Most electricity is created from burning fossil fuels or using nuclear energy. Both methods contribute to global pollution in many ways.

2. The energy sources that we are most dependent on—natural gas, oil and coal—are **nonrenewable**. This means that the supplies are limited. As human populations grow and more countries become industrialized, more energy is consumed. We must turn to **renewable** energy sources and eventually wean ourselves from the nonrenewable ones.

3. Many fossil fuels are controlled by companies or countries that may choose to make supplies costly or unreliable. One place we will feel the squeeze is in school budgets.

> **"The United States, with only 5 percent of the world's population, uses 23 percent of the world's energy resources."**
>
> David Bill, *Practical Home Energy Savings* (Snowmass, CO: Rocky Mountain Institute, 1991).

The good news is that there are solutions. Ways to conserve energy have been developed over the last 15 years. The best rely on technologies that use energy more efficiently to provide the same level of service. Other technologies that harness solar, wind, ocean, hydro power (water power) and geothermal energy (heat from deep within the earth) have progressed. All these sources of energy can be minimally polluting and infinitely renewable if used properly. **Infinitely renewable and less polluting energy sources do exist.** Their efficient use could produce enough energy to maintain our standard of living, according to experts like Amory Lovins of Rocky Mountain Institute. Our quality of life, in fact, would be improved, since we and the planet would be healthier for it.

Even better news is that energy conservation saves money. Environmental clean-up is often costly. The savings from conservation can be used to fund the transition to renewable energy, at the global level and locally, at your school.

Limited Resources

Fossil fuels are a result of millions of years of solar energy trapped by plants and tucked away in the earth. Over time, the heat and pressure of the earth have turned decayed organic matter into energy-rich fuels. When burned, fossil fuels release most of their stored chemical energy in the form of heat. But they also release air pollutants.

Fossil fuels—coal, oil and natural gas—have enabled industrialized society to enjoy a comfortable standard of living. But with this short-term advantage, we have learned of the long-term consequences:

◆ Air pollution
◆ Water pollution from acid rain, mining sludge and oil spills
◆ Land pollution from strip mining and acid rain
◆ Climatic changes (global warming)
◆ Declines in human health
◆ Damage to plant life from acid rain and the resulting destruction of wildlife habitat
◆ Economic and political disruption, such as the Persian Gulf war.

Obviously, we still need to use these fossil resources until cleaner, renewable and economical substitutes can be integrated into the marketplace. The public must call upon the local, state and federal governments to focus more attention on energy efficiency and renewable sources.

Nuclear Fission

Nuclear power uses a process called fission (splitting atoms) to produce energy. Naturally occurring radioactive elements are collected and concentrated to form a fuel. With the right amounts of radioactive materials, atoms are split apart and release great amounts of heat. The heat is used to convert water into steam and turn turbines, which make electricity. The steam recondenses into water and returns to be vaporized again.

This energy resource has the advantage of producing no carbon dioxide, and its fuel is plentiful. But it has some major disadvantages:

◆ **The waste from nuclear power plants is highly radioactive for thousands of years.**
◆ **There is no safe way to store radioactive waste.**
◆ **If one factors in government subsidies, nuclear power is extremely uneconomical.** (It has been called the most expensive way to boil water.)
◆ **Accidents can be catastrophic.** Just consider Chernobyl. This became a household word when, as a result of a 1986 accident at the power plant, more than 250,000 people within a 36-mile radius had to be permanently relocated. Radiation spread from the Soviet Union through Eastern Europe and Scandinavia to the British Isles. Lamb raised in England and Ireland, where cesium 137 (radioactive waste from Chernobyl) came down with the rain and settled in the soil, is still banned as a source of food. Each spring, with the regrowth of grass, cesium 137 shows up. When the mother ewe feeds on the grass, she consumes the radioactive waste, which becomes highly concentrated in her milk. She then passes this known carcinogen on to her baby. Areas of contamination from Chernobyl are still being discovered.

◆ **Once a nuclear power plant reaches the end of its life, it has to be entombed and guarded for generations or the entire facility must be dismantled and buried.** Waste sites must also be guarded.

We have chosen to emphasize these points because they are very powerful. Nuclear pollution in the form of radioactive waste or fallout can be lethal, not just for those residing nearby, but to all who inhabit the earth. It is impossible to guard completely against accidents. How can we choose this as an energy source after considering the possibility of such catastrophic and far-reaching effects?

The United States has been very lucky. The many accidents at nuclear plants in this country have been handled without significant releases of radioactivity. Several accidents, most notably the one at Three Mile Island in Pennsylvania, have narrowly avoided becoming major disasters. All reputable analysts acknowledge that there will be more accidents.

Acid Rain
Air pollution from vehicles, power plants and factories (sulfur dioxide and nitrogen oxide) combines with water and forms acidic compounds. These acids fall with fog, rain and snow and settle in surface water and on land.

Acid rain is formed when sulfur dioxide and nitrogen oxide emissions react with water vapor and oxidants that are already in the atmosphere to form acidic compounds. These compounds then fall to the ground in rain or snow and may also attach to dry airborne particles and fall to earth as acidic dust.

In small, confined ponds, lakes and streams, the water is made unusually acidic. If no natural alkaline compounds or flushing action (such as stream movement) is available to remove or neutralize the acidity, the water can become deadly to most life, such as fish, water birds, amphibians (turtles, frogs) and microscopic organisms.

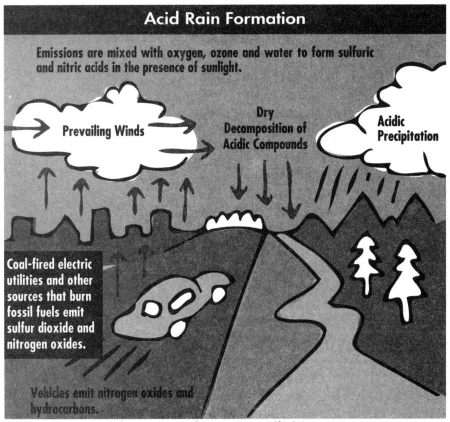

Acid Rain Formation

Emissions are mixed with oxygen, ozone and water to form sulfuric and nitric acids in the presence of sunlight.

Prevailing Winds

Dry Decomposition of Acidic Compounds

Acidic Precipitation

Coal-fired electric utilities and other sources that burn fossil fuels emit sulfur dioxide and nitrogen oxides.

Vehicles emit nitrogen oxides and hydrocarbons.

Source: United States Environmental Protection Agency, Acid Rain Program.

When acid rain falls on land, plants can be harmed if the soil does not have buffering alkaline substances. Forests in Canada, New England and Western and Eastern Europe have been damaged because of acid rain. When this destructive rain lands in urban areas, the acids corrode buildings, bridges, statues and cars.

More efficient use of fossil fuels generates less acid rain and thus gives nature more time to counteract its effects. The use of clean energy sources avoids this problem altogether.

Global Climate Change: The Greenhouse Effect

Naturally occurring carbon dioxide and water vapor in the earth's atmosphere slow heat loss into space, keeping the planet warm enough for life. Scientists call this phenomenon the greenhouse effect because the gases trap the heat on earth, just as the glass of a greenhouse traps heat inside. Without the earth's natural greenhouse gases the planet would be too cold for life. But human activities are adding more heat-trapping greenhouse gases [carbon dioxide, methane gas, nitrous oxide and chlorofluorocarbons (CFCs)] to the atmosphere. The result is that more heat remains on earth, thus raising temperatures.

There is considerable scientific debate on some of these points. What is known with a high degree of certainty is that increasing atmospheric levels of greenhouse gases will warm the atmosphere. But the climate is such a complicated system (interacting with oceans, land, forests, ice, air movement and so on) that scientists have yet to agree on the end results.

Carbon dioxide levels are rising because of fossil fuel combustion and deforestation.[1] Growing plants absorb carbon dioxide and store it. Plant decomposition releases carbon dioxide. We are presently cutting down our forests faster than we are replanting them so more carbon dioxide is being released than can be absorbed, thereby destroying the natural balance.

Many people believe temperatures will rise enough to cause dramatic changes by the middle of the next century. These could include melting ice caps, rising sea levels, changing global weather patterns and altered agriculture. Chaos is predicted. Others believe the earth will counter the effect of increased carbon dioxide, perhaps by increasing cloud cover, which would reflect more of the sun's heat.

Whatever the reality, it makes sense to avoid the risk through reducing carbon dioxide in our atmosphere by using energy more efficiently and by using less polluting energy sources. These measures will both save money and protect the environment in other ways.

Global warming is expected to increase air conditioner use enough to require 86 additional power plants in the United States by the year 2010 (costing $110 billion), which will in turn cause more global warming causing more air conditioner use...

Issues Review and Tracking: The Energy Newsbreif (IRT), Vol. 4, #9, June 1, 1989, Aspen CO.

To figure out how much carbon dioxide you are introducing into the atmosphere through your energy use, look at your energy bill. It will show you how much fuel you are using (gallons of oil, therms of natural gas, kilowatt-hours of electricity and so on). Multiply that number by the amount of carbon dioxide produced per unit of fuel as shown in the table below.

CO₂ Emissions from Different Energy Sources

	CO_2 Produced per Unit of Fuel	Pounds of CO_2 Produced per Million Btus
Fuel oil	26.4 lb. CO_2/gallon	190
Natural gas	12.1 lb. CO_2/therm	118
Gasoline	23.8 lb. CO_2/gallon	190
Coal (direct combustion)	2.48 tons CO_2/ton	210
Wood*	2059 tons CO_2/cord	216
Electricity (from coal)	2.37 lb. CO_2/kwh	694
Electricity (from oil)	2.14 lb. CO_2/kwh	628
Electricity (from natural gas)	1.32 lb. CO_2/kwh	388
Electricity (weighted national average, including all generation)	1.54 lb. CO_2/kwh	450

*If the wood is harvested on a sustainable basis, there is no net CO_2 emission because the growing trees absorb more CO_2 than is released when burning the wood.

Source: *Consumer Guide to Home Energy Savings*, 3rd ed., 1993, American Council for an Energy-Efficient Economy, Washington DC.

SUSTAINABLE SOLUTIONS

Building Energy Efficiency

In the 1970s, renewable energy and energy efficiency were national priorities in the United States. The rewards of this are felt every day:

◆ Efficiency gains made since 1973 are now saving the nation $100 to $200 billion annually.[2]

◆ The economy is 28 percent more energy efficient than it was in 1973.[3]

◆ Since 1973 the average fuel economy in cars has increased about 10 miles per gallon.[4]

Energy efficiency is the most immediate and cheapest energy solution and therefore should be the number 1 priority. Unfortunately, in 1986, when oil prices went down, the U.S. government abandoned its pursuit of efficiency. Nevertheless, quiet progress has been made. Our knowledge of which methods save the most energy and which are most economical has improved, and people are beginning to realize they can make a difference in environmental quality by applying this knowledge.

Energy efficiency:

◆ Reduces the amount of carbon dioxide entering the atmosphere, slowing global warming.

◆ Saves gas, oil, coal, uranium and money.

◆ Reduces energy needs immediately.

◆ Reduces the national deficit through lower oil imports.

◆ Promotes the use of renewable energy resources.

◆ Reduces dependence on unstable political regions.

If fossil fuels were used more efficiently, less pollution would result and supplies would last longer. Moreover, by using less, we pay less.

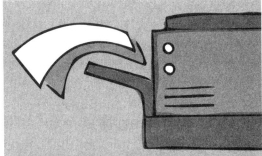

If 10 percent of office copiers had power-saving devices or were turned off when not in use, an estimated 7 billion kilowatt hours of electricity could be saved. That is the equivalent of 4 million barrels of oil a year.

EarthWorks Group, *50 Simple Things Your Business Can Do to Save the Earth* (Berkeley, CA: Earthworks Press, 1991), p. 17.

School Buildings

The first thing a school should do is organize it's energy data. This will put energy expenses in context. For example, energy data compared with other school budget items reveals that schools in California spend more per student on energy than on books and materials.[5] This kind of information will motivate administrators to take energy management more seriously. Organizing energy data is relatively easy to do. Follow the steps for calculating energy cost by hand presented in the box, Comparing Energy and Material Costs. This information will give student groups something to go to the principal or school board with so that an energy auditor might be hired.

Once a school is convinced that it is spending money for energy that could be better spent on education, an audit is the next step. An audit is a study done by an engineer or energy specialist to determine the best ways of improving the energy efficiency of buildings. The auditor inspects the building, measuring the temperatures, air movement, boiler or furnace efficiency, lighting use, thermostat settings and other indicators of energy usage. Then, usually

Source: Bonnie J. Cornwall, Senior Manager, California Energy Extension Service (CEES), personal correspondence, August 1994.

with the help of a computer, the auditor estimates which parts of the building are most wasteful and calculates the costs and potential savings of various **retrofits** the school could make. (A retrofit is any change that improves efficiency or function. Weather stripping leaky windows and insulating attics are typical, familiar retrofits.)

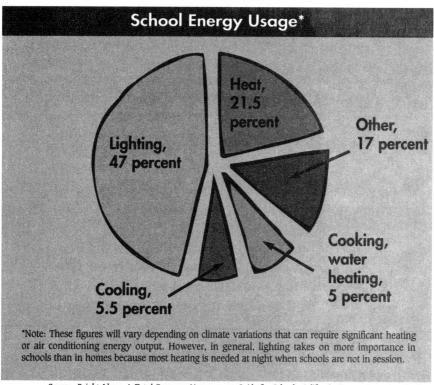

School Energy Usage*

Heat, 21.5 percent

Other, 17 percent

Lighting, 47 percent

Cooking, water heating, 5 percent

Cooling, 5.5 percent

*Note: These figures will vary depending on climate variations that can require significant heating or air conditioning energy output. However, in general, lighting takes on more importance in schools than in homes because most heating is needed at night when schools are not in session.

Source: *Bright Ideas: A Total Resource Management Guide for Schools*, California Energy Extension Service, Governor's Office of Planning and Research, 1989.

The School Energy Usage chart shows an approximate breakdown of energy consumption in schools. Notice that most energy is used for lighting.

After considering the feasibility of various retrofits, the auditor provides a detailed list of priorities for retrofitting the school. The most cost-effective retrofits will be listed first and provide the best return. One item may be more expensive than another, but if it brings greater savings, it can be more cost-effective. If the savings will never pay for the retrofit, it is not considered cost-effective. If the school does the most cost-effective retrofits first, it can be sure that there will be more money later to fund further energy efficiency improvements.

According to the California Energy Extension Service, which has sponsored approximately 150 school district energy conservation programs, the "key elements" listed at right have proved crucial for a successful energy program.

Finding a Reputable Energy Auditor

Someday energy auditors will be listed in the yellow pages of every phone book. (It's already worth a look.) Meanwhile, a good place to start is your state energy office. (See the state resources list in Chapter 20.) Some progressive cities have their own energy offices as well, such as Portland, OR; Minneapolis, MN; Austin, TX; and Berkeley, San Jose and Palo Alto, CA. Check the local phone book's government pages.

Key Elements for a Successful Energy Program

◆ Organize energy data.

◆ Build school board and top-level administrative support.

◆ Cultivate maintenance and operations support.

◆ Support "idea champions" at all levels.

◆ Set yearly goals.

◆ Appoint an energy coordinator.

◆ Conduct an energy survey or audit.

◆ Provide training for all staff.

◆ Integrate energy education with energy management.

◆ Provide incentives and recognition.

◆ Develop district and school energy teams.

◆ Make the program visible.

Source: *Bright Ideas: A Total Resource Management Guide for Schools*, California Energy Extension Service, Governor's Office of Planning and Research, 1989.

Beware of recommendations from heating and air-conditioning contractors who may have special arrangements with manufacturers that would bias them toward selling less efficient equipment.

There is a type of business that can meet the needs of groups such as schools. These are called Energy Service Companies (ESCo's). Often, they are HVAC (Heating, Ventilation, and Air Conditioning) contractors or manufacturers (such as Honeywell) that will audit your building and then pay for and install the necessary measures to make your building efficient. They are then paid back out of the energy savings.

Another source may be your local utility company. They vary from marketers, who will try to sell more electricity and gas, to active conservationists, who have solid, long-term programs to reduce energy use in their service territories. The sales-oriented utilities usually have extra capacity in their power plants and weak state regulators. The conservation-oriented utilities are often motivated by limited capacity (more demand than their power plants can produce) and stringent regulations on building new plants. Thanks to the work of envi-

ronmental groups like the Natural Resources Defense Council and the Conservation Law Foundation, some state regulations now allow utilities to make a profit on the energy they save for their customers. The utility companies in your area may provide auditing services, funding or referrals.

Schools should also check with the Association of Professional Energy Managers and the Association of Energy Engineers. (See the resource section at the end of this chapter.)

Convincing the School Board

An audit results in powerful tools to motivate school boards and administrators to take the most appropriate measures. Investing a small portion of its budget in this area will make the school more financially stable, and the reduced utility costs will be a potent reminder that savings may be possible when the budget comes up for review.

School energy conservation projects can also be funded through government agencies. The U.S. Department of Energy has a program called the Institutional Conservation Program that provides grants to schools to offset the costs of technical assistance, feasibility studies and retrofit installation. State energy offices administer this program as well as other programs that may help schools manage energy and link energy education with energy management. California's Energy Extension Service provides energy management technical services, which include an audit, lighting survey and education on ways people can save energy with simple behavioral changes. Pennsylvania's Energy Centers also have assistance programs. (See the state resources list in Chapter 20 for further information.)

If the school board can't be convinced to get an audit or apply for funding, teachers, students, staff and administrators can make a few low-cost or no-cost changes anyway. When board members see money left over in the utilities budget, they may well change their minds.

Maintenance. With shrinking school budgets, many schools don't have maintenance departments or even enough janitors; however, someone must maintain the place. Poorly maintained equipment wastes a lot of energy and money, adding to a downward spiral. Create a student "Energy Squad," and solicit parent volunteers and interested/available staff to help work with the maintenance crew.

"**W**e can say from experience that 10 to 15 percent can be saved with low or no cost actions, and up to 40 or even 50 percent with a concerted retrofit program. Organized energy data reveals which buildings have the greatest potential for saving and should be the first targets."

Bonnie J. Cornwall, Senior Manager, California Energy Extension Service (CEES), personal correspondence, August 1994.

First the basics:
- ◆ Fix broken windows.
- ◆ Patch big holes where air leaks in.
- ◆ Fix broken controls (e.g., thermostats).
- ◆ Replace broken thermostat covers ("vandal-proof").

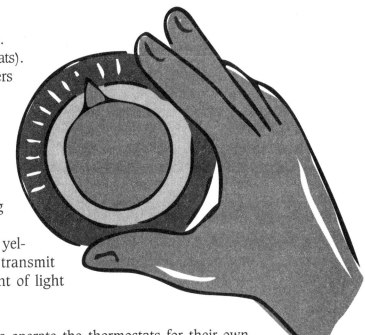

Then the preventive maintenance:
- ◆ Change furnace filters.
- ◆ Lubricate the heating, ventilation and air-conditioning systems.
- ◆ Clean coils (the copper tubing behind the air conditioner).
- ◆ Clean light fixtures and replace yellowed diffusers (they no longer transmit light well) to increase the amount of light coming from the fixtures.

Thermostats. If possible, let teachers operate the thermostats for their own classrooms and keep them off limits to others. This seems to be the most efficient way to control individual temperatures. The school should have a policy dealing with temperatures. Thermostats should not be operated like on/off switches. While students are in class, thermostats should be set at the lowest comfortable temperature on cold days and the highest comfortable temperature on hot days.

Automatic setback thermostats or time clocks turn the temperature down at a predetermined time and turn it back up before people arrive in the morning, so no one has to face a frigid room. The time clock can also be programmed to control temperatures during weekends, and with a 365-day time clock, during holidays. Make sure the person(s) operating the time clock know(s) how to program it and that it is not disconnected by frustrated users.

Holiday and Summer Shutdown. As simple as it seems, these no-cost measures are often overlooked. Turn off:
- ◆ Boilers/furnaces
- ◆ Pilot lights
- ◆ Icemakers
- ◆ Refrigerators
- ◆ Water coolers
- ◆ Water heaters
- ◆ Air-conditioning and ventilation systems
- ◆ Electric heaters and heat pumps
- ◆ Security lighting outdoors.

For more detail on a summer shutdown routine, the differences between summer and winter holiday shutdowns and fall start-up routines, see *Maintaining in the Nineties*, listed in the resource section at the end of the chapter.

Daylighting. Flip the light switch off, open the blinds and let the sun light the classroom whenever possible. There is usually too much light, not too little. So adjust blinds to deflect the light and reduce glare. The simplest way is to paint the ceiling white or another light, reflective color and then angle the blinds to bounce the light off the ceiling.

Use horizontal blinds on south-facing windows, where most direct light will enter, and vertical blinds on north-, east-, or west-facing windows. Painting the ground just outside the south windows also helps reflect indirect light into the room. Where they already exist, wash or repaint light-colored surfaces to increase indirect lighting throughout the building.

If people are skeptical about the amount of light that's getting to the student's desks, use a light meter to measure it. (Borrow one from a photo shop, if necessary.) Fifty foot-candles (measurement of illumination) should be plenty to read and write by. Advise those affected that this is generally accepted as sufficient. Walkways and other nonwork areas need considerably less.

Stop Drafts. Ask the students where the uncomfortable drafts are, search out the source of the cold air and seal the leak. This could mean weather-stripping leaky doors and windows, patching holes (even in internal walls) or stuffing backer rod (foam that fills cracks too wide for caulk alone) and caulk into cracks where the floor meets the wall. Fewer complaints from the cold spots mean the thermostat won't be turned up unnecessarily.

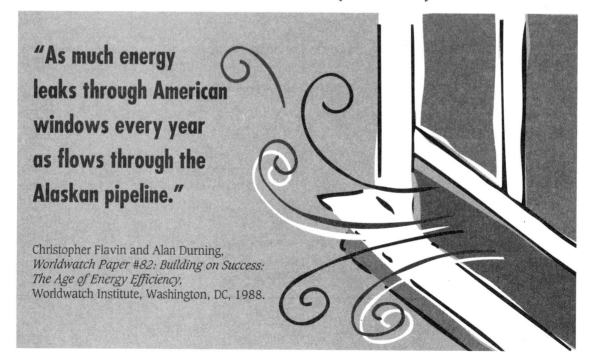

"As much energy leaks through American windows every year as flows through the Alaskan pipeline."

Christopher Flavin and Alan Durning,
*Worldwatch Paper #82: Building on Success:
The Age of Energy Efficiency*,
Worldwatch Institute, Washington, DC, 1988.

Water Heating. Heating water does not constitute a big portion of a school's energy budget, but the retrofits for it are inexpensive and pay for themselves quickly. The same methods you would use at home, work at school:

◆ Insulation jackets (or water heater blankets) should be put on water heaters to reduce heat loss. They are available from hardware stores.

◆ The temperature setting can be kept low (110°F) without compromising efficiency or comfort. Besides wasting money and energy, hot water increases corrosion, which reduces the life of the heater and can scald children's hands. Some dishwashers require hotter temperatures, which a booster heater can provide for less expense than heating the whole system to the needed level.

◆ When hot water will not be needed for a couple of days, turn the water heater temperature to the lowest setting, often marked "vacation." Better yet, install a timer to set back the temperature when hot water won't be needed.

◆ The addition of insulation to exposed hot water pipes will reduce heat loss. This is especially true if the system has a recirculating pump, which means hot water is continually flowing through the pipes. Check under the building (in the crawl space) or in the attic. Pipe wrap can be found at hardware stores.

◆ Replace high-flow showerheads in locker rooms with vandal-proof low flow ones.

◆ In school kitchens and bathrooms, install faucet aerators.

By the time the board sees the effects of these simpler retrofits and behavior changes, it will probably have saved enough money to hire an auditor. To be sure savings will be set aside for energy and environmental concerns, make a deal with the board in advance. A word of warning: A recent evaluation of savings from retrofits in California schools found that savings tripled after the first year. Administrations and maintenance staff may move slowly to incorporate all the recommendations, so savings won't necessarily show up in time for the next budget cycle.

More Expensive, but Worth It

This section lists retrofits an auditor is likely to recommend. But don't go by this list alone. It would be best to have a professional audit because each building, site and climate has its own way of affecting energy use.

Efficient Lighting. Get rid of incandescent light bulbs; they are probably the most wasteful energy guzzlers. Screw-in compact fluorescent lamps offer financial and environmental savings. They usually last 10 times longer than incandescent bulbs and are almost 4 times more energy efficient. Although they cost more initially (about $15 to $25 retail, often less where utilities offer rebates), in a high-use area the extra cost of using a compact fluorescent bulb can be made back in about 1 year from the energy savings.

Newer compact fluorescent bulbs no longer flicker or hum, and their color is similar to that of incandescent bulbs. But they vary in size and do not fit in all types of lamps and lighting

fixtures. With the right preparation, it can be educational and fun for students to retrofit their own classrooms simply by screwing in light bulbs. Calculating the yearly savings of compact fluorescents can blend math with social studies curricula. Compact fluorescent manufacturers are listed in the resource section at the end of this chapter.

"One 18-watt compact fluorescent bulb produces the same amount of light as a 75-watt incandescent bulb and lasts 13 times as long. Over its life, the compact fluorescent bulb will save emissions of about 500 pounds of carbon dioxide (one of the chief greenhouse gasses) and 5 pounds of sulfur dioxide, a greenhouse gas which also contributes to acid rain."

83 Ways to Save Energy Without Leaving Home, North Carolina Alternative Energy Corporation, Research Triangle Park, NC, 1991.

Yearly Savings of Compact Fluorescent Bulbs Calculation

Number of compact fluorescent bulbs	**X**	**hours used per day**	**X 2 =**	**annual savings**

Example:

4 lights x 6 hours per day x 2 = $48 per year

(57 watts x # of lights x hours/days x 365/1000 watts/kw x $0.08/kwh) +
(# lights x hours/day x 365/1,000 hours/bulb x $1) = watts saved per year.
Savings based on (75 minus 18) = 57 watts saved.

Source: Arizona Department of Commerce, Energy Office.

Another sure-bet retrofit involves the long-tube fluorescents used in overhead lighting. The newer T-8 size fluorescent tubes offer great savings over the traditional T-12s. Moreover, when the old ballasts fail, high-efficiency electronic ones should be installed. New electronic ballasts use 20 to 30 percent less energy and last longer.[6] Though they cost about twice as much initially, they have a lower life-cycle cost. Newer ballasts also prevent the flickering common with fluorescent bulbs. Be aware that the old ballasts and tubes usually contain toxic polychlorinated biphenyls (PCBs) and mercury, and should be treated as recyclable hazardous waste. (Call your school district for disposal instructions.)

Outdoor incandescents can be retrofitted with high-intensity-discharge (HID) lamps, such as high-pressure sodium. These bright lights are also good retrofits for gymnasiums. Exit signs can be cheaply converted to fluorescent with retrofit kits or the whole sign can be replaced with a no-maintenance LED sign for even greater savings. (See the resource section at the end of this chapter for the *Consumer Guide to Home Energy Savings*, which lists efficient lighting manufacturers.)

If burnt-out bulbs haven't been missed and safety is not threatened, consider "delamping." How much light is really needed? If a burnt-out bulb is replaced with an efficient one, it will still use energy.

School districts that have instituted night-time blackouts of their campuses have found that vandalism has not increased. In one district, vandalism decreased by 29 percent. Key lights, for example, near entry doors, can be put on motion sensors for emergency use and to alert police to trespassing. However, this is a very emotional issue and it is often difficult to convince people that it is safe. We are all still very afraid of the dark! But apparently, so are vandals. (For more evidence to bolster the argument, read *Maintaining in the Nineties*, p. 105, which is listed in the resource section at the end of this chapter.)

Heating System Replacements. When the old boiler goes, it's time to spend some money and it should be done right. One recommendation is to replace old central boilers with individual furnaces for each room, each controlled by the teacher. This strategy has shown dramatic savings. Stanton Elementary School (located in Castor Valley, CA) reduced natural gas use by approximately 50 percent after replacing a central boiler with individual room furnaces. These dramatic savings are due to the higher efficiency of the furnaces, combined with better control over room temperatures.

Lighting Controls. Smart switches can be used to save energy. They automatically switch off the lights when they're not needed. These include:
- ◆ **Occupancy sensors** or **motion detectors,** which measure infrared energy (heat) to determine whether anyone's in the room
- ◆ **Daylight controls,** which measure light levels to determine how much artificial light is needed and then turn on only that much.

If everyone in the building is not diligent about flipping switches (and they rarely are), these lighting controls save a lot of energy.

HVAC Controls. Optimizer controls check the outside temperature before deciding when to stop and restart the heating, ventilating and air-conditioning (HVAC) system. Other controls that may be part of an electronic energy management control system can set temperature ranges to cycle the system on and off. These controls are interactive or "smart" and may be complicated to program and operate. (They are usually PC based, so that school computers can run them.) But they are very worthwhile if the maintenance staff is qualified and trained to operate them.

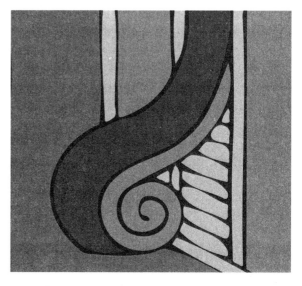

Insulation. Most buildings these days have some insulation. But where there is little or none (e.g., in the walls), it may be worthwhile to add more. Insulation reduces energy use by holding the heat in when it is cold outside and keeping the heat out when it is hot outside. Densely packed cellulose insulation blown into the outside walls is more economical than caulking and weather stripping. Find an insulation contractor who knows the technique, including how to seal the secret passages of air loss through walls to attics and crawl spaces (bypasses).

When Buying New Equipment and Appliances

When it is time to purchase any new equipment, make sure to buy the most energy-efficient models. To do this, look for the yellow energy consumption label and compare the amounts of energy used for different models. The brochures that engineers and contractors use when shopping for equipment should also contain efficiency information. The most efficient models are often more expensive to purchase but cheaper to operate because there are tremendous savings on utility bills. The higher initial cost will be paid back quickly.

Two resources that list the most efficient models of residential appliances are *Consumer Guide to Home Energy Savings* (found in bookstores) and *The Most Efficient Appliances* (available through the American Council for an Energy-Efficient Economy). (See the resource section at the end of this chapter.)

A report by E-Source (formerly Rocky Mountain Institute's Competitek program), *The State of the Art: Appliances*, has a section detailing the most energy-efficient office equipment, from copiers to computers. (See Rocky Mountain Institute in the resource section at the end of this chapter.)

Landscaping

Trees furnish many benefits to keep the environment productive and clean. They

◆ Provide shade and cooling
◆ Absorb carbon dioxide
◆ Release oxygen
◆ Retain moisture in soil
◆ Hold topsoil in place
◆ Provide food and shelter for wildlife
on your campus.

Trees planted in strategic locations around a building can help reduce many environmental problems. They can reduce the amount of solar energy that heats structures in the summer. Shade trees can reduce air-conditioning use by 20 to 50 percent. If there is no indoor air-conditioning, the extra shade will increase indoor comfort.

On the south and southwest sides of the buildings deciduous trees are best; on the north and northwest, evergreens are best. Deciduous trees lose their leaves in the winter, allowing sunlight to reach a building during the cooler seasons. Evergreens offer shade during the summer and act as windbreaks during winter storms.

"If planted in the proper location, trees and shrubs could reduce U.S. air-conditioning electricity use by as much as 50%."

H. Akabari et al., *The Impact of Summer Heat Islands on Cooling Energy Consumption and CO$_2$ Emissions*, Lawrence Berkeley Laboratory, Berkeley, July 1988.

Saving Paper Saves Resources

◆ The energy it took to create materials and transport them to your school is called embedded energy. Embedded energy is a one-time cost. Paper is an example of embedded energy that is of particular concern to schools.

◆ Americans use about 50 million tons of paper every day, or about 580 pounds per person. The average American uses 7 trees a year (in paper, wood and other products). In all, Americans use more than 1.5 billion trees a year.

◆ An EPA study concluded that using 1 ton of 100 percent recycled paper saves 4,100 kwh of energy (enough to power the average home for 6 months), saves 7,000 gallons of water and keeps 60 pounds of air-polluting effluents out of the atmosphere.

◆ Use both sides of the page, use scrap paper and don't use a huge sheet when a note pad will do. Pay attention to these guidelines when photocopying too. Make sure new copiers have an easy-to-use double-sided function.

David Assmann, *Environmentally Sound Paper Overview: The Essential Issues*, Conservatree Information Services, San Francisco, CA, 1992.

Transportation Efficiency

If there is anything more environmentally unsound than a single person driving a car to work every day, it is a person driving another person to school and then driving home alone. This means double the miles for each trip. This is what parents do when they drive their kids to school.

The school bus is a child's introduction to mass transit. Teachers, administrators and staff can set a great example by using the school bus. Their presence on board can moderate some of the rowdy behavior that sometimes occurs.

Consider coordinating efforts with municipal transit to avoid duplicating routes. Even if students ride the bus, they may not save energy if the routes aren't efficient. A standard bus with fewer than 20 passengers emits more air pollution per passenger mile than a single car! Use smaller buses or vans for less populated and after-school routes.

Some states and/or utilities offer financial help to schools to make their buses more efficient, especially those using alternative fuels. This is one way schools can take a leadership role with zero emission vehicles.

Students living nearby can be expected to walk or ride their bikes as long as there are safe routes. Parents, teachers and city officials can make bicycling and walking safer. Bike lanes to and from school should be provided at least within the radius not covered by bus routes. Bikes should be made secure at school. Providing this security may be as simple as placing the bike racks outside the principal's office rather than in a remote corner.

"Car traffic can accommodate about 750 passengers per meter-width of lane per hour, bicycles can carry 1,500 and rail can carry 9,000. One full train car can remove 100 cars from the road."

Ticket America, Washington, DC, 1994.

"If every driver in this country kept to the speed limit, we'd save 4.2 million gallons of gas every day."

"Driving Smart," Commuter Transportation Services, Inc., Los Angeles, CA, 1991.

Renewable Energy

Renewable energy resources offer many advantages over nonrenewable forms. Renewable resources are

◆ Abundant. Most areas of the world receive or contain some type of renewable energy resource.

◆ Clean or much less polluting than fossil fuels.

◆ Not likely to hide unexpected costs, such as health care or pollution cleanup.

◆ Usually sustainable and compatible with other finite resources, such as land, water and air.

In the United States, over the last decade, the government has provided many incentives to industries that use nonrenewable sources of energy. At the very least, equal incentives should be given to those who supply renewable sources of energy. Better yet, reducing incentives to use nonrenewable energy sources would also give renewable ones a fair chance. If renewable energy is allowed to reach its full potential, its contribution to the nation's energy use could rise from 8 percent to more than 50 percent by the year 2020, or sooner.[7] Schools can help spur the transition by educating the next generation about these possibilities and the need to find renewable, nonpolluting energy sources.

Solar Energy

Solar energy is abundant, clean, safe and inexhaustible. It can be captured right at the site where it is needed by the following means:

1. Solar cells for electricity

2. Solar collectors for hot water

3. Building design for heating.

Not all parts of the world receive enough solar radiation to make **solar electric cells** economical at present energy costs. But where the cost of running power lines is high, as in remote locations, or where little power is needed (e.g., calculators), solar electric systems are already very practical. Parking lot and walkway lights with built-in solar cells don't need underground wiring and can be found in hardware stores.

Today, millions of **solar water heaters** are in use in Japan, Israel, Australia and the United States. They are required by law for new buildings in northern Australia. Living facilities in Israel have them as routinely as Americans have one or two cars in their garages. The one drawback is that a building has only the amount of hot water that can be stored. At night, once it is used up, no more is available until late morning. Schools have the advantage of only needing hot water during the day, when it is most available.

Some schools already have solar water heating, although those systems installed during the heyday of solar tax credits in the 1970s may have been poorly designed or improperly maintained. But many such systems can be rehabilitated with professional attention. The Solar Rating and Certification Corporation is a nonprofit trade group intent on improving the reliability of solar systems that publishes listings of tested systems and component compatibility. (See the resource section at the end of this chapter.)

Schools with pools should consider **solar pool heaters**, for heating with fossil fuels is very expensive. Hot water stores a lot of energy. Once the water is heated, most of the solar energy can be retained through the night with an insulating pool cover, which should be used regardless of how the water is heated. Pool covers are available from pool supply stores and would make a great class gift from graduating students.

Passive solar building design is economical and should always be used in new construction. Solar energy will fall on the building regardless of design. Placing the windows in the right places will help trap solar energy at no additional cost. In the Northern Hemisphere, a building with most of its surface area facing west and south and with little or no vegetation cover absorbs more heat during the summer. Uncovered windows and little insulation in the attic and walls allow even more heat inside. In the winter, more heat can enter to warm the structure, but it will be lost at night without adequate insulation.

New buildings should be oriented to take advantage of the movement of the sun throughout the year. Place more windows on the east and north sides, with proper shading, weather stripping and R-value insulation. To add efficiency to windows in the south and west, appropriate vegetation should be planted for cover.

In new construction, **insulated windows** are a must. Double-glazed windows (2 layers of glass) or triple-glazed windows (3 layers) with argon gas sealed between the glass are called superwindows. Add a low-emissivity coating that bounces infrared radiation back into the room and these window can be more energy-efficient than a wall! Most of the major window manufacturers now carry low-emissivity and argon-filled windows.

Materials can be installed around the window to keep heat out or in. Outside, an awning made of cloth, metal or fiberglass can be attached over the window. Inside, curtains, shades or blinds can better insulate a room. Solutions for improving window efficiency can be found in *The Fuel Savers*. (See the resource section at the end of this chapter.)

Several good books on passive solar design are listed at the end of this chapter. The one most useful for schools is the *Energy-Efficient Design Guide for California Schools*. Although written specifically for southern California schools, many suggestions are applicable nationwide. The daylighting sections are particularly useful.

Use **alternative building materials** where possible in new construction and remodeling. A number of companies offer building materials made from discarded plant fibers, plastics and combinations of various traditional and untraditional materials. These recycled and low-tech materials often take less energy to produce than comparable standard materials. The single best resource is the handbook by the Center for Resourceful Building Technology. (See the resource section at the end of this chapter.)

Biomass

Biomass is plant matter, another form of indirect, stored solar energy. It includes a variety of materials, such as wood, agricultural waste, municipal sewage and aquatic plants. **Plant biomass** is a large resource available worldwide that can
 ◆ Be collected and used 24 hours a day.
 ◆ Be burned or converted into liquid fuels, such as methanol, biodiesel and ethanol for use in presently available vehicles.
 ◆ Burn more cleanly than other sources.
 ◆ Use plant materials otherwise considered waste.

Direct Combustion of Biomass (wood)

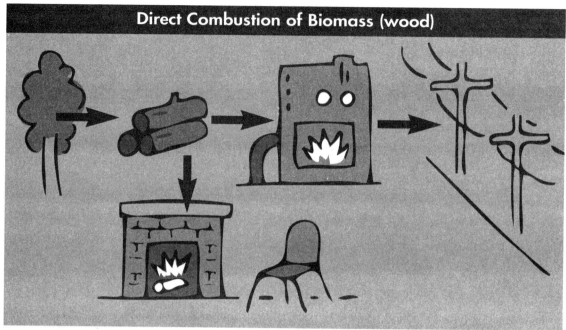

Source: United States Department of Energy, Conservation and Renewable Energy Inquiry and Referral Service.

Converting biomass into fuel has been given significantly more attention as nations work to reduce air pollutants. Some **biofuels** are becoming economical alternatives for diesel fuel. Vegetable oil, animal fats, used oils and fats, even algae, can be used to produce a diesel fuel substitute known as **biodiesel**. This fuel operates just as efficiently as petroleum diesel and meets the requirements of the Federal Clean Air Act. The emissions released contain less carbon and particulate matter and no sulfur; however, slightly more oxides of nitrogen are produced. At present biodiesel costs more than standard diesel, but to meet air emission standards, it may be the least expensive option.

There is a strong push in Europe for biodiesels. Many large companies are involved. Europe also produces biofuels from rapeseed oil (canola).

Imagine a School Bus That Doesn't Smell

A new methanol bus engine emits half as many oxides of nitrogen (NOx) as a standard two-stroke diesel engine. (Oxides of nitrogen are ingredients of acid rain and smog.) The heavy-duty engine also emits one-tenth the soot. When a diesel bus needs an overhaul, this new engine can be dropped in, and with a few changes to the fuel system it becomes a **methanol vehicle**. Even existing engines can be retrofitted with a kit sold by Detroit Diesel Corporation. (See the resource section of this chapter.)

Although the engine is actually less fuel efficient than standard engines, much of the noxious effect of using fossil fuels is remedied. If the methanol is made from biomass, even the carbon cycle is closed. That is, the same amount of carbon is absorbed by the plants as is released in burning the fuel. This means the fuel is not adding to global warming.

Wind Energy

Wind is the movement of air, which is caused by solar energy heating the planet. The equator receives the most heat, and the heated air rises. The void left behind is filled by cooler air from the north. As the heated air rises, it moves north to fill the void left by the cool air moving south. In the south, the process is reversed. Add the rotation and geographical differences of the earth and the result is wind.

Wind power is almost unlimited, free, clean, safe and renewable on a daily basis. But like solar energy, wind power is intermittent, so the electricity it generates must be stored or backed by renewable hydro or solar energy. A grid powered by these renewables is more reliable than a fossil and nuclear grid. Electricity storage is costly and inefficient. Also, the highest demand for electricity does not always occur when the wind is blowing. The sensible applications are those that don't have to be done at any particular time, so that the electricity generated does not have to be stored.

Another limitation for schools is location. Only certain sites with strong and steady winds can make windmills economical. Many of these are far from population centers. In rural areas, however, windmills are frequently used as water pumps, and the expertise for installing and maintaining them is available.

Geothermal Energy

Geothermal energy is produced when rocks deep below the earth's surface are heated by the high temperatures of the core. The heat from these rocks heat water or provide steam for running turbines. But geothermally rich areas—usually accompanied by volcanoes or geysers—are not the best locations for schools!

Ocean Energy

Ocean thermal and wave energy are two forms of renewable energy that are currently expensive and not appropriate for schools. **Tidal energy** may be economically feasible at about 2 dozen places in the world, where the gradient between rising and falling tides is large enough.

Conclusion

Each region has its own environmental conditions and endowments of energy resources. Solar energy is widely available. Many latitudes often have wind. People living near the meeting of tectonic plates have geothermal energy. Actually geothermal energy is available everywhere but is usually too deep to be used economically. Most regions have biomass. And most places have combinations of resources, plenty to satisfy their needs if the energy is used wisely.

SOLUTIONS: STUDENT PROJECTS

The previous sections discuss strategies to use energy more efficiently either by using less or by employing renewable sources. This section gives ideas for projects that will help students better understand and appreciate how energy is being used and how it can be saved. These projects will provide students with a way to help that can be rewarding, fun and exciting. This kind of involvement can give students a sense of belonging. Once people get involved in taking action, they are immediately empowered.

Lighting

Students can form energy patrol groups, survey their campus to find out where lighting improvements can be made and take their findings and recommendations to their school administration. It might be helpful to decide on a group name. A name helps promote unity and a feeling of belonging. One we have heard used is "Energy Busters." The manual, *Maintaining in the Nineties,* provides information that will help you do a lighting survey. (See the resource section at the end of this chapter.) Some state energy offices, such as Arizona, California, District of Colombia, Florida, Mississippi, Tennessee and Utah, offer support to school energy groups. The Arizona and California energy offices distribute a "How To" guide and video.

"When the Environmental Protection Agency switched to compact fluorescent bulbs, it cut electricity use, costs and power plant pollution by 57 percent."

EarthWorks Group, *50 Simple Things Your Business Can Do to Save the Earth* (Berkeley, CA: Earthworks Press, 1991), p. 44.

Students can involve their schools in a campaign launched by the EPA in 1991 called Green Lights. This campaign is designed to encourage major U.S. corporations and state and local governments to install energy-efficient lighting (such as compact fluorescent bulbs). Some of the businesses, governments and school boards that have joined the program are

- ◆ Bank of America
- ◆ Chevron
- ◆ Citicorp/Citibank
- ◆ Home Box Office
- ◆ Johnson & Johnson
- ◆ 3M
- ◆ Tufts University
- ◆ Walt Disney Studios

- ◆ State of Florida
- ◆ State of Nebraska
- ◆ City of Houston, Texas
- ◆ The Home Depot
- ◆ Xerox
- ◆ Polaroid
- ◆ Turner Broadcasting Systems
- ◆ Central Consolidated School District #22 in New Mexico

Students can contact these business to learn more or call the EPA at 202-382-6936 or 202-775-6650.

Bike, Walk and Bus Days

A great way to encourage participation in an energy-efficient transportation program is to give rewards. Set up a system for awarding points when anyone takes an efficient mode of transportation (walks, bikes, carpools, takes the bus or other public transportation). Points can then accumulate and be cashed in for prizes and/or awards (certificates and trophies). Local community vendors and businesses may be happy to donate the prizes and/or awards, thereby getting some great publicity and fostering community spirit.

Solar Ovens

One way for students to learn firsthand about the power and the effectiveness of solar energy is to build a solar oven. This is a very practical and simple project. The oven concentrates solar energy in a small area where the students will be able to cook or bake almost anything. It is simple to construct and really works, heating up to about 325 degrees.

For $5 you can receive a manual on how to make a solar oven with cardboard, newspaper, foil, string, glue, metal and glass. (See Solar Box Cookers International in the resources section at the end of this chapter.)

This is a lesson not only on how well paper works as an insulator, but also on energy-efficient cooking.

In 1991, kids in earth-saving clubs, classrooms and community groups joined together for the CO_2 Challenge. Youth from the coalition testified in front of Senators John Chafee and Al Gore at a Senate Special Children's Hearing on Global Warming. They presented 100,000 appeals urging then President Bush to commit the United States to a 20 percent reduction in CO_2 emissions. The youth and their families pledged to reduce carbon dioxide emission in their homes by 1 ton for the year using energy-saving actions.

Temperature Control

The following are some guidelines you can use to reduce the energy your school needs to keep everyone comfortable on the days that heating and cooling are necessary.

1. **To cut heating costs:**

◆ Wear layered clothes to school on particularly cold days so that the students and teachers can hang up their winter coats but still feel comfortable in the room when the thermostat is turned down to between 65 and 67 degrees.

◆ Raise money to plant trees on the windward side of the school to protect the classrooms and offices from cold winter winds.

2. **To cut cooling costs:**

◆ Raise money to plant trees around the buildings to increase shade. This reduces the amount of heat entering the buildings and the amount of air-conditioning required. If there is no air-conditioning, trees will improve comfort.

◆ For classrooms with no air-conditioning, try to go outside in the shade. If that is not an option, open the windows and doors, turn out the lights and use fans.

◆ For classrooms with individual air-conditioning units, hold class outdoors in the shade on particularly hot days.

◆ Special electrical outlet covers can seal electrical outlets to keep cooler or warmer air within the walls from leaking into the building. These covers have an automatic spring action to seal the plug opening when not in use, making it child-safe. Although they don't save much energy, the side benefit of increased safety makes this a good student project. Older students could retrofit kindergarten rooms.

High school students at 13 schools in Santa Cruz, California, conducted energy surveys of their schools and presented their recommendations to the school board. Retrofits were made and 6 months later the district realized astounding savings.

Projected savings are:

✔ $24,381 per year for Santa Cruz High School

✔ $160,666 per year for the district

✔ A net savings of $4,428,825 in 20 years.

Resources

Brochures/Papers/Reports

Cool Energy: The Renewable Solution to Global Warming
Union of Concerned Scientists
26 Church Street
Cambridge, MA 02238
617-547-5552

Directory of SRCC Certified Solar Collector and Water Heating System Ratings
Solar Rating and Certification Corporation
777 North Capitol Street NE, Suite 805
Washington, DC 20002-4226
202-383-2570

Energy Audit: A State-by-State Profile of Energy Conservation and Alternatives
Public Citizen
215 Pennsylvania Avenue SE
Washington, DC 20003
202-546-4996

Energy-Efficient Design Guide for California Schools
California Energy Commission
Publications Office
1400 10th Street
Sacramento, CA 95814
916-654-4287

Energy Options: Finding a Solution to the Power Predicament
National Issues Forums
100 Commons Road
Dayton, OH 45459-2777
513-434-7300

Energy Patrol Guide
California Energy Commission
Publications Office
1400 10th Street
Sacramento, CA 95814
916-654-4287

How to Organize Your Energy Data
California Energy Commission
Publications Office
1400 10th Street
Sacramento, CA 95814
916-654-4287

Maintaining in the Nineties: Energy Management for Maintenance and Custodial Staff
California Energy Extension Service
Publications Office
1400 10th Street
Sacramento, CA 95814
916-323-4388

Organizing Manual for "Renewables Are Ready": A Campaign of Education and Action
Union of Concerned Scientists
26 Church Street
Cambridge, MA 02238
617-547-5552

Recipes for an Effective Campus Energy Conservation Program
Union of Concerned Scientists
26 Church Street
Cambridge, MA 02238
617-547-5552

Renewable Energy: A National Directory of Resources, Contacts and Companies
Public Citizen's Critical Mass Energy Project
215 Pennsylvania Avenue SE
Washington, DC 20003
202-546-4996

Solar Industry Green Plan: A Call for Action
Solar Energy Industries Association
777 North Capitol Street NE
Washington, DC 20002
202-408-0660

Sustainable Energy
Renew America
1400 16th Street NW, Suite 710
Washington, DC 20036
202-232-2252

Worldwatch Paper 81: Renewable Energy: Today's Contribution, Tomorrow's Promise
Worldwatch Institute
1776 Massachusetts Avenue NW
Washington, DC 20036
202-452-1999

Worldwatch Paper 82: Building on Success: The Age of Energy Efficiency
Worldwatch Institute
1776 Massachusetts Avenue NW
Washington, DC 20036
202-452-1999

Worldwatch Paper 90: The Bicycle: Vehicle for a Small Planet
Worldwatch Institute
1776 Massachusetts Avenue NW
Washington, DC 20036
202-452-1999

Worldwatch Paper 111: Empowering Development: The New Energy Equation
Worldwatch Institute
1776 Massachusetts Avenue NW
Washington, DC 20036
202-452-1999

Books

Alternative Energy Source Book
John Schaeffer
Real Goods, 1992
966 Mazzoni Street
Ukiah, CA 95482

A New Power Base: Renewable Energy Policies for the Nineties and Beyond
Keith Lee Kozloff and Roger C. Dower
World Resources Institute, 1993
1709 New York Avenue NW
Washington, DC 20006

Consumer Guide to Home Energy Savings
Alex Wilson and John Morrill
American Council for an Energy-Efficient Economy, 1990
1001 Connecticut Avenue NW, Suite 801
Washington, DC 20036

Consumer Guide to Solar Energy
Scott Sklar and Kenneth Sheinkopf
Bonus Books, Inc., 1991
160 East Illinois Street
Chicago, IL 60611

Cooking with the Sun: How to Build and Use Solar Cookers
Beth Halacy
Morning Sun Press, 1992
P.O. Box 413
Lafayette, CA 94549

Cool Energy
Michael Brower
UCS Publications, 1992
26 Church Street
Cambridge, MA 02142

Cut Your Electric Bills in Half
Ralph J. Herbert
Rodale Press, 1986
33 East Minor Street
Emmaus, PA 18098

Energy Efficiency: Perspectives on Individual Behavior
Willett Kempton and Max Neiman
American Council for an Energy-Efficient Economy, 1987
1001 Connecticut Avenue NW, Suite 535
Washington, DC 20036

The Energy–Environment Connection
Jack M. Hollander
Island Press, 1992
1718 Connecticut Avenue NW, Suite 300
Washington, DC 20009

Energy and the Environment in the 21st Century
Jefferson W. Tester, David O. Wood and Nancy A. Ferrari
MIT Press, 1991
Massachusetts Institute of Technology
Cambridge, MA 02142

Energy Management and Conservation
Frank Kreith and George Burmeister
National Conferences of State Legislatures, 1993
1560 Broadway, Suite 700
Denver, CO 80202

Energy Policy in the Greenhouse: From Warming Fate to Warming Limit
Florentin Krause
Kogan Page Ltd., 1990
120 Pentonville Road
London, England N1 9JN

The Fuel Savers
Bruce N. Anderson
Morning Sun Press, 1991
P.O. Box 413
Lafayette, CA 94549

Natural Lighting
Eileen Haas
Solar Vision, 1982
Church Hill
Harrisville, NH 03450

Nuclear Madness: What You Can Do!
Dr. Helen Caldicott
Bantam Doubleday Dell, 1980
666 Fifth Avenue
New York, NY 10103

Nuclear Power Plants
Peter D. Dresser
Gale Research, Inc., 1993
835 Penobscot Building
Detroit, MI 48116

Passive Solar Buildings
J. Douglas Balcomb
MIT Press, 1992
Massachusetts Institute of Technology
Cambridge, MA 02142

Poisoned Power
John Gofman and Arthur Tamplin
Rodale Press, 1971
33 East Minor Street
Emmaus, PA 18098

Renewable Energy Sources for Fuels and Electricity
Laurie Burnham et al.
Island Press, 1993
1718 Connecticut Avenue NW, Suite 300
Washington, DC 20009

30 Simple Energy Things You Can Do to Save the Earth
John Javna, Seth Zuckerman and Chris Calwell
EarthWorks Group, 1990
1400 Shattuck Avenue, Suite 25
Berkeley, CA 94709

Solar Dictionary
Carl U. Breuning and Fred F. Evangel
The Energy Store, 1983
P.O. Box 1120
San Juan Pueblo, NM 87566

State of the Art Energy Efficiency
Edward Vine and Drury Crawley
American Council for an Energy-Efficient Economy, 1991
1001 Connecticut Avenue NW, Suite 535
Washington, DC 20036

Wind Power for Home and Business: Renewable Energy for the 1990s and Beyond
Paul Gipe
Chelsea Green Publishing Company, 1993
P.O. Box 130, Route 113
Post Mills, VT 05058-0130

Books for Youth

Electricity
Susan Mayes
Usborne Publishing Limited, 1989
83-85 Saffron Hill
London, England EC1 8RT

Energy and Power
Richard Spurgeon and Mike Flood
Usborne Publishing Limited, 1990
83-85 Saffron Hill
London, England EC1 8RT

Energy Resources
Robin Kerrod
Thomson Learning 1993
115 Fifth Avenue
New York, NY 10003

The Heat Is On: Facing Our Energy Problem
Shelley Tanaka
Firefly Books, 1991
P.O. Box 1325, Ellicot Station
Buffalo, NY 14205

Our Future at Stake
Citizen's Policy Center
New Society Publishers, 1985
4722 Baltimore Avenue
Philadelphia, PA 19143

Why Doesn't the Sun Burn Out?
Vicki Cobb
Lodestar Book/Dutton, 1990
375 Hudson Street
New York, NY 10014

Individuals/Companies/Organizations

Air Conditioning and Refrigeration Institute
1501 Wilson Boulevard
Arlington, VA 22209
703-524-8800
A trade group with information on efficient products.

Alliance to Save Energy
1725 K Street NW, Suite 509
Washington, DC 20006
202-857-0666
A nonprofit coalition of government, business, environmental and consumer leaders dedicated to increasing energy efficiency.

American Council for an Energy Efficient Economy (ACEEE)

1001 Connecticut Avenue NW, Suite 801
Washington, DC 200036
202-429-8873
ACEEE publishes a booklet *The Most Energy-Efficient Appliances.* Although generally geared to residential equipment, it is worth checking before making school purchases. Their publications catalog includes a variety of resources. Write or call:
ACEEE Publications
2140 Shattuck Avenue, Suite 202
Berkeley, CA 94704
510-549-9914

American Institute of Architects

1735 New York Avenue NW
Washington, DC 20006
800-365-ARCH
Publishes the *Environmental Resource Guide (ERG)*. A quarterly publication that provides subscribers with factual information on significant environmental impacts of building materials and construction practices, including life-cycle considerations and annotated bibliographies.

American Solar Energy Society

2400 Central Avenue, G-1
Boulder, CO 80301
303-443-3130
ASES promotes the use of solar energy technologies. Publishes *Solar Today* magazine, sponsors the National Solar Energy Conference and has regional chapters throughout the country.

Association of Energy Engineers

4025 Pleasant Dale Road, Suite 420
Atlanta, GA 30340
404-447-5083
A nonprofit internatinal professional society.

Association of Professional Energy Managers

100 Long Beach Boulevard
Long Beach, CA 90802
800-543-3563

Center for Resourceful Building Technology

P.O. Box 3866
Missoula, MT 59806
406-549-7678
CRBT is a nonprofit organization that encourages efficient resource and energy use within the building industry. Published *The Guide to Resource Efficient Building Elements*, a reference to suppliers of alternative and recycled building products.

Conservation Law Foundation Energy Project

62 Summer Street
Boston MA 02110
617-350-0990

Detroit Diesel Corporation

13400 West Outer Drive
Detroit, MI 48239
313-592-5000
This company manufactures methanol and natural gas engines. Retrofits some diesel engines to methanol and will also assist with the installation of both the methanol and natural gas engine.

Energy Efficient and Renewable Energy Clearinghouse (EREC)

P.O. Box 3048
Merryfield, VA 22116
800-523-2929; 800-233-3071 in Alaska and Hawaii
EREC gives out technical and general information on renewable energies and conservation.

Environmental Defense Fund (EDF)

257 Park Avenue South
New York, NY 10010
212-505-2100
One of the largest environmental action organizations, with 6 regional offices and more than 125,000 members. Pioneered the partnership of environmental science and law. The major issues EDF is working on are the greenhouse effect, wildlife and habitat, ozone depletion, saving the rainforests, acid rain, water, toxics, Antarctica and recycling. Publishes a newsletter called the *EDF Letter*.

Jade Mountain

P.O. Box 4616
Boulder, CO 80306-4616
800-442-1972
The *Jade Mountain Appropriate Technology News* contains a variety of energy-related products, including lighting, appliances, fans, solar, photovoltaics, water conservation supplies, insulation, gifts, toys and books.

Masters Corporation

P.O. Box 514
New Canaan, CT
203-966-3541
This organization puts out a catalog, *Environmental Outfitters,* that has been called an "architectural L.L. Bean."

McCracken Solar Company

329 West Carlos Street
Alturas, CA 96101
916-233-3175
Maker of solar stills since 1959. Through the process of distillation, heat is used to extract water from the air. A solar still uses the sun's energy to condense purified water for consumption, removing salts, minerals and volatile organic hydrocarbons.

Natural Resources Defense Council (NRDC)

40 West 20th Street
New York, NY 10011
212-727-2700
The NRDC is one of America's leading environmental protection organization and one of the most influential. Uses law and the regulatory process to shape public policy on a wide range of environmental issues. Through advocacy, education, litigation, lobbying, policy, publications and research the NRDC spreads awareness of critical environmental issues. Publishes a magazine called *The Amicus Journal*.

Philips Lighting Company

200 Franklin Square Drive
P.O. Box 6800
Somerset, NJ 08875-6800
908-563-3000
Manufacturer of light bulbs and a line of compact fluorescent bulbs.

Photocomm, Inc.

930 Idaho-Maryland Road
Grass Valley, CA 95945
800-223-9580
This organization bills itself as the country's largest distributor of solar-electric systems. Call to find closest source of its products and service. Publishes a catalog.

Real Goods Trading Company

966 Mazzoni Street
Ukiah, CA 95482
800-762-7325
Mail order catalog available with extensive supply of products for energy independence. Publishes *Alternative Energy Sourcebook,* a very comprehensive guide to energy sensible technologies.

Renew America

1400 16th Street NW, Suite 710
Washington, DC 20036
202-232-2252
Renew America gathers information on environmental problems and what's being done about them. Published *Sustainable Energy*, a report on the various renewable-energy resources and their potential in today's markets and in the near future.

Rising Sun Enterprises, Inc.

40 Sunset Drive, #1
Basalt, CO 81621
303-927-8051
This company has an informational pamphlet that gives facts and details on energy savings through the use of compact fluorescent bulbs and a catalog of these bulbs. Also does consulting with businesses on how to improve lighting efficiency.

Rocky Mountain Institute

1739 Snowmass Creek Road
Old Snowmass, CO 81654-9199
303-927-3851
A nonprofit research and education foundation whose goal is to foster efficient, sustainable use of resources as a path to global security. Publishes a number of informative papers and booklets.

Safe Energy Communications Council

1717 Massachusetts Avenue NW, Suite LL215
Washington, DC 20036
202-483-8491
Publishes viewpoints on energy efficiency and renewable energy alternatives.

Sage Advance Corporation

P.O. Box 23136
Eugene, OR 97402
503-485-1947
Markets passive solar hot water systems for residential and commercial uses.

Solar Box Cookers International

1724 Eleventh Street
Sacramento, CA 95814
916-444-6616.
Solar Box Cookers International offers manuals on how to make a solar oven and information covering solar cooking.

Southern Cellulose

6057 Boat Rock Boulevard
Atlanta, GA 30336
404-344-3590
Makes building insulation out of recycled telephone books. Cellulose can be 30 to 40 percent more efficient than fiberglass insulation, and there is no formaldehyde.

Union of Concerned Scientists

26 Church Street
Cambridge, MA 02238
617-547-5552
A nonprofit organization of scientists and other citizens concerned about the impact of advanced technology on society. Programs focus on national energy policy, national security policy and nuclear power safety. Published *Cool Energy*, a book by Michael Brower, on the future uses of nonrenewable and renewable energy resources.

Windstar Foundation

2317 Snowmass Creek Road
Snowmass, CO 81654
303-927-4777
The Windstar Foundation is a nonprofit educational organization that conducts research, develops demonstration projects and offers educational programs, all directed toward creating a healthy environment and a promising future.

Worldwatch Institute

1776 Massachusetts Avenue NW
Washington, DC 20036
202-452-1999
The Worldwatch Institute's mission is to research and publish information on global environmental issues to shape public opinion, policy and events. Publishes 2 periodicals, *State of the World* (annually) and *Worldwatch* (monthly).

Electromagnetic Fields

Chapter 8

CONTENTS

INTRODUCTION

Electromagnetic Terms Made Simple

Because of the complexity of this topic, we suggest that you familiarize yourself with the following terms:

◆ **Electromagnetic pollution**. This term is used when the electric and/or magnetic fields are stronger than levels some experts have considered safe to human health.

◆ **Electromagnetic field** (EMF). Made up of electric and magnetic fields. Magnetic fields radiate from the source whenever electricity is flowing or being "used." Electric Fields radiate from the source even if power isn't being used.

◆ **Frequency**. This is the rate of alternation and it is measured in **Hertz** (abbreviated Hz). Ranges of frequencies include high, low and extremely low.

◆ **High frequency (HF)** refers to the range of frequencies in the radio spectrum between 3 and 30 megaHertz.

◆ **Low frequency (LF)** refers to a radio frequency between 30 and 300 kiloHertz.

◆ **Extremely low frequency (ELF)** describes the electromagnetic spectrum extending from 0 to 1,000 cycles per second. ELF is by far the most common frequency to which we are exposed. The power frequency in the United States is 60 cycles per second and in Europe it is 50 cycles per second.

◆ **Direct current** flows in a constant direction. This type of current is produced by batteries, solar panels and power adapters.

◆ **Alternating current** changes direction 60 times per second (50 times per second in Europe and Asia). This creates electric and magnetic fields that "pulse back and forth."

◆ **Gauss**. This term denotes the strength of magnetic fields. We will be concerned with fields in the **milligauss** range, which is one-thousandth of a gauss.

The easiest way to understand the following basic electromagnetic terms is to think of the electricity as water.

◆ **Volts** measure electrical potential. Voltage is like the *pressure* of water.

◆ **Amps** is short for *amperes*, which is the amount of **current** flowing in a circuit. This is like the *volume* of water flowing past a particular point.

◆ **Watts** is a measure of the *power* of the flow in a circuit. Watts are calculated by multiplying the amount of electrons flowing (amps) by the pressure at which they are flowing (volts). Watts = amps multiplied by volts.

◆ **Cycles per second** is a measure of alternation or repetition. The simplest way to picture this is to imagine a wheel turning. Each time the wheel completes a turn, that is one cycle. The number of times this

> *"**T**he strength of magnetic fields are measured in a unit called gauss, named for the German scientist who investigated electrical properties in the eighteenth century."*
>
> "Electromagnetic Fields," *Environment*, New England Region, U.S. Environmental Protection Agency, Vol 3, No. 3, Spring 1993, p. 2.

occurs each second is the number of cycles per second, or the *frequency*. In the world of electricity and magnetism, cycles per second are called *Hertz* and are used to measure *wavelengths*. One wavelength is the same as one cycle and is measured from the beginning of one wave to the beginning of the next. Because all electromagnetic phenomena travel at the same speed, *the longer the wavelength, the lower the frequency*. Frequencies above 1,000 Hz are measured in kiloHertz, or kHz; frequencies above 1 million Hz are measured in megaHertz, or MHz. Therefore, 2 million Hz is written 2 MHz.

UNDERSTANDING THE DANGERS OF EMFs

Only in the last century were the conditions that now regularly expose many people to EMFs created. The potential hazards of EMF fields are measured statistically among certain populations by the increase in the number of cancer deaths. It takes time for the problem to show up, and it takes time for scientists to study the evidence and arrive at conclusions.

In 1992 congress passed a bill that allocated $65 million for a 5 year EMF research and public information program. The Department of Energy is to be held accountable for engineering research and the National Institute of Environmental Health Sciences is responsible for all health effects research and the communications component of the program. 1 million dollars each year is to be used for communication purposes.

"Congress Approves $65 Million EMF Research Program," *Microwave News*, (September/October 1992), p. 2.

Increasing evidence suggests that long-term exposure to some kinds of EMFs can cause cancer, leukemia, miscarriages, immune disorders and other health problems.[1]

The possible dangers of ELF magnetic fields come from chronic or frequent exposure. Attending school near power lines, sleeping under an electric blanket or working in front of a computer all day could all involve exposure to intense EMFs. Such exposure is beginning to be linked to various types of cancer. Because the risks of EMFs may be related to dosage, people living or working in strong EMF environments may be at much more risk. **Children may be at more risk because they are growing and electromagnetic pollution seems to affect the body's mechanisms that regulate cell growth**.

At this point there is no established safe level of EMF exposure because the conclusions of existing scientific research remain controversial. Do we have to choose between the convenience of electricity and our health?

How EMFs May Cause Cancer

Solid evidence now suggests that the dangers associated with EMF radiation arise from its interference with one or more of the basic cellular processes of life.[2]

Healthy cells communicate with their neighbors and regulate their activities based on the messages they receive. This information tells them what kind of cells to become. Cells also rely on this kind of communication to let them know that they have bumped into their neighbors and that it is time to stop reproducing. When populations of cells lose the ability to understand the signals that would normally tell them when to stop multiplying, they become "disorganized." This uncontrolled and undifferentiated growth results in what we call a tumor.

All life evolved with the approximately weak 10-Hz background magnetic field of the earth. Experiments with cells, animals and humans indicate that we use this 10-Hz field as a kind of clock. When experimental subjects are isolated from all time cues but are still exposed to this magnetic field, they stay on a rhythm similar to our 24-hour cycle. But if they are shielded from the earth's magnetic pulse, their sleeping and waking cycles lose regularity. Because this background pulse is comparatively weak, it is easily drowned out or confused by artificial fields that operate at similar or harmonic frequencies.[3]

This "confusion" of the basic timing mechanism of the cell, which is essential to life, is what seems to give rise to a host of superficially unrelated diseases.[4]

No. The problems arise from the way we are using electricity. Is there any way we can protect ourselves and our children from this risk? Yes. In many cases there are simple precautions that can greatly reduce exposure to these fields. (See "Minimizing Risks" on page 242.)

Where the Controversy Lies

There is a lot at stake in the fight over EMFs. Many powerful groups see their interests threatened by the emerging consensus that some of the common ways we use electricity and electromagnetic radiation might be hazardous to our health. The military, electric utilities and computer and television manufacturers all have contributed to studies that clearly have been aimed at trying to disprove any link between EMFs and the various forms of cancer they may cause. This is similar to the cigarette industry's attempts to disprove any link between smoking and cancer.

One of the most common ways of distorting the issue, which you would find in every utility paper on the subject of EMF hazards, is a reassuring graph comparing the strength of magnetic fields of common household appliance and tools with the "background" fields from transmission lines. This is a very misleading comparison. First, in many cases the measurements of the appliances were done as close to the source (the motor) as possible, which is not where you would stand or in some cases even could stand. Second, the dose you receive depends on how long you stand next to the machine, and most of us do not stand all day next to the blender or the back of the washing machine. However, if you live close to some transmission lines, you might be exposed to a 3- to 4-milligauss field *all the time* you are in and around your house. When seen in this light the charts in the utility pamphlet do not seem so reassuring.

The following chart, Typical Sources of EMFs in the School, relates the strength of magnetic fields one is exposed to at different distances from some common appliances.

Typical Sources of EMFs in the School

Appliance	Distance from Source		
	6 inches	1 foot	2 feet
Copy Machine	90	20	7
Fluorescent Lights	40	6	2
Electric pencil sharpeners	200	70	20
Video display terminals (PCs with color monitor)	14	5	2
Color TVs	–	7	2
Hand Mixer	100	10	1
Blenders	70	10	2
Microwave oven	200	40	10
Power saw	200	40	5
Drills	150	30	4

Source: *EMF In Your Environment*, EPA, 1992.

POTENTIAL HEALTH HAZARDS

Electromagnetic fields are being blamed for a wide range of health problems, such as miscarriages, birth defects, learning problems, many types of cancer and some immune disorders. In 1987 David Carpenter of the New York State Department of Health "estimated that 30 percent of all childhood cancer may be related to EMF exposure, amounting to a total of 2,000 children per year in the United States. According to Carpenter, roughly 4,000 of the nation's adults may also be affected."[5]

One study of electric power utility workers in East Texas routinely exposed to 60-Hz fields revealed an incidence of brain cancer 13 times that in a comparable unexposed group.[6] Sixty-hertz fields have also been shown to increase the growth rate of cancer cells dramatically and permanently by as much as 10 times, and statistical studies have demonstrated an increased risk of cancer for occupants of houses with wiring configurations that expose their inhabitants to EMF magnetic fields.[7]

It is very important for schools to consider that embryos and children may be particularly sensitive to carcinogens. Because the young are in periods of high growth, they are particularly susceptible to anything that disrupts the processes that regulate growth. Numerous reports have associated developmental defects with electromagnetic exposure.

Dosages Explained

Exposure to EMFs is called dosage because both the intensity of the field and the duration of the exposure are important. But EMFs may be different from other hazards that are measured in doses. Some evidence on EMFs suggests duration is more significant than intensity, particularly when it is repeated. In other words, a 1-gauss field for 1 week—168 gauss hours—would probably not be as harmful as a 10-milligauss field for 2 years, even though they are roughly equivalent in dosage terms.

POSSIBLE SOURCES OF EMFs ON YOUR CAMPUS

It is possible to reduce the risks of EMF exposure by following some inexpensive, commonsense precautions. Although magnetic fields are invisible, they are easy to detect with the right equipment. In fact, measuring these fields is the only way to be sure of their sources and strengths. Here is an opportunity for students to get involved. They can make an inventory of EMF sources around the campus, listing next to each one the kind of exposure it creates for those near it.

For a free listing of someone who can test your school for electromagnetic fields, write The National Electromagnetic Field Testing Association (NEFTA) 628-B Library Place, Evanston, IL 60201 or call 708-475-3696.

Using a meter is the only way to be sure about the strengths of fields. A number of meters for detecting magnetic fields are available, ranging in cost from $50 to $2,500. The Swedish government, which is the only government with laws protecting its citizens from EMFs, has set safety levels at 2.5 milligauss.[8]

MINIMIZING RISKS

How do we evaluate this threat and take effective action? Some actions, such as moving a school or suing the power company to make it move transmission lines, are very expensive. Others, such as keeping your bedside electric clock at least 3 feet from your body and not using an electric blanket, are easy and cost nothing. Avoidance of unnecessary risk is the wisest course, given the state of our knowledge of the health risks of EMFs.

The following describes the most common ways we are exposed to EMFs.

Computers

Most EMF radiation from monitors comes from the horizontal and vertical deflection coils which are on the cathode end of the cathode ray tube. Additional magnetic fields may come from the fly-back transformer which is usually mounted at the back of the computer. This may cause more EMF radiation from the back or sides of the monitor than from the front Older computers tend to be worse. Luckily, some newer monitors use wiring techniques that lower these fields.

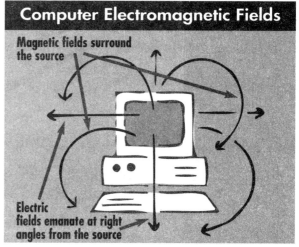

Computer Electromagnetic Fields

Magnetic fields surround the source

Electric fields emanate at right angles from the source

Source: *Electromagnetic Fields (EMFs) in the Modern Office*, The Labor Institute, NYC.

High emission computers and televisions both give off similar types of radiation, yet people sit closer to computers for longer periods of time. This is a serious problem. *It is best to sit at least 28 inches (approximately arm's length with fingers extended) away from a computer when it is on.*[9] Unfortunately, this is further than many children can reach. The field from the back and sides of an unshielded computer may also expose adjacent students. Until computers can be shielded or replaced with low emission monitors, the following sketch, Computer Spacing, illustrates the distance computer users should be from their computer screens and other computers.

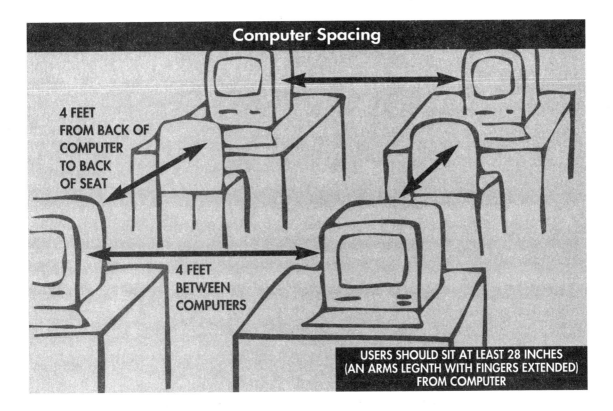

Computer Spacing

4 FEET FROM BACK OF COMPUTER TO BACK OF SEAT

4 FEET BETWEEN COMPUTERS

USERS SHOULD SIT AT LEAST 28 INCHES (AN ARMS LEGNTH WITH FINGERS EXTENDED) FROM COMPUTER

In 1986, Sweden's National Institute of Radiation Protection issued EMF guidelines for computers known as MPR I. Four years later they were revised to reduce field intensity and cover more field types. The present guidelines, known as MPR II, include standards for ELF and VLF magnetic fields, ELF and VLF electric fields, electrostatic charge and ionizing radiation. The Swedish Labor Union TCO (see resources) has established even tougher standards which have been unofficially adopted by some computer manufacturers. The TCO standard will probably by adopted as MPR III within the next few years.

When selecting a monitor and choosing between black and white or color you should be more concerned that the screen meets the most recent Swedish MPR II or TCO standards and not the older, less stringent guidelines (MRP I) than the difference between color or black and white. Both black and white and color monitors vary according to their manufacturer.

Shielding is available that is made out of special metal; it goes around the EMF emitting components, inside the plastic case, and provides protection from EMF's. Several suppliers of this shielding are listed in the resource section at the end of the chapter. Another type of shield fits over the computer screen; it may help with glare, electric fields and static electricity, but does not protect from magnetic fields.

VDTs emit both electric and magnetic fields. The magnetic field surrounds the monitor while the electric field is emitted in straight lines at right angles to the magnetic fields.[10] (See "Computer Electromagnetic Fields" illustration on page 242.)

Television Sets

It is important to stay at least 4 to 6 feet from a television set. The size of the picture tube is generally unrelated to the strength of the field provided.

Television sets emit a variety of frequencies, from the 60-Hz power frequency to radio frequencies in the megahertz range. When you are watching TV, the main sources of the radiation you are exposed to are the horizontal and vertical deflection coils. These fields are often found at a strength of 1 milligauss 4 to 6 feet in all directions from the set. The best way to determine safe distances is to measure with a meter.

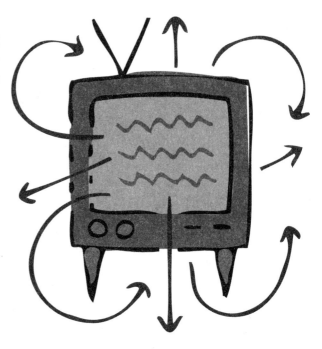

It is important to realize that these fields are not interrupted by most normal building materials, including walls. To avoid excessive exposure to EMFs, avoid putting a desk or work station on the other side of a wall with a TV set, a computer or any appliance that tests within the 1 milligauss range.

High-Tension Wires

Power lines and transformer substations present a more serious problem. It is not unusual to find readings as high as 7 to 10 milligauss at the base of some power poles. A small transformer station may produce a 3 milligauss field 50 feet away. The electrical feed into buildings

can also be a strong source (often as high as 10 milligauss on the inside of the wall).[11]

The best thing you can do in the case of these larger threats is to move away from them. If there are any high-tension or medium-tension wires within 500 feet of any part of your school, particularly parts of the campus where people spend long periods of time, EMFs should be measured and action should be taken where necessary.

High-tension and neighborhood distribution line cases that have been tried in the United States have met with poor results. Using the courts is costly and time-consuming. We recommend that you try to work with the power company without compromising safety. Some power companies have funds budgeted for low-cost field reduction. Most will also make changes if they are paid for by the school district.

Lighting and Heating

Unlike regular incandescent lighting, fluorescent lights create magnetic fields. These fields are not strong enough to be a hazard beyond 4 feet, and lighting usually is at least that distance from people; however, fluorescent tube desk lamps are an exception. Often these are quite close to the head of the person at the desk; it is probably wise to replace such lamps with ones that use incandescent bulbs. But using a compact fluorescent bulb and staying 2 feet from it will keep one safe from the magnetic fields and save energy as well.

Unless you have measured the magnetic field coming from an appliance (such an electric heater) and found it to be safe (less than 1 milligauss), you should assume that it is a fairly strong source of EMFs. It is possible to manufacture appliances so that they do not produce substantial amounts of EMF radiation. This is done by making sure that the electrical elements balance and cancel each other. Unfortunately, because EMF radiation is just beginning to be understood by the public, not many manufacturers are responding to it.

Stationary Appliances

Most of us do not stand in front of the refrigerator all day, and we stand next to the washer and dryer for relatively short periods. However, electric stoves are a strong source (5 to 7 milligauss in front) of EMF radiation.[12] If your cafeteria has an electric water heater or dishwasher, there may be a strong field near it. If the person working in the cafeteria is standing next to electric water heaters, dishwashers, refrigeration or other EMF sources, that person is at higher risk.

It is important to remember that the magnetic fields that stationary appliances create are not blocked by walls. To best understand this, take a meter that measures these emissions to the other side of a wall with a stationary appliance. You will most likely find a high reading.

Hand-Held Appliances

Many small appliances pass through our hands, such as hair dryers, shavers and power tools. Although these are fairly strong sources of EMFs (a hair dryer gives off more than 10 milligauss and an electric toothbrush between 7 and 10), most of these are not on and near us long enough to give a high dose.[13] However, if you work with any of these appliances on a daily basis, there is some cause for concern. The only remedy for this kind of exposure is to use them less, hold them as far away as possible and keep them turned off as much as you can.

Electric Clocks and Electric Blankets

Electric clocks and electric blankets are commonly used, and they are both strong sources of EMFs. Electric blankets, particularly older ones, often create fields of more than 10 milligauss.[14] Not using electric blankets, or using them to warm up the bed and then turning them off and unplugging the blanket when you get in bed, eliminates that hazard.

Those of us with electric clocks may sleep all night long with them very close to our heads. The field from an electric clock does not drop to less than 1 milligauss until the clock is at least 3 feet away.[15] Small, battery-operated clocks give you the functionality without the zap.

In 1993, Annie Raybuck's seventh-grade class at St. Mary School in Beaver Falls, Pennsylvania, participated in a contest sponsored by American Express. The class studied a power line proposed for Pennsylvania. In their report the students listed very specific details and statistics on the proposed 500,000 volt high-tension line. Their conclusion was, "We feel the utility companies should use alternative methods of power until there is conclusive evidence that neither man nor his environment will be harmed." The students wrote letters to Vice-president Al Gore and the Public Utility commissioners, who will vote on the power line issue. The class also made a presentation at the National EMR Alliance Conference in Pittsburgh.

RESOURCES

Brochures/Papers/Reports

Electric and Magnetic Fields: Measurements and Possible Effects on Human Health from Appliances, Power Lines and Other Common Sources
California Department of Health Services
2151 Berkeley Way, Room 704
Berkeley, CA 94704
415-540-2669

Electric and Magnetic Fields from 60 Hertz Electric Power: What Do We Know About Possible Health Risks?
Attn: EMF Brochure
Department of Engineering and Public Policy
Carnegie–Mellon University
Pittsburgh, PA 15213
412-268-2670

Electromagnetic Fields (EMFs): A Training Workbook for Working People
Labor Institute
853 Broadway, Room 2014
New York, NY 10003
212-674-3322

EMF News
Edison Electric Institute
701 Pennsylvania Avenue NW
Washington, DC 20004
202-508-5000

EMF in Your Environment: Magnetic Field Measurements of Everyday Devices
Superintendent of Documents
U.S. Government Printing Office
Washington, DC 20402
202-783-3238

Executive Summary: Childhood Leukemia Risks Associated with Exposure to Electric and Magnetic Fields
University of Southern California
School of Medicine
1420 San Pedro Street
Los Angeles, CA 90033
213-342-2000

A Guide to Managing EMF
Edison Electric Institute
701 Pennsylvania Avenue NW
Washington, DC 20004
202-508-5000

Making Sense of Our Measurements of Electric and Magnetic Fields
Department of Engineering and Public Policy
Carnegie–Mellon University
Pittsburgh, PA 15213
412-268-2670

Measuring Power Frequency Fields
Department of Engineering and Public Policy
Carnegie–Mellon University
Pittsburgh, PA 15213
412-268-2670

Microwave News
P.O. Box 1799
Grand Central Station
New York, NY 10163
212-517-2800

A School Teacher's and Administrator's Guide to EMF
Edison Electric Institute
701 Pennsylvania Avenue NW
Washington, DC 20004
202-508-5000

The VDT Book: A Computer User's Guide to Health and Safety
New York Committee for Occupational Safety and Health
275 Seventh Avenue, 25th Floor
New York, NY 10001
212-627-3900

Warning: The Electricity Around You May Be Hazardous to Your Health
Ellen Sugarman
Fireside — Simon and Schuster, 1992
Rockefeller Center
1230 Avenue of the Americas
New York, NY 10020

Books

The Body Electric
Robert Becker
Morrow, 1985
1350 Avenue of the Americas
New York, NY 10019

Cross Currents
Robert Becker
Tarcher Press, 1990
5858 Wilshire Boulevard
Los Angeles, CA 90036

Currents of Death
Paul Brodeur
Simon and Schuster, 1989
1230 Avenue of the Americas
New York, NY 10020

Deadly Deceit: Low-Level Radiation, High-Level Cover-up
Jay M. Gould
Four Walls Eight Windows, 1991
P.O. Box 548, Village Station
New York, NY 10014

The Great Power-Line Cover-up
Paul Brodeur
Little, Brown and Company, 1993
32 Beacon Street
Boston, MA 02108

Individuals/Companies/Organizations

Approach Technology
Department BR
P.O. Box 1045
Post Falls, ID 83854
800-955-6766 (Order Line)
Manufacturers of EMF Alert. An early audible detector of electromagnetic radiation designed for personal use.

Electro-Pollution Supply
John Banta
P.O. Box 3217
Prescott, AZ 86302
602-445-8225
Eectromagnetic testing and control, tools, supplies and information.

Get Safe! Inc.
P.O. Box 139, Department B
Fairfield, IA 52556
515-472-5551
Supplier of Elf Armor™ internal and external magnetic shields for computer monitors.

Holaday Industries
14825 Martin Drive
Eden Prairie, MN 55344
612-934-4920
Offers a complete line of sophisticated monitoring equipment for rent or purchase.

Information Ventures

1500 Locust Street, Suite 3216
Philadelphia, PA 19102-4321
215-732-9083
An EMF information clearinghouse that publishes 2 journals that deal with EMF research and effects.

Integrity Design and Research Corporation

296 West Ferry Street
Buffalo, NY 14213
716-882-9699

Narda Microwave Products

435 Moreland Road
Hauppauge, NY 11788
516-231-1700
Sells nonionizing monitor and measuring systems.

National EMR Alliance

Cathy Bergman
410 West 53rd Street, Suite 402
New York, NY 10019
212-554-4073
Supports local, regional and national efforts to reduce, mitigate and, where possible, eliminate hazardous exposures to electromagnetic radiation. Publishes a newsletter called *Network News* and *EMR Grassroots Handbook: A Guide for EMF Activists*.

NoRad Corporation

1160 E. Sand Hill Avenue
Carson, CA 90746
800-262-3260
The NoRad Shield has been independently tested and certified to be the most effective radiation-blocking shield on the market.

Safe Technologies

145 Rosemary Street
Needham, MA 02194
800-638-9121
Distributors of an affordable, easy-to-use hand-held gaussmeter.

Schaeffer Applied Technology

4378 East Aterton
Burton, MI 48519
800-366-5500
Rents and sells devices for measuring EMFs.

TRA Instruments

2257 South 11th East
Salt Lake City, UT 84106
800-582-3537
Manufactures the ELF Monitor.

The Science Room

Chapter 9

CONTENTS

INTRODUCTION

Hands-on science activities are an essential part of school science. Most educators agree that about 40 percent of science time should be spent doing hands-on activities.[1] Activities are important if students are to learn the processes of science and have the direct experiences that capture interest and maintain motivation. Science activities are truly the only way to learn the methods of science and to prepare for performance-based testing in science.

As with all activities where materials are handled, potential hazards exist. It is important that teachers be aware of these hazards and the maturity level of their students. Once the teacher understands these things, he/she will be better able to take the proper safety precautions.

Safety is an integral part of science instruction. Teachers must be trained to handle materials safely. If this is not possible, schools must seek an outside consultant, such as an environmental health technician. Your local school district, county or state education offices can provide qualified people. Police and fire departments or commercial disposal companies may also be available to provide services.

In addition to the need for safely using and disposing of hazardous substances, there are significant environmental concerns. Although the amount of chemical waste produced by science classes is much smaller than that from industry and municipalities, the science room is an excellent place for students to practice environmental responsibility and learn about the problems improper disposal of hazardous waste can cause. Each individual and institution contributes to pollution, and no matter how small the contribution, each bears responsibility for that part of the problem.

Modeling of environmentally responsible practices in science instruction includes learning to
   ◆ Resist dumping wastes into storm drains and sewers to avoid river and ocean pollution.
   ◆ Avoid mixing hazardous substances with the regular trash. If buried in a landfill, these substances may leach into groundwater that will eventually be used for drinking.
   ◆ Reduce solid wastes and conserve landfill space by reusing and recycling.
   ◆ Avoid using products or producing gases that will add to the concentration of chlorofluorocarbons, oxides of nitrogen, oxides of sulfur, carbon monoxide and ozone in the atmosphere. (This is a good place to explain why ozone is hazardous near the ground and beneficial in the atmosphere.)
   ◆ Avoid pollution from burning wastes. (This is an opportunity to introduce the incinerator controversy.)

Some teachers may also want to discuss the neutralization of chemicals, so that they are made safe for disposal.

This chapter looks first at creating a classroom that is connected with the natural world and then addresses the many ways to create a science room that fosters safer, healthier hands-on activities.

THE LIVING CLASSROOM

Too often when we teach science, we present it as something that is "out there." Natural systems are considered to be separate from the human experience. This approach removes us from an intimate connection with the natural environment and denies us the opportunity to develop a relationship with the earth that would define us as a strand in the web of life. Rather, we have made ourselves the observer, the insensitive controller of natural systems using earth's resources to meet our personal ends. By reducing the wonder of the interactions and interconnectedness of natural systems to textbook discussions, we sever the connection between our species and all that is living and nonliving on this earth.

We learn at a very early age to protect the things we most love, understand and have an intimate connection with. For example, a young boy will go up against the neighborhood bully who threatens his little brother. Although we ask our young students to protect natural resources, we offer little more than an artificial and distant connection with the environment. To convey a message about the preservation of natural systems and to cause it to come alive in the science classroom, we must allow students to experience nature firsthand. Students should understand that they have a place among the creatures of the earth, not as users, abusers, distant observers or even protectors, but as integral parts. When a student understands the necessity of coexistence with all organisms, that our survival depends on the survival of all, then science and the environment assume entirely new roles.

To make yours a living classroom you need only to walk out the door. Search the trees and bushes of your campus for birds, insects and other living creatures. Understand the nature of the trees and plants in your area. Are they indigenous to your region, or were they brought in from somewhere else? If they are native to the area, what traits facilitate their survival there? If they are not native, does it follow that the bugs who live there are native to a different location as well? If you are in a city, do you feel that the natural system is somewhere other than where you are? What is it you are trying to protect when you are asked to protect nature? Nature is in our national parks, nature centers and seashores, but it is also in our inner city, in the air we breathe, the ground we walk on and the water we drink. We need to teach respect for the rock, the river, the tree, whether it is in the inner city or in the middle of the wilderness.

As the science class experience becomes real and alive, students will desire to understand the phenomenon of our shared existence. With younger students, simply walk around the school grounds and collect and identify as many different things (leaves perhaps) as possible. Construct a book of who or what inhabits the area. Investigate the lives and daily activities of these small creatures. Teach the students that bugs are to be admired for their role in the web of life and not crushed under a heel or sprayed with a poison.

Hatching and releasing butterflies, maintaining ant farms and fish tanks, adopting a class pet from an animal shelter and finding it a home when school is over, and watching birds and recording sightings of them are just a few of the many activities that students of any age might enjoy and learn from.

In addition, Chapter 5 offers a significant hands-on connection with the earth that teaches much of what is discussed in textbooks. The resource section of this chapter lists books on teaching nature awareness.

DISSECTION AND ALTERNATIVE ACTIVITIES

Some states (and cities) have legislation governing the use of preserved animals in science classroom activities. In California, Pennsylvania and Florida, for instance, schools must inform students who morally object to dissection that they can be excused or provided with an alternative activity. Parental consent must be given for the student to be excused. The teacher may assign an alternative activity, to be cooperatively planned with the student. Neither the activity nor any examination can be punitive.

We suggest that the following questions be addressed:
- ◆ Are threatened species involved?
- ◆ Will a science activity be conducted in sufficient depth to justify its environmental expense? Remember that ecosystems are disrupted when a large number of animals

are removed from their habitat. Moreover, when the dissections are complete, the dumping of preserved animal carcasses creates more problems—hazardous waste and overcrowded landfills.

◆ Are bullfrogs being naturally replaced at the same rate at which they are collected for food and laboratory specimens? (One teacher wrote to us suggesting that science teachers have students figure out the rate at which frogs were being replaced.)

◆ Is it ethical to use any kind of animal in laboratory studies?

◆ Are certain activities appropriate to the age and emotional maturity of students? Activities that may be appropriate or even required in a high school physiology and anatomy class may be totally inappropriate with younger students.

◆ Are students sufficiently mature to participate in the activity with the requisite respect for the life forms involved? What is being taught by the casual dismemberment of an animal anyway? The importance of respecting and celebrating the contribution/gift other living things make to our lives should be stressed after completing a dissection.

> Sandra Larson, biology teacher and co-founder of the Connecticut Ethical Science Education Coalition, put it this way: "Biology means the study of life, and removing an animal from its habitat, cutting it up and throwing it away just doesn't teach respect for life."

Although dissection may help students understand the functions of internal structures and develop process-related laboratory skills, for most purposes alternatives are appropriate. If your class is advanced enough to benefit from a dissection, then perhaps the teacher should dissect the specimen, with the class merely observing. Furthermore, using live animals seems cruel and completely unnecessary!

Some alternatives to dissection include

◆ Studying reference books and charts.

◆ Drawing and labeling diagrams with names of systems, organs and tissues.

◆ Constructing models of organisms, systems, organs or tissues and labeling the parts.

◆ Writing papers on organisms, explaining the interrelationships of physiological systems, including organs, tissues and life processes.

◆ Using videotapes, films, computers and CD-ROM.

◆ Using a model.

Resources for further information on this topic are listed at the end of the chapter.

RISKS AND PROTECTION

Diseases That Can Result from Science Activities

Illnesses resulting from chemical exposures manifest in two ways:

◆ **Acute illness** is the result of a single exposure with a short period of time between exposure and development of symptoms.

◆ **Chronic illness** results from small exposures repeated over a longer period of time. It is more difficult to diagnose because the onset of symptoms is more gradual and may be mistaken for other maladies. Recovery may be slow and disability may be permanent.

Some chemicals that may be encountered in science programs are

◆ **Carcinogens** (substances that cause cancer). Some examples are ammonium dichromate, arsenic, asbestos fibers, benzene, soluble cadmium compounds, carbon tetrachloride, chloroform, soluble chromium compounds, ethylene dichloride, methylene chloride and soluble nickel compounds.

◆ **Mutagens** (substances that can cause cell mutations). An example is ethylene dichloride.

◆ **Teratogens** (substances that can damage an unborn fetus, causing birth defects). Some examples are aniline, ethylene dichloride, formaldehyde, soluble lead compounds, metallic mercury and soluble mercury compounds.

◆ **Poisons** (substances that kill, injure or impair an organism). Examples are soluble compounds of arsenic, mercury and lead.

◆ **Allergens** (substances that may cause difficulty in breathing or skin rashes). An example of an allergen is concentrated acetic acid.

At the beginning of the school year a letter should be sent home specifying some of the activities that could be hazardous to students with unusual sensitivities. Request a response if parents want the student excused from activities where these chemicals are used.

Why Children Are at Risk

Children are at particular risk because

◆ They may be affected by lower levels of exposure than adults.

◆ Their health risks can be greater because some toxic chemicals accumulate in the body over long periods of time.

◆ Their immune systems are not as well developed as those of adults.

◆ They may be more easily distracted and may not pay careful attention to safety precautions or instructions.

◆ They are less experienced than adults and more likely to behave unpredictably.

Laws and Regulations

Some areas of concern to science education are strictly governed by state and federal laws; some county ordinances and city codes may also apply. (See Chapter 17 for more detailed information.) Some examples include the following:

◆ Health and safety codes deal with the labeling, storage, transportation and disposal of chemicals.

◆ State education and health and safety codes are usually very specific on the use and specifications of approved eye protection devices.

◆ Although not a safety issue, student and parent sensitivities are taken into account in legislation dealing with the uses of animals in science instruction.

◆ State codes require that animals be housed and cared for in a humane manner.

Teachers and administrators should refer to *The California Science Safety Handbook for Secondary Schools*. Similar publications may exist in your state. Contact your state department of education for its science safety guidelines.

Laws concerned with science safety do not prevent districts and schools from enacting more restrictive policies and regulations. Although many chemicals were commonly used in classrooms at one time, new information indicates that some are no longer appropriate, particularly with younger children.

Staying current on which chemicals are no longer appropriate involves submitting lists of chemicals used in art, industrial arts and science classes to appropriate authorities for review and suggestions. Such authorities include the school chemical safety coordinator (as they have in the Los Angeles Unified School District) or the environmental health technician for the school district, who is called upon for consultation or advice in dealing with emergencies. If your school district does not have such a qualified person or is not providing guidelines, then contact state occupational and health agencies, fire departments or chemical safety officers at universities.

Current state and federal labeling laws require that

◆ **All chemicals be stored in their original containers** (unless they have been prepared in some way, such as being made into a solution).

◆ **Labels be legible.**

◆ **Hazards, precautions and first-aid procedures** be included on the labels of chemical containers.

◆ **The names and addresses of manufacturers be clearly indicated.**

◆ **Each site have a Material Safety Data Sheet (MSDS) on file for each regulated chemical.** The manufacturers must provide these on request. (Many chemicals come with these as a part of the package.)

◆ **All potentially hazardous equipment be clearly labeled with the hazard and precautions.** An example would be, "The laser beam is potentially damaging to the retina of the eye. Do not look into it or permit it to be reflected from shiny surfaces into the eye."

Some chemical labels include bar codes, useful for inventory. Some labels have color-coded areas to help place them in compatibility groups. (See "Storage Patterns, Compatibility and Appropriate Facilities" in the next section.)

SCIENCE ROOM SUPPLIES: SELECTION, STORAGE AND DISPOSAL

This section addresses the issues that need to be considered in the management of materials used in science teaching.

Environmental Quality

Our children's school environment can be safe or unsafe. It is the responsibility of our science educators to follow all precautions to ensure safety at school.

Some basic guidelines science educators should observe include the following:

◆ **Dispose of chemical wastes properly.**

◆ **Never permit eating or drinking when science materials are in the room.** Even though the substances in use may be harmless, good habits formed early may prevent a serious accident later.

◆ **Properly ventilate all experiments that produce unpleasant odors or potentially harmful gas or smoke.** No experiment is worth the risk presented by inhalation of dangerous substances. Generally, standards for proper ventilation are set by state school construction agencies. **The MSDS will not specify what kind of ventilation is necessary.**

◆ **Be sure exhausts do not discharge gas or smoke near the intake of a ventilation system.** Some essential experiments could be done outside.

◆ **Be sure solutions are purchased premixed or prepared by the teacher or a qualified aide.** If you buy powdered ingredients, the dust particles will be released into the air during mixing and can be dangerous to your eyes, lungs and skin.

◆ **When not in use, all school chemicals should be stored in a locked chemical storage area clearly marked "no unauthorized student admittance."** If there is glass on the door it should be covered so that no one can see inside the cabinet. (Sadly enough, this suggestion has resulted from legal cases involving dangerous chemicals or simple mischievousness.)

Choosing and Maintaining Science Supplies

Supplies should be purchased from reliable sources that provide both approved labels and an MSDS. It is best to order substances in unbreakable plastic bottles, but some companies now provide glass bottles that have been coated with plastic that will hold together if the glass is broken.

Inventory control is essential. Every item should have a "place" on a shelf. New stock should always be put behind old stock. It may be useful to label the shelf with the name of the item and the number of containers or packages that should be there. This can speed ordering and avoid unnecessary purchases.

Generally, no more than a year's supply should be purchased at a time. This is not always possible if the chemical is used in small quantities and has a long shelf life. Shelf-life information is valuable; when you label your shelves, be sure to include it. This will prevent waste and reduce disposal problems that result when containers are kept for too long and their contents begin to deteriorate.

Guidelines for Choosing Children's Science Supplies

Some general guidelines include the following:

◆ **Never order or use chemicals containing toxic heavy metals**, such as lead, cadmium, arsenic, chromium or mercury. These are dangerous to use and difficult to dispose of.

◆ **Be aware that toxic chemicals are harmful to your health and to the environment.** Teachers and students should ask themselves, "Is the use of toxics really necessary to complete this lesson?" What is the more important lesson to learn?

◆ **Order concentrated acids or bases only when facilities and knowledge are sufficient to permit safe preparation of dilute solutions; otherwise order only the solutions.** Concentrated acids and bases are toxic and generally not safe for students to handle until they are diluted.

◆ **Never obtain chemicals that produce reactions that cannot be quickly stopped.**

◆ **Use water-based solutions instead of organic solvents.**

◆ **Be sure that safety equipment, such as approved goggles, is available.**

◆ **Use colored stains and indicators known to be safe instead of identified toxins.** Chemical indicators are solutions or papers that have been impregnated with solutions that are used to show the presence or concentration of substances or chemical properties. Indicators may be colored or colorless. Examples of tests using indicators include those for pH, glucose, starch and amino acids.

Since few acceptable substitutes exist for many materials used in science, it might be better to eliminate certain activities.

Storage Patterns, Compatibility and Appropriate Facilities

Storage patterns are determined by compatibility groups of chemicals. Compatibility groups are based on chemicals that do not react together. Never store incompatible chemicals on the same shelf or in the same cabinet. One of the best references on compatibility groups is found in the Flinn Chemical Company catalog. Many other safety suggestions for schools are offered in this valuable reference. (See the resource section at the end of this chapter.)

Storing chemicals without attention to compatibility (such as in alphabetical order) is unacceptable. It may be difficult to find enough storage areas to accommodate all the compatibility groups, but you must at least identify these 8 areas:

1. Powdered metals, chemically active metals
2. Chemically active nonmetals, hydrogen peroxide, solid organic acids, bleach
3. Oxidizers
4. Liquid acids (except nitric)
5. Nitric acid
6. Ammonia solution, bases
7. Organic solvents (generally flammable), calcium carbide, solid organics
8. One generic group of everything not listed in one of the other groups

It is unsafe to have less than 8 compatibility groups unless no chemicals are present in some of the groups. Most compatibility schemes (including that of Flinn) have more than 8 groups. All groups may contain hazardous or potentially hazardous chemicals. The toxicity will vary, and some chemicals in some groups may be nontoxic. (Inclusion of any of the preceding chemical groups does not imply endorsement of their use in science instruction by the authors of this book.)

Flammable substances must be stored in approved cabinets. The most common and inexpensive type has 1-inch-thick plywood sides and a self-closing door. Thin-walled metal cabinets are totally inappropriate for storing flammable substances. A cabinet of this type in a fire becomes a bomb!

Hazardous Items Recommended for Immediate Disposal

Recent findings show that certain chemicals, once commonly used in science instruction, have lost their value. It is now recommended that they be removed from schools because of their hazardous properties.

The following chart recognizes the need for occasional use of more hazardous chemicals in senior high school. Some chemicals are not listed for grades 6 to 8 because they have no history of use at those grade levels. Schools and teachers should make it a point to stay informed about possible additions to this list. The Flinn catalog listed in the resource section is also a valuable source of additional information.

Chemicals that Should be Removed from Classrooms

Chemical	Grades 6–8	Grades 9–12	Hazard
Acetone (lacquer thinner)	X		F, P, I
Acids, strong or concentrated	X		C, P, R, I
Ammoniacal silver nitrate		X	U
Ammonium dichromate	X		I, C, D, R
Aniline (aniline hydrochloride)		X	P, F
Asbestos, sheet or powder	X	X	D
Benzene (benzol)	X	X	I
Benzidine		X	I
Benzoyl peroxide		X	U, I
Cadmium, soluble salts		X	P, I
Carbon tetrachloride	X	X	P
Chlordane (insecticide)	X		P
Chloroform (trichloromethane)	X	X	P, I
DDT	X		P
Diethyl ether (anesthetic)	X	1	F, U
Ethylene dichloride (1,2-dichloroethane)	X	X	F, I
Formaldehyde	X	2	P, I, F
Hydrazine		X	F, P, I
Mercuric oxide	X		P3
Mercury	X		P
Methyl chloride (methylene chloride)	X	X	P
Picric acid	X	X	U, F
Potassium hydroxide	X		C, P, I
Sodium azide		X	U
Sodium hydroxide (lye or drain cleaner)	X		C, P, I
Sodium hypochlorite (bleach)	X		C, P, I
2,4-D (herbicide)	X		P
2,4,5-T (herbicide)	X		P

Key to Hazardous Properties

C	=	Corrosive to skin or tissues
D	=	Harmful dust
F	=	Highly flammable
I	=	Irritant to skin, lungs or throat
P	=	Poisonous
R	=	Highly chemically reactive
U	=	Unstable or forms unstable compounds in storage, explosive
1	=	To be dated on receipt and not retained more than 12-18 months.
2	=	Not to be used for specimens to be handled. Recommended in dilute formula solutions only for classroom museum specimens in sealed jars. Other, less toxic alternatives that have a lower odor and produce less irritation are proprietary solutions sold by scientific supply companies. These are sold separately for on-site use or with biological specimens.
3	=	Very poisonous vapor may be produced when mercury or mercury compounds are heated.

Source: Gerald Garner, "Precautions with Chemicals," Publication #SC-865, Los Angeles Unified School District, Los Angeles, 1984.

As stated earlier in "Laws and Regulations," you should contact the chemical safety officer or environmental health technician in your school district. If your district does not have such qualified people, contact a state occupation or health department, your local fire department or a chemical safety officer at a nearby university.

Appropriate Disposal of Waste and Surplus

Governmental agencies can issue citations for excessive accumulation of waste, deteriorated chemicals and improper disposal. Schools and teachers should regularly dispose of waste and deteriorated chemicals.

Determine in advance which chemicals
- ◆ Can go in the trash.
- ◆ Can go down the drain.
- ◆ Must be accumulated and disposed of as hazardous waste.

Science educators must be aware of public agencies that will assist in disposal. School districts should provide for the safe disposal of chemical waste. If your district does not, see Chapter 13, "Taking Action." Other possibilities include the front section of your white pages, local universities, local manufacturers and commercial disposal companies. Assistance may also be available from local environmental organizations. (See the State Resource section in Chapter 20.)

The authors of this book strongly suggest that surplus chemicals be recycled. A school district program may exist; check with your administration. Teachers in the same school should combine their surpluses, and several schools could combine to hold a surplus materials swap meet. This could reduce disposal and result in cost savings, both in disposal and in the need to order new materials.

MAINTAINING A SAFE SCIENCE ROOM

Know the Ingredients

Manufacturers are required by the Occupational Safety and Health Administration (OSHA) to provide Material Safety Data Sheets (MSDS) for their workers on all products that contain toxic substances. The MSDS can be obtained by contacting the manufacturer. The address or phone number should be on the product label.

The MSDS will provide:
- ◆ The name of the chemical product
- ◆ Identification of any toxic ingredients
- ◆ A list of its physical properties
- ◆ Its fire and explosion data
- ◆ Its acute and chronic health hazards
- ◆ Clean-up information
- ◆ Precautions and protective equipment necessary with product usage

Whenever the properties of any products are in question, it is wise to contact the manufacturer and request the MSDS.

The MSDS will indicate when ventilation is needed but not the specific nature of ventilation required. This is another situation where a chemical safety officer needs to be contacted. It is generally assumed that a fume hood, porch or outdoor location is adequate. No chemicals should be used that require the use of respirators or breathing apparatus.

Safety Procedures

We have unfortunately become an intensely litigious society, and teacher liability has now become a very real concern. The responsibility of prudent and reasonable care now resides with the teacher. Reasonable care includes anticipating possible dangers and reminding students of safety instruction before each activity. This extends beyond the classroom to field trips and independent student projects. ERIC Clearinghouse for Science, Mathematics and Environmental Education (ERIC/CSMEE) has written a document on the topic and Flinn does workshops with science teachers that include the topic of liability. (Information on both organizations is listed in the resource section at the end of the chapter.)

The following list is about prevention, not about the solution of problems after they arise. This is obviously a very important consideration.

◆ **Good housekeeping is an essential part of science safety.** Constant awareness, regular clean-up and disposal, proper storage and good inventory procedures make significant contributions to the reduction of hazards.

◆ **Always substitute with the least toxic materials available.**

◆ **Do not use science supplies whose contents are unknown.**

◆ **Be very careful in taking donations.** Frequently, this results in someone else's problem becoming your own.

◆ **Properly dispose of old stuff!** Find out when it was ordered and when it was used last. If no one knows what the material is for or how it is used, you don't need it!

◆ **Be sure that proper disposal procedures are always followed.**

◆ **Post safety rules in the classroom.**

◆ **Remember that safety posters are effective.** This is even more true when they are student prepared.

◆ **Involve students in setting the rules.** Some teachers have had success making participation in science laboratory activities a privilege that can be temporarily withdrawn for irresponsible behavior.

◆ **Be sure that teachers or aides who prepare chemicals or solutions have the necessary knowledge, access to running water, ventilation, and protective clothing and equipment.**

◆ **Prohibit open shoes or sandals in the laboratory.**

◆ **Keep long hair up and out of the way to avoid open flames.** Hair doesn't have to come in direct contact with a flame to burn, especially when it is covered with a lot of hair care products.

◆ **Remember that the only eye protection devices approved for use in schools are splash goggles.** Those wearing contact lenses are strongly encouraged to wear goggles because liquid coming in contact with the eye can be drawn under the lens, resulting in damage before the lens can be removed and the eye washed.

Safety Items to Have in a Science Room

✔ At least 1 or 2 eyewash bottles

✔ Container of baking soda at each lab station

✔ Wool fire blanket

✔ Cat litter for application to chemical spills

✔ Separate container for broken glass

✔ Student-made safety posters

✔ Safety splash goggles

Inspection for potential hazards should be a regular activity. Even when funds are lacking for other purposes, items that could impair health and safety and result in liability must be quickly removed or fixed.

A careful inspection of science areas may disclose some or all of the following:

◆ Chemical bottles with labels written over
◆ Solutions stored in soft drink bottles
◆ Storage on shelves without proper barriers (necessary in times of natural disasters such as earthquakes)
◆ Bottles with broken or rusting caps
◆ Appliances with frayed electrical cords
◆ Bare light bulbs used as heaters
◆ Too many appliances connected with inadequate extension cords
◆ Homemade household voltage electrical equipment
◆ Improperly housed animals
◆ Students lacking in proper safety instruction

Science Activity Hazards

Common causes of accidents in science classes include

◆ **Animal bites.** These common accidents are usually the result of inadequate cages and insufficient supervision to prevent children from teasing animals and training them to bite objects inserted into the cage.
◆ **Burns.** These are generally from glass or metal that has been heated. Students heat glass tubing, put it down, do not realize how long it stays hot and forget which end they heated. Other burns result from hot liquids being ejected from test tubes when they are improperly heated.

More rare but of continuing concern is the possibility of accidents resulting from

◆ **Chemical poisoning through ingestion, breathing or skin contact.**
◆ **Corrosive chemicals.** Students, particularly younger ones, should handle only dilute solutions of chemicals. Science activities must be conducted with approved eye protection.
◆ **Electric shock.** Electrical equipment must be carefully maintained. Homemade equipment operating on 110 to 125 volts must never be assembled or used.
◆ **Eye damage from intense light.** No one should ever look directly at the sun during eclipses. When using lasers in the study of optics, follow appropriate precautions.
◆ **Poisonous plants and animals.** These must never be in schools. Instructions before and precautions during field trips are essential.
◆ **Water quality monitoring.** Rubber gloves need to be worn because of the potential danger from botulism and fecal coliforms.

RESOURCES

Hotlines

Dissection Hotline
1-800-922-FROG

Brochures/Papers/Reports

The Assessment of Hands-on Elementary Science Programs
North Dakota Study Group on Evaluation
George Hein, Editor
Center for Teaching and Learning
University of North Dakota
Grand Forks, ND 58202
701-777-2011

Safety in Academic Chemistry Laboratories, 5th Ed.
The American Chemical Society
Committee on Chemical Safety
1155 16th Street NW
Washington, DC 20036
202-872-4600

Science Framework for California Public Schools
California Department of Education
Bureau of Publications, Sales Unit
P.O. Box 271
Sacramento, CA 95812-0271
916-445-1260

Science Safety Handbook
California Department of Education
Bureau of Publications, Sales Unit
P.O. Box 271
Sacramento, CA 95812-0271
916-445-1260

Books

Bottle Biology
Mrill Ingram
Kendall/Hunt Publishing Company,1993
2460 Kerper Boulevard, P.O. Box 539
Dubuque, IA 52004-0539

Listening to Nature
Joseph Cornell
Dawn Publications, 1987
14618 Tyler Foote Road
Nevada City, CA 95959

Rapid Guide to Hazardous Chemicals in the Workplace
N. I. Sax and R. J. Lewis
Van Nostrand Reinhold, 1986
115 Fifth Avenue
New York, NY 10003

Safety in the Elementary Science Classroom
NSTA Publications Sales, 1978
1840 Wilson Boulevard
Arlington, VA 22201

Science Fairs and Projects
NSTA Publications Sales, 1988
1840 Wilson Boulevard
Arlington, VA 22201
#PB-15/1, Grades K-8.
#PB-15/2, Grades 7-12.

Science Safety for Elementary Teachers
Gary E. Downs and Jack A. Gerlovich
Iowa State University Press, 1983
2121 South State Avenue
Ames, IA 50014

Books for Youth

Biology for Every Kid: 101 Easy Experiments that Really Work
Janice VanCleave
John Wiley & Sons, Inc., 1990
605 Third Avenue
New York, NY 10158

Ecology: A Practical Introduction with Projects and Activities
Richard Spurgeon
Usborne Publishing, 1988
Usborne House, 83-85 Saffron Hill
London, England EC1N 8RT

Environmental Science: 49 Science Fair Projects
Robert L. Bonnet and G. Daniel Keen
Tab Books, 1990
13311 Monterey Lane
Blue Ridge Summit, PA 17294

How the Earth Works
John Farndon
Reader's Digest, 1992
Department 250
Pleasantville, NY 10570

More Science Activities
Smithsonian Institution, 1988
Galison Books
25 West 43rd Street
New York, NY 10036

Mr. Wizard's Supermarket Science
Don Herbert
Random House, 1980
201 East 50th Street
New York, NY 10022

Projects for a Healthy Planet: Simple Environmental Experiments for Kids
Sar Levine and Allison Grafton
John Wiley & Sons, Inc., 1992
605 Third Avenue
New York, NY 10158

Science Fairs with Style: A Comprehensive, Step-by-Step Guide to Running a Successful Science Fair Program
Jerry DeBruin
Good Apple, 1991
1209 Buchanan Street, Box 299
Carthage, IL 62321-0299

Sharing the Joy of Nature
Joseph Cornell
Dawn Publications, 1989
14618 Tyler Foote Road
Nevada City, CA 95959

Sharing Nature with Children
Joseph Cornell
Dawn Publications, 1979
14618 Tyler Foote Road
Nevada City, CA 95959

Individuals/Companies/ Organizations

Alternatives in Biology Education
333 Washington Street, Suite 850
Boston, MA 02108
617-523-2237
Provides teaching tools for alternatives to dissection.

Animal Legal Defense Fund
1363 Lincoln Avenue
San Rafael, CA 94901
415-459-0885

Provides a number of brochures and information sheets on the use of animals in science classes.

Carolina Biological Supply Company

2700 York Road
Burlington, NC 27215
910-584-0381, 800-334-5551
Publishes the Biology/Science Materials Catalog, an extensive catalog of biology and science materials, including a number of kits for solar energy studies, such as a miniature solar house and a solar oven. The catalog is published annually. Also available are models that replace living specimens.

E.R.I.C. Clearinghouse for Science, Mathematics, and Environmental Education

1929 Kenny Road
Columbus, Ohio 43210
614-292-6717
Sponsored by the Office of Educational Research and Improvement in the U.S. Department of Education. E.R.I.C. develops, maintains and makes accessible the world's largest education-related, bibliographic database. The clearinghouse has two monthly publications. Outreach and distribution resources include informational brochures, electronic services, direct sales, conference exhibits and materials and mailings.

Ethical Science Education Coalition (ESEC)

P.O. Box 16736
Stamford, CT 06905
203-872-8877
Conducts teacher workshops and maintains a resource center to aid teachers in finding dissection alternatives. ESEC has available a free booklet, *Beyond Dissection*, which lists alternative teaching tools and where to obtain them.

Flinn Scientific, Inc.

131 Flinn Street
Batavia, IL 60510
708-879-6900
Publishes a catalog reference manual annually.

National Association for Humane and Environmental Education

67 Salem Street
East Haddam, CT 06423
203-434-8666
A division of the Humane Society of the United States. Has a package, "Alternatives to Dissection," that includes 14 lesson plans that provide alternatives to some of the most common animal-related biology experiments and dissections. Publishes *KIND News*, a newspaper for children in grades 2-6. Each issue is accompanied by a 3-page teaching guide. Other services include consulting, workshops and conferences.

National Science Teachers Association (NSTA)

1840 Wilson Boulevard
Arlington, VA 22201
703-243-7100
The largest organization of science teachers in the world. Has approximately 50 funded projects in science education, publishes 5 award-winning journals and sponsors the Science Grasp Program, a workshop that fosters teaching of hands-on science in the elementary grades. NSTA also offers many awards for teachers and students.

New England Anti-Vivisection Society (NEAVS)

333 Washington Street
Boston, MA 02108
617-523-6020
Beyond Dissection offers a free booklet that lists alternative teaching tools and where to obtain them.

Student Action Corps for Animals (SACA)

P.O. Box 15588
Washington, DC 20003
202-543-8983
Publishes *SACA News,* a quarterly newsletter, and a booklet, *101 Non-animal Biology Lab Methods*.

Wisconsin Fast Plants

University of Wisconsin-Madison
Department of Plant Pathology
1630 Linden Drive
Madison, WI 53706
608-263-2634
Provides rapid-cycling plants for teaching tools in plant biology and reproduction, bee pollination, genetics, nutrition, ecology, seed saving and more.

Chapter 10

The Art Room

Chapter 10
CONTENTS

INTRODUCTION

When you choose art projects and stock an art room, consider the choices carefully. Many routinely used supplies are actually poisonous. Such materials not only are a hazard to the user but can be threatening to other people who use the room. Moreover, their disposal can be a threat to the environ-ment. Often less toxic or nontoxic alternatives are available, some of which are presented in this chap-ter. In addition, simple safety measures can elimi-nate unnecessary accidents and many potential health hazards. Suggestions for these will also be presented.

Students will carry the safety practices and respect for art supplies that they are taught in their early school years with them through life—in the class-room, workplace and home.

Art Room Risks

Children are at particular risk because

◆ Their bodies are smaller and will experience a greater exposure than those of adults.

◆ Their lungs are not as efficient, which puts them at greater risk from inhalation hazards.

◆ Their immune and nervous systems are still developing and are more vulnerable to toxicity.

◆ They have higher metabolic rates.

◆ They tend not to follow safety measures carefully (e.g., they put things in their mouths and do not wash up well).

◆ Greater absorption through the skin occurs if there are any cuts or sores, and, as we all know, children frequently have cuts and sores.

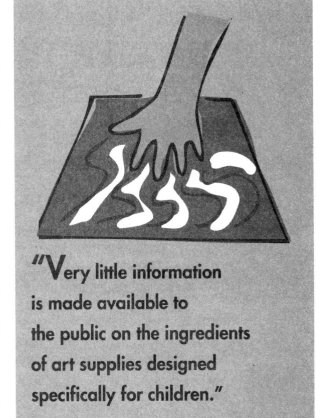

"**V**ery little information is made available to the public on the ingredients of art supplies designed specifically for children."

Lauren Jacobson, "Children's Art Hazards," The Natural Resources Defense Council, 1985.

The following story may personalize these issues:

After merely being in the kitchen where her parents were doing stained glass art work, an 18-month-old girl developed lead poisoning because lead fumes from soldering were in the air and dust.[1]

This case and many similar ones caused the Center for Disease Control to mention specifical-ly stained glass, pottery, casting lead toys, artists' paints and other crafts as sources of lead poisoning.[2]

Laws Protecting Children
California Health Laws

In June of 1987 California passed legislation (Education Code Section 32060) prohibiting the purchase of toxic art supplies for use in grades K through 6 and restricting their purchase for grades 7 through 12. As a result, the California State Department of Health Services published a very comprehensive 30-page list, "Art and Craft Materials Acceptable for Grades K through 6." The purchase of products for grades K thorough 6 is limited to those on the list. Evaluations were done by qualified toxicologists, who were solely concerned with the toxicity of the product. Products listed were not evaluated for such factors as skill level required for use, product quality or the hazards associated with accessory equipment. However, these factors do need to be evaluated at a school level before purchasing products. To obtain a copy of the list, refer to the resource section at the end of this chapter.

Labeling Laws

In November of 1990, the Labeling of Hazardous Art Materials Act went into effect. This law requires warning labels for all art and craft products that contain substances that can cause chronic illnesses. Labels are supposed to include a complete list of toxic ingredients and warnings about their long-term health dangers. The Consumer Product Safety Commission (CPSC) is responsible for enforcing this law. The CPSC can bring legal action to prohibit the purchase of materials considered hazardous for children in grades 1 through 6.

The Labeling of Hazardous Art Materials Act requires that labels include
- ◆ A warning statement of the hazard, such as, "Cancer agent! Exposure may cause cancer."
- ◆ Identification of any hazardous ingredients.
- ◆ Guidelines for safe use, such as, "Avoid inhalation/ingestion/skin contact," or, "Use NIOSH-certified mask for dusts/mists/fumes."
- ◆ The name, address and telephone number of the manufacturer or importer.[3]

The Art and Craft Materials Institute (ACMI), which has been certifying children's art supplies for more than 4 decades, sponsors a certification program to ensure proper labeling of art supplies. The seals shown below indicate that art material is nontoxic or properly labeled and that the product complies with the 1990 Labeling of Hazardous Art Materials Act.

Source: The Art and Creative Materials Institute, Inc., Boston, MA.

Public Interest Research Group Survey Results

Public Interest Research Group (PIRG) is a nonprofit organization dedicated to environmental quality and the common welfare. It is a national organization with state chapters. In June and July 1991 PIRG conducted a study to determine whether the requirements of the Labeling of Hazardous Art Materials Act were being met. The investigation found the following:

◆ Of 52 art products reviewed that contained toxic chemicals, 44 percent (or 23) failed to warn of the associated long-term health hazards.

◆ Different brands of similarly toxic products had differing labels (e.g., one warned of the long-term health hazards while another did not).

◆ Of the 150 toxic art supplies reviewed, only 36 percent (or 54) had a conformance statement on the label. Without this statement consumers cannot determine whether the product has been checked for toxic chemicals.

◆ Only 19 percent (or 10) of the 52 toxic art products reviewed printed a phone number on the product label, despite the law's requirement that a number be displayed so that consumers could contact the manufacturer for more detailed safety information.[4]

The Labeling of Hazardous Art Materials Act is definitely a step in the right direction, but it

◆ Is not being strictly enforced.
◆ Does not have an implementation plan.
◆ Does not require the elimination of toxic products in elementary schools.
◆ Does not establish guidelines for products that are acceptable.

YOUR ART ROOM

This section addresses the issues to be considered in choosing materials for all art projects.

Indoor Air Quality/Ventilation

Proper ventilation to the outdoors will solve many of the serious health hazards. As stated in The *Artist's Complete Health and Safety Guide* by Monona Rossol there are 2 basic types of ventilation, **comfort** and **industrial**.

Comfort ventilation is intended to keep people in buildings comfortable through either natural ventilation (naturally circulating air that exchanges indoor and outdoor air) or recirculating ventilation (fans and blowers used to circulate the air from room to room, with some exchange with outside air).

Industrial ventilation is intended to keep those who work with chemicals healthy. This is accomplished through either dilution ventilation (mixing contaminated air with clean air, generally using air inlets and outlets such as exhaust fans) or local exhaust ventilation (capturing the contaminants at their source, utilizing a hood, an air-purifier or an exhaust fan).

A ventilation system for the art room must be planned by an expert who is aware of all the types of work that will be done in the room and the gases, vapors and dusts that will be generated. The following steps should be observed in evaluating ventilation needs:

◆ Conduct an inventory to establish which materials and processes require ventilation. An open window will **never** be adequate for such materials.

◆ Eliminate those materials that are a problem. If this is impossible, then secure help/advice from the Science Department or from your local Department of Public Health.

For more information consult *The Artist's Complete Health and Safety Guide*, by Monona Rossol.

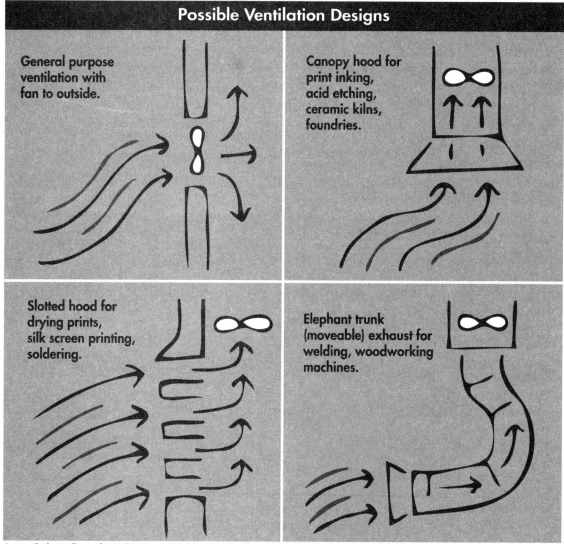

Possible Ventilation Designs

General purpose ventilation with fan to outside.

Canopy hood for print inking, acid etching, ceramic kilns, foundries.

Slotted hood for drying prints, silk screen printing, soldering.

Elephant trunk (moveable) exhaust for welding, woodworking machines.

Source: Charles Qualley, *Safety in the Artroom* (Worchester, MA: Davis Publications, Inc., 1987).

Choosing Art Supplies

A general rule for schools to follow when planning projects or purchasing supplies is to **buy only those supplies that clearly indicate all ingredients and where to write or call the manufacturer**. Unfortunately, some labels do not completely list all ingredients. Therefore, whoever purchases the supplies must follow up by obtaining the MSDS (Material Safety Data Sheet) from the manufacturer and by checking for any toxic ingredients. This information is vital for emergency treatment.

The following indicate danger and should be avoided:

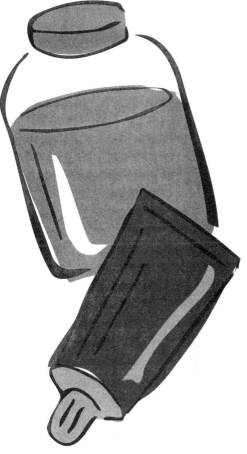

◆ Products whose labels say, "Use with adequate ventilation." This is too vague for safety and could mean anything from an open window to an isolated spray booth, depending on the amount of material used.

◆ Products whose labels list any of the contents as "trade secrets."

General Guidelines for Choosing Art Supplies

The following list of materials to be **avoided** was provided by the Center for Safety in the Arts:

◆ Dust or powders that can be inhaled or that can get in the eyes

◆ Organic solvents or solvent-containing products

◆ Aerosol spray cans, air brushes and so on

◆ Materials that stain the skin or clothing or that cannot be washed out

◆ Acids, alkalis, bleaches or other strong irritants or corrosive chemicals

◆ Supplies lacking a label with ingredients listed

◆ Instant papier-mache and modeling supplies older than 1977 may contain asbestos

◆ Oil paint with toxic pigments. Toxic solvents are required for clean-up and so adequate ventilation is a must. Unless nontoxic oil paint is specially ordered, regular oil paint is just too risky to use in schools.

Look for products bearing the PC-Certified Product Seal, the AP-Approved Product Seal or the Health Label (Nontoxic) Seal of the Arts and Crafts Material Institute shown on page 274.

Art Supply Substitutes

The following is a list of materials that should **never** be used in elementary schools and their less toxic substitutes. This list was provided by the Center for Safety in the Arts (with a few additions).

Dusts and Powders

◆ **Clay in dry form.** Powdered clay can be easily inhaled and contains free silica and possibly asbestos. Do not sand dry clay pieces or do other dust-producing activities.

✔ *Substitute:* Talc-free, premixed clay. Wet-mop or sponge surfaces after using clay.

◆ **Ceramic glazes or copper enamels.** These can be a source of lead, which is very toxic.

✔ *Substitute:* Water-based paints instead of glazes. Waterproof pieces with acrylic-based mediums.

◆ **Cold-water dyes, fiber-reactive dyes or other commercial dyes.**

✔ *Substitute:* Vegetable and plant dyes, such as food dyes, dry onion skins, tea, flowers and other vegetable materials. *Nature's Colors*, by Ida Grey, is a source of recipes for homemade natural dyes.

◆ **Powdered instant papier-mache mix.** This can send up dust that is easily inhaled. If it was manufactured before 1977, it may contain asbestos. The colored printing inks may also contain lead.

✔ *Substitute:* Make your own papier-mache from black-and-white newspaper with library or white paste. (If a child is sensitive to the newsprint ink or flour paste, nontoxic papier-mache is available at the art supply store.)

◆ **Powdered tempera paint**. This fine powder can send up dust that is easily inhaled. Some paints contain toxic pigments and preservatives.

✔ *Substitute:* Liquid tempera paint or paints that the teacher has premixed.

◆ **Pastels, chalks or dry markers that create dust.**

✔ *Substitute:* Crayons, oil pastels or dustless chalks.

Pigments are substances that give color to other materials, such as paints and inks. Pigments containing arsenic (A), cadmium (C) or lead (L) are toxic. The colors listed in the table below contain toxic pigments:

Common Names of Some Toxic Pigments	
Cadmium lemon (C)	Emerald green or Paris green (A, Copper)
Cadmium orange (C)	Flake white (L)
Cadmium red (C)	Flesh tint (L)
Cadmium yellow (C)	Foundation white (L)
Chrome deep (L)	Jaune brilliant (L)
Chrome lemon (L)	Magenta (A)
Chrome orange (L)	Mauve blue shade (A)
Chrome yellow (L)	Mauve red shade (A)
Cobalt violet (C)	Naples yellow (L,C)
Cremnitz white (L)	Transparent oxide of chromium (A)

Source: Household Hazardous Waste Project, "Guide to Hazardous Products Around the Home" (Springfield, MO: 1989) p. 145.

Solvents

◆ **Turpentine, shellac, toluene, rubber cement thinner or solvent-containing materials, such as solvent-based inks, alkyd paints and rubber cement.**

✔ *Substitute:* Water-based products only.

◆ **Solvent-based silk screen and other printing inks.** (Refer to the art glossary at the end of this chapter for a definition of solvent-based.)

✔ *Substitute:* Water-based silk screen inks, block printing or stencil inks containing safe pigments.

◆ **Aerosol sprays, spray paints and fixatives.**

✔ *Substitute:* Water-based paints with brushes, splatter techniques or pump spray bottles.

◆ **Epoxy, instant glue, airplane glue or other solvent-based adhesives.**

✔ *Substitute:* White glue, school paste or preservative-free wheat paste.

◆ **Permanent felt tip markers that may contain toluene or other toxic solvents.**

✔ *Substitute:* Water-based markers. (Always look at the label to see if other hazardous materials have been added.)

Toxic Metals

◆ **Stained-glass projects using lead came, solder and flux.**

✔ *Substitute:* Colored cellophane and black paper or tape to simulate lead.

◆ **Arsenic, cadmium, chrome, mercury, lead, manganese or other toxic metals** in pigments, metal fillings, metal enamels, glazes and metal casting. (Refer to the art glossary for definitions of metals.)

✔ *Substitute:* Approved materials only. Obtain ingredient information from the Material Safety Data Sheets on products that are inadequately labeled to be certain they are free of toxic metals.

Miscellaneous

◆ **Photographic chemicals.** These can cause many adverse health effects and are highly toxic as well as potentially mutagenic. Photographic processes should not be done in a grade school; at the secondary level they need to be supervised and carried out in a room with a professionally designed ventilation system. Contact with the skin and eyes should be avoided by using personal protective equipment, such as impermeable gloves and wraparound goggles.

✔ *Substitute:* Blueprint paper to make sun grams or use Polaroid cameras. (Refer to the art glossary for blueprint paper.) Students can learn a lot about photography without having to use toxic chemicals. Most photographers send film to a lab for developing.

◆ **Casting plaster may create dust that can be easily inhaled.** (Casting hands and body parts can result in serious burns.)

✔ *Substitute:* Sand castings. Any plaster mixing should be done outside or by the teacher in a separate, ventilated area.

◆ **Acid etches and pickling baths.**
   ✔ *Substitute:* No substitutes.
◆ **Scented felt tip markers.** These teach children bad habits about eating and sniffing art supplies.
   ✔ *Substitute:* Water-based markers.

Any projects requiring safety glasses, gloves or personal protective equipment are inappropriate for elementary classes.

Homemade Substitutes
Directions for Natural Dyes

Dyes can be made from fruit and vegetable juices. Think of any fruit or vegetable that stains your clothing as a good candidate for a natural dye. Blueberries, blackberries, coffee, plums, cranberries, flowers such as marigolds, onion skins, raspberries, strawberries and tea supply natural dyes. The easiest way to store and accumulate them over a period of time is in ice cube trays. When you open a can of beets, pour the juice into the ice tray. You can also take a fruit and/or vegetable, boil it and freeze the broth. To use it simply let the cube(s) thaw. (Unsweetened KoolAid makes a good dye for wool!)[5]

Natural Dyes	
For this color:	**Use one of these materials:**
Yellow	Goldenrod, sassafras flower, pomegranate rinds, onion skins, willow tree leaves, marigolds, orange peels
Red	Cherries, birch bark (gathered from the ground only)
Rose	Willow bark (gathered from the ground only)
Purple	Blackberries, elderberries
Blue	Red cabbage leaves, sunflower seeds
Green	Carrot tops, grass clippings, spinach, moss
Tan	Walnut shells, tea leaves, instant coffee

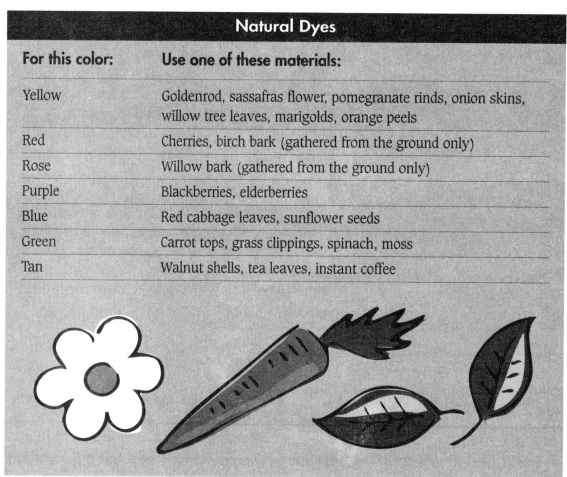

Source: Laurie Carlson, *Ecoart!: Earth-Friendly Art and Craft Experiences for 3-to 9-year-olds* (Charlotte, VT: Williamson Publishing, 1993), p. 16. 800-234-8791.

Recipe for Stovetop Modeling Dough

(This is a single recipe. It is better if doubled.)
1 cup flour
1 cup water (with food color added)
1/2 cup salt
1 tablespoon oil
2 teaspoons cream of tartar
Food coloring

Mix all ingredients together until they are smooth. Cook over medium heat (stirring constantly) until the mixture has a mashed-potato consistency. Knead on a lightly floured surface (while warm) until the desired consistency is reached.

Recipe for Modeling Clay

1 cup salt
1 cup cornstarch
1 cup flour
3/4 cup water
Juice dyes (optional)

Place salt, cornstarch and flour in a bowl. Mix to blend. Divide into 3 bowls for separate colors. Pour 1/4 cup water into the dry mixture in each bowl, followed by the juice dye, and stir until completely blended. Let rest for a few minutes. If the mixture is too dry, add a bit more water; if it is too moist, add more flour. Form into shapes. Place sculptures on a cookie sheet and bake at 250 degrees for 2 hours if you want to keep the artwork forever!

Options:
- ◆ Paint after pieces are baked and cooled.
- ◆ Add shells or other found objects to the clay before baking. Do not use plastic or other toxic materials that will melt.

Recipe for Finger Paints

1 cup cornstarch
1/2 cup cold water
1/3 cup finely grated soap bar
1 1/2 cups boiling water
Juice dyes

Place cornstarch in a bowl and stir in the cold water. Grate 1/3 cup of soap shavings from a bar of hand soap. (A kitchen grater will work.) Place in a separate, heat-resistant

bowl. Pour boiling water into the bowl with the soap shavings, stir until the soap has melted and pour the contents into the cornstarch mixture. Stir to blend. Let the mixture sit until it thickens, like finger-paint. Divide into separate bowls and stir in juice dyes for color.

Recipe for Papier-mache Mixture

2 cups flour
6 cups water
Newspapers (plain paper if the ink is a problem for some students), paper towels or other paper torn into strips about 1 inch wide and 6 inches long.

Put the 2 cups of flour into a mixing bowl and add the 6 cups of water. Stir this mixture with a spoon until it is smooth and pasty. To apply the mixture, either pull the paper strips through the mixture or paint it on with a brush. Each layer of wet paper strips needs to dry thoroughly before another is added.

Equipment
All students must be trained on safe usage of all class tools and equipment. A brief proficiency test should be given to ensure understanding. Do not rely on observation alone. Students who are physically or psychologically disabled will require special care and attention.

Keep such equipment as paper cutters, drills, sanders and heating elements in permanent locations. Put them away from the flow of traffic, with a clear sign outlining instructions for their safe use. These items should be used only by adults or under very careful adult supervision.

MAINTAINING A SAFE AND HEALTHY ART ROOM

A **safe** art room means no accidents, spills or splashes, in eyes or on skin, of substances that can burn or cause injury. A **healthy** art room means no exposure to toxic substances that damage health either acutely or chronically.

Know the Ingredients

Manufacturers are required by OSHA (Occupational Safety and Health Association) to provide Material Safety Data Sheets (MSDS) for their workers on all products that contain toxic substances. Purchasing agents for the school can get a copy of the MSDS by contacting the manufacturer. The address or phone number should be on the product label. The MSDS will give the name of the chemical product, of any toxic ingredients, its physical properties, its fire and explosion data, its acute and chronic health hazards and clean-up information. The sheet also indicates precautions and protective equipment necessary with product usage. Whenever any products are in question, it is wise to contact the manufacturer and request the MSDS.

Safety Procedures

◆ **Keep the art room clean, orderly and well lit.** It will be much safer this way!

◆ **Always substitute with the least toxic materials available.** (Refer to the section on art supply substitutes or the resource section of this chapter for more in-depth information.)

◆ **Do not use art supplies whose contents are unknown.** This should be noted particularly with supplies that have been donated, have been found or are old. Unless they have their original labels on them they should not be in your art room. Old supplies often contain such ingredients as lead compounds, mercury pigments and asbestos.

◆ **Establish safety rules and post them in the classroom.** They should address:
   •How materials and equipment must be handled.
   •Safety with regard to eye protection, clothing, jewelry and hair.
   •Proper clean-up guidelines.

◆ **Include students in establishing rules and the consequences if they are broken.**

◆ **Identify supplies requiring special waste disposal and establish procedures for safely disposing of them.** Your science department or custodial staff can be of considerable help. If there are no established methods for disposal, contact your school district for direction. Unopened containers, such as those containing lead glazes, should be returnable to the manufacturer.

◆ **Never put flammable materials, such as paint thinner and contaminated rags, into the regular trash.** The risks of fume inhalation and of fire are very serious.

The guidelines below will help you dispose of hazardous art supplies properly.

Disposal Tips for Hazardous Art Materials

◆ To prevent explosive or poisonous chemical reactions, never mix different waste products together in the same container.

◆ Follow disposal instructions on product labels. Do not remove labels!

◆ Recycle and reuse hazardous art materials whenever you can. For example, let paint particles settle in paint thinner, then use the clear thinner again. Donate usable materials to local artists or community organizations.

◆ Do not pour solvents down the drain! Pour nonpolluting liquids down the sink one at a time with lots of water.

◆ For hazardous art materials that require disposal, have your school hire a special waste hauler or take advantage of household hazardous waste collection programs in your community. Contact your local Public Works or Sanitation Department for more information.

Source: "Disposal Recommendations for Artists/Art Teachers," Hazard Evaluation System and Information Services, Berkeley, CA. 1989.

USE SIGNS!
◆ **Signs should list rules that are:**
  • Clear and concise
  • Placed strategically
  • Frequently relocated to avoid being overlooked
◆ **Signs describing all art supply inventory as either "nontoxic" or "possibly harmful—caution required" should be posted.**
◆ **Proper storage requirements and safe handling practices should be noted.**
Post handling and clean-up instructions where the supplies are stored.

Hazardous Art Materials

This list gives you a brief overview of the hazards associated with art materials. Refer to *The Artist's Complete Health and Safety Guide*, by Monona Rossol for more detail.

◆ **Jewelry making.** This is not a single craft, but many. It can include soldering, metals, metalworking, metal surface treatments, lapidary, enameling and plastics—to name a few! The inhalation of dust, particles and fumes is a major hazard with all these crafts. The use of high temperatures is also something to be concerned about.

◆ **Drawing.** Dust from pastels and charcoal can be inhaled. The fumes from aerosol spray fixatives can be toxic if there is not proper ventilation.

◆ **Painting.** Not all paints contain toxic pigments, but those with antimony, arsenic, benzene, cadmium, chromium, cobalt, lead, manganese, mercury and zinc are toxic.

◆ **Printmaking.** Unless water-based inks are used, there is a danger of exposure to toxic inks, solvents and acids. Cutting tools also can be dangerous.

◆ **Textiles.** Jute rope and burlap used in macramé can release irritating fibers and dust particles. If a student develops respiratory problems, a mask can be worn.

◆ **Dyeing and Batik.** Some dyes can damage the blood's ability to carry oxygen, and others cause severe allergies. The hazards of most dyes are unknown because only a few of the several thousand have been tested for long-term effects.

◆ **Stained-glass cutting.** This glass can be dangerous. Protective eye wear and gloves must be worn. The lead came that is used to piece the glass together is extremely toxic. Use only lead-free solder. Good ventilation to the outdoors and a fan are needed to remove soldering fumes.

◆ **Ceramics.** Powdered clay mixes contain silica, which can easily be inhaled if it escapes into the air. **Use only ready-mixed clays. Although it is more expensive, the risks of nonmixed clays are not worth taking.**

◆ Many **glazes** contain lead, lead frits and copper. You can obtain a list from *Safety in the Art Room* of glaze materials that should not be used in a school program. These include lead, arsenic, cadmium, nickel, beryllium, selenium and their compounds, and zinc chromate and any uranium compounds.

◆ **Kiln firing** presents problems because of the intense heat and the dangerous gases (e.g., carbon monoxide, sulfur dioxide and chlorine) that can be released. Manufacturers can be a good source of information on the ventilation needs of different models or contact the Center for Safety in the Arts. (See the resource section of this chapter for the address and phone number.)

Sickness and Art Activities

Teachers need to know if a student has particular sensitivities. They must make every effort to see that potentially high-risk exposure is avoided. For example, an asthmatic child should never be exposed to dust. Moreover, children taking medication should not be exposed to solvents. **Solvents should be avoided altogether**. (Use water as a solvent in water-based products.)

Health Risks

Research has shown that many children's art programs across the country use toxic materials. Some are known to be

- **Carcinogens** (cancer-causing agents).
- **Mutagens** (chemicals that can cause cell mutation).
- **Teratogens** (chemicals that can interfere with a developing fetus, causing birth defects).

Types of Illness

- **Acute illness** can result from a single exposure, with a short time between exposure and the development of symptoms. Depending on the nature of the material, the consequences of exposure can range from complete recovery to residual disability or death. Exposure to turpentine while painting can cause light-headedness, nausea, unconsciousness or death.

- **Chronic illness** results from small exposures repeated over time. It is more difficult to diagnose because the symptoms develop gradually and are often blamed on other causes. It may take a long time for adverse effects to subside. The result can be permanent disability. (Cancer is one example of chronic illness.)
- **Sensitivities and allergies** affect many people, and the young are particularly susceptible to many chemicals. These sensitivities manifest themselves most often as allergies. When a chemical causes an allergy in a large number of people, it is called a strong sensitizer. Examples of strong sensitizers include formaldehyde (discussed in Chapter 1); cold-water, fiber-reactive dyes, used in batik and tie-dying; and nickel, found in ceramic glazes.[6]

ART GLOSSARY

ACRYLIC-BASED PAINTS
Pigments are mixed in a resin solution or mineral spirits to make acrylic-based paints. These paints contain small amounts of formaldehyde and ammonia. Allergic reactions to acrylic paints can occur with children who are allergic to formaldehyde. Ammonia can cause eye, nose and throat irritations.

AEROSOL SPRAY
An aerosol spray disperses its product in tiny airborne droplets that are difficult to control. Two examples of art supplies that come in aerosol sprays are fixatives and spray paints. The mist from the spray can be inhaled into the lungs and quickly absorbed into the bloodstream. Risks vary according to ingredients in different sprays. Symptoms that can occur due to inhalation of aerosol fumes are headaches and lightheadedness.

ALKALIS
Most alkalis are solids that are dissolved in water. Alkalis are used in cleaning solutions, paint removers, dye baths, ceramic glazes and photographic developing baths. Alkalis can eat away or corrode other substances. Most alkalis are capable of burning the skin and eyes.

ALKYD PAINTS
Alkyd resins are a group of synthetic resins with high color retention. The paints usually have solvent bases and use plastic polymers as binders. These paints are more hazardous than oil-based paints because they contain large amounts of solvents.

ARSENIC
A metal-like substance recovered from copper smelter dust and processed into a white powder that is used as pigment in dyes, paints and ceramic glazes. Some side effects from exposure to arsenic include vomiting, diarrhea and skin irritation. Long-term health effects from arsenic include lung and skin cancer.

ASBESTOS FIBERS
Small, odorless, needle-like fibers that are hard to detect and, once airborne, are difficult to contain. Exposure to fibrous asbestos is regulated in the United States and Canada. In art materials asbestos can be found in kiln insulation, some white clays, old papier-mache, talc, French chalk and soapstone. Some adverse health effects caused by asbestos inhalation are asbestosis and cancer of the lung, liver, kidney and/or intestines.

BENZENE
An aromatic hydrocarbon that is carcinogenic, flammable and highly volatile. It should not be stored in any art room for any reason. Benzene can be found in dyes, resins, paint strippers and rubber cement. Contact with benzene can cause lightheadedness, disorientation, fatigue and loss of appetite. A possible long-term risk is leukemia.

BERYLLIUM

An industrial metal that can cause chronic lung disease and is believed to cause lung cancer. Beryllium is used in ceramic colorants, in some sculpture alloys and on nonsparkling metals. Short-term exposure to beryllium can cause inflammation of the respiratory tract, shortness of breath, weight loss, weakness, chest pain and a constant hacking cough.

BLUEPRINT PAPER

A chemically coated light-sensitive paper used to make copies of architectural, mechanical, electrical and theatrical design drawings. Small amounts of ammonia gas can be released in this process, which may be irritating to the nose, eyes and skin. It is important to have proper ventilation when using.

CADMIUM

A highly toxic metal that is used as a pigment. Cadmium produces a brilliant, reliable permanent color. Used in yellow, red or orange pigment for paints and dyes. Often found in solders, fluxes, ceramic glazes and enameling. Cadmium is a known carcinogen.

CASTING

The reproduction of an object by means of a mold. The original is formed with clay, wax or some other malleable material; then a molten liquid substance or metal (usually bronze) is poured into the mold casting.

CHALK

Chalk is calcium carbonate that acts as a binder for pigments. Dusty chalks release pigment and dust. To decrease exposure to dust, proper ventilation and a mask should be used. Dustless chalks are also available. Chalk is found in painting powders and pigments.

CHROMIUM

A highly toxic metallic element used as a pigment in paints, dyes, ceramic glazes and enameling. Can produce severe skin allergies and irritate the eyes and respiratory system. Chromium is a possible carcinogen.

COBALT

A moderately toxic element occurring in compounds that can maintain a strong blue coloring. Cobalt is used in ceramic glazes, paints and enameling. If it is inhaled asthma like symptoms and lung damage or pneumonia can occur. Other possible symptoms from contact with cobalt are mild skin, eye and respiratory irritation, vomiting or diarrhea.

COLD WATER DYES

A fiber-reactive dye used with batik and other dye processes. These dyes form a chemical bond with the fibers of the material, becoming an integral part of the cloth being dyed. Fiber-reactive dyes can cause respiratory allergies. With long-term exposure severe allergies can develop. When possible purchase the liquid dye instead of the powdered dye. Some alternatives are vegetable, plant or food dyes.

COPPER

A malleable metallic element that is used in metalwork, ceramics and enameling. Contact with copper can cause nausea, stomach pains, respiratory tract irritation and sinus congestion.

EPOXY

Most commonly known as an adhesive but also found in paints, inks, laminating, molding and casting. Epoxy is moderately toxic if it touches skin or eyes and if it is inhaled. Goggles, gloves and proper ventilation should be used as preventive measures with epoxy.

FLUXES

Substances used to promote fusing of metal. Fluxes are used with solders and stained glass. Some of the compounds are toxic, and all release toxic emissions when they are used. Some of the risks involved with fluxes include metal poisoning and highly hazardous fumes. Symptoms can include skin, eye and respiratory irritation, allergies and asthma. Precautions to take when using fluxes include wearing gloves and goggles, ensuring proper ventilation, choosing the safest materials by comparing MSDS information, never mixing different types of fluxes and following directions carefully.

GLAZE

Glazes used in ceramics are thin coatings fused to ceramic pieces by firing in a kiln. Glazes are a mixture of minerals, metallic elements, colorants and water that may include lead, cadmium, arsenic, uranium and zinc chromate. Some glazes are carcinogenic and highly toxic. Glazes are potentially hazardous at all stages of use, from mixing to the finished product.

INSTANT GLUE/SUPER GLUE

A cyanoacrylate glue that depends on a chemical reaction to provide adhesion. This type of glue is very hazardous when it comes in contact with skin or eyes. One of the greatest hazards is gluing parts of the body together. Children should not use this glue.

INSTANT PAPIER-MACHE

A molding material made of paper and a binder such as glue. This product is easy to use. Ingredients are finely ground from glossy magazines, newsprint or cellulose fillers and binders. It is most dangerous in its powdered form, because of easily inhaled dust. Use of regular torn newsprint and glue eliminates most dangers.

KILN

A specially designed oven for firing (baking) ceramics. When clays and glazes are fired, they release gases, vapors and fumes, including carbon monoxide, formaldehyde, sulfur dioxide, chlorine, fluorine and a host of toxic metals used in glazes and clay products. Carbon monoxide is emitted by all kilns during the firing process. Kilns should be used at night, when fewer people are around, and there should always be proper ventilation.

LEAD

A common industrial metal that causes severe health effects at relatively low levels. Found in pigments, paints, glazes, solder, stained glass materials, clays and enameling. Lead-based paint is the most common source of lead poisoning. Lead attacks the central nervous system, liver, kidneys and reproductive system, and it can cause brain damage and anemia. Symptoms include vomiting, listlessness, irritability, loss of appetite, weakness and hypertension. Other less toxic metals should always be used.

LEAD CAME

A thin, flat, grooved strip of lead used for binding together pieces of glass. Lead came is used in the stained glass process. It has the same health effects as those for lead.

LEAD FRITS

A ceramic glaze material usually containing a flux, silica and various other minerals. Lead frits are ground into a powder used to make glazes, enamels and paints. They have the same health effects as those for lead.

LIQUID TEMPERA PAINTS

Pigment(s) suspended in emulsions or mixtures of such substances as egg, oil or wax and mixed to a paste-like consistency. Egg and oil tempera can contain tetrachloroethane. Tetrachloroethane is highly toxic on contact with skin and when inhaled. This type of tempera paint is not recommended for use in schools.

MUTAGENS

A substance that permanently alters one's genetic structure (DNA) and may cause cancer. Mutagens can be found in pigments, dyes and solvents. Two examples of mutagens are lead and benzene.

PASTELS

A colored, pressed stick made from a dried paste of ground pigment mixed with gum water to hold it together. Pastels may contain toxic pigments. Inhalation of dust is the major hazard for people using pastels. Some alternatives are conte crayons, oil pastels or chalk.

PERMANENT MARKERS

Contains a mixture of dyes in a solvent that is inhaled. May contain toluene, xylene and other highly toxic solvents. Substitute water-based markers whenever possible.

PICKLING BATHS

A toxic method of cleaning metal in which the hot metal is immersed into an acid "bath" or solution. Pickling solutions are often mixtures of sulfuric and nitric acids. During pickling, a large amount of acid vapors and mist rise from the acid bath. Be sure to do pickling baths in a properly ventilated area and wear protective goggles, gloves and apron. An alternative, less hazardous mix of solutions is sodium bisulfate. Ventilation is still needed with sodium bisulfate.

RUBBER CEMENT

A temporary adhesive. A thick, gooey solution of gum rubber and hexane or other hydrocarbon solvents. Used to mask off areas that an artist wishes to leave untouched. Rubber cement is flammable and highly toxic. Inhalation of rubber cement can cause dizziness, numbness and paralysis. Use white or yellow glue whenever possible. If rubber cement is a must, always have adequate ventilation and wear a mask and gloves.

SAND CASTINGS

The casting of an object in a mold made of foundry sand. The sand is packed around a plaster cast of the original to form a negative mold. When this is dry, the molten metal (usually bronze) is poured into the mold to form a positive image. The sand is permeable and therefore allows gases and steam to escape. Proper ventilation is required to avoid inhaling fumes that can be harmful.

SELENIUM

A naturally occurring metallic element that is a common ingredient in pigments. Pigments are used in paints, dyes and glazes. Selenium is also used in photographic chemicals. Selenium is toxic in large concentrations and exposure to large amounts have been known to cause severe illness or even death.

SHELLAC

Shellac is a varnish made from an alcohol-soluble resin. It is a mild narcotic and is flammable. Shellac is also used in plaster casts as an undercoating for painted objects. It can be irritating to the eyes, nose and throat.

SILICA

Silicon dioxide, one of the earth's most common minerals, may constitute up to 60 percent of the elements used to make clay. Silica is used in ceramics, clay mixing, pigments and abrasives. When it is bonded with other elements, silica poses little threat. Silica can cause a chronic, disabling disease of the lungs and lung cancer.

SOLDER

A metal alloy used, when melted, for joining metal parts. Various metallic alloys that may contain lead, cadmium, zinc, arsenic, antimony, silver and tin are used in soldering. Long-term exposure can cause lung and kidney damage and lung cancer.

SOLVENT

An organic liquid chemical used to dissolve solid materials, grease and dirt. Used as a thinner for paints, varnishes, glues, adhesives and lacquers and to clean art tools, brushes, surfaces and hands. Solvents can be found in rubber cement, turpentine, permanent markers, oil paints and silk screen materials. Some examples of solvents are alcohol ketones (MEK), hydrocarbons (benzene, toluene, xylene, hexane, trichloroethane), glycol ethers (cellosolves) and acetones. Solvents are hazardous, volatile, flammable, corrosive and toxic. They are usually petroleum derived and readily evaporate. Exposure to solvents can cause the following symptoms: lung/throat irritation, dizziness, sleeplessness, nausea, vomiting and blurred vision.

SURFACE DECORATING

One of the most hazardous processes related to surface decorating is the etching or frosting of a surface using hydrofluoric acid. This process is used in enameling, stained glass and glass surface treatments. After prolonged use, severe pain and irreparable damage to skin tissues are possible.

THINNER

A volatile liquid solvent used to dilute solutions and substances. Examples of thinners are turpentine and mineral spirits that are used with paints and varnishes.

TOLUENE

A colorless, noncorrosive, highly volatile liquid used as a solvent. Toluene is used in oil-based paints, markers, inks, adhesives, model glues, thinners, silk screen inks and aerosols.

TOXIC PIGMENTS

A pigment is a finely powdered colored material. A toxic pigment is one that contains or is mixed with a toxic element, mineral or chemical. Many toxic pigments are also commonly known carcinogens and can be found in paints, printing inks, glazes and dyes. Many contain lead chromates. See cadmium, chromium, cobalt and zinc chromate for health risks and symptoms.

TURPENTINE

A pale yellow volatile solvent produced by tapping coniferous trees and distilling the various heavy viscous oleo-resins. Turpentine is used as a thinner and/or solvent. Turpentine is a skin irritant, a narcotic and a sensitizer.

ZINC

A bluish white metallic element used in pigments for paints, dyes, ceramic glazes and brazing metal. Exposure to zinc can cause rapid breathing, shivering, fever, chest and leg pains, and general weakness.

ZINC CHROMATE

A pigment that is not used in permanent painting because of its partial solubility in water and its tendency to turn green over time when subjected to light. Also known as zinc yellow or citron yellow. Zinc chromate is used in pigments for paints, dyes, ceramic glazes, enameling and stained glass. Zinc chromate is highly toxic and a suspected carcinogen.

This glossary of art terms was compiled from two sources: *Artist Beware* by Michael McCann PhD., C.I.H. and *The HarperCollins Dictionary of Art Terms & Techniques* by Ralph Mayer.

RESOURCES

Brochures/Papers/Reports

Art and the Craft of Avoidance: Toxic Art Supplies Lack Warnings Despite Federal Labeling Law
Public Interest Research Groups (PIRGS)
215 Pennsylvania Avenue SE
Washington, DC 20003
202-546-9707

Art and Craft Materials Acceptable for Grades K–6
The Art and Craft Toxicology Unit
Hazard Evaluation System
Occupational Health Branch
2151 Berkeley Way
Berkeley, CA 94704
510-540-2115

Children's Art Hazards
Natural Resource Defense Council
40 West 20th Street
New York, NY 10011
212-727-2700

Health Hazards in the Arts and Crafts
Society for Occupational and Environmental Health
1341 G Street NW, Suite 308
Washington, DC 20005

Books

Artist Beware
Michael McCann
Lyons & Burford Publishers,1992
32 West 21st Street
New York, NY 10010

Artist's Complete Health and Safety Guide
Monona Rossol
Allworth Press,1990
10 East 23rd Street
New York, NY 10010

Art Hardware
Steven L. Saitzyk
Watson-Guptill,1987
1515 Broadway
New York, NY 10036

Art Terms and Techniques
Ralph Mayer
HarperCollins,1969
10 East 53rd Street
New York, NY 10022

Health Hazards Manual for Artists
Michael McCann
Lyons & Burford Publishers,1994
32 West 21st Street
New York, NY 10010

Nature's Colors
Ida Grey
Robin and Russ Handweavers,1974
533 North Adams Street
McMinnville, OR 97128

Safety in the Artroom
Charles A. Qualley
Davis Publications, Inc.,1987
50 Portland Street
Worcester, MA 01608

Books for Youth

Ecoart
Laurie Carlson
Williamson Publishing Company, 1993
Box 185
Charlotte, VT 05445

Good Earth Art
Mary Ann F. Kohl and Cindy Gainer
Ecolokids,1991
3146 Shadow Lane
Topeka, KS 66601

Teachables II
Rhoda Redleaf
Toys 'n Things Press, 1987
906 North Dale Street
St. Paul, MN 55103

Teachables from Trashables
Rhoda Redleaf
Redleaf Press,1979
450 North Syndicate, Suite 5
St. Paul, MN 55104

Individuals/Companies/ Organizations

The Art and Creative Materials Institute, Inc. (ACMI)
100 Boylston Street, Suite 1050
Boston, MA 02116
617-426-6400
Sponsors a program for children's art supplies that certifies materials are nontoxic and meet voluntary standards of quality and performance. Provides a list of certified products for $2.

Arts, Crafts and Theater Safety
181 Thompson Street, Suite 23
New York, NY 10012-2586
212-777-0062
Provides educational information on safety and health for those involved in the arts.

Center for Safety in the Arts
5 Beekman Street, Suite 820
New York, NY 10038
212-227-6220
A national clearinghouse for research and education on hazards in the visual arts, performing arts, educational facilities and museums. They respond to telephone and written inquiries on art hazards. CSA offers lecture programs, workshops and an art hazards course. Another service offered is on-site or planning consultations for evaluation of facilities, new building or remodeling. CSA publishes the Art Hazards News.

Environmental Hazards Management Institute
10 Newmarket Road
P.O. Box 932
Durham, NH 03824
603-868-1496
A nonprofit environmental consulting corporation specializing in environmental and regulatory education and compliance assistance. It sells a ''Kidswheel on Household Hazardous Products'' that provides practical information on hazardous product identification, safety and less toxic alternatives in an easy-to-use slide-chart format.

**National Institute for Occupational
Safety and Health (NIOSH)**
1600 Clifton Road
Mail Stop D-32
Atlanta, GA 30333
800-356-4674
NIOSH researches safety and health problems in workplaces where toxic substances are used and then educates employers and workers. Also provides technical assistance and recommends standards for OSHA's adoption.

Chapter 11

Practicing Source Reduction

Chapter 11
CONTENTS

INTRODUCTION

Simple Ways to Reduce Waste

A simple and significant step each of us can take is to reduce the waste we generate. This is even better than recycling because we use less natural resources and energy. For example, when we buy a product that has no packaging, no paper (trees) or plastic (oil) has been used to pack it, no energy will be used to recycle it and no landfill will be needed for disposal. Reducing waste, or **source reduction,** is the ideal environmental choice.

Source reduction is also called precycling. Precycling involves (1) reducing the waste we create before we buy something or (2) using a product again and again **before** we recycle it.

Stores are the major source of the materials we buy that can end up in our waste stream. We practice source reduction when we make choices at the store that minimize the waste we generate.

Here are some easy ways we can reduce waste, or precycle, at the store:
- ◆ Buy reusable/durable products, not disposables.
- ◆ Buy items packaged in bulk, not those in single-serving sizes. Use concentrates when possible.
- ◆ Select items with packaging that can be recycled in your community.
- ◆ Buy products made with materials containing recycled content. Look for notations on packaging, such as "packaged in recycled paperboard" or "made with 40 percent postconsumer waste."
- ◆ Do not buy overpackaged products. Look for the same product with less or no packaging.
- ◆ Bring your own bag. Don't use a bag if you don't need one, and try to put all your purchases in one bag when you do.
- ◆ Buy only what you need.

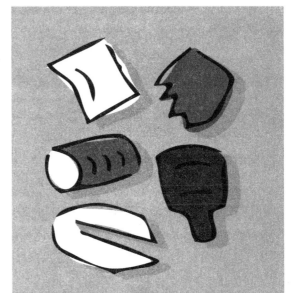

Americans produce more garbage than any other people on the planet: 7.6 billion tons of industrial waste and 160-180 million tons of municipal solid waste annually. Although we are only 5 percent of the world's population, we produce 50 percent of the world's waste.

U.S. PIRG Solid Waste Fact Sheet #1, Washington, DC, 1990.

Packaging Facts

Approximately one-third of the waste Americans send to the landfill is packaging.[1]

Seventy-five percent of the glass, 40 percent of the aluminum and 30 percent of plastics are used as packaging.[2]

Nearly $1 of every $10 that Americans spend for food and beverages pays for packaging.[3]

◆ If you must buy something or if you receive a gift that is overpackaged, write a letter to the manufacturers asking them to reduce their packaging and to include post-consumer waste wherever possible.

We can either create or reduce waste by the choices we make at home and at school. When we use something only one time or when we don't use it completely, we create waste. When we **reuse** it (instead of throwing a product away or even recycling it after only one use), we **reduce** waste, extend its life and save energy and natural resources. For example, if we use both sides of a piece of paper, 50 percent fewer trees are made into paper, 50 percent less energy is used to make paper and 50 percent less energy is used to recycle the extra piece of paper.

Here are simple things you can do to reduce waste, or precycle, at school:
◆ Use both sides of the paper for notes, printing and copying.
◆ Use any paper that has been printed on just one side for scratch paper.
◆ Think before you throw something away. Many paper products, such as envelopes and files, can be reused. (At the Center for Environmental Education we rarely purchase new oversized envelopes. We save and reuse the envelopes we receive.)
◆ Provide all faculty and administration with reusable mugs.
◆ Review your purchasing list. Eliminate unnecessary disposable items and replace them with reusable ones. You will quickly save money you would have had to spend to replace disposable goods.
◆ Review your purchasing list again to make sure you're buying only what you need.
◆ Give "old" supplies to a local thrift shop.
◆ Save and reuse packing and shipping materials.

Be creative! In the long run your school will save money by practicing source reduction. A good way to get started is to have a "Waste Awareness Day" at school. Designate a day for all students, teachers and staff to keep track of everything they throw away. Have each class, employees in the school office and the maintenance staff review the list of what they throw away and think of ways those items might have been used again or replaced with reusable products.

ZERO WASTE LUNCH

In a Zero Waste Lunch, reusables replace disposables. We'll review three student lunch programs. In the first program, students bring their own lunch. In the second program, students eat at a school cafeteria. In the third program, the school hires a vendor to bring food into the school.

Students Bring Their Own Lunches

Learning waste-free ways to pack their lunch will give students a hands-on experience every day and help them make the transition to waste reduction practices at home. The way students' lunches are packed can demonstrate waste reduction better than any other activity on campus.

Guidelines for Packing a Zero Waste Lunch

✔ DO NOT USE DISPOSABLES.

Use lunch boxes or fabric bags. There are many canvas and nylon bags on the market. The ideal choice is a canvas bag made from **organic cotton**, which is cotton grown from seed without pesticide exposure. The fabric is processed without toxic dyes, bleaches and unnecessary chemicals. Although organic cotton is still scarce, we list a source in the resource section at the end of this chapter. If organic cotton is not an option, our second choice is **green cotton**, which is cotton that is not grown organically but that uses no chemicals in processing the fabric. Students who bring paper bags should be encouraged to reuse them when possible. A ban on good bags in the garbage will help students be more aware of their reuse value.

✔ DO NOT USE PREPACKAGED SINGLE SERVING CONTAINERS.

Many parents buy prepackaged individual servings for convenience and for their "treat" value. But since each "treat" creates a single serving of waste, students should ask their parents to buy larger quantities of their favorites, such as raisins, yogurt, fruits, chips, apple sauce and desserts. Then individual servings can be packed in a reusable container. Students

> **In the United States we throw away 500,000 tons of garbage every day! That's enough trash in one day to fill about 92 million school lunchboxes.**
>
> Environmental Action Coalition, "Where Does All the Garbage Go?" Eco *News*, New York, 1992.

who bring individually packaged food should be asked to think of a way to reuse the containers/bags or to take them home.

✔ USE REUSABLE CONTAINERS.

Use durable plastic containers. Don't throw out plastic food containers such as margarine tubs and yogurt containers; reuse them over and over. Check the bottom for the plastic recycling code to be sure you can recycle them in your community when they eventually crack.

Also, water bottles, or PETE bottles, can be used again and again and then recycled once they crack. Bicycle bottles are not easily recycled, but they will outlast PETE bottles.

✔ USE RECYCLABLE PRODUCTS.

To qualify as a recyclable, the container must be recyclable on your campus or in your community. Aluminum is accepted everywhere. Metal juice cans are accepted at most recycling centers. But many plastic containers and juice boxes are not easy to recycle. (See Chapter 12 for more information about plastics and juice boxes.)

✔ DO NOT BUY NEW PLASTIC FOOD BAGS.

If you keep and reuse the bags in which food is wrapped, it may not be necessary to buy new plastic food storage bags at all. Some of our children have carried their sandwiches to school in the same bread bag for several months. We just turn them inside out, wipe with a soapy dishcloth or sponge, rinse and leave out to dry.

If food wrapping must be purchased, select unbleached wax paper or cellulose bags. Cellulose, which is made from wood pulp, is preferable. See the resource section at the end of this chapter for places to find these items.

✔ TAKE LEFTOVERS HOME .

Even leftover foods do not have to be garbage. Take leftovers home for the family pet or compost pile. (See Chapter 5 for ideas on starting a compost and/or vermicompost system at your school.)

✔ BRING CONTAINERS HOME .

Students should be taught to be responsible for the **full cycle** of their Zero Waste Lunch supplies. After all, the lunch and lunch supplies are theirs alone. By taking their containers home to wash and reuse, students will begin to realize how we are each responsible for the things we use and that materials aren't "finished" just because we are through using them for the moment.

A study conducted by the Minnesota Office of Waste Management (OWM) shows that products with the least packaging cut waste and save money. The following chart provides some examples:

The Price of Packaging

LESS WASTE	MORE WASTE
Orange Juice	
12-ounce can frozen concentrate	3-pack of 7.6-ounce ready-to-drink boxes
83% less waste by volume	
74% less waste by weight	
55% less expensive	
Raisins	
1.5-pound plastic bag	14 mini-snack boxes in bag
97% less waste by volume	
93% less waste by weight	
47% less expensive	
Chicken Noodle Soup	
Condensed can	Microwave single
46% less waste by volume	
46% less waste by weigh	
82% less expensive	
Toothpaste	
6.4-ounce tube	4.6-ounce pump
69% less waste by volume	
58% less waste by weight	
45% less expensive	
Pudding	
5.9-ounce instant box	Snack 6-pack
89% less waste by volume	
73% less waste by weight	
64% less expensive	
Cereal	
20-ounce box	3.67-ounce snack box
50% less waste by volume	
55% less waste by weight	
45% less expensive	
Noncarbonated Soft Drink	
0.13-ounce powder packet	6-pack plastic bottles
99% less waste by volume	
99% less waste by weight	
93% less expensive	
Precut Carrots	
Bulk bag	Prepacked plastic container
89% less waste by volume	
87% less waste by weight	
56% less expensive	
Milk	
1-gallon returnable	Half-gallon cardboard carton
99% less waste by volume	
95% less waste by weight	
4% less expensive	

Source: Minnesota Office of Environmental Assistance, St. Paul, MN, 1992.

Schools with Cafeteria Facilities

Although we strongly recommend that schools switch back to reusables, this may be unrealistic. We need to examine the use of permanentware and disposables in school cafeterias. What are the environmental impacts of using permanentware? What are the environmental impacts of using disposables? Is plastic or paper "better"? How do we decide which way to go? The following sections will help guide you toward the best answer for your school.

Permanentware

The environmentally ideal school cafeteria is one that serves food on permanentware (reusable trays, dishes, cups and utensils) and uses energy-grade and water-efficient industrial dishwashers.

Just 10 to 20 years ago most school cafeterias had dish-washing facilities and used permanentware. But when disposables entered the picture, many schools removed their existing dish-washing facilities and laid off the staff. School food service managers were sold on the notion that disposables were cheap, clean, convenient and labor efficient. Little thought was given to environmental or waste factors. Unfortunately, now that we know better, switching back to reusables in our school cafeterias can get very complicated and costly. School budgets have shrunk in recent years and everyone has become accustomed to the convenience of disposables. Redesignating the school cafeteria facilities for the storage, use and washing of permanentware entails

- ◆ Researching, purchasing and installing industrial-grade, energy-grade and water-efficient dishwashers.
- ◆ Purchasing reusable trays, plates, cups and utensils.
- ◆ Adding to cafeteria staff responsibilities or even adding new staff.

The environmental benefits of using permanentware are many. However, costs are also a factor for schools on tight budgets. Consider the following list of some of the benefits and costs of switching to permanentware:

Benefits	Costs
✔ Less trash going to landfill	✔ Initial costs to buy new dishes, cups, utensils and dishwashers
✔ Less consumption of natural resources (oil, wood)	✔ Ongoing costs of dish-washing staff and replacing broken items
✔ Reduced pollution associated with resource extraction, logging, manufacturing and transportation	
✔ Education of children about the value of resources and about the dangers of the throw-away mentality	

An environmental impact study conducted for the Portland, Oregon, Board of Education recommended converting from polystyrene disposableware to washable permanentware and concluded:

> When beginning the research for this report it became apparent that no one person or agency had undertaken an in-depth empirical study like this one. Yet a great deal of information in various forms is available. Some of it consists of theoretical studies using computer modeling; other information comes from limited empirical studies. All of it points in the same direction, namely, that conversion of permanentware from disposableware results in significant environmental savings.[4]

An additional report on the economic impacts of switching found permanentware to be a more expensive operational item.[5] The study was based on a variety of local factors, including labor costs, equipment costs and water and garbage rates. However, after reviewing both studies, the Portland board voted to phase in the permanentware system as the budget allowed.

Every school district must consider a different set of circumstances. Permanentware may not be more expensive in all schools. Some schools may have updated washers; others may need new equipment. Labor and disposal rates vary greatly by area. We hope you will find that the long-term environmental savings of permanentware in an educational institution far outweigh other considerations.

If the use of permanentware is not an option, you will want to figure out the most environmentally and economically sound way to serve food using disposables.

Polystyrene/Styrofoam

Polystyrene is often mistakenly referred to as Styrofoam, which is a trademark of Dow Chemical. Polystyrene is becoming more popular in food-serving facilities now because it is cheap, lightweight, sanitary and considered to be recyclable.

When we compare a moment's use of disposable polystyrene plates, cups, trays and plastic silverware to the long-term toll on our environment, it certainly makes sense to consider alternatives.

Some of the negative environmental impacts of polystyrene are:

◆ **The use of polystyrene teaches students to disregard our natural resources.** Serving students lunch on disposable tableware every day gives them the message that discarding something after only a few minutes of use is acceptable.

◆ **The success of polystyrene recycling is highly questionable.** Recycling polystyrene is technically possible, but it is difficult on a practical level. The National Polystyrene Recycling Company's goal is "to see that 25 percent of polystyrene used in food service and other packaging applications is recycled annually by 1995."[6] Because of limited recycling facilities, questionable markets for recycled plastic products and the prohibitive costs involved in collecting, sorting, cleaning, transporting and reprocessing, this goal may be unreachable.

◆ **Recycling polystyrene uses a lot of energy.** When it is trucked to the school every week or so, when it is trucked out to the recycling center (frequently over very long distances) and when it is put through the recycling process, energy must be expended.

◆ Although ozone-depleting chlorofluorocarbons (CFCs and HCFCs) have been eliminated from the manufacture of polystyrene foam, **the alternative, pentane, is known to create smog.**[7] It is also highly flammable and poses health hazards to workers.

◆ **Polystyrene is petrochemical based.** This means that the raw materials used to manufacture plastics come from oil and natural gas. These are fossil fuels that are **limited and nonrenewable natural resources.**

◆ Unlike glass and aluminum, postconsumer plastics used for food packaging cannot be made into the same product again. Thus, new polystyrene products are always being manufactured with all virgin material. This means **there will always be a need for virgin material.** For further explanation, please refer to Chapter 12.

"More than 45,000 tons of plastic waste are dumped in the world's oceans every year creating a serious threat to aquatic animals and fish. They can be trapped in or be strangled by plastic fishing nets, fishing line, plastic bags, or other plastic debris, or can die from ingesting them. Similarly, plastic litter on the land is a threat to wildlife."

Concern, Inc., "Household Waste: Issues and Opportunities," Washington, DC, 1989.

◆ In an EPA ranking **of the 20 chemicals whose production generates the most hazardous waste, 5 of the top 6 are chemicals commonly used in plastics.** In fact, polystyrene was ranked number 5.[8]

◆ **Polystyrene is a possible carcinogen and can leach from cups and plates into food, causing nerve damage in humans.**[9]

◆ **Exposure to polystyrene during the manufacturing can pose a hazard to workers.**[10] After only 5 years, workers in polystyrene plants have been known to develop liver damage while exposed to styrene concentrations considered safe by occupational health standards.[11]

◆ **Polystyrene is the fastest-growing component of our waste stream.** Polystyrene dishes are single-use items whose useful life can be measured in minutes! According to estimates, made in a 1989 Franklin Associates report, by the year 2000, polystyrene will make up 40 percent of landfill waste. Of grave concern is the fact that polystyrene is getting into our waterways and having a devastating effect on marine life.

◆ **Products that are being made with the recycled polystyrene waste contain less then 10 percent postconsumer material.** Moreover, the products being made are still not being sold in mass quantities. Some of these items include building insulation, food service trays, desk accessories, Frisbees and yo-yos.

◆ McDonald's Corporation has phased out the use of the polystyrene clamshell in favor of paper-based wraps that represent a reduction in packaging volume and environmental impact over the full life cycle of the package.

Paper

When considering disposables, many thoughtful consumers and environmental activists assume that paper is the best choice for the environment. After all, paper is made from trees, a renewable natural resource. However, we can also discover many harmful environmental effects from paper manufacturing and disposal.

Some of the environmental impacts of disposable paper goods follow.

◆ **The manufacture of a paper cup uses more raw material, more energy, more water and more chemicals and creates more pollution than that of a polystyrene cup.**[12]

◆ **Only one-sixth as much raw material is needed to make a polystyrene cup (petrochemical by-products) as is required to make a paper cup (wood pulp).**[13]

◆ **Logging trees by clear-cutting destroys forest ecosystems.** Erosion from logging pollutes streams and harms fish.

◆ **The manufacture of one paper cup uses about 12 times as much steam, 36 times as much electricity and twice as much cooling water as does that of one polystyrene foam cup.**[14]

◆ **The manufacture of a paper cup requires 97 percent more chemicals than does that of a polystyrene cup.**[15] During the pulping and bleaching process for paper cups, large amounts of chemicals are used, including chlorine, sodium hydroxide, sodium chlorate, sulfuric acid, sulfur dioxide and calcium hydroxide.

If Disposables Must Be Used

Does the choice between paper and plastic sound confusing? The point to remember is that both are single-use items whose useful life can be measured in minutes. Both paper and plastic pollute the environment. We should find ways to reduce our use of all disposables and replace them with permanentware and reusable containers. However, if disposables must be used, here are some suggestions to consider:

◆ **If you use paper products, we recommend paper plates, cups, napkins and towels made from unbleached and/or postconsumer materials.** Increasing consumer interest in environmental issues has caused manufacturers to respond with environmentally improved products. Paper plates, napkins and towels made from unbleached postconsumer materials are now commercially available. To meet strict health standards the manufacturers of recycled paper food service products have sandwiched the postconsumer content between inner and outer layers of virgin paper. (For a source please see the resource section at the end of this chapter.)

◆ **If you use polystyrene, establish an efficient recycling program.** You can use the State Resource List in Chapter 20 to find a recycling center or hauler near you that will accept polystyrene.

◆ **Make sure the entire school community is aware of the damaging effects that plastic and/or paper manufacturing, use and disposal have on the environment.**

Schools as consumers can send the message to the manufacturers of food service goods that they are concerned about the environmental impacts of these products both before and after their use. This is the best way to encourage manufacturers to invest in developing products that will be less harmful and less polluting.

Schools with a Vendor that Brings in Food

If your school vendor already serves on permanentware, congratulations! You are environmentally advanced. If paper napkins are being used, ask your vendor to consider switching to cloth ones or to napkins made from 100 percent postconsumer recycled-content, non-bleached paper.

If your vendor does not use permanentware, it should be required to develop a waste reduction plan that emphasizes reusable items and easily recycled packaging. Future vendor contracts should stipulate stringent waste reduction requirements.

We have 2 other alternatives we would like to suggest. First, if reusables are unmanageable but disposable paper products don't feel comfortable, try cloth napkins! Many foods can be set on or wrapped in cloth napkins—turkey or chicken dogs, pizza, veggie burgers, sandwiches, whole pieces of fruit and so on. The responsibility of laundering and returning the cloth napkins can rotate, or you can insist that your vendor make this part of his/her deal with your school. Explain that he/she will save money because it will be unnecessary to replace the disposables continually.

Our second alternative plan is to purchase reusable plastic containers with lids. See the resource section at the end of this chapter for companies that offer these materials. We wrote each student's name and grade on the lid and on the bottom of the containers with a permanent marking pen. Be sure to rough up the surface of the smooth plastic with sandpaper or an emery board so that the marker will stick to the surface. Otherwise, even permanent markers will wash off quickly. We sent flyers (see the sample) home with the students and asked the teachers to help us in our efforts. This plan worked beautifully as long as there were a few students and parents who cared about reducing waste enough to keep it going.

Please bring this reusable Hot Lunch Container

_____

(Fill in day(s) appropriate.)

In your reusable lunch container you should also bring:

> One cloth napkin
> One spoon and/or fork

It will be your responsibility to take your container home to be washed and ready for next time.

(These containers are dishwasher safe.)

We will no longer serve Hot Lunch on paper plates.

The school Environmental Club has organized this new system in its effort to save trees, water and energy.

Thank you for helping us!

The following is a sample of the note that we sent to all the teachers along with a stack of flyers:

Dear (teacher's name):

Please distribute the attached flyers. We will include a few extra copies, in case you need more.

It would be ever so helpful if you would make announcements reminding the kids to bring their hot lunch containers, napkin and spoon or fork to school.

Sincerely,

With every decision we all must try to **reduce** waste and extend the life of all that we have by **reusing**. Keep in mind that our choices are being modeled by our children, and they will keep these values with them their entire lives.

WHERE ELSE CAN YOU CUT WASTE?

Teachers and students can continually make changes on their campus. Once they begin to search for ways to reduce waste, many wonderful ideas that may affect attitudes and behaviors will present themselves. It is a great exercise to look at behaviors in a new way. The following are some new and old ideas for reducing waste on campus .

♦ Reuse boxes and envelopes.
♦ Wherever paper is generated, create collection boxes/bins for scratch paper.
♦ Use both sides of the paper whenever possible.
♦ Think twice before making numerous copies of exercises. Is there another way to present some of the information such as the chalkboard or the overhead projector?
♦ Install and use message boards for lounges/offices or classrooms to reduce paper waste.
♦ Designate one child per family to bring home school communications in order to cut down on duplication.
♦ Buy pens, crayons, paper and so on in bulk.
♦ Buy rechargeable batteries.

This list can go on and on. Get creative! It doesn't matter how much money we do or do not have. What matters is how we use our limited resources. The choice is yours. Should we think only about today and convenience, or should we look to the future?

310

RESOURCES

Brochures/Papers/Reports

Breaking the Waste Habit: A Guide to "Waste Reduction"
Channing L. Bete Company, Inc.
200 State Road
South Deerfield, MA 01373
413-665-7611

Cleaning Up: U.S. Waste Management Technology and Third World Development
World Resources Institute
1709 New York Avenue NW
Washington, DC 20006
800-822-0504

Environmental Shopping Guide
San Francisco Recycling Program
City Hall, Room 271
San Francisco, CA 94102
415-554-6193

Garbage: At the Grocery
Garbage Magazine
The Blackburn Tavern
2 Main Street
Gloucester, MA 01930
508-283-3200

Guide to Recycled Printing and Office Paper and Papers with Post-consumer Content
Californians Against Waste Foundation
926 J Street, Suite 606
Sacramento, CA 95814
916-443-8317

How to Make Waste Reduction and Recycling Happen in Your School
Washington State Department of Ecology
Waste Reduction, Recycling and Litter Control Program
P.O. Box 47600
Olympia, WA 98504-7600
206-407-6000

Making Less Garbage: A Planning Guide for Communities
Inform, Inc.
120 Wall Street, 16th Floor
New York, NY 10005
212-689-4040

The Next Frontier: Solid Waste Reduction
Community Environmental Council
930 Miramonte Drive
Santa Barbara, CA 93109
805-963-0583

Plagued by Packaging
New York Public Interest Group
9 Murray Street, 3rd Floor
New York, NY 10007
212-349-6460

Plastics in Municipal Solid Waste: A Primer
Environmental Planning and Education Services
10 Thoroughbred Trail
Penfield, NY 14526
716-671-9196

Put Waste in Its Place
Channing L. Bete Company, Inc.
200 State Road
South Deerfield, MA 01373
413-665-7611

Reducing, Recycling and Rethinking Garbage
Natural Resources Defense Council
40 West 20th Street
New York, NY 10011
212-272-2700

Sites for Our Solid Waste: A Guidebook for Effective Public Involvement
U.S. Environmental Protection Agency
Office of Solid Waste
441 G Street NW, Suite 51
Washington, DC 20548
202-512-3000 or 260-4610

Solid Waste: From Problems to Solutions—A Teacher's Handbook
Illinois Department of Energy and Natural Resources
325 West Adams, Room 300
Springfield, IL 62704-1892
217-785-2800

Solid Waste: Landfills
University cf Wisconsin-Madison
432 North Lake Street
Madison, WI 53706
608-262-0493

Waste Reduction Task Force: Final Report
McDonald's Environmental Affairs Department
McDonald's Plaza
Oak Brook, IL 60521
708-575-3000

A Week with Waste: A Five-Day Activity Packet for Teachers
California Integrated Waste Management Board
Office of Public Affairs and Education
8800 California Center Drive
Sacramento, CA 95826
916-255-2296

Books

The Garbage Primer
League of Women Voters of the United States, 1993
1730 M Street NW
Washington, DC 20036

Getting at the Source: Strategies for Reducing Municipal Solid Waste
World Wildlife Fund
The Island Press, 1991
1718 Connecticut Avenue NW, Suite 300
Washington, DC 20009

How Much Is Enough?
Alan Thein Durning
Earthscan Publications, Ltd., 1992
120 Pentonville Road
London, England N1 9JN

Rubbish! The Archaeology of Garbage
William Rathje and Cullen Murphy
HarperCollins, 1992
10 East 53rd Street
New York, NY 10022

War on Waste
Louis Blumberg and Robert Gottlieb
Island Press, 1989
1718 Connecticut Avenue NW, Suite 300
Washington, DC 20009

Wasting Away

Kevin Lynch
Sierra Club, 1990
730 Polk Street
San Francisco, CA 94109

Books for Youth

Buried in Garbage

Bobbie Kalman and Janine Schaub
Crabtree Publishing Company, 1991
350 Fifth Avenue, Suite 3308
New York, NY 10118

Environmental Awareness: Solid Waste

Mary Ellen Snodgrass
Bancroft-Sage Publishing, Inc., 1991
601 Elkcan Circle, Suite C-7
P.O. Box 355
Marco, FL 33969-0355

Garbage

Maria Fleming
Scholastic, Inc., 1992
555 Broadway
New York, NY 10012-3999

Garbage!

Evan and Janet Hadingham
Simon and Schuster, 1990
1230 Avenue of the Americas
New York, NY 10020

The Planet of Trash

George Poppel
Pandemonium Books/National Press, 1987
7508 Wisconsin Avenue
Bethesda, MD 20814

Reducing, Reusing and Recycling

Bobbie Kalman
Crabtree Publishing Company, 1991
350 Fifth Avenue, Suite 3308
New York, NY 10118

Trash!

Charlotte Wilcox
Carolrhoda Books, 1988
241 First Avenue
Minneapolis, MN 55401

What a Load of Trash

Steve Skidmore
The Millbrook Press, 1991
2 Old New Milford Road
Brookfield, CT 06804

Individuals/Companies/Organizations

Donnelley Marketing

1235 N Avenue
Nevada, IA 50201-1419
515-382-8202
To get off mailing lists write to this company and request that your name and address be removed from their lists.

Equifax Options

P.O. Box 740123
Atlanta, GA 30374-0123
404-885-8309
To get off mailing lists write to this company and request that your name and address be removed from their lists.

General Electric Company
GE Plastics
1 Plastics Avenue
Pittsfield, MA 01201
800-845-0600
General Electric is sponsoring a reusable milk bottle program with schools. The plastic bottles, made of Lexan® polycarbonate from GE's plastics unit, is a clear bottle similar to glass. After each use, the bottle is returned to the dairy, washed, refilled and used again— 100 times or more. After more than 100 uses, the bottles can be recycled for use in other high-volume products like automobile bumpers, computer housings, signs and building materials like roof shingles and clear decorator blocks.

James River Corporation
Sales Service Center
2410 North Hampton Street
Easton, PA 18042
800-257-9744
James River has introduced its Dixie Recycled® line of products, including hot and cold cups, clamshells, drink carriers and dispenser napkins. Products contain between 12 and 35 percent postconsumer waste.

Laserstar/LSI
23 Garfield Avenue
Woburn, MA 01801
617-932-8667 (inside MA)
800-432-9989 (outside MA)
Laser printer service, supplies and accessories. The firm will recycle laser printer cartridges. You can return yours and have it remanufactured or purchase one. The recycled or remanufactured cartridge is cheaper. In addition, Laserstar recycles the components of the cartridge that are not reusable.

Mail Preference Service
c/o Direct Marketing Association
P.O. Box 9008
Farmingdale, NY 11735-9008
212-768-7277
To get off mailing lists write to this company and request that your name and address be removed from their lists.

Metromail
901 West Bond
Lincoln, NE 65821
800-426-8901
To get off mailing lists write to this company and request that your name and address be removed from their lists.

National Demographics and Lifestyles
List Order Services
1621 18th Street, Suite 300
Denver, CO 80202-1294
800-525-3533
To get off mailing lists write to this company and request that your name and address be removed from their lists.

Packaging Company of America
18752 San Jose Avenue
City of Industry, CA 91788
818-912-2531 or 800-456-4725
Sells paper plates made with postconsumer materials.

P. Adelman
1050 Embury Street
Pacific Palisades, CA 90272
310-459-1319
Has organic cotton canvas lunch bags and t-shirts. Also provides logo imprinting.

R.L. Polk and Company
List Department
6400 Monroe Boulevard
Taylor, MI 48180
800-873-7655
To get off mailing lists write to this company and request that your name and address be removed from their lists.

Rubbermaid
1147 Akron
Wooster, OH 44691
216-264-6464
Rubbermaid makes very durable reusable containers that are readily available in most areas.

Seventh Generation
49 Hercules Drive
Colchester, VT 05446-1672
800-456-1177
Has cellulose bags, paper plates (with 100 percent recycled paper) and paper napkins (also with recycled content available). These items may be available through your local natural food store or food co-op. Ask the manager of your local grocery to stock them if they are not in the store.

Sterlite Corporation
198 Main Street
Townsend, MA 01469
508-597-8702
Compartmentalized plastic containers with covers that students can use to bring their lunch from home or for a hot lunch program.

Tupperware
P.O. Box 2353
Orlando, FL 32802
800-858-7221
Some schools have made a fundraiser out of promoting reusable containers with the help and encouragement of the Tupperware Company. The students take the orders, the school makes a profit and the Tupperware representative does most of the work. In the end, many more people will be using reusable containers. It is also important to note that Tupperware products carry a life-time guarantee. If they break, crack or scratch, Tupperware will replace them free of charge.

Chapter 12

The ABC's of Recycling

Chapter 12

CONTENTS

INTRODUCTION

The chart below shows a complete breakdown of America's annual trash by weight.

The recycling process entails collecting used products, reprocessing their components and then producing new products. Most recycled materials are used in new ways. For instance, plastic bottles are made into products such as carpets, jacket insulation and notebooks.

The used product that becomes part of a new product is called **postconsumer waste**. When we buy products made with postconsumer waste, the recycling process comes full circle and we have **closed the loop**. This means we have **bought recycled** and, in doing so we have helped create a market for the materials that have been collected.

What's in Our Trash?	
Paper products	40%
Yard waste	18%
Metals	9%
Plastic	8%
Food waste	7%
Glass	7%
Rubber, leather, textiles and wood	9%
Miscellaneous organic wastes	3%

* Total is over 100 because of rounding up.

Source: EPA

Why We Recycle

We recycle

- ◆ To conserve natural resources
- ◆ To conserve water and energy
- ◆ To reduce air, water, soil/land pollution
- ◆ To reduce litter
- ◆ To reduce the amount of waste clogging our landfills and extend the life of our limited landfills

Getting Started

The following is an outline of the steps you'll need to take to begin recycling on your campus:

1. Learn the different categories of recycled products.
2. Discover what recyclable materials are being used on your campus.
3. Find out what recyclable materials are accepted locally.
4. Find a hauler to take the recyclables to the recycle center.
5. Figure out how many bins you'll need, get them and label them.
6. Work with the campus maintenance crew on the collection program. (Find a pick-up area and figure out how to get the recyclables there.)
7. Educate everyone!
8. Buy recycled!

MATERIAL CATEGORIES

Paper
Virgin Materials vs. Postconsumer Materials

Recycling paper saves about 64 percent of the energy used to make it from virgin wood pulp.[1] This is particularly important because the paper industry is the largest single user of fuel and the third largest consumer of energy in the United States.

The U.S. is the largest consumer of paper in the world. In 1990, paper and paperboard consumption reached 86.5 million tons, or 690 pounds per person.

American Paper Institute, New York, NY.

Schools generate a tremendous amount of paper waste. In high schools this is comprised mostly of white ledger paper and computer paper, in middle schools it is mostly white paper and in elementary schools the waste comes generally from craft and mixed paper.

During a 6-month period, the following figures were obtained for the amount of waste paper recycled in Washington state schools. Remember that if this paper had not been recycled, it would have been thrown out.

- ◆ High school average: 3,160 lb, or 5.3 lb/student
- ◆ Middle school average: 2,192 lb, or 2.91 lb/student
- ◆ Elementary school average: 733 lb, or 1.41 lb/student

To convert these figures to a full 9-month school year average, increase them by 33 percent.

Paper recycling has become a well-established industry. Because government purchasing offices are demanding recycled products, many paper mills are investing in the equipment necessary to incorporate postconsumer waste. Many recycling companies will pay for the paper they collect from your school if you generate enough high-quality material. In recent years, the markets for lower grades of paper have also opened up. Mixed paper and magazines, which used to be thrown away, are now commonly accepted.

We must continue to even the competition between virgin materials and used materials. Virgin materials require more energy in the manufacturing process than used materials do. Although postconsumer waste paper is cheaper for the manufacturer to use, virgin materials are preferred because of tax advantages and government subsidies for mining and logging interests.

Three possible solutions to this misuse of our country's natural resources are to
- ◆ Eliminate government subsidies for mining and logging interests.
- ◆ Require manufacturers to pay a virgin materials tax.
- ◆ Provide manufacturers with incentives such as low-interest loans and tax breaks to encourage the use of postconsumer recycled materials.

Environmentalists fear that a tax would be only a token fee. Therefore, they support mandatory postconsumer content legislation. This would create a market for recycled paper materials.

Once the competition between virgin materials and used materials has been evened, the next step for incorporating postconsumer waste in the manufacturing processes is for Americans to buy, use and demand paper goods with postconsumer content. We must close the loop.

Categories of Paper Products
The following are categories of paper products:
- ◆ **White paper.** All white paper that is not glossy or coated, such as letter paper, copy paper and computer printout paper. There may be many colors of ink on the paper, often covering large areas. This does not matter. Of concern here is what the color of the paper was before the printing process.
- ◆ **Colored paper.** Uncoated, nonglossy colored paper.
- ◆ **Glossy or coated paper.** Magazines, catalogs, telephone books and paperback books. Although the paperback and telephone books do not have glossy or coated paper on the inside, they do contain glues and thus will contaminate other papers even if you tear off their covers.
- ◆ **Newspaper.** Some recyclers ask that the supplements and advertising inserts be removed and included with the glossy/coated paper. Fortunately, this is becoming a less common request.
- ◆ **Brown paper.** Brown bags and brown wrapping paper.
- ◆ **Corrugated cardboard.** Cartons and boxes made with 2 flat sheets and a ridged layer in between. Most services require that the boxes/cartons be broken down and flat.
- ◆ **Chipboard/paperboard.** Food container boxes, such as cereal boxes and egg cartons. Again, most services require that these be broken down and flat. If the inside of the box is gray, the box was made with recycled/postconsumer wastepaper. Don't worry, it can be recycled again.
- ◆ **Tissue.** Paper towels, paper napkins, toilet paper, facial tissues and diapers. While these products cannot be recycled, you can buy them with postconsumer recycled content.
- ◆ **Laminated paper.** Packaging in which the paper is bonded together with one or more other materials, such as plastic sheeting, metal foil or wax-coated paper. Some products packaged in laminated paper are milk in cartons, ice cream, hardware items in a blister pack, some juice cartons and microwave or frozen food packages.

The Recycling of a Drink Box

Drink boxes have been criticized for being difficult to recycle. In response, aseptic packaging manufacturers have helped communities create recycling programs for plastic-coated paper products. Because most juice boxes and milk cartons are used by students, recycling programs are being set up in schools. By late 1994, more than 1,800 schools in 20 states and 3 million homes in 16 states had recycling programs for these materials.

Giant hydrapulpers, which look like big kitchen blenders, are used to separate the plastic and foil layers from the paper pulp. The paper fiber is then sold to companies that make products like writing paper and facial tissue.

Despite industry efforts, only a small percentage of aseptic packaging is currently recycled. Remember, it is better to use refillable thermoses and easily recyclable beverage containers before grabbing a drink box. If your school is interested in recycling drink boxes and milk cartons, call the Aseptic Packaging Council at 800-277-8088.

Source: Fact Sheet, Aseptic Packaging Council, Washington, DC, 1994.

Most often these packages will never be recycled because the materials are extremely difficult and expensive to separate once they have been laminated or bonded together.

The most common example of laminated paper found in the schools is the juice or drink box. In the packaging world this box is called "aseptic" packaging. Let's take a quick glance at the life of the juice box. This will be a real eye-opener!

Aseptic packaging is made from aluminum foil, plastic sheeting (a petroleum by-product) and paperboard. These 3 materials are laminated together. Hazardous wastes and volatile pollution are standard by-products of producing the foil, plastic sheeting and paperboard. A considerable amount of natural resources and energy is used in the manufacturing process. And all drink boxes come with a disposable plastic straw in a disposable plastic wrapper. Thus, the **lifecycle** ("cradle to grave") of this single-serving, one-time-use item is very wasteful.

If left out in a field it would take an estimated 300 to 400 years for a drink box to decompose. In landfills, due to the lack of air and sunlight, no decomposing takes place. In the United States alone, **4 billion** drink boxes are consumed each year.[2]

Some possible alternatives are
  ◆ A reusable thermos
  ◆ A reusable plastic bottle made from a plastic that is recyclable in your community
  ◆ An easily recyclable aluminum can

The preceding 9 paper categories can serve only as a general guide because not all recycling centers follow the same guidelines. It is important that you check your recycling center to confirm exactly what materials are recyclable and how they must be sorted and bundled.

Recycling Paper Facts

It is estimated that nearly 50 percent of the nation's landfill space is now taken up by paper and paper products. A ton of paper made from 100 percent recycled wastepaper saves

✔ **17 trees** (this figure varies depending on tree size)

✔ **Enough energy to heat the average home for 6 months**

✔ **7,000 gallons of water**

✔ **60 pounds of air pollutants**

✔ **3 cubic yards of landfill space**

✔ **Taxpayer dollars that would have been used for waste disposal costs.**

Source: Debi Kimball, *Recycling in America* (Santa Barbara, CA: ABC-CLIO, Inc., 1992), pp. 49-50.

Metals

Virgin Materials vs. Postconsumer Material

Recycling metal is one of the most efficient ways to save nonrenewable resources. When metals are made from virgin materials, ore needs to be mined, refined, melted and cast into ingots to be made into new products. When metals are collected for recycling, they are crushed, shredded, melted, re-refined and poured into ignots. Metals are able to go through this process indefinitely without sacrificing any essential characteristics. Both steel and aluminum are 100 percent recyclable.

The environmental savings of using postconsumer materials compared to virgin materials are considerable:

◆ Recycling aluminum reduces the amount of virgin materials and energy needed by 95 percent. [3]

◆ Recycling steel reduces the amount of virgin materials used by 90 percent and energy needed by 74 percent.[4]

◆ For both aluminum and steel the amount of air pollution and water pollution produced when using raw materials decreases considerably when postconsumer materials are used.[5]

Recycling other metals such as zinc, iron, lead and copper is another way to stop the waste of more nonrenewable resources. These materials may be more difficult to recycle than steel and aluminum, but when disposing of them keep in mind that a scrap yard dealer may be interested in these metals.

323

Aluminum

The aluminum can is currently one of the most valuable commodities in the garbage pile. When it comes to recycling, the all-aluminum container (usually your soda can) is a marketing success story. This is a market where demand and supply are strong. Recovered aluminum cans represent considerable energy savings. For every can that is recycled, enough energy is saved to produce 19 more cans.[6] Every aluminum can should therefore be viewed as a commodity that represents stored energy.

Recycling Aluminum Can Facts

Every 3 months citizens of the United States throw away enough aluminum to rebuild our commercial air fleet.[7]

One recycled aluminum can saves enough energy to operate a TV set for 3 hours.[8]

Besides aluminum cans, other products made from aluminum are now recyclable. These include

- ✔ Aluminum pie pans and cooking dishes
- ✔ TV dinner trays
- ✔ Lawn chairs
- ✔ Gutters
- ✔ Storm doors
- ✔ Automobile parts

Reynolds Aluminum has centers nationwide (in conjunction with recycling centers) where these aluminum products can be taken for scrap recycling. These centers also have information about recycling copper and brass. Look under Reynolds Aluminum Recycling in your telephone book or call 800-228-2525 for a location near you.

Steel

Most recycling centers will accept steel cans, but usually they must be sorted from the aluminum. The best way to distinguish between the two is to use a magnet. If there is any pull at all, the container is steel or contains some steel.

Steel Recycling Facts

For every pound of steel cans recycled, enough energy is saved to light a 60-watt light bulb for more than 26 hours.

Steel cans and other steel products produced in the United States contain at least 25 percent recycled steel, with some containing 100 percent recycled steel.

Source: *A Few Facts About Steel: America's Most Recycled Material*, Steel Recycling Institute, Pittsburgh, PA, 1994.

Glass

Virgin Materials vs. Postconsumer Materials

Glass containers, such as jars and bottles, are completely recyclable, and the market for them is stable. Glass from light bulbs, drinking glasses and windows is not recyclable. Most glass container manufacturers currently use 25 to 30 percent recycled glass as "cullet."[9] (Cullet is the broken or refuse glass added to virgin glass in manufacturing glass containers.) Recycled glass (postconsumer glass/cullet) saves energy. When recycled cullet is used instead of virgin glass, the manufacturer can reduce the temperature at which the glass is fired by 200 degrees Farenheit.[10]

Glass Recycling

Glass food and beverage containers, such as the following, are easily recycled. (Remove lids and caps.)	The following materials cannot be recycled. Don't mix them with container glass.
Soda and beverage bottles	Light bulbs
Juice containers	Mirror and window glass
Food containers	Ceramic cups and plates
Ketchup bottles	Crystal and drinking glasses
	Clay flowerpots

Source: *Glass Recycling Made Easy*, Glass Packaging Institute, Washington, DC, 1990.

According to the Glass Packaging Institute, manufacturers should be using up to 50 percent recycled cullet within the next few years and hope to use 70 to 75 percent if supplies remain available.

Categories of Glass Products

Most recyclers require that glass be sorted as follows:

Clear (also called flint)
Brown (also called amber)
Green

Separate bins are necessary to avoid color contamination. Broken glass is tedious and dangerous to sort. Mixed glass is difficult for the recycler to sell and so has very little value. But don't panic, most of your collected glass will probably be clear and green, so 2 bins are usually adequate. We recommend a medium-sized cardboard box that is clearly labeled for brown glass and placed next to the clear and green glass bins. Once everyone is used to this system, you should find nicely sorted glass most of the time.

Some recyclers require that caps, lids and other attachments be removed.

> **Recycling Glass Facts**
>
> **Making new glass from old glass cuts mining wastes by 80 percent, water use by 50 percent and air pollution by 20 percent.**[*]
>
> **One recycled bottle saves enough energy to light a 100-watt light bulb for 4 hours.**[**]
>
> [*] EarthWorks Group, *50 Simple Things You Can Do to Save the Earth*, Earthworks Press, Berkeley, CA, 1989, pp. 62-63.
> [**] *Why Recycle*, TreePeople, Beverly Hills, CA, 1988.

Plastic

Virgin Materials vs. Postconsumer Materials

The same manufacturing procedure is used for both recycled plastics and virgin plastics. There is no by-product or waste from the production of plastic resins. It's a clean process and nothing is lost. Resin pellets are the end result. It's expensive to recycle plastics and that's why companies only use 25 percent recycled materials along with 75 percent of new plastic in their packaging.

Products that will have contact with food cannot contain postconsumer plastic waste. Plastic waste gets made into other products such as fiberfill.

Buying and Recycling Plastic

The good news is that manufacturers of plastic containers for beverages, food items, cleaning products, cosmetics and similar household goods are now labeling the containers with codes. Not only will this aid you in sorting for recycling, but it will also be a great guide when you shop. Assume that if the plastic container is not labeled with one of the codes, it will be very difficult, if not impossible, to recycle it. In this case look for that product in an alternative container that is locally recyclable. You will need to look carefully; often the code is molded into the plastic on the container bottom or side.

Categories of Plastic Products

1. **PETE (PET, or polyethylene terephthalate).** This is the easiest of all plastics to recycle and therefore the most valuable. This type of plastic is most commonly used to make large soft drink bottles. PETE soda bottles are redeemable in many states. This means that your recycling center will give you money when you turn them in.

Recycled bottles also find their way into about a third of the carpet made in the United States.

2. **HDPE (high-density polyethylene).** This is the second-easiest plastic to recycle. HDPE is used to make containers for milk, juice, laundry soap, motor oil, cottage cheese, vitamins and more. These recycled containers can be made into park benches, recycling bins, trash cans, flowerpots and new detergent bottles.

3. **PVC (vinyl/polyvinyl chloride) or V (vinyl).** PVC/V is used in construction materials, flooring, credit cards, garden hoses and nonfood containers. PVC/V contains a known human carcinogen (vinyl chloride) and is not currently used in many food containers other than those for cooking oil and the wrap on such perishables as lunch meats and cheese. Some water bottles are made of PVC/V. The Environmental Defense Fund recommends that you buy your water in another container, glass or PETE, to avoid leaching. PVC/V is not widely recycled; if mixed in with another type of plastic it can ruin an entire batch of recycled plastics. Also, if it gets too hot in the recycling process it can turn into hydrochloric acid and damage the recycling equipment.

4. **LDPE (low-density polyethylene).** LDPE is used for sandwich bags and the thin bags in the produce section of the grocery store, grocery bags, protective covers for dry cleaning and shrink wrapping for cassettes, CDs and many, many other products. Even if the bag does not have LDPE or the #4 code on it, it is still probably LDPE.

327

Plastic bags represent closed-loop recycling (rare in plastics); that is, they can be made into new plastic bags. But about 5 million tons of LDPE are used every year, and very little is recycled.[11] This is where precycling is a good idea. Avoid unnecessary use and reuse as many times as possible.

5. PP (polypropylene). PP is used for such packaging as bottle caps and lids, rope, twine and straws. In the United States we use about 3.5 million tons a year and a negligible amount is recycled.[12]

There is a need for creating a recycling program for propylene because
- ◆ Propylene is on the EPA's "worst toxics" list.
- ◆ Nickel (a toxic metal) is released when polypropylene is incinerated.

6. PS (polystyrene). PS is commonly called Styrofoam. It is used in coffee cups and other carry-out fast-food containers. PS has come to epitomize disposability in our culture. The pilot recycling programs and all their pitfalls are discussed in some detail under "Polystyrene/Styrofoam" in Chapter 11.

7. Other (all other resins). Typical containers made of other resins are those for ketchup and syrup bottles.

Categories 1 and 2 are the most commonly used plastics for containers, and most communities are now recycling them.

Plastic Recycling Facts

✔ Recycled PET is used to make deli and bakery trays, carpets and fiberfill and new bottles.

✔ Recycled HDPE is used to make bottles for laundry detergents, recycling bins, bags and motor oil bottles.

✔ Recycled vinyl becomes pipe, fencing and nonfood bottles.

✔ Recycled LDPE is used to make new bags and film plastic.

✔ Recycled PP becomes auto parts, carpets, industrial fibers and textiles.

✔ Recycled PS can be made into office accesories (scissors and rulers), cafeteria trays, toys and video cassettes.

Source: "Plastics in Perspective: Answers to Your Questions About Plastics in the Environment," American Plastics Council, Washington, DC, 1993.

GETTING STARTED

This section outlines the first 2 steps you must take to begin a campus recycling system. First, you must discover which materials your campus generates, learn which are recycled locally and decide which to collect. Second, you must establish how the recyclables will get from your campus to a recycling center.

Establish Campus Recyclables
Discover What Materials Your Campus Generates
The way to determine what recyclable materials are being thrown away on your campus is to speak with the campus maintenance workers and walk around looking inside the waste bins. The maintenance crew will have a pretty good idea of which materials are generated, who generates them and the quantity of each material.

Get a copy of your campus map. Take it with you when you go snooping into the waste bins. (You might need some gloves for this; it can get messy.) You can do 2 jobs at once if you mark down what materials are generated and where because in the section "Setting Up a Collection Program," we suggest that you map out recycle bin locations.

Discover Which Materials Are Recycled Locally
The following is a list of some resources that can help you discover who, in your area, offers hauling and/or recycling services:
1. State waste management board
2. State division of recycling
3. Your city hall can help you find out about:
   a. The city integrated solid waste management department
   b. The city sanitation department
   c. The city public works department
   d. The city conservation corps
   e. The department of conservation
4. The state department of public works
5. The state general services department
6. The state sanitation and solid waste division
7. Local recycling centers
8. Local environmental groups

These are possible departments that can offer assistance. Some of these are listed in the State Resource List in Chapter 20. The other offices, such as the city departments, can be found in the Yellow Pages. You can also call other schools and businesses in your area that are already recycling and find out where they are taking their recyclables and what materials are locally accepted. This might save you a lot of work.

Establish Who Will Haul Campus Recyclables

There are 2 ways of handling the removal of your sorted recyclables from the campus:

1. Hire a waste-hauling or recycling company.

2. Have volunteers load them in their cars and deliver them to the local recycling/buy-back center.

Many of the states that have legislation regarding redemption value on recyclables will require grocery stores to provide a collection center for the redeemable items.

Where Does Our Trash Go?

73% Landfilled   **14%** Incinerated   **13%** Recycled

Source: Jennifer Carless, *Taking Out the Trash* (Washington, DC: Island Press, 1992), p. 15.

"Incinerators, or waste-to-energy plants, recover between 1 and 10 percent of the energy value of solid waste, while recycling typically recovers 50 to 90 percent."

Conservatree Information Services, San Francisco, CA, 1993.

Please see the State Resource List in Chapter 20 to research your state's legislative guidelines regarding redemption. If your state has grocery store redemption centers, you will always have a convenient place that everyone drives to at least once a week to take your recyclables. These centers generally accept only cans, glass and some plastics and paper items.

Using Your Current Waste Hauler

It is easier and more efficient, and the rate of cooperation is higher if the recyclables are picked up from your school. First, you'll need to find out who is responsible for the campus solid-waste-disposal contract. Probably someone in the administration office or maintenance office will have this information. Whoever picks up the campus garbage may include the recyclables pick-up as a part of their service.

Although your current hauler may want to charge more, you should point out that the same amount of materials will still be hauled, but to 2 different locations—the landfill and the recycling center. At the landfill the hauler has to pay a tipping or dumping fee, but the recycling center pays the hauler. Try to work a deal. You'll surely develop negotiating skills!

If your garbage hauler does not offer this service and another hauler in the area offers both services, it may be time to renegotiate the hauling contract or switch to a new hauler.

Finding a New Waste Hauler

Before you start looking for hauling companies, it is a good idea to call other schools and businesses in your area that are already recycling and find out who they are using and which materials are locally accepted. This might save you a lot of work. But if this doesn't work, check your Yellow Pages. For haulers look under

- Waste Disposal
- Waste Paper
- Waste Reduction
- Recycling
- Rubbish

For your local recycling/buy-back center look under "Recycling Centers." In addition, we have listed some resources that can help you discover who in your area offers hauling and/or recycling services. You can find this information in the resource section at the end of this chapter or in the State Resource List in Chapter 20.

If it becomes necessary to research companies that haul both garbage and recyclables, there are some questions you may be asked and it's best to be prepared. Haulers want to know how much, by weight, you are generating of each recyclable material category. Your first approach should be to ask for a trial period in order to establish some realistic figures. Do plead your case. It is hard to say no to kids who are obviously trying to do something for the environment. You might even offer to try to get some publicity for their company in the local paper.

You are also going to need to ask whoever is handling the current waste-disposal contract the following questions:

- Who is picking up the garbage?
- Do they provide the dumpsters? Is there a rental fee?
- How many dumpsters will be needed and of what size?
- How often is the pickup?
- How much garbage, by weight, is your campus generating?
- Do the preceding figures include yard waste? This is important because yard waste can account for much of the weight and volume. We explore composting in Chapter 5, "School Gardens."
- How much does the service cost monthly?

The preceding information will help you compare the various services. The following questions are the ones you need to ask any new services you contact:

◆ Do they provide bins and/or dumpsters for recyclables and what are the rental and hauling fees?

◆ At what point (by volume) do the recyclables pay for the hauling/dumping fees? Many states are now paying a redemption fee for the recyclables. This means that it is possible for the recyclables to pay for their own hauling fees because the hauler will get money from the recycling/buy-back center when the materials are turned in.

◆ Would it be possible to cluster with other area schools?

It is important to note that you can always agree to do 2 or 3 aluminum drives per school year. This would be appealing to haulers. Schools have surprising resources. Just imagine all the children bringing in cans from home, neighbors, their parent's work and friends. Don't ever forget the power your school holds: Kid Power! Not too many adults will be able to ignore the efforts and enthusiasm of a young person.

If You Can't Find a Commercial Hauler

If a hauler won't take you on as a client for a trial period to discover what kinds of quantities your school will generate, there is still another way to get the recyclables from your campus to the recycling center. You will have to haul them yourself for an initial few months. Hence, the school families with station wagons and trucks will have to be called and asked to get involved.

At the recycling center they will weigh in everything you bring to them. If you keep track of this for 3 or 4 months, you will get a sense of the quantities your campus will generate of each material.

(If you are unable to secure a hauler do not be discouraged. At my children's school I hauled a trailer packed full once every month for 7 months. It wasn't easy, but it was worth it to get the whole program up and running. Now we have our local Conservation Corps picking up every other week, and it's great! Every school that has begun a recycling program has had to go through a breaking-in period. Don't give up. Once your local recycler, parents, teachers, maintenance crew and administration see how determined you are, things will begin to come together.)

School Pooling

Realistically, unless you are generating a large amount of recyclables, it may be difficult to have a pickup service. Another solution is to set up a cluster situation where several schools pool together all the recyclables at one location. By pooling your sorted recyclables, you will stand a better chance of meeting the minimums and the costs, if any, for dumpster rental or pickup.

SETTING UP A COLLECTION PROGRAM

Once you have established how the recyclables will get from your campus to a recycling center and what materials you will be collecting, the next steps are to

♦ **Determine what recycle bins are needed and where they will go.** It is best to begin with a campus map. For instance, paper will be generated in each classroom, the school offices, the library and at the copy machines and computer printers. Aluminum, plastic, glass and metals will be generated mostly near eating areas. (Don't forget the teachers' lounge.) Cardboard is pervasive. It will turn up everywhere.

The only accurate way to try to predict how many bins you'll need and where to put them is to walk around your campus and peek into the waste bins. The following are more specific guidelines for each material.

♦ **Get and label the bins.** Cardboard boxes are easy to find and collect and they work well indoors. For your outdoor collection sites you'll need durable containers. Bin labeling is vital to a successful program. Again, you will find more specific guidelines later.

♦ **Educate the students, faculty, administration and maintenance crew.** For your school to have a successful recycling system, it is very important that everyone on campus understand what defines each material category, how the system will work and that their cooperation is essential.

♦ **Assign responsibilities for bin maintenance.** This is a two-phase process. First you must monitor the bins to be sure that the materials are being collected properly. Second, you must work closely with campus maintenance to develop a system for getting all the recyclables to the pickup area.

Determine How Many Bins You Need

For recycling, well-labeled bins or boxes need to be set up around the campus wherever recyclables are generated. One of the most vital places to put your recycling bins is next to **all** trash cans. If you fail to do this many people will throw their recyclables away. Working with the custodial staff will help you.

Areas to consider for **paper** bins include
- ◆ Classrooms (particularly the art rooms)
- ◆ Offices
- ◆ Copy machines and computer printer areas
- ◆ The library

Areas to consider for **glass, plastic and metals** (aluminum and tin) bins include
- ◆ Next to existing trash bins
- ◆ The cafeteria
- ◆ The teachers' lounge
- ◆ Offices (many office workers eat at their desks)
- ◆ Play areas
- ◆ Sports facilities and auditoriums

Cardboard boxes need to be "broken down" or flattened and tied into bundles with twine. They will not fit into bins, so a designated area to store them can help keep things tidy.

Get the Bins You Need

If you are starting your collection/recycling program without any funding, here are some suggestions. Use your campus map to figure out how many bins you will need. Don't skimp on the number of bins because if it is too far for people to walk, they are not going to recycle. For paper you can simply use cardboard boxes. More durable bins will be necessary for all other recyclables because they can be messy and because many of their collection sites will be outdoors.

If your school has no funds to purchase durable bins, you can send notes home asking every family in the school to donate plastic garbage cans with lids. Or you can ask local businesses to help you by donating bins or the money to buy them.

If you have the funds to purchase recycle bins, here are a few companies that manufacture recycled plastic containers
- ◆ Rescue Earth (800-275-0660, in El Cajon, California)
- ◆ RecyCal Supply Company (800-927-3873, in Murrieta, California)
- ◆ REC Systems of Wisconsin (414-642-3363)
- ◆ Energy and Environmental Consultants of Michigan (800-968-9998)

Label Your Bins

Clarity is very important when you are labeling recycle bins. We have found that making signs (as mentioned later), attaching them to a stick and extending them above the top of the bin, close to eye level, works best. How you label your bins will affect the success of your collection program.

Some of the companies listed in "Get the Bins You Need" make signs for their bins. Be sure to ask that these signs are included as part of your purchase. It doesn't hurt to have 2 or even 3 signs on each bin. Besides, professionally produced signs will give your bins a very official look.

But student-made signs have special charm. Many schools have laminating machines. You can ask the art teacher to have a group of students design and create signs, then laminate them. Now they are permanent, reusable and weather proof.

Assign Responsibilities for Bin Maintenance

It is important to monitor carefully the recycle bins for the first few weeks and after long school holidays. It is best to give this responsibility to the students. They can learn a lot from the responsibility, and cooperation will be higher among peers. Monitoring the bins is important. For instance, if someone puts an aluminum can into the plastic bin, the materials will be "co-mingled." Most recycle centers do not want the materials co-mingled; they want them sorted by category. Otherwise the materials can get contaminated. So it is important that, at least initially, the bins be watched carefully.

Those assigned to monitor the bins should consider the following:
   ◆ Are the bins in the right place?
   ◆ Are the bins clearly labeled?
   ◆ Are the bins being used properly?

One school had "Deputy—Recycle Squad" badges made for the students to wear while they monitored the bins. This worked very well because the badges gave a sense of belonging, responsibility and pride. The rest of the students felt more comfortable putting their things into the bins because, with the squad members overseeing, they knew they were doing it right.

Many schools have found it works well when each class or grade is given "ownership" of one area of the recycling program. The areas that different groups can be assigned to are
   ◆ Sign making
   ◆ Monitoring of bins for correct usage
   ◆ Transport of recyclables to the pickup area

The next step is to work out how the recyclables will get to the pickup area. It is important not to allow the bins to get too full because they may become too heavy to carry. Work closely with the custodial staff to be sure they understand this new system and your dedication to its success.

You must look at your campus map carefully and see the most logical system for collection. Remember that the maintenance/custodial staff already have a system for trash collection and that they are the experts to turn to for advice. Every school will have its own special way of working this out.

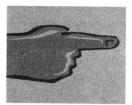

EDUCATE EVERYONE

None of this is going to happen unless the students, faculty, administration and maintenance staff are educated. Before you can begin educating, you must set up a meeting with all the people you think will support a campus recycling system. It will be crucial to have a representative from each of the following groups: the faculty, the parents and the student body. Then it is equally important to stay in touch with your administration and custodial staff. You should call yourselves something like the "Recycle Team" or the "Green Team."

At your first meeting, go through this chapter. Then your team will be ready to educate everyone else.

Keep in mind that it is always worthwhile to ask for ideas and suggestions, no matter whom you are speaking with. You will only benefit. You will get some good, helpful ideas and everyone will get more involved. Once a person participates in a conversation, she or he will feel a part of things. This is often called *empowering* or enabling others to join in a common cause. Anyone who feels a sense of ownership will work harder, and this is what you will need—dedication and involvement.

Besides empowering others and encouraging their participation, it is a very good idea to **reward those who help you along the way**. People love to be acknowledged for their work. Posting a list of names, announcing names and giving out awards will increase participation. This can be creative and fun.

Educating the Administration

It is important to let the school administration know that you want to start a campus recycling system. Some of the issues administrators may raise are discussed next.

Possible Unbudgeted Expenditures

Every school has a budget. One of your administrator's primary jobs is to operate the school within the budget. When you start talking about buying bins, contracting with haulers, and so on, the administration will immediately realize that this will take money. So it is important for you to have a clear idea of what your school's specific needs will be, that is, the number of bins that will be needed and the approximate hauling costs.

Try to establish right away whether the school will be able to fund a campus recycling system. If the answer is no, explain that there are several alternatives, including

- ◆ Involving parents
- ◆ Involving local businesses
- ◆ Coming to an agreement with a hauler
- ◆ Conducting campus aluminum can drives
- ◆ Organizing school car pooling
- ◆ Having bake sales
- ◆ Seeking help from an environmental organization. We have listed nationally based environment nonprofit organizations at the end of this chapter and in Chapter 18, plus you can check your local phone book for listings of those who are working in your area.

Campus Health and Safety

To ensure health and safety

- ◆ **Use gloves** when sorting through recycle bins. Not only can this be an unsanitary process, but there is a risk of cutting your hands on glass, aluminum cans or cracked plastic. (See the resource section of this chapter for a source for work gloves that fit children. You may also try the local garden store.)
- ◆ **Use bin lids.** Outdoor bins for food and drink containers need to be kept covered to avoid attracting insects and other pests.

How Recycling May Affect Your School

In considering the effect of the recycling system on other school systems ask the following questions:

- ◆ How will students find time in their already busy day to participate? The best way to handle this question is to have (if you don't already) a faculty member on your "Recycle Team." (See "Educating the Faculty.")
- ◆ How much help will be needed from the faculty members? Generally, administrators are reluctant to impose new responsibilities on their faculty, so this could be a touchy area. Be smart. Explain that you will need their guidance. Now is the time to mention that you want to be put on the agenda for the next faculty meeting.
- ◆ How much class time will be needed to introduce and maintain a recycling system? You will need 10 to 15 minutes at 2 school assemblies to introduce a recycling system and keep it in the minds of the students. Space these initial sessions within 3 to 4 weeks of each other. Then the upkeep should be as needed. Positive reinforcement will help if participation is low. Try to have constant announcements that tell how many trees are being saved, how much air pollution is being prevented and so on. The recycling center should be able to give you this information.

◆ **How will this new system affect established waste removal procedures?** If you already have a hauler, then you can answer this question. Although coordinating parents and/or school pooling can be big jobs, you must remember that others have had success. Recycling does become habit once it is established, as with any system. It's getting started that can be difficult.

Educating the Faculty

Once you have met with your school administration, you should meet with the faculty. The teachers will appreciate being informed before the student body is. So get yourself on the agenda for the next faculty meeting, or ask for a special meeting. Take examples of what can be recycled. It helps to have a hands-on demonstration. If it is too difficult to coordinate a meeting, circulate a memo.

Be sure to ask the teachers for their suggestions and ideas. Teachers are a valuable resource. Their advice can be very important and they will surely get more involved if they are asked for their thoughts. Remember that teachers are

◆ Old hands at planning activities.
◆ Familiar with school schedules, student schedules and their own schedules.
◆ The best people to ask about what is reasonable to expect of them and of the students.

Try to get at least one teacher on your recycle team as the faculty advisor. Plead for his or her help and explain how appreciative you will be. Once you are seen as serious, you are bound to get help.

Educating the Students

It is best to plan 2 presentations before the entire student body. These sessions should be within 3 or 4 weeks of each other. The first will be introductory; the second will be to review and point out any recurring problems. Don't forget to discuss the good, strong points and give out some compliments and thanks. Depending on the size of your school and the advice of your faculty or administration, you may need to address the student body in smaller groups or by grade levels.

At these assemblies you should bring examples of recyclables and labeled bins. This way everyone can get a mental picture of how things should be done. Explain the recycling system briefly and what steps are being taken to implement it. Be brief, clear and practical; this is not a subject that will hold students' attention for long. Let them know how they will be involved in making the program work. Always encourage questions.

It is important to keep your student body informed of any progress. It's a great idea to ask your recycle center for a "report card" every month. This information can be very useful and can contribute to the success of your campus recycle system. The report card will tell you, for example, how many trees your school has saved by recycling, how much air pollution was prevented by your schools' efforts and so on. People love to hear these kinds of facts. It makes them feel good about themselves—and they should! You might even try to set some goals as incentives for more participation.

Educating the Maintenance Crew

The maintenance crew or custodial staff will not be paid extra to do what will probably be more work. Keep in mind that their cooperation will be another vital element to the success of your recycling system. Therefore, you must be sure to show your appreciation whenever possible.

Ultimately, if the students help haul the recyclables to the pickup area, there will be much less garbage for them to transport. Try to convey this as well as the important educational process that they will be participating in with the rest of the school. Using some of the recycling facts to demonstrate how recycling really does make a difference through the energy and resources that will be saved can help convince them that the extra work is worth it.

Educating Parents

The students are the best educators for their parents, but you can help by placing an announcement in the school paper or sending home a note with the students that explains the new program. Invite them to join in. You may need their help to acquire bins and get the recyclables to the recycling center if you cannot find an adequate professional hauling program.

Troubleshooting

If you are working within a public school system and are finding resistance, remember you have representatives on the city council and in the state legislature. You can approach them with your plans. If it becomes necessary, call your local newspaper. The story of individuals, especially children or teenagers, trying to do something positive for the environment and meeting with resistance will surely grab their attention.

BUYING RECYCLED: CLOSING THE LOOP

Recycling is not the end of a process; it is the beginning of a new product. The cycle of recycling isn't complete until a new product is made from the recycled materials and that new product is used again. The used product that is remanufactured into the material for a new product is considered postconsumer waste.

The federal government buys more paper than any other institution in the country. In October 1993, President Clinton ordered the government to begin purchasing paper with high levels of postconsumer content. The executive order requires federal agencies to buy a variety of papers, such as computer, writing, copier and book paper, with at least a 20 percent postconsumer content .

Recycled Paper News, Vol. 4, No. 4, 1993.

The whole point of recycling is to make the most use of our natural resources, such as aluminum, paper and glass. Even plastic is made from one of our most precious natural resources—oil. When we leave our bottles, cans, paper and other materials at a recycling center, it's not the end for them. The recycled materials are cleaned and delivered to a manufacturer that uses them for new products.

It is important to realize that our part of the cycle doesn't end when we take our materials to the recycling center. **It is up to us to make sure we rebuy our recyclables after they've been made into new products.** When we buy products made from recycled materials using postconsumer waste, we help get the most use of our natural resources and we convince more manufacturers that we (consumers) want products made from recycled materials. This is also called **completing the cycle or closing the loop**. We should even write to manufacturers to let them know we prefer reused materials to new materials.

Right now, some manufacturers are worried that consumers (shoppers) won't buy products made from used or old materials. But aluminum, glass, paper, plastic and other materials are as good as new once they've been cleaned and processed. Manufacturers are also waiting to see how consistent the flow of materials from recycling centers will be. Before they invest in making their products with postconsumer waste, they want to be sure that the public is committed to recycling and buying recycled products.

Another good reason to buy products made from recycled materials is to help pay for our community collection programs, which are expensive to operate. Much of the funding for the programs comes from selling the recyclables/postconsumer materials to manufacturers. If manufacturers don't buy the materials, there will not be enough money to pay for the collection programs.

We need to reuse, recycle, remanufacture and re-buy.

To identify products that are made from recycled materials, look for labels that say something like the following:
- "Made from recycled materials."
- "This carton is made from recycled paperboard."
- "Contains 65 percent postconsumer waste."

Do not rely on the 3 "chasing arrows" recycling symbol for an indication of recycled content. This only symbolizes that the product is technically recyclable.

Some recycled materials are called **preconsumer materials**. These are manufacturing scraps that were never made into products for consumers. Buying products made from **postconsumer waste** is the best way to get the most from our natural resources and support our local collection programs.

RESOURCES

Hotlines

EPA National Solid Waste Hotline
800-424-9346

Steel Can Recycling Institute Hotline
800-876-SCRI

SWICH
800-67-SWICH
EPA funded information clearinghouse on recycling.

Brochures/Papers/Reports

Bergen County Recycling Marshal's Program for Elementary Schools
B.C.U.A. Resource Recovery Department
P.O. Box 122
Foot of Mehrhof Road
Little Ferry, NJ 07643
201-641-2552

Close the Loop: Guide to Recycled Products
Pennsylvania Resources Council
P.O. Box 88
Media, PA 19063
215-565-9131

Coming Full Circle: Successful Recycling Today
Environmental Defense Fund
257 Park Avenue South
New York, NY 10010
212-505-2100

Engines of Recycling: Strategies for Using Recycling to Drive Community Economic Development
Californians Against Waste Foundation
Recycling Economic Development Project
926 J Street, Suite 606
Sacramento, CA 95814
916-443-8317

Environmentally Sound Paper Overview: The Essential Issues
Conservatree
10 Lombard Street, Suite 250
San Francisco, CA 94111
415-433-1000

Guide to Recycled Products
Pennsylvania Resources Council
P.O. Box 88
Media, PA 19063
215-565-9131

How to Recycle Waste Paper
American Paper Institute
1111 19th Street NW, Suite 800
Washington, DC 20036
800-878-8878

How to Set Up a Local Program to Recycle Used Oil
U.S. Environmental Protection Agency
Solid Waste and Emergency Response
401 M Street SW
Washington, DC 20460
202-260-4610

How to Set Up a School Recycling Program
American Plastics Council
1275 K Street NW
Washington, DC 20005
800-2-HELP-90

Mining Urban Wastes: The Potential for Recycling

Worldwatch Paper 76
Worldwatch Institute
1776 Massachusetts Avenue NW
Washington, DC 20036
202-452-1999

1989-90 School Waste Reduction and Recycling Awards: Program Summary

Washington State Department of Ecology
Waste Reduction, Recycling and Litter
Control Program
P.O. Box 47600
Olympia, WA 98504-7600
206-407-6000

NAPCOR Community Guidebook

NAPCOR
100 North Tryon Street, Suite 3770
Charlotte, NC 28202
704-358-8882

No Time to Waste: Starting Waste Reduction, Recycling and Reuse Programs to Stop Incineration and Landfilling

New York Public Interest Research Group, Inc.
9 Murray Street
New York, NY 10007
212-349-6460

101 Practical Tips for Home and Work Recycling

The Windstar Foundation
2317 Snowmass Creek Road
Snowmass, CO 81654
303-927-4777

Paper: Linking People and Nature

American Paper Institute, Inc.
1250 Connecticut Avenue, Suite 360
Washington, DC 20036
800-878-8878

Paper Recycling Handbook

California Integrated Waste Management
Board
8800 Cal Center Drive
Sacramento, CA 95826
916-255-2296

Plastics in Perspective: Answers to Your Questions About Plastics in the Environment

American Plastics Council
1275 K Street NW, Suite 400
Washington, DC 20005
800-2-HELP-90

Recycling...the Answer to Our Garbage Problem

Citizen's Clearinghouse for Hazardous
Wastes, Inc.
P.O. Box 926
Arlington, VA 22216
703-237-2249

Recycling as Economic Development

Take It Back Foundation
15115 1/2 Sunset Boulevard, Suite C
Pacific Palisades, CA 90272
310-459-2377

Recycling Facts and Figures

Wisconsin Department of Natural Resources
Bureau of Information and Education
P.O. Box 7921
Madison, WI 53707
608-266-2711

Recycling: Getting Started

The Local Government Commission
909 12th Street, Suite 205
Sacramento, CA 95814
916-448-1198

Recycling Is More than Collections: Questions and Concerns from the Ground Up
League of Women Voters
1730 M Street NW
Washington, DC 20036
202-429-1965

Recycling at School
California Department of Conservation
Division of Recycling
1025 P Street, Room 401
Sacramento, CA 95814
916-323-3508

Recycling in School: A Teaching Tool
Pennsylvania Resources Council
P.O. Box 88
Media, PA 19063
215-565-9131

Recycling Works! State and Local Solutions to Solid Waste Management Problems
U.S. Environmental Protection Agency
Office of Solid Waste
401 M Street SW
Washington, DC 20460
202-260-4610

Report on Activities
Institute for Local Self-Reliance
2425 18th Street NW
Washington, DC 20009
202-232-4108

The Road to Recycling: New York City School Recycling Manual, the Complete "How-To" Guide
Environmental Action Coalition
625 Broadway
New York, NY 10012
212-677-1601

School Recycling Programs: A Handbook for Educators
U.S. Environmental Protection Agency
401 M Street SW
Washington, DC 20460
202-260-4610

Setting Up a Solid Waste Recycling Program in Schools
McDonald's Education Resource Center
3620 Swenson Avenue
P.O. Box 8002
St. Charles, IL 60174-7307
800-627-7646

Shopper's Guide to Recycled Products
Californians Against Waste Foundation
926 J Street, Suite 606
Sacramento, CA 95814
916-443-8317

The Solid Waste Mess: What Should We Do with the Garbage?
North American Association for
Environmental Education
Publications and Member Services Office
P.O. Box 400
Troy, OH 45373
513-676-2514

Solid Waste Recycling
Engineering Professional Development
University of Wisconsin—Madison
432 North Lake Street
Madison, WI 53706
608-262-0493

Waste: Choices for Communities
Concern, Inc.
1794 Colombia Road NW
Washington, DC 20009
202-328-8160

What You Should Know About Recycling
Channing L. Bete Co., Inc.
200 State Road
South Deerfield, MA 01373
413-665-7611

Books

Beyond 25 Percent: Materials Recovery Comes of Age
Teresa Allan, Brenda Platt and David Morris
Institute for Local Self-Reliance, 1989
2425 18th Street NW
Washington, DC 20009

Beyond 40 Percent: Record Setting Recyling and Composting Programs
Brenda Platt et al.
Institute for Local Self-Reliance, 1990
2425 18th Street NW
Washington, DC 20009

Collecting, Processing and Marketing Recyclables
Biocycle Staff
JG Press, 1990
419 State Avenue
Emmaus, PA 18049

15 Simple Things Californians Can Do to Recycle
Earthworks Group
EarthWorks Press, 1991
1400 Shattuck Avenue, # 25
Berkeley, CA 94709

Recycled Papers: The Essential Guide
Claudia G. Thompson
The MIT Press, 1992
Massachusetts Institute of Technology
Cambridge, MA 02142

Recycled Products Guide
M & F Case Company, 1991
335 Barton Street, P.O. Box 520
Pawtucket, RI 02860

Recycler's Handbook
Earthworks Group
EarthWorks Press, 1990
1400 Shattuck Avenue, # 25
Berkeley, CA 94709

Recycling in America
Debi Kimball
National Conference of State Legislatures, 1992
1560 Broadway, Suite 700
Denver, CO 80202

Recycling and Incineration: Evaluating the Choices
Richard Denison and John Ruston
Island Press, 1990
1718 Connecticut Avenue NW, Suite 300
Washington, DC 20009

Recycling Sourcebook
Thomas Cichonski
Gale Research, 1992
645 Griswold, Suite 835
Detroit, MI 48226-4094

Success in Recycling
Geoffrey Kessler and Stephen Dierkes
The Kessler Exchange, 1991
8910 Quartz Avenue
Northridge, CA 91324

Taking Out the Trash
Jennifer Carless
Island Press, 1992
1718 Connecticut Avenue NW, Suite 300
Washington, DC 20009

Books for Youth

Aunt Ippy's Museum of Junk
Rodney A. Greenblat
HarperCollins, 1991
10 East 53rd Street
New York, NY 10022

Earth to Matthew
Paula Danziger
Bantam Doubleday Dell, 1991
666 Fifth Avenue
New York, NY 10036

50 Simple Things Kids Can Do to Recycle
Earthworks Group
EarthWorks Press, 1994
1400 Shattuck Avenue, #25
Berkeley, CA 94709

From Trash to Treasure
Liza Alexander
Western Publishing Company, 1993
Golden Books
Racine, WI 53404

Here Comes the Recycling Truck!
Meyer Seltzer
Albert Whitman and Company, 1992
6340 Oakton Street
Morton Grove, IL 60053

Let's Talk Trash: The Kid's Book About Recycling
Kelly McQueen
Waterfront Books, 1991
85 Crescent Road
Burlington, VT 05401

Likeable Recyclables
Linda Schwartz
Learning Works, 1992
P.O. Box 6187
Santa Barbara, CA 93160

Recycle!
Gail Gibbons
Little, Brown and Company, 1992
34 Beacon Street
Boston, MA 02108

Recycling
Joan Kalbacken and Emilie Lepthien
Childrens Press, 1991
5440 North Cumberland Avenue
Chicago, IL 60656

Tons of Trash
Joan Rattner Heilman
Avon Books, 1992
1350 Avenue of the Americas
New York, NY 10019

Trash Bash
Judy Delton
Bantam Doubleday Dell, 1992
666 Fifth Avenue
New York, NY 10103

Where Does Our Garbage Go?
Joan Bowden
Doubleday, 1992
666 Fifth Avenue
New York, NY 10103

Individuals/Companies/ Organizations

Ambiance International
15327 Sunset Boulevard
Pacific Palisades, CA 90272
310-459-7138
Manufactures the Paper Pen, which has a barrel made of 100 percent recycled paper. The fittings are molded from recycled plastic materials, free of cadmium and lead. The pen is refillable.

American Recycling Market

P.O. Box 577
Ogdensburg, NY 13669
800-267-0707 or 315-471-0707
Produces "The Official Recycled Products Guide" (published twice a year) and "The Reporter" (a monthly newsletter). The guide is a source (thousands of listings) for the procurement of recycled products. "The Reporter" provides updated information on the recycling markets.

Californians Against Waste Foundation

926 J Street, Suite 606
Sacramento, CA 95814
916-443-5422
A nonprofit organization dedicated to creating a sustainable economy by promoting the reuse, recycling and renewal of our natural resources.

Dixon Ticonderoga Company

2600 Maitland Circle Parkway, Suite 200
Maitland, FL 32794-5106
800-824-9430
Produces Enviro Stiks, which contain only approved timber from renewable forests with 10 percent less wood than conventional pencils. Has a nontoxic, lacquer-free finish. Check for this at local stationery stores.

Earth Care Paper

966 Mazzoni Street
Ukiah, CA 95482-3471
800-347-0070
Earth Care has the widest and best selection of what's available in recycled office and school products.

Eberhard Faber

American EcoWriter
P.O. Box 2630
Lewisburg, TN 37091-9987
615-359-1583
The EcoWriter barrel is made from recycled newspaper and cardboard fibers instead of the traditional wood. Strength and durability are the same.

Eco Tech Recycled Products

14241 60th Street North
Clearwater, Florida 34620
800-780-5353
Catalog with a wide assortment of products made from recycled materials. Included are desktop accessories, binders/folders, office paper, paper products, flooring, parks and recreation equipment. The product descriptions list the amount of recycled content and postconsumer waste.

Gardener's Supply Company

128 Intervale Road
Burlington, VT 05401-2850
802-863-1700
Has work gloves for children ages 3 to 13.

Institute for Local Self-Reliance

2425 18th Street NW
Washington, DC 20009
202-232-4108
The institute works extensively in urban areas, focusing on the material, financial and human resources available for community economic development. It joins technical ingenuity with a sense of community to establish sustainable, environmentally sound forms of consumption and production.

National Recycling Coalition

1101 30th Street NW, Suite 305
Washington, DC 20007
202-625-6406
A coalition of recycling industries, government representatives, nonprofit groups and individuals that provide information on recycling and source reduction. NRC also promotes sound recycling laws and regulations.

Pimby Co

P.O. Box 240
Purdys, NY 10578
914-277-4315
Carry bulletin boards made from rubber tires and pens, pen holders, push pins, rulers, scissors and so on made with 70 percent postconsumer and 30 percent preconsumer content.

Recy-CAL Supply Company

40880B County Center Drive, Suite P
Temecula, CA 92591
909-695-5225
This company offers a full line of recycling containers. Its product line ranges from desktop/deskside trays, stackable bins and mobile recycling carts to recycling bags, shredders and accessories. Recy-CAL strives to sell products that have high postconsumer recycled content.

Chapter 13

How to Take Action

Chapter 13
CONTENTS

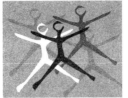

INTRODUCTION

One person can make a difference. It is easy to feel powerless because we are removed from our government and from the businesses that provide the products we depend on or enjoy. But many of the most significant changes in history have been the result of individuals who believed they could make a difference. Sometimes one person can effect change; other times many are required. So it is vital to realize that your voice counts and will be heard. **You can make a difference.**

This chapter's purpose is to discuss your potential as an individual to effect change. We want to provide you with some very basic guidelines, to empower you, so that you can influence those in positions of power.

One of the most important things to remember is that what you say and the way you say it will carry the most power if you speak from your heart. If you use your own words and personal experiences, you can't go wrong.

Remember too that solutions are not reached overnight. There is always a process and every step along the way, no matter how small, is essential to reach the final goal. By speaking out you will be an important part of the process of change.

> "**N**ever doubt that a small, highly committed group of individuals can change the world; indeed it is the only thing that ever has."
>
> Margaret Mead

RULES OF THUMB FOR EFFECTIVE COMMUNICATIONS

You can influence people in power by putting your ideas in writing. Letter writing is one of the most effective and least expensive ways to make your opinions count. If you don't feel you have time to sit down and write, a phone call is better than nothing. However, a phone call does not carry the same impact as a letter or provide a record of your efforts.

A form letter may be used but it is better to do your own. Writing a letter in your own words allows for a more accurate representation of how you feel and why. Moreover, it will be satisfying.

The following are some basic guidelines to ensure that your letter has maximum impact:

◆ **Be brief.** Be direct and to the point. Limit your letter to 1 page. Attach a news clip or concise fact sheet if appropriate.

◆ **Be specific.** Focus on a single issue. If you are writing to a member of Congress about a specific bill, include the bill number or a clear description of the issue.

◆ **Be personal.** Use your own words. Explain how the issue affects you, your family and your community.

◆ **Be informative.** If you have expertise or specific knowledge, share it. Your knowledge and experience are valuable.

◆ **Be constructive.** Be courteous. Don't just criticize. Give advice on how to change things for the better. Compliment the person you are writing to, if you can, on positive action taken in the past.

◆ **Always check your facts.** One inaccurate statement can invalidate your whole letter.

◆ **Be timely.** Make sure your message is received in time to make a difference.

◆ **Be selective.** Send your letter to the most appropriate person(s). When writing to members of Congress, stick to your own representatives.

◆ **Be neat.** Make sure your letter is legible. If no one can read it, your opinion isn't going to count.

◆ **Ask to be kept informed.** This shows your commitment and ensures that your letter has been duly noted.

◆ **Send others who support your opinion(s) copies of your letter(s).** It is important that others who are taking action know about you and your efforts.

> "Today, because of communications technology, children know as much as the wisest nobles knew in the past. When people were illiterate, they had to elect the lawyer or doctor or whoever had access to information or knowledge to represent them in government. But today the peasant has more information than the politicians, who lose their time in sterile partisan fighting. This kind of democracy is out of date."
>
> Jacques Cousteau

Get your whole class or school involved in a letter-writing campaign. Multiply the effect of your efforts by the number of students and/or faculty who participate. Involve them in the process; brainstorm ideas and vote on favorite topics.

You can simplify the guidelines as follows:

◆ Writers should introduce themselves and the problem they are writing about. They should explain what motivated them to sit down and write a letter.

◆ Back up your argument with facts.

◆ Offer solutions.

◆ Don't be afraid to use emotion to get your point across. You can be passionate without getting carried away.

◆ Express hope and ask to be kept informed.

◆ File copies of your letters and send copies to appropriate environmental groups for their records. If you are not sure which organization you should contact, please contact us at the Center for Environmental Education. We can help connect you with the right group.

◆ Send a copy to your local newspaper. Also, have your school newspaper cover the issue.

Sample Letter

Date
Name
Address

Dear Supermarket Manager or Restaurant Manager:

I am a 6th grade student at the local public elementary school. Our class has decided to write letters to our local businesses voicing our thoughts and feelings about an important issue. We are unhappy because it is so difficult to find organically grown produce in our community.

In our research, we found that most pesticides used on the food we eat and on the food that is grown for the livestock (cows, pigs, lambs and chickens) that we eat have never been tested. Many ingredients used in pesticides may cause cancer, birth defects and/or gene mutations. This is very scary for us. We think that we should be able to go to our local markets and buy food that does not have pesticides on it.

These pesticides also leach into our groundwater, so we not only eat them, but drink them as well. We also discovered that chemical fertilizers wash into our rivers, ponds and lakes and promote algae growth. If too much algae grows in these waterways, it chokes and kills fish and other aquatic life.

We have learned that there are a growing number of farmers who are trying to grow fruits and vegetables organically, without the use of pesticides or chemical fertilizers. We are writing to urge you to support these farmers by asking for organic produce.

Please call the Organic Foods Production Association of North America at 413-774-7511 today. Or write to them at P.O. Box 1078, Greenfield, MA 01301.

Thank you for your consideration and please keep me informed of your plans to provide organic foods.

Sincerely,

Your Name
Address

MAKE GOVERNMENT WORK FOR YOU

Politicians are very sensitive to what their constituents think. Since very few people take the time to write, your letter will represent hundreds of others. Legislators often vote according to public opinion. They listen to voters, especially those who write to them. It is their job to keep track of their constituents' views on important issues. They want to know why you are concerned and what you would like to see changed.

Government Fact Sheet

Always know your government officials' addresses and phone numbers. Be sure to have the correct spellings of their names. Keep a list of the following:

Local

✔ The county or city manager or mayor.

✔ Your local government representative (city council, county supervisor and so on).

✔ Dates of local elections.

✔ The candidates.

State

✔ The governor.

✔ The names of your state's other elected officials
   (attorney general, lieutenant governor and so on).

✔ Your state senator.

✔ Your state delegate, representative or assembly member.

   Get addresses and phone numbers for both State Capitol and local offices.

Federal

✔ The President and Vice-President.

✔ Your senators.

✔ The congressional district you live in.

✔ Your congressional representative.

   Get addresses and phone numbers for both Washington and local offices.

Although elected officials may not read your letters personally, their assistants will. Your views will be noted and any new information you provide will be passed on. Keep in mind that only 5 percent of congressional representatives are educated on any one issue, so don't feel as though you are writing to an expert. You may know more (and care more) about an issue than the representative does. If you speak from your heart, you can be sure that your passion will be noticed.

Don't get discouraged if your advice is not taken. If you receive a negative or noncommittal response, don't be afraid to write back. Politicians can always be persuaded to change their minds if enough constituents are persistent. **A survey of congressional staffers ranked spontaneous constituent mail first in effectiveness.** Telephone calls ranked second.

Pick up that pen and paper today and write your president, senator, congressperson or local elected official. Remember, they work for you!

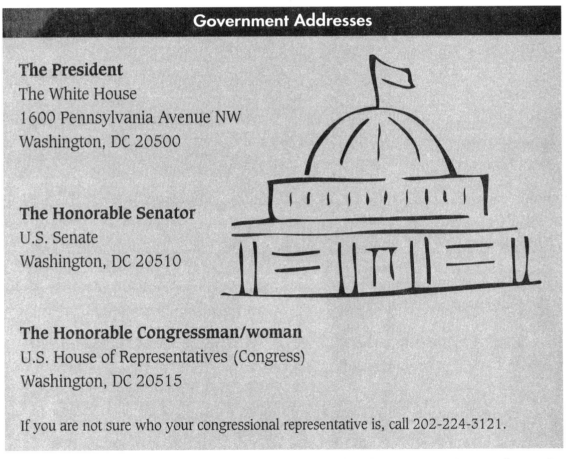

Government Addresses

The President
The White House
1600 Pennsylvania Avenue NW
Washington, DC 20500

The Honorable Senator
U.S. Senate
Washington, DC 20510

The Honorable Congressman/woman
U.S. House of Representatives (Congress)
Washington, DC 20515

If you are not sure who your congressional representative is, call 202-224-3121.

Be an active part of your local community. Get to know the environmental issues facing the community. Know who the people in power on these issues are (e.g., county board of supervisors, city council, department of transportation, coastal commissions) and write to them. See your white "community access" pages at the front of your local phone book.

CORPORATE ENVIRONMENT ABUSERS

Some of the worst environmental offenses are committed by big business. Look down the aisles in your local grocery store. Is all that packaging necessary? Find out if restaurants you go to recycle their waste. Find the problems and go to those who can do something. Start at the top; track down the company CEO or owner. Remember, every consumer is important to any business. Your letter could mean dollars lost or gained.

Sample C.E.O. Letter

Date

Name
Address

Dear:

While shopping at your store, I was unable to find any environmentally friendly cleaning products on your shelves. Most of the cleaners your store supplies contain harmful ingredients, such as toxic chemicals, phosphates and petrochemical by-products.

Cleaners containing these ingredients are dangerous to public health and the environment in manufacturing, use and disposal.

There are many effective nontoxic cleaning products on the market today. I have attached a list of suggested brands with this letter. I urge you to contact suppliers of these products and stock them in your stores.

Please give your customers an opportunity to buy products that help protect our environment and human health.

Thank you for your consideration and keep me informed of your plans.

Sincerely,

Your Name
Address

Letters that You Can Write to Reduce Waste

Check your daily mail. Write to all the companies that are sending unsolicited catalogs, advertisements or solicitations and ask to be taken off their mailing list immediately. Be sure to include the mailing label so they have your mailing code.

About 90 percent of the direct marketing companies in the United States belong to Direct Marketing. Write to them and request they remove your name from all mailing lists that are bought, sold or bartered.

Mail Preference Service
Direct Marketing Association
11 West 42nd Street
P.O. Box 3861
New York, NY 10163-3861

Sample: Get Off Junk Mail Lists

Date

Mail Preference Service
Direct Marketing Association
11 West 42nd Street
P.O. Box 3861
New York, NY 10163-3861

Dear Sir or Madam,

Please help us save trees. Americans receive 2 million tons of junk mail every year. The average American spends 8 months of his or her life just opening junk or unsolicited mail.

We are trying to stop all unsolicited mail immediately. Therefore, kindly remove our names from your mailing list. If your company sells, barters or gives away its mailing list, please remove our names from that list as well.

Your prompt attention to this matter is appreciated.

Thank you,

P.S. For your convenience, the mailing label is attached.

When you purchase a product that is unnecessarily overpackaged, write to the company. Let the company know you are looking for products without packaging or that are packaged in materials that have postconsumer recycled content. Be sure also to mention that these packaging materials should also be recyclable.

Sample: Overpackageing Letter

Date

Name
Address

Dear: (Company President or Customer Services Department)
Recently, I had _____ on my shopping list. When I found your product in the store, I was shocked by the tremendous amount of overpackaging. It is a statement about your company that I find very distasteful and I believe that many other customers share my concerns.

Americans are very wasteful. We are filling up our landfills with unnecessary product packaging and your company is contributing to the problem.

Please take steps to reduce the packaging of your products and to use recycled materials. By cutting down on waste, you will help conserve our precious natural resources. Until you change your packaging, I will buy products from other companies.

Thank you for your consideration.

Sincerely,

Your Name
Address

It is also a good idea to write those companies that are using resources efficiently and decreasing pollution in their business practices. Hearing positive responses from concerned citizens will let these companies know that consumers support their actions.

One positive example of big corporations trying to make less waste is provided by the two-way billing envelope. These envelopes have an extra flap tucked inside that can be used and sealed for a return mailing. This means that no envelopes are thrown out and waste is reduced. These are the kinds of changes everyone needs to make in order for our precious natural resources to continue to provide for our life-styles. Every bit will help.

USE THE MEDIA

There are many ways to use the media to further your cause. Letters to the editor in *The Los Angeles Times* alone are worth $3,000 in advertising space. Keep the local press informed of the environmental actions you and your school are taking. **Schools and students taking action are *always* newsworthy.**

Some basic guidelines for writing an effective "Letter to an Editor" are
- ◆ Share your concerns or opinions about the subject that you choose.
- ◆ Explain what prompted your concerns.
- ◆ Explain what the outcome will be if the situation isn't changed.
- ◆ Know exactly what you want to communicate to the reader.
- ◆ Know the facts.
- ◆ Propose solutions or alternatives and back them up.

Sample: Letter to the Editor

Date

Newspaper
Address

Dear Editor:

Every day, more than 62 million newspapers are printed in the United States. That's a lot of trees! The paper industry uses more than 26 million trees every year just to manufacture our Sunday papers. About 17 trees are needed to make 1 ton of newsprint. This process also uses 28 million Btus of energy, consumes 24,000 gallons of water and generates 176 pounds of solid waste and 120 pounds of water and air pollutants. When we throw away our newspapers, every ton takes up 3 cubic yards of landfill space for decades.

I feel strongly that all publishers should use recycled newsprint instead of virgin stock. Recycled newsprint reduces waste, preserves our forests, decreases pollution and saves energy and valuable landfill space. I urge you to follow the lead of the Chicago Sun-Times and the Los Angeles Times and print the _____ on recycled paper.

Thank you for your consideration.

Sincerely,

Your Name
Address
Telephone Number

Communicating information to the public requires knowing how to work with the media. Below are some tips for getting news coverage for your activities.

Media Tips

Writing a News Release
✔ Be brief and clear, 1 to 2 pages, typed and double-spaced.
✔ Give your release a title and a release date at the top of the page.
✔ Create a "hook" to make your story newsworthy.
✔ Incorporate a few quotes and a contact person.
✔ Send your release to the city editor of your newspaper and the assignment editor at radio and TV stations a few days before your event.

Organizing a News Conference
✔ Schedule your news conference early in the day (between 10:00 a.m. and noon is best).
✔ Try to have it on a slow news day.
✔ Hand out a press packet. This should include a copy of the press release and detailed background information about your group and your campaign.
✔ Be prepared. Plan for parking and security, have name tags, a podium, refreshments, visuals, restroom facilities and someone to greet and sign in those who attend.
✔ Make reminder phone calls to reporters the day before the event. Be brief and enthusiastic.
✔ Don't be discouraged if only a few reporters show up. No matter what the outcome, any news coverage will do a lot to help your efforts!

Pitch Your Story
✔ A news conference is not always the best way to get coverage for your event. Pitch your story to a specific reporter, editor or producer.
✔ Write a good pitch letter. Keep it short and interesting.
✔ Include background information on your group and your campaign.
✔ Follow up with a phone call.

Create a portfolio of news clips when stories start appearing!

Periodicals

Letter to the Editor
Time
Time/Life Building
Rockefeller Center
New York, NY 10020
Fax: 212-522-0601

Letter to the Editor
Newsweek
444 Madison Avenue
New York, NY 10022
Fax: 212-350-4120

Voices
U.S. News & World Report
2400 N Street NW
Washington, DC 20037-1196
Fax: 202-955-2685

Letter to the Editor
USA Today
1000 Wilson Boulevard
Arlington, VA 22229
Fax: 703-247-3134

Television

Audience Services
ABC
1330 Avenue of the Americas
New York, NY 10019

Audience Services
CBS
51 West 52nd Street
New York, NY 10019

Audience Services
NBC
30 Rockefeller Plaza
New York, NY 10019

Cable News Network (CNN)
1050 Techwood Drive NW
Atlanta, GA 30318

Public Broadcasting Company
Corporate Information
1320 Braddock Place
Alexandria, VA 22324-1698

When sending or faxing a letter to the editor, be sure to include your telephone number in case the editor has questions. Otherwise it may be impossible to print it.

Resources

Meaningful public involvement in decisions is possible only if all ideas are allowed to compete in the media marketplace. Started in 1976 by Professor Carl Jensen as an exercise for his mass media class at California's Sonoma State University, an annual national media research project announces its Top 10 Censored Stories for each year.

To nominate a story or to obtain more information, contact

Project Censored
Sonoma State University
Rohnert Park, CA 94928
707-664-2500

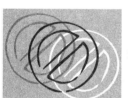

BOYCOTTING AND OTHER ACTIONS

Don't be quiet. If you know of an environmental atrocity or problem, spread the word! If writing letters doesn't lead to meaningful change, consider more drastic action. Before you make up your mind, be sure to consider the following:

◆ Do you have the time and energy to make a serious commitment?

◆ Do you have the support of others? Can you get your school's students, faculty, administration and parents to commit? Will other local schools join forces with you?

◆ Is there an environmental organization that would be willing to help you all the way?

◆ Do you have an articulate person(s) to elect as spokesperson(s)?

◆ Will you need funds to organize a campaign? If so, how much? Do you have any ideas for raising funds (e.g., bake sales, yard sales, art and craft fairs are some ideas that are certainly worth discussing).

Fundraising Ideas

✔ Sponsor fairs, dances, talent shows, auctions, movie screenings, car washes, and so on.

✔ Collect cans for recycling or sell T-shirts.

✔ Run a concession stand at school events. Sometimes restaurants and stores will donate food items if you give them free advertising.

✔ Groups can raise money from yard sales. Have members clean out their garages, bedrooms and attics of toys, clothes, books and other items that are collecting dust.

✔ Local businesses or people may donate money, time and/or materials to help with your project. Examples include printers and art stores. Businesses may offer the use of phones, fax machines and copiers.

✔ Good sources for funding requests are government agencies, corporations and foundations. Applying for grants can be time-consuming but worthwhile if you receive the money you asked for. The reference desk at the library should have information on foundation directories. Your city council member can help identify government funding and your local chamber of commerce can give you a list of corporations in your state.

Once you have really weighed the pros and cons, if you decide to persist, you must warn the company of your intentions to boycott if steps are not taken to rectify the situation. State your intentions and your goals clearly. Give them a chance to respond. Be fair and understand that businesses have concerns that must be taken seriously. Listen and consider a progressive plan of compromise where improvements are made on a specific schedule. Corporations are not always able to make sweeping changes quickly, but they may be willing to look ahead 2, 5 or 10 years and promise what they feel is possible.

Be sure to point out that the company has a choice. It can choose to receive good or bad publicity. You and your supporters hold the key to this corporation's future success. Suggest that the situation may be resolved happily if the company is willing to sit down and talk. Make it clear that you are reasonable and have good intentions.

Don't be fanatical. Hold on to your most important points, but, at the same time, prepare yourself and others to expect to compromise. Meeting in the middle is fine. Keep in mind that cooperation is something we have all tried to teach our children since preschool.

Get any agreement in writing. Have the owner or CEO sign it and make a media event of it. Say good things about the company if that is possible. Any step toward a safer future for the environment is worth being announced and celebrated.

If you are considering a boycott, the box to the right gives some suggestions to keep in mind.

Boycott Tips

◆ A boycott is never a first step. Try other actions first. Meet with officials of the company before you begin the boycott. Explain the changes you want from them, and start a boycott only if they are unwilling to make those changes.

◆ Boycotts rarely succeed right away. If you start a boycott, expect a long struggle. And starting it isn't enough. You'll need to keep up your efforts for weeks, months or longer to keep the boycott going.

◆ You'll need to explain the boycott over and over again as you convince more and more people to stop doing business with the company. Produce leaflets that explain why you are boycotting and what changes you want before you end the boycott.

◆ Boycotts are hard on a company's workers. They deserve an explanation of why you are boycotting. And don't be surprised if they respond to your actions with anger.

◆ Ask people to sign pledges that they will boycott the company until it makes the changes you want. Collect as many of these pledges as you can throughout the boycott. They are added ammunition in your efforts to make the company change its ways.

Source: Paul Fleisher, *Changing Our World: A Handbook for Young Activists,* Zephyr Press, Tucson, AZ, 1993, p. 114.

> *"Congress shall make no law... abridging the freedom of speech, or of the press; or the right of the people peaceably to assemble, and to petition the government for a redress of grievances."*

First Amendment, Constitution of the United States, 1791.

A petition is a piece of paper with signatures showing group support for your position. It's a great way to prove to school administrators, elected officials or corporate representatives that many people share your views. Below are some tips that will help you petition successfully.

Petitioning Tips

✔ Use the sample petition on the next page to gather signatures.

✔ Depending on your issue, good places to petition include your school, shopping malls or outside of theaters and grocery stores.

✔ If you are petitioning door to door, always have an adult with you. Never go alone!

✔ Remember that some people may not want to sign your petition. That's okay. Be polite and move on to the next person.

✔ Photocopy all pages of the petition after collecting signatures, in case the original is lost.

Sample Petition

Dear _____

We the undersigned believe _____

_____

and urge you to _____

_____

We oppose any measure that would endanger our environment.

AGREED TO BY THE FOLLOWING PEOPLE:

Name	Address/School	Phone
1.		
2.		
3.		
4.		
5.		
6.		
7.		
8.		
9.		
10.		
11.		
12.		

Source: Barbara A. Lewis, *The Kid's Guide to Social Action*, Free Spirit Publishing, Minneapolis, MN, 1991, p. 162.

The efforts made by America's young activists are starting to be recognized by organizations and government agencies. Some examples are:

Be Rewarded for Your Actions!

The President's Environmental Youth Awards Program

U.S. Environmental Protection Agency
Communications and Public Affairs
Washington, DC 20460
202-260-2080, or your regional EPA office.

Sebastian's Little Green Creative Arts Project

6109 DeSoto Avenue, Department C
Woodland Hills, CA 91367
818-999-5112 extension 260

Arbor Day Awards

National Arbor Day Foundation
211 North 12th Street
401 M Street SW
Lincoln, NE 68508
402-474-56-55

The Giraffe Project

P.O. Box 759
Langley, WA 98260
800-344-TALL
(206-221-7989 in
Washington state)

For more awards programs see Chapter 18.

RESOURCES

Action Alerts are a form of communication provided by many environmental organizations to their members in an effort to give them a concise account of the latest-breaking news/issues. They will often supply a sample letter and will always provide a name and address to contact regarding these issues. If there is any uncertainty, please feel free to call the Center for Environmental Education (CEE). We will get the necessary information and help make sense of it.

There are some very good general environmental publications that will keep you up-to-date with environmental issues. You will read about many things that are *sure* to drive you to your desk with pen and paper to **write**!

Hotlines

Federal Switchboard
202-245-6999

Legislation Hotline
202-225-1772
To find out about the status of legislation and dates of hearings you can call this number.

President's Message Line
202-456-1414

U.S. Capitol
202-224-3121

Brochures/Papers/Reports

Access EPA
U.S. Environmental Protection Agency
401 M Street SW
Washington, DC 20460
202-260-4610

Ahead of the Curve: Shaping New Solutions to Environmental Problems
Environmental Defense Fund
257 Park Avenue South
New York, NY 10010
212-505-2100

An Attainable Global Perspective
The American Forum for Global Education
120 Wall Street, Suite 2600
New York, NY 10005
212-742-8232

Conservation Can't Wait: How You Live, What You Do, What You Buy Makes a Difference
Marine World Africa USA
Marine World Parkway
Vallejo, CA 94589
707-644-4000

Earth Action Guide
Youth for Environmental Sanity
706 Fredrick Street
Santa Cruz, CA 95062
408-459-9344

Environmental Actions: Simple Things Women Are Doing to Save the Earth
Earthworks Press
1400 Shattuck Avenue, #25
Berkeley, CA 94709
510-841-5866

Investing in Children: Worldwatch Paper 64
Worldwatch Institute
1776 Massachusetts Avenue NW
Washington, DC 20036
202-452-1999

League of Conservation Voters National Environmental Scorecard
League of Conservation Voters
1707 L Street NW, Suite 550
Washington, DC 20036
202-785-8683

Preserving Our Future Today: Your Guide to the United States Environmental Protection Agency
U.S. Environmental Protection Agency
75 Hawthorne Street
San Francisco, CA 94105
415-744-1500

Regenerating the Environment: A Guide for Doers
Community Regeneration
Rodale Institute
33 East Minor Street
Emmaus, PA 18098
215-967-5171

Special Report: You Can Make a Difference
National Wildlife Federation
1400 Sixteenth Street NW
Washington, DC 20036-2266
202-797-6800

Sustainable Development: A Guide to Our Common Future
Global Tomorrow Coalition
1325 G Street NW, Suite 915
Washington, DC 20005-3104
202-628-4016

You Can Do It!
Canadian Wildlife Federation
2740 Queensview Drive
Ottawa, Ontario K2B 1A2
613-721-2286

Books

Blueprint for the Environment: A Plan for Federal Action
T. Allan Comp
Howe Brothers, 1989
P.O. Box 6394
Salt Lake City, UT 84106

Boundaries of Home
Doug Aberley
New Society Publishers, 1993
4527 Springfield Avenue
Philadelphia, PA 19143

Campus Ecology: A Guide to Assessing Environmental Quality and Creating Strategies for Change
April A. Smith and the Student Environmental Action Coalition
Living Planet Press, 1993
2940 Newark Street NW
Washington, DC 20008

Dear Mr. President: 100 Earth-Saving Letters
Marc Davenport
A Citadel Press Book, 1992
120 Enterprise Avenue
Secaucus, NJ 07094

Design for a Livable Planet
Jon Naar
Harper & Row, 1990
10 East 53rd Street
New York, NY 10022

Earth Right
H. Patricia Hynes
Prima, 1990
P.O. Box 1260PH
Rocklin, CA 95677

Environmental Career Directory
Bradley J. Morgan and Joseph M. Palmisano
Gale Research, 1993
835 Penobscot Building
Detroit, MI 48226

Environmental Jobs
Nicholas Basta
John Wiley and Sons, Inc., 1992
605 Third Avenue
New York, NY 10158-0012

Facing Our Future
Jim Cole
Growing Images, 1992
P.O. Box 2510
Novato, CA 94948

Fighting Toxics
Gary Cohn and John O'Connor
Island Press, 1990
1718 Connecticut Avenue NW, Suite 300
Washington, DC 20009

Helping Nature Heal
Richard Nilsen
Ten Speed Press, 1991
P.O. Box 7123
Berkeley, CA 94707

How to Heal the Earth in Your Spare Time
Acres U.S.A., 1990
Andrew Lopez
P.O. Box 8800
Metairie, LA 70011-8800

How to Make the World a Better Place
Jeffrey Hollender
Quill, 1990
1350 Avenue of the Americas
New York, NY 10019

How to Save the Children
Amy Hatkoff and Karen Kelly Klopp
Fireside, 1992
Simon and Schuster Building
Rockefeller Center
1230 Avenue of the Americas
New York, NY 10020

How to Save Your Neighborhood, City or Town
Maritza Pick
Sierra Club Books, 1993
730 Polk Street
San Francisco, CA 94109

How to Write to World Leaders
Rick Lawler
Avon Books, 1990
1350 Avenue of the Americas
New York, NY 10019

Making Things Happen: How to Be an Effective Volunteer
Joan Wolfe
Island Press, 1991
1781 Connecticut Avenue, NW, Suite 300
Washington, DC 20009

101 Ways to Save Money and Save Our Planet
The Green Group
Paper Chase Press, 1992
5721 Magazine Street, Suite 152
New Orleans, LA 70115

1,001 Ways to Save the Planet
Bernadette Valley
Ballantine Books, 1990
201 East 50th Street
New York, NY 10022

The Power of the People: Active Nonviolence in the United States
Robert Cooney and Helen Michalowski
New Society Publishers, 1987
4527 Springfield Avenue
Philadelphia, PA 19143

Save the Earth at Work
Steven Bennett
Bob Adams Publishing, 1991
260 Center Street
Holbrook, MA 02343

The Stop Junk Mail Book
Dorcas Miller
Georgetown Press, 1991
RFD 2, Box 535
Augusta, ME 04330

War Resisters' League Organizer's Manual
Ed Hedemann
War Resisters' League, 1986
339 Lafayette Street
New York, NY 10012

What Can I Do to Make a Difference?
Richard Zimmerman
Penguin Books, 1991
375 Hudson Street
New York, NY 10014

Books for Youth

Changing Our World: A Handbook for Young Activists
Paul Fleisher
Zephyr Press, 1993
P.O. Box 13448
Tucson, AZ 85732

Fifty Simple Things Kids Can Do to Save the Earth
Earthworks Group, 1990
1400 Shattuck Avenue, #25
Berkeley, CA 94709

Kid's Guide to Social Action
Barbara A. Lewis
Free Spirit, 1991
400 First Avenue North, Suite 616
Minneapolis, MN 55401

Kids Ending Hunger
Tracy Apple Howard
Andrews and McMeel, 1992
4900 Main Street
Kansas City, MO 64112

No Kidding Around! America's Young Activists Are Changing Our World and You Can Too
Wendy Schaetzel Lesko
Information USA, Inc., 1992
P.O. Box E
Kensington, MD 20895

Our Future at Stake
Citizen's Policy Center
New Society Publishers, 1985
4722 Baltimore Avenue
Philadelphia, PA 19143

Save the Earth: An Action Handbook for Kids
Betty Miles
Alfred A. Knopf, 1991
201 East 50th Street
New York, NY 10022

So You Love Animals: An Action-Packed Fun-Filled Book to Help Kids Help Animals
Zoe Weil
The American Anti-Vivisection Society, 1994
801 Old York Road, #204
Jenkintown, PA 19046-1685

The Student Environmental Action Guide
Earthworks Group
EarthWorks Press, 1991
1400 Shattuck Avenue, #25
Berkeley, CA 94709

Take Action
Ann Love and Jane Drake
Kids Can Press, 1992
29 Birch Ave
Toronto, Ontario M4V 1E2
Canada

365 Ways for You and Your Children to Save the Earth One Day at a Time
Michael Viner
Dove, 1991
Time, Inc.
Time and Life Building
Rockefeller Center
New York, NY 10020

A Vogt for the Environment
John Sailer
The Book Publishing Company, 1993
P.O. Box 99
Summertown, TN 38483

Individuals/Companies/ Organizations

Audubon Society
801 Pennsylvania Avenue SE
Washington, DC 20003
202-547-9009
Has regular action alerts for its members.

Concern, Inc.
1794 Columbia Road NW
Washington, DC 20009
202-328-8160
Works to broaden public participation in the protection of the environment, including recycling, pollution prevention and energy efficiency.

Earth Action Network
P.O. Box 5098
Westport, CT 06881
203-854-5559
Earth Action Network is a nonprofit organization that publishes **E Magazine**, a bimonthly publication that keeps readers informed about current environmental issues.

Friends of the Earth (FOE)
1025 Vermont Avenue NW, Suite 300
Washington, DC 20005
202-783-7400
A nonprofit environmental advocacy organization. FOE publishes a magazine that has an activist page with suggested actions.

Garbage Magazine
Dovetail Publishers
The Blackburn Tavern
2 Main Street
Glouchester, MA 01930
508-283-3200
An independent environmental quarterly.

Greenpeace
1436 U Street NW
Washington, DC 20009
202-462-1177
Has an activist network and sends out action alerts approximately every 3 months.

Public Interest Research Groups (PIRG)
218 D Street SE
Washington, DC 20003
202-546-9707
A National association of statewide environmental advocacy organizations. Publishes a newsletter, reports and action alerts.

Sierra Club
730 Polk Street
San Francisco, CA 94109
415-776-2211
Has regular action alerts for its members and it has an activist network. In its bimonthly magazine the club gives information on various actions people can take.

Student Conservation Association
P.O. Box 550
Charelstown, NH 03603-0550
603-543-1700
It has a monthly magazine called *Earth Work* that lists more than 100 internships, seasonal and permanent work opportunities, and careers.

Student Environmental Action Coalition (SEAC)
P.O. Box 1168
Chapel Hill, NC 27514-1168
919-967-4600
Has over 1,100 groups working on outreach to high school students. SEAC acts as a clearinghouse for information and references letting students know what is going on with environmental groups around the country.

20/20 Vision
1828 Jefferson Place NW
Washington, DC 20036
800-669-1782
Works to cut military spending and meet human and environmental needs. Has monthly action recommendations and bi-annual progress reports. Also publishes *Monthly Legislative Update*,

Working Assets
701 Montgomery Street, Suite 400
San Francisco, CA 94111-9474
800-788-0898
A long-distance company that donates 1 percent of your charges to nonprofit action groups. Each month it gives its customers background information on 2 pending issues and the names and phone numbers of political and business leaders to contact.

Chapter 14

Cleaning Products

Chapter 14

CONTENTS

INTRODUCTION

As defined in the Toxic Substance Control Act, a toxic substance is a "chemical or mixture of chemicals whose manufacturing, processing, distribution, use or disposal may present an 'unreasonable risk' to the environment."

As our bodies continually process and filter large quantities of chemical substances from a variety of sources, they can be easily overloaded. Unable to keep up this filtering process, the immune system weakens or breaks down. When this happens even minute amounts of a chemical can immobilize an individual and result in serious illness.

Chemical products can be found in many areas of our lives. Every day we depend on them to combat germs, mildew and odors; to remove stains; to clean our clothes; and more. Unfortunately, they can also cause life-threatening injury or illness as well as contaminate our air, land and water. Common chemical products contribute many toxic chemicals to our indoor environments. In many cases air pollution **inside** our schools, offices and homes can be far worse than outdoor air pollution.

Everyday products that we purchase at our neighborhood store are not necessarily safe. Such products as drain, oven, window and toilet cleaners; scouring powders (particularly those containing bleach); dish-washing and laundry detergents; disinfectants and deodorizers; degreasers; floor cleaners; strippers and finishers; and carpet shampoos belong to an increasingly long list of products with toxic chemicals that we are exposed to every day. The greatest exposure to toxic substances and hazardous waste begins in the home and extends to workplaces, hospitals, banks, restaurants, health clubs, movie theaters, sports stadiums, nursing homes, day-care centers and our **schools!**

Manufacturers should want to supply safer products. Consumers can take an active role by using cleaners that are safe for our children, pets, employees, maintenance crews and the environment. By buying and using only products with nontoxic ingredients, we will be sending a clear message to manufacturers.

There are healthy alternatives and this chapter will present them and their resources.

ADVERTISING

Many people perceive environmental products as time-consuming, inconvenient, more costly and less effective. This is not the case! Most environmentally friendly products

◆ Are less expensive. Those that cost more initially have a longer usable life and lower long-term operating costs, or both. Because they often come in concentrated form, once you dilute with water, they go further.

◆ Smell good (or at least better than those products with toxic ingredients).

◆ Are as effective as the toxic alternatives.

We are all influenced by advertising claims that chemical products are fast-acting, leave a fresh lemon or pine smell and are safe—especially when we see a baby crawling across a recently washed kitchen floor. Ads fail to mention the potential health risks associated with these products and their residues. In addition, we are bombarded by bright, colorful product labels with eye-catching graphics and words like All New, Improved or Fresh Smell.

Many new products are touting themselves as "Environmentally Friendly," "Safe," "Nontoxic," "Biodegradable" and "Recyclable"—but are they? Environmentalism has become a profitable marketing tool. No federal regulations and standards support these claims. How do we make an informed decision?

Two companies exist that can help consumers make wise choices. They are Green Seal and Scientific Certification Systems (SCS). Both companies test products for their impact on the environment and verify specific environmental claims made by manufacturers. The Green Seal certification mark is a blue globe with a green check, and the SCS certification mark is a blue earth with a green cross. In 1993, Green Seal released its "Environmental Standard for Household Cleaners," which is being used to evaluate and certify a number of cleaning products. Be sure to look for products that have Green Seal or SCS certification markings. For more information on these companies see the resource section at the end of this chapter.

"Green" advertising claims should be specific and supported by scientific documentation. The Environmental Advertising Claims chart on the following page will help you identify environmental marketing claims that may be unclear.

Environmental Advertising Claims

Claim	Considerations
Better for the environment	Too ambiguous to stand alone
Biodegradable soaps and detergents	Often applies to a limited number of product ingredients only. Some ingredients may break down into toxic elements. May ignore the rate at which chemicals build up in the environment.
Biodegradable paper and plastic	Often misleading; in landfills, rapid break down does not occur.
No CFCs	Implies that there are no other ozone-depleting chemicals present. Check this out. This claim is trivial if the product has been banned from using CFCs.
Dioxin free	In many cases, this claim would be more accurate if it read "no dioxins formed during production."
Environmentally friendly	Too vague, likely to imply more than what is intended.
Nontoxic	This claim generally pertains to the product's effects on human health, and does not generally refer to potential damage to the environment.
Photodegradable	Products labeled in this manner may not degrade once buried in a landfill.
Recyclable	A product may be theoretically recyclable, but this does not mean that facilities exist for such recycling in every area where the product is sold and used. Check out your options.
Safe for the atmosphere	Removal of CFCs is not enough to warrant this claim if, for example, the product contains other potential air pollutants, such as VOCs (volatile organic compounds). Read the label.

Source: *Distinguishing the Credible from the Incredible*, Scientific Certification Systems, Oakland, CA, 1993.

Labeling

Consumers have the right to know whether a product lives up to its advertising and labeling claims. Many product labels are seriously inadequate. The *Federal Hazardous Substances Act* requires that household products containing hazardous substances be labeled; however, it does not require the ingredients to be listed. Although the product may state "Poison," "Danger," "Corrosive" and/or "Flammable," the manufacturer is not required to specify the possible hazards or the long-term consequences of its use. The back of the packaging of a product may state, "If you have questions or comments about this product, please call," but how many of us actually phone? It is important for us to be aware that most labels

- Only list the "active" ingredient(s).
- Do not give the "secret" or "inert" ingredient(s).
- List only the short-term or acute side effects. Possible chronic and long-term dangers are usually not listed.
- Do not give correct disposal methods.

Many companies patent and market their products based on a secret ingredient. Secret ingredients need not be listed on the label, and most of the time the Environmental Protection Agency (EPA) and the Occupational Safety and Health Administration (OSHA) do not know what the secret ingredients are. OSHA was established in accordance with the Occupational Health and Safety Act of 1970 to set and enforce health and safety standards for workplaces through federal and state inspections.

Although manufacturers are required to list the active ingredients on labels, these ingredients can make up less than 1 percent of the product. The rest is usually a mixture of inert ingredients that, amazingly, are subject to very lax regulation. These inert ingredients are by no means safe. Many are carcinogenic (capable of causing cancer) and highly toxic. Hundreds of these ingredients are added to cleaning products to make them more spreadable, sprayable or slippery and less concentrated. Some common inert additives that cause heart and respiratory problems and disrupt the blood's ability to carry oxygen to the body's tissues are

- Methyl ethyl ketone (MEK)
- Xylene
- Phenol
- Numerous other solvents

Common Warnings on Cleaning Labels

The following are some common warnings on labels:

◆ Keep out of reach of children.

◆ Avoid contact with skin, eyes or clothing.

◆ May be fatal if swallowed.

◆ Corrosive—may produce chemical burns.

◆ Do not breathe vapor or fumes.

◆ Use in a well-ventilated area.

◆ May cause nausea, vomiting or diarrhea.

◆ Fumes are corrosive to metal.

◆ Do not use in commercial food areas.

◆ Keep away from heat, flame and sparks.

◆ Do not let pets or children near treated area.

The user is also advised to wear

◆ Respirator masks

◆ Safety goggles

◆ Rubber gloves

◆ Well-soled shoes or rubber boots

◆ Protective covering for all skin areas

◆ No contact lenses

One can see from reading these lists how difficult it can be to assess the true dangers. **Some products, even when used carefully and when the label's warnings are strictly followed, are hazardous.** When these products are used carelessly, they can cause irreparable harm. Because of the vast array of chemicals to which we are now exposed every day, we are living among health risks we cannot even assess.

Since warning labels are usually written in English and rarely in any other language, it is important to consider that some of those who use these products cannot read the warnings. This puts their lives and the lives of those around them in danger.

TESTING

When a corporation or institution purchases a chemical product, the Right-to-Know Act requires that a Material Safety Data Sheet (MSDS) be included (see the form on next page). If the MSDS is missing, request one. Actually, it is a good idea to obtain MSDSs from a number of manufacturers before purchasing any products. This will help you make informed decisions about a product, its content, possible hazards, disposal needs and more.

MATERIAL SAFETY DATA SHEET
(Prepared according to OSHA 29CFR 1010, 1200)

PRODUCT NAME

SECTION 1. MANUFACTURER/DISTRIBUTOR INFORMATION

PREPARED BY: _____ on DATE: _____ FOR: (Company Name) _____

ADDRESS: _____ EMERGENCY PHONE: _____

_____

_____

SECTION 2. INGREDIENT INFORMATION

_____

_____

_____

_____

_____

SECTION 3: PHYSICAL AND CHEMICAL CHARACTERISTICS

BOILING POINT: _____ SPECIFIC GRAVITY: _____ VAPOR PRESSURE: _____

SOLUBILITY IN WATER: _____ APPEARANCE: _____ ODOR: _____

SECTION 4. FIRE AND EXPLOSION HAZARD DATA

FLASH POINT: _____ FLAMMABLE LIMITS: _____

EXTINGUISHING MEDIA: _____

SPECIAL FIRE FIGHTING PROCEDURES: _____

_____

UNUSUAL FIRE AND EXPLOSION HAZARDS: _____

_____

D.O.T. CLASSIFICATION: _____

SECTION 5. REACTIVITY DATA

STABILITY: _____ INCOMPATIBILITY (Materials to Avoid): _____

_____

HAZARDOUS PRODUCTS OF DECOMPOSITION: _____

HAZARDOUS POLYMERIZATION: _____

SECTION 6. HAZARD DATA

PRIMARY ROUTES OF ENTRY: (Inhalation, skin absorption, etc.) _____

_____

HEALTH HAZARDS: _____ ORAL TOXICITY: _____ INHALATION: _____

EYE IRRITATION: _____ PRIMARY SKIN IRRITATION: _____

CARCINOGENICITY: _____ SIGNS AND SYMPTOMS OF EXPOSURE: _____

_____

EMERGENCY AND FIRST AID PROCEDURES: EYES _____ SKIN _____

INGESTION _____

SECTION 7. SPECIAL PROTECTION INFORMATION

RESPIRATORY PROTECTION: _____ PROTECTIVE GLOVES: _____

EYE PROTECTION: _____ PROTECTIVE CLOTHING: _____

VENTILATION: _____

SECTION 8. SPECIAL PRECAUTIONS AND SPILL/LEAK PROCEDURES

STEPS TO BE TAKEN IF SPILLED OR RELEASED: _____

WASTE DISPOSAL: _____

PRECAUTIONS TO BE TAKE IN HANDLING AND STORAGE: _____

_____

The Right-to-Know Act also requires that MSDSs be on file in the purchaser's office and be made available to employees who want to know more about the products they work with or are likely to be exposed to. The MSDS should include the following information:

◆ Accurate contents and ingredients
◆ Physical/chemical data
◆ Health hazards (including possible side effects)
◆ Application and safety precautions or requirements
◆ Spill and leak procedures
◆ Reaction/flammability information

MSDSs also include what is known as the LD-50 (lethal dose-50) rating. **This is the calculated dose of a substance that is expected to cause the death of 50 percent of an experimental animal population through ingestion or absorption of the product.** Products that result in a death rate of 49 percent are still considered and labeled safe.

Unfortunately, the LD-50 rating system measures only the acute toxicity (exposure to a large dose of a toxic substance over a short period of time) and overlooks levels of chronic exposure (repeated exposure to a substance over a long period of time) that may cause health problems.

It is important to note that the most common way that large chemical companies determine a product's toxicity and achieve this rating is through animal testing.

EFFECTS ON CHILDREN

Because each individual is likely to have a different threshold of tolerance for toxics, it is difficult to calculate the risk factor of toxic chemicals. **It is widely known that children are particularly susceptible to toxics, much more so than adults, because of their size, body weight, rapid growth development and increased respiratory rates.** Proportionally, they ingest and inhale a greater percentage of a given toxic substance than an adult in the same situation. Children are closer to low surfaces, where the chemical products are applied, and their playing habits put them into direct contact with these toxics.

Higher concentrations of chemicals are found in children, and their bodies are less able to clean themselves of the toxics than are those of adults, because children have lower levels of the enzymes needed. Toddlers at day-care centers and children at schools are frequently in direct contact with chemicals in every room, from those on carpets and floors to those used in locker rooms and bathrooms. Often classroom carpets are cleaned or treated before the start of a schoolday and students are exposed to high levels of these toxins throughout the day in a room with little or no ventilation.

Exposure to these toxins can affect a student's behavior, ability to concentrate, academic performance and general health. Toxins can greatly increase the risk of Reye's syndrome and have been associated with increases in leukemia and other forms of cancer.

WHAT ARE CORPORATIONS DOING?

Some major corporations have begun to realize that the long-term costs of creating, using and disposing of highly toxic chemical cleaners and solvents, combined with the negative impacts on workers and the environment, are unacceptable.

Realizing that it is preferable to deal with a problem before it becomes one, businesses and regulators are increasingly directing their efforts toward pollution prevention rather than clean-up. Many corporations have started programs to redesign their manufacturing and processing plants in order to create less waste and pollution—and save money.

3M (Minnesota Mining and Manufacturing) launched its 3P Program (Pollution Prevention Pays) in the 1970s and has since saved millions of dollars by substituting chemicals, including cleaners and solvents, with less toxic alternatives. General Dynamics has switched from using the highly toxic substance 1,1,1-trichloroethane to Simple Green (a spray cleaner) for cleaning metal parts and submarine assemblies prior to painting. Side effects of 1,1,1-trichloroethane include dizziness, poor coordination and

loss of consciousness. General Dynamics' goal is to substitute less toxic solvents whenever possible. John Kirkland, Environmental Resource Manager at the Groton, CT, shipyard stated, "We began looking at the impact of these materials on employees, the community and the environment and making changes wherever we could."

Many other large companies have also developed effective pollution prevention programs. Westinghouse has ACT ("Achievements in Clean Technology"), Dow Chemical has WRAP ("Waste Reduction Always Pays"), Chevron has SMART ("Save Money and Reduce Toxics"). Lockheed, Merck, Johnson & Johnson, WMX Industries (Waste Management) and Phillip Morris have also established rigorous corporate objectives of reducing their use of toxic chemicals and replacing them with safer alternatives.

WHAT CAN YOUR SCHOOL DO?

Schools and campus grounds are bombarded by the extensive use of industrial chemical cleaning products. Schools are also extremely restricted by their budgets. A school's primary concern when choosing and purchasing products is cost. Although product effectiveness, toxicity, safety and testing are important, they have not been primary concerns. This may be because those who are making the purchasing decisions do not realize how dangerous chemical cleaning products are. In order to save growing children from exposure to toxic chemicals, it is important that we all become more imformed.

When a school decides to change to a line of nontoxic cleaning products, it is often because of the passion and drive of a single person, a select few, or a hard working alternative cleaning products distributor. These individuals do the research, price out the alternatives and make presentations to the school administrators.

When comparing the long-range impacts of using chemical cleaning products versus nontoxic cleaning products, the results show that **it is economically wiser to use environmentally safe products once the *hidden cost* of using toxic chemical cleaners has been considered.** To compare cleaners properly we must factor in the following *hidden costs*:

◆ Initial purchase
◆ Training
◆ Proper disposal
◆ Insurance premiums
◆ Worker's compensation claims from maintenance employees who have been injured by toxic chemicals due to misuse, spills or improper disposal
◆ The effects of these chemicals on administrators, students and teachers
◆ Days lost because of sickness caused by chemical use
◆ The effects of these chemicals on the environment

Despite budget frustrations, most alternative cleaning product companies are excited by the opportunity to help a school change to environmentally safe cleaning products.

If your school is not using environmentally safe products and needs extra funding to make the switch, call your local Chamber of Commerce and ask if the businesses in your neighborhood will allow you to come and speak at their next meeting. If you are unsure about what to say, read your favorite excerpts from this chapter! There is a good chance that at least one of the local businesses will be willing to contribute the needed funds. It is safe to assume that prices will drop as the demand builds.

Training

Once a school has purchased or decided to purchase a new line of cleaning products, proper training of the maintenance staff in the correct use, handling and disposal will help reduce costs in a number of areas.

When choosing a cleaning product, schools should also look for one that will be the easiest for their maintenance crews to work with. It should not be labor intensive. It should require minimal mixing, thus reducing spills and the improper mixing of chemicals. And it should produce minimal waste, thus reducing improper disposal.

The number one ingredient in many of these products has been water. In the past, large amounts of time, money and natural resources have been needlessly wasted by shipping large quantities of a product across the country. Concentrates, ounce for ounce, use resources much more efficiently. They eliminate the need for shipping water and they reduce product waste. Because concentrates have become more popular, many cleaning products are now available in this form.

What Can Teachers and/or Students Do?

◆ Examine awareness and attitudes about toxics in your community. Will these beliefs help or hinder your efforts to create change?

◆ Examine the kinds of products currently being used in your school and at home.

◆ A good project for a science class might be to research and compare the effectiveness of a variety of common cleaning products, nontoxic alternatives and homemade remedies. For example, the substitution of lemon juice for highly toxic metal cleaners is simple, is inexpensive, and produces results, especially on copper and brass, that are very impressive.

◆ When you make the switch from toxic to nontoxic cleaners, you must be sure that the toxics are properly disposed of. If you allow the toxic cleaning products to remain on campus, there is always a chance that the custodial crew will slip back into using them. Although there are many reasons for avoiding toxic cleaners, change is always met with some resistance and you must allow for that.

◆ Discover whether your community sponsors a hazardous waste collection day. If not, contact a community that does and learn how to sponsor one in your area. Encourage your community to establish such a service.

◆ Locate and contact local community services that handle toxic wastes and create a resource listing for your community (hospitals, product safety bureaus, government health departments, automobile repair shops and so on).

◆ Inform your community about what you have learned through a flyer or newsletter, public meetings or the local newspaper.

◆ Convince your friends, parents and school to purchase and use safe, nontoxic products.

ENVIRONMENTAL EFFECTS

Chemical products not only are dangerous to humans, but can be devastating for the environment. Often the manufacturing process of a product and its "afterlife" have far greater impacts on the environment than we see.

Chemical cleaners pollute the air and water during manufacture, while in use and after disposal. The cumulative impact of the disposal of small quantities to the landfill or down the drain has become a very serious problem. These chemicals can cause damage to sewage treatment plants and septic systems, and they can contaminate groundwater supplies. Water treatment facilities are frequently overloaded and are often unable to treat or remove certain chemicals completely. They are then discharged in the wastewater, contaminating our lakes, rivers and oceans.

Many of our conventional chemical products are petroleum based and contain ammonia, phosphates, surfactants, hydrochloric acid and chlorine bleach, as well as heavy metals such as zinc, iron, lead, arsenic, copper, mercury and silver, to name just a few. Most of these products are known carcinogens. For a list of some common chemicals and cleaners to look out for and a sampling of their physiologic and environmental hazards see page 389.

Detergents

Phosphates are a common additive in laundry detergents because they rinse away cleanly without leaving "soap scum," soften water and improve a detergent's performance. However, approximately 20 to 60 percent of all phosphates found in waste treatment plants come from detergents and are not completely removable.[1] Thus, they end up in local rivers, lakes, estuaries and so on.

Acting as a natural fertilizing agent for algae, the decomposing phosphates promote an explosive growth of algae that chokes other aquatic life as it competes for oxygen. These water systems are quickly transformed into swamps and bogs. Although many states have banned or limited phosphates, they are still widely used in many detergents.

In light of the preceding discussion, it makes sense for all states to ban phosphates. You can discover if your state allows their use by calling your regional EPA office (see the resource section of Chapter 17). If your state does allow phosphates in detergents, voice your opposition by writing to manufacturers and your state and federal officials. See Chapter 13 for more information on how you can take action.

Surfactants (surface-active agents) are another common ingredient in detergents. A surfactant is a chemical that reduces the surface tension of water, helping to penetrate other substances and cut grease. Surfactants are responsible for lifting dirt off fabrics during the wash cycle. Like phosphates, they are not completely broken down during the water treatment process, and their organic compounds, dissolved salts and foam are released into waterways, where they compete with aquatic life for needed oxygen.

Solvents

Solvents come in a variety of compounds (usually liquids) and are used to dissolve a solid material. Water is a solvent. (Our favorite!) Solvents are organically based, evaporate quickly and leave little or no residue. Many are also extremely hazardous, flammable, corrosive and toxic. These fall into the following general categories:

- ◆ Alcohols (ethanol, methanol, isopropyl)
- ◆ Ketones (acetone, methyl ethyl ketone—MEK)
- ◆ Aliphatic hydrocarbons (gasoline, kerosene, hexane)
- ◆ Aromatic hydrocarbons (benzene, styrene, toluene, xylene)
- ◆ Chlorinated hydrocarbons (methylene chloride, tetrachloride, 1,1,1-trichloroethane/trichloroethylene)
- ◆ Glycol ethers/cellosolves (butyl)

Look for these compounds in the following:
- ◆ Paints
- ◆ Thinners
- ◆ Degreasers
- ◆ Dry-cleaning fluids
- ◆ Furniture polish
- ◆ Floor strippers
- ◆ Spot removers
- ◆ Rug cleaners
- ◆ All-purpose cleaners and many other chemical products

These solvents must be used with the utmost care!

Deodorizers and Disinfectants

As popular and easy to use as deodorizers and disinfectants are, they are incredibly toxic and virtually unnecessary. Many are expensive and loaded with toxic chemicals, such as phenol, formaldehyde, cresol, glycols, methylene chloride and dichlorobenzene. These "air fresheners" employ a host of chemicals to "mask" unpleasant odors, in exchange for promis-

es of spring breezes, fall foliage and a myriad of other seasonal smells and flower mixes. Rarely do these products solve an odor problem. Many also contain a nerve-deadening agent that desensitizes your sense of smell while coating your nasal passages with an oily film. They can irritate the eyes, nose and throat and can cause vomiting, numbness, nausea, convulsions and cold sweats. More serious side effects include respiratory tract irritations, memory loss, paralysis and damage to the central nervous system, liver and kidneys.

Many deodorizers and air fresheners are packaged in aerosol cans. When they are used, a fine mist containing these chemicals is released into the air, where they are inhaled easily into the lungs and absorbed quickly into the bloodstream. Also, many of the gases used as propellants in the aerosol cans are hydrocarbons, which are highly flammable and even explosive when exposed to heat or pressure. If you use such products, purchase them in a nonaerosol form (e.g., in a spray pump bottle).

Most disinfectants should be avoided unless you are trying to control a serious or contagious illness. A clean, well-ventilated building rarely is in need of such products. If there is an odor problem, one should consider what is producing the odor and eliminate it. Some questions to consider include the following:
- ◆ Is the area clean?
- ◆ Has mold developed?   .
- ◆ Have surfaces been thoroughly cleaned that have had food on them?
- ◆ Do the filters in the ventilation system need replacing?

Also consider
- ◆ Opening windows on a regular basis.
- ◆ Placing an open box of baking soda near the odor source or using it as a preventive measure.

Other solutions might include putting out a dish of hot vinegar, buying a plant or, for more industrial areas, using zeolite. (For more information see Chapter 1.)

Some Toxics to Avoid

CHEMICAL	USE	PHYSICAL EFFECT
Ammonia	Glass cleaners, all-purpose cleaners	Rash and skin irritation; chemical burns; eye irritation , irritation of lungs and other mucous membranes. Causes and intensifies respiratory problems, including asthma.
Chlorine	Bleach, scouring powders	Vomiting, circulatory collapse, delirium, erosion of mucous membranes, respiratory tract irritation.
Cresol	Deodorizers, disinfectants	Absorbed through skin and mucous membranes. Damage to liver, kidneys, lungs, pancreas, spleen and the central nervous system.
Ethylene glycols (glycol ethers) (butyl cellusolve)	Common industrial solvents	Nausea, vomiting, abdominal pain, dehydration, weakness, possible coma. Central nervous system depressant, can cause symptoms of mental illness.
Lye	Drain cleaners, oven cleaners	A corrosive poison. Eats through skin. If ingested, eats through internal tissues, causing irreparable damage. Severe damage to eyes, nose and throat. Damaging to septic systems.
Methyl ethyl ketone (MEK)	Industrial solvent	Irritating to eyes, skin, throat, mucous membranes. Long-term effects include memory loss, headaches, numbness of extremities and slowed reaction time.
Perchloroethylene	Carpet cleaners, spot removers	Carcinogenic. Nausea, loss of appetite, dizziness. Central nervous system depressant.
Trichloroethylene	Rug cleaners, spot removers, floor polishes	Air and water contaminant. Carcinogenic, mutagenic, corrosive. Respiratory distress, liver and kidney poisoning. Poor concentration and coordination, nausea, paralysis.

CONSIDERATIONS WHEN BUYING CLEANING PRODUCTS

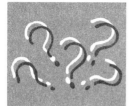

When evaluating the purchase of cleaning products, ask yourself the following questions:

◆ Do I really need this product?

◆ Is there a safer alternative?

◆ Is the product nontoxic? Biodegradable? How do I know?

◆ Will this product do the job?

◆ Is the product usable for more than a single task?

◆ Does it contain ingredients like ammonia, acids, phosphates or other toxics listed in the preceding section? Read the label for contents and warnings.

◆ Is this product tested on animals? (Is it cruelty-free?)

◆ Does it provide a phone number for obtaining further information?

◆ Is the product packaging made with recycled materials? Is the packaging recyclable?

◆ How will I dispose of the product when I'm finished? If it can't go down the drain, go out with the trash or be recycled safely, why am I buying it?

◆ Is it a product that is safe for growing children, teachers, administrators and maintenance workers to inhale or touch?

◆ Am I completely satisfied that the health of the students and other occupants of the building will not be adversely affected by its use?

Remember always to buy only the amount you need.

IMPORTANT TIPS FOR CLEANING SAFETY

◆ **Do not use more of a product than is recommended.** When you use a concentrate, be sure to follow the instructions for diluting it. Using more of a product does not make the product more effective. At best, you may not achieve the desired result; at worst, excessive quantities may be extremely dangerous and toxic. (For example, an undiluted all-purpose cleaner used to clean walls might actually strip the paint off altogether!)

◆ **Do not mix chemicals together.** Many products that are harmless by themselves undergo chemical reactions when mixed. Some combinations can be incredibly toxic and may be fatal. (Chlorine bleach and ammonia, for example, form deadly gases when mixed.)

◆ **Do not ignore warning signs or possible side effects.**

◆ **Always wear protective clothing, gloves and masks if suggested.**

◆ **Remember to keep the work area well ventilated.**

◆ **Do not eat or drink while working with cleaning products.**

◆ **Always read the label thoroughly and follow the instructions.**

◆ **Do not leave a product unattended or unsealed.**

◆ **Store safely.**

◆ **When disposing of a product, check to see if it is empty.** If it is not, see if someone else is interested in using the product.

◆ **Always keep the product in its original container with all labels.**

ENVIRONMENTALLY SAFE ALTERNATIVES

So how do we find products that are as effective as the toxic products but better for ourselves, our families and our environment? A number of books are available that explain how to make home made, natural cleaners. A number of environmentally safe alternative products also can be purchased through your local health food store or by mail. Environmentally safe cleaners for industrial use are available from a number of fine companies. (See the resource section of this chapter.)

Remember, if we all purchase, use and dispose of products wisely, these actions will make a difference on a local as well as a global level.

For those of you who want to make your own, here are 5 basic cleaners:

SPRAY CLEANER
✔ 1 teaspoon borax
✔ 2 tablespoon vinegar
✔ 1/4 teaspoon vegetable-oil-based liquid soap
✔ 2 cups very hot water
✔ spray bottle
Combine ingredients in the spray bottle and add very hot tapwater. Shake the bottle gently until the borax is dissolved. Then just spray and wipe!

SCOURING POWDER
✔ 2/3 cup baking soda
✔ 1/3 cup borax
This combination not only scours but also disinfects.

WINDOW WASH
✔ 1 cup vinegar
✔ 1 cup water
✔ spray bottle
Shake this up a little and use just as you would a commercial brand.

FLOOR CLEANER
✔ 1 cup vinegar
✔ 1 pail water
Use this formula in your pail and just mop as you normally would.

TOILET BOWL CLEANER
✔ 1 cup of borax
✔ 1/4 cup of vinegar or lemon juice
Pour ingredients into the bowl and let sit for a few hours; then scrub and flush.
Adapted from Annie Berthold-Bond, *Clean & Green* (Woodstock, NY, Ceres Press, 1990).

For those of you who do not want to make your own cleaners the following recommendations come straight from the author.

FLOORS: Ecover liquid floor soap or, for hard-to-clean spots, EarthSake Natural Solvent Spotter. For wood floors, Murphy's Oil Soap.

WINDOWS: Earth Rite glass cleaner and EarthSake glass and window cleaner.

STUDENTS' DESKS: EarthSake Natural Solvent Spotter.

LAUNDRY: For upper schools with gym and swimming facilities, Seventh Generation Ultra Laundry Powder. For spots, White Wizard Spot Remover and All-Purpose Cleaner.

DISHES: Seventh Generation Ultra Laundry Powder. This can be used for both laundry and dishes.

TOILETS, TUBS AND SHOWERS: Ecover Cream Cleaner and/or EarthSake Basin, Tub and Tile Cleaner.

MOLD AND MILDEW REMOVER: EarthSake Mold and Mildew Remover.

GENERAL: Citrasolve and Simple Green.

RESOURCES

Brochures/Papers/Reports

Choose to Use Nontoxic Alternative for a Safer, Healthier Home
Pennsylvania Resources Council
P.O. Box 88
Media, PA 19063
215-565-9131

Ecover: An Introduction to Environmental Problems of Cleaning Products
Ecover
P.O. Box SS
Carpenter Road
Thilmont, NY 12565
518-672-0190

The Natural Home Handbook
Rodale Press, Inc.
33 East Minor Street
Emmaus, PA 18098
215-967-5171
More than 100 safer ways to pest-proof, clean and maintain your home.

Shopping Guide for Caring Consumers
People for the Ethical Treatment of Animals (PETA)
P.O. Box 42516
Washington, DC 20015
301-770-7444
Listing of cruelty-free companies and their products and where you can find them.

Books

Clean & Green
Annie Berthold Bond
Ceres Publishing, 1990
P.O. Box 87
Woodstock, NY 12498

Consumer's Dictionary of Household, Yard and Office Chemicals
Ruth Winter
Crown, 1992
201 East 50th Street
New York, NY 10022

The Green Consumer
John Elkington, Julia Hailes and Joel Makower
Penguin Group, 1990
375 Hudson Street
New York, NY 10014

The Green Consumer Supermarket Guide
John Elkington, Julia Hailes and Joel Makower
Penguin Group, 1991
375 Hudson Street
New York, NY 10014

The Green Pages
The Bennet Information Group
Random House, 1990
201 East 20th Street
New York, NY 10022

The Green Supermarket Shopping Guide
John F. Wasik
Warner Books, 1993
1271 Avenue of the Americas
New York, NY 10020

Guide to Hazardous Products Around the Home
Beth Impson, editor
Household Hazardous Waste Project, 1989
1031 E. Battlefield, Suite 214
Springfield, MO 65807

Hazardous Substances Resource Guide
Richard Pohanish
Gale Research, 1992
835 Penobscott Building
Detroit, MI 48226-4094

The Nontoxic Home and Office
Debra Lynn Dadd
Jeremy P. Tarcher, Inc., 1992
11150 North Olympic Boulevard, Suite 600
Los Angeles, CA 90064

The Nontoxic Home: Protecting Yourself and Your Family from Everyday Toxics and Health Hazards
Debra Lynn Dadd
Jeremy P. Tarcher, Inc., 1986
11150 North Olympic Boulevard, Suite 600
Los Angeles, CA 90064

Nontoxic and Natural: How to Avoid Dangerous Everyday Products and Buy or Make Safe Ones
Debra Lynn Dadd
Jeremy P. Tarcher, Inc., 1984
11150 North Olympic Boulevard, Suite 600
Los Angeles, CA 90064

Poisoning Our Children: Surviving in a Toxic World
Nancy Sokol Green
The Noble Press, Inc., 1991
213 West Institute Place, Suite 508
Chicago, IL 60610

Shopping for a Better Environment
Lawrence Tasady
Meadowbrook Press, 1991
Simon and Schuster
1230 Avenue of the Americas
New York, NY 10020

Individuals/Companies/Organizations

AFM Enterprises, Inc.
1960 Chicago Avenue, Suite E7
Riverside, CA 92507
909-781-6860
Full line of cleaning products, stains, paints, strippers, sealers and adhesives for the chemically sensitive, immune-deficient and environmentally aware. No animal testing, no formaldehyde, no petrochemicals. Home and industrial. Free catalog.

Association of Vermont Recyclers
P.O. Box 1244
Montpelier, VT 05601
802-229-1833
"Teaching Toxics: Creating Solutions to Household Pollution" and "Teacher's Resource Guide to Recycling and Solid Waste Education"

Benckiser Consumer Products, Inc.
Corporate Center 1
55 Federal Road
P.O. Box 1991
Danbury, CT 06813-1991
203-731-5000
Makers of EarthRight Cleaning Products. Nontoxic, biodegradable, recyclable and cruelty-free!

Buckeye International, Inc.
Mark Gindling, Director of Research
2700 Wagner Place
Maryland Heights, MO 63043
800-321-2583
Cleaners, detergents, degreasers, disinfectants and floor/carpet products. Made from recycled products, also recyclable. Very competitive prices. Directions and right-to-know information printed on all materials in English and Spanish. A 24-hour emergency hotline number listed on all MSDS. Has implemented programs in southern California schools.

Council on Economic Priorities (CEP)
30 Irving Place
New York, NY 10003
212-420-1133
Educates the American public and provides incentives for corporations to be responsive to the social concerns of their employees, investors and consumers. Publishes *Shopping for a Better World*, a guide for socially responsible supermarket shopping that is updated annually.

The Ecology Center
2530 San Pablo Avenue
Berkeley, CA 94762
510-548-2220
The center provides fact sheets on alternative household cleaners.

Ecolo International
739 North West Bypass
Springfield, MO 65802
417-865-6260
Manufactures an environmentally friendly cleaning product line called Naturally Yours. These products are excellent for use in homes, schools and commercial facilities.

Ecover
P.O. Box SS
Carpenter Road
Thilmont, NY 12565
518-672-0190
Continually researches and tries to produce the most effective and ecologically safe cleaning products.

Environmental Health Coalition
1717 Kettner Avenue, Suite 100
San Diego, CA 92101
619-235-0281
Dedicated to the prevention and clean-up of toxic pollution that threatens human health and the environment. Disseminates information to create social policy change.

Enviro-Clean
30 Walnut Avenue
Floral Park, NY 11001
800-466-1425
Full line of Enviro Care, Green Earth and numerous other cleaning products. Retail, wholesale and bulk pricing. Free catalog. Hospitals, businesses, schools and home use.

Green Seal
1250 23rd Street NW, Suite 275
Washington, DC 20037-1101
202-331-7337
An environmental labeling organization that identifies least harmful products in the same category. Has begun a program for universities and high schools to obtain these products. Also available for teachers and administrators is a handout on how to save the environment.

Harvey Universal, Inc.
1805 West 208th Street
Torrance, CA 90501
800-800-3330
Manufactures a line of nontoxic
cleaners called Harvey's.

Planet
10114 McDonald Park Road, Suite 204C-16
Rural Route 3
Sidney, British Columbia, Canada V81 3X9
604-656-9436
Manufacturers of nontoxic dishwashing and
laundry soap.

Real Goods
966 Mazzoni Street
Ukiah, CA 95482-3471
800-762-7325
Catalog of environmentally friendly products.

Scientific Certification System (SCS)
The Ordwau Building
One Kaiser Plaza, Suite 901
Oakland, CA 94612
510-832-1415
800-ECO-FACTS (Consumer Hotline)
A scientific research and auditing firm
designed to help consumers determine which
products have what environmental impact.

Seventh Generation
49 Hercules Drive
Colchester, VT 05446-1672
800-456-1177
Catalog of "Products for a Healthy Planet."

Shaklee Corporation
444 Market Street
San Francisco, CA 94111
800-SHAKLEE
Full line of cleaning products for industrial
and home use. Clients include Esprit clothing, day-care centers, schools, colleges and
universities.

Sunshine Makers, Inc.
15922 Pacific Coast Highway
Huntington Harbor, CA 92649
800-228-0709
Makers of **Simple Green**, a concentrated,
nontoxic, biodegradable, phosphate-free,
petroleum-free, water-based and nonflam-
mable all-purpose cleaner in a recyclable
plastic bottle. Used as oil dispersant during
Exxon Valdez spill.

Washington Toxics Coalition
4516 University Way NE
Seattle, WA 98105
206-632-1545
A nonprofit group working to reduce reliance
on toxic chemicals. Promotes alternative
products and techniques that are nontoxic
and environmentally sound.

Personal Hygiene

Chapter 15

CONTENTS

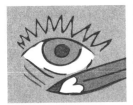

INTRODUCTION

Personal care items are responsible for severe damage to our environment. From toothpaste to tampons, the products we use to keep ourselves clean, fresh and pretty contribute substantially to pollution. What's more, some may damage your health.

Fortunately, there are alternative ways to take care of yourself and protect the environment at the same time. The following pages discuss some of these ways.

SMILE!

Some brands of toothpaste may contain formaldehyde, plastic resins, saccharin and fluoride, all of which are considered possible carcinogens. Most chemical ingredients in toothpaste only improve the taste and appearance of the toothpaste.

Fluoride is the most controversial toothpaste additive. As quoted by George L. Waldbott in *Fluoridation: The Great Dilemma,* "No other procedure in the history of medicine has been praised so highly nor at the same time condemned so thoroughly."[1]

The U.S. National Toxicology Program (NTP) issued a report in February 1990 that found "equivocal" evidence linking fluoride to cancer. One experiment had the following results: "Out of 180 male rats who drank fluoridated water, 80 were given the high dose of 79 parts per million (ppm). Three developed osteosarcoma, a rare bone cancer."[2] However, one analyst interpreted the committee's conclusion as follow: "If fluoride presents any risks to the public at the levels to which most of us are exposed, those risks are so small that they have been impossible to detect."[3] Another fluoride researcher, Dr. John A. Yiamouyiannis, says the committee's results "provide clear evidence that fluoride is a carcinogen."[4] A pathologist and former science director of the National Health Federation, Dr. Yiamouyiannis unveiled for Congress in 1977 his controversial study that found people living in the nation's 10 largest fluoridated cities suffered 15 percent more cancer than those living in the 10 largest nonfluoride areas. This conflicting information is confusing, but it may be best to err on the side of caution.

Fluoride is also suspected of causing damage to the human immune system, and it may affect the nervous system, even causing psychological and behavioral problems in some cases. Some researchers think it may cause fetal damage; others believe fluoride interferes with enzyme action in our bodies. Fluoride may also play a role in many common maladies, including arthritis, ulcers and migraine headaches.

Both sides of the fluoridation debate agree on three points:

1. You can get too much fluoride.

2. The line between fluoride's beneficial and harmful effects is very fine.

3. Sensitivity to fluoride can vary dramatically from person to person.

Steve Coffel, "The Great Fluoride Fight," *Garbage* (May/June 1992), p. 37.

The benefits of fluoride are also under scrutiny. Most dentists agree that fluoride is helpful in preventing cavities and that it may help strengthen children's growing teeth. But the American Dental Association now says the reduction in tooth decay from fluoride use is only 25 percent, not the 60 percent originally reported.[5] And taking in too much fluoride can cause fluoride poisoning, leading to bone and kidney damage, as well as dental fluorosis, a condition that causes pitted, discolored, brittle teeth. Concerned that children might be getting too much fluoride, the National PTA reversed its endorsement in 1991, after backing its use since 1952. The association is now calling for "further research to assure the safety of our children and to determine unknown risks."[6]

The information about the risks and benefits of fluoride is too extensive to print in detail here, but a few things seem clear. Most of us get as much fluoride as we need through water, food and other sources. We don't need additional fluoride in our toothpaste and mouthwash. Some evidence also suggests that some people may be particularly sensitive to fluoride and should therefore limit their intake.

Thanks to increased consumer demand, you can purchase fluoride-free toothpaste at most drug and grocery stores. Read the labels carefully before you buy, and choose the most natural products. One choice is Tom's of Maine, which also uses a recyclable aluminum tube for its natural toothpaste. Or forget toothpaste altogether. Baking soda with water makes a great alternative: It's additive-free, will clean and whiten your teeth and is less expensive.

PACK IT UP

When it comes to toothpaste, dental floss or any product you buy, consider the packaging. Most personal care items are overpackaged. Consider a typical purchase of makeup foundation. The makeup comes

- In a tiny glass bottle
- Encased in plastic
- Surrounded by corrugated cardboard
- Stuffed (along with advertising inserts) into a paperboard box
- Shrink-wrapped in plastic film
- Secured and decorated with metallic adhesive stickers.

Then the salesperson wraps it in tissue paper and puts it in a bag. What a waste!

Excessive packaging ends up in the landfill without bringing any benefit to the consumer. We shouldn't tolerate it. Try to do your part. Patronize companies that care enough to use minimal amounts of packaging materials with recycled content. Some companies even feature complete recycling programs. For example, Origins and The Body Shop recycle empty bottles when customers return them to the cosmetics counter. Other companies offer products with creative packaging, like J. R. Liggett's bar shampoo, which is shaped like a bar of soap and comes in a small cardboard box instead of a plastic bottle.

If an item is overpackaged, send the manufacturer a letter of complaint. You might even want to return the excessive packaging along with your letter. (See Chapter 13, "How to Take Action.") Don't buy that product again until the company cleans up its act. Buy non-perishable items, such as dental floss, in large sizes. It's often more economical and you'll be doing your part to cut down on waste.

KEEPING NATURALLY CLEAN AND FRESH

Soap, shampoo, deodorant, depilatories, dusting powder and perfume are often environmental hazards. The problem is chemicals. Most personal care products start with a chemical base or use many synthetic ingredients. (Just read the labels!) Compared to all-natural products, these items almost always require more energy to produce, create more pollution in the manufacturing process and deplete the earth of more resources.

Some chemically based products are bad not only for the earth, but for your body. **Chemicals applied to the skin are absorbed through the pores into the bloodstream,** so using a deodorant containing aluminum or a "cosmetic puff" saturated with dye is just another way of feeding your body a toxic chemical.

Why do manufacturers use chemicals and extra additives? This is a good question. Some chemicals are preservatives, designed to give products a longer shelf life. Others are stabilizers, to keep ingredients from separating. Still others change the way the product looks, like dyes that color toothpaste blue. Chemicals may make products last longer and look "better," but they don't necessarily make a difference in the way the product works. If you're willing to shake a bottle now and then when it separates and give up a few color choices, you may be able to get along without most chemical additives. Here's what to look for:

Soap and Shampoo

Most shampoos are safe for most consumers. However, the chemically sensitive consumer may suffer allergic reactions and eye or skin irritation. Some shampoo brands contain potentially carcinogenic ingredients, such as formaldehyde, triethanolamine (TEA) and diethanolamine (DEA). Stay away from shampoos that also contain BNPD (2-bromo-2-nitropropane-l,3-diol), which can decompose and form nitrates and formaldehyde. And beware of the following: Food Dye & Color (FD & C) red No. 4, FD & C yellow No. 10 and coal tar—all potential carcinogens.[7]

Homemade Alternatives

Astringent
◆ Use tea tree oil.
◆ Brew strong chamomile or mint tea.

Cleansing Grains
◆ Grind almond to a fine powder.
◆ Grind aduki beans to a fine powder.
For both mix some powder with water until you have a paste and rub it on your face.

Facial Masks
◆ Peel and slice half of a cucumber. Puree in a blender or food processor. Mix with one tablespoon of plain yogurt. Leave on your face for 20 minutes.
◆ Make a paste of oatmeal and water. Apply and leave on until completely dry. Remove by rubbing with your fingers. Rinse.

Lip Color
◆ Rub a raw beet over your lips.

Shampoo
◆ Mix one-quarter cup olive, avocado or almond oil with a cup of liquid castile soap and one-half cup of distilled water.

Hair Conditioner
◆ Saturate your hair with olive oil, sesame or corn oil. Wrap your hair with aluminum foil and apply hot damp towels for 10 minutes. Wash your hair.

Source: Debra Lynn Dadd, *Nontoxic, Natural, and Earthwise* (Los Angeles: Jeremy P. Tarcher, Inc., 1990), pp. 174-218.

You will have the best choices of truly natural shampoos and other products by shopping in health food stores. Natural soap products are vegetable-based, not petroleum-based. Fragrances should be made of natural oils and can be scented with flowers and herbs. Herbal extracts and plant proteins are great natural ingredients for hair conditioners and kinder to our ecology than the man-made versions.

Fragrance

Perfumes and aftershaves are a mixture of natural essential oils, aroma chemicals and solvents in a base of alcohol. Some of these ingredients can cause problems with coordination; headaches; nausea; numbness; eye, nose and throat irritation; and even depression in exceptional cases. An example of this is toluene, a toxic chemical used in perfume. "According to the EPA, toluene was detected in every fragrance sample collected for a report in 1991."[8]

Many of the chemicals used in fragrances are designated as hazardous waste disposal chemicals.[9] "According to the Food and Drug Administration, fragrances are responsible for 30 percent of all allergic reactions to cosmetics. Seventy-two percent of asthmatics have respiratory symptoms related to perfume."[10]

Natural fragrances, used either as perfumes or as enhancements for other personal care items, are made from the juices and extracts of flowers, fruits and herbs, just as they have been for centuries. Pure essential oils from real plants are becoming more available in health food stores. These are the concentrated oils of herbs. They have a very distinctive smell and one drop goes a long way.

Lotions, Creams and Sunscreens

Typically, skin creams (even baby oils) contain petroleum and additives. Lanolin or sheepwool can be contaminated with trace amounts of pesticides with which the sheep are dipped. But cosmetics companies are beginning to catch on. Some of the most natural products are the best. Aloe vera and vitamin E can heal and repair skin burns, scrapes and scratches. Oils from fruits and seeds (look for safflower, avocado or orange oil) are great moisturizers.

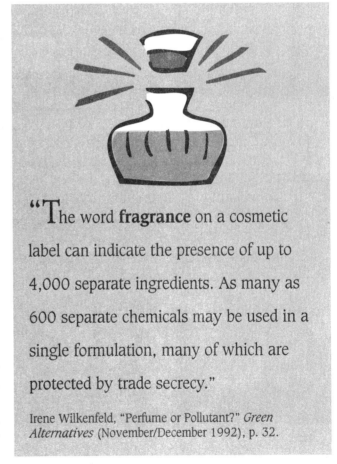

"The word **fragrance** on a cosmetic label can indicate the presence of up to 4,000 separate ingredients. As many as 600 separate chemicals may be used in a single formulation, many of which are protected by trade secrecy."

Irene Wilkenfeld, "Perfume or Pollutant?" *Green Alternatives* (November/December 1992), p. 32.

The importance of a good sunscreen cannot be overemphasized. According to the National Cancer Institute, the occurrence of melanoma, an often fatal form of skin cancer associated with sun exposure, increased 89.5 percent between 1973 and 1990.[11] "The *Archives of Dermatology* reports that using an SPF 15 sunscreen during the first 18 years of life may reduce by 78 percent the lifetime incidence of non-melanoma skin cancer."[12]

Keep in mind, not all sunscreens are equally effective. Some only block out short-wave

ultraviolet radiation (UVB), which damages the skin's surface. Others block longer-wave ultraviolet radiation (UVA), which penetrates deeper into the skin. The best protection comes from sunscreens that block both UVB and UVA rays. Chemical-free sunscreens use titanium dioxide and zinc oxide, which are physical barrier-type sunscreens and are excellent UVB/UVA blockers. However, for the naturalist, coffee and pansy extracts are also terrific natural sunscreens.

The simplest measure is to keep out of the direct sun during its peak hours, between 10 a.m. and 3 p.m. Seek out the shade. You may even end up preferring it there.

Deodorants

Although the U.S. government banned the use of chlorofluorocarbons (CFCs), aerosol spray cans continue to contribute to the deterioration of the ozone level. CFC substitutes, such as propane, butane and isobutane, interact with our environment just like hydrocarbons from a car's exhaust pipe. They mix with nitrogen oxide and sunlight to form smog.

Spray cans are not only harmful to our environment, but they also are wasteful. Much of what you spray ends up in the air or on the floor, rather than on your body.

Refillable deodorants and antiperspirants that are petroleum- and alcohol-free are available in health food stores or directly from the distributor. (See the resource section at the end of this chapter for companies.)

Deodorant crystals are simple to use and they really work. Formed into attractive shapes of various sizes, they are made of natural salts. All you need to do is dampen them with warm water and rub them under your arm. Or try all-natural deodorants made with aloe vera and other ingredients. These resemble the more familiar stick and roll-on deodorants but are aluminum-free. Finally, baking soda is a natural antiperspirant. Use it after your bath or shower, just as you would talcum powder. All these options really do work!

Powders

Natural products companies claim that talc-based powders can be contaminated with asbestos and may cause cancer.[13] Talc-based powder can irritate the lungs if inhaled. According to the World Health Organization, however, the data are not extensive enough to be conclusive. In any case, alternative powders made from sago palm flour, calendula or other natural ingredients can keep skin smooth without toxic effects.

Cotton Balls and Swabs

Cotton swabs made with plastic sticks are manufactured using petroleum. Use double-tipped swabs with wooden sticks, as they require less energy than plastic.[14] "Cosmetic puffs," found in drugstores, are often made of synthetic materials and may contain harmful dyes. Use pure cotton balls labeled "100 percent cotton" instead. Unbleached cotton or cotton bleached without chlorine is best of all. (See the resource section at the end of this chapter.)

Depilatories and Shaving Supplies

Depilatories (agents used for removing hair) are full of chemicals, and their labels warn you not to use them on certain body areas because of their harsh effects.

Although some natural versions are available, shaving cream is another additive-laden product.

Men's shaving products are infamous for causing problems for perfume-sensitive people. Moreover, these products can produce indoor air pollution because of the high proportion of moderately toxic alcohols they contain. Also, canned shaving cream is pressurized with the same hydrocarbons that contribute to ground-level smog. Some shaving soaps contain TEA, which can form carcinogenic substances and be absorbed through the skin.

Natural alternatives are the classic ceramic shaving mug with a bristle brush and natural glycerin cake soaps, or use shaving cream in a tube.

Disposable razors are a landfill disaster. According to one report, Americans use 2 billion of these nonrecyclable "conveniences" each year![15] Razors in which only the blade is replaced are considered better because the metal blades can be recycled.

LET'S TALK COSMETICS

The cosmetics industry presents alluring images of youth and beauty—flawless skin, full heads of hair, softer hands and longer nails. This $20 billion industry, with some 20,000 different products sold annually, is regulated by a division of the FDA that employs only 27 people.[16] According to Ruth Winter, author of *The Consumer's Dictionary of Cosmetic Ingredients*, the cosmetics industry spends less than half of 1 percent of its annual budget on cosmetic safety surveillance. "The 156-page Federal Food, Drug and Cosmetic Act of 1938, which regulates this product group, contains only 1 page on cosmetics. In essence, this industry is largely self-regulated. Most of the information consumers receive about cosmetics comes from advertising."[17] The following chart gives a breakdown of how consumers spend money on beauty products.

Consumer Spending for (Toxic) Beauty Products	
Hair dyes (slightly to moderately toxic)	$4.1 billion
Nail polish (moderately to very toxic)	$704 million
Nail polish remover (moderately to very toxic)	$125 million
Perfumes (moderately toxic)	$9.9 billion
Permanent wave preparations (moderately to extremely toxic)	$808.5 million

Reprinted with permission from the July/August 1990 issue of *Garbage* the Practical Journal for the Environment.

Increasing evidence indicates that many cosmetics contain toxic materials. For instance, formaldehyde, a common ingredient in nail products, can affect the central nervous system and has been shown to cause cancer in laboratory animals. Nail polishes and strengtheners commonly contain other known dangers such as:

- ◆ Carcinogens
- ◆ Allergens
- ◆ Nervous system depressants
- ◆ Chemicals that irritate or abrade the skin

When you apply nail polish, you are applying harsh toxic chemicals directly onto your body. Although some doctors believe that these ingredients don't penetrate enough to have much effect, others say that it is possible that trace amounts can enter into your body.

Approximately 30 million Americans dye their hair.[18] Even though hair dyes are popular, study after study has consistently shown that the use of synthetic dyes can increase the risk of cancer. Hair dyes, permanents and straighteners contain chemicals that can enter the bloodstream through the scalp. Believe it or not, some are proven carcinogens and some damage genetic material. Synthetic dyes are commonly contaminated by, or even made with, heavy metals.

Certainly if you want to dye your hair, experimenting with natural dyes is worth a try. Although some claim the natural dyes don't work very well, others say that dyes obtained from plants give more natural-looking highlights and do not damage the hair at all.

Makeup foundation, blushes, eye shadows and lipsticks are more often than not mixed with harmful dyes, allergens and fragrances that enter your body through the pores in your skin.

It is horrifying to consider that using cosmetics might contribute to cancer, chronic diseases and even chromosomal damage. But using unsafe cosmetics is not simply a matter of individual health. The policies and practices of many cosmetic companies affect all of us, whether we use their products or not.

Although many have changed their practices there are still cosmetic companies that needlessly test their products on animals, conducting experiments for results that frequently

Major Alternatives to Animal Testing

Microorganisms. Bacteria and fungi can be used to measure specific genotoxic effects, since it is easy to detect changes in their genetic makeup.

Epidemiologic data. Investigations of specific groups of people who have been exposed to a known substance. Some of these studies have discovered carcinogenicity as early as the eighteenth century.

In vitro studies. It is possible to use living cells or organs for tests instead of the whole animal.

Computer models. In some cases, mathematical and computer models can supplement information from in vitro testing.

Invertebrates. Certain aspects of invertebrate physiology are similar to that of mammals, which makes them useful in toxicity testing.

Source: Bill Breen, "Why We Need Animal Testing," *Garbage* (May 1993), p. 44.

could be obtained by other means. Such tests are cruel, unnecessary and out of keeping with respect for life on earth.

The good news is that many cosmetic companies now refuse to test their products on animals and sometimes include this information on their labels. **However, product labeling is not fail-safe. Even companies that do not perform animal tests may be obtaining ingredients from other companies that do.**

To make good educated choices, begin by reading the ingredients of every product you buy. By law, this information must be listed on the package, in descending order of content by weight. (In other words, if water is listed first, the product contains more water by weight than anything else.) It may be wise to avoid items with artificial dyes and colors, metal, petroleum-based additives and other synthetic chemicals.

Fortunately, more cosmetic companies are beginning to recognize their responsibility to protect the consumer and the environment. The result is safer, purer and more natural products that are better for your health and better for our ecology. And because natural ingredients are often less likely to cause allergic reactions, these more socially conscious products may prove to be better for beauty as well.

Some companies that have made a dedicated commitment to natural, safe, environmentally responsible products are

- ◆ Aubrey Organics
- ◆ Aveda
- ◆ Body Shop
- ◆ Origins
- ◆ Ida Grae
- ◆ Dr. Hauschka
- ◆ Logona
- ◆ Paul Mitchell
- ◆ Paul Penders
- ◆ Sebastian
- ◆ VitaWave

At the end of this chapter is a list of recommended companies. Look for products by these manufacturers when you shop. You can purchase them with confidence that you are buying natural colors and preservatives.

"Perhaps the most innovative industry trend is the sourcing of native plants harvested by indigenous people for cosmetic ingredients. Aveda Corporation recently located a red dye used by a Kenyan tribe that may replace a synthetically derived cosmetic color. And a Body Shop hair conditioner contains oil from nuts harvested by the Kayapo, a Brazilian rainforest tribe. A number of manufacturers also donate some of their proceeds to environmental, cultural and animal protection organizations. In an industry devoted to surface appearances, it's refreshing to see that some changes are more than skin deep."

Leslie Purdue, "The Green Cosmetics Revolution," *E—The Environmental Magazine* (November/December 1992), p. 50.

THE TRUTH ABOUT TAMPONS

Your Health and the Environment

Fifty to seventy percent of American women use tampons.[19] Although tampons look like they are pure white sterile cotton, the principal fiber ingredient for most brands is viscise-rayon.[20] "Deodorant" tampons are doused with fragrance chemicals, some strings are coated with wax and most tampons are treated with a surfactant to improve absorbency.

Lillian Yin, head of the Ob-Gyn-Devices branch of the FDA, commented, "There are a whole lot of other things in there."[21] Unfortunately, according to the cosmetics industry and the FDA, these "other" things are secret ingredients and not for public knowledge.

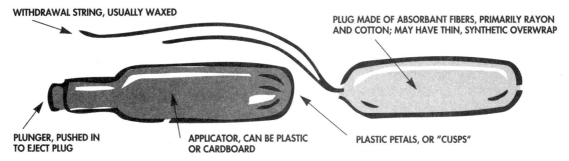

WITHDRAWAL STRING, USUALLY WAXED

PLUG MADE OF ABSORBANT FIBERS, PRIMARILY RAYON AND COTTON; MAY HAVE THIN, SYNTHETIC OVERWRAP

PLUNGER, PUSHED IN TO EJECT PLUG

APPLICATOR, CAN BE PLASTIC OR CARDBOARD

PLASTIC PETALS, OR "CUSPS"

Plastic tampon applicators are environmentally harmful. Plastic is produced from petroleum and is not biodegradable. These applicators will be with us indefinitely, tons and tons of them. Women flush them down toilets by the millions, so that they frequently clog up our sewage systems. As if that is not bad enough, millions of these plastic applicators end up on our beaches and in our rivers and lakes. This is pollution at its worst! Not only are they unattractive (and embarrassing), but they can be deadly to fish, birds and other wildlife that mistake them for food and choke to death.

The paper used in tampons is bleached. The bleaching process leaves a tiny dioxin residue which women then put into direct contact with their mucous membranes. (Dioxin is a confirmed carcinogen.)

The fibers, the covers, the deodorants, even the strings have all been associated with health and environmental risks. Toxic shock syndrome (TSS) still affects one in 100,000 women.[22] TSS, a potentially fatal condition, is believed to be caused when superabsorbent tampons allow a toxin to be released by a bacteria commonly present in women's bodies. But according to the Center for Disease Control, TSS has decreased since the most superabsorbent tampons were removed from the marketplace. More prevalent are cases of diarrhea, rash and fever, which may be milder versions of TSS, and incidents of internal irritation, dryness, ulceration and infection suffered by thousands of women due to tampon use.

Alternatives

The real truth about tampons is that you don't need to use them. Alternatives are available that are ecologically sound and better for your health. Whichever product you choose, it's important to put sanitation first. During your menstrual period, keep your body clean and always change or clean your supplies frequently to avoid an unhealthy buildup of bacteria.

Whatever you choose, keep in mind these conclusions. No menstrual product is thoroughly regulated by the FDA. Over the generations, women have used everything from papyrus to wool, commercial tampons to quartered kitchen sponges—and lived to tell the tale. And finally, plastic applicators are a huge, unnecessary waste.

Disposable Pads

We suggest not using the popular, plastic-coated, gelling chemical-filled, talc-laden, perfumed pads that line grocery store shelves. They are full of chemicals and are bad for our landfills (especially the pads that come with their own plastic disposal cases). The baby powder used in some pads may not be as benign as it sounds. "A World Health Organization (WHO) document on talc and cancer cites a study that 'suggested an approximate doubling of the risk of ovarian cancer among women after perennial use of talc.' The theory has been around for a decade but WHO considers the data to be inadequate to draw any conclusions."[23] Furthermore, as with tampons, extra-absorbent pads are associated with TSS in a small number of cases.

However, there are environmentally better disposable pads and panty liners on the market. Products from such companies as Today's Choice (available in health food stores) and Seventh Generation (available by mail) sell pads and liners in various sizes. The best for our health and the environment are those made of chlorine-free pulp, sheathed with 100 percent cotton and packaged in recycled-cardboard boxes.

Washable Pads

Reusable cloth pads are even better for the environment, and many swear that they are also more comfortable and absorbent. Look for machine-washable flannel. Some will fold over panties, others use snaps, Velcro fasteners or belts. Organic-cotton menstrual pads are also now available. This is cotton that is grown entirely without toxic pesticides, using no bleach or dye during the process. These pads are machine washable, soft and very absorbent. (See the resource section at the end of this chapter for ordering information.)

Menstrual Cup

In the early 1950s the "tasset" first appeared on the market and got rave reviews from medical professionals. Having appeared on and off the market since that time, the cup is now available through The Keeper. (See the resources section at the end of this chapter.) This is a small rubber cup with a loop on the bottom that serves as a handle. Placed at the bottom of the vagina, it collects flow and can be reused after rinsing.

Gynaseal

The gynaseal is a diaphragm-like contraceptive that also collects menstrual flow. This relatively new device was developed in Australia. It can be worn for 24 hours at a time and is reusable. Ask your gynecologist about it.

Sea Sponges

Sea sponges can be inserted during menstruation to absorb flow, rinsed and then reused. They are simple to use and ecologically responsible, but they may involve some health risks. Occasionally, natural sponges harbor residual bacteria, fungi, chemicals and other materials from their ocean homes that may not be welcomed by your body.

However, the sea sponge is linked to **less than** 1 percent of menstrual TSS cases.[24] It is available at food co-ops and health food stores. Or it can be ordered by mail from InterNatural. (See the resource section at the end of this chapter.)

Tampon of Choice

Natracare, a product of Bodywise, is a tampon without an applicator. It is 100 percent first-grade cotton, bleached with chlorine and contains no optical whiteners. It is packaged in recycled materials, and each purchase of the product contributes to the Fund for Nature organization. Natracare is available in health food stores.

OVERPOPULATION AND BIRTH CONTROL

The earth has limited resources. Yet we continue to increase our population as if these resources will last forever. The United States adds approximately 2 million people per year to the Earth's population through surplus births.[25] In the United States approximately one million teenage girls become pregnant each year with about 30,000 under the age of 15.[26] How do we begin to combat this problem?

Health clinics that encourage abstinence and dispense birth control advice, sex education and contraceptives to junior and senior high school students are a possible answer. These are very personal choices that each of us must face on our own terms, yet **it is vital to understand that if present growth rates continue, our population will double in the next 40 years.**

Every 30 seconds 136 babies are born and 48 people die, causing a net increase of 88 new inhabitants. This works out to approximately 93 million new people each year.

Arthur Haupt and Thomas T. Kane, "Population Handbook," 3rd ed. Population Reference Bureau, Inc., Washington, DC, 1991.

Although the United States comprises only 5 percent of the world's population, we consume 25 percent of its energy.[27] This problem is the basis for all the serious environmental problems we face today. Each of us can help preserve what we have by choosing to limit the number of babies we conceive and by using our natural resources wisely.

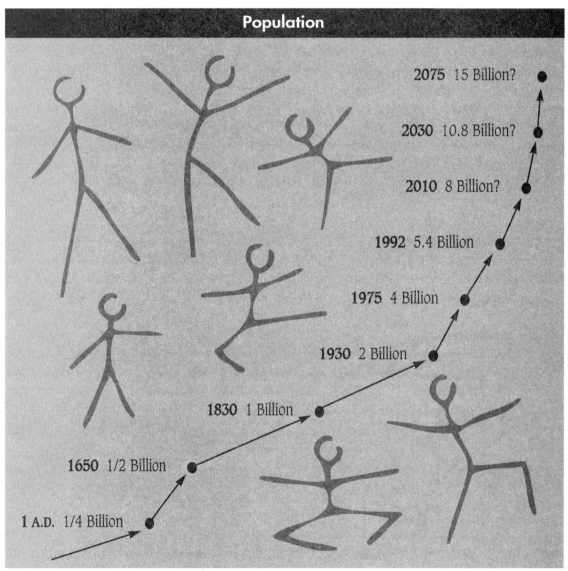

Source: The Population Education Committee, *The Real Fire,* Los Angeles, CA, 1992.

There are many options for birth control. Choosing a method should be a personal decision between you, your partner and your physician. If you do not have a private physician, there are clinics in every community that provide professional counseling and guidance in this area. One nationally based organization is Planned Parenthood. Check your local telephone directory.

A WORD ABOUT "DRY CLEANING"

Dry cleaning uses solvents to remove oil stains from clothes. The most commonly used solvent today, perchloroethylene, or "perc," has a long list of problems. It is a hazardous air pollutant, so emissions of perc are strictly regulated. It can cause health problems in humans that include central nervous system depression and liver damage. And it is very harmful to aquatic life.

Try to keep your dry cleaning to a minimum. Make sure your clothes really must be dry-cleaned. According to the FDA, even trace amounts of commercial dry-cleaning fluid can cause cancer. Many articles of clothing that are labeled "dry-clean only" can actually be washed by hand and dried flat. Spot cleaning with mild soap and water can remove some stains in between trips to the dry cleaners.

One company, Ecoclean, is offering dry cleaners a way to operate without solvents. Instead of perc, Ecoclean relies on a variety of methods using water and nontoxic soaps that are carefully chosen according to the fabric. Known as "multi-process wetcleaning," the approach includes steam cleaning, spot removing, handwashing, gentle machine washing, vacuuming and tumble drying (which is effective for removing loose dirt). The EPA has studied the Ecoclean approach and found it to be "technically feasible and economically competitive" with perc dry cleaning.

Check with your cleaners and encourage them to investigate dry cleaning with nontoxic techniques.

RESOURCES

Brochures/Papers/Reports

Stop the Waste: Women Taking Action on Sanitary Products and Diapers
The WEED Foundation (Women and the Environments Education and Development Foundation)
736 Bathurst Street
Toronto, ON M5S 2R4
Canada
416-516-2600

Books

The Green Consumer
John Elkington, Julia Hailes and Joel Makower
Penguin Group, 1990
375 Hudson Street
New York, NY 10014

The Green Consumer Supermarket Guide
John Elkington, Julia Hailes and Joel Makower
Penguin Group, 1991
375 Hudson Street
New York, NY 10014

The Green Pages
The Bennet Information Group
Random House, 1990
201 East 20th Street
New York, NY 10022

The Green Supermarket Shopping Guide
John F. Wasik
Warner Books, 1993
1271 Avenue of the Americas
New York, NY 10020

The Nontoxic Home and Office
Debra Lynn Dadd
Jeremy P. Tarcher, Inc., 1992
11150 North Olympic Boulevard, Suite 600
Los Angeles, CA 90064

The Nontoxic Home: Protecting Yourself and Your Family from Everyday Toxics and Health Hazards
Debra Lynn Dadd
Jeremy P. Tarcher, Inc., 1986
11150 North Olympic Boulevard, Suite 600
Los Angeles, CA 90064

Nontoxic and Natural: How to Avoid Dangerous Everyday Products and Buy or Make Safe Ones
Debra Lynn Dadd
Jeremy P. Tarcher, Inc., 1984
11150 North Olympic Boulevard, Suite 600
Los Angeles, CA 90064

Sustaining the Earth: Choosing Consumer Products That Are Safe for You, Your Family and the Earth
Debra Dadd-Redalia
Hearst Books, 1994
1350 Avenue of the Americas
New York, NY 10019

Individuals/Companies/Organizations

If you can't find the products mentioned in the chapter at your local stores, check with women's organizations and health food stores for likely retailers. Or you may wish to order by mail. The following is a list of several companies you can contact:

Alba Botanica
P.O. Box 12085
Santa Rosa, CA 95406
800-347-5211
Specializes in shaving cream and facial and body care products.

Aroma Vera, Inc.
P.O. Box 3609
Culver City, CA 90231
800-669-9514
Pure oils as an alternative to perfume.

Aubrey Organics
4419 North Manhattan Avenue
Tampa, FL 33614
800-282-7394
Natural hair and skin care products.

Aura Cacia
P.O. Box 399
Weaverville, CA 96093
800-437-3301
Naturally scented oils that can be used as an alternative to perfume.

Auromere
1291 Weber Street
Pomona, CA 91768
909-629-8255 or 629-0108
Body care products from India.

Autumn Harp
51 Pine Street
Bristol, VT 05443
802-453-4807
Petroleum-free lip balm, talc-free baby powder and cosmetics.

Aveda
4000 Pheasant Ridge Drive
Minneapolis, MN 55449
800-328-0849
Hair and skin care products plus color cosmetics.

The Body Shop
45 Horsehill Road
Cedar Knolls, NJ 07927
201-984-9200
800-541-2535
Cosmetics, hair, skin and body care products.

Borlind of Germany
P.O. Box 130
New London, NH 03257
603-526-2076
Skin care products.

Desert Essence
9510 Vassar Avenue, Unit A
Chatsworth, CA 91311
818-709-5900
Specializes in Tea Tree oil deodorant, toothpaste, lip balm and other personal products.

Ecoclean
180 West 80th Street
New York, NY 10024
212-769-1777
Nontoxic dry-cleaning technique.

Ida Grae Natural Cosmetics
424 Laverne Avenue
Mill Valley, CA 94941
415-388-6101
Natural cosmetics.

Internatural
P.O. Box 1008
Silverlake, WI 53170
800-446-4903
Herbs, cosmetics, sea sponges and other green products.

The Keeper
Box 20023
Cincinnati, OH 45220
513-631-0077
Manufactures and sells the menstrual cup.

Kiss My Face
144 Main Street, Box 224
Gardiner, NY 12525-0224
800-262-5477
Natural cosmetics and moisturizers.

Leydet Oils
P.O. Box 2354
Fair Oaks, CA 95628
916-965-7546
Natural aromatic oils that can be used as perfume alternatives.

The Living Source
7005 Woodway Drive, Suite 214
Waco, TX 76712
800-662-8787
Personal health products.

Logona
554-E Riverside Drive
Ashville, NC 28801
800-648-6654
Personal care products.

Many Moons
P.O. Box 166
Boulder Creek, CA 95006
604-382-1588
Menstrual pads.

National Antivivisection Society
53 West Jackson, Suite 1550
Chicago, IL 60604
312-427-6065
Learn more about animal testing. Publishes a "Personal Care with Principle" guide to choosing "cruelty-free" cosmetics and household products.

Natracare
191 University Boulevard, #219
Denver, CO 80206
303-320-1510
Distributors of a tampon made from 100 percent first-grade cotton that is not bleached with chlorine and contains no optical whiteners.

Original Swiss Aromatics
P.O. Box 6842
San Rafael, CA 94903
415-459-3998
Perfume alternatives.

Orjene
5-43 48th Avenue
Long Island City, NY 11101
800-88-ORJENE
Body and skin care products.

Paul Mitchell
John Paul Mitchell Systems
P.O. Box 10597
Beverly Hills, CA 90213-3597
310-276-7957
Hair and skin care products.

Paul Penders ~ Naturally You
1340 Commerce Street
Petaluma, CA 94954
800-473-6337
Natural hair and skin products.

Planned Parenthood Federation of America
National Headquarters (Check your Yellow Pages for a local office.)
810 7th Avenue
New York, NY 10019
212-541-7800
The nation's oldest and largest voluntary reproductive health care organization. It is dedicated to the principle that every individual has a fundamental right to choose when or whether to have children.

Rachel Perry
9111 Mason Avenue
Chatsworth, CA 91311
800-966-8888
Cosmetics, hair and skin care products.

Sebastian International
P.O. Box 4111
Woodland Hills, CA 91367
818-999-5112
Hair and skin care products.

Seventh Generation
49 Hercules Drive
Colchester, VT 95446
800-456-1177
A variety of environmental products.

Shivani
P.O. Box 377
Lancaster, MA 01523
800-237-8221
Cosmetics, perfume, hair and skin care products.

Sisterly Works
7006 Highway 21
Erberon, IA 52225
319-439-5451
Sea sponges and reusable menstrual pads.

Tom's of Maine
Railroad Avenue
P.O. Box 710
Kennebunk, ME 04043
207-985-2944
Natural personal care products such as deodorant and toothpaste.

Weleda
P.O. Box 249
Congers, NY 10920
914-268-8572
Natural body care products.

Women's Choice
P.O. Box 245
Gabriola, BC V0R 1X0
Canada
604-247-8433
Menstrual and incontinence pads.

Zero Population Growth (ZPG)
1400 16th Street NW, Suite 320
Washington, DC 20036
202-332-2200
A national nonprofit membership organization that works to achieve a sustainable balance of population, resources and the environment, both in the United States and worldwide.

Chapter 16

Preschool/ Day Care

Chapter 16

CONTENTS

INTRODUCTION

As any preschool or day-care teacher knows, working with very young children is both an opportunity and a challenge. Because young children are extremely receptive to the wonders of the earth, they are almost always eager to learn about and protect our environment. This desire helps the environmental educator, but children's energy needs to be guided. Consider the age group and specific needs of the children you are working with and remember that anything can be simplified so that it is understandable by children of all ages.

Young children imitate the behavior of adults. Actions communicate values and attitudes. Casual conversations affect a child's perception of everyday activities. If a teacher says, "We can use the back side of this piece of paper," this tells a child that it is important not to throw items away indiscriminately. Many things can be reused or recycled. A bin for reusable paper in the classroom reinforces the importance of reusing and recycling.

Using wisdom as a guide to decision making places responsibility for actions on the individual. This approach allows children to weigh their behavior and consider the outcome of their actions.

Whether you are planning nutrition, starting a recycling campaign or developing instructional materials at your preschool, paying attention to the special concerns of these future environmentalists will be important to your success.

It is not hard to turn your preschool classroom into a model of environmental commitment. Some schools have already done it. The Country Day School in McLean, Virginia, is a great example. This school has an entire shed full of materials that would have been thrown away but are destined instead for many creative art and craft projects. Eight natural playgrounds, a nature trail and a fitness trail turn the outdoor campus into a living classroom.

Right now your recycling shed may be a small cupboard, and your natural playground may be only a potted plant in the corner. But as your students and their parents begin to appreciate the environmental education you are providing, their enthusiasm will grow. In time and with careful planning, you can build a playground paradise, especially if parents and local businesses are willing to help.

In the meantime, here are some ideas that you can use immediately with very little money. We think you'll enjoy them!

CLASSROOM RECYCLING AND LEARNING TO REUSE

Make your concern for the earth an integral part of the preschool. Your young students will be happy to use recycling bins if they are attractive, well marked and well located. Preschoolers love to sort and separate items, especially when you make it simple. Use separate bins for plastic milk bottles, paint bottles, glass juice bottles and similar items wherever possible. If your school is composting for a garden, a bin for food waste can also be kept in the classroom and emptied daily into the compost pile. (No dairy or other animal products should go into this bin. See Chapter 5.)

Children will happily help the teacher pick up litter, recycle used containers and handle other simple tasks. You might assign such work to the children on a "V.I.P." rotating basis to reinforce the idea that caring for the earth's resources is an important responsibility.

The faculty at the McClean Country Day School stocks the following items in the recycling shed: boxes, bread tags, cardboard tubes, catalogues, computer paper, containers, corks, bottle caps, egg cartons, fabric scraps, film canisters, foil packaging, gift wrap, tissue paper, junk mail, stickers, lids, tops, metal cans, packaging materials (i.e., Styrofoam and bubble wrap), pantyhose, plastic spray bottles, ribbon, yarn, sewing notions, shirt and stocking cardboard, stationery, food trays and food baskets. (No wonder they need a shed!)

NUTRITION

Learning by Doing Can Be Fun and Delicious

Mid-morning and mid-afternoon snack times are ideal for introducing preschoolers to nutritious, healthy eating. All the foods you serve should be pesticide-free. If organic fruits and vegetables are too expensive to purchase, consider growing your own, because children can also learn to appreciate the source of food. If your school doesn't have a garden, you can use big indoor pots to grow such delicious snack items as cherry tomatoes and strawberries. Sugar snap peas are another great choice. Even the pod is edible, and kids love to pop them open. If you must buy nonorganic food, make sure it is washed thoroughly before serving to remove any harmful pesticide residue.

For those who have the space, a more ambitious outdoor garden can be a great learning experience for preschoolers, as well as an economical source of food. Do be careful to keep safety concerns in mind. Many gardening tools are too sharp or heavy for small children to use. (Small shovels and hoes are safe when closely supervised.) Also, unless they are wearing gardening gloves, preschoolers should be kept away from compost piles, which can harbor unsafe bacteria. (See the resources section of Chapter 12 for a source for gloves.)

When you are buying snack foods, avoid grapes. Not only are they often grown with harmful pesticides, but they can cause children to choke. Remember, preschoolers enjoy bland foods. If you choose whole grain crackers without salt, rice cakes or juice-sweetened animal crackers, children will soon learn how delicious low-salt, low-fat items can be. If you want to add some extra flavor and nutrition, try a yogurt dip with the crackers.

Activities permit young children to learn by doing and to have fun at the same time. The following are some creative ideas you may want to try:
- ◆ Take a field trip to the local supermarket or a roadside farmer's market and buy some vegetables your students have never tried. Eat them when you return.
- ◆ Play the salad bowl game by drawing a big circle on the floor (the salad bowl). Each child jumps in and tells what ingredient he or she is.
- ◆ Plant some fast-growing vegetables in individual pots. Try beans, peas and radishes. Also, it is fun to watch sprouts grow in a jar.
- ◆ Put foods into a box and see if the kids can identify them by feel, smell or the sound they make when you shake the box. Then talk about how foods grow.
- ◆ Teach your preschoolers about the food pyramid. (See Chapter 4 for nutrition information.)
- ◆ Environmentally aware kids may want to learn what pollution and pesticides can do to all these foods. (Chapter 3 provides information that you can adapt to the preschool level.)

Reusables vs. Disposables

When you serve snacks, remind children of the difference between reusables and disposables. If your school cannot accommodate dishwashing, have the children bring a mug and cloth napkin from home each day. You'll find some very good reasons to avoid disposables in Chapter 11. Share these arguments with your young students. When they learn how wasteful it is to throw away paper products, they'll feel proud to provide their own tableware. This daily routine will help promote cleanliness and responsibility.

THE PRESCHOOL CURRICULUM

Recycling and other environmental concerns are ideal subjects for the preschool curriculum because of the way young children learn. Educators tell us that from ages 2 to 7, children respond best to several specific learning methods: (1) hands-on demonstrations, (2) activities requiring interaction with other children and adults, (3) ideas that invite value judgments ("good things," "bad things") and (4) learning through the 5 senses (sight, smell, touch, taste and hearing).

You can easily tailor recycling instruction and activities to correspond to these various preschool learning styles, and, in the process, turn your young charges into lifetime recyclers. Several of the following ideas are already successfully used in preschools. Plus you'll probably come up with some of your own. Of course, the average preschooler has a short attention span, so, except for the field trips, these activities are designed to take only a few minutes of classroom time.

Hands-on Demonstrations

◆ Leave a few disposable items outside, exposed to the elements. Let the children observe how some materials (newspapers) decompose and how others (e.g., juice boxes) do not.

◆ Use magnets to determine which cans are aluminum and which are steel.

◆ Show children examples of recyclable materials and the products that can be made from them. (See Chapter 12 for examples of this.)

Interactive Activities

◆ Have the students, as a group, separate recyclable materials and put them into classroom collection bins.

◆ Take a field trip to the recycling center.

◆ Using gloves pick up litter at the park. (See the resource section of Chapter 12 for a source for gloves.)

◆ Ask children to bring recyclable newspapers or cans to school from their homes.

Value Judgments

◆ Have a "fun test": Line up samples of consumer choices and have the kids shout out "Helpful!" or "Hurtful!" after each one. Some examples are (a) an item with plastic wrap and cardboard vs. the same item with just a price sticker, (b) individual servings vs. bulk buying and (c) a juice box vs. reusable water bottle.

◆ Ask children to survey their homes for "helpful" and "hurtful" environmental examples. Examples are (a) cloth napkins vs. paper napkins, (b) paper towels vs. cloth rags and (c) canvas shopping bags vs. paper or plastic from the store.

◆ Preschoolers love to shout out answers to questions. Ask them, as a group, questions that they can answer with "Hurtful!" and "Helpful!" Some examples of questions to ask are

✔ Is recycling helpful or hurtful?
✔ When people don't recycle it is helpful or hurtful?
✔ Using disposables is?
✔ Reusing is?

Learning Through the Five Senses

◆ Have children feel different types of paper. Can they guess by touching which are recyclable?

◆ Point out how air pollution looks, smells, even tastes. Don't forget noise pollution. (Do they hear it?)

◆ How does a material change when it's recycled? Does it look different? Does it feel different? Does it smell different?

And don't forget to use the senses to educate on the elements of the natural world. Nature-study field trips are an excellent way to enjoy the earth and to learn the value of working to save it.

ADAPTING TRADITIONAL MATERIALS AND METHODS

As you survey your program with an eye toward including environmental instruction, take a look at all the traditional classroom activities. At story time or during music, you can easily include stories and songs about preserving, understanding and enjoying the earth.

Here's a song from a great book by Christine Berman and Jacki Fromer, *Teaching Children About Food*. Sing it to the tune of "Twinkle Twinkle":

Carrots, peas and broccoli, vegetables are good for me.
For my snack and in my lunch, veggie sticks are great to munch.
Carrots, peas and broccoli, vegetables are good for me.

Play the "Name Game" about endangered species:

Whale, whale, Bo-bale, Banana-fanana Fo-fale,
Me, My Mo-male Whale!
Baboon, Baboon, Bo-baboon, Banana-fanana Fo-faboon,
Me, My, Mo-maboon Baboon!

You can also make environmental references when reading any children's book. Point out how clean the air looks in the pictures, or mention that you hope that the girl in the book will put her carton in the recycling bin when she's finished with her milk.

Outdoor activities, including nature walks, are ideal opportunities to teach children about the earth and the life cycles of plants and animals. Ask children to share their observations with their classmates. Some teachers keep a classroom "diary" of student news or weather reports. These could be expanded to include nature observations or reports on how many cans were recycled by the class or how many animal homes were discovered on the walk. Preschool children are amazingly receptive to science lessons, if they are presented in a simple and interesting way. Animals, people, plants and food are all appropriate subjects for short lessons and close observations that will capture children's attention and help them begin to see how all natural life acts, reacts and interacts.

Many arts and crafts activities use recycled objects and materials from nature to great practical and artistic effect. Children will be especially proud of these projects if they have collected the raw materials themselves.

Use waste products to make classroom supplies and materials. Some ideas include

◆ Crayon containers from recycled coffee cans

◆ Building blocks from rinsed and dried milk cartons covered with contact paper

◆ Musical "instruments" from pie plates, bottle caps or oatmeal boxes

When planning an arts and crafts project, think ahead. Try to make the finished product something that the children or their parents will proudly save, display or use. Otherwise your carefully recycled materials may be destined to end up in the trash after all, this time in a nonrecyclable condition.

PRESCHOOL ART

Keep in mind that children 5 years old and younger have their own special ways of handling materials. Because they're likely to eat the finger-paints and spill the glue, nontoxic supplies are a must. Paints made from organic dyes and flour-based pastes are a natural choice for this age group.

When you're using or purchasing art supplies, keep in mind **the "3 R's," reduce** waste, **reuse** materials and **recycle** to produce new products. Children are often happy to use the unused sides of mail, memos and computer printouts, so you shouldn't have to purchase expensive drawing paper except for very special projects. Pieces of cardboard used to package shirts and stockings are also good choices for drawings. Styrofoam trays (the kind used for food packaging) make excellent little canvases for collages, paintings and reliefs.

You can stretch some brands of poster paints by diluting them with liquid starch. Experiment until you find out what formula works best. You'll be saving money and conserving resources. (Refer to Chapter 10 for recipes of good homemade art supplies from materials that are nontoxic.)

Here are some things you can make from recycled materials:

◆ Sock puppets. After you've made sock puppets out of recycled materials, turn them into classroom environmental experts. With the children's help, they can lecture the other puppets about recycling and the like.

◆ Winter paperweights made from baby food jars filled with water and "snow." Use tiny pieces of used foil. (They won't float on top if you add one drop of dishwashing liquid to the water.)

◆ A ring toss using plastic coffee can tops to toss into a box.

◆ Binoculars made by stapling 2 toilet paper rolls together and then tying a string to them to make a strap.

◆ A great bed for a baby doll. Decorate a shoe box, then make a blanket out of old clothing. Even Goldilocks would say, "It's just right!"

◆ "New" crayons with a fun shape. You can use broken crayons to make them. Put pieces of the same color in a muffin tin cup and remelt them at 400 degrees. When they cool, you have "new" crayons with a shape that little kids love to use.

◆ Crazy eggheads. Cut toilet paper rolls into half-inch sections. Stand an empty eggshell in each one. Let the children paint them to look like faces. Put a damp cotton ball inside, sprinkle it with alfalfa seeds, place it in a sunny place and keep the cotton damp. When the seeds sprout, your eggheads will need a haircut!

◆ Recycled paper. Tear several sheets of paper into 1 inch squares and soak them in water overnight. The next day, put a 1/2 cup of soaked paper in a blender and fill it with water from the soaking container. Blend for 30 seconds to separate the wood fibers. (You'll be able to see the fibers with a magnifying glass.) Suspend an old

window screen over the sink and pour the pulp onto it. Place a layer of newspaper over the pulp and press out the excess water. Turn the screen and newspaper over and set it on a table. Slowly lift off the screen, and press out more water with fresh newspaper. Repeat the pressing on both sides, peel off the damp (outer) newspaper and let your recycled (sandwiched) paper dry.

◆ Another good project is to demonstrate why clean water is so important to life. Gather a bunch of white flowers and put them in a vase with water. Add a squirt of food coloring. In a few days, when you see the flowers turn color, you'll know why water pollution is dangerous: Water and the chemicals in it become part of all living things.

◆ Make collages out of trash. In a California preschool, one class collected litter from the campus and then used it to make a mural collage celebrating the benefits of recycling. It made the kids proud and attracted attention to an important idea at the same time.

HEALTH, SAFETY AND ENVIRONMENTAL ISSUES

A prime health hazard for preschoolers is the sun. With the depletion of the ozone layer in the earth's atmosphere, our children are exposed to dangerous ultraviolet rays that can cause precancerous damage to their skin. Sun block should be used whenever children are outdoors and reapplied frequently when they are perspiring.

Regularly applying sun block on preschoolers will provide them with immediate protection, and encourage them to build a life-long habit.

If you can, plan your outdoor areas to include shady sections, where children can stay out of the brightest sun. Your students will still need sunscreen, but they'll be more comfortable when they have a beautiful, green place to cool off and relax. Before long, they'll also be delighted by the birds and animals attracted to the greenery. The more children have a chance to interact with nature and appreciate its wonders, the more regard they will have for the earth and all its inhabitants.

Pesticides are a serious source of danger for children. Preschoolers in particular are prone to placing their fingers in and around their mouths, thereby ingesting whatever residue of chemicals they may have touched with their hands. A pesticide-free campus is thus extremely important for preschoolers.

Be absolutely certain that your preschool classrooms contain no walls, baseboards, furniture or toys painted with lead-based paint (see Chapter 1). Remember also to use nontoxic, biodegradable cleaning supplies (which, of course, should be kept locked out of reach of your curious, active, young students) (see Chapter 14).

Every year we hear horror stories of toys that turn out to be lethal weapons, built from sharp, jagged parts or containing tiny parts that are small enough for children to swallow. Older toys can be a danger if they have lead paint on them. You can protect your students from these dangers by using only well-constructed, durable toys from reliable manufacturers or craftsmen. It's certainly all right to accept donations of hand-me-down toys, but remember always to put safety first. Check for peeling paint and for rough and broken edges before you add any toy to your school collection.

Most preschool teachers agree that the best toys are the classic ones, such as dolls made from natural materials, trucks and building blocks made of wood and soft fabric balls stuffed with cotton. As awareness of the importance of environmentalism grows, some manufacturers have begun to make new, ecology-oriented toys. Some of these toys are both fun to play with and educational. Many are beautifully designed, but not all are appropriate for preschoolers. In particular, some of the science kits contain glass plates or tiny objects that could be dangerous. Try to evaluate every product with an eye to safety. Save the microscopes and chemistry sets for the older children or use them for a teacher-only demonstration.

RESOURCES

There isn't room in this chapter to share all the wonderful craft projects, ideas for utilizing community resources and helpful information about preschoolers that you'll eventually want to know about but the following books, videos and pamphlets provide a good start for your own research.

Books

A Child Goes Forth: A Curriculum Guide for Preschool Children
Barbara J. Taylor
Macmillan Publishing Company, 1991
866 Third Avenue
New York, NY 10022

Creative Food Experiences for Children
Mary T. Goodwin and Gerry Pollen
Center for Science in the Public Interest, 1990
1875 Connecticut Avenue NW, Suite 300
Washington, DC 20009-5728

Earth Book for Kids
Linda Schwartz
Learning Works, 1990
P.O. Box 6187
Santa Barbara, CA 93160

Earthways: Simple Environmental Activities for Young Children
Carol Petrash
Gryphon House, 1992
3706 Otis Street
Mt. Rainer, MD 20712

Eat, Think and Be Healthy
Paula Klevan Zeller and Michael F. Jacobson
Center for Science in the Public Interest, 1987
1875 Connecticut Avenue NW, Suite 300
Washington, DC 20009-5728

Everyone Wins: Cooperative Games and Activities
Sambhava and Josette Luvmour
New Society, 1990
4527 Springfield Avenue
Philadelphia, PA 19143

Fostering a Sense of Wonder During the Early Childhood Years
Ruth A. Wilson
Greyden Press, 1993
2020 Builders Place
Columbus, Ohio 43204-4885

Hands-on Nature
Jenepher Lingelbach
Vermont Institute of Natural Science, 1986
Church Hill Road
Woodstock, VT 05091

Hug a Tree and Other Things to Do Outdoors with Young Children
Robert E. Rockwell, Elizabeth A. Sherwood and Robert A. Williams
Gryphon House, 1983
3706 Otis Street
Mt. Rainer, MD 20712

The Kids' Nature Book: 365 Indoor/Outdoor Activities and Experiences
Susan Milord
Williamson Publishing, 1989
P.O. Box 185
Charlotte, VT 05445

Meals Without Squeals
Christine Berman and Jacki Fromer
Bull Publishing Company, 1991
P.O. Box 208
Palo Alto, CA 94302-0208

More Teaching Kids to Love the Earth
Marina Lachecki and James Kasperson
Pfeifer-Hamilton, 1995
210 West Michigan
Duluth, MN 55802-1908

My First Nature Book
Roger Priddy
Alfred A. Knopf, 1990
201 East 50th Street
New York, NY 10022

In a Pumpkin Shell
Jennifer Storey Gillis
Storey Communications, 1992
Schoolhouse Road
Pownal, VT 05261

Recipes for Recycling
Dorothy McCormick
The Country Day School, 1992
6418 Georgetown Pike
McLean, VA 22101

Recyclopedia
Robin Simons
Houghton Mifflin Company, 1976
222 Berkeley Street
Boston, MA 02116

Resources for Creative Teaching in Early Childhood Education
Bonnie M. Flemming and Darleen F. Hamilton
Redleaf Press, 1992
450 North Syndicate, Suite 5
St. Paul, MN 55104

Sharing the Joy of Nature
Joseph Cornell
Dawn Publications, 1989
14618 Tyler Foote Road
Nevada City, CA 95959

Sharing Nature with Children
Joseph Cornell
Dawn Publications, 1979
14618 Tyler Foote Road
Nevada City, CA 95959

Snips and Snails and Walnut Whales
Phyllis Fiarotta with Noel Fiarotta
Workman Publishing Company, 1975
708 Broadway
New York, NY 10003

Take 'Em Along: Sharing Wilderness with Your Children
Barbara Euser
Cordilera Press, 1987
P.O. Box 3699
Evergreen, CO 80439

Teaching Children About Food: A Teaching and Activities Guide
Christine Berman and Jacki Fromer
Bull Publishing Company, 1991
P.O. Box 208
Palo Alto, CA 94302-0208

Trails, Tails and Tidepools in Pails
Docents of Nursery Nature Walks
Nursery Nature Walks, 1992
P.O. Box 844
Pacific Palisades, CA 90272

Audio Cassettes

Kids love music, and audio cassettes are a wonderful way of teaching young children important concepts. Here is a list of our favorite cassettes:

All in This Together
The Singing Rainbows
Sisters' Choice
1450 Sixth Street
Berkeley, CA 94710
510-524-5804

Aunt Merriwether's Adventures in the Backyard
Kaye Ballard and Tim Heath
The Nature Company
P.O. Box 188
Florence, KY 41022-0188
800-227-1114

Celebrate Earth
Center Stage Children's Theatre Group
Center Stage Productions
1289 Bartlein Court
Menasha, WI 54952
800-553-4058

Dirt Made My Lunch
The Banana Slug String Band
Music for Little People
P.O. Box 1460
Redway, CA 95560

Evergreen Everblue
Raffi
MCA Records, Inc.
70 Universal City Plaza
Universal City, CA 91608
818-777-4000

Head First and Belly Down
The Singing Rainbow Youth Ensemble
The Singing Rainbows
Sisters' Choice
1450 Sixth Street
Berkeley, CA 94710
510-524-5804

I'm Blue
Michael Mish
Mish Mash Music
P.O. Box 3477
Ashland, OR 97520
503-482-6578

The Magic Stone and Other Stories
Michael Mish
Mish Mash Music
P.O. Box 3477
Ashland, OR 97520
503-482-6578

Put on Your Green Shoes
Various Artists
Sony Kids' Music and Video
550 Madison Avenue
New York, NY 10022-3211
800-257-3880

Save the Animals, Save the Earth
Lois Skiera-Zucek
Kimbo
Box 477
Long Branch, NJ 07740
908-229-4949

To Save the Planet
Center Stage Children's Theatre Group
Center Stage Productions
1289 Bartlein Court
Menasha, WI 54952
800-553-4058

We Can Change
Michael Mish
Mish Mash Music
P.O. Box 3477
Ashland, OR 97520
503-482-6578

Individuals/Companies/ Organizations

Wildwood School
Box 9290
Aspen, CO 81612
(303) 925-5678
An environmental arts preschool named for
the magical place Rat and Mole went to visit
in the English children's story Wind in the
Willows. It is set among beaver ponds and
dense willow and evergreen trees near the
Roaring Fork River and the approach to
Independence Pass.

Chapter 17

Environmental Regulatory Compliance

Chapter 17

CONTENTS

INTRODUCTION

Since the enactment of the National Environmental Policy Act (NEPA) in 1969, the scope and complexity of environmental law have expanded greatly. Today environmental regulations affect virtually every aspect of public administration and business throughout the United States and many foreign countries. U.S. environmental laws now govern everything from the quality of the air we breathe to the disposal of hazardous waste. In this chapter we will take a brief look at the main U.S. environmental laws and regulations at the federal and state levels.

However, before we get started, it is important to understand the environmental law-making process. Environmental laws are made at both the federal and state levels. At the federal level, a bill is drafted and introduced to the Senate or the House of Representatives. From here the bill makes its way to committee, where merits are evaluated. Usually after considerable debate and rewriting, if the bill is successful, it makes its way to the floor of the Senate or House, where it is openly debated and voted on. If it passes the House and Senate, the bill goes to the president for his signature. Once it is signed it becomes law.

The new law then goes on to a specific governmental agency, such as the U.S. Environmental Protection Agency (EPA), where it serves as the guiding document for environmental regulations. The following chart reveals just how active this process has been in the past 20 years.

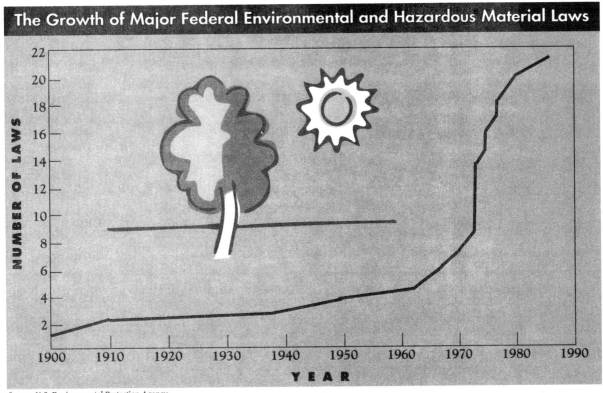

Source: U.S. Environmental Protection Agency.

Newly adopted federal regulations often become the model for state laws and regulations. States that do not have comparable (or federally required) environmental laws and regulations must follow federal guidelines.

The environmental laws that we discuss in this chapter include the following:
- ◆ The National Environmental Policy Act (NEPA)
- ◆ The Clean Air Act (CAA)
- ◆ The Clean Water Act (CWA)
- ◆ The Safe Drinking Water Act (SDWA)
- ◆ The Resource Conservation and Recovery Act (RCRA)
- ◆ The Comprehensive Environmental Response, Compensation and Liability Act (CERCLA)
- ◆ The Emergency Planning and Community Right-to-Know Act (EPCRA)
- ◆ The Toxic Substances Control Act (TSCA)
- ◆ The Federal Insecticide, Fungicide and Rodenticide Act (FIFRA)
- ◆ The Occupational Safety and Health Act (OSHA)

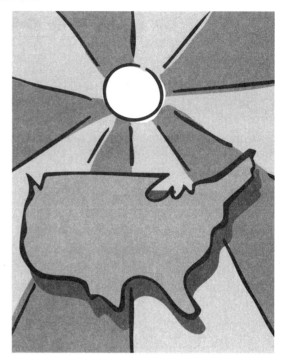

These 10 acts constitute the majority of environmental legislation in the United States today. Other industrialized countries have similar laws.

THE NATIONAL ENVIRONMENTAL POLICY ACT

NEPA, passed in 1969, really started the ground swell of environmental regulatory compliance we see today. It provided for 3 very important elements:
1. National environmental policies and goals
2. Federal environmental action
3. Establishment of the Council on Environmental Quality (CEQ)

NEPA requires all federal agencies to consider the environmental effects of their proposed actions.

THE CLEAN AIR ACT

From its original form in 1967 the Clean Air Act has undergone many legislative changes (amendments). The CAA works toward ensuring that the air we breathe is safe. It sets numerous standards for commercial and industrial air emissions, controlling the amount of pollutants that may be discharged. These are referred to as National Ambient Air Quality Standards, or NAAQS. Under the NAAQS, the following pollutants are regulated:

1. Sulfur dioxide (SO_2)
2. Nitrogen oxides (NO_X)
3. Carbon monoxide (CO)
4. Ozone
5. Lead
6. Particulate matter

The CAA also regulates the release of over 180 toxic compounds, and this number is expected to grow as new data become available. And the CAA requires treatment technologies for manufacturing emissions to ensure that air quality goals are met and maintained.

THE CLEAN WATER ACT

The Clean Water Act of 1977 has also undergone many changes and amendments. This act seeks to protect the quality of our lakes, rivers and bays. The CWA provides for regulation of toxic pollutant discharges into surface waters.

Central to the CWA is the National Pollutant Discharge Elimination System (NPDES) program, which establishes a very precise means of controlling what may be discharged into the surface waters of virtually every state in the country. The CWA regulates discharges originating from publicly owned treatment works (POTWs). This act also provides for the regulation of hazardous substance spills and the release of petroleum products storage facilities in proximity to surface waters.

Under the 1987 amendments, the Clean Water Act also regulates "nonpoint source" pollution, that is, run-off from agriculture and urban areas. These sources include pesticides, animal droppings, litter, motor oil and other pollutants that can contaminate bodies of water because they are not treated through municipal sewage treatment plants.

THE SAFE DRINKING WATER ACT

In 1974 Congress passed the Safe Drinking Water Act (SDWA) to ensure the quality of the water we drink. Central to this legislation was the establishment of National Primary and Secondary Drinking Water Standards. These standards ensure that the water we drink from both surface and ground-water sources is safe. These drinking water standards are referred to as maximum contaminant levels (MCLs). (MCLs are often used as guidelines for other areas of environmental regulation governing various aspects of hazardous and nonhazardous waste disposal.)

Specific standards have already been set for a large number of chemicals. The primary and secondary drinking water standards regulate specific volatile organic compounds, inorganic compounds, microbiological organisms, radionuclides (radioactive nuclides) and other properties of drinking water like color and odor. Public drinking systems are required to test their water regularly for the presence of these compounds. This information is available through your Public Works Department or local Water Quality Control Board.

RCRA

THE RESOURCE CONSERVATION AND RECOVERY ACT

The Resource Conservation and Recovery Act (RCRA, pronounced Reck-Ra) is one of the most important and far-reaching environmental laws ever passed. RCRA provides for the comprehensive management of hazardous waste from "cradle to grave." The following chart provides a general summary of the process, beginning with the EPA in Washington, DC.

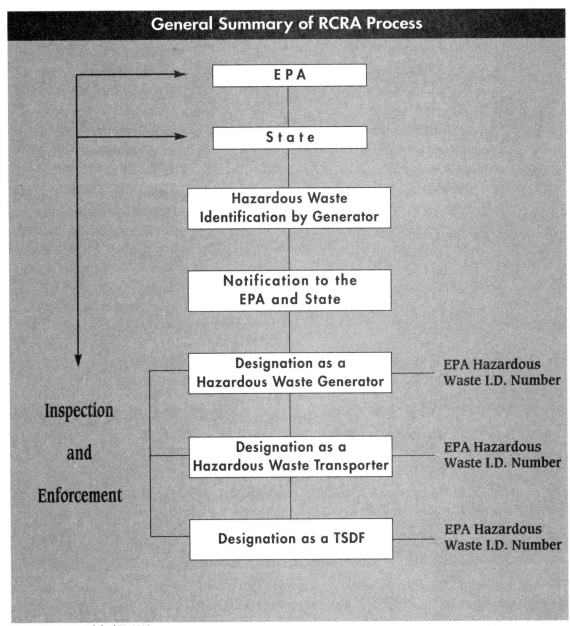

General Summary of RCRA Process

EPA

State

Hazardous Waste Identification by Generator

Notification to the EPA and State

Inspection and Enforcement

Designation as a Hazardous Waste Generator — EPA Hazardous Waste I.D. Number

Designation as a Hazardous Waste Transporter — EPA Hazardous Waste I.D. Number

Designation as a TSDF — EPA Hazardous Waste I.D. Number

Source: Tim Varney, Lakeland FL, 1994.

The EPA is able to track hazardous waste from its origin (the generator) to its ultimate disposal site, the treatment, storage and disposal facility (TSDF) which is responsible for treating and disposing of wastes. Under RCRA these wastes are required to be tightly regulated.

All hazardous waste must be identified accurately by the respective generator. This entails classifying the waste into 4 broad categories as follows:

1. Ignitability
2. Corrosivity
3. Reactivity
4. Toxicity.

If the waste falls into any one of these categories, the law requires that it be classified as hazardous. Most important, if you generate a regulated hazardous waste, you are responsible for it, even after treatment and disposal, forever.

Generators of hazardous waste are divided by law into 3 broad categories based on the volume of waste generated each month. These categories are as follows:

1. Large quantity generator [1,000 kg (kilograms) or more per month]
2. Small quantity generator [< 1,000 kg but > 100 kg per month]
3. Very Small quantity generator [< 100 kg per month]

These categories govern the complexity of compliance. Regardless of the category you are in, you must accurately characterize and dispose of your waste in accordance with the law. The RCRA also provides for the management of above- and below-ground petroleum and chemical storage tanks. Leaking underground petroleum storage tanks alone are believed to be responsible for 200,000 contaminated sites across the United States. Violation of RCRA may result in fines up to $25,000 per day per violation and criminal penalties may include imprisonment.

CERCLA THE COMPREHENSIVE ENVIRONMENTAL RESPONSE, COMPENSATION AND LIABILITY ACT

The Comprehensive Environmental Response, Compensation and Liability Act (CERCLA), passed in 1980, is commonly known as the "Superfund." Unlike RCRA, which regulates all *current* hazardous waste generators, CERCLA provides for the discovery, assessment and clean-up of *uncontrolled and/or abandoned* hazardous materials disposal sites throughout the United States and some foreign countries.

The EPA has been systematically ranking contaminated sites across the United States according to the level of hazard. This list of Superfund sites is referred to as the National Priority List

(NPL). More than 1,000 sites are on the NPL and another 20,000 are under review.

Legal liability for corporations and individuals under CERCLA is the most demanding of all environmental laws. This law provides for retroactive liability. When someone is found to be a contributor to hazardous materials disposed of at an NPL site, they are liable in the past, present and future, along with everyone else involved. They may be required to pay a pro-rated share for clean-up, legal fees, fines and any environmental or personal damages.

Like RCRA, CERCLA provides tough civil and criminal penalties for those who violate this environmental law. Fines may be up to $25,000 per day or per violation and, depending on the violation, criminal penalties may include imprisonment.

THE EMERGENCY PLANNING AND COMMUNITY RIGHT-TO-KNOW ACT

In 1986 Congress amended Superfund and created the Emergency Planning and Community Right-to-Know Act (EPCRA, pronounced Ep-Kra). This legislation created an extensive inventory and reporting system aimed at all companies storing listed hazardous chemicals.

EPCRA requires all states to establish the following:
◆ A State Emergency Response Commission (SERC)
◆ Emergency planning districts
◆ Local emergency planning committees (LEPC).

EPCRA provides for extensive reports from all regulated industries. Reporting may be divided into 3 general categories as follows:

1. A list of all hazardous chemicals in quantities of 10,000 pounds or greater and all extremely hazardous substances in quantities of 500 pounds or greater
2. All accidental releases of chemicals in excess of reportable-quantity (RQ) thresholds
3. All continuous releases of listed chemicals equal to or in excess of reporting thresholds.

The respective company must also provide detailed technical information about its chemicals and where on the property they are stored. Material Safety Data Sheets (MSDS) may suffice for the technical data about each chemical.

This information must be regularly updated. Of particular note, however, is the fact that this information is readily available to the public through the LEPC, SERC or EPA. This is a major source of information about what a particular facility has stored on-site, has accidentally released to the environment or continues to release as a result of an industrial process. Public access to this information has many industries concerned.

Failure to comply with the EPCRA can result in fines up to $25,000 per day or per violation and, depending on the violation, criminal penalties may include imprisonment.

TSCA THE TOXIC SUBSTANCES CONTROL ACT

The Toxic Substances Control Act (TSCA, pronounced TOS-KA) was passed in 1976. The primary goal of this act is to regulate the manufacture and distribution of chemicals in all forms. In this regard, it requires the following of affected industries:

1. Toxicity testing for risks to human health
2. Record keeping and reporting
3. Export notification
4. Import certification
5. Plans for manufacture, sale and disposal

Industries producing chemicals for sale must supply a material safety data sheet (MSDS) upon request. (See Chapter 14 for a sample MSDS.)

TSCA also provides for the special regulation of the following hazardous substances:

1. Asbestos
2. Chlorofluorocarbons (CFCs)
3. Hexavalent chromium
4. Metal-working fluids
5. Polychlorinated biphenyls (PCBs)

All these substances, except CFCs, are strictly regulated because of their toxicity. CFCs have recently come under strict regulation because of their role in atmospheric pollution and the resultant damage to the ozone layer.

THE FEDERAL INSECTICIDE, FUNGICIDE AND RODENTICIDE ACT

FIFRA

The Federal Insecticide, Fungicide and Rodenticide Act (FIFRA) of 1947 is one of the oldest pieces of environmental legislation. However, FIFRA plays a rather minor role in the overall scheme of environmental protection when compared to other laws. Over the years, FIFRA has been amended and now provides for

1. Labeling
2. Registration of insecticide, fungicide or rodenticide
3. Chemical content, action and effectiveness
4. Control of production and distribution
5. Environmental fate and potential health threat
6. Removal, recall and disposal
7. Integration with other areas of environmental regulation

THE OCCUPATIONAL SAFETY AND HEALTH ACT

OSHA

The Occupational Safety and Health Act (OSHA) of 1970 and subsequent amendments have made a major impact on the health and safety of the work force. If there is a central defining element to OSHA, it would have to be the General Duty Clause. Found in Section 5(a), this requires employers to *"furnish to each of his [or her] employees employment and a place of employment which are free from recognized hazards that are causing or likely to cause death or serious physical harm to his (or her) employees."*

In 1970 when OSHA was passed, there were well over 14,000 work-related fatalities in the United States. This number has declined steadily to a current rate of approximately 10,000 per year.

OSHA provides for a very broad range of regulatory compliance in the workplace, including the following:

1. Employee training
2. Personal protective equipment
3. Medical monitoring
4. Engineering controls
5. Hazardous materials safety
6. Written plans and programs
7. Regular inspections
8. Detailed record keeping and reporting

CLOSING THOUGHTS

The important thing to remember about environmental regulatory compliance is that it no longer applies just to big corporations. Individuals can be held liable for an environmental or health and safety transgression, even if they are employees (in either the private or the public sector). Without question, the most important areas of regulatory enforcement involve the disposal of hazardous wastes and/or the release of hazardous and toxic materials into the environment. (If you are in doubt about what to do, call your local Department of Environmental Protection or Pollution Control. See the EPA listings at the end of this chapter.)

Unfortunately, comprehensive monitoring and enforcement of environmental laws go beyond the resources of federal government. Although the struggle to discover and penalize environmental violators will continue and will help clean up and maintain our resources, manufacturers and citizens both need to do their part. Everyone should take responsibility for his/her contribution to the problem of environmental pollution. Everyone should also take responsibility for discovering violations of these protective acts.

WHERE TO GO FOR HELP AND INFORMATION

EPA Public Information Services

EPA Public Information Center (PIC)
Public Information Center, 3404
U.S. Environmental Protection Agency
401 M Street SW
Washington, DC 20460
Visitors Center and Tours
202-260-1077
Operational Support/Telephone and Mail Requests
202-260-7751

EPA Publications and Information Center (EPIC)
Labat Anderson, Inc.
11029 Kenwood Road, Building 5
Cincinnati, OH 45242
513-489-8190

Regional EPA Offices

EPA Region 1: *Connecticut, Maine, Massachusetts, New Hampshire, Rhode Island, Vermont*
JFK Federal Building
Boston, MA 02203

General number	617-565-3420
External Affairs	617-565-2713
Hazardous Waste Ombudsman	617-573-5700
Small Business Ombudsman	617-565-3617
Public Information Center	617-565-3357
Unleaded Fuel Hotline	617-565-4996

EPA Region 2 : *New Jersey, New York, Puerto Rico, Virgin Islands*
26 Federal Plaza
New York, NY 10278

General Number	212-264-2657
External Programs/Public Affairs	212-264-2515
Hazardous Waste Ombudsman	212-264-3384
Small Business Ombudsman	212-264-7584
Public Information Center	716-285-8842
RCRA and Superfund Hotline	800-346-5009

EPA Region 3 : *Delaware, District of Columbia, Maryland, Pennsylvania, Virginia, West Virginia*
841 Chestnut Street
Philadelphia, PA 19107

General Number	215-597-9800
External Affairs/Public Affairs	215-597-6938
Hazardous Waste Ombudsman	215-597-8181
Small Business Ombudsman	215-597-9807
General Information Hotline	800-438-2474

EPA Region 4: *Alabama, Florida, Georgia, Kentucky, Mississippi, North Carolina, South Carolina, Tennessee*
345 Courtland Street, NE
Atlanta, GA 30365

General Number	404-347- 4727
Hazardous Waste Ombudsman	404-347-7603
Small Business Ombudsman	404-347-7109
Public Affairs/Public Information Center	404-347-3004

EPA Region 5: *Illinois, Indiana, Michigan, Minnesota, Ohio, Wisconsin*
77 West Jackson Boulevard
Chicago, IL 60604

General Number	312-353-2000
Public Affairs	217-782-5562
General Information Hotline	312-886-7935
Hazardous Waste Ombudsman	312-886-7455
Small Business Ombudsman	312-353- 2072

EPA Region 6: *Arkansas, Louisiana, New Mexico, Oklahoma, Texas*
1445 Ross Avenue, Suite 1200
Dallas, TX 75202

General Number	214-665-6444
External Affairs	214-665-2200
Hazardous Waste Ombudsman	214-665-6701
Small Business Ombudsman	214-665-2203
Environmental Emergency Hotline	214-665-2222

EPA Region 7: *Iowa, Kansas, Missouri, Nebraska*
726 Minnesota Avenue
Kansas City, KS 66101

General Number	913-551-7000
Public Affairs	913-551-7003
Hazardous Waste Ombudsman	913-551-7050
Small Business Ombudsman	913-551-7336
General Information Hotline	800-223-0425
Emergency Response	913-236- 3778

EPA Region 8: *Colorado, Montana, North Dakota, South Dakota, Utah, Wyoming*
999 18th Street, Suite 500
Denver, CO 80202

General Number	303-293-1603
External Affairs	303-293-1119
Public Affairs Branch	303-293-1120
Hazardous Waste Ombudsman	303-293-1720
Small Business Ombudsman	303-294-1111
Emergency Response Hotline (24 Hours)	303-293-1788
(Within region)	800-424-8802
General Information Hotline	800-227-8917

EPA Region 9: *Arizona, California, Hawaii, Nevada, American Samoa, Guam, Trust Territories of the Pacific*
75 Hawthorne Street
San Francisco, CA 94105

General Number	415-744-1305
External Affairs	415-744-1015
Public Affairs	415-744-1585
Hazardous Waste Ombudsman	415-744-1730
Small Business Ombudsman	415-744-1635
Emergency Response Team	415-744-2000

EPA Region 10: *Alaska, Idaho, Oregon, Washington*
1200 Sixth Avenue
Seattle, WA 98101

General Number	206-553-1200
External Affairs	206-553-1107
Hazardous Waste Ombudsman	206-553-2782
Small Business Ombudsman	206-553-1138
General Information Hotline	800-424-4372

RESOURCES

Hotlines

U.S. EPA Toxic Substance Control, Assistance Information Service
202-554-1404
Provides information on federal regulations of toxics and can refer questions to the appropriate EPA department.

U.S. EPA Emergency Planning and Community Right-to-Know (EPCRA) Hotline
800-535-0202
Provides regulatory, policy and technical information about EPCRA.

U.S. EPA Safe Drinking Water Hotline
800-426-4791
Information on drinking water safety.

Brochures/Papers/Reports

Chemicals in Your Community: A Guide to the Emergency Planning and Community Right-to-Know Act
U.S. Environmental Protection Agency
OS-120
401 M Street SW
Washington, DC 20460
202-260-7751

Clean Water Act Briefing Paper
U.S. Public Interest Research Group (U.S. PIRG)
215 Pennsylvania Avenue SE
Washington, DC 20003
202-546-9707

The Federal Insecticide, Fungicide and Rodenticide Act as Amended and Highlights Brochure
U.S. Environmental Protection Agency
Office of Pesticide Programs
401 M Street SW
Washington, DC 20460
202-260-7751

Legislative Requirements Under the Clean Air Act Amendments of 1990
National Conference of State Legislatures
1560 Broadway, Suite 700
Denver, CO 80202
303-830-2200

101st Congress in Review: The Clean Air Act Amendments of 1990
National Conference of State Legislatures
1560 Broadway, Suite 700
Denver, CO 80202
303-830-2200

State Asbestos Programs: Related to the Asbestos Hazard Emergency Response Act
National Conference of State Legislatures
1560 Broadway, Suite 700
Denver, CO 80202-5140
303-830-2200

Toxic Chemical Provisions of the Clean Air Act
Air and Waste Management Association
P.O. Box 2861
Pittsburgh, PA 15230
412-232-3444

Books

Environmental Assessment
R. K. Jain et al.
McGraw-Hill, 1993
1221 Avenue of the Americas
New York, NY 10020

Guide to State Environmental Programs
Deborah Hitchcock Jussup
BNA Books Distribution Center, 1990
300 Raritan Center Parkway
P.O. Box 7816
Edison, NJ 08818-7816

Legal Responses to Indoor Air Pollution
Frank B. Cross
Quorum Books, 1990
88 Post Road West
Westport, CT 06881

The Threat at Home: Confronting the Toxic Legacy of the U.S. Military
Seth Shulman
Beacon Press, 1992
25 Beacon Street
Boston, MA 02108

Toxic Struggles: The Theory and Practice of Environmental Justice
Richard Hofrichter
New Society Publishers, 1993
4527 Springfield Avenue
Philadelphia, PA 19143

Individuals/Companies/Organizations

Environmental Law Institute
1616 P Street NW, 2nd Floor
Washington, DC 20036
202-328-5150
Advances environmental protection by improving law, management and policy. Researches current issues and educates professionals and citizens about the nature of these issues.

League of Conservation Voters (LCV)
1707 L Street NW, Suite 550
Washington, DC 20036
202-785-8683
A nonpartisan political arm of the environmental movement. For more than 24 years, LCV has provided voters across the country with their representatives' environmental record in Congress. Publishes annually the National Environmental Scorecard as well as special committee scorecards to distinguish "green" members from those who work against environmental protection and conservation.

Natural Resources Defense Council (NRDC)
40 West 20th Street
New York, NY 10111
212-727-2700
A nonprofit membership organization, staffed by lawyers and scientific specialists, that employs litigation and public advocacy on a wide range of environmental issues. Acts as a watchdog over government agencies and supplies vital scientific information to the public.

Sierra Club Legal Defense Fund
180 Montgomery Street, Suite 1400
San Francisco, CA 94104-4209
415-627-6700
A nonprofit, public-interest law firm, created
to bring lawsuits on behalf of environmental
and citizen organizations to protect the
environment.

**U.S. Department of Justice,
Environment and Natural Resources
Division**
10th Street and Constitution Avenue NW
Room 2143
Washington, DC 20530
202-514-2701
The responsibilities of this division include
litigation involving the protection and
enhancement of the American environment
and wildlife resources; the acquisition,
administration and disposition of public
land, water and mineral resources. Also
responsible for safeguarding Indian rights
and property.

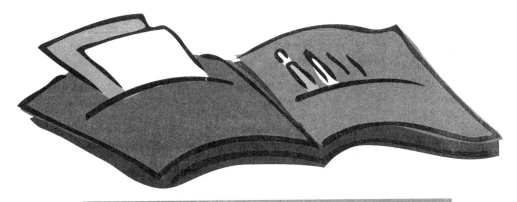

Resources

Student and Teacher Environmental Education Activities

Chapter 18

CONTENTS

INTRODUCTION

The **Student/Teacher Activities** and **Grants and Awards** listings in this chapter have been created to be used by a wide spectrum of readers, from those just starting out with involvement in environmental concerns, to those who are seasoned environmentalists. The alphabetically arranged records provide addresses and telephone numbers.

The **Student/Teacher Activities** section also offers a brief description for each entry and uses the following categories for quick reference.

- Youth Clubs
- Fundraising Ideas
- Expeditions and Camps
- Projects and Activities
- Energy
- Waste

- ECO Heroes
- Field Trips
- Atmosphere
- Rainforests
- Water
- Workshops

- Sponsorship Organization
- Internships and Careers
- Nature and Wildlife
- Speakers Bureaus
- Membership Organization
- Classroom Materials and Activities

To find out about local programs, look in your own backyard. All urban areas have one or more of the following valuable resources: Natural History Museums, Zoos, Aquariums, Botanical Gardens and/or Arboretums. Your local yellow pages will have telephone numbers and addresses for these places. Another valuable resource is your local library, which may have information on environmental events and activities in your area.

The **Grants and Awards** section uses the following categories:

- Student and Youth Awards
- Grants for Projects and Activities
- Scholarships

- Awards for Teachers
- Grants for Educators
- Activist Awards

An excellent resource for researching environmental grants and funding is the Environmental Data Research Institute in Rochester, New York (716-473-3090). They publish *The Environmental Grantmaking Foundations,* which profiles environmental grantmakers and is updated each year.

Some excellent books offering valuable information on fundraising are *The Principal's Guide to Grant Success* by David G. Bauer. This guide provides a step-by-step approach for developing a system to attract grant funds. Also by Mr. Bauer are *Grantseeking Primer for Classroom Leaders*, a guide that explains how to get the inside information needed before proceeding with a grant application, and *The Fund-Raising Primer,* an introductory book for individuals concerned with raising funds for nonprofit organizations.

The Center for Environmental Education is constantly updating these listings and would love to hear about new programs. We hope that you find this information valuable in your pursuit to further explore environmental issues.

STUDENT/ TEACHER ACTIVITIES

Academic Study Associates, Inc.
355 Main Street, P.O. Box 38
Armonk, NY 10504
914-273-2250
• Expeditions and Camps
• Workshops
Offers precollege enrichment programs to high school students. A variety of courses are available, including environmental studies and community service.

Academy of Natural Sciences
1900 Benjamin Franklin Parkway
Philadelphia, PA 19103-1195
215-299-1020
• Atmosphere
• Projects and Activities
• Water
A pioneer in watershed research for over 30 years.

Acorn Designs
5066 Mott Evans Road
Trumansburg, NY 14886
607-387-3424
• Fundraising Ideas
• Waste
Offers student groups a way to spread the word about the environment and raise money at the same time.

Activism 2000 Project
Encouraging Youth Initiative Through Participation
1632 Ridout Road
Annapolis, MD 21401
410-757-6595
• ECO Heroes
• Workshops
Their primary mission, "kids should be seen and heard," assists with finding organizations and information needed to run a successful campaign.

Adamsville School
400 Union Avenue
Bridgewater, NJ 08807
908-526-6440
• Youth Clubs
• Fundraising Ideas

• Rainforests
A fifth-grade class created a cookbook with recipes from countries with rainforests. Money raised was sent to indigenous people in these countries.

Adirondack Life Science Institute
Skidmore College
Saratoga Springs, NY 12866
518-584-5000, ext. 2624
• Expeditions and Camps
Offers 1-week courses to students in grades 7 through 9.

Adirondack Outdoor Education Center
HCO 1 Box 35, Piolet Knob Road
Katskill Bay, NY 12844
518-656-9462
• Field Trips
• Expeditions and Camps
• Nature and Wildlife
Outdoor adventures and environmental education programs on the shore of Lake George are offered to school groups, colleges, adults and families.

Adopt-A-Beach
California Coastal Commission
45 Fremont Street, Suite 2000
San Francisco, CA 94105
415-904-5210
• Sponsorship Organization
• Field Trips
• Classroom Materials and Activities
• Water
• Waste
This program promotes conservation awareness, recycling and litter abatement through community involvement, environmental awareness and stewardship.

Adopt-A-Beach School Assembly Program
The Malibu Foundation
1527 North Genesee Avenue
Los Angeles, CA 90046
213-650-8143
• Sponsorship Organization
• Field Trips
• Projects and Activities
• Water
• Waste
• Speakers Bureaus
An environmental education effort that shows K through 8 students the way to a cleaner marine environment.

Adopt-A-Stream Foundation
P.O. Box 5558
Everett, WA 98206
206-388-3487
• Sponsorship Organization
• Membership Organization
• Workshops
• Water
Promotes environmental education and stream enhancement while offering support and guidance to those "adopting" a stream.

Adopt-A-Watershed
P. O. Box 356
Hayford, CA 96041
916-628-5334 or 4608
• Sponsorship Organization
• Projects and Activities
• Water
Plays a major part in the training of watershed restoration, monitoring and assessment that is necessary for future forest management.

African Wildlife Foundation
1717 Massachusetts Avenue NW
Washington, DC 20036
202-265-8394
• Membership Organization
• Nature and Wildlife
Works with Africans promoting grassroots programs in conservation, wildlife management and management of threatened areas.

Alaska Conservation Foundation
430 West 7th Avenue, Suite 215
Anchorage, AK 99501
907-276-1917
• Membership Organization
• Projects and Activities
• Waste
• Nature and Wildlife
Meets the funding needs and provides technical assistance to grassroots groups throughout the state.

Alberta Global Education Project, Summer Institute
11010-142 Street
Edmonton, AB, Canada T5N 2R1
403-453-2411
• Workshops
This institute explores the theoretical and practical applications of global education in a retreat setting.

Alliance for Acid Rain Monitoring (ALLARM)
James Center, Dickinson College
Carlisle, PA 17013
717-245-1573
• Projects and Activities
• Water
Students run workshops, recruit community members to become water site monitors. Created the largest data base of water quality levels in the state.

Alliance for Children's Trust Foundation (ACT)
Environmental Science Parks
10477 Riverside Drive
Toluca Lake, CA 91602
818-762-7082
• Field Trips
• Projects and Activities
Environmental Science Parks are a place for children of multicultural backgrounds to plant, maintain and harvest orchards and gardens.

Alpine Conference
Boise State University
1487 Olympus Point
Pocatello, ID 83201
208-385-3490
• Expeditions and Camps
• Workshops
Workshops bring educators and youth group leaders together, using the outdoors to teach environmental responsibility and stewardship.

America the Beautiful Fund
219 Shoreham Building
Washington, DC 20005
202-638-1649
• Classroom Materials and Activities
• Membership Organization
• Projects and Activities
• Waste
Gives recognition, technical support and small seed grants to those interested in helping beautify their communities.

American Anti-Vivisection Society (AAVS)
Animalearn
801 Old York Road, Suite 204
Jenkinstown, PA 19046-1685
215-887-0816
• Internships and Careers
• Workshops
• Projects and Activities

• Nature and Wildlife
• Speakers Bureaus
Offers programs, presentations (in the tri-state area) and resources on human and environmental issues for students in the sixth grade through the college level.

American Association of Zoological Parks and Aquarium
Oglebay Park
Wheeling, WV 26003
304-242-2160
• Sponsorship Organization
• Classroom Materials and Activities
• Membership Organization
• Nature and Wildlife
Offers several brochures on various wildlife issues.

American Birding Association (ABA)
P.O. Box 6599
Colorado Springs, CO 80934
800-850-2473
• Membership Organization
• Nature and Wildlife
A source of information, contacts, outings, volunteer opportunities and much more for beginner and veteran birders.

American Cave Conservation Association
P.O. Box 409
Horse Cave, KY 42749
502-786-1466
• Field Trips
• Membership Organization
• Nature and Wildlife
A national nonprofit association dedicated to the protection of caves, groundwater and karstlands (underground caves).

American Cetacean Society
P.O. Box 2639
San Pedro, CA 90731-0943
310-548-6279
• Field Trips
• Expeditions and Camps
• Membership Organization
• Water
• Nature and Wildlife
• Speakers Bureaus
Working to protect whales and dolphins through education, conservation and research.

American Community Gardening Association
325 Walnut Street
Philadelphia, PA 19106
215-625-8250
• Membership Organization
• Projects and Activities
Encourages local self-reliance through education, recreation and hands-on experience.

American Environmental Outfitters
242 Noble Road
Clarks Summit, PA 18411
800-397-0292
• Sponsorship Organization
• Fundraising Ideas
Allows students to raise money for specific projects and helps spread environmental awareness and action.

American Farmland Trust
1920 N Street NW, Suite 400
Washington, DC 20036
202-659-5170
• Sponsorship Organization
• Membership Organization
• Projects and Activities
• Nature and Wildlife
Founded to undertake projects to rescue our nation's endangered farms.

American Forests
1515 P Street NW
Washington, DC 20005
800-545-TREE or Membership Hotline
800-873-5323
• Fundraising Ideas
• Classroom Materials and Activities
• Projects and Activities
• Nature and Wildlife
Educates people about the vital role that forests and trees play in our lives. Offers help restoring damaged ecosystems through the Global ReLeaf Program.

American Friends Service Committee (AFSC)
1501 Cherry Street
Philadelphia, PA 19102
215-241-7000
• Sponsorship Organization
Dedicated to aiding developing countries while advocating peace and civil rights.

American Hiking Society
Volunteer Vacations
P.O. Box 86
North Scituate, MA 02060
617-545-7019
• Field Trips
• Expeditions and Camps
• Projects and Activities
• Nature and Wildlife
Needs summer volunteers to help preserve America's parks and forests.

American Horse Protection Association, Inc.
1000-29th Street NW, Suite T-100
Washington, DC 20007
202-965-0500
• Sponsorship Organization
• Membership Organization
The only national nonprofit organization dedicated to the protection of horses and burros, both wild and domestic.

American Oceans Campaign
725 Arizona Avenue, Suite 102
Santa Monica, CA 90401
310-576-6162
• Membership Organization
• Water
A nonprofit organization dedicated to the restoration and preservation of America's oceans.

American Society for the Prevention of Cruelty to Animals (ASPCA)
424 East 92nd Street
New York, NY 10128
212-876-7700
• Classroom Materials and Activities
• Membership Organization
• Nature and Wildlife
Has a youth magazine called *Eye on Animals* that will feature stories submitted by youth.

American Water Works Association
6666 West Quincy Avenue
Denver, CO 80235
303-794-7711
• Projects and Activities
• Water
Developed the booklet *Water Can Be Fun! How to Create a Successful Science Fair*.

Animal Issues and Environment Club
Scott Intermediate High School
Eighth and Olive Streets
Coatesville, PA 19320
610-380-1625
• Youth Clubs
• Sponsorship Organization
• Projects and Activities
Publishes a newsletter, participates in Adopt-A-Whale and Adopt-A-Manatee programs, and hosts a vegetarian tasting party for school faculty.

Animal Rights Club (ARC)
Salem High School
44 Geremony Drive
Salem, NH 03079
603-893-7069
• Youth Clubs
• Nature and Wildlife
Organizes boycotts of companies that use animals for testing and educates students about factory farming.

Animal Rights Network
456 Monroe Turnpike
Monroe, CT 06468
203-452-0446
• Classroom Materials and Activities
• Membership Organization
• Nature and Wildlife
An organization offering a broad range of materials and information about animals and environmental issues.

Animal Tracks
26 West Center Street, Suite 203
Fayetteville, AR 72701
501-444-0901
• Classroom Materials and Activities
• Nature and Wildlife
This teaching guide uses animals to help kids understand different environmental problems and to develop solutions.

Appalachian Mountain Club
Pinkham Notch Visitor Center
P.O. Box 298BZ
Gorham, NH 03581
603-466-2721
• Field Trips
• Expeditions and Camps
• Membership Organization
• Workshops
• Projects and Activities
• Nature and Wildlife
Pursues an aggressive conservation

agenda while encouraging responsible recreation.

Arbor Day Institute
P.O. Box 81415
Lincoln, NE 68501-1415
402-474-5655
• Workshops
Fosters better tree care and stewardship of our environment through education.

Arcadia Institute of Oceanography
P.O. Box 89
Kittery, ME 03904
Summer: 207-276-9364; Winter: 207-439-2733
• Internships and Careers
• Field Trips
• Expeditions and Camps
• Water
• Nature and Wildlife
Serves as the base of operations for a field-oriented Summer Camp in Marine Studies. For ages 11 to 18.

Art for Our Environment
The Bali Project
188 Gravatt
Berkeley, CA 94705
415-841-6450
• Projects and Activities
• Waste
A group of concerned professionals whose purpose is to teach recycling through cross-cultural community based art projects.

Arts and Technologies for Youth, Inc.
856 Glen Arbor
Encinatas, CA 92024
619-944-0403
• Youth Clubs
• Workshops
• Projects and Activities
• Waste
Provides multidisciplinary art education programs that focus on environmental awareness for homeless and underserved youth throughout San Diego County.

Aspen Global Change Institute
Ground Truth Studies Project
100 East Francis
Aspen, CO 81611
303-925-7376

- Classroom Materials and Activities
- Membership Organization
- Atmosphere
- Energy
- Workshops
- Projects and Activities
- Water
- Waste
- Rainforests
- Nature and Wildlife

Teaches students through scientific observation about the changing global environment.

Associated Oregon Forestry Clubs
Student Leadership Center
700 Pringle Parkway SE, Suite 602
Salem, OR 97301
503-378-5596
- Internships and Careers
- Nature and Wildlife

Trains individuals to become involved in leadership and skill development activities in their schools, community and throughout the state.

Association of Forest Service Employees for Environmental Ethics (AFSEEE)
P.O. Box 11615
Eugene, OR 97440
503-484-2692
- Sponsorship Organization
- Membership Organization

Recommends reorganizing the U.S. Forest Service.

Association of Vermont Recyclers (AVR)
P.O. Box 1244
Montpelier, VT 05601
802-229-1833
- Classroom Materials and Activities
- Membership Organization
- Workshops
- Waste
- Speakers Bureaus

Offers teacher training workshops, in-class programs, implementation assistance and resources.

Astro Camp
P.O. Box 1360
Claremont, CA 91711
714-949-0687
- Field Trips
- Expeditions and Camps
- Atmosphere

- Nature and Wildlife

An outdoor education camp suited for grades 4 through 9.

B. Gunther and Company
4742 Main Street
Lisle, IL 60532
708-969-5595
- Fundraising Ideas
- Waste

Offers a wide range of products made from 100 percent recycled plastic, such as clipboards, rulers and yo-yo's. Will imprint on any of the items.

Ballona Lagoon Marine Preserve
P.O. Box 9244
Marina Del Rey, CA 90295-9244
310-306-5078
- Classroom Materials and Activities
- Field Trips
- Speakers Bureaus

Ballona Lagoon Marine Preserve gives free tours of one of the last wetlands in the Los Angeles area.

Bamfield Marine Station
Marine Biology for Teachers
Bamfield, BC, Canada V0R 1B0
614-728-3301
- Workshops

A marine workshop held in early July.

Bat Conservation International
Adopt-A-Bat
P.O. Box 162603
Austin, TX 78746
512-327-9721
- Sponsorship Organization
- Membership Organization
- Nature and Wildlife

Protects bats and their unique habitats worldwide by educating people about their importance.

Beam Me Up, Scotty: There's No Life on Earth
Environmental Committee, Student Council
Lafayette Senior High School, 400 Reed Lane
Lexington, KY 40503
606-281-0300
- Youth Clubs
- ECO Heroes
- Sponsorship Organization
- Projects and Activities
- Waste

- Speakers Bureaus

Trista Claxon was concerned about the lack of environmental education at her school, so she created a program which had 3 parts: education, contests and action.

Beyond Beef
1130 17th Street NW, Suite 300
Washington, DC 20036
202-775-1132
- Youth Clubs
- Internships and Careers
- Speakers Bureaus
- Membership Organization

Works to educate the public about the beef industry.

Biodiversitas Foundation
Tropical Rainforest Fund
P.O. Box 60223
Palo Alto, CA 94306
- Sponsorship Organization
- Rainforests

One of the most successful scientifically based environmental organizations in Brazil, with projects addressing conservation issues.

Bishop Ireton Environmental Awareness Club
Bishop Ireton High School
201 Cambridge Road
Alexandria, VA 22314
703-751-7606
- Youth Clubs
- Waste

Participates in contests with other high schools to see who can recycle the most and organizes the school's Earth Week celebration.

Borneo Big Home Project
1137 Hearst Avenue, Suite D
Berkeley, CA 94702
510-649-8460
- Projects and Activities
- Rainforests

Furthers rainforest preservation and indigenous rights in Sarawak, Malaysia.

Brooklyn Botanic Garden
1000 Washington Avenue
Brooklyn, NY 11225-1099
718-622-4433
- Field Trips
- Expeditions and Camps

- Membership Organization
- Workshops
- Nature and Wildlife

Programs include a Children's Garden and a Discovery Center with interactive exhibits and a Discovery Garden for preschool explorations.

Brooklyn Center for the Urban Environment (BCUE)

Tennis House, Prospect Park
Brooklyn, NY 11215-9992
718-788-8500
- Sponsorship Organization
- Field Trips
- Expeditions and Camps
- Membership Organization
- Workshops
- Water
- Nature and Wildlife

Focuses on urban environmental education, offering school programs for K through 12.

Brookside Nature Center

Maryland National Capital Park and Planning Commission
1400 Glenallan Avenue
Wheaton, MD 20902
301-946-9071
- Field Trips
- Expeditions and Camps
- Nature and Wildlife

Offers a hands-on children's discovery room, exhibits about native wildlife, live animal exhibits and bird feeding stations.

Browning Ferris Industries of Ohio, Inc.

Environmental Education Center
2415 Glendale-Milford Road
Cincinnati, OH 45241
513-769-3055 or 513-771-4200
- Field Trips
- Workshops
- Waste
- Speakers Bureaus

Developed environmental education curriculum geared to children in grades 4 through 6. Teacher workshops offered.

Bruce Rosen

721 Enchanted Way
Pacific Palisades, CA 90272
310-459-2818
- ECO Heroes

Reduces the amount of good but technically "expired" food ending up in the landfills by distributing donations of food to the needy.

Budongo Forest Project

58 Banbury Road
Oxford, England OX2 6QS
0-865-274700
- Sponsorship Organization
- Rainforests
- Nature and Wildlife

Studies the forest's chimpanzees and the effects of past selective logging on the structure of the forest and on its wildlife.

Bugs Are My Business

Steve Kutcher
1801 Oakview Lane
Arcadia, CA 91006
818-836-0322
- ECO Heroes
- Classroom Materials and Activities
- Nature and Wildlife
- Speakers Bureaus

A trained biologist who brings his bugs to local schools for presentations.

Butterfly Lovers International

220 Montgomery Street, Suite 2811
San Francisco, CA 94104
415-864-1169
- Sponsorship Organization
- Projects and Activities

Founded to protect butterflies and educate the public about their endangered status.

Buy Back the Dacks

P.O. Box 492
Canton, NY 13617
802-434-4077
- Sponsorship Organization

A fund designed to raise money from individuals, companies, environmental groups and others in order to purchase Adirondack lands.

Cabrillo Marine Aquarium

3720 Stephen White Drive
San Pedro, CA 90731
310-548-7563
- Field Trips
- Workshops
- Projects and Activities
- Water
- Nature and Wildlife

- Speakers Bureaus

Dedicated to promoting knowledge and awareness of marine life in southern California.

Cadette Girls Scout Troop #5314

P.O. Box 752
Gatesville, TX 76528
- Youth Clubs

Attempting to increase environmental awareness in the troop and the community.

California Environmental Project

Adopt-A-Canyon and Eco-Teams
2032 Eden Avenue
Glendale, CA 91206
818-500-1025
- Sponsorship Organization
- Field Trips
- Projects and Activities
- Waste
- Nature and Wildlife

Dedicated to the restoration and preservation of natural areas throughout California.

California Foundation for Agriculture in the Classroom

Cream of the Crop Newsletter
1601 Exposition Boulevard
Sacramento, CA 95815
916-924-4380
- Classroom Materials and Activities
- Workshops

Dedicated to bringing the world of agriculture into the California school system.

California Museum of Science and Industry

IMAX Theater, Our Urban Environment
700 State Drive
Los Angeles, CA 90037
Museum 213-744-7400; IMAX Cinema 213-744-2014
- Field Trips
- Atmosphere
- Energy
- Projects and Activities
- Water
- Waste
- Rainforests
- Nature and Wildlife

Environmental education is the major topic for California's Museum of Science and Industry.

Callaway Winery
32720 Rancho California Road
Temecula, CA 92591
909-676-4001
• ECO Heroes
• Water
• Waste
Has done what it can to eliminate toxic substances from its wine-making process.

CALPIRG
11965 Venice Boulevard, Suite 408
Los Angeles, CA 90066
310-397-3404
• Internships and Careers
• Membership Organization
• Atmosphere
• Energy
• Projects and Activities
• Water
• Waste
• Nature and Wildlife
Does research and advocacy work in a variety of areas.

CalStart
3601 Empire Street
Burbank, CA 91505
818-565-5600
A nonprofit consortium of public and private entities dedicated to creating an advanced transportation industry in California.

Camp Allen: The Discovery Program
Route 1, Box 426
Navasota, TX 77868
409-825-7175
• Expeditions and Camps
• Workshops
• Nature and Wildlife
Provides hands-on educational experiences that enhance classroom learning.

Camp Ertan
1969 DeMille Drive
Los Angeles, CA 90027
213-666-1900
• Expeditions and Camps
Was created to provide an opportunity for abused children to experience the outdoors at a summer camp.

Camp Somerhill
Something Different
20 Huntley Road, P.O. Box 295

Eastchester, NY 10709
914-793-1303 or 800-488-6415
• Expeditions and Camps
Offers sessions to kids 7 to 17. Offers nature studies.

Camp Watonka in the Poconos
P.O. Box 356
Paupack, PA 18451
717-857-1401
• Expeditions and Camps
This program combines science education with traditional camp activities to provide a fun and educational camp experience for boys ages 7 to 15.

Campus Canyon Elementary School
Environmental Impact Committee
15217 Monroe Avenue
Moorpark, CA 93021
805-529-4693
• ECO Heroes
• Sponsorship Organization
• Projects and Activities
• Rainforests
Has the only parent volunteer environmental enrichment program in its district.

Campus Green Vote
1601 Connecticut Avenue NW, Suite 440
Washington, DC 20009
202-778-6133
• Youth Clubs
Trains students on influencing environmental policy through the electoral process and is developing an on-line computer network.

Canada–El Salvador Education and Development Association
El Salvador Excursion
366 Adelaide Street East, Suite 477
Toronto, ONT, Canada M5A 3X9
Phone 416-367-1986
• Workshops
Visitors will meet human rights and church groups, visit schools and rural areas.

Cape Cod Museum of Natural History, The
P.O. Box 1710, Route 6A
Brewster, MA 02631
508- 896-3867
• Sponsorship Organization

• Field Trips
• Expeditions and Camps
• Membership Organization
• Water
• Nature and Wildlife
A nonprofit educational research center dedicated to promoting environmental appreciation and sustainable living.

Care and Restore the Earth (CARE)
Blue Ridge Middle School
P.O. Box 222
Purcellville, VA 22132
703-338-6820
• Youth Clubs
• Sponsorship Organization
• Nature and Wildlife
Participates in an Adopt-An-Endangered-Animal program.

Caretakers of the Environment International Headquarters
Global Forum for Environmental Education
Nassauplein 8
1815 Gmalkmaar, Netherlands
(31) 2-11-85-02
• Membership Organization
• Workshops
• Waste
• Nature and Wildlife
An international network of secondary schools active in environmental education.

Caretakers of the Environment International/USA
2216 Schiller Avenue
Wilmette, IL 60091
708-251-8935
• Youth Clubs
• Membership Organization
• Projects and Activities
A network for high school students, offering guidelines on how to set up a group and a list of potential projects.

Cascade Wildlife Rescue
P.O. Box 5079
Eugene, OR 97405
503-935-5923
• Classroom Materials and Activities
• Nature and Wildlife
Dedicated to the science of wildlife rehabilitation, specializing in predatory mammals native to North America.

Catalina Island Marine Institute
P.O. Box 796
Avalon, CA 90704
213-510-1622
- Field Trips
- Expeditions and Camps
- Nature and Wildlife

Offers the opportunity to study the beautiful land and underwater world of Santa Catalina Island.

Center for Children's Environmental Literature
Nature's Course Newsletter
3603 Norton Place NW
Washington, DC 20016
202-362-1409
- Classroom Materials and Activities
- Workshops
- Projects and Activities
- Speakers Bureaus

An organization committed to reconnecting children to the natural world with educational literature.

Center for Environmental Education
881 Alma Real Drive, Suite 300
Pacific Palisades, CA 90272
310-454-4585
- Classroom Materials and Activities
- Projects
- Workshops
- Speakers Bureaus
- Internships and Careers

Multitopic resource library dedicated to furthering environmental education in all disciplines in schools throughout the continent.

Center for Environmental Study
Tree Amigos
3516 NE 155th Street
Grand Rapids, MI 49503
616-771-3935
- Sponsorship Organization
- Workshops
- Projects and Activities
- Rainforests
- Nature and Wildlife

The Tree Amigos Program is a special cross-cultural program of the center and uses trees as our common bond in the environment.

Center for Global Education
Augsburg College
731 21st Avenue South

Minneapolis, MN 55454
612-330-1159
- Expeditions and Camps
- Membership Organization
- Workshops

Provides education on issues related to global justice through experiential travel seminars.

Center for Marine Conservation
National Marine Debris Information Office
1725 DeSales Street NW, Suite 500
Washington, DC 20036
202-429-5609
- Classroom Materials and Activities
- Projects and Activities
- Water
- Nature and Wildlife

Dedicated to the health and protection of marine wildlife and their habitat. Developed curriculum for grades K through 12.

Center for Respect of Life and the Environment
2100 L Street NW
Washington, DC 20037
202-778-6133
- Youth Clubs

Fosters an ethic of compassion toward all sentient beings and respect for the integrity of nature.

Center for Talented Youth
Johns Hopkins University
Academic Programs Department
3400 North Charles Street
Baltimore, MD 21218
410-516-0337
- Expeditions and Camps

A residential summer camp for gifted students in grades 5 through 11 designed to help them to grow socially and emotionally.

Centerstage Productions
1289 Bartlein Court
Menasha, WI 54952
800-553-4058
- Fundraising Ideas
- Workshops
- Projects and Activities

Work for the environment is achieved mainly through the touring and distribution of its original environmental musical "To Save the Planet."

Central Park Conservancy
The Arsenal, Central Park
New York, NY 10021
212-860-1311
- Field Trips
- Classroom Materials and Activities
- Workshops
- Projects and Activities
- Nature and Wildlife

Promotes park-based educational programs and workshops for students, teachers and schools throughout the city.

Central Utah Outdoor Education Workshop
Gooseberry Guard Station, Fishlake National Forest
P.O. Box 534
Richfield, UT 84701
801-896-6441
- Workshops
- Nature and Wildlife

Educators and youth group leaders experience activities to promote understanding and respect of our natural resources.

Charmlee Natural Area Park and Nature Center
Nature Center Associates
2577 Encinal Canyon Road
Malibu, CA 90265
310-457-7247
- Nature and Wildlife

Facilities include a Nature Center/Museum, live oak woodlands, coastal sage scrub and grassy meadows.

Chewonki Foundation Inc.
Route 2, Box 1200
Wiscasset, ME 04578
207-882-7323
- Expeditions and Camps

Offers environmental science and outdoor education programs year-round for teenagers and adults.

Children and Trees Project
Shanta, Via Abri
Auroville, TN 605101
- Sponsorship Organization

A nonprofit educational research organization.

Children for a Safe Environment
Kory Johnson

517 East Roanoke, Apartment A
Phoenix, AZ 85004
602-279-5001
• ECO Heroes
In 1986, when Kory was 8, her 17-year-old sister died because her mother drank contaminated wellwater when she was pregnant. Kory decided to take a stand against pollution.

Children for Old Growth
P.O. Box 1090
Redway, CA 95560
707-923-3009
• Youth Clubs
• Projects and Activities
• Nature and Wildlife
Through newsletters, letter-writing campaigns, books and videos, they inspire children of all ages to get involved in saving forests.

Children for the Green Earth
307 North 48th Street
Seattle, WA 98103
• Youth Clubs
• Sponsorship Organization
• Nature and Wildlife
Helps connect children in various countries around the theme of trees and environmental education through a Tree Planting Partnership.

Children Now
2001 South Barrington, Suite 100
Los Angeles, CA 90025
310-268-2444 or 800-CHILD44
• Projects and Activities
An advocacy organization that speaks out for our children.

Children's Aid International
Angel Care
1420 Third Avenue, P.O. Box 83220
San Diego, CA 92138-3220
619-235-0095 or 800-842-2810
• Sponsorship Organization
• Membership Organization
• Water
Founded to assist Vietnamese Boat People. Their mission's scope broadened to include the policy of "giving children a chance" to fulfill their potential.

Children's Alliance for Protection of the Environment, Inc. (CAPE)
P.O. Box 307

Austin, TX 78767
512-476-2273
• Youth Clubs
• Membership Organization
• Projects and Activities
• Water
• Waste
• Nature and Wildlife
An international nonprofit youth organization dedicated to the building of a strong children's environmental movement by offering environmental action plans.

Children's Beach House, Inc.
128A Senatorial Drive
Greenville Place
Wilmington, DE 19807-2638
302-655-4288
• Expeditions and Camps
• Water
• Nature and Wildlife
Serves Delaware's special children with 2 programs: a summer resident camp and a coastal environmental education program.

Children's Earth Fund
Box 2335, 40 West 20th Street
New York, NY 10011
212-727-4505
• Youth Clubs
• Atmosphere
• Energy
• Projects and Activities
Offers kids information and opportunities to take coordinated environmental action.

Children's Rainforest U.S.A.
P.O. Box 936
Lewiston, ME 04243-0936
207-784-1069
• Youth Clubs
• Sponsorship Organization
• Fundraising Ideas
• Rainforests
Promotes awareness of and education about rainforests.

Chisholm Elementary
300 Colorado
North Enid, OK 73701
405-237-5645
• Youth Clubs
• ECO Heroes
• Rainforests
Fourth-grade students made coloring

books about rainforest animals and wrote more than 100 letters to the president and members of Congress asking them to help save rainforests.

Christian Miller
Sea Turtle Protectionist
One Leaman Lane
Palm Beach, FL 33480
• ECO Heroes
• Nature and Wildlife
Since 1985 Christian Miller has been patrolling the beaches of Palm Beach to protect the sea turtles who live and make their nests there.

Cities In Schools (CIS)
Communities in Schools
401 Wythe Street, Suite 200
Alexandria, VA 22314
703-519-8999
• Sponsorship Organization
• Membership Organization
• Projects and Activities
• Water
The nation's largest nonprofit dropout-prevention program bringing services directly to schools so that they are accessible to students.

Citizen Exchange Council
12 West 31st Street, 4th Floor
New York, NY 10001
212-643-1985
• Workshops
Conferences designed to maximize students' interaction while enriching their study of world history and environmental science.

Citizen's Clearinghouse for Hazardous Waste, Inc.
P.O. Box 6806
Falls Church, VA 22040
703-237-CCHW
• Projects and Activities
• Waste
An Environmental Justice Center that organizes and educates people to fight for the clean-up of hazardous waste landfills and stop the siting of new ones in their communities.

Citizen's Environmental Coalition
Toxics in Your Community Newsletter
33 Central Avenue
Albany, NY 12210
518-462-5527

- Sponsorship Organization
- Membership Organization
- Atmosphere
- Projects and Activities
- Water

A nonprofit coalition of New York individuals and groups working to eliminate toxic contamination of homes, schools, workplaces and the environment.

Citizens for a Better Environment

122 Lincoln Boulevard, Suite 201
Venice, CA 90291
310-450-5192
- Atmosphere
- Waste
- Speakers Bureaus

Working to create an ecological and democratic future for California that prevents and reduces toxic pollution.

Citizens Opposing a Polluted Environment (COPE)

1908 Tenth Street
Berkeley, CA 94710
415-548-0861
- Membership Organization
- Atmosphere
- Projects and Activities
- Waste
- Speakers Bureaus

Advocates pollution prevention as the most effective way of protecting our environment from industry-generated hazardous waste.

City of Los Angeles Wastewater Youth Education Program

650 South Spring Street
Los Angeles, CA 90014
213-847-9564
- ECO Heroes
- Field Trips
- Workshops
- Water
- Waste

For students and teachers to learn about reclaimed water use in wetlands for the benefit of migratory animals.

CityKids Foundation

57 Leonard Street
New York, NY 10013
212-925-3320
- Projects and Activities
- Water

Develops an understanding between people of all racial, socioeconomic and cultural backgrounds.

Clean Campus Committee

Alhambra High School
101 South Second Street
Alhambra, CA 91801
818-308-2342
- Youth Clubs
- Waste

This student group coordinates the school's paper and aluminum can recycling program, plus plants trees and shrubs around the school.

The Cleanfleet Project

Battle Memorial Institute
505 King Avenue
Columbus, OH 43201-2693
614-424-4062

Cleanfleet helps guide regulatory agencies and public officials in an attempt to replace diesel and gasoline with "cleaner" fuels.

Climate Protection Institute

5833 Balmoral Drive
Oakland, CA 94619
510-531-0100
- Atmosphere
- Projects and Activities

Publishes *Greenhouse Gas-ette* and develops public education materials about changes in global climate.

Clinton Middle School

The Raptor Center
311 West Broad Street
Clinton, TN 37716
615-457-3451
- Youth Clubs

This group of middle school students received the Bush Gardens Award for work in rehabilitating injured wildlife.

The Cloutier Agency

7201 Melrose Avenue
Los Angeles, CA 90046
213-931-1323
- ECO Heroes
- Waste
- Nature and Wildlife
- Speakers Bureaus

Hair, makeup and wardrobe stylists raise awareness and gain attention for environmental issues.

Coalition for Clean Air

Smog: What and Where
122 Lincoln Boulevard, Suite 201
Venice, CA 90291
310-450-3190
- Atmosphere
- Speakers Bureaus

Dedicated to returning healthy air to southern Californians through education, research and advocacy.

Coastcamp —Teen Marine Mammal Studies Camp

Marine Mammal Center
Marin Headlands, GGNRA
Sausalito, CA 94965
415-289-7330
- Expeditions and Camps
- Water
- Nature and Wildlife

Offers summer programs for students ages 7 to 17 who visit marine research, study and education sites.

College of the Atlantic, Allied Whale

Finbacks–Whale Adoption Program
105 Eden Street
Bar Harbor, ME 04609
207-288-5644
- Sponsorship Organization
- Nature and Wildlife

Focuses on solving human and ecological problems.

Colorado Environment Magazine

Colorado Confluence
442 Emerson Street
Denver, CO 80218
303-744-3672
- Projects and Activities

Appears as an insert in the Rocky Mountain News the first Friday of every month.

Common Ground Farm Project

Peace Maker Center
2300 Caesar Avenue South
Minneapolis, MN 55404
612-724-3129
- Projects and Activities

A farm where inner-city kids learn organic gardening while growing food for their community.

Common Ground Garden Program

Gardening Angels
2615 South Grand Avenue, Suite 400

Los Angeles, CA 90007
213-744-4345
• Projects and Activities
Provides workshops and materials on grassroots leadership and conflict-resolution skills.

Community Action International Alliance
Community Action Tours
110 Maryland Avenue NE, Suite 505
Washington, DC 20002
202-547-2640
• Projects and Activities
Offers an environmental activism educational program for inner-city high school students in the DC area.

Compost King: Howard Westley
525 Gretna Green Way
Los Angeles, CA 90049
• ECO Heroes
• Waste
• Speakers Bureaus
A concerned citizen trying to educate people about composting and bees.

Concerns About Kid's Environment (CAKE)
29 Pine Street
Freeport, ME 04032
207-865-6263
• Youth Clubs
• Atmosphere
• Projects and Activities
• Waste
An environmental action network for young people. Training workshops for facilitators are offered.

Conservation International
RAP Team
1015 18th Street NW, Suite 1000
Washington, DC 20036
202-429-5660
• ECO Heroes
• Fundraising Ideas
• Projects and Activities
• Rainforests
• Nature and Wildlife
A group of scientists who are learning everything they can about "hot spots."

Conservation Law Foundation
62 Summer Street
Boston, MA 02110-1008
617-350-0990
• Internships and Careers

• Membership Organization
Founded to improve resource management, environmental protection and public health throughout New England.

Co-op America
Save the Rainforests
2100 M Street NW, Suite 403
Washington, DC 20037
202-872-5307
• Sponsorship Organization
• Fundraising Ideas
• Rainforests
Has developed a strategy to save rainforests by replanting and reforesting logged areas and empowering indigenous peoples.

Cornell Laboratory of Ornithology
159 Sapsucker Woods Road
Ithaca, NY 14850
607-254-BIRD
• Membership Organization
• Nature and Wildlife
Through the study of individual bird species, scientists frequently avert environmental damage.

Cory Dunne
1220 Mountainview Drive
Aspen, CO 81611
• ECO Heroes
• Energy
• Waste
Instituted the "Kids for a Better World" campaign, co-found Aspen's E.A.R.T.H. and has been a speaker for several organizations.

Costa Rica... Naturally
California State University
Northridge Department of Biology
18111 Nordhoff Street
Northridge, CA 91330
818-885-3352
• Expeditions and Camps
• Workshops
• Rainforests
This program consists of a 14-day field class in Central America to study the biology and ecology of tropical forests.

Cousteau Society
Dolphin Log
930 West 21st Street
Norfolk, VA 23517
804-627-1144

• Membership Organization
• Water
Dedicated to the protection and preservation of the quality of life for present and future generations.

Crayon Power
P.O. Box 34
Bloomfield, NJ 07003
201-338-9575
• Classroom Materials and Activities
• Membership Organization
• Projects and Activities
• Rainforests
Environmental education organization established to help elementary school children turn their interest in the environment into positive action.

Creative Learning Center
P.O. Box 3204
Sewanee, TN 37375
615-598-2122
• Energy
Their primary goal is to give students a comprehensive understanding of the world's ecological crises.

Crossroads School for Arts and Sciences
Camp Crossroads
1229 4th Street
Santa Monica, CA 90401
310-458-7300 or 213-465-1184
• Expeditions and Camps
Believes that the fun and excitement of summer camp is a natural way to enrich kids with knowledge of the world around us.

Cultural Conservancy
P.O. Box 5124
Mill Valley, CA 94942
415-491-1948
• Membership Organization
To preserve and protect the essential role of native people in preserving environmental integrity and biological diversity.

Cultural Survival International
Action for Cultural Survival and Cultural Survival Quarterly
215 First Street
Cambridge, MA 02142
617-621-3818
Has helped indigenous people and eth-

nic minorities deal as equals in their encounters with industrial society.

Cynthia Tanguilig
School Recycling Club
3 Comstock Place
Charleston, WV 25314
• ECO Heroes
• Waste
Cynthia Tanguilig formed a Recycling Club that became the largest and smoothest-running student organization in the school.

Dade County Public Schools
Environmental Education Newsletter Update
6161 NW 2 Court
Miami, FL 33127-1259
• Classroom Materials and Activities
• Projects and Activities
Intended to help teachers and administrators stay informed about environmental education opportunities in Dade County Public schools.

...Dear World, Inc.
1510 Oxford Avenue
Austin, TX 78704
512-467-9598
• Speakers Bureaus
An astonishing collection of children's artwork and astute observations about nature and the environment from around the world.

Defenders of Wildlife
Defenders Magazine
1101 Fourteenth Street NW, Suite 1400
Washington, DC 20005
202-682-9400
• Membership Organization
• Nature and Wildlife
A national nonprofit educational organization founded to protect and preserve wildlife and their habitats.

The Denver Museum of Natural History
2001 Colorado Boulevard
Denver, CO 80205
303-370-6321
• Internships and Careers
• Field Trips
• Expeditions and Camps
• Atmosphere
• Energy

• Water
• Nature and Wildlife
Offers school tours and classes, children's workshops, overnight camp-ins and the WOW (Worlds Of Wonder) van.

Devil's Punchbowl Natural Area Park and Nature Center
28000 Devil's Punchbowl Road
Pearblossom, CA 93553
805-944-2743
• Field Trips
• Nature and Wildlife
One of the most spectacular geological formations in California.

Dian Fossey Gorilla Fund
Adopt-A-Gorilla
45 Inverness Drive, Suite B
Englewood, CO 80112-5480
303-790-2349
• Sponsorship Organization
• Membership Organization
• Nature and Wildlife
Dr. Dian Fossey founded the Digit Fund to protect and study endangered mountain gorillas.

Discovery Camp
National Arbor Day Foundation
100 Arbor Avenue
Nebraska City, NE 68410
402-873-9347
• Expeditions and Camps
Offers an opportunity to introduce young people to stewardship principles and provides a chance for nature exploration for ages 9 to 12.

Dolphin Defenders
United Church Neighborhood Houses
Dignity House
812 North Union Boulevard
St. Louis, MO 63108
314-361-8400
• Youth Clubs
• Fundraising Ideas
• Membership Organization
• Projects and Activities
• Water
• Waste
• Nature and Wildlife
Uses a unique method of fundraising by selling stock in the group.

Dome Project, Inc.
Developing Opportunities Through

Meaningful Education
486 Amsterdam Avenue
New York, NY 10024
212-724-1780
• Workshops
• Projects and Activities
Works with at-risk and disadvantaged youngsters to build self-worth and work towards positive educational goals.

Donnelly-Colt Catalog
Progressive Resources for Grassroots Organizing and Fundraising
Box 188
Hampton, CT 06247
203-455-9621 or 800-553-0006
• Fundraising Ideas
Great fundraising items: buttons, t-shirts, stickers, bumper stickers, posters and more.

E2: Environment and Education
881 Alma Real Drive, Suite 118
Pacific Palisades, CA 90272
310-573-9608
• Classroom Materials and Activities
• Energy
• Workshops
• Water
• Waste
Developed a curriculum for middle and secondary school students.

E2 Environmental Enterprise
4223 Glencoe Avenue
Marina Del Rey, CA 90292
310-827-1217
• Water
• Waste
E2's mission is to help "green" businesses by providing them with consultation services.

Earth Academy
Laidlaw Environmental Services, Inc.
220 Outlet Pointe Boulevard
Columbia, SC 29210
800-845-1019 or 803-798-2993
• Classroom Materials and Activities
• Workshops
• Waste
• Speakers Bureaus
Teaches about recycling and ways of reducing household hazardous waste.

Earth Action Club
142 Darwin Street

Santa Cruz, CA 95062
408-423-8749
• Youth Clubs
• Membership Organization
• Projects and Activities
A group of people taking care of the earth through community service in schools.

Earth Beat Press
P.O. Box 33852, Station 'D'
Vancouver, BC, Canada V6J 4L6
604-736-6931
• Classroom Materials and Activities
Publishes several workbooks and dictionaries for children to help them understand their world and the problems in their environment.

Earth Care Paper, Inc.
P.O. Box 14140
Madison, WI 53714
608-223-4024
• Fundraising Ideas
• Waste
Catalog of recycled products. Offers fundraising opportunities.

Earth Day 2000
A Consumer Clearinghouse for the Environmental Decade
116 New Montgomery Street, Suite 530
San Francisco, CA 94105
415-495-5987
• Waste
Acts as an environmental consumer clearinghouse and watchdog.

Earth Endeavors
Video and Educational Projects
881 Alma Real Drive, Suite 300
Pacific Palisades, CA 90272
310-319-9503
• Sponsorship Organization
• Membership Organization
• Projects and Activities
• Water
• Speakers' Bureaus
A video production group offering a public speaking program and mentorship/internship opportunities for high school and university students.

Earth First!
Earth First Journal
P.O. Box 1415
Eugene, OR 95440

503-741-9191
• Membership Organization
• Atmosphere
• Energy
• Water
• Waste
• Rainforests
• Nature and Wildlife
A radical environmental group consisting of autonomous groups around the United States and world.

Earth Force
1501 Wilson Boulevard, 12th Floor
Arlington, VA 22209
703-243-7400
• Youth Clubs
Based upon the principles that youth can benefit the environment through actions learned and thereby become more responsible adult decision makers.

Earth Foundation
Texas Rainforest Action Group
5002 Morningside
Houston, TX 77005
713-699-8010
• Sponsorship Organization
• Fundraising Ideas
• Expeditions and Camps
• Water
• Rainforests
Established to empower educators and students to change the current collision course of the Earth's ecosystems.

Earth Island Institute
300 Broadway, Suite 28
San Francisco, CA 94133
415-788-3666
• Sponsorship Organization
• Membership Organization
• Atmosphere
• Projects and Activities
• Water
• Speakers Bureaus
Concerned with fundamental environmental problems and their solutions. Publishes a wide array of environmental books and magazines.

Earth Kids Organization (EKO)
P.O. Box 3847
Salem, OR 97302
503-363-1896
• Youth Clubs
• Projects and Activities

Operates the Earth Kids Network BBS (Bulletin Board System).

Earth Ninos
Humphrey Avenue School
500 South Humphrey Avenue
Los Angeles, CA 90022
213-263-6958
• Youth Clubs
Offers an after-school program and participates in tree planting, environmental education lessons, students educating students and beach clean-ups

Earth Preservation Fund
3516 NE 155th Street
Seattle, WA 98155
206-365-0686
• Field Trips
• Expeditions and Camps
• Projects and Activities
• Nature and Wildlife
Explores ways in which travelers can assist global conservation and support the well-being of local peoples.

Earth Service Corps
Metrocenter YMCA
909 4th Avenue
Seattle, WA 98104
206-382-5013 or 800-733-YESC
• Membership Organization
• Workshops
• Water
• Speakers Bureaus
Empowers young people to be effective, responsible global citizens.

Earth Service, Inc.
The Environment and Our Personal Behavior Assemblies
2401 Colorado Boulevard, Suite 170
Santa Monica, CA 90404
310-829-9190
• Speakers Bureaus
Fosters a personal and corporate environmental ethic through programs which reinforce all person's contributions to environmental stewardship.

Earth Spirit
Earth Spirit On-line—The Environmental Computer Network
2425 Colorado Avenue, Suite 204
Santa Monica, CA 90404
310-582-8228
ES On-line (310) 264-4785

- Workshops
- Projects and Activities

Dedicated to informing, entertaining and involving people in environmental appreciation. Earth Spirit (ES) On-line is an environmental computer network.

Earth Team

Soil Conservation Service, (USDA)
California Office
2121 C Second Street
Davis, CA 95616
800-THE-SOIL or 916-449-2848
- Internships and Careers

Volunteers work at land conservation projects, field surveys, schools and nonprofit organizations.

Earth Trust Foundation

EarthWays Projects of Earth Trust Foundation
20110 Rockport Way
Malibu, CA 90265
310-456-3534
- Workshops
- Projects and Activities
- Water

Encourages personal awareness and social responsibility from a global perspective through community involvement.

Earth's Birthday Project

The Penny Drive
170 Joralem Street
Brooklyn, NY 11201
800-698-4438
- Fundraising Ideas
- Projects and Activities
- Rainforests

A national network of elementary school teachers that promotes an annual celebration as a way to give children opportunities to care for the Earth.

Earthbound

Environmental Creations
266 Village Green Boulevard, Suite 206
Ann Arbor, MI 48105
313-994-7958
- Fundraising Ideas

A catalog of jewelry, t-shirts, notecards and more with environmental messages. Donates funds to organizations worldwide.

Earthlands

Institute for Environmental Awareness, Inc.
39 Glasheen Road
Petersham, MA 01366-9715
508-724-3428
- Internships and Careers
- Expeditions and Camps
- Membership Organization
- Workshops

A community-based organization promoting responsibility for everyday actions.

Earthminders

Partners in Environmental Education
Maine Department of Environmental Protection, State House Station 17
Agusta, ME 04333
207-287-7688
- Workshops
- Projects and Activities

A coalition of nonprofit groups, state agencies and businesses united to promote environmental education in Maine.

EarthSave Foundation

706 Frederick Street
Santa Cruz, CA 95062-2205
408-423-4069
- Membership Organization
- Atmosphere
- Energy
- Workshops
- Projects and Activities
- Water
- Waste
- Rainforests
- Nature and Wildlife
- Speakers Bureaus

Spreads the message that the healthiest way to eat is also the most economical, the most compassionate and the least environmentally destructive.

Earthstewards Network

P.O. Box 10697
Bainbridge Island, WA 98110
206-842-7986
- Field Trips
- Membership Organization
- Workshops
- Projects and Activities

Network of people that promotes conflict resolution, environmental youth service and global networking. Publishes a network directory.

Earthwatch

EarthCorps
680 Mount Auburn Street
P.O. Box 403
Watertown, MA 02272
617-926-8200
- Internships and Careers
- Field Trips
- Expeditions and Camps
- Membership Organization
- Nature and Wildlife

Offers the public, opportunities to work side by side with distinguished field scientists and scholars.

Eaton Canyon Natural Area Parkland Nature Center

1750 North Altadena Drive
Pasadena, CA 91107
818-398-5420
- Field Trips
- Nature and Wildlife

Contains displays of local flora and fauna, ecosystem concepts and a Naturalist Room with live animals and natural history objects.

Ebersole Environmental Education and Conference Center

Lansing School District
3400 Second Street
Wayland, MI 49348
616-792-6294
- Field Trips
- Expeditions and Camps

Provides residential hands-on environmental education programs for elementary students throughout Michigan.

Eco-Carpool

Florida Kids for Clean Air
Nob Hill Elementary School
Sunrise, FL 33322
305-572-1240
- Youth Clubs
- Atmosphere
- Projects and Activities

A school-wide car pool project. Offers a packet with sample forms and step-by-step instruction on how to set up a car pool in your school.

Eco-Home

4344 Russell Avenue
Los Angeles, CA 90027
310-662-5207
- Field Trips
- Energy

- Workshops
- Water
- Waste

An environmentally sound, energy-efficient, economical house that serves as a model to others.

Eco-Kids Club

Avon Books
Box 767
Dresden, TN 38225
- Youth Clubs
- Membership Organization

Learn how to make a difference in your neighborhood, through a newsletter.

Eco Warrior: Peacefully Protecting the Web of Life on Earth Newsletter

Eco Education
275 East Fourth Street
St. Paul, MN 55101
612-222-7691
- Youth Clubs
- Classroom Materials and Activities
- Speakers' Bureaus

Somebody who knows basic ecology and actually does something about it in a peaceful way.

EcoCity Society

9523 Jasper Avenue
Edmonton, AB, Canada T5H 3V2
403-429-3659
- Projects and Activities

A nonprofit organization that educates and advocates for an ecologically sustainable city.

Ecol-O-Kids

3146 Shadow Lane
Topeka, KS 66604
913-232-4747 or 800-423-7202
- Fundraising Ideas
- Energy
- Workshops
- Projects and Activities
- Water
- Rainforests
- Nature and Wildlife

Catalog of books, games, videos, music toys, puppets, balls and more for the green classroom. Everything is "kid-tested."

Ecologia (Ecologists Linked for Organizing Grassroots Initiatives and

Action)
Box 199
Harford, PA 18823
717-434-2873
- Membership Organization
- Atmosphere
- Projects and Activities
- Water

A global network helping people who are suffering from the devastating environmental effects of Soviet history.

Ecology Center

417 Detroit Street
Ann Arbor, MI 48104
313-761-3186
- Field Trips
- Classroom Materials and Activities
- Membership Organization
- Projects and Activities
- Water
- Waste

Has educational activities and programs that bring hands-on environmental education to the youth of southeast Michigan.

Ecowatch

Great American Opportunities, Inc.
P.O. Box 305142
Nashville, TN 37230-5142
800-251-1542
- Fundraising Ideas

A fundraising program for schools.

Education for Life Foundation

Ananda School
14618 Tyler Foote Road
Nevada City, CA 95959
916-292-3775
- Workshops

A private school for grades K through 9 that teaches how to be a friend and live in harmony with the earth. Workshops are available for teachers.

Education for the People

1806 T Street NW
Washington, DC 20009
202-235-0041
- Youth Clubs

Offers resources for evaluating environmental impacts of campus research dollars and opposing corporate control of education.

Educational Video Center (EVC)

Y.O. TV (Youth Organizers Television)

60 East 13th Street, 4th floor
New York, NY 10003
212-254-2848
- Classroom Materials and Activities
- Projects and Activities

A nonprofit media center dedicated to empowering inner city youth through the creative use of media.

Educator's Rainforest Workshops

International Expeditions, Inc.
801 Devon Place
Alexandria, VA 22314
800-669-6806 or 703-549-6626
- Expeditions and Camps
- Rainforests
- Workshops

Teachers can explore a tropical rainforest while attending a workshop led by scientists, researchers and environmental educators.

Educators for Social Responsibility

23 Garden Street
Cambridge, MA 02138
617-492-1764
- Membership Organization
- Workshops
- Classroom Materials and Activities

Creates and disseminates new ways of teaching for responsible participation in shaping a better world. Training opportunities for teachers are offered.

El Dorado Nature Center

7550 East Spring Street
Long Beach, CA 90815
310-421-9431, ext. 3415
- Field Trips
- Classroom Materials and Activities
- Workshops
- Projects and Activities
- Nature and Wildlife
- Speakers Bureaus

Student nature programs and teacher workshops are offered.

Endangered Species Project

E-205 Fort Mason Center
San Francisco, CA 94123
415-921-3140
- Projects and Activities
- Nature and Wildlife

Assists new endangered species campaigns by helping campaigners develop documentary evidence for public education.

Enviro Cop
P.O. Box 952
Williamsville, NY 14231
• ECO Heroes
• Waste
• Speakers Bureaus
A 7-foot character with a costume made of trash visits schools and puts on a show about cleaning up the environment.

Environmental Action Coalition
625 Broadway, 2nd Floor
New York, NY 10012
212-677-1601
• Membership Organization
• Projects and Activities
• Waste
• Workshops
Promotes recycling and waste prevention in NYC. Developed a "how to" guide for schools and communities.

Environmental Action Foundation
Environmental Action Magazine
6930 Carroll Avenue, Suite 600
Takoma Park, MD 20912
301-891-1100
• Membership Organization
• Energy
• Waste
Works for strong state and federal environmental laws and assists grassroots organizations.

Environmental Association for Great Lakes Education (EAGLE)
3547 Haines Road
Duluth, MN 55811
218-722-2421
• Membership Organization
• Water
Promotes community awareness in order to protect and preserve the Great Lakes ecosystem.

Environmental Awareness Society
Middletown High School South
501 Nutswap Road
Middletown, NJ 07748
908-671-3850
• Youth Clubs
• Nature and Wildlife
• Speakers Bureaus
Members teach environmental lessons at a local elementary school. Plus sponsors a weekly Wilderness program.

Environmental Children's Organization
2477 Point Grey Road
Vancouver, BC, Canada V6K 1A1
604-738-6956
• Youth Clubs
• Membership Organization
Hopes to inform young people about the power their opinions can have on the environment and affect actions for a better world.

Environmental Concern, Inc.
WOW! The Wonders of Wetlands Curriculum
P.O. Box P
St. Michaels, MD 21663
410-745-9620
• Workshop
• Nature and Wildlife
Holds a series of professional courses on wetlands available to educators, college and graduate students as well as government personnel.

Environmental Defense Fund (EDF)
257 Park Avenue South
New York, NY 10010
212-505-2100
• Membership Organization
• Nature and Wildlife
Environmental Defense Fund tries to apply both technical and legal skills to the solution of environmental problems facing humanity and wildlife.

Environmental Education Associates
Borrowed Time
1211 Connecticut Avenue NW, Suite 812
Washington, DC 20036
202-296-4572
• Energy
• Workshops
• Waste
Workshops and materials developed are targeted to secondary-level teachers, but lessons can be shaped to fit students at any level.

Environmental Education Association of Indiana
3516 NE 155th Street
Greenfield, IN 46140
317-326-3117
• Membership Organization

• Workshops
An organization whose purpose is to coordinate, expand and strengthen conservation education programs in Indiana.

Environmental Education for Preschoolers
EARTHWORM Newsletter
Bowling Green State University
College of Education
Bowling Green, OH 43403
419-372-7278
• Classroom Materials and Activities
• Projects and Activities
• Speakers Bureaus
An international network of individuals interested in linking young children and the world of nature.

Environmental Exchange
1718 Connecticut Avenue NW, Suite 600
Washington, DC 20009
202-387-2182
• Membership Organization
A national nonprofit organization with a clearinghouse of information that provides members with access to environmental problem solvers.

Environmental Hazards Management Institute (EHMI)
Earth Express Newsletter
P.O. Box 932, 10 Newmarket Road
Durham, NH 03824
603-868-1547
• Fundraising Ideas
• Membership Organization
• Projects and Activities
A nonprofit environmental education institute with a reputation for building working partnerships to benefit the environment.

Environmental Litigation Fund
P.O. Box 10836
Eugene, OR 97440
503-683-1378
• Projects and Activities
• Workshops
Provides information and holds conferences for activists about the use of various statutes to enforce environmental laws.

Environmental Opportunities
P.O. Box 788

Walpole, NH 03608
603-756-4553
• Internships and Careers
A monthly listing of environmental
jobs throughout the United States.

Environmental Preservation, Inc.
Friends of the Forest, Friends of the
Ocean, Wolf Sponsorship
250 Pequot Avenue
Southport, CT 06490
203-255-1112
• Sponsorship Organization
• Fundraising Ideas
• Classroom Materials and Activities
• Projects and Activities
• Rainforests
• Nature and Wildlife
A cause-conscious marketing company
whose primary focus is to create non-
traditional funds for its nonprofit con-
servation partners.

Environmental Resource Center
411 East 6th Street
Ketchum, ID 83340
208-726-4333
• Classroom Materials and Activities
An umbrella organization for many
projects, with a small public library of
videos, books, curriculum and other
materials.

Environmental Schools
P.O. Box 381
Ocean Park, ME 04063
207-934-7374
• Internships and Careers
• Field Trips
• Expeditions and Camps
A nonprofit, educational organization
that offers residential programs to stu-
dents throughout New England, New
York and parts of Canada.

**Environmental Youth Alliance
(EYA)**
202-1650 Duranleau Street
Vancouver, BC, Canada V6H 3S4
604-737-2258
• Youth Clubs
• Expeditions and Camps
A nonprofit group of young people
working together toward environmen-
tal and social change.

Environmentally Sound
Project R.E.S.P.E.C.T. (Realizing

Expectations through Situations that
Produce Esteem, Confidence, and
Training)
P.O. Box 1620
Agoura Hills, CA 91376
818-597-8733
• Waste
A youth-run group organizing such
events as concerts, comedy shows,
dance shows, motivational seminars
and environmental Pic-up/Pic-nic
days.

The Environmentors Project
5301 Broad Branch Road NW
Washington, DC 20015
202-363-0200
• Projects and Activities
• Sponsorship Organization
Matches volunteer experts with high
school students to develop environmental science projects.

**Envirowaste Management
Program**
Division of N.I.A., Inc.
P.O. Box 266277
Kansas City, MO 64126-6277
816-241-8315 or 800-527-9537
• Internships and Careers
• Workshops
• Waste
Teaches practical use of biological and
physical sciences, environmental laws
and regulations, pollution prevention
and waste management.

Espace Natural Regional
Club Nat'
17 Rue Jean Roisin
59800 Lille, France
31-20-60-60-60 Telecopie: 31-60-69-
36, Telex: 120049
• Youth Clubs
• Sponsorship Organization
A children's organization in France
committed to respecting and protecting
nature through actions.

Exploration Summer Program
124 High Rock Lane
Westwood, MA 02090
617-283-3785
• Expeditions and Camps
Offers courses taught by college students dedicated to sharing their knowledge, experience and love of learning
with campers.

**F.A.C.E.: Fundamental Action to
Conserve Energy**
75 Day Street
Fitchburg, MA 01420-4335
508-345-5385
• Projects and Activities
• Waste
Conducts recycling audits and helps
schools set up recycling programs.

Falcon Magazine
P.O. Box 1718
Helena, MT 59624
800-582-2665
• Projects and Activities
A "just for kids" magazine sponsored
by a group of governmental agencies,
education associations and nonprofit
organizations.

Flagstaff Unified School District #1
Environmental and Outdoor Education
3285 East Sparrow Avenue
Flagstaff, AZ 86004
602-527-6000
• Expeditions and Camps
Offers an outdoor environmental camp
as part of their environmental education curriculum.

**Flat Rock Brook Nature
Association**
Flat Rock Brook
443 Van Nostrand Avenue
Englewood, NJ 07631
201- 567-1265
• Field Trips
• Expeditions and Camps
• Workshops
• Nature and Wildlife
Dedicated to maintaining a natural
wildlife sanctuary that educates about
the ecosystems and wildlife at Flat
Rock Brook.

Floresta
Adopt-A-Farmer
21809 Highway 18, P.O. BOX 1362
Apply Valley, CA 92307
619-240-3220 or 800-842-2243
• Sponsorship Organization
Providing farmers in the Dominican
Republic with agricultural training and
small loans.

**Florida Foundation for Future
Scientists (UF-FAIS)**
Student Science Training Program

University of Florida
111 Norman Hall, P.O. Box 117035
Gainesville, FL 32611
904-392-2310
• Expeditions and Camps
Offers a 4- and 8-week summer program for students in eighth through twelfth grade.

Florida Marine Conservation Corps
Adopt-A-Dolphin
160 Elaine Road
West Palm Beach, FL 33413
407-793-9647
• Sponsorship Organization
• Field Trips
• Expeditions and Camps
• Water
• Nature and Wildlife
A nonprofit marine conservation, research and educational organization founded to protect and preserve Florida's Treasure Coast.

Food from the Hood
Crenshaw High School
5010 11th Street
Crenshaw, CA 90043
213-296-5370
• Youth Clubs
• ECO Heroes
• Projects and Activities
The first student-run natural food company in the country. Proceeds are turned into college scholarships for participating students.

Food Not Bombs
3145 Geary Boulevard, Suite 12
San Francisco, CA 94118
415-330-5030
• Membership Organization
Provides food for people who do not qualify for government support.

Fort Myers High School
River Week
2635 Cortez Boulevard
Fort Myers, FL 33901
813-334-2167
• ECO Heroes
• Classroom Materials and Activities
• Projects and Activities
• Water
Begins with a field trip to a tributary of the local river and then does follow up research and work on preserving the health of their river.

Four Corners School of Outdoor Education
Department BZ, P.O. Box 1029
Monticello, UT 84535
807-587-2516
• Internships and Careers
• Field Trips
• Expeditions and Camps
• Workshops
• Nature and Wildlife
Offers field trips focusing on the natural and human history of the Colorado Plateau.

4-H Environmental Stewardship Program
7100 Connecticut Avenue
Chevy Chase, MD 20815
301-961-2800 or 961-2840
• Youth Clubs
• Projects and Activities
• Nature and Wildlife
Recruits young people to become our nation's environmental stewards through hands-on educational experiences.

Friends of Animals
P.O. Box 1244
Norwalk, CT 06856-1244
203-866-5223
• Membership Organization
• Nature and Wildlife
An international nonprofit organization working to reduce and eliminate the suffering inflicted by humans on animals.

Friends of Environmental Education Society of Alberta (FEESA)
10150-100 Street, 9th Floor
Edmonton, AB, Canada T5J 0P6
403-421-1497
• Atmosphere
• Workshops
• Water
• Waste
Offers teacher training workshops on environmental education in Alberta.

Friends of Hanauma Bay
University of Hawaii
Sea Grant College Program
1000 Pope Road, MSB 226
Honolulu, HI 96822
808-956-2870
• Water

• Nature and Wildlife
• Field Trips
Educates visitors about island reef ecosystems and promotes responsible stewardship.

Friends of Sea Lions Marine Mammal Center
Adopt-A-Seal and Adopt-A-Sea Lion
20612 Laguna Canyon Road
Laguna Beach, CA 92651
714-494-3050
• Sponsorship Organization
• Water
• Nature and Wildlife
A nonprofit volunteer organization dedicated to educating the public and helping sick and wounded sea lions or seals in southern California.

Friends of the Big Wood River
P.O. Box 4411
Ketchum, ID 83340
• Water
To prevent environmental abuses to the Big Wood River, friends educate the public whenever possible and work with state officials.

Friends of the Earth
218 D Street SE
Washington, DC 20003
202-544-2600
• Membership Organization
• Projects and Activities
• Nature and Wildlife
An international nonprofit networking agency of grassroots organizations that educate people on issues and events happening around the world.

Friends of the Los Angeles River (FOLAR)
P.O. Box 292134
Los Angeles, CA 90029
213-223-0585
• Water
• Membership
• Projects and Activities
FOLAR's mission is to revitalize and protect the Los Angeles River and its tributaries.

Friends of the River
128 J Street
Sacramento, CA 95814
916-442-3155
• Water

• Membership
Dedicated to saving California's rivers.

Friends of Trees
P.O. Box 40851
Portland, OR 97240
503-775-1829
• Membership Organization
• Nature and Wildlife
Promotes the planting, care and protection of urban trees as a means of strengthening neighborhoods and renewing the environment.

The Garden Project
35 South Park
San Francisco, CA 94107
415-243-8558
• Projects and Activities
• Nature and Wildlife
A special horticultural program in which San Francisco County Jail convicts work an organic garden and sell the produce to local restaurants.

Gardens for Kids
6223 Poppy Peak Drive
Los Angeles, CA 90042
213-344-9397
• Projects and Activities
A Los Angeles-based nonprofit group that uses gardening to teach young people about nature and environmental stewardship.

The Gateway Pacific Foundation
Earth Train USA
P.O. Box 1668
Orinda, CA 94563
510-254-9101
• Youth Clubs
• Expeditions and Camps
Selected youth leaders from around the world travel by train, stopping in communities to inspire others to take action and work for a healthier future.

Genesee River Valley Project
Rochester Public School #6
595 Upper Falls Boulevard
Rochester, NY 14605
716-546-7780
• ECO Heroes
• Water
• Field Trips
To solve low attendance, low test scores and morale problems teachers

turned to hands-on learning experiences through intensive field studies.

Girl Scouts of America
830 Third Avenue
New York, NY 10022
212-940-7500
• Youth Clubs
• Membership Organization
• Projects and Activities
Published a guidebook entitled *Earth Matters: A Challenge for Environmental Action*.

Global Action and Information Network (GAIN)
575 Soquel Avenue
Santa Cruz, CA 95062
408-457-0130
• Internships and Careers
• Projects and Activities
Provides support to members so they can take action on environmental protection and sustainable development. On-line via EcoNet.

Global Corps
4455 Torrance Boulevard, Suite 237
Torrance, CA 90503
800-775-GLOBAL or 310-530-2905
• Workshops
• Projects and Activities
An international network of information, education, communication and action committed to building a new future for our global community.

Global Habitat Project
Greentrail
745 Atlantic Avenue, 9th floor
Boston, MA 02111
617-526-9480
Dedicated to increasing environmental education opportunities for young people ages 10 to 18 in the Boston area.

Global Kids
Global Action Project (GAP)
561 Broadway, Sixth Floor
New York, NY 10012
212-226-0130
• Youth Clubs
• Workshops
A school-based program that focuses on global issues and world cultures, promoting a sense of community in the classroom.

Global Kidz
4880 Lower Roswell Road, Suite 630
Marietta, GA 30067
800-743-2774 or 404-992-1062
• Youth Clubs
• Membership Organization
• Projects and Activities
An environmental program for children that combines self-esteem with the care of the earth.

Global Response
Environmental Action Network
P.O. Box 7490
Boulder, CO 80306-7490
303-444-0406
• Atmosphere
• Projects and Activities
A network of dedicated letter writers helping to meet the challenge of protecting our global environment.

Global Rivers Environmental Education Network (GREEN)
216 South State Street, Suite 4
Ann Arbor, MI 48104
313-761-8142
• Membership Organization
• Workshops
• Projects and Activities
• Water
Develops and refines environmental monitoring programs, and distributes curricula and resource materials. Over 120 countries are involved.

Global Tomorrow Coalition
Globescope Americas
1325 G Street NW, Suite 915
Washington, DC 20005-3104
202-628-4016
• Internships and Careers
• Workshops
Dedicated to making sustainable development the cornerstone of decision making in the United States.

Global View, Inc.
Ecokids and Earth Scope
2901 Connecticut Avenue NW, Suite B-4
Washington, DC 20008
202-667-5968
• Classroom Materials and Activities
• Rainforests
Believes in the power of children to lead by example in environmental issues.

G.L.O.B.E.: Global Learning and Observation to Benefit the Environment
325 Broadway
Boulder, CO 80303
303-938-2065
• Energy
• Nature and Wildlife
• Projects and Activities
Announced by Vice-president Al Gore on Earth Day 1994 as an effort to involve students in scientific studies to protect the environment.

Gompers Outdoor Learning Laboratory
1005 47th Street
San Diego, CA 92102
619-263-2717
• Youth Clubs
• ECO Heroes
• Energy
Teachers, students and parents transformed an abandoned lot into an outdoor learning laboratory.

Good Knight Campaign for Protection of Children and Earth
National Missing Child Search Society
8200 Professional Place, Suite 106
Landover, MD 20785
301-577-7755
• Membership Organization
This organization attempts to prevent victimization of children and empower them to protect each other and the earth.

Goodwill Industries of Southern California
Students Against Violating the Environment (SAVE)
342 San Fernando Road
Los Angeles, CA 90031
213-343-9927
• Projects and Activities
Supplies Los Angeles high school students with bags to collect different kinds of recyclables during the week of Earth Day.

The Gorilla Foundation
Allan G. Sanford Gorilla Preserve
Maui, Hawaii
P.O. Box 620-240
Woodside, CA 94062
415-831-8505
• Sponsorship Organization

• Rainforests
• Nature and Wildlife
Is establishing a large, secluded sanctuary for families of endangered gorillas.

Gould League
Platypus Creek Club
Genoa Street, Moorabbin 3189
P.O. Box 446
Prahran, Australia 3181
03-532 0909
• Youth Clubs
• Membership Organization
Focuses on environmental education and ecologically sustainable development, focusing on ways kids can help the environment.

Graduation Pledge Alliance
P.O. Box 4439
Arcata, CA 95521
707-826-3011
• Projects and Activities
"I Pledge to investigate thoroughly and take into account the social and environmental consequences of any job opportunity I consider."

Grand Canyon Field Institute
Natural History Association
P.O. Box 399
Grand Canyon, AZ 86023
602-638-2485
• Expeditions and Camps
Dedicated to enhancing the understanding and enjoyment of the Grand Canyon through educational programs.

Great Smoky Mountains Institute
Naturalist and Educator Weeks
Route 1, Box 700
Townsend, TN 37882
615-448-6709
• Workshops
• Nature and Wildlife
Features artistic presentations, environmental education lessons, hikes, natural history sessions, nighttime wildlife census and more.

Greater Los Angeles Zoo
Zoo Camp
5333 Zoo Drive
Los Angeles, CA 90027
213-663-4819 tours, 213-666-5133 presentations, 213-664-1100 wildlife savers

• Field Trips
• Classroom Materials and Activities
• Workshops
• Projects and Activities
• Nature and Wildlife
Has many on-site and outreach programs available to teachers and students.

Greater Newark Conservancy
Living Laboratories, Weatherwatch and Eco-Act
303-9 Washington Street
Newark, NJ 07102
201-642-4646
• Field Trips
• Classroom Materials and Activities
• Projects and Activities
Has 3 programs within its youth education program: Living Laboratories, Weatherwatch and Eco-Act.

Green Corps
1109 Walnut Street, 4th Floor
Philadelphia, PA 19107
215-829-1760
• Internships and Careers
• Projects and Activities
A grassroots organization dedicated to training and working with young environmentalists.

Green Earth Fundraising Programs
P.O. Box 950
Santa Cruz, NM 87567
800-880-1915
• Fundraising Ideas
This program offers environmental fundraising alternatives.

Green Education Development Fund
P.O. Box 30208
Kansas City, MO 64112
816-731-9366
• Projects and Activities
The Green Education and Development Fund is a national educational group associated with the emergence of a green political movement in the United States.

The Green Group
Green Kid Club
164 Cortleigh Boulevard
Toronto, ON, Canada M5N 1P5
416-487-4767
• Youth Clubs
A program in which students help their

family make simple but important changes in lifestyle to conserve and preserve our environment.

Green Logic: The Environmental Catalog
P.O. Box 2988
Santa Cruz, CA 95063
800-473-3645
• Fundraising Ideas
Provides opportunities for schools to make money and make a difference by promoting environmentally friendly products.

The Green River Preserve
Green River Road, P.O. Box 1000
Cedar Mountain, NC 28718
704-324-5832 (winter) or 704-885-2250 (summer)
• Expeditions and Camps
• Nature and Wildlife
Sessions open to students in grades 4 through 8, in ecology, botany, zoology, ornithology, forestry, entomology, Indian lore and pottery.

Greener Pastures Institute
P.O. Box 2190
Pahrump, NV 89041-2190
702-382-4847 or 800-688-6352
• Fundraising Ideas
Developed a fun and educational tool for changing habits and attitudes about ecological issues, a book of eco-citations and commendations.

Greenpeace International
1436 U Street NW
Washington, DC 20009
202-462-8817
• Membership Organization
• Projects and Activities
• Nature and Wildlife
Greenpeace is an international environmental organization dedicated to preserving the earth and the life it supports.

Global Habitat Project
Greentrail: A Kids' Summer Guide to Environmental Activities in Boston
745 Atlantic Avenue, 9th floor
Boston, MA 02111
617-526-9480
• Field Trips
• Expeditions and Camps
Provides information on activities for

youth to get involved in, from hiking to museums to riding public transportation.

Greenworks
Envirolopes
P.O. Box 1926
Portland, OR 97207
503-234-2893
• Fundraising Ideas
• Waste
Envirolopes are made of recycled paper and attached with a glue strip to used envelopes so they may be reused.

Groundwater Foundation
Water Festival Workshop
P.O. Box 22558
Lincoln, NE 68542
402-434-2740
• Workshops
• Water
• Speakers' Bureaus
Sponsors the Water Festival Workshop, which shares information on successful water education and activities.

Group for the South Fork
117 Main Street
Bridgehampton, NY 11932
516-537-1400
• Membership Organization
• Workshops
• Water
Advocates protection of the environment, rural character and quality of life on the South Fork.

Gulf of Mexico Program
Mote Marine Laboratory
Building 1103, Room 202
Stennis Space Center, MS 39529
601-688-1519
• Sponsorship Organization
• Classroom Materials and Activities
Established to develop and implement a strategy to protect, restore and maintain the health and productivity of the Gulf of Mexico.

Hamilton County Department of Environmental Services
Spencer's Team News
Solid Waste Division
1632 Central Parkway, Room 202
Cincinnati, OH 45210
513-763-4638

• Waste
This local newsletter, for students in grades 3 through 6, has information on environmental activities and education.

Harmony Foundation
Environmental Values Education
Lester B. Person College of the Pacific
560 Johnson Street, Suite 209
Victoria, BC, Canada V8W 3C6
604-380-3001
• Workshops
Teacher workshops explore environment and development issues and their classroom applications.

Hawaii Preparatory Academy
P.O. Box 428
Kamuela, HI 96743-0428
808-885-7321
• ECO Heroes
• Water
Offers environmental education programs in their college preparatory curriculum.

Hawk Mountain Sanctuary
RD 2 Box 191
Kempton, PA 19529
610-756-6961
• Internships and Careers
• Field Trips
Environmental Education Internship incorporates both field work and research.

Hawkwatch International, Inc.
Protecting Raptors and Our Environment
P.O. Box 35706
Albuquerque, NM 87176-5706
505-255-7622
• Sponsorship Organization
• Membership Organization
Monitors and protects hawks, eagles and falcons and their habitats.

Headlands Institute
Golden Gate National Recreation Area
Building 1033
Sausalito, CA 94965
415-332-5771
• Workshops
• Speakers Bureaus
• Classroom Materials
Designs programs utilizing Marin Headlands to complement curricula and to meet individual teachers needs.

Heal the Bay
1640 Fifth Street, Suite 204
Santa Monica, CA 90401
310-394-4552
• Membership Organization
• Water
• Speakers Bureaus
Using research, education, outreach
and policy to make Santa Monica Bay
and California's coastal waters safe
and healthy.

**Heart of the Rockies Adventure
Program**
Rocky Mountain National Park
Estes Park, CO 80517
303-586-2371
• Field Trips
• Workshops
Offers K through 12 programs related
to Estes Park's natural resources.
Workshops and guidebooks available
for teachers.

**Heartland All Species
Project**
201 Westport Road
Kansas City, MO 64111
816-756-5686
• Workshops
• Projects and Activities
• Nature and Wildlife
Offers several projects, including art,
theater, history and other educational-
ly oriented programs.

**Heartland Peaks
Workshop**
2500 West Flamingo
Nampa, ID 83651
800-632-6586, ext. 3490
• Expeditions and Camps
• Workshops
• Nature and Wildlife
Allows educators to learn new meth-
ods of bringing environmental educa-
tion into the classroom.

Help Our World (HOW)
Columbia School
345 Plainfield Avenue
Berkeley Heights, NJ 07922
908-474-1600
• Youth Clubs
• ECO Heroes
• Projects and Activities
Encourages an active participation in
environmental solutions.

Help Save Our Environment
421 Linebrook Road
Ipswich, MA 01938
508-356-0152
• Youth Clubs Atmosphere
• Workshops
• Projects and Activities
Students and adults from around the
globe studying acid rain and its effects.

Hidden Villa
26870 Moody Road
Los Altos Hills, CA 94022
415-948-4690
• Field Trips
• Expeditions and Camps
Engages children and adults in hands-
on, innovative programs emphasizing
environmental awareness and multicultural understanding.

**High Schools Organized to Protect
the Environment (HOPE)**
42 Eames Street
Providence, RI 02906
401-789-3692
• Atmosphere
• Projects and Activities
• Waste
• Rainforests
• Nature and Wildlife
HOPE was organized by 24 Rhode
Island high schools with the goal to set
up an environmental conference.

Homeless Garden Project
P.O. Box 617
Santa Cruz, CA 95061
408-426-3609
• Field Trips
• Projects and Activities
• Speakers Bureaus
Provides a therapeutic context for
homeless people through meaningful
labor in an organic garden.

**Household Hazardous Waste
Project (HHWP)**
University of Missouri Extension
1031 East Battlefield, Suite 214
Springfield, MO 65807
417-889-5000
• Classroom Materials and Activities
• Atmosphere
• Projects and Activities
• Water
• Waste
Develops and promotes education and

action concerning household hazardous products.

How on Earth! (HOE!)
P.O. Box 3347
West Chester, PA 19381
717-529-8638
• Classroom Materials
A quarterly newsletter for and by
youth who support compassionate,
ecologically sound living.

Hulbret Outdoor Center
The Aloha Foundation
RR1, Box 91A
Fairlee, VT 05045
802- 333-9840
• Field Trips
• Expeditions and Camps
Personal growth, community responsi-
bility and environmental awareness
are the essence of this center.

Human Environment Center
1001 Connecticut Avenue NW, Suite
827
Washington, DC 20036
202-331-8387
• Internships and Careers
• Membership Organization
• Workshops
Internship programs place
Washington, DC, area minority high
school students with environmental
agencies.

Human Rights Watch
National Headquarters
485 Fifth Avenue
New York, NY 10017
212-972-8400
Monitors and promotes human rights
in 70 countries worldwide.

**Humane Society of the Desert:
Orphan Pet Oasis**
P.O. Box 798
North Palm Springs, CA 92258
619-329-0203
• Membership Organization
Saves numerous animals every year.
Publishes a newsletter.

**Humane Society of the United
States**
National Association for Humane and
Environmental Education
67 Salem Road

East Haddam, CT 06423-1736
203-434-1940
• Classroom Materials and Activities
• Membership Organization
• Projects and Activities
• Nature and Wildlife
Student action guide explains how to take action and start a school group to help the environment and protect animals from inhumane treatment.

Human-I-Tees

The Environmental Tee Shirt Company
19 Marble Avenue
Pleasantville, NY 10570
914-741-2424 or 800-A-PLANET
• Fundraising Ideas
This organizaton's goal is to help student groups increase environmental awareness through fundraisers.

Idaho Wildlife Rescue Center

P.O. Box 2471
Ketchum, ID 83340
208-726-1919
• Nature and Wildlife
A rehabilitation unit caring for injured and orphaned wildlife until they can be released back to the wild.

Illinois Department of Energy Education Development (ILEED)

Camp K.E.E.P., Energy Intern Program, Kilowatt Kids
ILEED/ENR 325 West Adams, Room 300
Springfield, IL 62704-1892
800-526-0844 or 217-785-3412
• Youth Club's
• Internships and Careers
• Expeditions and Camps
• Energy
Has various programs teaching students how saving energy saves money and helps the environment.

Indigenous Environmental Network

P.O. Box 485
Bemidji, MN 56601
218-751-4967
• Membership Organization
• Workshops
• Waste
Serves as a grassroots alliance to help indigenous people stand up to policy that contaminates their land, water and air.

Inherit the Earth

P.O. Box 814
Crawfordsville, IN 47933
• Membership Organization
• Nature and Wildlife
A local grassroots organization connected to humane and environmental awareness action groups worldwide.

Inland Seas Education Association

101 Dame Street
Suttons Bay, MI 49682
616-271-3077
• Field Trips
• Membership Organization
• Water
• Nature and Wildlife
Promote the study and conservation of the Great Lakes ecosystem by taking high school students out on the water.

Institute for Earth Education

Talking Leaves Newsletter
Cedar Cove
Greenville, WV 24945
304-832-6404
• Workshops
Creates adventuresome, magical educational programs. Publishes a newsletter full of timely events, programs and activities.

Institute for Environmental Education

18554 Haskins Road
Chagrin, OH 44023-1823
216-543-7303 or 800-484-7949
• Workshops
Improves the environmental quality of life through a variety of educational programs, workshops and seminars around the country.

Institute for Global Communications

Peace Net, Eco Net, Conflict Net
18 De Bloom Street
San Francisco, CA 94017
415-442-0220
• Energy
• Projects and Activities
• Water
• Rainforests
Comprises a worldwide computer communications system dedicated solely to environmental preservation, peace and human rights.

Institute for International Cooperation and Development

Plant Trees in Africa
P.O. Box 103-X
Williamstown, MA 01267
413-458-9828
• Internships and Careers
• Workshops
Students and teachers travel to different countries planting trees, vegetables and flowers, teaching children and agricultural workers.

International Development Research Center

Summer Institute in Costa Rica
Box 8500
Ottawa, ON, Canada K1G 3H9
613-236-6163
• Workshops
Helps high school and postsecondary educators meet scientists working on the most pressing problems of developing countries.

International Pen Friends

P.O. Box 65, Homecrest Station
Brooklyn, NY 11229
718-769-1785
• Youth Clubs
• Projects and Activities
Provides an international channel of communication so people can learn to understand, respect and live in harmony with each other.

International Planned Parenthood Federation

Under 20 Clubs
902 Broadway, 10th floor
New York, NY 10010
212-995-8800
• Youth Clubs
Reaches teenagers with messages addressing issues of family planning, drug and alcohol use, nutrition and hygiene.

International Student Trade, Environment and Development Program

P.O. Box 13208
Minneapolis, MN 55414
612-379-3905
• Youth Clubs
Helps students organize around free trade negotiations related to environmental quality. Publishes the *Campus Action Guide to Free Trade*.

International Wildlife Coalition
Whale Adoption Project
P.O. Box 388, 634 North Falmouth
Highway
North Falmouth, MA 02556-0388
508-564-9980
• Sponsorship Organization
• Nature and Wildlife
Humpback whale adoption programs.
Adopters receive a quarterly newsletter.

Island Institute
Whale Camp
4004 58th Place SW
Seattle, WA 98116
206-938-0345
• Field Trips
• Expeditions and Camps
• Nature and Wildlife
Operates a variety of residential marine
science programs for individuals and
groups.

Ivan Siemens
The Hungry Lunch, Starpower
Simulation
Box 538
Bon Accord, Canada T0A OKO
• ECO Heroes
• Classroom Materials and Activities
• Water
Increases awareness about world
hunger and the disparity in access to
resources.

Izaak Walton League of America
Save Our Streams Program (SOS)
1401 Wilson Boulevard
Level B
Arlington, VA 22209
301-548-0150
• Sponsorship Organization
• Water
• Nature and Wildlife
• Membership Organization
• Classroom Materials and Activities
Gets people involved in improving the
water quality of local streams.

**Jane Goodall Institute for Wildlife
Research, Education and
Conservation**
Roots and Shoots Club and Adopt-A-
Chimpanzee
P.O. Box 599
Ridgefield, CT 06877
203-431-2099

• Youth Clubs
• Sponsorship Organization
• Membership Organization
• Nature and Wildlife
Committed to studying and protecting
chimpanzees and mobilizing young
people around the world to care for
their immediate environment.

Jennifer Kyer
421 Oradell Avenue
Oradell, NJ 07649
• ECO Heroes
Jennifer Kyer worked with her principal
to develop a recycling program at her
school that is still operating today. She
welcomes letters.

Jim Morris Environmental T- Shirts
P.O. Box 831
Boulder, CO 80306
303-444-6430
• Fundraising Ideas
Offers fundraising opportunities for
schools and environmental groups.

**Joining Animals and Man/Woman
(JAM)**
The George School
Newtown, PA 18940
215-579-6589
• Youth Clubs
• Speakers Bureaus
Eliminated veal from the school menu
and currently arranges for animal
rights speakers.

Jon Jay
Treecyclers
1933 Grace Avenue, Suite 2
Hollywood, CA 90068
213-876-8575
• ECO Heroes
• Projects and Activities
A one-man organization dedicated to
planting live Christmas trees in local
parks, schools and canyons. Hires "at
risk" neighborhood kids to help.

Journey's End Farm Camp
Box 136, RD 1
Newfoundland, PA 18445
717-689-2353
• Expeditions and Camps
A hands-on summer camp for ages 7
to 12 in a farm setting that emphasizes
peace, simple living and environmental
concerns.

Kate Budd
Students Aware of the Value of Earth
(SAVE)
4738 Gardenville Road
Pittsburgh, PA 15236
• Youth Clubs
• ECO Heroes
• Waste
Received the prestigious Rachel Carson
Award given to high school students
who have contributed to environmental awareness.

**Keewaydin Environmental
Education Center**
Lake Dunmore
Salisbury, VT 05766
802- 352-9011
• Workshops
• Expeditions and Camps
Provides residential environmental
education programs for school groups,
grades 4 through 8.

Kevin Bell
1818 Tumbleweed Road
Fallon, NV 89406
• ECO Heroes
• Water
Kevin's water research earned him the
"Youth Conservationist of the Year" for
Nevada and the President's
Environmental Youth Award.

Keystone Science School
Box 8606
Keystone, CO 80435-7998
303-468-5824
• Expeditions and Camps
• Workshops
• Nature and Wildlife
Educational programs focus on natural
sciences and colorful cultural history of
the Colorado Rockies.

**Kids C.U.E. (Kids for Cleaning Up
the Environment)**
10120 West Fair Avenue
Littleton, CO 80127
303-972-1930
• Eco Heroes
• Projects and Activities
A nonprofit environmental newspaper
written and illustrated by kids for kids.

Kids Against Junk Food
Center for Science in the Public Interest
1875 Connecticut Avenue NW, Suite 300

Washington, DC 20009
202-332-9110 ext. 387
• Youth Clubs
• Membership Organization
• Atmosphere
A national organization of youth interested in improving children's eating habits.

Kids Against Pollution (KAP)
Tenakill School
P.O. Box 775
Closter, NJ 07624
201-784-0668
• Youth Clubs
• ECO Heroes
• Atmosphere
• Membership Organization
Founded in 1987 by a fifth-grade class, a worldwide student network that empowers youth to help the environment.

Kids for a Clean Environment (Kids F.A.C.E.)
Earth Flag
P.O. Box 158254
Nashville, TN 37215
615-331-7381 or 800-952-3223
• Youth Clubs
• ECO Heroes
• Projects and Activities
Helps local grassroots clubs get started on cleaning up their environment by providing tips.

Kids for Nature
The Nature Company
750 Hearst Avenue
Berkeley, CA 94710
800-227-1114
• Youth Clubs
• Membership Organization
• Waste
• Nature and Wildlife
Members receive the quarterly newsletter *TerraTopia Times,* plus many other educational and fun items.

Kids for Saving Earth
P.O. Box 47247
Plymouth, MN 55447
612-525-0002
• Youth Club's
• Sponsorship Organization
• Fundraising Ideas
• Membership Organization

• Energy
• Rainforests
Educates and empowers children of all ages worldwide to take positive, peaceful actions that help the environment.

Kids for the Earth
Davis Middle School
350 Gramatan Avenue
Mount Vernon, NY 10552
914-665-5120
• Youth Clubs
• ECO Heroes
• Projects and Activities
A group of seventh and eighth graders who started many successful environmental programs in their school and community.

Kids Save the Planet
(formerly, Kids Save the Ozone Project)
P.O. Box 471
Forest Hills, NY 11375
718-997-7837
• Youth Clubs
• ECO Heroes
• Membership Organization
• Atmosphere
• Energy
• Water
• Waste
• Nature and Wildlife
Helped pass a law stopping auto repair shops from releasing CFCs. Has grown to 200 national chapters working on many projects.

Kids Speak Workshops
808 Second Avenue
Fayetteville, TN 37334
615-433-8871
• Workshops
• Speakers Bureaus
Holds workshops throughout the year.

Kidseeds Garden Club and Kidseeds Garden Kit
N K Lawn and Garden Company
P.O. Box 1974
Young America, MN 55594-1974
• Youth Clubs
• Projects and Activities
• Classroom Materials
Helps educate youngsters in gardening and natural science. Offers kids gardening products.

Kimbark Elementary School
18021 Kenwood Avenue
San Bernardino, CA 92407
909-880-6641
• ECO Heroes
Has been recognized as a national role model for their integration of environmental education throughout the school.

The Kindness Club
65 Brunswick Street
Fredericton, New Brunswick, E3B 1G5
506-459-3379
• Youth Clubs
• Membership Organization
• Nature and Wildlife
• Classroom Materials and Activities
Teaches children to respect and be kind to all living things and to understand the environment.

Kiwanis Camp Wyman
600 Kiwanis Drive
Ereka, MO 63025
314-938-5245
• Expeditions and Camps
Offers a summer nature program for kids ages 8 to 16.

L.A. Harvest
Greening Exchange Newsletter
1611 South Hope Street, 2nd floor
P.O. Box 151226
Los Angeles, CA 90015
213-742-0429
• Projects and Activities
Helps reshape the environmental, economic and aesthetic status of Los Angeles through community-based gardening and horticulture.

L.A. Shares
3224 Riverside Drive
Los Angeles, CA 90027
213-485-1097
• ECO Heroes
• Classroom Materials and Activities
• Waste
Donations of reusable office furniture and art supplies to nonprofit groups in Los Angeles County. Schools are eligible for art materials only.

L.A. Works
351 South La Brea Avenue, Suite 202
Los Angeles, CA 90036
213-465-4095

• Projects and Activities
Committed to revitalizing Los Angeles by making it easier for people to get involved in their communities through volunteer projects.

Lake Michigan Summer Institute for Teachers
Wisconsin Department of Natural Resources
1819 Harwood Court
Sun Prairie, WI 53590
618-264-6282
• Workshops
For teachers of grades 4 through 10.

Hands on Biodiversity: Networking Students and Their Biomes
Lake Ridge Academy
37501 Center Ridge Road
North Ridgeville, OH 44039
216-327-1175
• Projects and Activities
Links 5 high school classes in different environmental regions via Internet. Students share ecological/scientific data.

Lake Upsata Guest Ranch
Box 6
Ovando, MT 59854
800-594-7687
• Expeditions and Camps
• Water
• Nature and Wildlife
Guests at the ranch participate in wildlife programs presented by top wildlife biologists.

Land Stewardship Project
14758 Ostlund Trail North
Marine on St. Croix, MN 55047
612-433-2770
• Membership Organization
• Projects and Activities
• Nature and Wildlife
Works to encourage a national farming ethic. Has a number of educational programs and resources.

Land Trust Alliance
1319 F Street NW, Suite 501
Washington, DC 20004-1106
202-638-4725
• Membership Organization
• Projects and Activities
• Nature and Wildlife
Works to save critical open areas in communities for future generations. There are more than 1,000 of these groups at work in all 50 states.

Leaf It to Us
P.O. Box 184
Menam, ID 83434
208-754-4934
• Fundraising Ideas
• Projects and Activities
• Nature and Wildlife
Helps youth organize tree-planting programs in their communities.

Leave No Trace!
National Outdoor Leadership School
288 Main Street
Lander, WY 82520
307-332-6973
• Expeditions and Camps
• Waste
• Nature and Wildlife
• Workshops
Has pioneered the teaching and development of practical conservation techniques designed to minimize impact on wilderness areas.

Legacy International
Route 4, Box 265
Bedford, VI 24523
703-297-5982
• Expeditions and Camps
Legacy offers summer programs for youth ages 15 to 18 ranging from environmental topics to the performing arts while putting their idealism into action.

Let's Get Growing
1900 Commercial Way
Santa Cruz, CA 95065
408-464-1868
• Classroom Materials
• Projects and Activities
A catalog of curriculum, kits and science supplies for kids of all ages.

Life Lab Science Program
1156 High Street
Santa Cruz, CA 95064
408-459-2001
• Workshops
• Classroom Materials
A hands-on garden-based science education program for elementary school students. Teacher training workshops are offered.

Lighthawk
P.O. Box 8163
Santa Fe, NM 87504
505-982-9656
• Membership Organization
• Atmosphere
• Water
• Waste
• Rainforests
• Speakers Bureaus
An environmental Airforce. Sparrow, the youth outreach program, brings environmental issue into classrooms.

Lincoln Filene Center
Tufts University
Medford, MA 02155
617-628-5000 ext. 2400
Publishes the *Guide to Environmental Programs in New England Colleges and Universities*. Also provides environmental leadership training.

Living Earth Learning Project
P.O. Box 2160
Boston, MA 02106
617-367-8687
• Workshops
• Projects and Activities
• Nature and Wildlife
Offers a series of educational programs about animal and environmental issues for all grades. Teacher workshops are available.

Lizard Lady North
2448 Great Highway 1
San Francisco, CA 94116
• Projects and Activities
• Rainforests
• Speakers Bureaus
The Lizard Lady brings her reptile road show to schools, summer camps and birthday parties.

Lloyd Center for Environmental Studies
P.O. Box 87037
South Dartmouth, MA 02748
508-990-0505
• Field Trips
• Workshops
• Nature and Wildlife
A nonprofit education and research facility that focuses on coastal issues.

Lloyd's Pets and Reptiles
20929 Pioneer

Lakewood, CA 90715
310-924-3115
• Nature and Wildlife
• Speakers Bureaus
Offers hands on classroom encounters with snakes, lizards, tarantulas, frogs, scorpions and iguana.

Los Angeles Children's Museum
Club Eco
310 North Main Street
Los Angeles, CA 90012
213-687-8801
• Field Trips
Club Eco is an interactive kids' clubhouse designed so visitors come away with a greater awareness of their urban environment.

Los Angeles Conservation Corps
2824 South Main Street
Los Angeles, CA 90007
213-749-3601
• Projects and Activities
• Internships and Careers
Employs and educates young people between the ages of 18 and 23 to perform community improvement and conservation projects.

Los Angeles Natural History Museum
Educational Division, Adventures in Nature
900 Exposition Boulevard
Los Angeles, CA 90007
213-744-3534
• Field Trips
• Expeditions and Camps
• Nature and Wildlife
• Internships and Careers
Provides exhibits, classes and other activities that promote ecological awareness. An apprenticeship program trains students in research methods.

Magic Basket
4025 Laskey Road
Toledo, OH 43623
419-475-6042
• Classroom Material
• Speakers Bureaus
A nature-based curriculum using puppets that believe that children are the key to the success of recycling, and conserving living beings in our world.

Make-A-Difference Day
U.S.A. Weekend
1000 Wilson Boulevard
Arlington, VA 22229
703-276-6432
• Projects and Activities
Make-A-Difference Day, October 22, is a chance to do something to help your local community.

Malibu Foundation
Adopt-A-Beach School Assembly Program
1257 North Genesee Avenue
Los Angeles, CA 90046
213-650-8143
• Field Trips
• Water
• Waste
• Speakers Bureaus
A nonprofit organization dedicated to the health of our planet through education in the schools and the media.

Mammal Marine Stranding Center
P.O. Box 773, 3625 Brigantine Boulevard
Brigantine, NJ 08203
609-266-0538
• Membership Organization
• Nature and Wildlife
A nonprofit organization dedicated to rescuing, rehabilitating and releasing stranded marine mammals and sea turtles.

Manomet Bird Observatory
The Birder's Exchange
81 Point Road, Box 1770
Manomet, MA 02345
508-224-6521
• Sponsorship Organization
• Membership Organization
• Nature and Wildlife
Donates equipment and exchanges information between North American birders and Latin American birders.

Marine and Aquatic Teacher Education
Ohio State University Sea Grant College Program
1314 Kinnear Road, Room 1541
Columbus, OH 43212-1194
614-292-8949
• Workshops
• Nature and Wildlife
• Water

Offers teacher and student workshops on marine wildlife and ecosystems.

Marine Education Program
Los Angeles County Office of Education
9300 Imperial Highway
Downey, CA 90242-2890
310-922-6330
• Field Trips
• Classroom Materials and Activities
• Nature and Wildlife
• Speakers Bureaus
An umbrella for several Los Angeles environmental education programs.

Marine Science Institute
Marine Science Mobile
500 Discovery Parkway
Redwood City, CA 94063-4715
415-364-2760
Provides interdisciplinary education that cultivates a responsibility for the environment both on-site and through a Marine Science Mobile that visits schools.

Marine Science Teacher Education Program (M-STEP)
UCLA Marine Science Center
405 Hilgard Avenue
Los Angeles, CA 90024-1606
310-206-8247
• Internships and Careers
• Workshops
Eighty teachers from the Los Angeles Unified School district (grades 5 through 12) initially participated in the UCLA Marine Science Teacher Education Program intensive 6-week course in interdisciplinary marine science.

Master Recycler Composter Program
Waste Watchers
18410 Muncaster Road
Derwood, MD 20855
301-590-9638
• Classroom Materials and Activities
• Projects and Activities
• Waste
Educates teens to spread awareness about solid waste to elementary school students.

Matthew Mazer and Keith Schiller
The Yosemite Fund

155 Montgomery Street, Suite 1104
San Francisco, CA 94104
415-434-1782
• ECO Heroes
• Nature and Wildlife
• Fundraising Ideas
Thought up having license plates picturing Yosemite National Park. Money raised goes to preservation and restoration of the park.

Mayaquest
Center for Global Environmental Education, Hamline University
529 South 7th Street, Suite 310
Minneapolis, MN 55415
612-349-6606 or 800-919-MAYA
• Classroom Materials and Activities
• Expeditions and Camps
A bicycle expedition that takes 12-year-olds through Central and South America to discover new information about the Mayan world.

Meadowcreek Environmental Education Center
P.O. Box 100
Fox, AR 72051
501-363-4500
• Field Trips
• Expeditions and Camps
• Workshops
Offers education programs, tours, workshops, family retreats, youth camps and teacher training programs.

Miami Valley Earth Central
Good Choices Newsletter
P.O. Box 401
Spring Valley, OH 45370
513-862-6100
• Workshops
• Projects and Activities
• Water
• Speakers Bureaus
A clearinghouse of environmental education information and water quality workshops.

Milton Academy Mountain School
Rural Route 1, Box 123 F
Vershire, VT 05079-9722
802-685-4520
• Workshops
High school juniors and seniors spend a semester living and working on an organic farm while maintaining a full academic load.

Mohican School in the Out-of-Doors, Inc.
21882 Shadley Valley Road
Danville, OH 43014
614-599-9753
• Field Trips
• Expeditions and Camps
Offers outdoor environmental education to more than 70 Ohio school districts each year.

Monterey Bay Aquarium
886 Cannery Row
Monterey, CA 93940-1085
408-648-4800
• Internships and Careers
• Field Trips
• Classroom Materials and Activities
• Workshops
• Water
• Nature and Wildlife
Promotes stewardship of Monterey Bay and the ocean environment through innovative exhibits, public education and scientific research.

Mote Marine Laboratory
1600 Thompson Parkway
Sarasota, FL 34236
813-388-4441
• Sponsorship Organization
• Membership Organization
• Water
•Nature and Wildlife
An independent research center with several outreach programs and teacher training.

Mountains Education Program
2600 Franklin Canyon Road
Beverly Hills, CA 90210
310-858-3834
• Internships and Careers
• Field Trips
• Expeditions and Camps
• Projects and Activities
• Nature and Wildlife
Operates 4 programs: Share and Care Naturalist Program, the Mountain Parks Information Service, the Recreation Transit Program and the Urban Naturalists in Training Program.

M.S. Creations
P.O. Box 83
Bolivar, MO 65613
417-326-7736

• Classroom Materials
Newsletter focusing on science and nature materials for children ages 2 through 13.

National Anti-Vivisection Society (NAVS)
3516 NE 155th Street
Brookfield, WI 53005-9976
800-888-NAVS
• Membership Organization
• Nature and Wildlife
Has sought to eliminate animal use in biochemical research, product testing and education.

National Association of Service and Conservation Corps
Youth Corps
666 Eleventh Street NW, Suite 500
Washington, DC 20001
202-737-6272
• Internships and Careers
• Membership Organization
Conservation and service corps programs, serving 20,000 young people annually across the country.

National Audubon Society
Audubon All Species Day,
The Expedition Institute
700 Broadway
New York, NY 10003
212-979-3000
• Field Trips
• Expeditions and Camps
• Membership Organization
• Workshops
• Projects and Activities
• Nature and Wildlife
Supports grassroots level of environmental protection. Offers trips, camps and workshops.

National Energy Education Development
The NEED Project
P.O. Box 2518
Reston, VA 22090
703-860-5029
• Internships and Careers
• Membership Organization
• Energy
• Projects and Activities
A national network dedicated to providing comprehensive energy programming.

National Gardening Association

Gardens for All—Helping Young Minds
Grow, Grow Lab
180 Flynn Avenue
Burlington, VT 05401
802-863-1308
• Membership Organization
• Workshops
• Projects and Activities
The association's mission is to help people become successful gardeners while encouraging stewardship of the earth.

National Geographic Society

World Magazine
1145 17th Street NW
Washington, DC 20036-4688
800-638-4077
• Membership Organization
• Nature and Wildlife
Junior members receive an official Junior Member Card as well as a t-shirt transfer emblem and *World Magazine*.

National Outdoor Leadership School

288 Main Street
Lander, WY 82520-3128
307-332-6973
• Internships and Careers
• Expeditions and Camps
A nonprofit private school whose mission is to be the best source for wilderness leadership skills that protect the environment.

National Science Teachers Association (NSTA)

1840 Wilson Boulevard
Arlington, VA 22201
703-243-7100
• Membership Organization
• Workshops
The largest organization of science teachers in the world united to improve science teaching, curriculum and professional growth.

National Sports Center for the Disabled

P.O. Box 36
Winter Park, CO 80482
303-726-5514
• Field Trips
• Expeditions and Camps
Offers a variety of programs and outdoor activities for physically challenged individuals.

National Toxics Campaign

37 Temple Place, 4th Floor
Boston, MA 02111
617-232-4014
• Membership Organization
• Workshops
• Projects and Activities
• Waste
Committed to curbing the nation's excessive use and careless disposal of toxic chemicals. Has a Social Action Packet to help youth get involved.

National Tree Trust

1120 G Street NW, Suite 770
Washington, DC 20005
202-628-TREE
• Projects and Activities
Helps local volunteer groups with growing, planting and maintaining trees in rural communities, urban areas and along the nation's highways.

National Wildlife Federation

1400 16th Street NW
Washington, DC 20036-2266
202-797-5445
• Membership Organization
• Nature and Wildlife
• Workshops
• Projects and Activities
• Classroom Materials
Works for clean air, pure water, endangered species and the wise use of natural resources. Has a catalog of resources and outdoor programs.

Native American Rights Fund

1506 Broadway
Boulder, CO 80302
303-447-8760
• Sponsorship Organization
Fighting to save what is left of Native Americans' sacred sites.

Natural Guard

2631 Durham Road
North Guilford, CT 06437
203-457-1302
• Membership Organization
• Projects and Activities
A nonprofit environmental organization created to help organize chapters in underprivileged neighborhoods and communities.

Natural Resources Career Camp

U.S. Department of Agriculture Forest
Service

1420 Maud Street, P.O. Box 988
Poplar Bluff, MO 63901
314-785-1475
• Internships and Careers
• Expeditions and Camps
Working to increase African-Americans' awareness of career opportunities in the field of conservation and natural resource management.

Natural Resources Defense Council (NRDC)

40 West 20th Street
New York, NY 10011
212-727-4474
• Membership Organization
• Projects and Activities
• Expeditions and Camps
Dedicated to protecting America's natural resources through scientific and legal channels.

Nature Center Associates of Los Angeles County

1750 North Altadena
Pasadena, CA 91107
818-398-5420
• Internships and Career
• Nature and Wildlife
Working to provide a variety of educational programs and services at county nature centers and other natural areas in Los Angeles County.

Nature Conservancy

Adopt-An-Acre Program
1815 North Lynn Street
Arlington, VA 22209
703-841-5300 or 800-628-6860
• Sponsorship Organization
• Field Trips
• Expeditions and Camps
• Membership Organization
• Rainforests
• Nature and Wildlife
A nonprofit national organization working to preserve rare plants and animals by purchasing their habitats for protection.

Nature Institute

Discovery 1994
P.O. Box 462
Alton, IL 62002
618-463-0766
• Expeditions and Camps
• Membership Organization
A nonprofit organization dedicated to

the preservation of natural heritage. Offers a summer camp for students in grades K through 7.

New Forests Project
The International Center
731 Eighth Street SE
Washington, DC 20003
202-547-3800
• Rainforests
Stems rainforest destruction by teaching Third World farmers innovative agro-forestry techniques and providing seeds and seedlings.

New Jersey School of Conservation (SOC)
Montclair State College
1 Wapalanne Road
Branchville, NJ 07826
201-948-4646
• Internships and Careers
• Classroom Materials and Activities
• Workshops
Operates as a field campus. This is the largest center for environmental studies in the Western Hemisphere.

New York Cares
116 East 16th Street, Sixth floor
New York, NY 10003
212-228-5000
• Projects and Activities
A volunteer corps that unites skilled and motivated volunteers with organizations that need them.

New York State Department of Environmental Conservation
Adopt-A-Wetland Stewardship Program
Office of Natural Resources
Wildlife Resources Center
Delmar, NY 12054
518-439-0198
• Sponsorship Organization
• Projects and Activities
• Nature and Wildlife
Gives volunteers the opportunity to improve the environmental quality of New York wetlands.

New York Turtle and Tortoise Society
162 Amsterdam Avenue, Suite 365
New York, NY 10023
212-459-4803
• Membership Organization
• Nature and Wildlife
Focuses on the preservation of habitat, as well as the humane treatment of turtles and tortoises.

New York Zoological Society (NYZS)
Wildlife Conservation Society
180 Fifth Street and Southern Boulevard
Bronx, NY 10460
718-220-5100
• Sponsorship Organization
• Membership Organization
• Rainforests
• Nature and Wildlife
Combines education with ecological and biological studies. Works to breed endangered species and preserves habitats on 5 continents.

Newfound Harbor Marine Institute
Seacamp
Box 170, Route 3
Big Pine Key, FL 33043
305-872-2331
• Workshops
• Nature and Wildlife
• Water
Seacamp provides an excellent outdoor teaching area for this field-oriented marine science program.

North American Association for Environmental Education (NAAEE)
P.O. Box 400
Troy, OH 45373
Phone or Fax 513-676-2514
• Internships and Careers
• Classroom Materials and Activities
• Membership Organization
• Workshops
Offers workshops, conferences, awards, networking opportunities and a newsletter for educators interested in environmental education.

North Cascades Institute
2105 Highway 20
Sedro Woolley, WA 98284
206-856-5700
• Workshops
• Camps
• Projects and Activities
• Classroom Materials and Activities
Provides hands-on environmental edu-

cation for children, adults and teachers. Elderhostel programs for seniors.

North East Trees
4701 Olson Street
Los Angeles, CA 90041
213-221-1778
• Sponsorship Organization
• Projects and Activities
Dedicated to planting and caring for urban forests in Northeast Los Angeles.

Northwestern State University
Advance Program for Young Scholars
124 Russell Hall
Natchitoches, LA 71497
318-357-4448
• Expeditions and Camps
An advanced program for seventh through eleventh graders, offering biology, ecology, chemistry, social sciences, humanities and others.

Nova Scotia Global Education Project
Nova Scotia Teachers Union
Tom Parker Building, 3106 Dutch Village Road
Halifax, NS, Canada B3L 4L7
902-577-5621
• Workshops
An in-service support program for teachers, helping them to deliver established curriculum in an active and creative way.

Nursery Nature Walks
1440 Harvard Street
Santa Monica, CA 90404
310-998-1151
• Field Trips
• Expeditions and Camps
• Nature and Wildlife
An independent, nonprofit organization with volunteers leading walks for families with infants, toddlers and preschoolers to nature areas.

Oak Knoll Animal Rights Club
The Oak Knoll School
44 Blackburn Road
Summit, NJ 07901
908-522-8100
• Youth Clubs
Sponsors trips to local animal shelters and raises money for animal rights efforts.

Oceanic Society Expeditions
Fort Mason Center, Building E
San Francisco, CA 94123
800-326-7491 or 415-441-1106
• Field Trips
• Expeditions and Camps
Promotes low-impact travel and
research programs. All proceeds go to
environmental research and conserva-
tion projects.

**Offer Versus Serve and Food
Choices**
227 SW Pine Street, Third Floor
Portland, OR 97204
503-227-1326 or 503-378-3569
• Classroom Material and Activities
• Waste
A new effort to reduce the amount of
food thrown away in school cafeterias.

Officer Snook Program
2550 Douglas Road, Suite 300-A
Coral Gables, FL 33134
305-443-3343
• ECO Heroes
• Water
Started as a high school project, this
program later developed into a national
outreach program of the U.S. Coast
Guard.

Offspring Urban Farms
Dignity of Man Foundation
8133 San Pedro
Los Angeles, CA 90003
213-243-8262
• Internships and Careers
Incarcerated teens at Camp Holton
work with the land, growing organic
produce. The program provides on-the-
job training for teens.

**Okeanos Ocean Research
Foundation, Inc.**
Adopt-A-Seal, Whale or Sea Turtle
P.O. Box 776, 278 East Montauk
Highway
Hampton Bays, NY 11946
516-728-4522
• Sponsorship Organization
• Membership Organization
• Nature and Wildlife
Activists are working to protect the
endangered turtles.

Olympic Park Institute
HC 62 Box 9T

Port Angeles, WA 98362
206-928-3720
• Field Trips
• Workshops
Conducts environmental education
courses at the historic Rosemary Inn in
Olympic National Park.

On Target Marketing
Wildlife Note Cards
P.O. Box 565
Cavalier, ND 58220
800-267-2349
• Fundraising Ideas
Fundraising with wildlife note cards.

One Voice
Adopt-A-Family Program
1228 15th Street, Suite C
Santa Monica, CA 90404
213-458-9961
• Sponsorship Organization
A nonprofit organization helping fami-
lies living at the poverty level.

One World Work Force (OWWF)
P.O. Box 3188
La Mesa, CA 91944-3188
619-270-5438
• Expeditions and Camps
Unites conservation research and species
protection scientists with volunteers.

Open Charter School
6085 Airdrome Street
Los Angeles, CA 90035
213-937-6249
• ECO Heroes
• Fundraising Ideas
Fifth- and sixth-grade students created
an environmental calendar that
addresses a key environmental issue
each month.

Operation Brightside
601 West Jefferson Street, City Hall
Louisville, KY 409202-2728
502-222-1433
• Classroom Material and Activities
An activity book for preschool children
designed to help them discover that
they are part of a large, interconnected
and diverse world.

Operation Clean Sweep
200 North Spring Street
Los Angeles, CA 90012
213-485-6651

• Projects and Activities
• Waste
Created to deal with the problems fac-
ing city life, such as litter and graffiti.
The program depends on volunteers.

Origins Natural Resources
767 Fifth Avenue
New York, NY 10153
212-572-4423
• ECO Heroes
• Energy
• Waste
Cosmetics developed with a commit-
ment to the preservation of earth, ani-
mals and the environment.

The Outdoor School
Los Angeles County Office of
Education
9300 East Imperial Highway
Downey, CA 90242-2890
213-922- 6334
• Field Trips
• Expeditions and Camps
Offers seasonal experiences extending
beyond the classroom, including pre-
trip activities, preparation and follow-
up activities.

**Outward Bound Urban Resources
Initiative**
Yale School of Forestry and
Environmental Studies
205 Prospect Street
New Haven, CT 06511
203-432-6570
• Internships and Careers
• Expeditions and Camps
• Projects and Activities
A collaboration between Outward
Bound and Yale University, working
with urban youth to develop environ-
mental solutions for local problems.

Oxfam America
26 West Street
Boston, MA 02111-1206
617-482-1211
• Sponsorship Organization
Funds self-help development and dis-
aster relief projects in poor countries in
Africa, Asia, the Caribbean and the
Americas.

**Pacific Palisades High School
Environmental Club**
Adopt-A-School Program

15777 Bowdoin Street
Pacific Palisades, CA 90272
310-454-4585
• Youth Clubs
Prototype for the Center for Environmental Education's Adopt-A-School program. Club members make environmental presentations on a monthly basis to local elementary schools.

Pacific Whale Foundation
Adopt-A-Whale
101 North Kiheli Road, Kealia Beach Plaza, Suite 25
Maui, HI 96753
808-879-8860
• Sponsorship Organization
• Field Trips
• Expeditions and Camps
• Membership Organization
• Nature and Wildlife
• Internships and Careers
A nonprofit conservation and research organization that brings the wonder of the oceans to schools and individuals around the world.

Pathways at Amherst College
Academic Study Associates
355 Main Street, P.O. Box 38
Armonk, NY 10504
914-273-2250
• Expeditions and Camps
Pathways offers courses in human biology, entrepreneurship and environmental studies to grades 7 through 9.

Peace Child
Rescue Mission: Planet Earth
The White House
Buntingford, Herts, UK SG9 9AH
(+44) 76 327 4459
Rescue Mission USA
11426/28 Rockville Pike, #l00
Rockville, MD 20852, USA
• Youth Clubs
• Projects and Activities
Rescue Mission: Planet Earth (English and Spanish), a sustainable development textbook written by youth sponsored by the United Nations.

Peacemakers, Inc.
P.O. Box 375
Purcell, OK 73080
405-527-5356
• Workshops

• Youth Clubs
A multicultural, nonprofit organization that empowers youth to take a stand against self-destruction.

People Against Chimpanzee Experiments (PACE)
59A Tisbury Road
Hove, UK BN3 3BL
011-44-273-77-25-42
• Sponsorship Organization
• Membership Organization
• Nature and Wildlife
Set up by volunteers as a Charitable Trust, to abolish medical experiments on chimpanzees.

People for Animal Welfare (PAW)
1659 NW 109th Street
Clive, IA 50325
• Youth Clubs
Created Day Care Day, through which money from baby-sitting is donated to a local animal shelter.

Performing and Fine Artists for World Peace
Earth-Friendly Schools International
P.O. Box 261
Lihu'e, HI 96766
808-246-2463
• Projects and Activities
• Waste
A program that challenges schools to become green.

Phoenix Recycling, Inc.
Phoenix School Recycling Programs
35 Capers Way
Pawley Island, SC 29585
800-866-3954
• Projects and Activities
• Waste
Schools in Ohio and Michigan can earn $1 a pound for recycling plastic grocery bags.

Physicians for Social Responsibility
1101 Fourteenth Street NW
Washington, DC 20005
202-785-3777
• Membership Organization
• Projects and Activities
Conducts studies assessing health risks of past and future weapons production and clean-up activities and generates petitions to politicians.

Pine Jog Environmental Education Center
Florida Atlantic University
College of Education
6301 Summit Boulevard
West Palm Beach, FL 33415
407-686-6600
• Field Trips
• Expeditions and Camps
• Water
• Nature and Wildlife
Provides awareness and appreciation of the natural world while instilling a sense of stewardship for the earth and its inhabitants.

Placerita Canyon Nature Center
19152 West Placerita Canyon Road
Newhall, CA 91321
805-259-7721
• Internships and Careers
• Field Trips
• Expeditions and Camps
• Workshops
• Projects and Activities
• Nature and Wildlife
Offers exciting and informative activities for the entire family.

Plan International U.S.A.—Kids for Kids
Child Reach
155 Plan Way
Warwick, RI 02886-1099
800-556-7918
• Sponsorship Organization
• Membership Organization
A humanitarian organization linking caring sponsors with needy children and their families in other countries.

Plant-A-Tree, Grow-A-Friend
633 South College
Fort Collins, CO 80524
303-244-2877
• Projects and Activities
• Water
• Nature and Wildlife
Dedicated to all stewards of the earth who are showing gratitude to the earth for the abundance it provides.

Plant-it 2000
6547 North Academy, Suite 475
Colorado Springs, CO 80918
719-481-8390
• Sponsorship Organization
• Projects and Activities

• Nature and Wildlife
Works to plant indigenous trees world-wide and educate people about the benefits of tree plantings.

Pocono Environmental Education Center
RD 2, Box 1010
Dingmans Ferry, PA 18238
717-828-2319
• Field Trips
• Expeditions and Camps
• Workshops
Advances environmental awareness, knowledge and skills through environmentally focused programs.

Point Bonita YMCA Outdoor Education Conference Center
Building 981, Fort Barry
Sausalito, CA 94965
415-331-9622
• Field Trips
• Expeditions and Camps
• Workshops
• Water
Offers outdoor education programs to students from northern California and Reno, Nevada, area.

Point Reyes Educational Programs
Point Reyes National Seashore Association
Point Reyes, CA 94956
415-663-1200
• Field Trips
• Expeditions and Camps
• Workshops
• Nature and Wildlife
Educates people about the coastal environment.

Points of Light Foundation
P.O. Box 66534
Washington, DC 20035
202-223-9186
• Membership Organization
•Projects and Activities
An independent, nonprofit organization that enables leaders to use their influence to mobilize others.

Pok-O-MacCready Outdoor Education Center
112 Mountain Road
Willsboro, NY 12996
518-963-7967
• Field Trips

• Expeditions and Camps
• Water
Offers residency outdoor education programs studying in the Adirondacks.

Polystyrene Ban in West Milford Schools
67 Highlander Drive
West Milford, NJ 07480
201-697-3918
• Youth Clubs
• ECO Heroes
• Projects and Activities
• Waste
Tanja Vogt organized students to demand a ban of polystyrene trays at her school.

Preserving the Earth and Conserving the Environment (PEACE)
Oldenburg Academy
Main Street
Oldenburg, IN 47036
812-934-4440
• Youth Clubs
• Waste
Coordinated the school's recycling program and conducted educational programs at local elementary schools.

Programme for Belize
Massachusetts Audubon Society
208 South Great Road
Lincoln, MA 01773
617-259-9500
• Fundraising Ideas
• Rainforests
A nonprofit group in Belize working to purchase and protect 230,000 acres of the country's tropical rainforests.

Progressive Animal Welfare Society (PAWS)
P.O. Box 1307
Lynwood, WA 98046
206-743-3845
•Membership Organization
•Nature and Wildlife
A nonprofit animal protection agency with a newsletter.

Progressive Student Network
3411 West Diversey, Suite 18
Chicago, IL 60647
312-227-4708
• Youth Clubs
A student network focusing on the

intersections between environmental quality, racism and militarization.

Project City Camp
Pillsbury Neighborhood Services, Inc. and The Urban Environmental Education Coalition (UEEC)
1701 Oak Park Avenue North
Minneapolis, MN 55411
612-377-7000
• Expeditions and Camps
• Energy
• Water
• Waste
A focused experience created to help inner-city youth explore their urban environment.

Project Earth
Environmental Fundraisers
RR 1, Box 168C
Cold Spring, NY 10516
800-IM4-ERTH
• Fundraising Ideas
Provides many environmentally responsible fundraising programs.

Project Environment
Thomas Perlmutter and Associates
3812 Waterford Way
Calabasas, CA 91302
818-591-3060
• Fundraising Ideas
• Waste
Links a fundraising program for southern California schools with quality environmental curriculum.

Project L.I.F.E. (Life in the Flagstaff Environment)
Camp Colton
3285 East Sparrow Avenue
Flagstaff, AZ 86004
602-527-6000
• Expeditions and Camps
• Nature and Wildlife
Every sixth-grade student in the Flagstaff School District has the chance to spend a week on the western slopes of the San Francisco Peaks.

Project Learning Tree (PLT)
A Project of the American Forest Foundation
1111 19th Street NW, Suite 780
Washington, DC 20036
202-463-2462
• Workshops

- Classroom Materials
- Nature and Wildlife

An education program designed to use the forest as a "window" into the natural world while raising awareness and knowledge of the world.

Project P.E.O.P.L.E. (People Educating Other People for a Long-lasting Environment)
River Trails Middle School
P.O. Box 932
Mount Prospect, IL 60070
708-298-1750
- Youth Club
- Membership Organization
- Projects and Activities

An Illinois nonprofit corporation created by students who wanted to make a difference in saving the earth by forming a chain of action and education.

Project Step and Hollywood Beautification Team
L.A. Free Clinic
8405 Beverly Boulevard
Los Angeles, CA 90048
213-653-8622
- ECO Heroes
- Internships and Careers

Works to beautify the Hollywood community by employing homeless youth or youth in danger of becoming homeless in short-term day-labor jobs.

Project WET National Headquarters
Montana State University, Culbertson Hall
Bozeman, MT 59717-0057
406-994-5392
- Workshops
- Water
- Classroom Materials

Interdisciplinary water resource education program for grades K through 12 with workshops throughout the United States.

Project W.I.Z.E. (Wildlife Inquiry Through Zoo Education)
Survival Strategies Summer Institute
Bronx Zoo Education
Department/International Wildlife Park
Bronx, NY 10460
212-220-5131 or 800-937-5131
- Workshops

Participants (seventh- through ninth-grade teachers) spend 1 week at the Bronx Zoo while receiving training and life science materials.

Project Wild National Headquarters
5430 Grosvenor Lane
Bethesda, MD 20814
301-493-5447
- Classroom Materials and Activities
- Workshops
- Nature and Wildlife

An interdisciplinary program emphasizing wildlife as a way to understand our responsibilities to all living things.

Project Yes!
East Bay Conservation Corps
1021 Third Street
Oakland, CA 94607
510-891-3917
- Youth Clubs
- Internships and Careers
- Expeditions and Camps
- Projects and Activities

Puts middle school youth in the Alameda and Contra Costa counties to work serving their communities.

Prospect High School Animal Rights Club
Prospect High School
801 West Kensington Road
Mount Prospect, IL 60056
708-255-9700
- Youth Clubs

This club adopted a snow leopard at a local zoo and collects petitions against companies that test on animals.

Rails-to-Trails Conservancy
1400 Sixteenth Street NW, Suite 300
Washington, DC 20036
202-797-5400
- Membership Organization
- Nature and Wildlife

A nonprofit corporation dedicated to converting abandoned railroad corridors into public trails around the country.

Rainforest Action Network (RAN)
450 Sansome, Suite 700
San Francisco, CA 94111
415-398-4404
- Sponsorship Organization
- Internships and Careers
- Membership Organization

- Rainforests
- Speakers Bureaus

A nonprofit activist organization working internationally to protect the world's rainforests and support the rights of indigenous people.

Rainforest Alliance
270 Lafayette Street, Suite 512
New York, NY 10012
212-941-1900
- Sponsorship Organization
- Fundraising Ideas
- Membership Organization
- Projects and Activities
- Rainforests

An international nonprofit organization dedicated to the conservation of the world's endangered tropical forests.

Rainforest Preservation Foundation
P.O. Box 820308
Fort Worth, TX 76182
800-460-RAIN or 817-284-5884
- Sponsorship Organization
- Rainforests

Raises funds to purchase and preserve rainforest land in Para, Brazil. Also, educates Brazilians on how to live sustainably on rainforest lands.

Raptor Center
Adopt-A-Raptor
1920 Fitch Avenue
St. Paul, MN 55108
612-624-4745
- Sponsorship Organization

The Adopt-A-Raptor program helps The Raptor Center rehabilitate a sick or injured bird and set it free in the wild.

Real Goods Trading Corporation
Real Goods for Real Kids on Real Planets
966 Mazzoni Street
Ukiah, CA 95482
800-762-7325
- Fundraising Ideas

Works with environmental nonprofit organizations to provide earth-friendly merchandise to students for fundraisers.

Real World Science
Springfield College
Alden Street
Springfield, MA 01109
413-748-3111

- Expeditions and Camps
Open to students in grades 6 through 9 offering courses in science, human ecology and science problems

Recover
Austin High School
1625 Danville Road, SW
Decatur, Al 35601
205-552-3060
- Youth Clubs
- Waste
Responsible for implementing a school-wide paper-recycling program.

Recycle Rex School Education Program
EarthSpirit
2425 Colorado Avenue, Suite 204
Santa Monica, CA 90404
310-582-8228
- Classroom Materials and Activities
- Waste
- Speakers Bureaus
An assembly presentation about recycling with educational materials.

Recyclery and Education Center
Browning-Ferris Industries of California
1601 Dixon Landing Road
Milpitas, CA 95035
408-262-1401
- Field Trips
- Waste
Offers fascinating information about recycling and the history of garbage, as well as hands on exhibits for students to explore.

Refuse Industry Productions, Inc. (RIPI)
The Public Awareness People
P.O. Box 1011
Grass Valley, CA 95945
916-274-3092 or 800-576-3092
- Classroom Materials and Activities
- Waste
A team of solid-waste professionals and educators who provide public awareness and educational materials via a catalog.

Rhapsody in Green
11648 Ventura Boulevard
Studio City, CA 91604
213-654-5821
- Field Trips
- Projects and Activities

- Nature and Wildlife
Works in various areas of southern California restoring habitats and harvesting fruit for the needy.

Ribbon International
235 East 22nd Street, Suite 11J
New York, NY 10010
212-689-0048
- Classroom Materials and Activities
- Projects and Activities
An ever-growing number of pictures, sewn or painted on fabric, showing what individuals love most and want to protect.

Rock Eagle 4-H Center
Rock Eagle Fort Center
350 Rock Eagle Road
Eatonton, GA 31024-9599
706-485-2831
- Field Trips
- Nature and Wildlife
A nonprofit service for elementary and middle school children that teaches all academic subjects by using the outdoors as a living laboratory.

Rocky Mountain Nature Association
Rocky Mountain Seminars
Rocky Mountain National Park
Estes Park, CO 80517
303-586-1258
- Field Trips
- Workshops
- Nature and Wildlife
Presents a variety of outdoor classes in Rocky Mountain Park.

Roger Tory Peterson Institute of Natural History
110 Marvin Parkway
Jamestown, NY 14701
716-665-2473
- Expeditions and Camps
- Projects and Activities
- Workshops
- Nature and Wildlife
Conducts workshops, conferences and projects that promote nature in education.

Roundhouse Marine Studies Lab and Aquarium
Oceanographic Teaching Stations
P.O. Box 1
Manhattan Beach, CA 90266

310-379-8117
- Field Trips
- Water
Promotes the study of the oceans, tidelands and beaches of southern California and the impact of human populations.

Rutabaga Ranch
7953 McGroarty Street
Sunland, CA 91040
818-353-3144
An innovative program designed to teach math and science in a hands-on, outdoor learning environment.

Sacred Land Film Project
P.O. Box C-151
La Honda, CA 94020
415-747-0685
- Energy
- Projects and Activities
Has produced environmental films.

Safari Club International
American Wilderness Leadership School (AWLs)
4800 West Gates Pass Road
Tucson, AZ 85745
602-620-1220
- Expeditions and Camps
- Workshops
Offers a national/international outdoor instructional program that concentrates on natural resource conservation.

Safe Sets Recycling Corporation
2210 Wilshire Boulevard, Suite 314
Santa Monica, CA 90403
310-319-9433
- Waste
Donates to schools, art centers and nonprofit organizations materials the entertainment industry would otherwise send to the landfills.

San Dimas Canyon Nature Center and Park
1628 North Sycamore Canyon Road
San Dimas, CA 91773
714-599-7512
- Field Trips
- Nature and Wildlife
Offers a variety of plant and animal communities, nature trails, a Nature Center and a large raptor rehabilitation flight cage.

San Francisco Bay Bird Observatory
P.O. Box 247
Alviso, CA 95002
408-946-6548
• Internships and Careers
• Field Trips
• Expeditions and Camps
• Membership Organization
• Workshops
• Nature and Wildlife
Dedicated to research, wildlife management and environmental education in the San Francisco Bay region. Offers bird identification classes.

San Francisco Zoo
San Francisco Zoological Gardens, Adopt-An-Animal, Adopt-An-Acre
1 Zoo Road
San Francisco, CA 94132
415-753-7073
• Sponsorship Organization
• Field Trips
• Workshops
• Rainforests
• Nature and Wildlife
Dedicated to promoting activity-based science teaching in the areas of biology, ecology and conservation.

Santa Monica Baykeeper
P.O. Box 10096
Marina Del Rey, CA 90295
310-305-9645 or 1 800-HELPBAY
• ECO Heroes
• Projects and Activities
• Water
• Waste
• Speakers Bureaus
The Baykeeper program hopes to rid the Santa Monica Bay of pollution and keep it safe for humans and wildlife.

Save America's Forests
4 Library Court SE
Washington, DC 20003
202-544-9219
• Projects and Activities
Forest preservation network coordinating letter-writing campaigns and lobbying efforts to prevent ancient forests from being destroyed.

Save the Animals
Spring Valley High School
Route 59
Spring Valley, NY 10977

914-577-6500
• Youth Clubs
Visits local animal shelters to exercise and bathe the animals.

Save the Manatee Club
500 North Maitland Avenue
Maitland, FL 32751
800-432-Join or 407-539-0990
• Sponsorship Organization
• Water
• Nature and Wildlife
Working to save the endangered manatee.

Save the Rainforest
Dodgeville High School
912 West Chapel
Dodgeville, WI 53533
608-935-9435
• Youth Clubs
• Fundraising Ideas
• Expeditions and Camps
• Workshops
• Projects and Activities
• Rainforests
Raises funds for rainforest conservation and operates summer rainforest ecology courses in Latin America for teachers and high school students.

Save the Redwoods League
114 Sansome Street, Room 605
San Francisco, CA 94104
415-362-2352
• Sponsorship Organization
• Membership Organization
• Nature and Wildlife
Acquires Coast Redwood and Giant Sequoia forestland for protection in Redwood National Park and in other public parks and preserves.

Save the Whales
Whales on Wheels
1426 Main Street, Unit E
Venice, CA 90291
310-392-6226 or 800-WHALE-OK
• Sponsorship Organization
• Classroom Materials and Activities
• Membership Organization
• Water
• Nature and Wildlife
• Speakers Bureaus
Dedicated to educating people about marine mammals, their environment and their preservation.

Save the World's Animals from Torment (SWAT)
Pentucket Regional High School
22 Main Street
West Newbury, MA 01985
508-363-5507
• Youth Clubs
Writes protest letters to companies that still test on animals and distributes animal protection information.

Save What's Left
Coral Springs High School
7201 West Sample Road
Coral Springs, FL 33065
305-344-3412
• Youth Clubs
• ECO Heroes
• Membership Organization
• Water
• Nature and Wildlife
Empowers young people to make positive environmental changes in their communities and has more than 800 clubs in the Florida area.

Sawtooth Workshop
412 Hillcrest Road
Burley, ID 83318
208-678-3903 or 208-384-9902
• Workshops
This workshop offers a unique hands-on experience with methods and strategies for understanding contemporary environmental issues.

"School to School" International Secretariat
Via Torino 44-20123
Milano, Italy
02-72000512
• Classroom Materials and Activities
Creates communication between Italians aged 12 to 16 with students around the world and allows exchange of environmental information.

Sci-Link
1509 Varsity Drive
Raleigh, NC 27606
919-515-5290
• Classroom Materials and Activities
• Atmosphere
• Water
• Waste
An innovative 2-year project linking scientists, teachers and students to

translate current scientific knowledge into teaching practices.

Science Adventures
15467 Chemical Lane
Huntington Beach, CA 92649
800-472-4362 or 714-895-3966
- Field Trips
- Camps
- Classroom Materials and Activities
- Workshops
- Speakers Bureaus

An organization of science professionals dedicated to providing hands-on science enrichment for elementary schools.

Science Technology Society (STS)
Science Education Center, Department of Curriculum and Instruction
Southern Illinois University
Carbondale, IL 62901
618-453-4216
- Classroom Materials and Activities
- Energy
- Workshops
- Waste

A curriculum development project designed to help students learn the similarities and differences between science, technology and society.

Sea Shepherd Conservation Society
Sea Shepherd Log Newsletter
1314 Second Street
Santa Monica, CA 90401
310-394-3198
- Internships and Careers
- Water
- Speakers Bureaus

An all-volunteer international marine conservation agency dedicated to enforcing international laws protecting marine mammals.

Sea Turtle Survival League/Caribbean Conservation Corporation
Adopt-A-Turtle
P.O. Box 2866
Gainesville, FL 32602-2866
800-678-7853
- Sponsorship Organization
- Nature and Wildlife

Provides information on sea turtles and works to preserve them through an Adopt-A-Turtle program.

Sea World of California
1720 South Shore
San Diego, CA 92109-7795
619-226-3834
- Field Trips
- Classroom Materials Activities
- Expeditions Camps
- Projects Activities
- Water
- Speakers Bureaus

Offers a program in which students can learn about ecology, animal behavior and conservation.

Seacamp
Box 170
Route 3
Big Pine Key, FL 33043
305-872-2331
- Expeditions and Camps
- Water
- Nature and Wildlife

Dedicated to the education of youth in marine science.

Seattle Audubon Society
Finding Urban Nature
8028 35th Avenue
Seattle, WA 98115
206-523-4483
- Field Trips
- Projects and Activities

Children explore nature in their own neighborhoods while developing abilities to observe, use scientific tools and work with data.

Sebastian International
Little Green Poetry and Art Contest
6109 De Soto Avenue
Woodland Hills, CA 91367
818-999-5112, ext. 260
- ECO Heroes
- Projects and Activities
- Waste
- Rainforests

A beauty-care company that sponsors an international art contest for children ages 5 to 15. Winners get to visit the Amazon rainforest.

Seeds Foundation
Sustainability Education Leadership Forums
S-440
10169 104th Street
Edmonton, AB, Canada T5J 1A5
403-424-0971

- Workshops

Hold conferences on Environmental Education.

Seeds of Change
Native Scholar Program
P.O. Box 15700
Santa FE, NM 87506-5700
800-957-3337 or 505-986-0366 to place an order
- Classroom Materials and Activities
- Projects and Activities

Seeds of Change is a biodiversity company offering a large variety of 100 percent certified organically grown seeds.

Sharing Nature Foundation
14618 Tyler Foote Road
Nevada City, CA 95959
916-292-3893
- Workshops

Offers workshops based on the writings of Joseph Cornell.

Shaver's Creek Environmental Center
Penn State University
201 Mateer Building
University Park, PA 16802
814-863-2000
- Field Trips
- Expeditions and Camps
- Projects and Activities
- Workshops
- Nature and Wildlife

Provides a variety of educational and recreational opportunities for visitors.

Sierra Club
Conservation Opportunities, Outing Programs
730 Polk Street
San Francisco, CA 94109
415-776-2211
- Internships and Careers
- Expeditions and Camps
- Projects and Activities
- Nature and Wildlife

Offers volunteer opportunities for conservation activities, national and international outings for members and urban outings.

Sierra Institute
University of California Extension
740 Front Street, Suite 155
Santa Cruz, CA 95060

408-427-6618
• Expeditions and Camps
Attracts students from all around the country interested in using the outdoors as a field study classroom.

Sierra Student Coalition
Sierra Club
223 Thayer Street, Suite 2
Providence, RI 02906
401-861-6012 or 415-923-5510 Help Line
• Youth Clubs
• Membership Organization
• Nature and Wildlife
Dedicated to making students the most effective, responsible activists they can be. Provides environmental leadership training programs.

Sigurd Olson Environmental Institute
Northland College
Ashland, WI 54806
715-682-4531, ext. 223
• Field Trips
• Expeditions and Camps
• Membership Organization
• Workshops
• Projects and Activities
• Nature and Wildlife
An outreach program to the western Lake Superior region consisting of problem-solving workshops, research, projects and resources.

Simian Lodge
Adopt-A-Monkey
5581 Thomas Road
Bath, NY 14810
607-776-9014
• Sponsorship Organization
Takes in unwanted, abused and elderly monkeys and provides them with the best possible treatment.

Skipping Stones Magazine
P.O. Box 3939
Eugene, OR 97403-0939
503-342-4956
• Projects and Activities
• Membership Organization
• Nature and Wildlife
A multiethnic children's magazine. Each issue contains a teacher's guide and suggestions for activities.

Smogbusters
South Coast Air Quality Management
21865 East Copely Drive
Diamond Bar, CA 91765-4182
800-252-4666 or 714-396-2000
• Atmosphere
• Projects and Activities
• Nature and Wildlife
• Classroom Materials and Activities
Aids students with science projects and provides information on smog.

Solar Box Cookers International
1724 11th Street
Sacramento, CA 95814
916-444-6616
• Membership Organization
• Atmosphere
Promotes using solar energy instead of burning wood for cooking.

Solar Now
421 Linebrook Road
Ipswich, MA 01938
508-356-0152
• ECO Heroes
• Energy
• Workshops
• Projects and Activities
A collaboration between organizations dedicated to the research and promotion of photovoltics.

Sonoma State University
Earthlab
Department of Environmental Studies and Planning
1801 Cotati Avenue
Rohnert Park, CA 94928
707-664-2306
• Internships and Careers
• Energy
Offers environmental baccalaureate degree.

Sort, Inc. (Save Our Trash)
16744 Park Circle Drive
Chagrin Falls, OH 44022-1050
216-543-9777
• Fundraising Ideas
• Waste
Provides information and educational resources to ensure success for waste management and recycling programs. Great fundraising ideas.

Southern College of Technology
School of Architecture

1100 South Marietta Parkway
Marietta, GA 30060
404-528-7253
• Youth Clubs
Students invented a game called "Kinder City" for young children. The winner of the game is the person who saves the most trees and animals.

Southern Regional Youth Environmental Summit (Y.E.S.)
P.O. Box 24496
Nashville, TN 37202
615-895-1123
• Youth Clubs
• Workshops
The summit is presented by youth who teach other young people that they can make a difference.

Southern Utah Wilderness Alliance (SUWA)
1417 South 1100 East
Salt Lake City, UT 84105-2423
801-486-3161
• Membership Organization
Seeks to give the people of southern Utah a voice in deciding the fate of one of America's most magnificent landscapes.

Spencer's Team News
Hamilton County Department of Environmental Services
Solid Waste Division
1632 Central Parkway, Room 202
Cincinnati, OH 45210
513- 763-4638
• Projects and Activities
• Waste
Designed for students in third through sixth grades. Students can become a member by implementing waste reduction.

Stewards of the Earth
598 North Fairview Avenue
Goleta, CA 93117
805-967-7369
• Projects and Activities
• Nature and Wildlife
• Speakers Bureaus
Published *From the Good Earth*, a book about agriculture, and makes presentations about traditional and organic agriculture.

Stonyfield Farms
Adopt-A-Cow
10 Burton Drive
Londonderry, NH 03053
603-437-7594
• Sponsorship Organization
• Nature and Wildlife
Their "Adopt-A-Cow" program fosters
an appreciation for farm life and a
healthy planet.

Stormy Williams
3813 Fiftieth Street West
Rosemond, CA 93560-6489
• ECO Heroes
• Waste
Stormy Williams has been the driving
force behind closures and clean-ups
of two dozen toxic sites in
Rosemond.

Stream Team
Washington Public Works Department
Water Resources Program
P.O. Box 1967
Olympia, WA 98507
206-753-8598
• Projects and Activities
• Workshops
• Water
Projects that enhance streams, lakes
and wetlands through water monitor-
ing and action projects in the Thurston
County watershed.

**Student Action Corps
for Animals
(SACA)**
P.O. Box 15588
Washington, DC 20003
202-543-8983
• Membership Organization
• Projects and Activities
• Nature and Wildlife
Provides opportunities for students to
exchange ideas and empowers young
people to work for animal protection.

Student Action Union
P.O. Box 456
New Brunswick, NJ 08903
Unlisted
• Youth Clubs
• Projects and Activities
Coordinates direct action campaigns
around college democracy and labor
unions as well as environmental
health and quality issues.

**Student Advocates for a Green
Earth (SAGE)**
Bay Area Action
667 Marion Avenue
Palo Alto, CA 94301
408-447-2153
• Youth Clubs
A network of high school environmen-
talists in the San Francisco Bay area.

**Student Animal Rights
Activists of Huntington
(SARAH)**
Huntington High School
Oakwood and McKay Road
Huntington, NY 11743
516-673-2001
• Youth Clubs
Sponsors vegetarian potluck dinners,
sets up animal rights information
booths and is raising funds for plastic
dissection frogs for the school.

**Student Conservation Association
(SCA)**
Conservation Career Development
Program
2524 16th Avenue South
Seattle, WA 98144
206-324-4649
• Internships and Careers
Works to educate young people to be
future environmental leaders.

**Student Environmental Action
Coalition**
P.O. Box 1168
Chapel Hill, NC 27514-1168
919-967-4600
• Youth Clubs
• Projects and Activities
A national network of independent
high school and university student
groups concerned with environmental
issues.

**Student Pugwash
USA**
1638 R Street NW, Suite 32
Washington, DC 20009
202-328-6555 or 800-WOW-a-PUG
• Internships and Careers
• Membership Organization
• Workshops
Recent college graduates give high
school students a better understanding
of the social and ethical implications of
science and technology.

**Students Acting for the
Environment (SAFE)**
Francis Howell High School
7001 Highway 94 South
St. Charles, MO 63304
314-441-0050
• Youth Clubs
• Sponsorship Organization
• Water
• Waste
Participates in cleaning up area lakes
and streams.

**Students Against Animal Cruelty
(SAAC)**
Mother Theo Guerin High School
90001 West Belmont Avenue
River Grove, IL 60171
708-453-6233
• Youth Clubs
• Sponsorship Organization
• Nature and Wildlife
Collects pet supplies for local animal shel-
ters and works to stop animal cruelty.

**Students Against Cruelty to
Animals (SACA)**
Norcross High School
Norcross, GA 30071
404-448-3674
• Youth Clubs
SACA collects food and supplies for
local humane shelters. Younger stu-
dents work on animal protection
issues.

**Students Against the Violation of
the Earth (SAVE)**
Opelika High School
1700 Lafayette Parkway
Opelika, AL 36801
205-745-9715
• Youth Clubs
• Sponsorship Organization
• Water
Cleans up a local stream and works to
beautify the local community.

**Students Aware of the Vanishing
Environment (SAVE)**
Gulf Breeze High School
675 Gulf Breeze Pkwy
Gulf Breeze, FL 32561
904-932-5388
• Youth Clubs
• Water
• Waste
Circulated a petition to have a commu-

nity bike path created. Also participates in beach clean-ups and plans Earth Day Festival.

Students for Environmental Action (SEA)
Lakeland High School Environmental Club
58 Carey Street
Mahopac, NY 10541
914-628-1671
• Youth Clubs
• Fundraising Ideas
• Rainforests
Holds an annual environmental fair for elementary students.

Student's Environmentally Concerned United to Restore Earth (SECURE)
West 8463 Street, RD #11
Delavan, WI 53115
Unlisted
• Youth Clubs
Works on 3 projects: an education program for elementary students, rainforest conservation and school recycling program.

Students Watching Over Our Planet Earth (SWOOPE)
Los Alamos National Laboratory
MS J447
Los Alamos, NM 87545
505-667-8950
• Youth Clubs
An education program for grades K through 12 where students gather data and send the information to a database for scientists and agencies.

Stuyvesant International Summer Institute
New York Institute of Technology, Long Island
Bowling Green Station, Box 843
New York, NY 10274
800-292-4452
• Expeditions and Camps
The science camp is open to students in grades 5 through 12.

Summer Discovery Camp
Keystone Science School, P.O. Box 8606
Keystone, CO 80435
303-468-5824
• Expeditions and Camps

Offers environmental and science programs for kids ages 9 through 13.

Summerscape
Georgia Institute of Technology
Center for Education Integrating Science, Math and Computing
Atlanta, GA 30332
404-894-8994
• Expeditions and Camps
Offers 2-week environmental, science and math courses for students in grades 7 through 9.

SUNY at Fredonia
Pathways of the Math and Sciences Summer Program
Thompson Hall, E282
Department of Education
Fredonia, NY 14063
716-673-3521
• Expeditions and Camps
Offers math, ecology, environmental, geology and mineralogy programs for minority students in grades 6 through 8.

Super Science Red Magazine
Scholastic Publishing
730 Broadway
New York, NY 10003
201-939-8050
• Projects and Activities
A children's magazine created with support from the National Science Foundation, published 8 times during the school year.

Support the United Nations Campaign (SUN)
2401 Lincoln Boulevard, 2nd Floor
Santa Monica, CA 90405
310-392-6562
• Sponsorship Organization
• Internships and Careers
• Membership Organization
• Projects and Activities
• Speakers Bureaus
Promotes United Nations goals and standards for peace, human rights and the environment. Provides community outreach.

Surfrider Foundation
122 South El Camino
San Clemente, CA 92672
310-393-7775
• Field Trips
• Water

• Nature and Wildlife
• Speakers Bureaus
Works to preserve and protect coastal environment through hands-on programs dealing with water quality, beach access and surf protection.

Take Back the Coast! Campaign
213 D Street, SE
Washington, DC 20002
202-544-2600
• Membership Organization
• Projects and Activities
• Water
A coalition of Friends of the Earth and grassroots organizations working to protect the nation's coasts through education, advocacy and networking.

Taking Responsibility for the Earth Everyday (TREE)
Roger Bacon High School
4320 Vine Street
Cincinnati, OH 45217
513-641-1300
• Youth Clubs
• Waste
Began a campaign to reduce the amount of junk mail and coordinates the school's recycling program.

Talent Identification Program (TIP)/Scientific Field Studies
Duke University
Box 90747
Durham, NC 27708
919-684-3847
• Expeditions and Camps
Precollege programs give talented high school students a chance to make the most of their summer. Field studies use outdoors classrooms.

Tarlton Foundation
Adopt-A-Whale, Sea Camp, Project Ocean, The Whale Bus
1160 Battery Street, Suite 360
San Francisco, CA 94111
415-433-3163
• Sponsorship Organization
• Field Trips
• Classroom Materials and Activities
• Workshops
• Projects and Activities
• Water
• Nature and Wildlife
• Speakers Bureaus

Offers marine science programs to better educate 6- to 14-years-olds.

Teaching KATE (Kids about the Environment)

Coalition for Natural Resource Education
82 Camp Long Road
Aiken, SC 29801
803-649-9512
• Classroom Materials and Activities
• Expeditions and Camps
• Water
• Nature and Wildlife
Provides children with stimulating, outdoor learning experiences about the ecology and the stewardship of our natural resources.

Teaching Zooquarium Project

Baldwin High School
155 Highway 49 West
Milledgeville, GA 31061
912-453-6429
• Internships and Careers
• Classroom Materials and Activities
• Projects and Activities
• Nature and Wildlife
A student-run Zooquarium where students apply for positions and take training courses for certification before they can care for the animals.

Team Rainforest

P.O. Box 10075
Berkeley, CA 94709
510-548-1710
• Sponsorship Organization
• Fundraising Ideas
• Projects and Activities
• Workshops
• Rainforests
Protects the planet's rainforests and provides opportunities for young people while acting on behalf of the rainforests.

TEAMS —Total Energy Action Management in Schools Program

National Energy Foundation
5225 Wiley Post Way, Suite 170
Salt Lake City, UT 84116
801-539-1406 or 800-616-TEAM to enter
• Classroom Materials and Activities
• Energy
• Projects and Activities
Encourages middle school students to explore energy use and its impact on the environment by developing energy efficiency policies for their schools.

Teenagers Against Cruelty to Animals (TACTA)

South Grand Prairie High School
301 Warrior Trail
Grand Prairie, TX 75051
214-264-4731
• Youth Clubs
TACTA collected more than 300 pounds of pet food for shelter animals and provides an animal awareness information.

Teens Restoring Earth's Environment (Tree, Inc.)

P.O. Box 2812
Boise, ID 83701
1-208-338-PINE (7463)
• Youth Clubs
• Membership Organization
Established by and for students, enabling them to act upon their concerns about our rapidly deteriorating environment.

Tennessee Students Against Pollution (TSAP)

802 Warrior Drive
Murfreesboro, TN 37129
615-890-6450
• Youth Clubs
• Membership Organization
A statewide network through which educators and students will be able to work together on environmental issues.

Terrene Institute

American Wetlands Month
1717 K Street NW, Suite 801
Washington, DC 20006
202-833-8317
• Classroom Materials and Activities
• Projects and Activities
• Water
• Nature and Wildlife
Aims to increase public awareness of wetlands while encouraging people to enjoy and protect them.

Terrific Kids/Arms Partnership

2421 East Johnson Street
Madison, WI 53705
608-246-4493
• Speakers Bureaus
A model volunteer program for the enhancement of learning, with special emphasis in science.

Teton Science School

P.O. Box 68
Kelly, WY 83011
307-733-4765
• Expeditions and Camps
• Workshops
• Nature and Wildlife
Once a dude ranch, now offering year-round programs for people of all ages.

Think Earth

5505 East Carson Street, Suite 250
Lakewood, CA 90713
310-420-6814
• ECO Heroes
• Classroom Materials and Activities
A consortium of 13 businesses developed the Think Earth Curriculum kits, free to southern California schools.

Thompson Island Outward Bound Education Center

Box 127
Boston, MA 02127-0002
617-328-3900
• Expeditions and Camps
Renowned for outdoor learning adventures. Launched a nationwide initiative to improve public schools and the lives of young people in urban communities.

Through Children's Eyes, Inc.

386 Longview Place
Thousand Oaks, CA 91360
805-373-6200
• Projects and Activities
• Field Trips
A nonprofit organization using photography as an educational tool with gifted and talented elementary school children.

Ticket America Campaign

Greenhouse Crisis Foundation
1130 17th Street NW, Suite 630
Washington, DC 20077-6572
202-466-2823
• Projects and Activities
Part of the National Gas Guzzler Campaign, a long-term initiative that seeks to alter our nation's love affair with the automobile.

Tiffin Centre for Conservation
Nottawasaga Conservation Authority
Highway 90, Rural Route 1
Angus, ON, Canada L0M 1B0
705-424-1485
• Field Trips
• Nature and Wildlife
Serves to increase knowledge, understanding and appreciation of our natural environment by offering outdoor environmental education.

Timber Wolf Alliance
Adapt-A-Wolf Pack Program
Sigurd Olson Environmental Institute
Northland College
Ashland, WI 54806-3999
715-682-1223
• Membership Organization
• Nature and Wildlife
• Classroom Materials and Activities
Promotes education about wolf ecology, continuing wolf population monitoring and habitat management programs.

Timber Wolf Information Network
Adopt-A-Wolf Pack Program
East 110 Emmons Creek Road
Waupaca, WI 54981
715-258-7247
• Sponsorship Organization
• Internships and Careers
• Nature and Wildlife
Educates teachers, student groups, citizen groups and families about the recovery of the wolves in Wisconsin and Michigan's Upper Peninsula.

Tomorrow's Morning Weekly Newspaper
11466 San Vicente Boulevard
Los Angeles, CA 90049
Subscriptions: 800-365-2881; Office: 310-826-5187
• Projects and Activities
Features articles, letters, cartoons and commentary for the young on current events going on around the world.

Topanga-Las Virgenes Resource Conservation District
122 North Topanga Canyon Boulevard
Topanga, CA 90290
310-455-1030
• Field Trips
• Water
Offers educational programs for stu-

dents grades K through 12 utilizing 3 conservation education field programs.

Trailside Discovery
519 West Eighth Street, Suite 201
Anchorage, AK 99501
907-561-5437
• Expeditions and Camps
• Nature and Wildlife
A summer nature education program for ages 4 through 18. Focuses on environmental education, the natural sciences and outdoor skills.

Trash Museum
Hackensack Meadowlands
Development Commission's
Environment Center
Two DeKorte Park Plaza
Lyndhurst, NJ 07071
201-460-8300
• Field Trips
• Waste
The nation's first museum devoted to trash gives visitors a sense of being deep inside a landfill.

Tree Musketeers
136 Main Street
El Segundo, CA 90245
800-473-0263
• Youth Clubs
Founded by a group of young people dedicated to saving the environment through their own actions.

TreePeople
12601 Mulholland Drive
Beverly Hills, CA 90210
818-753-4600
• Internships and Careers
• Workshops
• Projects and Activities
• Nature and Wildlife
• Speakers Bureaus
Offers citizen forester training, school programs, community outreach and volunteer opportunities.

Trees for Life
1103 Jefferson
Wichita, KS 67203
316-263-7294
• Sponsorship Organization
• Membership Organization
• Projects and Activities
• Nature and Wildlife
Dedicated to restore environmentally

damaged forests, to feed the hungry and to assist people of developing countries.

Trees for Mother Earth
P.O. Box 1491
Chinle, AZ 86503
602-674-3258
• Sponsorship Organization
• Membership Organization
Through this program high school students help plant fruit trees and other trees on Navajo lands.

Treetops-in-the-Forest
Davy Crockett National Forest
809 East Coral
Grand Prairie, TX 75051
214-262-2816
• Expeditions and Camps
• Workshops
Offers teacher environmental education courses, student environmental education workshops and creative arts camps.

Tropical Rainforest Education Program (TREP)
4646 Shenandoah
St. Louis, MO 63110
314-771-2885
• Classroom Materials and Activities
• Rainforests
• Speakers Bureaus
Provides accurate and current educational information about tropical educators at national institutions.

Trust for Public Land
1116 New Montgomery Street, Fourth Floor
San Francisco, CA 94105
415-495-4014
• Sponsorship
A leading national nonprofit organization dedicated to protecting land for the public's use and enjoyment.

Tualatin High School
Eco Warriors
22300 SW Boones Ferry Road
Tualatin, OR 97062
503-598-2810
• Youth Clubs
• Waste
Implemented a waste prevention program that reduced solid waste by 38,800 pounds and saved the school more than $13,600 a year.

20/20 Vision

1828 Jefferson Place NW
Washington, DC 20036
202-833-2020 or 800-669-1782
• Membership Organization
• Projects and Activities
Works to cut military spending by contacting policy analysts in national and local organizations to find the best actions tailored to where you live.

21st Century News (21 CN)

P.O. Box 42286
Tucson, AZ 85733
602-327-9555
• Sponsorship Organization
• Projects and Activities
A media arts and educational organization for at-risk multicultural youth between the ages of 8 and 18.

Tybee Island 4-H Center

University of Georgia Cooperative
Extension Service
9 Lewis Avenue
Tybee Island, GA 31328
912-786-5534
• Field Trips
• Expeditions and Camps
Serves as an educational center for students in grades 3 through 8 on coastal and marine ecosystems.

U.S. Environmental Protection Agency

Expedition Opportunities
U.S. Environmental Protection Agency, Suite A-107
Washington, DC 20460
202-260-5810
• Field Trips
• Expeditions and Camps
Has been sending research teams of scientists, teachers and students to investigate issues of environmental concern around the world for 15 years.

U.S. Forest Service Volunteers

P.O. Box 96090
Washington, DC 20090-6090
202-720-8732
• Internships and Careers
Welcomes all interested individuals and groups who wish to contribute toward improving our nation's natural resources.

U. The National College Magazine

American Collegiate Network, Inc.
1800 Century Park East, Suite 820
Los Angeles, CA 90067
310-551-1381
• ECO Heroes
• Projects Activities
A magazine devoted to issues facing college students. Published 9 times a year. Articles are written by college students nationwide.

Unified Sewerage Agency of Washington County

River Rangers
155 North First Avenue, Suite 270
Hillsboro, OR 97124
503-648-8621
• Classroom Materials and Activities
• Projects and Activities
• Water
• Waste
An interactive environmental education program that involves students in learning about water issues.

Union of Concerned Scientists

26 Church Street
Cambridge, MA 02238
617-547-5552
• Projects and Activities
• Membership
• Speakers Bureaus
Dedicated to advancing responsible public policies in areas where technology plays a critical role.

United Earth

55 East 75th Street
New York, NY 10021
212-517-7776
• Classroom Materials and Activities
• Projects and Activities
Encourages people and nations to join together for a sustainable future through global school programs, volunteer youth networks and more.

United National Indian Tribal Youth (UNITY)

P.O. Box 25042
Oklahoma City, OK 73125
405-424-3010
• Youth Clubs
• Internships and Careers
• Membership Organization
A national nonprofit organization serving the individual and collective needs

of American Indian and Alaskan native youth.

United States Public Interest Research Group (U.S. PIRG)

215 Pennsylvania Avenue SE
Washington, DC 20003-1155
202-546-9707
• Youth Clubs
• Membership Organization
• Speakers Bureaus
College student-based organizations doing research, advocacy and education on consumer and environmental issues around the country.

United States Student Association (USSA)

815 15th Street NW, Suite 838
Washington, DC 20005
202-347-USSA
• Youth Clubs
• Projects Activities
The only student lobby in Washington DC, voicing student concerns on issues affecting education.

University of Saskatchewan Extension Division

Saskatoon, SK, Canada S7N 0W0
306-966-5539
• Expeditions and Camps
• Workshops
• Nature and Wildlife
The Summer Ecology Day Camp for Kids engages children (ages 8 to 14) in science and environmental issues. The Wilderness and Ecology Summer Camps for Teachers and Other Adults offers various ecology programs.

Urban Options

405 Gove Street
East Lansing, MI 48823
517-337-0422
• Membership Organization
• Energy
• Waste
A nonprofit energy and environmental science organization, specializing in energy efficiency, healthy homes and composting.

Urban Peace Trees

P.O. Box 10697, Department TL
Bainbridge Island, WA 98110
206-842-7986
• Youth Clubs

• Projects and Activities
International youth corps that works to re-green inner cities.

Utah Society for Environmental Education
230 South 500 East, Suite 280
Salt Lake City, UT 84102
801-328-1549
• Membership Organization
The Society's goal is to produce a citizenry that is environmentally knowledgeable, with the ability to apply that knowledge appropriately.

Vasquez Rocks Natural Area Park
Nature Center Associates
10700 West Escondido Canyon Road
Agua Dulce, CA 91350
805-268-0840
• Field Trips
• Nature and Wildlife
This 745-acre park, located in the high desert near Agua Dulce, features unusual rock formations and Tataviam Indian archaeological sites.

Vegetarian Education Network (VE• Net)
How on Earth! (HOE!)
P.O. Box 3347
West Chester, PA 19381
717-529-8638
• Youth Clubs
• Projects and Activities
• Nature and Wildlife
A unique quarterly newsletter for and by youth who support compassionate, ecologically sound living.

Vegetarian Resource Group
Vegetarian Journal
P.O. Box 1463T
Baltimore, MD 21203
410-366-8343
• Membership Organization
• Projects and Activities
Educates the public about vegetarianism and the interrelated issues of health, nutrition, ecology, ethics and world hunger.

Venice Action Committee
804 Main Street
Venice, CA 90291-3218
310-399-6690
• ECO Heroes
• Field Trips

• Speakers Bureaus
A volunteer organization dedicated to making Venice a cleaner, safer and prettier place to live. It sponsors the weekly Venice farmers market.

Vermont Institute of Natural Science
Environmental Learning for the Future
RR 2 Box 532
Woodstock, VT 05091
802-457-2779
• Classroom Materials and Activities
• Workshops
• Waste
Volunteers attend monthly workshops, then present information to children that encourages environmental awareness.

Vegetarian Society
P.O. Box 34427
Los Angeles, CA 90034
310-839-6207
• Membership Organization
Teaches that vegetarianism is good for one's health and can reduce world hunger and save the earth from global warming.

Visions United —Can You Hear Us Project
P.O. Box 52367
Atlanta, GA 30355
404-892-3992
• Projects and Activities
• Rainforests
Committed to letting kids speak out about preserving their earth through a series of environmental art and literacy projects.

Voices for a Viable Future
P.O. Box 22903
Alexandria, VA 22304
703-461-3393
• Workshops
• Speakers Bureaus
Offers lecture program motivating people to become spokespersons for change.

W.I.L.D.
P.O. Box 8397
Van Nuys, CA 91409
818-781-4421
• Expeditions and Camps
• Nature and Wildlife

Offers outings in winter and summer to deserts and mountains. All trips are designed to enrich wilderness experience.

Wahsega 4-H Center
Route 8, Box 1820
Dahlonega, GA 30533
706-864-2050
• Field Trips
At Camp Wahseg students in grades 3 through 8 put classroom knowledge into practical application in the outdoor setting.

The Washington Center
1101 Fourteenth Street NW, Suite 500
Washington, DC 20005
800-486-8921
• Internships and Careers
Offers internships designed to provide work experience in environmental law, lobbying, energy policy and recycling while earning college credit.

Watchfire Productions
P.O. Box 917
Woodacre, CA 94973
415-488-1715
• Classroom Materials and Activities
• Rainforests
Produces environmental music videos to educate and motivate the public concerning issues such as rainforest destruction.

West Branch Middle School
P.O. Box 637
West Branch, IA 52358
319-643-5324
• Classroom Materials and Activities
• Projects and Activities
Incorporates environmental education into each grade level with a variety of programs designed to strengthen critical thinking.

West Michigan Environmental Action Council
WMEAC Yikes
1432 Wealthy Street SE
Grand Rapids, MI 49506
616-451-0351
• Youth Clubs
• Classroom Materials and Activities
• Membership Organization
• Projects and Activities

Does environmental education out-reach through numerous programs.

Western Canada High School
641 17th Avenue SW
Calgary, AL, Canada T25 OB5
403-228-5363
• Youth Clubs
Raised money for rainforest conservation, started a paper-recycling project and teaches environmental awareness to younger students.

GRANTS AND AWARDS

AAVS Student Animal Advocate Award
The American Anti-Vivisection Society
801 Old York Road, Suite 204
Jenkintown, PA 19046-1685
215-887-0816
• Student and Youth Awards

Acts of Kindness Towards Animals Poster Contest
American Humane Association
9725 East Hampden Avenue
Denver, CO 80231
303-695-0811
• Student and Youth Awards

Administrator's Awards Program—Pollution Prevention Award
Environmental Protection Agency
401 M Street SW
Washington, DC 20460
202-260-2090
• Awards for Teachers
• Student and Youth Awards

America the Beautiful Fund
2l9 Shoreham Building
Washington, DC 20005
202-638-l649
• Awards for Teachers
• Student and Youth Awards
• Grants for Projects and Activities

Amway "Class Act" Environmental Challenge Awards
Creative Resources, Inc.
220 Lyon Street NW, Suite 567
Grand Rapids, MI 49503-2210
616-698-7566
• Awards for Teachers
• Student and Youth Awards

Annenberg/CPB Math and Science Project
901 E Street NW
Washington, DC 20004
(202) 879-9711
• Awards for Teachers

Arbor Day Awards
National Arbor Day Foundation
211 North 12th Street

Lincoln, NE 68508
402-474-5655
• Awards for Teachers
• Student and Youth Awards

Award for Outstanding Contributions to Research in Environmental Education
North American Association of Environmental Education
P.O. Box 400
Troy, OH 45373
513-676-2514
• Awards for Teachers

Award for Outstanding Service to Environmental Education
North American Association of Environmental Education
P.O. Box 400
Troy, OH 45373
513-676-2514
• Awards for Teachers

B.E.S.T. Environmental Education Programs in Al. (Beep) Awards
Center for Environmental Research and Service/EEAA
Troy State University
Troy, AL 36082
800-642-2377
• Student and Youth Awards
• Grants for Educators
• Grants for Projects and Activities

Bausch & Lomb Honorary Science Award and Scholarship
1 Lincoln 1st Square
Rochester, NY 14604
716-338-5174
• Student and Youth Awards

Bill Rosenberg Award
P.O. Box 22213
Alexandria, VA 22304
703-823-8951
• Student and Youth Awards

California Foundation for Agriculture in the Classroom Teacher Awards
1601 Exposition Boulevard, FB 16
Sacramento, CA 95815
916-924-4380
• Awards for Teachers

Chevron –Times Mirror Magazines Conservation Awards
P.O. Box 7753
San Francisco, CA 94120
415-894-6083
• Grants for Projects and Activities

Brower Fund
Earth Island Institute
300 Broadway, Suite 28
San Francisco, CA 94133
415-788-3666
• Grants for Projects and Activities

Earth Kids Organization
P.O. Box 3847
Salem, OR 97302
503-363-1896
• Awards for Teachers
• Student and Youth Awards

Earthguard Award
Wisconsin Association for
Environmental Education
7290 County MM
Amherst Junction, WI 54407
715-346-2796
• Student and Youth Awards

Earthwatch Expeditions Student Scholarship Program
680 Mt. Auburn Street
P.O. Box 403R
Watertown, MA 02172
617-926-8200, ext. 136
• Scholarships

Eddie Bauer's "Heroes for the Earth" Award
15010 NE 36th Street
Redmond, WA 98052
206-882-6100
• Awards for Teachers
• Student and Youth Awards
• Grants for Projects and Activities

Environmental Pride Awards
Los Angeles Magazine
1888 Century Park East, Suite 920
Los Angeles, CA 90067
310-557-7592
• Activist Awards

Equal Education in Arts, Math, Science, and the Environment
Newman's Own, Inc.
246 Post Road East
Westport, CT 06880

203-222-0136
• Grants for Projects and Activities

Firestone Firehawks—Advocates for Ecology
209 7th Avenue North
Nashville, TN 37219
615-244-1818
• Student and Youth Awards

The Giraffe Project
P.O. Box 759
Langley, WA 98260
206-221-7989
• Student and Youth Awards

The Goldman Environmental Prize
Goldman Environmental Foundation
One Lombard Street, Suite 303
San Francisco, CA 94111
415-788-9090
• Grants for Projects and Activities

Great Explorations in Math and Science
L H S GEMS
Lawrence Hall of Science
Berkeley, CA 94720
510-642-7771
• Grants for Educators

Great Lakes Protection Fund
35 E. Wacker Drive, Suite 1880
Chicago, IL 60601
312-201- 0660
• Grants for Projects and Activities

Inherit the Earth Award
Connecticut College
270 Mohegan Avenue
New London, CT 06320-4196
203-439-2000
• Grants for Projects and Activities

Los Angeles the Beautiful
404 South Bixel Street
Los Angeles, CA 90017
213-482-1665
• Student and Youth Awards
• Grants for Projects and Activities

National Association of Conservation Districts
408 East Main
P.O. Box 855
League City, TX 77574-0855
800-825-5547
• Awards for Teachers

National Conservation Achievement Awards Program
National Wildlife Federation
1400 Sixteenth Street NW
Washington, DC 20036-2266
202-797-6800
• Awards for Teachers
• Student and Youth Awards

National Energy Education Development (The NEED Project)
P.O. Box 2518
Reston, VA 22090
703-860-5029 or 800-875-5029
• Student and Youth Awards
• Educator Grants

National Environmental Education Awards
Environmental Protection Agency
Environmental Education Division
401 M Street SW
Washington, DC 20460
202-260-4965
• Teacher Awards

National Environmental Education and Training Foundation
915 15th Street NW, Suite 200
Washington, DC 20005
202-628-8200
• Grants for Educators
• Grants for Projects and Activities

National 4-H Conservation of Natural Resources Award
National 4-H Council
7100 Connecticul Avenue
Chevy Chase, MD 20815
301-961-2800
• Scholarships

National Science Education Leadership Association
Max McGraw Foundation
P.O. Box 380057
East Hartford, CT 06138-005
• Scholarships

National Youth Garden Grant
National Gardening Association
180 Flynn Avenue
Burlington, VT 05401
802-863-1308
• Student and Youth Awards
• Project and Activity Grants

Nature Educator of the Year Awards
Roger Tory Peterson Institute of Natural History
110 Marvin Parkway
Jamestown, NY 14701
716-665-2473
• Awards for Teachers

Neighborhood Service to America Award
National Association of Neighborhoods
1651 Fuller Street NW
Washington, DC 20009
202-332-7766
• Grants for Projects and Activities

New England Anti-Vivisection Society Creative Arts Competition
333 Washington Street, #850
Boston, MA 02108-5100
617-523-6020
• Student and Youth Awards
• Scholarships

New Explorers Science Teachers Awards Program
General Learning Corporation
60 Revere Drive
Northbrook, IL 60062-1563
708-205-3000
• Awards for Teachers

Phillips Environmental Partnership Awards (PEP Awards)
PEP Program
16 D1 PB
Bartlesville, OK 74004
405-744-7233
• Awards for Teachers
• Student and Youth Awards
• Projects and Activity Grants
• Educator Grants

A Pledge and a Promise Environmental Awards
Anheuser-Busch Theme Parks Environmental Awards
7007 Sea World Drive
Orlando, FL 32821
407-363-2389
• Student and Youth Awards

The President's Environmental Youth Awards Program
401 M Street SW
Washington, DC 20460
202-382-4454

• Student and Youth Awards
• Grants for Projects and Activities

President's Youth Service Awards
P.O. Box 310
New Castle, DE 19720
202-606-8070, ext. 123
• Student and Youth Awards

Reader's Digest American Heroes in Education
Reader's Digest Road
Pleasantville, NY 10570-7000
914-238-1000, ext. 5352
• Awards for Teachers
• Grants for Projects and Activities

Renew America Awards
Searching for Success
1400 Sixteenth Street NW, Suite 710
Washington, DC 20036
202-232-2252
• Awards for Teachers
• Student and Youth Awards

Safe Neighborhood Parks Proposition of 1992
Los Angeles County Regional Park and Open Space District
433 South Vermont
Los Angeles, CA 90020
213-738-2961
• Grants for Projects and Activities

Sebastian's Little Green Creative Arts Project
The International Children's Campaign to Save the Environment
6109 DeSoto Avenue, Department C
Woodland Hills, CA 91367
818-999-5112, ext. 260
• Student and Youth Awards

Seiko Youth Challenge
1234 Summer Street
Stamford, CT 06905
800-323-1550
• Student and Youth Awards

Take Pride in America National Awards Program
Keep America Beautiful, Inc.
P.O. Box 1339
Jessup, MD 20794-1339
Unlisted
• Student and Youth Awards
• Teacher Awards

Teens Making a Difference
KCET Community Outreach/Life and Times
4401 Sunset Boulevard
Los Angeles, CA 90027
213-665-6067
• Student and Youth Awards

Tapestry Grants
Toyota/National Science Teachers Association
1742 Connecticut Avenue NW
Washington, DC 20009
202-328-5800
• Awards for Teachers
• Educator Grants
• Project Activity Grants
• Student and Youth Awards

United Earth
55 East 75th Street
New York, NY 10021
212-223-0890
• Awards for Teachers
• Student and Youth Awards

United Nations Global 500 Awards
United Nations Environment Program
Room DC2-803
New York, NY 10017
212-963-1234
• Awards for Teachers
• Student and Youth Awards

Urban Forestry Grant Program
California Department of Forestry and Fire Protection
2524 Mulberry Street
Riverside, CA 92501
909-782-4140
• Grants for Projects and Activities

USDA/Forest Service, Urban and Community Forestry Department
201 14th Street SW
Washington, DC 20090
202-205-1689
• Grants for Projects and Activities

Vegetarian Resource Group
606 Old Crossing Drive
Baltimore, MD 21203
410-366-8343
• Student and Youth Awards

The Volvo Environment Prize
AB Volvo
Department 654 VHK

S-405 08 Gothenburg, Sweden
46-31-594433
• Grants for Projects and Activities

Walter E. Jeske Award
North American Association of
Environmental Education
P.O. Box 400
Troy, OH 45373
513-676-2514
• Teacher Awards

Westinghouse Science Talent Search
Science Service, Inc.
1719 N Street
Washington, DC 20036
202-785-225
• Scholarships

Wildlife and Fisheries Scholarships
National 4-H Council
7100 Connecticut Avenue
Chevy Chase, MD 20815
301-961-2800
• Scholarships

The Windstar Youth Award
The Windstar Foundation
2317 Snowmass Creek Road
Snowmass, CO 81654-9198
303-927-4777
• Student and Youth Awards
• Scholarships

Wisconsin Teacher of the Year Awards
Wisconsin Department of Natural
Resources
I and E, Box 7921
Madison, WI 53707
608-264-6280
• Awards for Teachers

World Environment Day Youth Poster and Essay Contest
United States Committee for United
Nations Environmental Program
2013 Que Street NW
Washington, DC 20009
202-234-3600
• Student and Youth Awards

Young Activist Campaign Contest
American Anti-Vivisection Society
801 Old York Road, #204
Jenkintown, PA 19046
215-887-0816

• Student and Youth Awards

Youth Awards Program for Energy Achievement
Illinois Department of Energy and
Natural Resources
325 West Adams Street, Room 300
Springfield, IL 62704
217-524-5454
• Student and Youth Awards

Youth Energy Awards
California Energy Extension Service
1400 Tenth Street
Sacramento, CA 95814
916-323-4388
• Student and Youth Awards

Chapter 19

Resources

Environmental Education Materials

Chapter 19
CONTENTS

INTRODUCTION

To understand the global ramifications of the life-style and business choices they will make as adults, today's children must learn about the intricacies of life on earth. Once exposed to a river teaming with life, they will be able to grasp the tragedy of a river killed by pollution. Once they understand that the brown they see along the horizon is there because people put it there, they may also realize that people can make it better. There are solutions. Some solutions are obvious, but most are more evasive. To find these solutions we must understand the problems, because today's children will be tomorrow's leaders.

Environmental education has been around since the 1940s, but it is now recognized that it must go beyond the classroom and into our daily lives, taking into account economic, social, political and ecological issues and looking at how these interact and depend upon one another.

Should environmental education be a single subject with its own textbook, or should it be integrated into other disciplines? If it is presented on its own, environmental education becomes another required subject in an already crowded school plan. If environmental topics are infused into other subjects, students will learn how they affect all aspects of life.

To date there is no nationally mandated environmental curriculum in the United States. However, the National Environmental Education Act (NEEA), passed in November 1990, requires the EPA to set up an Office of Environmental Education. Through this new office the EPA must develop environmental education standards and regulations. The EPA is now responsible for stimulating and supporting environmental education and environmental educators.

To face the future with hope for a healthy life for all living things on earth, we will need a proactive, environmentally literate population. The following list of environmental education materials that can be adapted to all disciplines of study (cross-curricular) in whatever way best suits individual teachers' needs and desires is designed to achieve this goal. We have compiled this list by diligently searching the country and speaking with many teachers, individuals and organizations. Teachers have visited our office and offered a review of every piece of material listed. All the titles on the list were seen to have some value to a teacher in the grade levels indicated.

Best wishes in your pursuit of educating our children as they grow into global citizens!

EDUCATIONAL MATERIALS

Action

C.A.P.E. Program Guide
Grades: K–6
C.A.P.E., 1992
P.O. Box 307
Austin, TX 78767
512-476-2273
This guide assists educators or adults who want to help children set up a club and begin environmental action projects.

Ecology Action Workbook and Dictionary
Grades: 6–12
Earth Beat Press, 1991
250 H Street, P.O. Box 8110-729
Blaine, WA 98230
604-736-6931
Raises environmental consciousness through activities such as how to write an effective letter, how to start an ecology club and how individual action can make a difference.

Social Action Projects in Alberta Schools
Grades: K–12
Alberta Global Education Project, 1992
11010 142nd Street
Edmonton, Alberta, Canada T5N 2RI
403-453-2411
Twenty-five projects with fascinating facts and planned activities. Some of the projects deal with the environment.

Thinking Globally and Acting Locally
Grades: 5–12
ERIC: Clearinghouse for Science, Mathematics and Environmental Education, 1982
Ohio State University
1200 Chambers Road, Room 310
Columbus, OH 43212
614-292-6717
Students become involved with tangible community actions that have a positive effect on improving the world environment while stressing similarities between cultures.

Atmosphere

Connection: The Living Planet: The Air Around Us
Grades: 3–5
Ginn Publishing Canada, Inc., 1993
P.O. Box 261 Tonawanda
New York, NY 14151-0261
800-361-6128
Exploring weather, changing climates and ozone issues through stories, poems and hands-on activities.

Earth, Moon and Stars
Grades: 5–9
Great Explorations in Math and Science, 1986
Lawrence Hall of Science, University of California—Berkeley
Berkeley, CA 94720
510-642-7771
Understanding earth in relation to the sun, stars and moon. Activities include making star maps and studying ancient models of the world.

Icewalk School Kit
Grades: 6–12
Amway International, USA, 1993
7575 East Fulton Road
Ada, MI 49355
616-676-6000
Learning about the atmosphere through modules that include videos, readings for students and activity sheets.

Look to the Sky
Grades: 4–12
Good Apple, Inc., 1988
1204 Buchanan Street, P.O. Box 299
Carthage, IL 62321-0299
800-435-7234
Activities include photographing objects in the sky. Contains 12 pairs of illustrated sky charts, mythological characters and foldout charts.

Nature Scope: Astronomy Adventures
Grades: K–8
National Wildlife Federation, 1986
1412 Sixteenth Street NW
Washington, DC 20036-2266
800-432-6564
Interdisciplinary activities in astronomy. The curriculum develops under-standing of the natural world and the skills to make responsible decisions.

Saving Our Planet Series: Air
Grades: 1–3
Good Apple, Inc., 1992
1204 Buchanan Street, P.O. Box 299
Carthage, IL 62321-0299
800-435-7234
Basic understanding of environmental problems developed through hands-on activities, reading comprehension and activity sheets.

Saving Our Planet Series: Air
Grades: 4–7
Good Apple, Inc., 1992
1204 Buchanan Street, P.O. Box 299
Carthage, IL 62331-0299
800-435-7234
Background information on air pollution issues with hands-on activities that focus on protecting air quality and solutions to current problems.

Acid Rain

Acid Precipitation Learning Materials
Grades: 6–12
The Acid Rain Foundation, 1985
1410 Varsity Drive
Raleigh, NC 27606
919-828-9443
Acid rain explained through the earth and social sciences. Activities, teacher guidelines, objectives, tests and materials are included.

Acid Rain
Grades: 6–12
Great Explorations in Math and Science, 1990
Lawrence Hall of Science, University of California—Berkeley
Berkeley, CA 94720
510-642-7771
Study of causes and effects of acid rain. Students find solutions, conduct experiments, play games and hold town meetings.

The Acid Rain Curriculum
Grades: 4–8
The Acid Rain Foundation, 1986
1410 Varsity Drive

Raleigh, NC 27606
919-828-9443
Acid rain explored through art, language, math, science and social studies. This curriculum includes lessons, worksheets, quiz, poster and pH paper.

Acid Rain Curriculum Set
Grades: 6–12
The Acid Rain Foundation, 1986
1410 Varsity Drive
Raleigh, NC 27606
919-828-9443
Exploring acid rain issues through interdisciplinary activities and tests that can be integrated into a curriculum.

Acid Rain Quiz
Grades: 4–8
The Acid Rain Foundation, 1985
1410 Varsity Drive
Raleigh, NC 27606
919-828-9443
Thirty worksheets reinforce concepts and vocabulary of an acid rain study.

The Acid Rain Reader
Grades: 4–8
The Acid Rain Foundation, 1989
1410 Varsity Drive
Raleigh, NC 27606
919-828-9443
This guide provokes thought about the effect acid rain has on the environment through questions. Offers a general overview and glossary of acid rain.

Acid Rain: Science Projects
Grades: 5–12
The Acid Rain Foundation, 1987
1410 Varsity Drive
Raleigh, NC 27606
919-828-9443
Activities use the scientific method, which includes tests for pH balance, logarithms and study of the effects of acid rain on plants and microorganisms.

Acid Rain: A Student's First Sourcebook
Grades: 4–8
U.S. Environmental Protection Agency, 1990
Public Information Center, PM-211B
401 M Street SW
Washington, DC 20460
202-260-2049

The background, concepts, definitions, activities and experiments in this sourcebook help students understand the problems and solutions to acid rain.

Acid Rain: A Teacher's Guide
Grades: 4–12
National Wildlife Federation, 1985
1412 Sixteenth Street NW
Washington, DC 20036-2266
800-432-6564
This guide explains the causes of acid rain, the problems and what to do about them. Students study the Clean Air Act, follow a bill through Congress and learn how to write an action letter.

Acid Rain Word Find
Grades: 4–8
Acid Rain Foundation, 1985
1410 Varsity Drive
Raleigh, NC 27606
919-828-9443
Thirty worksheets that reinforce concepts and vocabulary concerning acid rain.

Air Pollution

Air Education Unit
Grades: K–3
Wisconsin Department of Natural Resources
P.O. Box 7921
Madison, WI 53707
608-266-2711
Motivating activities with units on air, air pollution and what can be done to help stop air pollution.

Air Pollutants' Effects on Forests, Vol. 1
Grades: 4–12
The Acid Rain Foundation, 1990
1410 Varsity Drive
Raleigh, NC 27606
919-828-9443
Interdisciplinary activity workbook helps students develop an awareness of trees in the forest.

Air Pollutants' Effects on Forests, Vol. 2
Grades: 4–12
The Acid Rain Foundation, 1990

1410 Varsity Drive
Raleigh, NC 27606
919-828-9443
Interdisciplinary activity workbook helps students develop an awareness of the effects of air pollution on trees and forests.

Breakthroughs: Strategies for Thinking: Smog, Sore Throats and Me?
Grades: 3–6
Zaner-Bloser, Inc., 1992
2200 West Fifth Avenue, P.O. Box 16764
Columbus, OH 43216-6764
800-421-3018
The lessons cover what causes dirty air, how dirty air affects your health and how people can keep the air clean.

Environmental Impact of Cars
Grades: 5–12
Courseware Solutions, Inc., 1991
100 Lombard Street, Suite 404
Toronto, Ontario, Canada M5C 1M3
416-863-6116
Includes communication, science, geography and math activities with reproducible student worksheets.

Environmental Resource Guide: Air Quality
Grades: 6–8
Air and Waste Management Association, 1991
P.O. Box 2861
Pittsburgh, PA 15230-2861
412-232-3444
Weather, climate, air pollutants, acid deposition, ozone and indoor air quality are explored in a series of fact sheets and activities that can be integrated into an existing curriculum.

Let's Clear the Air About Air (Pollution, That Is): The Eco Badge Lesson Book
Grades: K–12
Vistanomics, 1992
230 North Maryland Avenue, Suite 310
Glendale, CA 91206-4261
818-409-9157
Ozone and air pollution articles, activities, handouts for all school levels, plus an eco badge, eco filters, color charts and more.

Our Only Earth Series: Our Troubled Skies
Grades: 4–12
Zephyr Press, 1990
3316 North Chapel Avenue, P.O. Box 13448
Tucson, AZ 85732-3448
602-322-5090
Provides an integrated science, language arts and social studies program consisting of eight classroom activities. Activities can last from one month to a year.

Smog Check: For a More Colorful World
Grades: K–6
California Bureau of Automotive Repair, 1994
10240 Systems Parkway
Sacramento, CA 95827
916-255-4360
Informs students about the automobile pollution problem in California and what each can do to help clean the air.

Climate

The Effect of Lake Erie on Climate
Grades: 11–12
Ohio Sea Grant College Program, 1990
Ohio State University
1314 Kinnear Road
Columbus, OH 43212-1194
614-292-8949
Student and teacher guides investigate air temperatures, density and movement, changing winds and other implications of Lake Erie on the economy of northern Ohio.

Knowledge Tree on Global Climate
Grades: 7–12
Climate Protection Institute, 1989
5833 Balmoral Drive
Oakland, CA 94619
510-531-0100
Students learn about global climate change using the computer.

Global Warming

Atmospheric Carbon Dioxide and the Greenhouse Effect
Grades: 9–12

National Technical Information Service, 1989
Department of Commerce
Springfield, VA 22161
703-487-4600
Informational booklet written in a clear and concise manner on atmospheric carbon dioxide and the greenhouse effect.

Beat the Heat: The CO_2 Challenge
Grades: 5–8
Scholastic, Inc., 1991
555 Broadway
New York, NY 10012
800-325-6149
Background information on global warming with class activities, a pledge and certificate for kids, a petition and a list of energy-saving products and resources.

Global Warming and the Greenhouse Effect
Grades: 7–11
Great Explorations in Math and Science, 1990
Lawrence Hall of Science, University of California—Berkeley
Berkeley, CA 94720
510-642-7771
Includes teacher's guide plus lab experiments, instructions for building a greenhouse model and a Global Warming game.

Global Warming: Impacts and Solutions
Grades: 9–12
Stanford Program on International and Cross-cultural Education (SPICE), 1990
300 Lasuen Street
Littlefield Center, Room 14
Stanford, CA 94305-5013
415-725-1480
HyperCard stack tour of global-warming issues for social studies, government or science courses. Supplementary guide includes role play, small group activities, pretests and more.

Global Warming: Meeting a Global Challenge Through Individual Action
Grades: 5–12
Schlitz Audubon Center

1111 East Brown Deer Road
Milwaukee, WI 53217
414-352-2880
Science experiment activities with objectives and procedures clearly stated. Motivates students by demonstrating the principles of global warming.

Global Warming Social Studies Activities
Grades: 5–8
Climate Protection Institute, 1991
5833 Balmoral Drive
Oakland, CA 94619
510-531-0100
Informative facts and statistics on global warming. Ideas for fun activities and intercurricular games.

Global Warming: Understanding the Forecast
Teachers' Resource Manual
Grades: 6–12
American Museum of Natural History Education Department, 1992
Central Park West at 79th Street
New York, NY 10024
212-769-5304
Based on AMNH exhibition—The History of the Earth's Climate and Possible Future Impacts of Human Population on Its Climate. A self-guided tour of the exhibition plus classroom activities appropriate for science, social studies, math and English classes.

The Greenhouse Effect and Global Warming
Grades: 10–12
Enterprise for Education, 1991
1320 A Third Street, Suite 202
Santa Monica, CA 90401
310-394-9864
Greenhouse effect and global warming—its causes, adaptation and abatement are explained. Student booklet comes with accompanying teacher's guide.

Ground Truth Studies Teacher Handbook
Grades: 4–12
Aspen Global Change Institute, 1992
100 East Francis Street
Aspen, CO 81611
303-925-7376
Interdisciplinary activity-based guide

to the greenhouse effect, biodiversity, ozone depletion and watersheds.

Weather

Nature Scope: Wild About Weather
Grades: K–8
National Wildlife Federation
1412 Sixteenth Street NW
Washington, DC 20036-2266
800-432-6564
Hands-on activities and interdisciplinary curriculum encourage nature appreciation and develop skills needed to make responsible decisions about the environment.

Weather in Action
Grades: 4–6
National Geographic Society, 1990
17th and M Street NW
Washington, DC 20036
800-368-2728
Telecommunications-based science curriculum includes investigation, collaboration, geography, computer skills and critical thinking.

Weather Study Under a Newspaper Umbrella
Grades: 4–10
How the Weather Works, 1989
1522 Baylor Avenue
Rockville, MD 20850
301-762-SNOW
Interdisciplinary activities show the importance of weather in our lives. Additional teaching aids include newspaper/magazine articles, photos, advertisements and other media.

Biodiversity

Biodiversity: The Florida Story
Grades: 3–6
Florida Department of Education, 1991
325 West Gaines Street
Tallahassee, FL
800-542-FREE
Background information and activity sheets focus on the diversity of living things and their habitats.

Conservation

Conservation Projects
Grades: K–12
Chesapeake Bay Foundation, 1991
162 Prince George Street
Annapolis, MD 21401
301-268-8816
Projects include sediment control, water conservation, lifestyle analysis, adopting a stream, habitat improvement and energy conservation.

Conservation Seeds
Grades: K—2
Missouri Department of Conservation, Education Programs, 1990
P.O. Box 180
Jefferson City, MO 65102-0180
314-751-4115
Heightens awareness of nature and conservation. Easy-to-follow activities to tie into existing curriculum. Includes several posters.

Preserving America's Wilderness
Grades: 7–9
Knowledge Unlimited, Inc., 1992
P.O. Box 52
Madison, WI 53701-0052
800-356-2303
Activity designed to accompany a unit in land conservation. Includes film, discussion guide, audio tape, glossary and review quiz.

Energy

Breakthroughs: Strategies for Thinking: Fuel Today...Gone Tomorrow?
Grades: 3–6
Zaner-Bloser, Inc., 1992
2200 West Fifth Avenue, P.O. Box 16764
Columbus, OH 43216-6764
800-421-3018
Lessons on fossil fuels, nuclear energy and other energy sources. Material is factual with illustrations and photos.

Energy Conservation Education: An Action Approach
Grades: 3–8
Council on the Environment, Inc., 1983

51 Chambers Street, Room 228
New York, NY 10007
212-566-0990
Addresses the teaching of energy and electricity conservation in the classroom.

Energy Conservation: Experiments You Can Do
Grades: 3–6
Edison Electric Institute, 1986
701 Pennsylvania Avenue NW
Washington, DC 20004-2696
202-508-5424
Experiments dealing with heating, air conditioning, hot water, appliances, lighting and energy sources of the future.

Energy Conservation: Student Activities
Grades: 5–12
New York Energy Education Project, 1988
New York Education Department, Room 232M EB
Albany, NY 12234
518-474-3852
Activities teach students about home energy conservation and engine care for saving gasoline.

Energy Smarts Team Training Manual
Grades: 3–8
Oregon State University Extension Energy Program, 1993
800 Northeast Oregon Street, #450
Portland, OR 97232-2162
503-731-4104
Suggestions for saving energy and programs for schools that will save money and help protect the environment in the process.

How to Save Energy
Grades: 1–5
Channing L. Bete Company, 1992
200 State Road
South Deerfield, MA 01373
800-628-7733
A coloring and activities book on saving energy.

Manipulative Energy Activities
Grades: 7–8
Louisiana Department of Natural Resources, Energy Division, 1987

P.O. Box 44156
Baton Rouge, LA 70804-4156
505-342-1399
Scientific concepts presented in a way that enable students to gather and interpret information as if they obtained it themselves.

Offalot
Grades: K–1
Energy Source Education Council, 1988
5505 East Carson Street, Suite 250
Lakewood, CA 90713-3093
310-420-6814
Teaches energy conservation and safety practices in the home. Kit includes teacher's guide, hand puppet, audio cassette, cards and poster.

Saving Our Future
Grades: 6–12
Los Angeles Department of Water and Power
Educational Services, Public Affairs Division, 1991
P.O. Box 111, Room 1514
Los Angeles, CA 90051-0100
213-481-4085, ext. 6358
Interdisciplinary activities that maintain or extend the quality and quantity of the earth's natural resources.

Turn Out Those Lights! Here Comes the Energy Patrol
Grades: 4–8
Arizona Department of Commerce Energy Office, 1992
3800 North Central Avenue, Suite 1200
Phoenix, AZ 85012
800-352-5499
Students learn about energy and leadership skills simply by being responsible for monitoring rooms to ensure that lights are turned off when not in use.

Water

Admiral Splash
Grade: 4
Metropolitan Water District of Southern California, 1993
Supervisor of Education Programs
P.O. Box 54153
Los Angeles, CA 90054-0153

213-250-6739
Activities and materials to help students develop strong water-related habits and attitudes. Also available in Spanish.

Adopt-A-Stream: Teacher's Handbook
Grades: 9–12
Delta Laboratories, Inc., 1987
P.O. Box 435
Pittsford, NY 14534
916-567-4000
Contains detailed instructions for a variety of environmental quality tests, and data evaluation.

California Smith
Grade: 6
Metropolitan Water District of Southern California, 1993
Supervisor of Education Programs
P.O. Box 54153
Los Angeles, CA 90054-0153
213-250-6739
Discusses the importance of water—where we get it, how nature recycles it, how it is distributed in California and its quality.

California's Water Problems
Grades: 7–12
Water Education Foundation, 1989
717 K Street, Suite 517
Sacramento, CA 95814
916-444-6240
Role-playing scenarios designed to give students first-hand experiences at working out solutions to real-life water problems.

Don't Be a Waterhog, School Education Packet
Grades: K–6
Los Angeles Department of Water and Power, 1991
P.O. Box 111, Room 1514
Los Angeles, CA 90051-0100
213-481-4085, ext. 6358
Packet includes a water conservation checklist, water saver's pledge, certificate of appreciation, book list, water awareness games and science activities.

From Rain to Drain: Water for the Santa Clara Valley
Grades: 6–12

Santa Clara Valley Water District, 1992
5750 Alameda Expressway
San Jose, CA 95118
408-265-2600
Provides a foundation of basic water education with an emphasis on conservation. Some activities are nonscience in their orientation.

The Geography of Water
Grades: 4–8
Metropolitan Water District of Southern California, 1989
Supervisor of Education Programs
P.O. Box 54153
Los Angeles, CA 90054-0153
213-250-6739
Water conservation unit dealing with elevations, physical features, precipitation, population, industry and agriculture, as well as moving and using water in California.

Investigating Streams and Rivers
Grades: 5–12
Global Rivers Environmental Education Network, 1992
721 East Huron Street
Ann Arbor, MI 48104
313-761-8142
Activities designed to encourage students to investigate and take action regarding local streams and rivers.

Official Captain Hydro Water Conservation Workbook
Grades: 4–8
Innovative Communications, 1992
207 Coggins Drive
Pleasant Hill, CA 94523
510-944-0923
Covers all aspects of water use and conservation. Includes activities and exercises addressing the short- and long-term problems of water use. Also available in Spanish.

A Sense of Water
Grades: K–6
Southern Arizona Water Resources Association, 1984
48 North Tucson Boulevard, Suite 106
Tucson, AZ 85716
602-881-3939
Lessons and activities focus on living in a desert for an understanding of the limitations and possibilities with water.

Splash!
Grades: 2–5
American Water Works Association, 1990
6666 West Quincy Avenue
Denver, CO 80235
303-974-7711
Activities cover water conservation issues.

Water and Me
Grades: K–3
National Association of Conservation Districts, 1994
P.O. Box 855
League City, TX 77574-0855
713-332-3402
Promotes water awareness and conservation. Activities cover recycling water, water pollution and environmental and water careers.

Water Conservation Garden Activity Book
Grades: 4–8
Western Municipal Water District, 1992
450 Alessandro Boulevard
Riverside, CA 92508
714-780-4170
Activities and lesson plans that study water conservation as it relates to plants and landscaping. Also available in Spanish.

Water Is Valuable
Grades: K–2
New York City Department of Environmental Protection, 1990
Office of Intergovernmental Relations and Public Affairs
1 Center Street, Room 2454
New York, NY 10007
212-669-3381
This workbook uses writing, drawing, coloring and math to show how water is used, its importance and ways to conserve it.

Water Is Your Best Friend
Grades: 2–4
Los Angeles Department of Water and Power, 1982
P.O. Box 111, Room 1514
Los Angeles, CA 90051-0100
800-342-5397
Can be used as a science unit or with other curriculum. Lesson plans on the water cycle, water conservation and water reclamation with coloring book and posters.

Water: The Lost Treasure
Grades: 5–8
Water Pollution Control Federation, 1990
Public Education Department
601 Wythe Street
Alexandria, VA 22314-1994
800-666-0206
Activities motivate students to save water in everyday life. Kit includes a teacher's guide, student guides and a video.

Water: The Resource that Gets Used and Used for Everything
Grades: 5–8
American Water Resources Association, 1990
5410 Grosvenor Lane, Suite 220
Bethesda, MD 20814-2192
703-904-1225
Activities and discussion questions use a poster depicting water use in a typical town. Students learn about the earth's water distribution.

Water for Santa Clara County
Grades: 6–12
Santa Clara Valley Water District, 1986
5750 Alameda Expressway
San Jose, CA 95118
408-265-2600
Promotes wise use of water through multidisciplinary activities. Teacher's guide includes step-by-step procedures and bonus spin-off suggestions.

The Water Sourcebook
Grades: 3–5
Water Environment Federation, 1993
601 Wythe Street
Alexandria, VA 22314
703-684-2400
Hands-on activities and experiments develop awareness, knowledge and skills for sound water use decisions.

Water in Your Hands
Grades: 4–10
Soil and Water Conservation Society, 1990
7515 NE Ankeny Road
Ankeny, IA 50021-9764
800-THE-SOIL

Designed to improve student's understanding of water and their place in the hydrologic cycle. Lessons are based on learning cycle strategies. Also in Spanish.

Water Watchers
Grades: 6–9
Massachusetts Water Resources Authority, 1983
Charleston Navy Yard
100 First Avenue
Charlestown, MA 02129
617-242-6000
Water conservation lessons for science and social studies classes. Includes activities and worksheets and a teacher's guide.

Water Wisdom
Grades: 4–8
Alameda County Office of Education, 1990
313 West Winton Avenue
Hayward, CA 94544-1198
510-887-0152
Sequential lessons about water, plants and animals; water routes, rights and responsibilities; plus the impact of too much or too little water.

Water Wisdom
Grades: 9–12
Massachusetts Water Resources Authority, 1990
Charleston Navy Yard
100 First Avenue
Charlestown, MA 02129
617-242-7110
Water conservation education program that has students inspect school water.

Water Wizards: School Program on Water Conservation
Grades: 3–4
Massachusetts Water Resources Authority, 1985
Charleston Navy Yard
100 First Avenue
Charlestown, MA 02129
617-242-7110
Explores water cycles, drinking sources, how water reaches and leaves our homes, water use and water conservation.

WET (Water Education for Teachers)
Grades: K–12
North Dakota State Water Commission, 1990
900 East Boulevard
Bismarck, ND 58505-0850
701-224-4989
Hands-on learning that develops in students an awareness of water as an essential, precious and managed resource.

Ecosystems

Adopting a Wetland: A Northwest Guide
Grades: 7–12
Adopt-A-Stream Foundation, 1989
P.O. Box 5558
Everett, WA 98206
206-388-3487
Exploring the wetlands of the Pacific Northwest and ways to preserve them. Useful to educators visiting wetlands with students for the first time.

Connection: The Living Planet: The Web of Life
Grades: 3–5
Ginn Publishing Canada Inc., 1993
P.O. Box 261 Tonawanda
New York, NY 14151-0261
800-361-6128
Information and activities on how all things are interconnected, their balance in nature and the preservation of ecosystems.

Fragile Frontiers: The Ends of the Earth
Grades: K–12
Minnesota Conservation Federation, 1991
1034 South Cleveland Avenue
St. Paul, MN 55116
612-690-3077
Background information plus activities for students on the arctic and antarctic ecosystems. Includes a teacher's guide.

Freshwater Marsh Habitat Pac
Grades: 4–7
National Institute for Urban Wildlife, 1980
P.O. Box 3015

Shepardstown, WV 25443
304-876-6146
Sampling methods, model marsh building and the study of food webs are used to illustrate the importance of marshes and their ecological problems.

The Galapagos Jason Curriculum
Grades: 4–12
National Science Teacher's Association, 1991
1742 Connecticut Avenue NW
Washington, DC 20009
202-328-5800
Interdisciplinary unit on the Galapagos Islands explores its geology, currents, climate, biodiversity, food webs, evolution and more, through activities, worksheets, readings and simulation games.

It Begins with a Watershed...and Its People
Grades: K–6
U.S. Department of Agriculture, Soil Conservation Service, 1993
Washington, DC 20050
202-205-8333
Activities and presentation material cover the issues of water quality, wetlands, flood damage and water conservation.

Nature Scope: Discovering Deserts
Grades: K–8
National Wildlife Federation, 1989
1412 Sixteenth Street NW
Washington, DC 20036-2266
800-432-6564
Interdisciplinary curriculum with hands-on activities that encourages nature appreciation and develops skills needed to make responsible decisions about the environment.

Nature Scope: Wading into Wetlands
Grades: K–8
National Wildlife Federation, 1992
1412 Sixteenth Street NW
Washington, DC 20036-2266
800-432-6564
Interdisciplinary curriculum with hands-on wetland activities encourage nature appreciation and responsible decision-making skills about the environment.

Observing an Aquarium
Grades: K–5
Delta Education, Inc., 1988
P.O. Box 915
Hudson, NH 03051
603-889-8899
Activities show how to set up an aquarium and give instructions on how to observe the natural habitat of water plants and animals in a local pond or a stream.

Pond Life
Grades: K–6
Delta Education, Inc., 1988
P.O. Box 915
Hudson, NH 03051
603-889-8899
Students set up a pond-life habitat and observe the interactions. Kit includes maintenance information for the activities and ordering instructions.

Pond Study Kit
Grades: 6–12
Young Entomologists' Society Inc., 1993
1915 Peggy Place
Lansing, MI 48910
Thorough study of entomology. Includes insect identification guide and lap desk with detailed labeled illustrations of insects.

Rescue the Reef
Grades: 3–6
Nature Company, 1993
P.O. Box 188
Florence, KY 41022
800-227-1114
Examines the plant and animal life of reefs, how they are formed, environmental threats they face and what can be done to save them.

The Stream Scene: Watersheds, Wildlife and People
Grades: 6–12
Oregon Department of Fish and Wildlife, 1992
P.O. Box 59
Portland, OR 97207
503-229-5403
Activities offer a look at watersheds from many perspectives. Background information for the teacher can be used as a reading assignment for students.

Teacher's Guide to Coral Reef Teaching
Grades: 7–9
The World Wildlife Fund, 1986
1250 24th Street NW
Washington, DC 20037-1175
202-293-4800
Includes a coloring book, slide program and game about the Caribbean coral reef ecosystem. Also available in Spanish.

Trans-Antarctica: Bringing Antarctica into Your Classroom
Grades: K–12
Target Stores, 1990
33 South Sixth Street, P.O. Box 1392
Minneapolis, MN 55440-1392
612-370-6073
Students learn about the antarctic ecosystem by studying the trip of two men going across antarctica using only dogsleds. Adjustable to all grade levels.

Wetlands Affect You and Me
Grades: 4–9
Department of Natural Resources
P.O. Box 30028
Lansing, MI 48909
517-373-2329
Marine science activities that show how to help the environment. Easily reproducible.

Wetlands Are Wonderlands
Grades: 6–8
University of Illinois
4-H Marine Education Series
4-H Youth Program, 1991
65 Mumford Hall
1301 West Gregory Drive
Urbana, IL 61801
217-782-6370
Basic information about wetlands is provided through aquatic science activities that help the environment.

Wetlands Conservation and Use Issue Pac
Grades: 4–7
National Institute for Urban Wildlife, 1982
P.O. Box 3015
Shepardstown, WV 25443
304-876-6146
Students learn about wetland habitats and wildlife/human impact on wetlands in the United States through field trips, activities and surveys. Findings can be reported in the *Wetlands Gazette*.

Wetlands Protectors: Guarding Our Wild and Watery Lands
Grades: 5–9
California Aquatic Science Education Consortium, 1994
Department of Education
University of California—Santa Barbara
Santa Barbara, CA 93106
805-893-2739
Activities for groups interested in observing and conserving wetlands. Assistance provided to group leaders in selecting and planning the activity.

Wetlands: Water, Wildlife, Plants and People
Grades: K–6
U.S. Geological Survey/Branch of Distribution, 1992
P.O. Box 25286, Denver Federal Center
Denver, CO 80225
303-236-7477
On one side of this poster is a large colorful picture, the other side contains information and activities on wetlands.

WOW! The Wonders of Wetlands Educator's Guide
Grades: K–12
Environmental Concern, Inc., 1991
P.O. Box P
St. Michaels, MD 21663
410-745-9620
Indoor and outdoor wetland activities that cover all aspects of wetlands. Teacher's guide included.

EMFs

A Teaching Unit on Electromagnetic Waves
Grades: 7–12
Los Angeles Department of Water and Power
Educational Services, Public Affairs Division, 1991
P.O. Box 111, Room 1514
Los Angeles, CA 90051-0100
213-481-4085, ext. 6358
Lectures, demonstrations, activities and lab experiments that explore electrical charges, magnetic fields and possible/known health risks.

Your Guide to Understanding EMF
Grades: 6–9
The Culver Company, 1991
316 Merrimac Street
Newbury Port, MA 01950
800-428-5837
Introduces electric and magnetic fields, ways to reduce exposure and controversy surrounding them. Accompanied by teacher's guide.

Endangered Species

America's Endangered Wildlife
Grades: 4–9
Elsa Wild Animal Appeal, 1982
P.O. Box 4572
North Hollywood, CA 91617-0572
818-761-8387
Ecological and wildlife themes are stressed in this kit.

Audubon All Species Day
Grades: 4–6
National Audubon Society, 1993
700 Broadway
New York, NY 10003
212-979-3000
Activities designed to teach students about endangered species and basic ecology concepts.

Connection: The Living Planet: Endangered Wildlife
Grades: 3–5
Ginn Publishing Canada Inc., 1993
P.O. Box 261 Tonawanda
New York, NY 14151-0261
800-361-6128
Ideas, activities and photo illustrations encourage students to think about endangered wildlife. A word list appears at the end of the book.

Discovering Endangered Species: A Nature Activity Book
Grades: K–5
Dog-Eared Publications, 1990
P.O. Box 620863
Middleton, WI 53562-0863
608-831-1410
The activities in this book drive the

imagination and artistic talents of students as they expand their understanding of extinction and conservation.

Endangered Animals
Grades: 3–5
Wildlife Education Ltd.—Zoo Books, 1984
3590 Kettner Boulevard
San Diego, CA 92101
800-477-5034
Endangered animals, their habitats, why we need them and how they can be saved are taught using puzzles, games, quizzes and more.

Endangered Animals
Grades: 6–8
Wildlife Education Ltd.—Zoo Books, 1984
3590 Kettner Boulevard
San Diego, CA 92101
800-477-5034
Endangered animals, their habitats, why we need them and how they can be saved are taught using puzzles, games, quizzes and more.

Endangered Animals: Zoo Books
Grades: 3–7
Wildlife Education Ltd.—Zoo Books, 1993
3590 Kettner Boulevard
San Diego, CA 92101
800-477-5034
Discusses why we need plants and animals; why animals need homes, food and water; and the causes of animal extinction.

Endangered Species Activity Book: A Teacher Resource
Grades: 4–11
Courseware Solutions, Inc., 1991
100 Lombard Street, Suite 404
Toronto, Ontario, Canada M5C 1M3
416-863-6116
Activities about endangered species using language, mathematics and problem-solving skills.

Endangered Species Issue Pac
Grades: 4–7
National Institute for Urban Wildlife, 1980
P.O. Box 3015
Shepardstown, WV 25443

304-876-6146
Students study a critical habitat and partake in a town where they act as informed and responsible citizens to help protect species.

Endangered Species: We're All in This Together
Grades: K–8
Golden State Wildlife Federation, 1992
2530 San Pablo Avenue, #D
Berkeley, CA 94702
510-848-2211
Activities look at endangered species and why they are in trouble.

Nature Scope: Endangered Species Wild and Rare
Grades: K–8
National Wildlife Federation, 1989
1412 Sixteenth Street NW
Washington, DC 20036-2266
800-432-6564
Interdisciplinary hands-on activities encourage nature appreciation and problem-solving skills.

Our Only Earth Series: Endangered Species: Their Struggle to Survive
Grades: 4–12
Zephyr Press, 1990
3316 North Chapel Avenue, P.O. Box 13448
Tucson, AZ 85732-3448
602-322-5090
One part of a 7-part series. Provides an integrated science, language arts and social studies program that can run from 1 month to 1 year. Real-life issues are addressed.

Protecting Endangered Species
Grades: 4–8
EDC Publishing, 1990
10302 East 55th Place
Tulsa, OK 74146
800-475-4522
Introduces the students to the threat faced by wildlife and what can be done to keep more species from extinction.

Protecting Forest Wildlife
Grades: 3–6
American Teaching Aids, 1993
6442 City West Parkway
Prairie Eaton, MN 55344-7718
612-946-0046
Reproducible activities about dozens of

endangered animals who live in the jungle or forest.

Who's Endangered on Noah's Ark? Literary and Scientific Activities for Teachers and Parents
Grades: K–12
Teacher Ideas Press
A Division of Libraries Unlimited, Inc., 1992
P.O. Box 6633
Englewood, CO 80155-6633
303-770-1220
Pertains to animals that are or have been endangered. Suggested activities include art, literature, writing and drama.

Energy

Alternative Energy Sources: Experiments You Can Do
Grades: 9–12
Edison Electric Institute, 1992
701 Pennsylvania Avenue NW
Washington, DC 20004-2696
202-508-5424
Activities teaching about different types of energy.

Brightland
Grades: 1–2
Energy Source Education Council, 1987
5505 East Carson Street, Suite 250
Lakewood, CA 90713-3093
310-420-6814
Introduces basic energy concepts emphasizing the importance of energy conservation.

California Challenge!
Grade: 4
California Energy Extension Service, 1989
1400 Tenth Street, Room 209
Sacramento, CA 05814
916-323-4388
Addresses energy, what it is, where we get it, how we use it and how we can conserve it.

Careers in Conservation and Renewable Energy
Grades: 5–8
Conservation and Renewable Energy

Inquiry and Referral Service, 1985
P.O. Box 8900
Silver Springs, MD 20907
800-523-2929
Information about careers in energy,
including such activities as word hunts
and quizzes.

Conserve and Renew

Grades: 4–6
Sonoma State University Energy
Center, 1990
1800 East Contati Avenue
Rohnert Park, CA 94928
707-664-2880
Offers cooperative learning activities in
energy conservation and renewables
as a unit or to complete existing curricula.

Earth Express

Grades: 4–8
EHMI—Environmental Hazards
Management Institute, 1993
10 Newmarket Road
Durham, NH 03824
603-868-1496
Newsletter for kids working to make a
difference in our environment.
Activities about energy sources.

EcoAction Activities

Grades: 4–6
National Energy Foundation, 1993
5160 Wiley Post Way, Suite 200
Salt Lake City, UT 84116
801-539-1406
Unique and fun activities that can be
used as supplementary material to
already existing energy and environmental units.

Efficiency of Electric Appliances

Grades: 4–8
Enterprise for Education, 1978
1320-A Santa Monica Mall
Santa Monica, CA 90401
310-394-9864
Students learn the efficiency of household electrical appliances by conducting experiments.

Electro Juice

Grades: 8–12
Pacific Gas and Electric, Educational
Services, 1992
77 Beale Street, Room 2825
San Francisco, CA 94106-9900

415-972-5416
Provides information about potential
electrical hazards and an understanding of how to avoid and deal with
these hazards.

Energy Activities for the Primary Classroom

Grades: K–3
California Energy Extension Service,
1985
1400 Tenth, Room 209
Sacramento, CA 95814
916-323-4388
Activities, experiments and games
demonstrate the importance of energy
and what it is. Lists energy-related
career options.

Energy in American History

Grades: 6–9
Energy Source Education Council,
1987
5505 East Carson Street, Suite 250
Lakewood, CA 90713-3093
310-420-6814
Overview of the role of energy in
American history and its impact.
Includes lessons and a film.

Energy Bridges to Science, Technology and Science

Grades: 6–9
Florida Energy Office, 1991
2740 Centerview Drive
Tallahassee, FL 32399
904-488-2475
Energy production, solar power and
conservation are explored through lab
experiments and worksheets.
Teacher's guide included.

Energy Choices and Challenges

Grades: 6–8
Energy Source Education Council,
1988
5505 East Carson, Suite 250
Lakewood, CA 90713-3093
310-420-6814
Emphasis on energy technologies and
issues makes this unit adaptable to science and social science classes.
Materials are field tested and revised.

Energy Crunch

Grades: 6–12
Energy Source Education Council,
1985

550 East Carson Street, Suite 250
Lakewood, CA 90713-3093
310-420-6814
Energy issues are presented through
the story of an energy sleuth, working
on an "energy crunch" case. Research
and critical thinking skills are utilized.

Energy Futures: A Guide for Energy Educators

Grades: K–2
New York Energy Education Project,
1988
New York Education Department,
Room 232M EB
Albany, NY 12234
518-474-5215
Innovative and motivating suggestions
for teachers organizing a unit on energy. A list of software programs and
guest speakers are also offered plus a
student activity book.

Energy Math

Grades: 1–6
Gold Country Energy Extension Center
El Dorado County Office of Education
6767 Green Valley Road
Placerville, CA 95667
A set of materials that will assist in
integrating primary math and physical
science curricula with respect to an
energy theme.

Energy Matters

Grades: 3–7
Ontario Ministry of Energy, 1992
56 Wellesley Street West, 9th Floor
Toronto, Ontario, Canada M7A 2B7
416-323-4321
Activity book that explains different
energy concepts such as how energy
changes form, where energy comes
from, where energy goes and energy
conservation.

Energy: Multidisciplinary Activities for the Classroom

Grades: K–6
National Energy Foundation, 1986
5160 Wiley Post Way, Suite 200
Salt Lake City, UT 84116
801-539-1406
Activities with reproducible illustrations analyze the sources, forms, applications, economic impacts, conservation and management of energy.

Energy 90s: Learning About Science Technology and Society

Grades: 7–11
Enterprise for Education, 1989
1320-A Third Street, Suite 202
Santa Monica, CA 90401
310-394-9864
Colorful graphics illustrate energy concepts for students. There are no activities to demonstrate concepts.

Energy 90s: Teacher's Resource Book

Grades: 8–11
Enterprise for Education, 1989
1320-A Third Street, Suite 202
Santa Monica, CA 90401
310-394-9864
Integrated energy activities address fundamentals of energy—fossil fuel, nuclear and renewable—as well as the economics and conservation of energy.

Energy and Safety: Science Activities for Elementary Students

Grades: K–2
New York Energy Education Project, 1988
New York Education Department, Room 232M EB
Albany, NY 12234
518-465-6251
Lessons and activities on potential hazards associated with the use of energy.

Energy Skill Builders

Grades: 3–5
Enterprise for Education, 1987
1320-A Third Street, Suite 202
Santa Monica, CA 90401
310-394-9864
Designed to enhance science instruction and to help teacher's achieve a greater understanding of today's energy issues.

Energy, Technology and Society

Grades: 8–12
National Energy Foundation, 1990
5160 Wiley Post Way, Suite 200
Salt Lake City, UT 84116
801-539-1406
Includes a resource book with 5 teaching units, a computer software package, a video tape offering background information and student fact sheets.

Enermagic: The Energy Magazine for Kids

Grades: K–6
MacIntyre Media Limited, 1993
30 Kelfield Street
Rexdale, Ontario, Canada M9W 5A2
416-245-7800
Comic book full of energy facts and tips.

4-H Home Conservation Guide

Grades: 4–12
California Energy Extension Service, 1988
1400 Tenth Street, Room 209
Sacramento, CA 05814
916-323-4388
Collection of hands-on activities that teach home energy conservation.

Let's Explore Energy

Grades: 4–8
Channing L. Bete Company, 1986
200 State Road
South Deerfield, MA 01373
800-628-7733
An information and activity book teaching energy issues, such as where it comes from and why it is important to explore new energy sources.

Let's Get Energized: Energy Education for After-School Enrichment

Grades: K–6
Pacific Gas and Electric, Educational Services, 1989
77 Beale Street, Room 2825
San Francisco, CA 94106-9900
415-972-5416
Songs, poems, experiments, crafts and activities designed for after-school programs.

Let's Learn About Energy and the Environment

Grades: 2–4
Channing L. Bete Company, 1988
200 State Road
South Deerfield, MA 01373
800-628-7733
Information and activity book teaching the importance of wise energy use and a commitment to protect the environment.

N.E.E.D. Project

Grades: 5–10
The N.E.E.D. Project, 1992
P.O. Box 2518
Reston, VA 22090
703-860-5029
A wide array of fun, exciting and creative lessons and activities such as debates, plays, talk shows and energy games.

New York Energy Education Project

Grades: 7–8
New York Science, Technology and Society Education Project
New York State Education Department, RM 232-MEB
Albany, NY 12234
518-473-9741
Students learn about energy conservation and various types of nonrenewable and renewable resources through readings and worksheets.

Nuclear Energy: Student Activities

Grades: 4–12
New York Energy Education Project, 1988
New York Education Department, Room 232M EB
Albany, NY 12234
518-473-9741
Information and activities on the atom, radioactivity, nuclear energy, radioactive waste and nuclear choices for the future.

Our Only Earth Series: The Energy Crisis

Grades: 4–12
Zephyr Press, 1990
3316 North Chapel Avenue, P.O. Box 13448
Tucson, AZ 85732-3448
602-322-5090
Part of a 7-part series that provides an integrated science, language arts and social studies program using real-life issues in activities that can run from 1 month to 1 year.

Plan It for the Planet!

Grades: 4–6
Scholastic, Inc., 1993
555 Broadway
New York, NY 10012
800-325-6149
Hands-on activities about solar power and how to move America toward a clean energy future.

Power Switch
Grades: 5–6
Energy Source Education Council, 1987
5505 East Carson Street, Suite 250
Lakewood, CA 90713-3093
310-420-6814
This unit features 10 lessons, a video-tape, class poster, quizzes and information on the history of energy and energy sources.

Science Activities in Energy
Grades: 1–6
Arizona Department of Commerce Energy Office, 1991
3800 North Central Avenue, Suite 1500
Phoenix, AZ 85012
800-352-5499
Workbook of activities such as word and picture puzzles and suggested experiments. Also provides energy information. Pages are easily reproducible.

Science Activities in Energy
Grades: 3–12
U.S. Department of Energy, 1980
Technical Information Center
P.O. Box 62
Oak Ridge, TN 37830
615-576-2268
Experiments that illustrate principles and problems related to energy and its development, use and conservation.

Science Activities in Energy
Grades: 9–12
Arizona Department of Commerce Energy Office, 1991
3800 North Central Avenue, Suite 1500
Phoenix, AZ 85012
800-352-5499
Workbook of activities such as word and picture puzzles and suggested experiments. Also provides energy information. Pages are easily reproducible.

Science Alive! Unit 1: Energy Flow
Grades: K–12
Science Oriented Learning, 1988
1324 Derby Street
Berkeley, CA 94702
510-644-2054
A bilingual, multicultural science and social studies program. Activities teach energy flow, cycles, communities, interdependence and change.

Science Study Skills Program: People, Energy and Appropriate Technology
Grades: 9–12
National Science Teacher's Association, 1983
1742 Connecticut Avenue NW
Washington, DC 20009
202-328-5800
Explores the relationship between energy, technology and the environment. Students will discover how energy decisions made today will affect future technologies.

Simple Experiments on Magnetism and Electricity
Grades: 7–10
Edison Electric Institute, 1988
701 Pennsylvania Avenue NW
Washington, DC 20004-2696
202-508-5424
Experiments that teach magnetism and electricity.

S.I.R.S. Digest: Energy
Grades: 6–9
Social Issues Resources, Inc., 1990
P.O. Box 2348
Boca Raton, FL 33427-2348
407-994-0079
A collection of articles on energy sources, technological developments, the link between technology and resources and the development of new energy sources.

Student Energy Patrol: Saving Energy, Money and Planet Earth
Grades: K–8
California Energy Extension Service, 1992
1400 Tenth, Room 209
Sacramento, CA 95814
916-323-4388
Students become active problem solvers for a real environmental issue by monitoring the school's electric use and examine strategies to reduce use.

Teach with Energy!
Grades: K–3
National Energy Foundation, 1990
5160 Wiley Post Way, Suite 200
Salt Lake City, UT 84116
801-539-1406
Thirty-one interdisciplinary energy lessons with 15 supplemental activities. Also provides background information to answer student questions.

Teach with Energy!
Grades: 4–6
National Energy Foundation, 1990
5160 Wiley Post Way, Suite 200
Salt Lake City, UT 84116
801-539-1406
Thirty-one interdisciplinary energy lessons with 15 supplemental activities. Also provides background information to answer student questions.

Top Hit Energy Lesson Plans
Grades: K–12
National Energy Foundation, 1986
5160 Wiley Post Way Suite 200
Salt Lake City, UT 84116
801-539-1406
The activities illustrate the importance of energy and how it affects our quality of life and leisure time through songwriting, poetry, art and other activities.

Understanding Electricity
Grades: 1–6
National Energy Foundation, 1989
5160 Wiley Post Way, Suite 200
Salt Lake City, UT 84116
801-539-1406
A collection of activities that teach about electricity and its role and effect in the community. Activities will enhance an existing energy curriculum.

Wind, Water, Fire and Earth
Grades: 9–12
National Science Teacher's Association, 1986
1742 Connecticut Avenue NW
Washington, DC 20009
202-328-5800
Interdisciplinary energy lessons designed to be easily incorporated into existing curricula. Also included are handouts, diagrams and information sheets.

Fuel

Breakthroughs: Strategies for Thinking: Are We Unplugging the World?
Grades: 3–6
Zaner-Bloser, Inc., 1992
2200 West Fifth Avenue, P.O. Box 16764
Columbus, OH 43216-6764
800-421-3018
Describes and explains electricity with definitions, illustrations and paper and pencil activities.

Coal Education Resource Kit
Grades: 5–6
Illinois Department of Energy and Natural Resources, 1993
Office of Coal Development and Marketing
325 West Adams Street, Room 300
Springfield, IL 62704
217-782-6370
This education kit on coal includes lessons, supplemental activities, a video and a poster.

Dinosaurs and Power Plants: Energy from the Past into the Future
Grades: 5–8
New Jersey Department of Environmental Protection
Public Participation and Education Office, 1992
CN 402
Trenton, NJ 08625
609-777-4322
Students learn about energy while developing critical thinking skills. In addition to a lesson plan and activity guide, reproducible graphics are included.

Fossil Fuel Junction
Grades: 3–4
Energy Source Education Council, 1989
5505 East Carson Street, Suite 250
Lakewood, CA 90713-3093
310-420-6814
Lesson ideas, a poster, quizzes and information covering fossil fuels and the importance of conservation are offered.

Fossil Fuels
Grades: 4–12
New York Science Technology and Society Education Project, 1988
Room 678 EBA
Albany, NY 12234
518-473-5556
Complete student activities with teacher information section covers all aspects of fossil fuels, the history and the future.

Power Lifelines for Los Angeles
Grades: 5–9
Los Angeles Department of Water and Power, 1987
P.O. Box 111, Room 1514
Los Angeles, CA 90051-0100
213-367-1345
Activity teaching electricity—how it is made, measured and used; where it comes from and why it is important to conserve it.

Where the Little Light Bulb Gets Its Juice Activity Book
Grades: K–3
Los Angeles Department of Water and Power, 1987
P.O. Box 111, Room 1514
Los Angeles, CA 90051-0100
213-481-4085 ext. 6358
Information and activity book explains where energy is made and how it travels to your home.

Renewable Energy

Renewable Energy Activities for the Middle Grades
Grades: 5–9
Florida Solar Energy Center, 1990
300 State Road 401
Cape Canaveral, FL 32920-4099
305-783-0300
Teacher developed renewable energy experiments and activities include building a solar box cooker and a device that can measure wind speeds. Incorporates science and social studies research.

Renewable Energy Fact Sheets
Grades: 7–12
Solar Energy Industries Association, 1992
777 North Capitol Street NE, Suite 805
Washington, DC 20002
202-408-0660
Fact sheets and activities cover study of the economics, benefits and effects of biomass, solar, photovoltaics, ocean, water and wind power.

Renewable Energy—Student Activities, Revised Edition
Grades: 4–12
New York Energy Education Project, 1988
New York Education Department, Room 232M EB
Albany, NY 12234
Renewable energy objectives, procedures and motivational activities. Background, evaluation and reference information included.

Renewables Are Ready: A Guide to Teaching Renewable Energy
Grades: 6–12
Union of Concerned Scientists, 1991
26 Church Street
Cambridge, MA 02238
617-547-5552
A guidebook on renewable energy technologies. Classroom activities, project suggestions, ideas for student-led action campaigns and resources.

Renewables Are Ready: Slide Show
Grades: 6–12
Union of Concerned Scientists, 1992
26 Church Street
Cambridge, MA 02238
617-547-5552
Slides/script look at wind, geothermal, hydroelectric, solar energy, biomass, biogas fuel and related transportation issues. Supplementary facts and case studies.

Science Projects in Renewable Energy and Energy Efficiency
Grades: 5–12
National Energy Foundation, 1991
5160 Wiley Post Way, Suite 200
Salt Lake City, UT 84116
801-539-1406
Looks at scientific experiments on renewable energy. Includes technology descriptions, project ideas and resource information.

Wind Energy Comes of Age
Grades: 6–12

American Wind Energy Association, 1992
777 North Capitol Street NE, Suite 805
Washington, DC 20002
202-408-8988
Presents the past, present and future hopes of wind generation through colorful tables, graphs and figures.

Solar Energy

Hot Water and Warm Homes from Sunlight
Grades: 4–8
Great Explorations in Math and Science, 1986
Lawrence Hall of Science
University of California—Berkeley
Berkeley, CA 94720
510-642-7771
Guide to understanding the uses and potential of solar energy and the issues surrounding dependence on oil and natural gas. Solar heating experiments.

The Solar Box Cooker Leader's Manual
Grades: 5–12
Solar Box Cookers International, 1991
1724 11th Street
Sacramento, CA 95814
916-444-6616
Gives basic directions for making and using solar box cookers and presents a global view of solar cooking.

Solar Energy
Grades: 5–8
Delta Education, Inc., 1988
P.O. Box 915
Hudson, NH 03051
603-889-8899
Hands-on activities and worksheets for investigating solar energy collection strategy and use.

Solar Science Projects
Grades: 9–12
Governor's Office of Energy Resources
270 Washington Street SW, Suite 615
Atlanta, GA 3-334
404-656-5176
Experiments use basic solar energy principles to research problems, build model solar homes and collectors,

study solar water heating and the production of electricity.

Sunny Side Up, Jr.
Solar Activities in Science
Grades: K–5
Florida Solar Energy Center, 1984
300 State Road 401
Cape Canaveral, FL 32920-4099
305-783-0300
Learn more about solar energy with common throw-away materials. That's all that's needed for these experiments and activities.

Food/Nutrition

California's First People: Their Search for Food
Grades: 4–8
Green Oak Publishing, 1990
472 Greensboro Court
Claremont, CA 91711
Respect for the natural world and Indian culture is emphasized in these games, maps, illustrations and information.

Energy, Food and You (elementary grades)
Grades: K–8
Washington State Office of Environmental Education, 1991
17011 Meridian North
Seattle, WA 98133
206-542-7671
Interdisciplinary curriculum guide and activities look at energy, food systems and the international, environmental and economics impacted by food choices.

Energy, Food and You (secondary grades)
Grades: 7–12
Washington State Office of Environmental Education, 1978
17011 Meridian North
Seattle, WA 98133
206-542-7671
Interdisciplinary curriculum guide and activities look at energy, food systems and the international, environmental and economics impacted by food choices.

Exploding the Hunger Myth
Grades: 11–12
The Institute for Food and Development Policy, 1987
145 Ninth Street
San Francisco, CA 94103
415-864-8555
Lessons and activities with background information, reading and handouts that reproduce. Hunger pretest, audio-visual materials, books and periodicals.

Food First Curriculum
Grades: 4–8
The Institute for Food and Development Policy, 1984
145 Ninth Street
San Francisco, CA 94103
415-864-8555
Explores food production, hunger, politics of food and more. Activities include debates, interviews, journal keeping, plays, poetry and songs.

Food for Thought
Grades: 7–12
Zero Population Growth, 1989
1400 16th Street NW, Suite 320
Washington, DC 20036
202-332-2200
Students "populate" regions, observe disparities of population, wealth, arable land and diet and experience the resulting problems. Teaching activity guide.

Foodworks
Grades: 4–8
Addison Wesley Publishing, 1987
Jacob Way
Reading, MA 01867
800-447-2226
Food activities, games and facts. Topics include fish farming, secret life of seeds, eating habits of a python and creating a hydroponic garden.

Global Food Web
Grades: 6–12
Rock Eagle 4-H Center, 1990
350 Rock Eagle Road, NW
Eaton, GA 31024
404-485-2831
Project looks at the environment, food supply and human nutrition. Aims to lead students toward "thinking globally and acting locally."

Healthy Choices for Kids

Grades: 1–5
Healthy Choices Nutrition Education
Program, 1993
P.O. Box 550
Wenatchee, WA 98807
509-663-9600
Based on the U.S. dietary guidelines.
Complete with activities, work sheets
and lessons.

Healthy Eating Pyramid

Grades: 7–12
Center for Science in the Public
Interest, 1993
1875 Connecticut Avenue NW, Suite
300
Washington, DC 20009
202-332-9110
Teacher's Guide has activities and a
do-it-yourself pyramid that can be
reproduced for students. Creativity and
fun encouraged.

Understanding Vegetarianism

Grades: 1–6
Vegetarian Society of Colorado, 1992
P.O. Box 6773
Denver, CO 80206
303-777-4828
Lessons help students understand vegetarianism and vegetarian life styles
with an emphasis on nutrition and
social studies.

Vitamin C Testing

Grades: 6–9
Great Explorations in Math and
Science, 1988
Lawrence Hall of Science
University of California—Berkeley
Berkeley, CA 94720
510-642-7771
By testing juices for vitamin C, stu-
dents learn about chemistry, nutrition
and the effects that the treatment of
food has on nutritional value.

Gardening/ Landscaping/Plants

Bottle Biology: Wisconsin Fast Plants

Grades: 3–12
Kendall-Hunt Publishing Co., 1993
4050 Westmark Drive, P.O. Box 1840

Dubuque, IA 52004-1840
800-228-0810
An idea book full of ways you can use
plastic soda bottles and other recyclable materials to teach about science
and the environment.

Breakthroughs: Strategies for Thinking: Plants and People as Partners

Grades: 3–6
Zaner-Bloser, Inc., 1992
2200 West Fifth Avenue, P.O. Box
16764
Columbus, OH 43216-6764
800-421-3018
Lessons and activities on the interdependence of plants and people.

Children's Gardens

Grades: K–13
Common Ground Garden Program,
1990
2615 South Grand Street, Suite 400
Los Angeles, CA 90007-2668
213-744-4341
A field manual for a successful garden
plus classroom activities.

Classroom Plants

Grades: 3–6
Delta Education, Inc., 1988
P.O. Box 915
Hudson, NH 03051
603-889-8899
Students learn about plants by growing and caring for them in the classroom. Supplemental activities that can
be staggered throughout the school
year are offered.

From Seed to Plant

Grades: 3–6
Delta Education, Inc., 1988
P.O. Box 915
Hudson, NH 03051
603-889-8899
Offers activities and discussions that
teach seed classification, planting, care
for plants and more.

Gardening Fun

Grades: K–4
Fearon Teacher Aids, 1992
P.O. Box 280
Carthage, IL 62321
217-357-3900
Hands-on activities introduce basic

botany. Background information and
fascinating facts are added to enhance
activities and discussions.

The Growing Classroom

Grades: K–6
Addison Wesley Publishing, 1990
Jacob Way
Reading, MA 01867
800-447-2226
Full year science and nutrition curriculum with indoor and outdoor garden
experiential activities. Includes planting guides and materials list.

Growing with Gardening: A 12-Month-Guide for Therapy, Recreation and Education

Grades: 3–8
University of North Carolina Press,
1989
P.O. Box 2288
Chapel Hill, NC 27515/2288
919-677-0977
Guide to horticulture, reference materials and ideas on how to use gardening
to teach.

Growing Ideas

Grades: 4–8
National Gardening Association
Quarterly
180 Flynn Avenue
Burlington, VT 05401
802-863-1308
Provides instructional ideas, horticultural information and a forum for
exchange among teachers using classroom gardening.

GrowLab: Activities for Growing Minds and a Complete Guide to Growing in the Classroom

Grades: 4–9
National Gardening Association, 1991
180 Flynn Avenue
Burlington, VT 05401
802-863-1308
Offers comprehensive "how-to" information for indoor gardening.
Plus activities that stimulate science
inquiry and turn curiosity about living
things into learning experiences.

Guide to Kids' Gardening

Grades: 4–10
National Gardening Association, 1990
180 Flynn Avenue

Burlington, VT 05401
802-863-1308
Provides activities that will involve students in all facets of gardening and make growing food a lively, surprise-filled experience.

Let's Grow
Grades: K–6
Storey Communications, Inc., 1989
Schoolhouse Road RD#1, Box 105
Pownal, VT 05261-9990
802-823-5811
Year-round gardening projects and adventures that teach a love and knowledge of nature while instilling good gardening principles.

Planting Seeds, Growing Minds
Grades: K–6
California Association of Nursery Men, 1992
4620 Northgate Boulevard, Suite 155
Sacramento, CA 95834
916-567-0200
Curriculum with hands-on experiments and extension activities designed to teach the basic needs and concepts of seeds, plants, flowers and trees.

Plants: Improving Our Environment
Grades: 4–6
Soil and Water Conversation Society, 1987
7517 NE Ankeny Road
Ankeny, IA 50021-9764
800-THE-SOIL
Activities designed to examine the importance of plants.

Power of the Flower
Grades: K–6
Instructor Magazine
555 Broadway
New York, NY 10012-3999
800-544-2917
Activities which explore the function of flowers in plant life cycles and investigates a flower's connection to other living things.

Teaching Ideas: Pesticide Awareness and the Concept of Integrated Pest Management (IPM)
Grades: 9–12
Northwest Coalition for Alternatives to Pesticides, 1989

P.O. Box 1393
Eugene, OR 97440
503-344-5044
Science and social studies classes look at pesticide use, possible hazards and alternatives. Adaptable for home economics and health classes.

General/Global

All in This Together
Grades: 4–10
Practice Hall Science, 1991
4350 Equity Drive
Columbus, OH 43228
800-848-9500
Audio cassette of ecology songs. Accompanied by teacher/reference guide with relevant questions and listing of related organizations.

Audubon Adventures
Grades: 3–6
National Audubon Society, Biannual Publication
700 Broadway
New York, NY 10003
212-979-3000
Bimonthly newspaper for students, with teacher's guide that includes background information and activity ideas.

Beyond the Classroom
Grades: K–9
Massachusetts Audubon Society, Educational Resources, 1991 Revised
South Great Road
Lincoln, MA 01773
617-259-9500, ext. 7250
Exploration activities that involve students in the science of the world around them and introduces them to the interactions of nature.

Blue Plant
Grades: 3–12
Office of Education, National Air and Space Museum, 1990
Smithsonian Institute
Washington, DC 20560
202-357-1300
Supplements the IMAX film by same name. Resources and activities for art, science, geography, geology, literature, math and social studies classes.

Breakthroughs: Strategies for Thinking: Polymers, Pollution and People
Grades: 5–10
Zaner-Bloser, Inc., 1992
2200 West Fifth Avenue, P.O. Box 16764
Columbus, OH 43216-6764
800-421-3018
Students learn about the development and use of synthetics (plastics) and their role in society.

California Challenge
Grades: K–12
The American Forum for Global Education, 1993
45 John Street, Suite 908
New York, NY 10038
212-742-8232
Activities include developing and discussing issues relevant to global education, population, hunger, life in developing nations, water and energy.

California Class Project
Grades: 6–9
California Department of Education
Bureau of Publications, Sales Unit
P.O. Box 271
Sacramento, CA 98512
916-445-1260
An interdisciplinary hands-on program covering real life environmental issues while promoting students to use critical thinking skills.

California State Environmental Education Guide
Grades: K–6
Alameda County Office of Education, 1988
313 West Winton Avenue
Hayward, CA 94544-1198
510-887-0152
Instructional units and action-oriented, hands-on projects addressing various environmental issues. The guide integrates concepts from the California State Framework.

A Child's Place in the Environment
Grades: 1–6
Konocti Unified School District
Lake County Office of Education, 1994
1152 South Main Street
Lakeport, CA 95453
707-263-7249

Interdisciplinary thematic lessons that guide students through environmental awareness, value analysis, problem solving and action projects.

Children's Literature: Springboard to Understanding the Developing World

Grades: 3–8
UNICEF Canada, 1988
443 Mt. Pleasant Road
Toronto, Ontario, Canada, M4S 2L8
416-482-4444
Guide for how to use children's literature to teach global understanding, empathy and cooperation.

CNN Newsroom

Grades: 5–12
Turner Educational Services, Daily
One CNN Center, P.O. Box 105366
Atlanta, GA 30348-5366
800-344-6219
A daily 15-minute news program highlighting different global themes. Daily classroom guides with activities, class projects and homework assignments are available through electronic mail.

Cobblestone Publishing, Inc.

Grades: 4–8
Cobblestone Publishing, Inc., 1992
28 Main Street
Peterborough, NH 03458
603-924-7209
Magazines on the environment with accompanying teacher's guide and activities.

Completing the Cycle

Grades: K–3
Indiana Department of Education, 1991
Room 229, State House
Indianapolis, IN 46204-2798
317-232-6610
Covers conservation, preservation, ecology, resource management, solid waste and recycling through activities that relate to daily life.

Connections

Grades: 5–6
National Center for Appropriate Technology, 1980
Publications, Box 3838
Butte, MT 59701

406-494-4572
Technology, conservation, transportation, renewable resources, organic gardening and more is covered in lessons, activities, homework assignments and quizzes.

Connections: Guide to a Healthy Environment with Teacher's Manual

Grades: 3–7
Eco Education, 1994
275 East Fourth Street, Suite 821
St. Paul, MN 55101
612-222-7691
Students learn how their decisions and actions affect other creatures by studying ecosystems, the atmosphere, pollution, habitat destruction, deforestation and population.

Consider the Earth

Grades: 4–8
Teacher Ideas Press, Inc., 1989
Libraries Unlimited, Inc.
P.O. Box 6633
Englewood, CO 80155-6633
800-237-6124
Students discover and learn about the different aspects of the environment through action-oriented activities.

Decisions, Decisions: The Environment: The Science and the Politics of Protecting Our Planet

Grades: 9–12
Tom Snyder Productions, Inc., Educational Software, 1991
90 Sherman Street
Cambridge, MA 02140
617-876-4433
In this multidisciplinary curricula, students use problem-solving skills, computer activities, critical reading and writing to deal with an environmental dilemma.

Discover the World: Empowering Children to Value Themselves, Others and the Earth

Grades: P–6
New Society Publishers, 1990
4527 Springfield Avenue
Philadelphia, PA 19143
215-382-6543
Empowers children to value themselves, others and the earth by developing an awareness of the environ-

ment and other cultures through discussions, activities and charts.

E2

Grades: 6–12
E2: Environment and Education, 1992
881 Alma Real Drive, #118
Pacific Palisades, CA 90272
310-573-9608
Students investigate human health, resource consumption and environmental issues at their school and take action for improvement.

Earth Academy

Grades: K–12
Laidlaw Environmental Service, Inc., Rev. 1992
220 Outlet Point Boulevard
Columbia, SC 29210
800-845-1019
A video, study guide and activities teach students about recycling, household hazardous waste, lifestyles that create waste and environmental career opportunities.

Earth Angels Environmental Education Unit

Grades: 3–6
Earth Angels Environmental Education Program
64 Prince Arthur Avenue
Toronto, Ontario, Canada M5R 1B4
416-767-9300
An activity-based, interdisciplinary program teaching environmental studies.

Earth Child

Grades: K–6
Council Oak Books, 1991
1350 East Fifteenth Street
Tulsa, OK 74120
800-583-4995
Games, stories, activities and experiments about the earth's water cycle, trees, endangered species, food chain, habitats and animals.

Earth Day 1990

Grades: K–6
U.S. Environmental Protection Agency, 1991
26 West Martin Luther King Drive
Cincinnati, OH 45268
513-569-7771

Activities and information for special Earth Day classes and/or celebrations.

Earth Day 1990 Lesson Plan and Home Survey

Grades: K–6
Earth Day 1990
116 New Montgomery Street, Suite 530
San Francisco, CA 94105
415-495-5987
Classroom lessons, home survey and action guide to help students better understand issues of water, toxics, energy, transportation and solid-waste recycling.

Earth Day 1990 Lesson Plan and Home Survey

Grades: 7–12
Earth Day 1990
116 New Montgomery Street, Suite 530
San Francisco, CA 94105
415-495-5987
Classroom lessons, home survey and action guide to help students better understand issues of water, toxics, energy, transportation and solid-waste recycling.

Earth Forever

Grades: K–6
Indiana Department of Education, 1993–94
State House, Room 229
Indianapolis, IN 46204-2798
317-232-6610
Includes teacher's guide and activities that participating Indiana schools engaged in during 1993 and 1994.

Earth Matters: A Challenge for Environmental Action

Grades: 1–12
Girl Scouts of the U.S.A., 1990
420 Fifth Avenue
New York, NY 10018-2702
212-852-8000
Information and activities about how humans impact earth's life support systems and the critical environmental issues that affect us.

Earth Matters: Studies for Our Global Future

Grades: 9–12
Zero Population Growth, 1991

1400 16th Street NW, Suite 320
Washington, DC 20036
202-332-2200
Interdisciplinary activities, lab experiments, debates and games help students critically evaluate and develop solutions for environmental, social and economic issues.

Earth Science Activities

Grades: 2–8
Prentice Hall Science, 1986
Route 9W
Englewood Cliffs, NJ 07632
800-922-0579
Hand-on activities covering ecology issues that help develop problem-solving and critical-thinking skills.

Earth Trek...Explore Your Environment

Grades: 6–9
U.S. Environmental Protection Agency
Office of Communications and Public Affairs, 1990
Public Information Center, PM-211B,
401 M Street SW
Washington, DC 20460
202-260-2049
Activity oriented lessons that address water, air, land, pesticides, toxic substances and environmental laws.

Earth: Voices of a Planet

Grades: 4–8
Earth Music Productions, 1990
P.O. Box 68
Litchfield, CT 06759
Teacher's guide to musical selections by Paul Winter which pay tribute to all 7 continents, the oceans, mountains and deserts.

Earthbeat

Grades: K–12
Intellimation, 1990
130 Cremona Drive, P.O. Box 1922
Santa Barbara, CA 93116-1922
805-968-2291
TV series highlighting people and their efforts to solve environmental problems. Teacher's guide offers demonstrations, field trips and class projects.

Earthways: Simple Environmental Activities for Young Children

Grades: K–3
Gryphon House, Inc., 1992

3706 Otis Street, P.O. Box 275
Mt. Ranier, MD 20712
800-638-0928
Crafts and seasonal activities that increase environmental awareness and respect for nature. Students learn to connect products they use with their original source.

Earthwatching 3

Grades: 4–12
University of Wisconsin—Madison
Institute for Environmental Studies, 1990
550 North Park Street, Room 15, Science Hall
Madison, WI 53706
608-263-3185
Explores the atmosphere, the biosphere, waste, water, energy, agriculture, urban growth, nutrition, technology, plants, animals and how they all interrelate.

Earthwise

Grades: K–6
Carolrhoda Books/Lerner Publication Company, 1993
241 First Avenue North
Minneapolis, MN 55401
800-328-4929
This curriculum covers environmental issues at home, at play and at school. Classroom projects, hands-on activities, handouts, homework and lists of supplemental materials are offered.

Ecology

Grades: 4–8
EDC Publishing, 1989
10302 East 55th Place
Tulsa, OK 74146
800-475-4522
Activities and experiments investigating the science of ecology, environmental problems and solutions.

Ecology Discover Activity Kit

Grades: 4–8
Prentice Hall, Education Division, 1989
Route 9W
Englewood Cliffs, NJ 07632
800-922-0579
Classroom and field activities cover recycling, population, the food web, energy and communities. Kit comes with ready-to-use worksheets.

Ecology: Earth's Living Resources

Grades: 6–12
Prentice Hall Science, 1993
Route 9W
Englewood Cliffs, NJ 07632
800-922-0579
Integrated learning system contains Spanish and English audiotapes, activity book, test book and lab manual.

Ecology: Exploring Planet Earth

Grades: 6–12
Prentice Hall Science, 1993
Route 9W
Englewood Cliffs, NJ 07632
800-922-0579
Integrated learning system contains Spanish and English audiotapes, activity book, test book and lab manual.

EcoSense It's Elementary! An Economic Environmental Learning Kit

Grades: 2–6
Business Economics Education Foundation, 1993
123 North Third Street, Suite 504
Minneapolis, MN 55401
612-337-5252
Looks at how our use of the environment is linked to economic decision making. Activities for many subject areas.

Education Goes Outdoors

Grades: K–9
Addison Wesley Publishing, 1986
Jacob Way
Reading, MA 01867
800-447-2226
Outdoor language adventures, schoolyard math investigations, art activities and explorations in social studies and science foster a sensitivity to the environment.

Educator's Earth Day Sourcebook

Grades: K–6
U.S. Environmental Protection Agency, 1990
Public Information Center, PM-211B
401 M Street SW
Washington, DC 20460
202-475-7751
Offers background information and suggested activities that show students how they can make a difference in protecting the environment.

Educator's Earth Day Sourcebook

Grades: 7–12
U.S. Environmental Protection Agency, 1990
Office of the Administrator
Washington, DC 20460
202-475-7751
Offers background information and suggested activities that show students how they can make a difference in protecting the environment.

Energy, Economics and the Environment

Grades: 6–9
Indiana Department of Education
State House, Room 229
Indianapolis, IN 46204-2798
317-232-6610
Offers background information, teacher instructions and activities on waste reduction, air pollution and energy.

Energy, Economics and the Environment

Grades: 9–12
Indiana Department of Education
State House, Room 229
Indianapolis, IN 46204-2798
317-232-6610
Offers background information, teacher instructions and activities on water pollution, forest management, renewable energy resources and global warming.

EnviroKids Celebrate the Environment

Grades: K–3
Alberta Environment Education, 1991
Oxbridge Place, 12th Floor
9820 106th Street
Edmonton, Alberta, Canada T5K 2J6
403-427-6310
Reproducible activity worksheets covering various environmental issues.

Environment: Event—Assessments—Response

Grades: 9–12
N and N Publishing Company, Inc., 1993
18 Montgomery Street
Middletown, NY 10940
914-342-1677
Lectures, demonstrations, activities and lab experiments look at electrical charges, magnetic fields and the possible and known health risks.

Environment on File

Grades: 3–12
Facts on File, 1991
460 Park Avenue South
New York, NY 10016
212-683-2244
A guide to issues relating to the environment, a reference source of images and text for photocopying and a foundation for developing tests.

Environment: A Kindergarten Unit

Grade: K
Carol Eliuk—Kids for Saving Earth
40 Samor Road
Toronto, Ontario, Canada M6A 1J6
Activities that develop an awareness of the environment and solutions to environmental problems.

Environmental Activities for Teaching Critical Thinking

Grades: K–12
ERIC: Clearinghouse for Science, Mathematics and Environmental Education, 1990
Ohio State University
1200 Chambers Road, Room 310
Columbus, OH 43212
614-292-6717
Presents ideas of choices and competing interests. Encourages critical thinking and problem solving.

Environmental Education Activity Guide

Grades: K–8
American Forests, 1993
P.O. Box 2000
Washington, DC 20013
202-667-3300
Activities accompanied by helpful background information.

Environmental Education Guide

Grades: K–12
Alameda County Office of Education, 1981
313 West Winton Avenue
Hayward, CA 94544-1198
510-887-0152
Provides background information, program structure and activities for promoting a better understanding of the diversity and interdependence of life systems.

Environmental Experiments...From Edison

Grades: 6–12
Edison Electric Institute, 1990
701 Pennsylvania Avenue NW
Washington, DC 20004-2696
202-508-5424
Science projects and activities that could fit into lessons for science, conservation, earth science or biology.

The Environmental Math Workbook

Grades: 4–11
Courseware Solutions, Inc., 1992
100 Lombard Street, Suite 404
Toronto, Ontario, Canada M5C 1M3
416-863-6116
Workbook of activities that utilize math skills to solve environmental problems.

Environmental Science Activities Kit

Grades: 7–12
Center for Applied Research in Education, 1993
West Nyack, NY 10995
212-698-7000
Activities on environmental topics with summaries, extension activities, discussion questions and background information.

ESPN Team Up to Clean Up

Grades: 4–8
ESPN's Cable in the Classroom
ESPN Inc., 935 Middle Street
Bristol, CT 06010
203-585-2000
Encourages environmental awareness and team action to protect the planet. Projects cover transportation, water quality and acid rain issues.

Everybody's Beautiful

Grades: 9–12
Alberta Global Education Project, 1992
11010 142 Street
Edmonton, Alberta, Canada T5N 2RI
403-453-2411
Global environment unit designed for English classes. Lessons emphasize social responsibility, equality and justice, the environment and empowerment for the future.

The Evolution Book

Grades: 5–8
Workman Publishing Company, Inc., 1986
708 Broadway
New York, NY 10003
212-254-5900
Students hold town council meeting where they are encouraged to act as informed and responsible citizens helping to protect living species.

Exploring the Environment Weekly Reader

Grades: 2–6
Weekly Reader Corp., 1993
P.O. Box 2791
Middletown, CT 06457-9291
203-638-2400
Hands-on activities support an understanding of the earth's resources as finite and encourages their preservation.

Exploring the Third World: Development in Africa, Asia and Latin America

Grades: 8–12
The American Forum for Global Education, 1987
45 John Street, Suite 908
New York, NY 10038
212-732-8606
Lessons cover political, social, industrial and environmental development issues facing the third world and how they affect population, food, forest and trade. Teacher's guide and map are included.

Finding the Balance for Earth's Sake

Grades: 9–12
Breakwater Books, 1993
100 Water Street, P.O. Box 2188
St. John's, Newfoundland, Canada A1C 6E6
709-722-6680
Through this guide and field study, students learn about basic ecological concepts, the scientific method, field research and global and local issues.

Fostering a Sense of Wonder During the Childhood Years

Grades: P–4
Greyden Press, 1993
2020 Builders Place

Columbus, OH 43204
614-488-2525
Activities foster a sense of wonder and appreciation for the natural world. Resources listed.

From the Mountains to the Sea: A Journey in Environmental Citizenship

Grades: 7–12
Ministry of Supply and Services, 1992
165 University, Suite 701
Toronto, Ontario, Canada M5H 3B8
416-860-1611
Describes various environmental concerns for the forests, wilderness and waterways that house animals, plants, birds and fish. Activities and puzzles.

Geology: Self-directed Study Units

Grades: K–8
Zephyr Press, 1983
3316 North Chapel Avenue, P.O. Box 13448
Tucson, AZ 85732-3448
602-322-5090
A self-directed unit promoting critical and creative thinking while researching the world of geology. Activities emphasize language and critical thinking skills.

Global 2000 Kit

Grades: 8–12
Zero Population Growth, 1982
1400 16th Street NW, Suite 320
Washington, DC 20036
202-332-2200
Designed for independent study, each unit contains a summary of an environmental topic with activities that can be done individually or in teams.

Global Alert: Understanding the Environmental Problems Facing Our Planet

Grades: 5–8
Good Apple, Inc., 1992
1204 Buchanan Street, P.O. Box 299
Carthage, IL 62321-0299
800-435-7234
Reproducible word and drawing puzzles developed in accordance with Bloom's higher level of thinking on various environmental issues.

Global Ecology Handbook

Grades: 6–12

Global Tomorrow Coalition, 1990
1325 G Street NW, Suite 1010
Washington, DC 20005-3104
202-628-4016
A comprehensive interdisciplinary
guide to sustaining the Earth's future.
A supplement to the PBS video series
"Race to Save the Planet."

Global Environment: Resource Handbook

Grades: 7—12
Alberta Global Education Project, 1991
11010 142nd Street
Edmonton, Alberta, Canada T5N 2RI
403-453-2411
Focuses on developing analytical and
critical awareness skills of students
and fosters a sense of global citizen-
ship.

Global Issues Education Set

Grades: K–12
Global Tomorrow Coalition, 1990
1325 G Street NW, Suite 1010
Washington, DC 20005-3104
202-628-4016
Educates students on global issues and
stresses interdependence on global
ecosystems through hands-on activities, worksheets, group discussions,
role-playing and individual creativity.

Global Science

Grades: 9–12
Kendall-Hunt Publishing, 1991
4050 Westmark Drive
Dubuque, IA 52002
800-258-5622
Multidisciplinary curriculum analyzes
interaction between humans and the
environment. Emphasis on direct student involvement in lab-type activities.

Good Planets Are Hard to Find

Grades: 6–8
Earth Beat Press, 1989
250 H Street, P.O. Box 8110-729
Blaine, WA 98230
604-736-6931
An information guide, dictionary and
action book that can be read as text.
Promotes the concept of one person
making a difference.

Grassroots Convention 1989 Song Book

Grades: K–12

People United for Environmental
Justice, 1989
P.O. Box 926
Arlington, VA 22216
703-276-7070
Songs vary from some standard folk
songs to new politically oriented
songs.

Great Beginnings in Environmental Education

Grades: P–12
Tennessee Environmental Education
Association, 1991
Smoky Mountains Institute at Tremont
Townsend, TN 37882
615-448-6709
Hands-on activities focusing on nature
and nature's processes. All activities
have been field tested.

Green Box

Grades: K–6
Humbolt County Office of Education,
1989
Attn: Curriculum and Staff
Development Department
901 Myrtle Avenue
Eureka, CA 95501
707-445-7000
Uses a system called Open Access,
where emphasis is placed on self-
determined investigations of the
school, community, wilderness and
world. Problem solving, conceptualiza-
tion experiences and communication
skills are developed and used.

Hands-on Environmental Science Activities

Grades: 6–12
Alpha Publishing Company, 1991
1910 Hidden Point Road
Annapolis, MD 21401-9720
410-757-5404
Activities and games on ecology, energy, conservation, populations, pollution, politics and economics.

The Home We Share

Grades: K–6
Alberta Environment Education, 1991
Oxbridge Place, 12th Floor
9820 106th Street
Edmonton, Alberta, Canada T5K 2J6
403-427-6310
An environmenal education program
focusing on the general aspects of the

environment. Each activity has two
parts, a discussion and follow-up
activities.

HOPE: Seeing Our World Through New Eyes

Grades: 1–6
AGA Khan Foundation, 1990
Waterpark Place, 10 Bag Street, Suite
610
Toronto, Ontario, Canada M5J 298
416-364-2532
Multimedia exhibition to increase
awareness and understanding of inter-
national development and the role the
Canadians play in this process.

Hug a Tree and Other Things

Grades: Pre K–6
Gryphon House, Inc., 1983
3706 Otis Street, P.O. Box 275
Mt. Ranier, MD 20712
800-638-0928
Uses natural environments for learning
language, spatial and mathematical
relationships. Suggested activities will
organize and expand outdoor experiences.

Impact!

Grades: K–6
Environmental Literacy Group, 1990
33770 Woodland Drive
Evergreen, CO 80439
303-674-3853
Multidisciplinary examination and
exploration of world environmental
problems. Critical and creative projects
are integrated in each unit.

In Response to That...An Environmental Education Tool

Grades: K–12
Amy Siedman-Tighe, 1992
5105 Velvet Lane
Culver City, CA 90230
310-280-0385
Lessons utilize humorous photos to
motivate students through laughter.
Environmental education proposal and
urban greening guides are included.

Integrating Environmental Education into the Curriculum Painlessly

Grades: 2–7
National Educational Service, 1992
1610 West Third Street

Bloomington, IN 47402
812-336-7701
Projects integrate environmental issues with math, language and science. Vocabulary, background information and follow-up activities are provided.

Interdependence in the Global Environment

Grades: 9–12
Alberta Global Education Project, 1989
11010 142nd Street
Edmonton, Alberta, Canada TAN 2R1
403-453-2411
Social studies unit examines the impact of colonialism on the Third World. Lessons focus on consequences of development and future alternatives.

The Kids Care Book: 50 Class Projects That Help Kids Help Others

Grades: 4–6
KIDS C.A.R.E., 1991
P.O. Box 1400K
Dayton, OH 45413-8005
Worksheet activities focus on various ecological topics and related problems and solutions.

Kid's Ecology Book: Good Planets Are Very Hard to Find

Grades: 3–5
Earth Beat Press, 1991
250 H Street, P.O. Box 8110-729
Blaine, WA 98230
604-736-6931
In dictionary format but can be read as a text. Complex ecological problems simplified and presented in a way that empowers students.

Learning and Caring About Our World

Grades: K–6
Warren Publishing House, Inc., 1990
P.O. Box 2250, Dept. B
Everett, WA 98203
206-353-3100
Introduces the wonders of the world—land, air and water—through games, songs, experiments, art and language activities.

Let's Clean Up Our Act

Grades: K–12
National Wildlife Federation, 1994

1412 Sixteenth Street NW
Washington, DC 20036-2266
800-432-6564
A published newsletter with activities and environmental tips. Covers waste management, air pollution and water pollution.

Living Lightly on the Planet, Vol. I

Grades: 7–9
Schlitz Audubon Center, 1985
1111 East Brown Deer Road
Milwaukee, WI 53217
414-352-2880
Students discover limits to growth through exploration of global population and land issues. Activities promote creative thinking and problem-solving skills.

Living Lightly on the Planet, Vol. 2

Grades: 10–12
Schlitz Audubon Center, 1985
1111 East Brown Deer Road
Milwaukee, WI 53217
414-352-2880
Helps students to apply knowledge of ecological concepts to interactions with the land. Activities infuse environmental issues into science and social studies classes.

Manure, to Meadow, to Milkshakes

Grades: K–6
The Trust for Hidden Villa, 1986
26870 Moody Road
Los Altos, CA 94022
415-949-8644
Ideas for sharing the natural world with children through humorous and motivational activities that relate experiences to their own lives.

My Earth Book

Grades: 1–4
Learning Works, Inc., 1991
P.O. Box 6187
Santa Barbara, CA 93160
800-235-5767
Puzzles, pictures, projects, games and facts on littering, packaging, recycling, water pollution, endangered animals and conservation.

Nature Conservancy Student Stewardship Program

Grades: 7–12
Institute for Environmental Education,

1978
18554 Haskins Road
Chagrin Falls, OH 44023-1823
216-543-7303
Students gather information and are asked to protect and maintain a Nature Conservancy preserve. Environmental and scientific concepts, plus analytic and field-oriented skills are learned.

Nature Scope: Geology the Active Earth

Grades: K–8
National Wildlife Federation, 1988
1412 Sixteenth Street NW
Washington, DC 20036-2266
800-432-6564
Interdisciplinary hands-on activities that encourage nature appreciation and develop skills needed to make responsible decisions about the environment.

Nature's Course

Grades: K–8
Center for Children's Environmental Literature, 1992–93
3603 Norton Place NW
Washington, DC 20016
202-966-6110
Teaches educators how to encourage children to explore the wonders of nature through literature, art and hands-on experiences.

Our Environment

Grades: 3–6
Educational Impressions, Inc., 1991
210 Sixth Avenue, P.O. Box 77
Hawthorne, NJ 07507
201-423-4666
Promotes critical and creative thinking on environmental issues.

Our Only Earth Series: War: The Global Battlefield

Grades: 4–12
Zephyr Press, 1990
3316 North Chapel Avenue, P.O. Box 13448
Tucson, AZ 85732-3448
602-322-5090
A program of activities including science, language arts and social studies that address real-life issues and propose solutions. Part of a series.

Our Planet, Our Home

Grades: 3–11

Zephyr Press, 1992
3316 North Chapel Avenue, P.O. Box 13448
Tucson, AZ 85732-3448
602-322-5090
Builds understanding of the interrelationships on earth. Emphasis placed on process, conversation and experience rather than "correct" answers.

Our Threatened Environment
Grades: 4–12
Knowledge Unlimited, Inc., 1990
P.O. Box 52
Madison, WI 53701-0052
800-356-2303
Lessons, activities and multimedia materials provide the skills needed to identify, research, analyze and debate the environmental threats to our planet.

Planet Earth
Grades: 4–8
EDC Publishing, 1991
10302 East 55th Place
Tulsa, OK 74146
800-475-4522
Comprehensive introduction to our environment and its processes. Imaginative projects, experiments and activities cover physical geography, climate and population.

Pollution
Grades: 1–6
Delta Education, Inc., 1989
P.O. Box 915
Hudson, NH 03051
603-889-8899
Activities and worksheets help to develop an awareness of the effects of pollution on the air, water, land, plants, fish, animals and humans.

Primary Science Sampler
Grades: K–3
The Learning Works, 1980
P.O. Box 6187
Santa Barbara, CA 93160
800-235-5767
Looks at heat and cold, animals, human senses, natural forces, plants and cooking chemistry. Background information, vocabulary, experiments and puzzles are included.

The Private Eye
Grades: K–12

The Private Eye Project, 1992
7710 31st Avenue NW
Seattle, WA 98117
206-784-8813
Investigative hands-on program about the drama and wonder of looking closely at the world, thinking by analogy, changing scale and theorizing.

Protecting Our Planet
Grades: K–1
Good Apple, Inc., 1992
1204 Buchanan Street, P.O. Box 299
Carthage, IL 62321-0299
800-435-7234
Activities discuss air, land and water. Children are shown how they can become part of the solution by protecting the planet. Includes a poster, songs and a short dramatic play.

Protecting Our Planet
Grades: 1–3
Good Apple, Inc., 1991
1204 Buchanan Street, P.O. Box 299
Carthage, IL 62321-0299
800-435-7234
Activities discuss air, land and water. Children are shown how they can become part of the solution by protecting the planet. Includes a poster, songs and an environmental board game.

Protecting Our Plant
Grades: 4–8
Good Apple, Inc., 1991
1204 Buchanan Street, P.O. Box 299
Carthage, IL 62321-0299
800-435-7234
Uses puzzles, word games, projects and experiments to promote an understanding of global warming, waste, air pollution and water pollution.

Put on Your Green Shoes: An All-star Album Dedicated to Healing the Planet
Grades: K–12
Cherry Lane Music Company, 1993
P.O. Box 430
Port Chester, NY 10573
914-937-8601
Guide contains the music and words for songs plus a special game and activity section. Comes with a compact disc.

Race to Save the Planet
Grades: 7–12

Annenberg/CPB Collection, 1990
P.O. Box 2345
South Burlington, VT 05407-2345
800-LEARNER
Video series presents global perspective on the declining state of our planet. A study guide prepares students to evaluate and view programs critically and examine solutions.

Reaching for Connections: Creative Exploration of Nature with Young Children, Vol. 2
Grades: P–5
Schlitz Audubon Center, 1991
1111 East Brown Deer Road
Milwaukee, WI 53217
414-352-2880
Activities designed to reinforce in young children a positive connection with nature by promoting an understanding and appreciation of it.

Real Science, Real Decisions: A Collection of Thinking Activities from the Science Teacher
Grades: 7–11
National Science Teacher's Association, 1990
1742 Connecticut Avenue NW
Washington, DC 20009
202-328-5800
Activities examine new technologies and pose questions that should be considered. Students will analyze such topics as acid rain, animal rights and chemical warfare.

Regeneration: You and Your Environment
Grades: K–12
Rodale's Press Regeneration Project, 1987
33 East Minor Street
Emmaus, PA 18098
610-967-5171
Encourages students to look for strengths and capabilities, instead of problems and weaknesses. Activities provide experiences that nurture a sense of wonder.

Regional Environmental Education Program: Adaptations
Grade: 3
Schuylkill Center for Environmental Education, 1991
8480 Hagy's Mill Road

Philadelphia, PA 19128
215-482-7300
Sequential lessons and activities.
Adaptations look at ways animals,
plants and habitats adjust to environmental conditions.

Regional Environmental Education Program: Communities

Grade: 2
Schuylkill Center for Environmental
Education, 1991
8480 Hagy's Mill Road
Philadelphia, PA 19128
Sequential lessons and activities. Studies
different habitats to discover what
makes them a community. Students
build their own microcommunity.

Regional Environmental Education Program: Communities

Grade: 6
Schuylkill Center for Environmental
Education, 1991
8480 Hagy's Mill Road
Philadelphia, PA 19128
215-482-7300
Sequential lessons and activities. Takes
a deeper look at human and wilderness
communities and how they interact.

Regional Environmental Education Program: Cycles

Grade: 5
Schuylkill Center for Environmental
Education, 1991
8480 Hagy's Mill Road
Philadelphia, PA 19128
215-482-7300
Sequential lessons and activities.
Teaches about various environmental
cycles such as air, nutrients and water.

Regional Environmental Education Program: Energy

Grade: 4
Schuylkill Center for Environmental
Education, 1991
8480 Hagy's Mill Road
Philadelphia, PA 19128
215-482-7300
Sequential lessons and activities. A
close-up look at energy—what is it,
where it comes from and why we need
to conserve it.

Regional Environmental Education Program: The Five Senses

Grade: K
Schuylkill Center for Environmental
Education, 1991
8480 Hagy's Mill Road
Philadelphia, PA 19128
215-482-7300
Sequential lessons and activities. Puts
an ecological spin on the senses of
sight, hearing, touch, smell and taste.
Also introduces children to the environment and recycling.

Regional Environmental Education Program: Plants and Animals

Grade: 1
Schuylkill Center for Environmental
Education, 1991
8480 Hagy's Mill Road
Philadelphia, PA 19128
215-482-7300
Sequential lessons and activities.
Teaches children the difference
between living and nonliving things,
plants and animals and looks at their
habitats, needs, human impact and
extinction.

Robots of Cave Alpha: Creating a Livable Land

Grades: 5–10
Soil and Water Conservation Society,
1986
7515 NE Ankeny Road
Ankeny, IA 50021-9764
800-THE-SOIL
Activities, teacher's guide and cartoon
booklet focus on human beings—their
needs, actions and effects on the environment.

Schoolyard Science

Grades: 2–4
Good Year Books, 1991
Scott, Foresman and Company
1900 East Lake Avenue
Glenview, IL 60025
708-729-3000
Uses the outdoor science classroom.
Each activity includes teacher information and a student lab sheet.

Science Experiences

Grades: 3–8
Addison Wesley Publishing, 1990
Jacob Way
Reading, MA 01867
800-447-2226
Offers interdisciplinary activities and

problem-solving skills to engage student in an integrated approach.

Science Sampler

Grades: 4–8
The Learning Works, 1980
P.O. Box 6187
Santa Barbara, CA 93160
800-235-5767
Units on temperature, animals, human
senses, natural forces, plants and
cooking chemistry. Each unit includes
background information, vocabulary,
experiments and puzzles.

Science Through Children's Literature

Grades: K–3
Libraries Unlimited, Inc.
Teacher Ideas Press, Inc., 1989
P.O. Box 6633
Englewood, CO 80155-6633
800-237-6124
Alternative approach to teaching elementary science using fictional children's literature that is factually correct.

The Secret of Life on Earth

Grades: 3–6
World Wildlife Fund, 1993
1250 24th Street NW, Suite 500
Washington, DC 20037
202-293-4800
Activities illustrate our reliance on
plants and how they have evolved
specific adaptations to survive in virtually every habitat on earth.

Sidewalk Field Trips

Grades: 1–2
Delta Education, Inc., 1986
P.O. Box 915
Hudson, NH 03051
603-889-8899
Adventures in exploring worlds of scientific discovery available in local
communities. Lessons and worksheets
look at the interaction of the living and
physical world.

Sidewalk Field Trips

Grades: 3–4
Delta Education, Inc., 1986
P.O. Box 915
Hudson, NH 03051
603-889-8899
Adventures in exploring worlds of scientific discovery available in local

communities. Lessons and worksheets look at the interaction of the living and physical world.

Sidewalk Field Trips
Grades: 5–6
Delta Education, Inc., 1986
P.O. Box 915
Hudson, NH 03051
603-889-8899
Adventures in exploring worlds of scientific discovery available in local communities. Lessons and worksheets look at the interaction of the living and physical world.

Spaceship Earth: A Global Geography
Grades: 8–12
South Carolina E-TV Marketing, 1991
2712 Millwood Avenue
Columbia, SC 29250
800-553-7752
Students are encouraged to feel they are on a mission in a spaceship as they view each of the videos. Teacher and viewer guides include discussion questions.

The Study of Ecology: Learning to Love Our Planet
Grades: K–8
Zephyr Press, 1984
3316 North Chapel Avenue, P.O. Box 13448
Tucson, AZ 85732-3448
602-322-5090
Interdisciplinary guide helps to develop and empower students to action through activities covering ecosystems, pollution and population.

Sunship Earth: An Earth Education Program Getting to Know Your Place in Space
Grades: 4–9
The American Camping Association, Inc., 1979–89
5000 State Road 67 North
Martinsville, IN 46151-7902
800-428-2267
Complete 5-day program helps kids understand how their world functions through exploration of their five senses.

Target Earth
Grades: K–6
Kids for Saving Earth Group, 1992

P.O. Box 47247
Plymouth, MN 55447
Motivational activities encourage clear understanding of environmental issues.

Teachable Moments
Grades: 7–12
Las Palomas de Taos, 1990
P.O. Box 3194
Taos, NM 87571
505-758-9456
Suggested activities, discussions and projects that stimulate critical thinking and learning about the environment.

Teacher's Guide to "World Resources 1990–91"
Grades: 9–12
World Resources Institute, 1990
1709 New York Avenue NW
Washington, DC 20006
202-638-6300
Bi-annual guide offers current accessible environmental information. Designed to enhance science, social studies, geography, global studies or environmental curriculum.

Teacher's Guide to "World Resources 1992–93"
Grades: 9–12
World Resources Institute, 1992
1709 New York Avenue NW
Washington, DC 20006
202-638-6300
Bi-annual guide offers current accessible environmental information. Designed to enhance science, social studies, geography, global studies or environmental curriculum.

Teaching About Global Issues: Population, Health, Hunger, Culture, Environment
Grades: 7–12
American Forum for Global Education, 1993
45 John Street, Suite 908
New York, NY 10038
212-732-8606
Compilation of selected parts of curriculum considered "oldies, but goodies." Most of the lessons appeared previously in either "Intercom" or another curriculum guide.

Teaching Guide for the Environmental Databook
Grades: 7–12
The World Bank, 1993
1818 H Street NW
Washington, DC
202-477-1234
Presents statistics on countries with a population of more than one million and looks at how this affects the quality of the environment and economic development.

Think Earth: Environmental Education Program
Grades: K–6
Educational Development Specialists, 1991
5505 East Carson Street, Suite 250
Lakewood, CA 90713-3093
310-420-6814
Lessons show how to conserve natural resources, reduce waste and minimize pollution. Program includes teacher's guide, story and practice cards, posters and a video.

This Land Is Sacred
Grades: 3–7
North Carolina Wildlife Resources Commission, 1992
512 North Salisbury Street
Raleigh, NC 27604
919-733-7123
Video and teacher's guide with classroom activities that are based on Chief Seattle's famous speech about respecting the natural environment.

Training Student Organizers Curriculum
Grades: 7–12
Council on the Environment, Inc., 1990
51 Chambers Street, Room 228
New York, NY 10007
212-566-0990
Projects and lessons address energy conservation, solid waste, water, air, open space preservation, noise pollution, nuclear energy and transportation.

3-2-1 Contact Extras
Grades: 3–7
Children's Television Workshop, 1991
P.O. Box 660002
Scotts Valley, CA 95067-0002

800-321-7511

Video series exploring environmental issues. Activities let students analyze social issues relating to science and technology and introduces them to careers.

TreePeople Environmental Education Materials

Grades: K–12
TreePeople, 1991
12601 Mulholland Drive
Beverly Hills, CA 90210
818-753-4620
Activities concentrate on tree/nature awareness and recycling/waste reduction. Includes teacher notebook and activity sheets.

Tuning the Green Machine: An Integrated View of Environmental Systems

Grades: 9–12
Institute for Environmental Education, 1978
18554 Haskins Road
Chagrin Falls, OH 44023-1823
216-543-7303
Interdisciplinary guide to making responsible decisions that affect the environment. Guidelines for cleaning up and further prevention activities are offered.

TVA World of Resources

Grades: 6–8
Tennessee Valley Authority
Water Quality Department Library,
Haney Building 2C
1101 Market Street
Chattanooga, TN 37402-2081
615-751-7338
Supplementary for existing curricula teaches environmental concepts of interdependence, change, adaptation, energy flow and diversity.

Vision Changers: Totally Clean = Totally Cool

Grades: 5–8
Earth Day Canada/Vision Changer Project, 1991
2 Bloor Street West, Suite 100-209
Toronto, Ontario, Canada M4W 3E2
416-924-4449
Six-week program where children define their own preferred world view. Empowers and influences their actions, creativity and thinking.

Water, Stones and Fossil Bones

Grades: 4–8
National Science Teacher's Association, 1991
1742 Connecticut Avenue NW
Washington, DC 20009
202-328-5800
Teacher-tested, hands-on activities help to explore physical and chemical changes of the earth's past, solar systems, geology, water, weather and air.

Weather, Electricity, Environmental Investigations

Grades: 4–8
The Learning Works, 1982
P.O. Box 6187
Santa Barbara, CA 93160
800-235-5767
Activities cover interrelated areas of weather, energy and waste. Students learn to investigate, develop and implement practical solutions to environmental problems.

What on Earth You Can Do with Kids: Environmental Activities for Every Day of the School Year

Grades: K–6
Good Apple, Inc., 1991
1204 Buchanan Street, Box 299
Carthage, IL 62321-0299
800-435-7234
Year-long focus on the environment includes activities, experiments and art projects. Black-and-white illustrations for easy reproduction.

What You Can Do to Save the Planet

Grades: K–12
Intellimation, 1990
130 Cremona Drive, P.O. Box 1922
Santa Barbara, CA 93116-1922
805-968-2291
Activity guide with video that emphasizes what individuals can do to make a difference concerning environmental problems.

Woodsy Owl Environmental Education Leader's Kit

Grades: K–3
USDA Forest Service, 1989
Woodsy Owl Campaign, P.O. Box 1963
Washington, DC 20013
202-720-8732

Lessons use multisensory, multidisciplinary approach to environmental awareness, problems and solutions.

People/Places

Environmental Portraits: People Making a Difference for the Environment

Grades: 4–6
Good Apple, Inc., 1993
1204 Buchanan Street, P.O. Box 299
Carthage, IL 62321-0299
800-435-7234
Biographical profiles and activities that entail writing, thinking and reading-comprehension skills. Encourages students to explore their own interests.

Keepers of the Animals: Native American Stories and Wildlife Activities for Children

Grades: K–6
Fulcrum Publishing, Inc., 1991
350 Indiana Street, Suite 350
Golden, CO 80401
800-992-2908
Native American stories and multidisciplinary activities introduce the wonders of wildlife, ecology, habitat and natural history.

Keepers of the Earth: Native American Stories and Environmental Activities for Children

Grades: K–6
Fulcrum Publishing, Inc., 1989
350 Indiana Street, Suite 350
Golden, CO 80401
800-992-2908
Multidisciplinary stories and activities introduce students to the earth and Native American cultures. Activities explore the environment.

Population

Adventures in Population Education

Grades: 4–12
Zero Population Growth, 1984
1400 16th Street NW, Suite 320
Washington, DC 20036
202-332-2200

Hands-on cross-curricular activities introduce basic population concepts. Simulations, games and other group activities make the concepts more understandable.

Cairo Bound
Grades: 7–12
Izaak Walton League of America, 1994
1401 Wilson Boulevard, Level B
Arlington, VA 22209-2318
703-528-1818
Multidisciplinary, event-based curriculum that introduces the purpose and process of the 1994 United Nations International Conference on population and development held in Cairo.

Connections: Linking Population and the Environment
Grades: 6–12
Population Reference Bureau, 1991
1875 Connecticut Avenue NW, Suite 520
Washington, DC 20009-5728
202-483-1100
Worksheets, resource lists and activities compliment the articles on population in the Student Resource Guide.

Development Data Book: Guide to Social and Economic Statistics with a Comprehensive Data Table
Grades: 8–12
The World Bank, 1988
1818 H Street NW
Washington, DC
202-477-1234
Presents economic statistics on countries with populations of more than 1 million and changes they are bringing about in the world. Includes teacher's guide.

Elementary Population Activities Kit
Grades: K–8
Zero Population Growth, 1980
1400 16th Street NW, Suite 320
Washington, DC 20036
202-332-2200
Hands-on activities demonstrate population and environmental concepts. Kit provides data sheets, copy masters, Ranger Rick reprint and cassette tape.

For Earth's Sake: Lessons in Population and the Environment

Grades: 6–10
Zero Population Growth, 1989
1400 16th Street NW, Suite 320
Washington, DC 20036
202-332-2200
Designed to increase an understanding of population and environmental issues and promote individual responsibility. Activities include games, simulations and field trips.

Kenya: A Country in Transition
Grades: 9–12
Zero Population Growth, 1987
1400 16th Street NW, Suite 320
Washington, DC 20036
202-332-2200
Students in social studies and science classes explore the effects of rapid population growth through discussion questions and hands-on activities.

Making Connections: Linking Population and Environment
Grades: 3–6
Population Reference Bureau, 1992
1875 Connecticut Avenue NW, Suite 520
Washington, DC 20009-5728
202-483-1100
Students study the link between population and the environment. Geography, math and communication activities focus on resource use.

Our Only Earth Series: Our Divided World: Poverty, Hunger and Overpopulation
Grades: 4–12
Zephyr Press, 1990
3316 North Chapel Avenue, P.O. Box 13448
Tucson, AZ 85732-3448
602-322-5090
Part of a series. Provides an integrated science, language arts and social studies program. Activities that can run from 1 month to 1 year address real-life issues and propose solutions.

Population Handbook
Grades: 6–12
Population Reference Bureau, 1991
1875 Connecticut Avenue NW, Suite 520
Washington, DC 20009-5728
202-483-1100
This booklet provides information on

all aspects of population and how it affects the environment.

Population Images
Grades: 7–12
United Nations Fund for Population Activities, 1987
One United Nations Plaza
New York, NY 10017
212-906-5000
Students study urban and rural populations, birth and death rates and the interrelationship of resource consumption and population growth.

Teenage Parents: A Global Perspective
Grades: 7–12
Population Reference Bureau, 1989
1875 Connecticut Avenue NW, Suite 520
Washington, DC 20009-5728
202-483-1100
Overview of the health, social, psychological, economic and demographic effects of teenage parenting worldwide.

USA by Numbers
Grades: 9–12, C
Zero Population Growth, 1988
1400 16th Street NW, Suite 320
Washington, DC 20036
202-332-2200
Compilation of current and historic data on demographic, socioeconomic and environmental trends in the United States, with hands-on activities.

World Population
Grades: 4–12
Zero Population Growth, 1990
1400 16th Street NW, Suite 320
Washington, DC 20036
202-332-2200
Video presents effective graphic simulation of the history of human population growth. Activity and discussion guide included.

World Population: Towards the Next Century
Grades: 9–12
Population Reference Bureau, 1989
1875 Connecticut Avenue NW, Suite 520
Washington, DC 20009-5728
202-483-1100
Workbook activities covering current

and projected population patterns and their consequences on society and the environment.

Zero Population Growth: Hope for Future Generations

Grades: 7–12
Current Affairs, 1980
346 Ethan Allan Highway, P.O. Box 426
Ridgefield, CT 06877
Filmstrip with accompanying audio tape focuses on the causes and effects of pollution in industrialized and less developed countries.

Rainforests

Adopt an Acre in the Children's Rainforest: Give the Earth a Birthday Present!

Grades: 4–7
Earth's Birthday Project, 1992
170 Joralem Street
Brooklyn, NY 11201
800-698-4438
The Earth's Birthday Project, the Nature Conservancy and students join together to save Latin American rainforests. Students raise money to adopt rainforest acres.

Breakthroughs: Rainforests: The Lungs of the Earth?

Grades: 4–6
Zaner-Bloser, Inc., 1989
2200 West Fifth Avenue, P.O. Box 16764
Columbus, OH 43216-6764
800-421-3018
Lessons on the importance of rainforests, their destruction and the rainforest water cycle.

Connection: The Living Planet: The Remarkable Rainforest

Grades: 3–4
Ginn Publishing Canada Inc., 1993
P.O. Box 261 Tonawanda
New York, NY 14151-0261
800-361-6128
Articles and activities on the rainforest.

Exploring the Rainforest: Activities, Reproducibles and Patterns

Grades: 1–5

Copycat Press, 1991
P.O. Box 081546
Racine, WI 53408-1546
414-634-0146
Construct a rainforest in your classroom. Discuss biodiversity and the importance of preserving rainforests.

Global ReLeaf World Forests: Striking a Balance Between Conservation and Development

Grades: 5–12
American Forests, 1993
P.O. Box 2000
Washington, DC 20013
202-667-3300
Lessons and activities teach interrelations, interdependence, stability, change and human responsibility for tropical forests.

Jungles: From Streets to the Rainforest

Grade: 8
Alberta Global Education Project, 1990
11010 142nd Street
Edmonton, Alberta, Canada T5N 2RI
403-453-2411
Explores the environmental impact of development in Brazil and the Amazon rainforest. Develops mapping skills.

More Than Trees!/Mas Que Arboles!

Grades: 7–9
The World Wildlife Fund, 1983
1250 24th Street NW
Washington, DC 20037-1175
202-293-4800
Teaches the basic ecology of rainforests and the problem of deforestation. Available in Spanish.

Nature Scope: Rain Forests Tropical Treasures

Grades: K–8
National Wildlife Federation, 1989
1412 Sixteenth Street NW
Washington, DC 20036-2266
800-432-6564
Interdisciplinary hands-on activities encourages nature appreciation and develops skills needed to make responsible environmental decisions.

Our Only Earth Series: The Future of Our Tropical Rainforests

Grades: 4–12

Zephyr Press, 1990
3316 North Chapel Avenue, P.O. Box 13448
Tucson, AZ 85732-3448
602-322-5090
Part of a series. Provides an integrated science, language arts and social studies program of activities that address real-life issues.

The Rainforest Book

Grades: 4–8
Natural Resources Defense Council, 1990
P.O. Box 1400
Church Hill, MD 21690
800-327-1400
Provides lesson plans and activities that give a view of tropical rainforests. Students learn about the diversity of rainforests and their endangerment.

The Rainforest Connection

Grades: 3–8
Janet Peterson, 1989
5917 Hempstead Road
Madison, WI 53711
608-262-7419
Activities, riddles, treasures hunts and a simulation game introduce students to issues facing tropical rainforests.

Rainforest: Help Save Their Layers of Life

Grades: K–12
National Wildlife Federation, 1993
1412 Sixteenth Street NW
Washington, DC 20036-2266
800-432-6564
Includes discussions and activities covering the layers of life in the tropical rainforest.

Rainforests: Kids for Conservation

Grades: K–12
Marine World Africa, USA Marine World Foundation, 1989
Marine World Parkway
Vallejo, CA 94589
707-644-4000, ext. 434
Worksheets, flashcards, activities and conservation focuses on rainforest destruction and its effects.

Treasures of the Rainforest

Grades: 5–9
The Lifetime Learning Systems, 1990
79 Sanford Street

Fairfield, CT 06430
203-259-5257
Activities build awareness of rainforest destruction and show students how to become involved in saving them.

Tree Amigos Program
Grades: 5–9
Center for Environmental Study, 1992
143 Bostwick NE
Grand Rapids, MI 49503
616-771-3935
Promotes greater awareness of the role trees and forests play in the global environment.

Tropical Rainforest: An Activity Guide for Teachers
Grades: 4–12
Educational Resources, 1992
Science Museum of Minnesota
30 East 10th Street
St. Paul, MN 55101
612-221-9488
Designed to accompany the IMAX film, "Tropical Rainforest." This activity packet can be used separately.

Tropical Rainforest Curriculum
Grades: 4–8
Earthwatch, 1992
680 Mt. Auburn Street, P.O. Box 403
Watertown, MA 02272
800-776-0188
Activities and games for all school subjects (even PE). Compiled by teachers who have visited rainforests.

Tropical Rainforest: A Disappearing Treasure, Teacher Manual and Student Activities
Grades: K–12
Prentice Hall Science, 1979
Route 9W
Englewood Cliffs, NJ 07632
800-922-0579
Designed to augment the Smithsonian Institute's traveling exhibition "Tropical Rainforest: A Disappearing Treasure." Some activities can be done without the exhibit.

Tropical Rainforest Education Program
Grades: K–12
Tropical Rainforest Education Program, 1989
4646 Shenandoah

St. Louis, MO 63110
314-771-2885
Multidisciplinary slideshow and lessons examine the political, social and environmental issues of rainforests.

Tropical Rainforest Food Web Game
Grades: 3–8
Floyd Sandford, 1992 (3rd ed.)
Coe College Biology Department
Cedar Rapids, IA 52402
319-399-8576
An interactive role-playing game to help educate students about the plants, animals and interrelationships in the Amazon rainforest.

Tropical Rainforests and the Indiana Connection
Grades: 6–10
Indiana Department of Natural Resources
Division of Forestry, 1991
402 West Washington Street, Room 296
Indianapolis, IN 46204
317-232-4105
Gives students information and experiences with their own native forests so that they can relate this knowledge to tropical forests.

Vanishing Rainforests Education Kit
Grades: 2–6
World Wildlife Fund, 1988
P.O. Box 4866, Hampden Post Office
Baltimore, MD 21211
301-338-6951
Introduction to the rainforest. The teacher's manual contains background information and discussion of conservation and global environmental issues. Poster and video are included.

Recycling

Beautiful Junk
Grades: K–12
Fearon Teacher Aids, 1990
P.O. Box 280
Carthage, IL 62321
217-357-3900
Creative ways to recycle boxes, cans,

flyers and other throwaways. Includes ideas for games, gifts, musical instruments and science experiments.

Beautiful Junk 2: More Creative Classroom Uses for Recyclable Materials
Grades: 1–6
Fearon Teacher Aids, 1993
P.O. Box 280
Carthage, IL 62321
217-357-3900
Creative ways to recycle boxes, cans, flyers and other throwaways. Includes ideas for games, gifts, musical instruments and science experiments.

Beyond Recycling
Grades: K–4
Desert Rose Productions, 1992
1775 Corydon Avenue
Winnipeg, Manitoba, Canada R3N 2A6
204-489-3400
Activities that teach young students what recyclables become after they get recycled.

Captain Conservation: All About Recycling
Grades: K–2
National Geographic Society, 1992
17th and M Streets NW
Washington, DC 20036
800-368-2728
Improves reading skills and builds vocabulary while describing how paper, glass, aluminum, plastic and organic materials can be recycled. Available in Spanish.

CURB: Clean Up...Recycle Brookhaven!
Grades: K–6
Town of Brookhaven, 1988
3233 Route 112
Medford, NY 11763
516-451-6222
Worksheets, activities and project ideas designed to make the study of recycling interesting.

Don't Waste Waste
Grades: 4–6
Environmental Action Coalition, 1982
625 Broadway
New York, NY 10012
212-677-1061
Activities explain solid waste manage-

ment, natural resource depletion and recycling. Lessons are divided into the different school disciplines.

Education and Recycling: Educator's Waste Management Resource and Activity Guide 1991

Grades: 2–12
California Department of Conservation, Division of Recycling, 1991 (rev. annually)
Resource Center
801 K Street, MS 18-55
Sacramento, CA 95814
916-445-1490
Multidisciplinary activities that teach waste management issues, natural resources and conservation.

Education and Recycling: Educator's Waste Management Resource and Activity Guide 1992

Grades: K–12
California Department of Conservation, Division of Recycling, 1992
Resource Center
801 K Street, MS 18-55
Sacramento, CA 95814
916-445-1490
Multidisciplinary recycling and waste management activities.

Education and Recycling: Educator's Waste Management Resource and Activity Guide 1994

Grades: K–12
California Department of Conservation, Division of Recycling, 1994
Resource Center
801 K Street, MS 18-55
Sacramento, CA 95814
916-445-1490
Multidisciplinary recycling and waste management activities.

The Fourth R

Grades: K–12
Wisconsin Department of Natural Resources, 1990
Bureau of Information and Education
P.O. Box 7921
Madison, WI 53707
608-266-2711
Teachers helped develop this booklet that will help schools reduce, reuse and recycle.

The 4th R: Recycling Curriculum

Grades: K–5
San Francisco Recycling Program, 1986
Solid Waste Program
1145 Market Street, Suite 401
San Francisco, CA 94103
415-554-3411
Lessons and activities about waste reduction, reuse and recycling. This curriculum has been tested in San Francisco Unified School District classrooms.

Garbology: Recycling in Schools: A Guide to Accompany the Television Program Full Circle

Grades: 5–12
Environmental Media, 1991
P.O. Box 1016
Chapel Hill, NC 27514
919-933-3003
Student learn how a landfill operates and investigate soil and water conservation.

The Great Glass Caper

Grades: 4–6
Glass Packaging Institute, 1990
1627 K Street NW, Suite 800
Washington, DC 20006
202-887-4850
Activities describing how glass is made and recycled.

KIDS C.A.R.E.: A Crosscurricular Environmental Program

Grades: 4–6
Mead Corporation, 1991
Courthouse Plaza Northeast
Dayton, OH 45463
513-459-3501
Worksheets offer activities that illustrate an ecological problem or idea for solution. Activities can be completed individually, as group projects or as homework.

Let's Learn About Recycling

Grades: K–6
Channing L. Bete Company, 1992
200 State Road
South Deerfield, MA 01373
800-628-7733
An information and activities book.

Let's Recycle

Grades: K–12

U.S. Environmental Protection Agency, 1980
Public Information Center, PM-211B,
401 M Street SW
Washington, DC 20460
202-475-7751
Activity-oriented lesson plan used to teach children about a city recycling program in Massachusetts.

Likable Recyclables

Grades: 1–12
Learning Works, Inc., 1992
P.O. Box 6187
Santa Barbara, CA 93160
800-235-5767
Ways and reasons to reuse and recycle. Turn bags, bottles, boxes and cans into toys, games and art objects.

McHenry Co. Schools Recycling Lessons Ideas: Background Information

Grades: K–8
Illinois Department of Energy and Natural Resources, 1989
325 West Adams Street, Room 300
Springfield, IL 62704
217-785-2800
Lessons and worksheets address waste and waste reduction. Plus background information for teachers.

Nature's Recyclers Activity Guide

Grades: K–12
Wisconsin Department of Natural Resources, 1990
P.O. Box 7921
Madison, WI 53707
608-266-2711
Activities such as games, crafts, songs and plays are intended to help teach people about natural recycling and cycles in nature.

Operation Separation Presents...A Recycling Curriculum

Grades: K–6
Onondaga County Resource Recovery Agency, 1992 (rev.)
100 Elwood Davis Road
North Syracuse, NY 13212-4312
315-453-2866
This curricula focuses on recycling, composting and waste reduction using factsheets, handouts, vocabulary and other multidisciplinary activities.

Operation Separation Presents...A Recycling Curriculum
Grades: 7–12
Onondaga County Resource Recovery Agency, 1992 (rev.)
100 Elwood Davis Road
North Syracuse, NY 13212-4312
315-453-2866
This curricula focuses on recycling, composting and waste reduction using factsheets, handouts, vocabulary and other multidisciplinary activities.

Plastics in Perspective
Grades: 7–12
Illinois Department of Energy and Natural Resources
Office of Recycling and Waste Reduction, 1991
325 West Adams Street, Room 300
Springfield, IL 62704-1892
217-524-5454
Lessons and activities look at solid waste management from 1960 through 1990 and examine what causes plastics to degrade in the environment.

R.A.Y.S.—Recycle and You Save
Grades: K–6
San Diego Department of Public Works, Solid Waste Division, 1987
5555 Overland Avenue; MS 0383
San Diego, CA 92123-1295
619-974-2661
A collection of lessons that can be done independently.

Recycle Now!
Grades: 4–6
California Department of Conservation, Division of Recycling, 1989
Resource Center, 801 K Street, MS 18-55
Sacramento, CA 95814
916-445-1490
A recycling education program for kids in California

Recycle Team: Waste Reduction and Recycling Education Program
Grades: 1–6
Southeast Regional Laboratory, 1992
4665 Lampsen Avenue
Los Alimitos, CA 90720
310-598-7661
Lessons instruct students to be part of the solution to the waste problem by preaching to others and by practicing waste reduction.

Recycle This!
Grades: 7–12
DOW Chemical Company, 1990
2040 DOW Center
Midland, MI 48674
800-441-4369
Musical video and an informational booklet about how recycling can help protect the environment, save energy, reduce waste and conserve resources.

Recycled: Mobius Curriculum: Understanding the Waste Cycle
Grades: 4–6
Browning-Ferris Industries, Inc., 1990
P.O. Box 3151
Houston, TX 77253
800-BFI-8100
Worksheets and activities introduce waste disposal and recycling issues while encouraging participation in and development of solutions.

Recycling: Games and Quizzes
Grades: 3–6
Wisconsin Department of Natural Resources
P.O. Box 7921
Madison, WI 53707
608-266-2711
Mazes, crossword puzzles, word searches and quizzes about recycling.

Recycling Lesson Plans
Grades: K–12
Pennsylvania Department of Environmental Resources, 1991
25 West Third Street, P.O. Box 88
Harrisburg, PA 17120
717-787-9870
Lessons explore recycling as a method of waste management.

Recycling: Mining Resources from Trash
Grades: K–6
Cornell University Resource Center, 1990
#7 Cornell Technology and Business Park
Ithaca, NY 14850
607-255-2091
Games and activities that teach students how to sort trash for recycling.

Recycling Our Available Resources (R.O.A.R.)
Grades: 4–8
Illinois Department of Energy and Natural Resources
Office of Recycling and Waste Reduction, 1991
325 West Adams Street, Room 300
Springfield, IL 62704-1892
217-524-5454
Teaches recycling through puppetry. Instructions for 2 puppet shows and suggestions for waste recycling projects are given.

The Recycling Study Guide
Grades: 4–12
Wisconsin Department of Natural Resources, 1989
Bureau of Information and Education, P.O. Box 7921
Madison, WI 53707
608-266-2711
Provides lessons that are designed to help instill an awareness of the importance of recycling as a method of waste management.

Recycling in Your School Makes Good Sense
Grades: 4–8
Cornell University Resource Center, 1989
#7 Cornell Technology and Business Park
Ithaca, NY 14850
607-255-2091
Slide-show presentation focuses on implementing a paper recycling program. Explains where resources come from, why we need to recycle and how to get started.

Recycling's No Puzzle
Grades: 4–7
Pennsylvania Resources Council, 1987
25 West Third Street, P.O. Box 88
Media, PA 19063
215-565-9131
A collection of puzzles about recycling.

Reusable Math
Grades: 1–9
Pennsylvania Resources Council, 1992
25 West Third Street, P.O. Box 88
Media, PA 19063
215-565-9131
Lessons give practice in arithmetic

concepts—such as visualizing quantities, areas and volume in concrete terms—by relating these concepts to trash habits and recycling.

Rex and Regina: The Recycling Robots Present a Lesson for Living
Grades: 3–8
Louisiana Department of Natural Resources, 1987
P.O. Box 44156
Baton Rouge, LA 70804-4156
504-342-1399
Lessons, worksheets, diagrams, tips for shopping and a "Who's in My Garbage" school play.

San Jose Beautiful
Grades: K–5
San Jose Beautiful, 1989
333 West Santa Clara Street, Suite 800
San Jose, CA 95113
408-277-5208
Lessons and cross-curricular activities look at where waste comes from, why it's a problem and what we can do about it.

Spike and His Friends Recycle
Grades: K–4
Pennsylvania Resource Council, 1983
25 West Third Street, P.O. Box 88
Media, PA 19063
215-565-9131
A story book about recycling includes puzzles using vocabulary words about recycling.

Steel: America's Most Recycled Material
Grades: 5–8
Lifetime Learning Systems, 1990
79 Sanford Street
Fairfield, CT 06430
203-259-5257
Students learn the how and why of recycling and the role they can play in their community's recycling effort.

Wee Recyclers
Grades: K–1
Wisconsin Department of Natural Resources, 1992
2421 Darwin Road
Madison, WI 53704
608-266-2621
Activities include puppet shows, stories

and games to teach recycling. Suggests take home follow-up actions.

Worms Eat Our Garbage
Grades: 4–8
Flowerfield Enterprises, 1993
10332 Shaver Rd.
Kalamazoo, MI 49002
616-327-0108
Interdisciplinary curriculum presents the concept of worms eating garbage and activities that go beyond the worm bin and into the real world.

Soil/Agriculture

Conserving Soil
Grades: 6–9
National Association of Conservation Districts, 1990
P.O. Box 855
League City, TX 77574
800-825-5547
The program has a balance of indoor and outdoor lessons about soils. Students will use the skills of mathematics, science, English and social studies.

Dracons Visit the Earth to Study Food and the Land
Grades: 4–6
Soil and Water Conservation Society, 1984
7417 NE Ankeny Road
Ankeny, IA 50021-9764
800-THE-SOIL
Cartoon booklet and teacher's guide with activities to help students learn about land and food production.

Erosion
Grades: 3–6
Delta Education, Inc., 1990
P.O. Box 915
Hudson, NH 03051
603-889-8899
Activities and worksheets address how weathering and erosion are changing the features of the earth's surface.

Lines on the Land
Grades: 5–8
National Association of Conservation Districts, 1991
P.O. Box 855
League City, TX 77574

800-825-5547
Through activity-oriented lessons students discover concepts, form opinions and become more informed about soil conservation.

The Living Soil: A Renewable Resource: A Science Module
Grades: 7–12
Weigl Educational Publishers, Ltd., 1991
2114 College Avenue
Regina, Saskatchewan, Canada S4P 1C5
306-569-0766
Highlights soil issues through case studies, activities and profiles of people who work in soil research.

Primary and Junior Activities
Grades: K–8
Ontario Ministry of Agriculture and Food
Rural Organizations and Services Branch, Agriculture in the Classroom Program
Toronto, Ontario, Canada
416-326-3400
Looks at Ontario's agriculture to make students aware of the processes involved in producing the food eaten on a daily basis.

Project Stewardship Minnesota
Grades: 6–12
Minnesota Office of Environmental Education, 1990
300 Centennial Office Building, 658 Cedar Street
St. Paul, MN 55155
612-296-2723
Curriculum of soil and water stewardship activities. Provides a review of principles and promotes critical analysis of decisions about resource use.

Saving Our Planet Series: Land
Grades: 1–3
Good Apple, Inc., 1992
1204 Buchanan Street, Box 299
Carthage, IL 62321-0299
800-435-7234
Hands-on activities, worksheets and reading comprehension lessons offer a basic understanding of the environment and land erosion.

Saving Our Planet Series: Land
Grades: 4–7
Good Apple, Inc., 1992
1204 Buchanan Street, Box 299
Carthage, IL 62321-0299
800-435-7234
Hands-on activities, worksheets and reading comprehension lessons offer a basic understanding of the environment and land erosion.

Show You Care with Buddy Bear: Celebrating Soil and Water Stewardship
Grades: K–1
National Association of Conservation Districts, 1993
P.O. Box 855
League City, TX 77574-0855
713-332-3402
Lessons and activities explain how to take care of soil and water.

The Story of Land: Its Use and Misuse Through the Centuries
Grades: 4–6
Soil and Water Conservation Society, 1985
7515 NE Ankeny Road
Ankeny, IA 50021-9764
800-THE-SOIL
Activities and a cartoon book address the fact that humans depend upon the land for their well being.

Toxics

About Hazardous Products in the Home: A Guide to Proper Use and Disposal
Grades: 6–12
Channing L. Bete Company, 1992
200 State Road
South Deerfield, MA 01373
800-628-7733
Explains hazardous products in the home, how to use them properly and how to dispose of them safely.

The Hazard House
Grades: 5–8
California Department of Toxic Substances Control, 1992
Education and Information Unit, P.O. Box 806
Sacramento, CA 95812

916-324-1214
Through the use of a computer disk, students will learn the dangers of toxics as well as ways to protect their health and the environment.

Household Hazardous Materials Pollution Solutions Starts at Home
Grades: 6–9
San Diego Regional Household Hazardous Materials Program (n.d.)
450 A Street, Suite 500
San Diego, CA 92101
619-235-2111
Multidiscipline curriculum encourages students to use knowledge and skills acquired in regular course work to investigate an environmental problem.

Household Toxics
Grades: 5–6
Municipality of Anchorage, Solid Waste Services, 1989
1111 East 56th Avenue, P.O. Box 196650
Anchorage, AK 99519-6650
907-561-1906
Educates students on the everyday use of hazardous products in the home and the consequences of not properly disposing these products.

Nature Scope: Pollution Problems and Solutions
Grades: K–8
National Wildlife Federation, 1990
1412 Sixteenth Street NW
Washington, DC 20036-2266
800-432-6564
Interdisciplinary, hands-on activities that encourage an appreciation of nature and the skills needed to make responsible environmental decisions.

Teaching Toxics: Creating Solutions to Household Pollution
Grades: K–12
Association of Vermont Recyclers, 1992
P.O. Box 1244
Montpelier, VT 05601
802- 229-1833
Interdisciplinary activity guide on household hazardous products—what they are, where they come from and how to dispose of them.

Toxics in My Home? You Bet!
Grades: K–3
Local Government Commission, 1984
909 12th Street, Suite 205
Sacramento, CA 95814
916-448-1198
Curriculum on household toxics designed to introduce students to the potential hazards of common products used in the home. Available in Spanish.

Toxics in My Home? You Bet!
Grades: 4–6
Local Government Commission, 1984
909 12th Street, Suite 205
Sacramento, CA 95814
916-448-1198
Curriculum on household toxics designed to introduce students to the potential hazards of common products used in the home. Available in Spanish.

Toxics in My Home? You Bet!
Grades: 7–8
Local Government Commission, 1984
909 12th Street, Suite 205
Sacramento, CA 95814
916-448-1198
Curriculum on household toxics designed to introduce students to the potential hazards of common products used in the home. Available in Spanish.

Toxics in My Home? You Bet!
Grades: 9–12
Local Government Commission, 1984
909 12th Street, Suite 205
Sacramento, CA 95814
916-448-1198
Curriculum on household toxics designed to introduce students to the potential hazards of common products used in the home. Available in Spanish.

Toxics: Taking Charge
Grades: 4–6
Alameda County Office of Education, 1989
313 West Winton Avenue
Hayward, CA 94544-1198
510-887-0152
Lessons focus on the use and environmental effects of toxic household cleaning products.

Trees/Forests

Breakthroughs: Strategies for Thinking: Forest Fires
Grades: 3–5
Zaner-Bloser, Inc., 1992
2200 West Fifth Avenue, P.O. Box 16764
Columbus, OH 43216-6764
800-421-3018
Includes lessons and activities on the benefits and dangers of forest fires.

City Trees: A Curriculum Guide to Our Urban Forest
Grades: K–12
Friends of the Urban Forest, 1993
512 Second Street, 4th Floor
San Francisco, CA 94107
415-543-5000
This curriculum uses trees growing right outside the classroom as a laboratory to explore the physical environment and community.

City Trees, Country Trees
Grades: K–12
Environmental Action Coalition, 1980
625 Broadway
New York, NY 10012
212-677-1061
Multidisciplinary curriculum that makes teachers and students more aware of their immediate environment, rural or urban.

Forests Forever
Grades: 9–12
Alberta Global Education Project, 1991
11010 142 Street
Edmonton, Alberta, Canada T5N 2R1
403-453-2411
Integrates global environmental awareness with particular attention to forests.

Global ReLeaf
Grades: 4–8
American Forests, 1991
P.O. Box 2000
Washington, DC 20013
202-667-3300
Lesson plans show how conservation of energy combined with the ability of trees to use carbon dioxide can combat global warming.

The Green Scene
Grades: 4–8
University of Arizona
School for Renewable Natural Resources, 1990
BioSciences East, Room 325
Tucson, AZ 85721
602-621-7255
Games and activities explain problems forests are having and show how students can help with forest preservation.

Grow Your Own Tree
Grade: 2
National Arbor Day Foundation, 1991
100 Arbor Avenue
Nebraska City, NE 68410
402-474-5655
Uses filmstrips, audio cassettes, activities and posters to teach the value and importance of trees and environmental responsibility.

Introduction to Forestry in Florida
Grades: 8–10
Florida Division of Forestry,
Environmental Education Unit, 1992
3125 Conner Boulevard
Tallahassee, FL 32399-1650
904-488-6591
Activities show how to map, measure and maintain urban and rural forests. The history, management and future of Florida's forests are discussed.

The Magical City Forest
Grades: K–6
TreePeople, 1994
12601 Mulholland Drive
Beverly Hills, CA 90210
818-753-4620
Activity-based curriculum has students examining their role as healers in the urban ecosystem by studying the cycles of the forest (air, water, carbon and energy).

Nature Education Kits: What Leaf Is It?
Grades: K–9
Young Naturalist, 1990
1900 North Main
Newton, KS 671114
316-283-4103
Students will classify leaves, using a leaf key; design their own leaf key; collect, press and preserve leaves;

and artistically portray leaves in different ways.

Nature Scope: Trees Are Terrific
Grades: K–8
National Wildlife Federation, 1985
1412 Sixteenth Street NW
Washington, DC 20036-2266
800-432-6564
Interdisciplinary, hands-on activities that encourage an appreciation of nature and help students make environmentally responsible decisions.

Plant a Tree for Life
Grade: 5
Florida Division of Forestry,
Environmental Education Unit, 1991 (rev. annually)
3125 Conner Boulevard
Tallahassee, FL 32399-1650
904-488-6591
Helps students to understand the importance of trees and the effects of global warming on climate, plants, animals and humans.

Protecting Trees and Forests
Grades: 3–6
EDC Publishing, 1991
10302 East 55th Place
Tulsa, OK 74146
800-475-4522
Text and illustrations introduce conservation of trees and forests and outline threats that face trees.

Seed to Seedling
Grades: K–6
Sacramento Tree Foundation, 1991 (2nd ed.)
201 Lathrop Way, Suite F
Sacramento, CA 95815
916-924-8733
Activities provide many hands-on learning experiences as students nurture an acorn into an oak tree.

Share and Care Naturalists Notebook
Grades: 2–10
Mountains Education Program, 1990
27300 Waycross Drive
Calabasas, CA 91302
818-880-0664
Through hands-on activities, students nurture an acorn into a young oak tree and gain awareness, understanding

and appreciation of the important role oaks play.

Spruce Up America
Grades: K–6
Adirondack Teacher Center, 1993
P.O. Box 327
Paul Smiths, NY 12970
518-327-5012
Teaches the importance of trees in our environment and the care needed for their survival. Activities include caring for a tree and a tree-planting ceremony.

Spruce Up America
Grades: 7–12
Adirondack Teacher Center, 1993
P.O. Box 327
Paul Smiths, NY 12970
518-327-5012
Teaches the importance of trees in our environment and the care needed for their survival. Activities include caring for a tree and a tree-planting ceremony.

Stick on Overlays: The Caretakers
Grades: 4–6
Trees Are for People, 1979
629 South Rancho Santa Fe, Suite 334
Lake San Marcos, CA 92069
619-744-4220
Introduces students to the basic concepts of conservation and forest use.

Tree Celebrations
Grades: K–4
Plant a Tree, Grow a Friend, Inc., 1993
633 South College Avenue
Fort Collins, CO 80524
All the songs, stories, poems and activities focus on celebrating the birth of nature and trees.

TreePeople: Environmental Leadership Teacher Activity Notebook
Grades: K–12
TreePeople, 1982
12601 Mulholland Drive
Beverly Hills, CA 90210
818-753-4620
Activities center on trees and nature awareness but also cover food packaging, litter, waste reduction and global warming.

Trees Are Terrific
Grade: 5

National Arbor Day Foundation, 1989
100 Arbor Avenue
Nebraska City, NE 68410
402-474-5655
The focus is on observation and classification skills through tree identification and ecological interdependence.

Trees for Life
Grades: K–5
Tree for Life, 1991
1103 Jefferson
Wichita, KS 67203
316-263-7294
Complete tree-planting kit and educational materials.

The Wild Wild World of Old Growth Forests
Grades: 4–12
Wilderness Society, 1990
1424 Fourth Avenue, Suite 816
Seattle, WA 98101
206-624-6430
Lessons with background information and activities introduce students to old growth forests.

Parks

Teacher's Guide to Craters of the Moon
Grades: 3–6
Craters of the Moon Natural History Association, Inc., 1992
P.O. Box 29
Arco, ID 83213
208-527-3257
Craters of the Moon is a national monument in Idaho. This guide can enhance a field trip or contribute to classroom study.

Urban Issues

Beastly Neighbors
Grades: 4–8
Delta Education, Inc., 1981
P.O. Box 915
Hudson, NH 03051
603-889-8899
Activities and expeditions for students to explore the "wild" world around them, even in a high-rise apartment.

The City Kid's Field Guide
Grades: 4–8
Delta Education, Inc., 1989
P.O. Box 915
Hudson, NH 03051
603-889-8899
Shows how species have learned to survive in human-made surroundings. Includes tips for finding and observing wildlife.

Connection: The Living Planet: Earth Friendly Cities
Grades: 3–5
Ginn Publishing Canada Inc., 1993
P.O. Box 261 Tonawanda
New York, NY 14151-0261
800-361-6128
Looks at the evolution of cities and suggests how they should be planned for the future to be more earth-friendly.

Growing Greener Cities
Grades: 5–8
American Forests, 1992
P.O. Box 2000
Washington, DC 20013
202-667-3300
Lessons and activities are designed to teach students about the vital role trees and parks play in cities.

Living with Insects in the Big City
Grades: K–3
Citizens for a Better Environment, 1987
501 Second Street, Suite 305
San Francisco, CA 94701
415-243-8373
Students learn about urban insect ecology and safe pest management.

Living Lightly in the City, Vol. I
Grades: K–3
Schlitz Audubon Center, 1983
1111 East Brown Deer Road
Milwaukee, WI 53217
414-352-2880
Action-oriented activities inspired by urban children to stimulate exploration of their surroundings and develop a positive image of themselves and their environment.

Living Lightly in the City, Vol. 2
Grades: 4–6

Schlitz Audubon Center, 1992
1111 East Brown Deer Road
Milwaukee, WI 53217
414-352-2880
Action-oriented activities that include land use, water resources, transportation, nature in cities and the Native American philosophy.

Obis Human Impact Modules
Grades: 4–7
Delta Education, Inc., 1981
P.O. Box 915
Hudson, NH 03051
603-889-8899
Outdoor activities involve students in investigating impact effects and the decision-making process of dealing with impact concerns.

A Place to Live
Grades: 2–4
National Audubon Society, 1990
700 Broadway
New York, NY 10003
212-979-3000
Lessons and activities help students observe, improve, respect and protect the city environment. Available also in Spanish.

Urban Areas Habitat Pac
Grades: 4–9
National Institute for Urban Wildlife, 1982
P.O. Box 3015
Shepardstown, WV 25443
304-876-6146
Designed to educate students about wildlife habitats and resource management. Includes lesson plans, activities, a student observation log and teacher background information.

Walking: A Realistic Approach to Environmental Education
Grades: 3–8
Council on the Environment, Inc., 1977
51 Chambers Street, Room 228
New York, NY 10007
212-566-0990
Lessons and activities involve classes taking walking tours in the vicinity of the school, concentrating on pollution sources and nature.

Waste

Classroom Activities: Maine Waste Management Agency
Grades: K–12
Maine Waste Management Agency, Office of Waste Reduction and Recycling, 1989
State House Station 154
Augusta, ME 04333
800-662-4545
Hands-on activity oriented program includes topics such as recycling, bartering, paper making and composting.

Don't Let a Good Thing Go to Waste
Grades: 2–5
Plastic Bag Information Clearinghouse, 1993
1817 East Carson Street
Pittsburgh, PA 15203
412-381-8890
Activities emphasizing thinking skills for making difficult choices.

4 R's Project
Grades: 9–12
Florida Department of Education, 1990
325 West Gaines Street
Tallahassee, FL 32399
904-487-7900
A supplementary resource for integrating solid waste and recycling education in existing curriculum.

Garbage
Grades: 1–4
Scholastic, Inc., 1992
555 Broadway
New York, NY 10012
800-325-6149
Lessons and activities suggest hands-on methods for taking action. Students conduct trash research, a "biodegradable" experiment, participate in a recycling skit, plus more.

Garbage in America
Grades: K–12
Refuse Industry Productions, Inc., 1982
P.O. Box 1011
Grass Valley, CA 95945
800-535-9547
Covers full spectrum of solid-waste

issues, incorporating math, science, art and English into the lessons.

The No Waste Anthology: A Teacher's Guide to Environmental Activities
Grades: K–12
California Department of Toxic Substance Control, 1993
400 P Street, P.O. Box 806
Sacramento, CA 95812-0806
916-322-0476
Compilation of interdisciplinary, action-oriented and field-tested activities covering natural resources, pollution and waste.

Solid Thinking About Solid Waste
Grades: 6–9
Kraft General Foods, 1993
Three Lakes Drive
Northfield, IL 60093-2753
708-646-2000, 800-323-0768
Provides information about the complex problems related to solid waste.

The Solid Waste Crisis: Issues and Arguments
Grades: 6–8
Knowledge Unlimited, Inc., 1992
P.O. Box 52
Madison, WI 53701-0052
800-356-2303
Supplemental activity for solid waste studies. Contains filmstrip, audio tape, discussion guide, glossary, quiz and extension activities.

Trash Goes to School
Grades: K–12
Cornell University Resource Center, 1991
#7 Cornell Technology and Business Park
Ithaca, NY 14850
607-255-2091
A set of 7 IBM WordPerfect disks that have activities on solid waste issues.

Trash Monster Environmental Education Kit
Grades: 5–6
California Department of Education, 1980
Bureau of Publications, Sales Unit,
P.O. Box 271
Sacramento, CA 95802
916-445-1260

Interdisciplinary introduction to solid waste concepts, problems, solutions and personal practices.

Trash Today, Treasure Tomorrow
Grades: K–6
Governor's Recycling Program, 1990
Office of State Planning
2 1/2 Beacon Street
Concord, NH 03301
603-271-1098
Addresses the solid waste problems of New Hampshire and the nation. Contains hands-on group activities and games.

Waste: A Hidden Resource
Grades: 7–12
Keep America Beautiful, 1988
Mill River Plaza, 9 West Broad Street
Stamford, CT 06902
203-323-8987
Activities, factsheets, lessons and simulation games cover solid waste management, hazardous waste and municipal waste.

What About Waste
Grades: 4–8
Cornell University Resource Center, 1990
#7 Cornell Technology and Business Park
Ithaca, NY 14850
607-255-2091
Lessons introduce waste issues through activities that heighten awareness of the natural world.

Woodsy's Wastewise
Grades: 4–8
Cornell University Resource Center, 1991
#7 Cornell Technology and Business Park
Ithaca, NY 14850
607-255-2091
Provides information on solid waste, landfills, recycling, composting and disposal of hazardous materials with accompanying activities and slide show.

Hazardous Waste

Hazardous Wastes from Homes
Grades: 3–12
Enterprise for Education, 1991
1320 A Third St. #202
Santa Monica, CA 90401
310-394-9864
Information on which products are considered hazardous waste, how to dispose of them safely and what can be done about them at home.

Hazardous Waste and You
Grades: 5–8
Ontario Waste Management Corporation, 1990
2 Bloor Street West, 11th Floor
Toronto, Ontario, Canada M4W 3E2
800-268-1178
Designed to make students aware of hazardous waste and related issues.

Hazardous Waste and You
Grades: 10–12
Ontario Waste Management Corporation, 1990
2 Floor Street West, 11th floor
Toronto, Ontario, Canada M4W 3E2
416-923-291822111
Makes students aware of hazardous waste and related issues. Provides an understanding of Ontario's waste situation.

Waste Management

Actions Speak Louder Than Words: The Social and Environmental Impact of Solid Waste
Grades: 6–10
Illinois Department of Energy and Natural Resources
Office of Recycling and Waste Reduction, 1991
325 West Adams Street, Room 300
Springfield, IL 62704-1892
217-524-5454
Explores the social and environmental implications and limitations on technological development pertaining to the production and management of solid waste.

All Trashed Out
Grades: K–6
Illinois Department of Energy and

Natural Resources
Office of Recycling and Waste Reduction, 1992
325 West Adams Street, Room 300
Springfield, IL 62704-1892
217-524-5454
Includes hands-on solid waste management activities that integrate math, science and social studies.

A-Way with Waste
Grades: K–12
Department of Ecology, 1990 (3rd ed.)
3190 160th Avenue SE
Bellevue, WA 98008-5452
206-649-7043
Addresses how waste management affects the environment with activities promoting actions for solving waste problems. Has been tested in Washington state schools.

Borrowed Time
Grades: 5–12
Environmental Education Association, 1992
1211 Connecticut Avenue NW, Suite 812
Washington, DC 20036
202-296-4572
A waste management curriculum kit which addresses recycling, source reduction, incineration and landfilling.

Breakthroughs: Strategies for Thinking: Too Much Trash?
Grades: 3–6
Zaner-Bloser, Inc., 1992
2200 West Fifth Avenue, P.O. Box 16764
Columbus, OH 43216-6764
800-421-3018
Looks at where trash goes, what happens when trash is not properly disposed and how people can learn to dispose of trash correctly.

Breakthroughs: Strategies for Thinking: Where Does Garbage Go?
Grades: 3–6
Zaner-Bloser, Inc., 1992
2200 West Fifth Avenue, P.O. Box 16764
Columbus, OH 43216-6764
800-421-3018
Examines how people get rid of trash

and offers solutions to the problem of garbage disposal.

**Closing the Loop:
Integrated Waste Management
Activities for School
and Home**
Grades: K–12
Institute for Environmental Education, 1993
18554 Haskins Road
Chagrin Falls, OH 44023-1823
216-543-7303
Utilizes hands-on activities so teachers and students can relate lessons to school, home and life situations.

**Closing the Loop:
Integrated Waste Management
Activities for School
and Home**
Grades: K–8
Institute for Environmental Education, 1993
18554 Haskins Road
Chagrin Falls, OH 44023-1823
216-543-7303
Utilizes hands-on activities so teachers and students can relate lessons to school, home and life situations.

**Closing the Loop:
Integrated Waste Management
Activities for School and Home**
Grades: 9–12
Institute for Environmental Education, 1993
18554 Haskins Road
Chagrin Falls, OH 44023-1823
216-543-7303
Utilizes hands-on activities so teachers and students can relate lessons to school, home and life situations.

The Conserving Classroom
Grades: 3–6
Metro Regional Environmental Education Council, 1990
Minnesota Environmental Education Board
Box #5, DNR Building, 500 Lafayette Road
St. Paul, MN 55155-4004
612-772-7900
A collection of activities that are to be used daily throughout the year. The focus is on classroom solid waste issues.

A Curriculum Activities Guide to Solid Waste and Environmental Studies
Grades: K–12
Institute for Environmental Education, 1973
18554 Haskins Road
Chagrin Falls, OH 44023-1823
216-543-7303
Activities involve students in solid waste investigations in both rural and urban settings while addressing the problems and solutions.

EcoSense: An Economic Environmental Learning Kit
Grades: 7–12
Minnesota Council on Economic Education, 1992
510 First Avenue North, North Butler Building, Suite 409
Minneapolis, MN 55403
612-337-5252
Teaches students about the environmental impact consumers have on waste management.

Here Today, Here Tomorrow...Revisited
Grades: 4–8
New Jersey Department of Environmental Protection, 1990
Division of Solid Waste Management
CN 414, 401 East State Street
Trenton, NJ 08625
609-777-4322
Covers solid waste management issues, specifically those in New Jersey. Activities include skits, puzzles, poetry, product promotion and redesigning product packaging.

Ohio Science Workbook: Litter Prevention and Recycling
Grades: 9–12
Ohio Academy of Science, 1991
1500 West Third Avenue, Suite 223
Columbus, OH 43212-2817
614-488-2228
Information and research activities on litter prevention, recycling and the effects of these issues on the state of Ohio and the nation.

A School Based Waste Minimization and Education Program
Grades: K–12

Institute for Environmental Education, 1991
18554 Haskins Road
Chagrin Falls, OH 44023-1823
216-543-7303
Interdisciplinary lessons provide an examination of solid waste and management issues. Includes factsheets, charts and handouts.

Solid Waste Activity Packet
Grades: K–6
Illinois Department of Energy and Natural Resources, 1990
325 West Adams Street, Room 300
Springfield, IL 62704
217-785-2800
Activities provide an integrated approach to incorporating solid waste management issues into all school subjects.

Super Saver Investigators
Grades: K–6
Institute for Environmental Education, 1988
18554 Haskins Road
Chagrin Falls, OH 44023-1823
216-543-7303
Interdisciplinary activity guide on solid waste and natural resources.

Take Me to Your Litter
Grades: K–4
Pennsylvania Resource Council, 1978
25 West Third Street, P.O. Box 88
Media, PA 19063
215-565-9131
Bilingual story about littering with a song and instructions on how to build a model of the main character, a robot from outer space.

Teacher's Resource Guide for Solid Waste and Recycling Education
Grades: K–12
Association of Vermont Recyclers, 1989
P.O. Box 1244
Montpelier, VT 05602
802-229-1833
A comprehensive interdisciplinary curriculum and activity on solid waste.

Trash Conflicts: A Science and Social Studies Curriculum on the Ethics of Disposal
Grades: 5–7

Educators for Social Responsibility, 1993
23 Garden Street
Cambridge, MA 02138
617-492-1764
Includes suggestions for demonstrating disposal methods in the classroom and role-playing activities.

Waste Away
Grades: 4–8
Vermont Institute of Natural Sciences, 1989
P.O. Box 86
Woodstock, VT 05091
802-457-2779
Multidisciplinary activities investigate trash problems and solutions. Includes worksheets, handouts, trash survey and information for starting a school recycling program.

Waste Management Software
Grades: 9–12
Keep America Beautiful, 1987
Mill River Plaza, 9 West Broad Street
Stamford, CT 06902
203-323-8987
Programs teach and test various concepts relating to waste management through quizzes and games.

Waste in Place
Grades: K–8
Keep America Beautiful, 1990 (3rd ed.)
Mill River Plaza, 9 West Broad Street
Stamford, CT 06902
203-323-8987
Interdisciplinary program focusing on litter prevention and solid waste management issues.

Woodsy Resource Gold Mine
Grades: 4–8
Cornell University Resource Center, 1989
#7 Cornell Technology and Business Park
Ithaca, NY 14850
607-255-2091
Slide show introduces and examines waste management and the importance of reducing and recycling our garbage.

Waste Reduction

Come Along to Trash to Treasure Land
Grades: P–5
EHMI—Environmental Hazards Management Institute, 1993
10 Newmarket Road
Durham, NH 03824
603-868-1496
Coloring book and puzzles regarding recycling.

Composting to Reduce the Waste Stream: A Guide to Small Scale Food and Yard Waste Composting
Grades: 10–12
Northeast Regional Agricultural Engineering Service, 1991
152 Riley-Robb Hall, Cooperative Extension
Ithaca, NY 14853
607-255-7654
Guidebook for starting educational programs on composting. Covers the composting process, how to construct and maintain a compost pile and compost use.

Composting: Wastes to Resources
Grades: 3–12
Cornell University Resource Center, 1990
#7 Cornell Technology and Business Park
Ithaca, NY 14850
607-255-2091
Designed to help those who want to set up a composting project for youths. Includes procedure and design ideas.

Garbage Reincarnation
Grades: 4–12
Sonoma County Community Recycling, 1986
P.O. Box 1375
Santa Rosa, CA 95402
707-584-8666
Curriculum includes activities, glossary and a bibliography related to recycling and materials conservation.

Let's Reduce and Recycle
Grades: K–12
U.S. Environmental Protection Agency, 1990
Public Information Center, PM-211B,

401 M Street SW
Washington, DC 20460
202-475-7751
This curriculum covers problems associated with solid waste. Includes activities, glossary, list of state agencies and resources.

Reduce, Reuse, Recycle Alaska
Grades: K–12
Alaska Department of Environmental Conservation
Pollution Prevention Program, 1990
3601 C Street, Suite 1334
Juneau, AK 99503
907-563-6529
Includes student worksheets for outdoor exploration and a science-oriented activities handbook.

Solid Waste: From Problems to Solutions
Grades: 3–5
Illinois Department of Energy and Natural Resources, 1990
325 West Adams Street, Room 300
Springfield, IL 62704
217-785-2800
Background information and activities address the issue of solid waste management, source reduction, recycling, incineration and landfills.

A Week with Waste
Grades: K–12
California Integrated Waste Management Board, 1992
Office of Public Affairs and Education
8800 Cal Center Drive
Sacramento, CA 95826
918-255-2296
Activity packet on solid waste reduction, consumer product packaging, reusing and recycling and stewardship through personal choices.

The Wizard of Waste Environmental Education Kit
Grades: 2–3
California Department of Education, 1980
Bureau of Publications, Sales Unit,
P.O. Box 271
Sacramento, CA 95802
916-445-1260
Lessons, a filmstrip, a poster and tests introduce students to solid waste con-

cepts of identifying recyclable solid waste and improving personal habits.

Water

Adopting a Stream: A Northwest Washington Handbook
Grades: 7–12
Adopt-A-Stream Foundation, 1991
P.O. Box 5558
Everett, WA 98206
206-388-3487
Provides an overview of streams and their watersheds. Gives a detailed outline of adopt-a-stream projects that can be done anywhere.

All About Water
Grades: K–3
Metropolitan Water District of Southern California, 1991
Supervisor of Education Programs,
P.O. Box 54153
Los Angeles, CA 90054-0153
213-250-6739
Interdisciplinary activities related to water conservation, the water cycle and water use.

Always a River: Supplemental Environmental Education Curriculum on the Ohio River and Water
Grades: K–12
U.S. Environmental Protection Agency, 1991
26 West Martin Luther King Drive
Cincinnati, OH 45268
513-569-7771
Interactive, hands-on activities with background information designed to engage students in an investigation of the Ohio River.

Appreciating Your Great Lakes: A Guide for Developing Educational Projects
Grades: 6–12
Illinois/Indiana Sea Grant Program, Cooperative Extension Service, 1989
University of Illinois, 65 Mumford Hall
1301 West Gregory Drive
Urbana, IL 61501
217-333-9448
Activities about the Great Lakes and environmental issues.

Aquatic Activities for Youth
Grades: 3–7
David Green Youth Coastal Education Program, 1980
21 South Grove Street
East Aurora, NY 14052
716-652-7874
Introductory Leader's Guide with activities that include starting a fish aquarium, raising worms, calculating stream flow and more.

Breakthroughs: Strategies for Thinking: Water—Enough for Everyone?
Grades: 3–6
Zaner-Bloser, Inc., 1992
2200 West Fifth Avenue, P.O. Box 16764
Columbus, OH 43216-6764
800-421-3018
Lessons and activities about water use, water cycle, water problems and who is responsible for the world's water problems.

The California Water Story
Grades: 4–6
Water Education Foundation, 1992
717 K Street, Suite 517
Sacramento, CA 95814
916-444-6240
Helps students develop critical thinking and mapping and graphing skills through lessons, worksheets, tests, posters and a filmstrip/audio cassette.

Connection: The Living Planet: Water in Our World
Grades: 3–5
Ginn Publishing Canada, Inc., 1993
P.O. Box 261 Tonawanda
New York, NY 14151-0261
800-361-6128
Discusses the importance of water in our world, contemporary problems with water and possible solutions.

A Curriculum Activities Guide to Watershed Investigations and Environmental Studies
Grades: 9–12
Institute for Environmental Education, 1973
18554 Haskins Road
Chagrin Falls, OH 44023-1823
216-543-7303
Examines the hydrologic cycle, human

activity, ecological perspective and social and political factors through hands-on activities in the classroom and community.

Earth: The Water Planet
Grades: 6–10
National Science Teacher's Association, 1992
1742 Connecticut Avenue NW
Washington, DC 20009
202-328-5800
Students investigate how water shapes our planet and our daily lives through hands-on experiments, role-playing activities and water conservation.

Gee-Wow! Adventures in Water Education
Grades: 4–8
Ecology Center of Ann Arbor, 1991
417 Detroit Street
Ann Arbor, MI 48104
313-761-3186
Video with study guide containing suggested activities. Covers topics such as groundwater; water and the government and the trouble with trash.

Geography: Reflections on Water: Teacher's Handbook
Grades: K–12
National Geographic Society, 1992
17th and M Streets NW
Washington, DC 20036
800-368-2728
Activities, lesson plans and posters help students become aware of water issues that affect them directly.

The Great Lakes in My World
Grades: K–8
Lake Michigan Federation, 1989
59 East Van Buren, Suite 2215
Chicago, IL 60605
312-939-0838
Interdisciplinary activity workbook with stories, games, plays and maps introducing students to the Great Lakes environment, its history and geology.

Great Minds? Great Lakes!
Grades: 7–11
U.S. EPA—Great Lakes National Program Office, 1990
230 South Dearborn Street
Chicago, IL 60604
312-353-2117

Background information, discussion points and hands-on activities introduce the Great Lakes.

H2O—2010
Grades: 9–12
Water Education Foundation, 1992
717 K Street, Suite 517
Sacramento, CA 95814
916-444-6240
Designed to get students thinking about the issues that revolve around water and its use in California. Includes a video that is a great starting point.

Indiana's Water Riches
Grades: 4–8
Purdue University, 1992
Dept. 4-H/Youth, Media Distribution Center
301 South 2nd Street
West Lafayette, IN 47901-1232
317-494-6795
A video, activities, experiments and a board game focus on water issues.

A Journey Down the Colorado River Aqueduct
Grades: 5–8
Metropolitan Water District of Southern California, 1994
Supervisor of Education Programs
P.O. Box 54153
Los Angeles, CA 90054-0153
213-250-6739
A map of the aqueduct, a crossword puzzle and an activity about water use in the home.

Living in Water
Grades: 4–6
National Aquarium in Baltimore
Department of Education and Interpretation, 1989 (2nd ed.)
501 East Pratt Street
Baltimore, MD 21202-3194
410-576-3887
Lessons and worksheets offer scientific study of water, aquatic environment and life in both marine and freshwater habitats.

The Magic of Water
Grades: K–6
California Department of Water Resources, 1986
P.O. Box 942836

Sacramento, CA 94236-0001
916-653-1097
Hands-on water science activities.

Mississippi Waters
Grades: 7–11
Mississippi Headwaters Board, 1991
Cass County Court House, 300 Minnesota Avenue
Walker, MN 56484
218-547-3300
Includes a video and study guide with background information, maps, charts and photos that explore 10,000 years of the history and culture of the Mississippi River.

Our Great Lakes Connection
Grades: K–8
University of Wisconsin—Madison Environmental Resources Center, 1985
1450 Linden Drive
Madison, WI 53706
608-262-2106
Activities are designed to teach students about the Great Lakes. Includes maps, readings and game boards.

Peter's Magical Water Journey: A Flannel Board Story
Grades: 2–4
California Department of Water Resources, 1987
P.O. Box 942836
Sacramento, CA 94236-0001
916-653-1097
Teaches the importance of water, where it comes from and why we should use it wisely.

A Primer on Water: Questions and Answers
Grades: 5–8
Environment Canada, Enquiry Center, 1992 (3rd ed.)
Ottawa, Ontario, Canada K1A 0H3
819-997-2800
Students study water's physical characteristics, its availability above and below the ground plus how it is managed in Canada and the Great Lakes.

Project Water Science
Grades: 7–12
Water Education Foundation, 1991
717 K Street, Suite 517
Sacramento, CA 95814
916-444-6240

General science unit on the chemistry of water and how water relates to the environment. Includes lab experiments and activities and water trivia fact cards.

Project Waterworks: Teacher's Resource Workbook
Grades: 6–12
American Water Works Association, 1990
6666 West Quincy Avenue
Denver, CO 80235
303-974-7711
Computer-based curriculum with activities to explore water resource management, chemistry, water conservation and water science.

River Cutters
Grades: 6–9
Great Explorations in Math and Science, 1989
Lawrence Hall of Science
University of California—Berkeley
Berkeley, CA 94720
510-642-7771
Study of how erosion, river characteristics, pollution and humans have impacted on rivers. Students will chart rivers, construct dams and create toxic waste dumps.

Rivers Curriculum Project: Biology
Grades: 9–12
Southern Illinois University, 1993
Box 2222
Edwardsville, IL 62026
618-692-3799
Involves students forming a "River Watch" network and completing in-depth studies on local river systems for biology class.

Rivers Curriculum Project: Chemistry
Grades: 9–12
Southern Illinois University, 1993
Box 2222
Edwardsville, IL 62026
618-692-3799
Curriculum involves students forming a "River Watch" network and completing in-depth studies on local river systems for chemistry class.

Rivers Curriculum Project: Earth Science
Grades: 9–12

Southern Illinois University, 1993
Box 2222
Edwardsville, IL 62026
618-692-3799
Curriculum involves students forming a "River Watch" network and completing in-depth studies on local river systems for earth science class.

Rivers Curriculum Project: Geography

Grades: 9–12
Southern Illinois University, 1993
Box 2222
Edwardsville, IL 62026
618-692-3799
Curriculum involves students forming a "River Watch" network and completing in-depth studies on local river systems for geography class.

Rivers Curriculum Project: Language Arts

Grades: 9–12
Southern Illinois University, 1993
Box 2222
Edwardsville, IL 62026
618-692-3799
Curriculum involves students forming a "River Watch" network and completing in-depth studies on local river systems for language arts class.

Rivers and Streams Habitat Pac

Grades: 4–7
National Institute for Urban Wildlife, 1981
P.O. Box 3015
Shepardstown, WV 25443
304-876-6146
Students will examine water habitats, water conservation and allocation of water resources. Activities include a field trip to explore the area bordering streams and rivers and following a river.

Saving Our Planet Series: Water

Grades: 1–4
Good Apple, Inc., 1992
1204 Buchanan Street, Box 299
Carthage, IL 62321-0299
800-435-7234
Focuses on reading and a hands-on approach to the environmental problem of water pollution and conservation practices.

Saving Our Planet Series: Water

Grades: 4–7
Good Apple, Inc., 1992
1204 Buchanan Street, Box 299
Carthage, IL 62331-0299
800-435-7234
Focuses on reading and a hands-on approach to the environmental problem of water pollution and conservation practices.

Teacher's Guide for Hands-on Water Activities

Grades: 1–6
California Department of Water Resources, 1986
P.O. Box 942386
Sacramento, CA 94236-0001
916-653-1097
Experiments teach students about the technical aspects of water.

Water Activities to Encourage Responsibility

Grades: 4–6
Wisconsin Department of Natural Resources, 1992
Bureau of Information and Education
P.O. Box 7921
Madison, WI 53707
608-266-2711
Promotes water awareness through activities that include environmental career-role playing.

Water Activities Manual

Grades: 6–8
Ventura County Water Conservation Program, 1989
8005 Victoria Avenue
Ventura, CA 93009
805-654-2440
Water activities and discussions.

Water Education

Grades: K–6
International Office for Water Education, 1992
Utah Water Research Laboratory
Utah State University
Logan, UT 84322
801-750-3186
Background water information and activities include student experiments, teacher demonstrations, reference study and field experiences.

Water Fun

Grades: K–3
Los Angeles Department of Water and Power, 1982
P.O. Box 111, Room 1514
Los Angeles, CA 90051-0100
213-481-4085, ext. 6358
Booklet with word games, puzzles and stories about water. Teacher's Guide supplies background information and tips/ideas for activities.

Water Highways

Grades: 9–12
Metropolitan Water District of Southern California, 1990
Supervisor for Education Programs
P.O. Box 54153
Los Angeles, CA 90054-0153
213-250-6739
Provides an overview of the southern California water supply system. Lessons were developed for use in science classes.

Water: The Liquid of Life

Grade: 5
Illinois Environmental Protection Agency, 1991
2200 Churchill Road, P.O. Box 19276
Springfield, IL 62794-9276
217-782-3397
Lesson module covers water pollution, human dependency on water, the hydraulic cycle, water treatment and more.

Water Matters: Everyday, Everywhere, Every Way

Grades: K–12
Geography Education Program, 1993
1145 17th Street NW
Washington, DC 20036
202-775-6577
Covers the basics of the water cycle, issues of water quality and conservation.

Water Play

Grades: K–12
Project Water/East Bay Municipal Utility District, 1992
375 11th Street
Oakland, CA 94607
510-835-3000
Teaches students how they can conserve water and make a difference.

Water Precious Water

Grades: 2–6
Aims Education Foundation, 1988
5629 East Westover Street
P.O. Box 7766
Fresno, CA 93747
209-255-4094
Hands-on instructional curriculum
includes activities about water issues
and concepts.

Water Related Teaching Activities

Grades: K–12
ERIC: Clearinghouse for Science,
Mathematics and Environmental
Education, 1977
Ohio State University
1200 Chambers Road, Room 310
Columbus, OH 43212
614-292-6717
Experiment type activities that demon-
strate concepts relating to water in a
fun and motivational way.

Water Tradeoffs

Grades: 9–12
Metropolitan Water District of Southern
California, 1990
Supervisor of Education Programs
P.O. Box 54153
Los Angeles, CA 90054-0153
213-250-6739
Provides an overview of how water
management and distribution have
affected the economy of California.
Lessons are designed for social science
classes.

Water: A Unified Science Supplement

Grades: 9–12
University of New York, 1991
The State Education Department
Bureau of Curriculum
Albany, NY 12234
518-474-5992
Provides detailed information about
water, specifically in New York State.

Water for You and Me

Grades: K–4
The Central Utah Water Conservancy
District, 1990 (rev.)
355 West 1400 South
Orem, UT 84058

801-226-7100
Lessons and activities create an appreciation of water's role in human survival. Pre- and post-tests are provided.

Wet and Wild Water

Grades: 4–8
Indiana Department of Education,
1992
Room 229, State House
Indianapolis, in 46204-2798
317-232-9141
Crosscurricular activities about water.

Woods and Water

Grades: 4–6
Environmental Action Coalition, 1984
625 Broadway
New York, NY 10012
212-677-1601
Unique forestry curriculum focusing on
the connection between forests and
water supplies for large metropolitan
areas.

Coastal Ecology

Changing Chesapeake: An Introduction to the Natural and Cultural History of the Chesapeake Bay

Grades: 4–9
U.S. Fish and Wildlife Service, 1991
180 Admiral Cochrane Drive, Suite
535
Annapolis, MD 21401
410-974-3195
Includes illustrations, background
information, activities, discussion
questions, maps, diagrams and ideas
for follow-up activities.

Estuaries and Tidal Marshes Habitat Pac

Grades: 4–7
National Institute for Urban Wildlife,
1981
P.O. Box 3015
Shepardstown, WV 25443
304-876-6146
Students discover estuaries and
tidal/salt marshes and learn of their
importance to humans through
lessons, activities and poster.

Drinking Water

Drinking Water: Quality on Tap

Grades: 7–12
League of Women Voters of Michigan,
1991
200 Museum Drive
Lansing, MI 48933-1997
514-484-5383
Information about drinking water
sources and conservation. The packet
includes a video, study guide and
viewer handouts.

The Story of Drinking Water

Grades: 4–9
American Water Works Association,
1992
6666 West Quincy Avenue
Denver, CO 80235
303-974-7711
Includes information, class activities, a
comic book and activity worksheets on
topics of groundwater, the water cycle,
household plumbing and water conservation.

The Tapwater Tour

Grades: 6–9
LaMotte Company, 1989
P.O. Box 329
Chestertown, MD 21620
800-344-3100
Experiments for teaching the concepts
of water treatment and other compo-
nents of drinking water.

Groundwater

ERIC Reports: Groundwater Resources and Educational Activities for Teaching

Grades: 7–9
CBIS Federal, Inc., 1989
7420 Fullerton Rd., Suite 110
Springfield, VA 22153-2852
800-443-3742
Activities on groundwater.

The Groundwater Adventure

Grades: 5–9
New Dimension Media, 1987
85803 Lorane Highway
Eugene, OR 97405

800-288-4456
Examines industrial, agricultural and residential groundwater pollution, contamination prevention and groundwater cleanup.

Groundwater: A Critical Resource

Grades: 6–8
National Science Teacher's Association, 1993
1742 Connecticut Avenue NW
Washington, DC 20009
202-328-5800
Offers basic understanding of the hydrologic cycle and aquifers. Includes a poster with activities, facts and statistics about groundwater.

Groundwater: The Hidden Resource

Grades: K–6
U.S. Geological Survey/Branch of Distribution, 1992
P.O. Box 25286, Denver Federal Center
Denver, CO 80225
303-236-7477
A poster about groundwater with information and activities on the back side.

Groundwater Study Guide

Grades: 6–9
Wisconsin Department of Natural Resources, 1990
Bureau of Information and Education, P.O. Box 7921
Madison, WI 53707
608-266-2711
Activity sheets, diagrams, overhead projections, map and posters help students examine groundwater issues.

Groundwater: A Vital Resource, Student Activities

Grades: K–12
Tennessee Valley Authority, 1986
Water Quality Department Library
Haney Building, 2C, 1101 Market St.
Chattanooga, TN 37402-2081
615-751-7338
Activities aim to instill in students the value of groundwater. Topics covered include water distribution in soils, water quality and the community's impact.

Oceans/Seas

Guide to Marine Ecology Research

Grades: 9–12
Alameda County Office of Education, 1974
313 West Winton Avenue
Hayward, CA 94544-1198
510-887-0152
Examines ecological problems in bays and estuaries.

Marine Biology: Ecology of the Sea

Grades: K–8
Zephyr Press, 1992 (rev.)
3316 North Chapel Avenue, P.O. Box 13448
Tucson, AZ 85732-3448
602-322-5090
Activities (for independent study or classroom use) look at the relationship between organisms that make up the food chain and the mysteries of the ocean floor.

Marine Ecology Research Project: Elementary Education

Grades: K–6
Alameda County Office of Education, 1981
313 West Winton Avenue
Hayward, CA 94544-1198
510-887-0152
Interdisciplinary activities, experiments, arts projects and field trips on the marine environment.

Marine Ecology Research Project: Junior High Curriculum

Grades: 7–9
Alameda County Office of Education, 1981
313 West Winton Avenue
Hayward, CA 94544-1198
510-887-0152
Interdisciplinary lessons about the marine environment. The guide is filled with worksheets, activities, experiments, arts and crafts projects and field trips.

Nature Scope: Diving into Oceans

Grades: K–8
National Wildlife Federation, 1989
1412 Sixteenth Street NW
Washington, DC 20036-2266
800-432-6564
Hands-on interdisciplinary activities that encourage nature appreciation and responsible environmental decisions.

The Ocean Book

Grades: 3–8
Center for Marine Conservation, 1989
1725 Desales Street, Suite 500
Washington, DC 20036
202-429-5609
A comprehensive approach to the study of the ocean environment and marine life. The material is hands-on and broad in scope.

Our Only Earth Series: The Ocean Crisis

Grades: 4–12
Zephyr Press, 1990
3316 North Chapel Avenue, P.O. Box 13448
Tucson, AZ 85732-3448
602-322-5090
Provides an integrated science, language arts and social studies program concerning real-life issues and solutions. Part of a series.

The Problem's Deep

Grades: K–6
National Geographic Society, World Magazine, 1993
17th and M Streets NW
Washington, DC 20036
800-368-2728
Information and puzzles regarding ocean pollution.

Save Our Seas

Grades: K–12
Center for Marine Conservation, 1993
1725 Desales Street, Suite 500
Washington, DC 20036
202-429-5609
Addresses the importance of the marine environment, the problem of marine debris and how individuals can be part of the solution.

Water Pollution

Alaska Oil Spill Curriculum

Grades: K–3
Prince William Sound Science Center, 1990
P.O. Box 705

Cordova, AK 99574
907-424-5800
Hands-on independent and group activities with maps, diagrams and illustrations.

Alaska Oil Spill Curriculum
Grades: 4–6
Prince William Sound Science Center, 1990
P.O. Box 705
Cordova, AK 99574
907-424-5800
Hands-on independent and group activities with maps, diagrams and illustrations.

Alaska Oil Spill Curriculum
Grades: 7–12
Prince William Sound Science Center, 1990
P.O. Box 705
Cordova, AK 99574
907-424-5800
Hands-on independent and group activities with maps, diagrams and illustrations.

Beneath the Shell
Grades: 1–10
New Jersey Department of Environmental Protection, 1991
Office of Communications and Public Education, CN 402
Trenton, NJ 08625
609-777-4322
Information, classroom activities and field excursions explore human activity and New Jersey's waterways. Main focus is on nonpoint source pollution.

Breakthroughs: Strategies for Thinking: Are We Killing Our Lakes?
Grades: 3–6
Zaner-Bloser, Inc., 1992
2200 West Fifth Avenue, P.O. Box 16764
Columbus, OH 43216-6764
800-421-3018
Lessons cover the life cycles of lakes and what people can do to protect them.

Breakthroughs: Strategies for Thinking: The Muddy River, the Sticky Sea and Me?
Grades: 3–6

Zaner-Bloser, Inc., 1992
2200 West Fifth Avenue, P.O. Box 16764
Columbus, OH 43216-6764
800-421-3018
Lessons explain why we need clean water, how water gets polluted and some solutions to water pollution.

Clean Water: Student Information Kit
Grades: 5–8
America's Clean Water Foundation, 1991
750 First Street NE, Suite 911
Washington, DC 20002
202-898-0902
A curriculum on water issues.

A Curriculum Activities Guide to Water Pollution and Environmental Studies: Volumes 1, 2 and 3
Grades: 9–12
Institute for Environmental Education, 1973
18554 Haskins Road
Chagrin Falls, OH 44023-1823
216-543-7303
Students will study watersheds, social and political actions influencing environmental quality and human impact on these systems.

Environmental Resource Guide: Nonpoint Source Pollution Prevention
Grades: 6–8
Air and Waste Management Association, 1992
P.O. Box 2861
Pittsburgh, PA 15230-2861
412-232-3444
Factsheets and activities explore the relationship between land use and water quality, specifically nonpoint source water pollution.

Field Manual for Water Quality Monitoring
Grades: 5–12
William B. Stapp, 1992
2050 Delaware Avenue
Ann Arbor, MI 48103
Students will use a variety of data collection techniques to conduct water quality tests and use this information

to devise actions to raise the water quality in their own communities.

My World, My Water and Me!
Grades: 3–5
New Jersey Department of Environmental Protection, 199
Office of Communications and Public Education, CN 402
Trenton, NJ 08625
609-777-4322
Activities enhance student awareness of the waste water pollution problem through water analysis and evaluation, and encourage solutions.

Officer Snook
Grades: 1–4
7-Dippity, Inc., 1992
2550 Douglas Road, Suite 300-A
Coral Gables, FL 33134
305-661-8901
Looks at water pollution and its effect on animals, plants and humans. Includes both a slide show and video.

Oil Spill
Grades: 11–12
Ohio Sea Grant College Program, 1987
Ohio State University
1314 Kinnear Road
Columbus, OH 43212-1194
614-292-8949
Teacher and student guides with background information and activities concerning the causes and effects of oil spills and the methods used to clean them up.

Surface Water
Grades: 5–9
New Dimension Media, 1988
85803 Lorane Highway
Eugene, OR 97405
800-288-4456
Activities and lessons examine the water cycle, surface water, pollution, water quality issues and how to prevent water pollution.

Turning the Tide on Trash: A Learning Guide on Marine Debris
Grades: 5–8
U.S. Environmental Protection Agency, Office of Water, 1992
Public Information Center, PM-211B
401 M Street SW
Washington, DC 20460

202-475-7751

Activities teach about the sources and effects of marine debris.

Water Quality

Grades: 9–12
Metropolitan Water District of Southern California, 1990
Supervisor of Education Programs
P.O. Box 54153
Los Angeles, CA 90054-0153
213-250-6739
Lessons provide an overview of the southern California water supply system and a grasp of some factors that affect the quality of their water supply.

Water Quality Monitoring Program

Grades: 7–12
Pennsylvania Bureau of State Parks, 1985
Environmental Education and Interpretive Section
2150 Herr Street
Harrisburg, PA 17103-1626
800-673-2757
Designed for use in science classes. Lessons focus on the topic of water quality as it applies to a public water supply system.

Water Quality Series

Grades: 10–12
Tennessee Valley Authority
Environmental Education Section, 1992
Forestry Building, Ridgeway Road
Norris, TN 37828
615-632-1599
Describes equipment used by water quality professionals to collect samples and offers instructions for students to make their own. There are guidelines for organizing a cleanup.

Water, Water Everywhere

Grades: 7–12
Hach Company, 1991/1993
P.O. Box 389
Loveland, CO 80539
800-227-4224
Combines readings, discussions and hands-on science activities to explain the variables affecting water quality.

Water Wise

Grades: 5–6
New York Department of Natural

Resources, 1989
#7 Resource Center, Cornell University
Ithaca, NY 14850
607-255-2090
Focuses on the water cycle, the aquatic environment and the causes, effects and prevention of water pollution.

Water Treatment

How Do We Treat Our Wastewater?

Grades: 5–8
U.S. Geological Survey/Branch of Distribution, 1992
P.O. Box 25286, Denver Federal Center
Denver, CO 80225
303-236-7477
Offers activities and a poster showing how wastewater is treated.

Wastewater Treatment

Grades: 7–9
Water Pollution Control Federation, 1989
Public Education Department
601 Wythe Street
Alexandria, VA 22314-1994
800-666-0206
Wastewater treatment activities, demonstrations, tests and reading assignments. Includes a video to be used with the lessons.

Wastewater Treatment Unit

Grades: 7–9
New Dimension Media, 1987
85803 Lorane Highway
Eugene, OR 97405
800-288-4456
Activities, lessons and a video examine the complete wastewater treatment process.

Wildlife

The City Kid's Field Guide

Grades: K–6
Vermont Institute of Natural Sciences, 1989
P.O. Box 86
Woodstock, VT 05091
802-457-2779
Information and activities for students

to study animal habitats, adaptations, life cycles and designs of nature.

Classroom Creature Culture

Grades: K–12
National Science Teacher's Association, 1986
1742 Connecticut Avenue NW
Washington, DC 20009
202-328-5800
Explains how dozens of species have learned to survive in their human-made surroundings. Tips for finding and observing wildlife.

A Curriculum Activities Guide to Birds, Bugs, Dogs and Weather and Environmental Studies

Grades: K–12
Institute for Environmental Education, 1973
18554 Haskins Road
Chagrin Falls, OH 44023-1823
216-543-7303
Uses birds, bugs and dogs to study the environment. Activities advance from simple observations to bird banding and operating a weather station.

Developed Lands: Restoring and Managing Wildlife Habitats

Grades: 5–8
National Institute for Urban Wildlife, 1991
P.O. Box 3015
Shepardstown, WV 25443
304-876-6146
Data and activity sheets offer practical approaches to enhancing the recreational, aesthetic, educational and ecological value of urban, suburban and other developed lands.

Helping Wildlife: Working with Nature

Grades: 3–8
Wildlife Management Institute, 1990
1101 14th Street NW, Suite 725
Washington, DC 20005
202-371-1808
Teaches the basic ecological concepts associated with natural resources and wildlife management. Also examines what wildlife managers do.

Hunting and Wildlife Management Issue Pac

Grades: 4–7

National Institute for Urban Wildlife, 1981
P.O. Box 3015
Shepardstown, WV 25443
304-876-6146
Introduces wildlife survival, the role of predators in natural ecosystems and how biologists estimate wildlife populations.

Make Room for Monsters and Wildlife on the Land
Grades: 4–12
Soil and Water Conservation Society, 1982
7515 NE Ankeny Road
Ankeny, IA 50021-9764
800-THE-SOIL
Activities designed to help teach the basic concepts of wildlife and land conservation. Includes a cartoon and teacher's guide.

Nature Puzzlers
Grades: 9–12
Libraries Unlimited, Inc.
Teacher Ideas Press, 1989
P.O. Box 3988
Englewood, CO 80155-3988
800-237-6124
Mental puzzles encourage students to use scientific methods and cognitive skills to find answers to strange, mysterious or bizarre occurrences in the natural world.

Nature Scope: Wild and Crafty
Grades: K–8
National Wildlife Federation, 1988
1412 Sixteenth Street NW
Washington, DC 20036-2266
800-432-6564
Hands-on interdisciplinary activities that encourage nature appreciation and responsible environmental decisions.

Predators of the World
Grades: 4–10
Elsa Wild Animal Appeal, 1977
P.O. Box 4572
North Hollywood, CA 91617-0572
818-761-8387
Factual information, activities and posters on predatory animals.

Project WILD
Grades: K–12
Project WILD, 1983

5430 Grosvenor Lane
Bethesda, MD 20814
301-493-5447
Teaches students about people, wildlife and the environment. Activities are designed for easy integration into school subjects and different skill levels.

Project WILD (elementary)
Grades: K–6
Project WILD, 1987
5430 Grosvenor Lane
Bethesda, MD 20814
301-493-5447
This interdisciplinary program emphasizes wildlife management, conservation and ecological systems while promoting awareness, appreciation and responsible behavior for the environment.

Project WILD (secondary)
Grades: 7–12
Project WILD, 1987
5430 Grosvenor Lane
Bethesda, MD 20814
301-493-5447
This interdisciplinary program emphasizes wildlife management, conservation and ecological systems while promoting awareness, appreciation and responsible behavior for the environment.

The Web of Life
Grades: 1–6
American Society for the Prevention of Cruelty to Animals (ASPCA), 1993
424 East 92nd Street
New York, NY 10128
212-876-7700 ext. 4400
This easy to use lesson plan instills in children a respect for all animals.

Wildlife Conflicts Issue Pac
Grades: 4–7
National Institute for Urban Wildlife, 1990
P.O. Box 3015
Shepardstown, WV 25443
304-876-6146
Examines what happens between wildlife and humans. Introduces students to the conflicts that can occur between wildlife and people, why they arise and how to reduce or avoid these conflicts through appropriate management plans.

Wildlife Trade Education Kit
Grades: 3–12
World Wildlife Fund, 1989
P.O. Box 4866, Hampden Post Office
Baltimore, MD 21211
301-338-6951
Activities designed to teach the basic concepts of wildlife and land conservation as a part of the on-going curriculum.

Animals

Animals in Action
Grades: 5–9
Great Explorations in Math and Science, 1986
Lawrence Hall of Science
University of California—Berkeley
Berkeley, CA 94720
510-642-7771
Provides activities for humanely observing, investigating and experimenting with the patterns and puzzles of animal behavior.

Animals in the Classroom
Grades: K–12
Addison Wesley Publishing, 1989
Jacob Way
Reading, MA 01867
800-548-4885
Provides activities for responsible and humane ways to observe, investigate and experiment with the patterns and puzzles of animal behavior.

Animal Defenses
Grades: P–2
Great Explorations in Math and Science, 1986
Lawrence Hall of Science
University of California—Berkeley
Berkeley, CA 94720
510-642-7771
Explores why and how animals have to protect themselves from predators.

Best Friends
Grades: K–6
AKC Public Education Department, 1990
51 Madison Avenue
New York, NY 10010
800-152-8355
Activities focus on students' responsibilities to their pets, to each other, to their families and to their community.

Biological Diversity: Makes a World of Difference

Grades: 4–6
The National Park Service, 1989
Midwest Regional Office
1709 Jackson Street
Omaha, NE 68102-2571
402-221-3471
Contains hands-on activities designed to make children aware of the importance of maintaining a biologically diverse world.

Build a Bat House

Grades: 6–12
Canadian Wildlife Federation, 1990
2740 Queensview Drive
Ottawa, ON, Canada K2B 1A2
613-721-2286
Instructions for building a bat house, taking a few hours and using some simple tools. Includes some facts about bats.

Case Study: Wildlife on the Road

Grades: 7–12
Current Affairs Films, 1979
346 Ethan Allan Highway, P.O. Box 426
Ridgefield, CT 06877
203-431-0421
Filmstrip and booklet explaining how roads have a profound impact on animals, both positive and negative.

Discovering Wolves: A Nature Activity Book

Grades: K–6
Dog-Eared Publications, 1990 (4th edition)
P.O. Box 620863
Middleton, WI 53562-0863
608-831-1410
Contains background information and word and picture games on wolves.

Educator's Activity Book About Bats

Grades: 6–12
Bat Conservation International, 1991
P.O. Box 162603
Austin, TX 78716
512-327-9721
Activities about bats.

Environmental Awareness: Wildlife

Grades: 6–12

University of Connecticut Cooperative Extensions Services, 1993
The University of Connecticut
Storrs, CT 06268
203-486-3336
Activities describe basic principles and ways to study wildlife.

Mapping Animal Movements

Grades: 5–9
Great Explorations in Math and Science, 1987
Lawrence Hall of Science
University of California—Berkeley
Berkeley, CA 94720
510-642-7771
Students explore loss of animal habitat due to logging, farming, industry, recreation, pollution and other factors through research on movement patterns of wild animals.

Mountain Gorilla Preservation in Our Endangered World

Grades: 7–9
Diane Fossey Gorrila Foundation, 1992
45 Inverness Drive East, Suite B
Englewood, CO 80112-5480
303-790-2349
Contains preplanning and teaching activities, interdisciplinary projects and various resources for studying mountain gorillas.

Nature Scope: Amazing Mammals, Parts 1 and 2

Grades: K–8
National Wildlife Federation, 1986
1412 Sixteenth Street NW
Washington, DC 20036-2266
800-432-6564
Interdisciplinary hands-on activities encourage nature appreciation and responsible environmental decisions.

North American Predators

Grades: K–12
Elsa Wild Animal Appeal, 1976
P.O. Box 4572
North Hollywood, CA 91617-0572
unlisted
Studies groups of animals through projects, games, group activities and a large wall poster "The Role of the Predator."

Wonder of Wolves: A Story and Activities

Grades: 3–5
Roberts Rinehart, Inc., Publishers, 1989
5455 Spine Road, Mezzanine
Boulder, CO 80301
303-652-2921
Fictional story about the bond between Indians and wolves, plus activities that can be done at school or home.

Birds

Bluebirds in New York: 4-H Members' Guide

Grades: 4–8
Cornell Cooperative Extension, 1989
214 Central Avenue
White Plains, NY 10606
914-285-4620
Activities include instructions on building a nesting box and observing bluebird behavior. A crossword puzzle is included.

A Home for Pearl

Grades: 3–5
U.S. Fish and Wildlife Service, Publications Unit, 1993
Arlington Square Building, Room 130
18th and C Streets NW
Washington, DC 20240
202-208-5634
Activities and a video that teach about wildlife habitats.

Migratory Birds Issue Pac

Grades: 4–7
National Institute for Urban Wildlife, 1981
P.O. Box 3015
Shepardstown, WV 25443
304-876-6146
Students learn about bird migration, how they navigate, how to identify birds in flight and play a board game charting the migration of whooping cranes.

Nature Scope: Birds, Birds, Birds

Grades: K–8
National Wildlife Federation, 1985
1412 Sixteenth Street NW
Washington, DC 20036-2266
800-432-6564

Interactive hands-on activities encourage nature appreciation and responsible environmental decisions.

Fish/Aquatic Life

Discovering Salmon: A Learning Activity Book
Grades: K–6
Dog-Eared Publications, 1990 (4th printing)
P.O. Box 620863
Middleton, WI 53562-0863
608-831-1410
Contains background information, word and picture games about salmon.

F.I.S.H. Habitat Education Program
Grades: K–12
F.I.S.H. Habitat Education Program, 1992
2501 SW First Avenue, Suite 200
Portland, OR 97201-4752
503-326-7025
Articles, resource lists, brochures, lessons and activities on fish habitats.

Fish Ways (Elementary)
Grades: K–8
Canadian Ministry of Natural Resources
Fisheries Education Unit, 1991
5th Floor, ICI House
90 Shepard Avenue East
Toronto, Ontario, Canada M2N 3A1
416-314-2000
Teacher's manual of activities on fish and fishery management for primary/junior level classes.

Fish Ways (Secondary)
Grades: 7–12
Canadian Ministry of Natural Resources
Fisheries Education Unit, 1991
5th Floor, ICI House
90 Shepard Avenue East
Toronto, Ontario, Canada M2N 3A1
416-314-2000
Teacher's manual of activities on fish and fishery management for secondary level classes.

Great Lakes Fishing in Transition
Grades: 6–8
Michigan Sea Grant College Program,

1984
2200 Bonisteel Boulevard
Ann Arbor, MI 48109
313-764-1138
An interdisciplinary problem-solving, action-oriented curriculum that explores the Great Lakes through an in-depth study of its fishery.

Lake Erie...Build a Fish to Scale!
Grades: K–6
Ohio Sea Grant College Program, 1991
Ohio State University
1314 Kinnear Road
Columbus, OH 43212-1194
614-292-8949
Teaches about the different parts of a fish, how to assemble a fish model and classify a fish according to various fish characteristics.

Mapping Fish Habitats
Grades: 5–10
Great Explorations in Math and Science, 1987
Lawrence Hall of Science
University of California—Berkeley
Berkeley, CA 94720
510-642-7771
Provides activities for building, maintaining and observing a classroom aquarium.

Nutrients in the Great Lakes
Grades: 11–12
Ohio Sea Grant College Program, 1991
Ohio State University
1314 Kinnear Road
Columbus, OH 43212-1194
614-292-8949
Students learn to simulate aquatic habitats using lake water and goldfish in glass jars and observe the effects of nutrient loading and nutrient limitation on aquatic life.

Project WILD Aquatic
Grades: K–12
Project WILD, 1983, 1987
5430 Grosvenor Lane
Bethesda, MD 20814
301-493-5447
Designed to involve students with creative and engaging hands-on activities for individual and group learning.

Save Our Schools
Grades: 3–6

F.I.S.H. Habitat Education Program, 1992
2501 SW First Avenue, Suite 200
Portland, OR 97201-4752
503-326-7025
Lessons and activities focus on fish habitat preservation, specifically the impacts of wetland loss, pollution and dams.

Insects

Butterflies Abound
Grades: K–4
Addison Wesley Alternative Publishing Company, 1993
P.O. Box 10888
Palo Alto, CA 94303-9843
415-854-0300
An integrated curriculum that follows the caterpillar metamorphose into a butterfly.

Butterflies and Moths
Grades: 3–6
Delta Education, Inc., 1988
P.O. Box 915
Hudson, NH 03051
603-889-8899
Activities and worksheets help students observe the growth and development of butterflies through a series of stages.

Buzzing a Hive
Grades: 1–3
Great Explorations in Math and Science, 1987
Lawrence Hall of Science
University of California—Berkeley
Berkeley, CA 94720
510-642-7771
Activities and lessons allow students to explore the honeybee's social behavior, communicating style and hive environment.

Earthworms
Grades: 6–10
Great Explorations in Math and Science, 1989
Lawrence Hall of Science
University of California—Berkeley
Berkeley, CA 94720
510-642-7771
Students observe, measure, predict,

interpret and infer a variety of information about earthworms.

Family Science Adventure Kit: Western Backyard Jungles

Grades: 2–5
Acorn Naturalists, 1991
17300 East 17th Street, Suite J-236
Tustin, CA 92680
714-838-4888
Contains everything necessary for students to explore a backyard garden or local park and discover all the creatures (especially insects) that live there.

Hide a Butterfly

Grades: P–K
Great Explorations in Math and Science, 1986
Lawrence Hall of Science
University of California—Berkeley
Berkeley, CA 94720
510-642-7771
Students will create a mural of paper flowers, birds and butterflies and learn about butterflies through observation, comparison and matching.

Nature Scope: Incredible Insects

Grades: K–8
National Wildlife Federation, 1984
1412 Sixteenth Street NW
Washington, DC 20036-2266
800-432-6564
Interdisciplinary hands-on activities encourage students to make responsible environmental decisions with regard to nature.

Nature Scope: Incredible Insects Discovery Pac

Grades: K–8
National Wildlife Federation, 1988
1412 Sixteenth Street NW
Washington, DC 20036-2266
800-432-6564
Interdisciplinary hands-on activities encourage students to make responsible environmental decisions with regard to nature.

Teacher and Student Insect Identification Study Guide

Grades: 6–12
Young Entomologist's Society, Inc., 1991
1915 Peggy Place

Lansing, MI 48910-2553
517-887-0499
A study guide and concise reference for insect identification.

Things that Creep and Crawl

Grades: K–12
Instructor Magazine, 1993
555 Broadway
New York, NY 10012-3999
800-544-2917
Students will observe earthworms, arthropods and other insects and discover why these species are plentiful in the spring.

Marine Mammals

Discovering Marine Mammals: A Learning and Activity Book

Grades: K–6
Dog-Eared Publications, 1990
P.O. Box 620863
Middleton, WI 53562-0863
608-831-1410
Contains background information and word and picture games about marine mammals.

Marine Mammals of the World

Grades: 3–6
Elsa Wild Animal Appeal, 1986
P.O. Box 4572
North Hollywood, CA 91617-0572
818-761-8387
Newsprint booklets and a poster featuring the great whales, dolphins, porpoises, seals, sea lions, walrus, and manatee.

Whale Preservation

Grades: 5–9
S & S Learning Materials Limited, 1993
P.O. Box 306
Niagara Falls, NY 14302
800-463-6367
Current facts, lesson plans and activities address the conservation and preservation of whales, dolphins and porpoises.

Whales of the World

Grades: 4–10
Whale Adoption Project, 1990
634 North Falmouth Highway

P.O. Box 388
North Falmouth, NY 02556
508-548-8328
Whales, dolphins and porpoises are introduced through activity sheets that involve reading comprehension, analytical thinking and creative writing.

Wyland the Artist and "Save the Whales" Workbook

Grades: 3–12
Suzanne Garnier—Weythman Productions, 1992
19700 Fairchild, Suite 300
Irvine, CA 92715
714-660-9223
Workbook with interdisciplinary activities and questions supplement a video that portrays people who are doing something to create positive changes.

Reptiles/ Amphibians

Frog Math: Predict, Ponder, Play

Grades: K–3
Great Explorations in Math and Science, 1992
Lawrence Hall of Science
University of California—Berkeley
Berkeley, CA 94720
510-642-7771
Students learn to observe, predict, describe, classify, estimate and develop strategies with frogs that turn into mathematical principles at the touch of a hand.

Nature Scope: Digging into Dinosaurs

Grades: K–8
National Wildlife Federation, 1984
1412 Sixteenth Street NW
Washington, DC 20036-2266
800-432-6564
Interdisciplinary hands-on activities encourage students to appreciate nature and to make responsible environmental decisions.

Nature Scope: Let's Hear It for Herps and Reptiles

Grades: K–8
National Wildlife Federation, 1987
1412 Sixteenth Street NW
Washington, DC 20036-2266

800-432-6564
Interdisciplinary hands-on activities encourage students to appreciate nature and to make responsible environmental decisions.

EDUCATOR REFERENCES

Acorn Naturalists: 1993–94 Field Guide to Science and Environmental Education Resources
Acorn Naturalists, 1993
17300 East 17th Street, Suite J-236
Tustin, CA 92680
714-838-4888
Descriptive reviews and photographs of 726 inexpensive, hands-on resources for science and environmental education programs.

Addendum to Green Print for Minnesota Schools: A Guide for Integrating Environmental Education
Minnesota Department of Environmental Education, 1993
Capitol Square Building
550 Cedar Street
St. Paul, MN 55155
612-297-2228
Provides teachers with the methods to integrate environmental education into their curriculum. It uses an outcome-based philosophy and methods.

Alternative Energy: A Guide to Free Information for Educators
Center for Renewable Resources 1985
1001 Connecticut Avenue NW, Suite 638
Washington, DC 20036
202-466-6880
A directory of free education materials including both lessons and nontechnical background references on energy.

Bergen County Recycling Marshal's Program for Elementary Schools
Bergen County Utilities Authority, 1987

P.O. Box 122, Foot of Mehrhof Road
Little Ferry , NJ 07643
201-641-5341
This manual was developed to help school administrators, teachers and/or parents to set up a recycling program tailored to meet their specific needs.

California Endangered Species Resource Guide
California Department of Education, 1993
Bureau of Publications, Sales Unit, P.O. Box 271
Sacramento, CA 95812-0271
916-445-1490
Provides a list of endangered, rare and threatened plants and animals as well as government agencies and organizations involved in species preservation.

California Environmental Education Guide (Grades K–3)
Alameda County Office of Education, 1988
313 West Winton Avenue
Hayward, CA 94544-1198
510-887-0152
This guide provides teachers of kindergarten through 3rd grade with background information, program structure and activities for environmental education.

California Environmental Education Guide (Grades 4–6)
Alameda County Office of Education, 1988
313 West Winton Avenue
Hayward, CA 94544-1198
510-887-0152
This guide provides 4th- through 6th-grade teachers with background information, program structure and activities for environmental education.

California Environmental Education Guide (Grades 7–9)
Alameda County Office of Education, 1988
313 West Winton Avenue
Hayward, CA 94544-1198
510-887-0152
This guide provides 7th- through 9th-grade teachers with background information, program structure and activities for environmental education.

California Environmental Education Guide (Grades 10–12)
Alameda County Office of Education, 1988
313 West Winton Avenue
Hayward, CA 94544-1198
510-887-0152
This guide provides 10th- through 12th-grade teachers with background information, program structure and activities for environmental education.

The Canadian Environmental Education Catalog
Pembina Institute for Appropriate Development, 1991
Box 7558 Drayton Valley
Alberta, Canada T0E 0M0
403-542-6272
A complete listing of Canadian environmental education resources available.

Catalog of Aquatic Science Education
California Aquatic Science Education Consortium, 1993
Department of Education
University of California–Santa Barbara
Santa Barbara, CA 93106
805-893-2739
This catalog contains information on products and services offered by members of the California Aquatic Science Education Consortium.

Catalog of Water Quality Educational Materials
Tennessee Valley Authority, 1991
Water Quality Department Library, Haney Building 2C
1101 Market Street
Chattanooga, TN 37402-2081
615-751-7338
Lists many free brochures, factsheets, pamphlets, curriculum materials and posters available from TVA.

Clearing Magazine: Environmental Education in the Pacific Northwest
Creative Educational Networks
19600 South Molalla Avenue
Oregon City, OR 97045
503-656-0155
Designed to be a source of information and inspiration for developing in students an awareness and understanding of our environment.

Clearinghouse for Science, Mathematics and Environmental Education (ERIC)

Ohio State University
College of Education and School of Natural Resources
1200 Chambers Road, 3rd Floor
Columbus, OH 43212
800-USE-ERIC
ERIC is a system of 16 clearinghouses for science, math and environmental education materials (EE).

Coastal and Marine Educational Resources Directory for the San Francisco Bay Area

California Coastal Commission, 1990
45 Fremont, Suite 2000
San Francisco, CA 94105-2219
415-904-5200
A guide to organizations that provide information and resources on marine and coastal education.

Community Education: A Resource and Planning Guide

Wisconsin Department of Public Instruction, 1992
Publication Sales Drawer 179
Milwaukee, WI 53293-0179
800-243-8782
Offers information on how to set up an active community education program.

Computer-Aided Environmental Education

North American Association for Environmental Education (NAAEE), 1990
P.O. Box 400
Troy, OH 45374
513-339-6835
Contains articles organized into 4 major content areas: environmental hypermedia (including interactive videodisks), environmental simulation/modeling, interactive software and telecommunications.

The Council for Environmental Education

University of Reading
London Road
Reading, UK RG1 5AQ
Provides a national resource center and reference library available to members of the organization, researchers and environmental educators.

Current Literature and Curriculum Guides

Institute for Environmental Education
18554 Haskins Road
Chagrin Falls, OH 44023-1823
216-543-7303
A list of educational materials offered by the Institute for Environmental Education.

The Daedalus Education Foundation

Daedalus Education Foundation
12702 Via Cortina, Suite 201B
Del Mar, CA 92014
619-793-0411
An educational organization dedicated to training individuals and groups to care for the environment.

Designing an Environmental Curriculum: A Process

University of New York, 1984
The State Education Department
Bureau of Curriculum Development
Albany, NY 12234
518-474-5890
Offers a process to cut through the bewildering mass of approaches, information and resources that have amassed concerning the environment.

Directory of Great Lakes Educational Materials

International Joint Commission, Great Lakes Regional Office, 1991
Information Services
P.O. Box 32869
Detroit, MI 48232-2869
313-226-2170
This directory identifies materials that can be used in teaching about the Great Lakes ecosystem.

A Directory of Selected Environmental Education Materials

IIED-NA World Resources Institute, 1988
1709 New York Avenue NW, Suite 700
Washington, DC 20006
202-638-6300
Provides sources of readily available materials that may be used to plan education programs on conservation.

Discovery Network's Educator Guide

Destination Discovery, 1993
7700 Wisconsin Avenue NW
Bethesda, MD 20814
800-321-1832
A guide to the education programs offered on the Discovery Channel and activities that teachers can do with their classes.

Earth Keepers

The Institute for Earth Education, 1987
P.O. Box 288
Warrenville, IL 60555
The goal of the Earthkeepers program is to turn out youngsters who possess some basic ecological understanding and good feelings about the earth.

Ecoline: Together Foundation for Global Unity

University of Vermont Environmental Program
130 South Willard Street
Burlington, VT 05401
802-862-2030
Information on the Ecoline program that includes a database logging the efforts and results of environmental and humanitarian projects around the world.

EcoNet: The Environmental Computer Network

Institute for Global Communications
18 de Bloom Street
San Francisco, CA 94107
415-442-0220
EcoNet is a computer network for individuals and organizations that want to stay on top of worldwide environmental issues.

Educating Young People About Water: A Guide to Goals and Resources

University of Wisconsin–Madison
Institute for Environmental Studies
550 North Park Street, Room 15
Science Hall
Madison, WI 53706
608-263-31-85
This guide is for professionals who design and develop water quality training programs and curricula and for coordinators of water education programs.

557

Electricity in Education
Edison Electric Institute, 1992
701 Pennsylvania Avenue NW
Washington, DC 20004-2696
202-508-5000
Describes a series of 8 publications
that provide students with a wide variety of simple experiments that teach
them about electricity.

**Elementary Teachers Guide to Free
Curriculum Materials, 1991**
Educators Progress Services, Inc.,
1991
214 Center Street
Randolph, WI 53956
414-326-3126
Intended to help teachers select current
and relevant materials. This guide
includes a section specifically on environmental education.

**Elementary Teachers Guide to Free
Curriculum Materials, 1992**
Educators Progress Services, Inc.,
1992
214 Center Street
Randolph, WI 53956
414-326-3126
Intended to help teachers select current
and relevant materials. This guide
includes a section specifically on environmental education.

**Elementary Teachers Guide to Free
Curriculum Materials, 1993**
Educators Progress Services, Inc.,
1993
214 Center Street
Randolph, WI 53956
414-326-3126
Intended to help teachers select current
and relevant materials. This guide
includes a section specifically on environmental education.

**Energy Education
Resources**
Energy Information Administration,
National Energy Information Center
U.S. Department of Energy, 1994
Washington, DC 20585
202-586-8800
A list of available free or low-cost
energy related education materials for
primary and secondary students and
educators. This list is updated once a
year.

Environmental Connections
Earth Information Center
P.O. Box 387
Springfield, IL 62705-0387
A magazine that is published bimonth-
ly during the school year. The maga-
zine is a resource full of environmental
information for educators.

**Environmental Education About
the Rainforest**
University of Michigan, School of
Natural Resources, 1984
Wildland Management Center
430 East University
Ann Arbor, MI 48109
313-764-0478
A handbook for educators to teach the
values of tropical moist forests.

**Environmental Education
Bibliography: Resources for the
Elementary Teacher in the
Outdoors Classroom**
Environmental Institute for
Technology Transfer, 1994
University of Texas
Box 19050, Arlington Geoscience
Building, Room 142
Arlington,TX 76019-0050
817-273-2300
Helps teachers access environmental
education materials.

**Environmental Education
Compendium for Integrated Waste
Management**
California Integrated Waste
Management, 1993
Office of Public Affairs and Education
8800 Cal Center Drive
Sacramento, CA 95826
916-323-4388
A compendium of integrated waste
management educational materials
that explain the strengths and weak-
nesses of existing waste management
curricula.

**Environmental Education
Compendium for Water Resources**
California Department of Water
Resources, 1992
P.O. Box 942386
Sacramento, CA 94236-0001
916-653-1097
A compendium of water education
materials that explain the strengths

and weaknesses of existing water
resources curricula.

**Environmental Education
Compendium for Energy Resources**
California Energy Extension Service,
1992
1400 Tenth Street, Room 209
Sacramento, CA 95814
916-323-4388
A compendium of energy educational
materials that explain the strengths
and weaknesses of existing energy
resources curricula.

**Environmental Education Guide
for Teachers**
Institute for Environmental Education,
1974
18554 Haskins Road
Chagrin Falls, OH 44023-1823
216-543-7303
The material is organized as suggestions to teachers on how they might
integrate community studies into their
present courses.

**Environmental Education in the
Portland Area**
Portland Metropolitan Service District
(METRO), 1991
600 NE Grand Avenue
Portland, OR 97232
503-797-1700
This report provides information on the
status of environmental education programs in the Portland metropolitan
area.

**Environmental Education for
Preschoolers**
Dr. Ruth Wilson
Bowling Green State University
Bowling Green, OH 43403
A network of over 300 individuals
interested in linking young children
and the world of nature.

**Environmental Education
Materials for Teachers of Young
People (Grades K–12)**
U.S. Environmental Protection Agency,
1991
Public Information Center, PM-211B
401 M Street SW
Washington, DC 20460
202-475-7751
A list of materials available from pri-

vate and public sector organizations that was compiled by the U.S. Environmental Protection Agency.

Environmental Education Resource Guide
Friends of the Earth, 1991
218 D Street SE
Washington, DC 20003
202-544-2600
A guide to various environmental education programs and resources.

Environmental Education: Teacher Resource Handbook
The Kraus Organization Limited, 1993
358 Saw Mill River Road
Millwood, NY 10546-1035
914-762-2200
Provides information on the background of environmental education (EE) curriculum, as well as information on publications, standards and special EE materials for K–12.

Environmental Media Catalog
Environmental Media, 1994
P.O. Box 1016
Chapel Hill, NC 27514
919-933-3003
A comprehensive field guide to the education media and production and distribution services offered by environmental media.

EPA Journal
U.S. Environmental Protection Agency, 1991
Office of Communications and Public Affairs
Washington, DC 20460
202-475-7751
The September/October 1991 issue focuses on environmental education. It looks at the EPA's mandate on promoting environmental education.

Essential Leanings in Environmental Education
North American Association for Environmental Education (NAAEE), 1990
P.O. Box 400
Troy, OH 45373
513-339-6835

Covers concepts necessary for environmental literacy and is intended to help design and review educational activities and programs that teach about the environment.

Florida Resources in Environmental Education (FREE)
Florida Department of Education, 1994
325 West Gaines Street
Tallahassee, FL 32399-0400
904-488-7451
Is an on-line clearinghouse of Florida-based environmental education material, programs and information. All services are free to Florida teachers.

The 4-H Traveling Energy Troupe Final Report
North Carolina Alternative Energy Corporation Community Program, 1988
P.O. Box 12699
Research Triangle Park, NC 27709
919-549-9046
A report on the impact of a play about energy performed by a touring theater group. Information on how the show was produced is provided.

Getting Started: A Guide to Bringing Environmental Education into Your Classroom
National Consortium for Environmental Education and Training, 1994
School of Natural Resources and Environment
University of Michigan
Ann Arbor, MI 48109-1115
313-763-1312
A collection of stories about everyday teachers who initiated not-so-everyday environmental programs in their classrooms and schools.

Global Education: Entry Points into the Curriculum
Alberta Global Education Project
11010 142 Street
Edmonton, Alberta, Canada T5N 2RI
403-453-2411
For teachers and librarians who want to integrate global education concepts into existing curricula.

Global Rivers Environmental Education Network (GREEN)
216 South State Street, Suite 4
Ann Arbor, MI 48104
313-761-8142
Describes the Global Rivers Environmental Education Network (GREEN), a group of citizens from all over the world sharing their concerns about water quality on a computer network.

A Glossary of Selected Terms of Conservation, Ecology and Resource Use
Missouri Department of Conservation Education Programs, 1992
P.O. Box 180
Jefferson City, MO 65102-0180
314-751-4115
An assortment of explanations and interpretations for words most likely to appear in publications not intented for professional use.

Great Teaching in the One Computer Classroom
Tom Snyder Productions, Inc., 1991
90 Sherman Street
Cambridge, MA 02140
617-876-4433
Shows how one computer can help ease the teacher's administrative burden, enliven classroom presentations, spark discussions, foster cooperative learning and much more.

Greatest Hits of Environmental Education
California Department of Education 1993
Bureau of Publications, Sales Unit, P.O. Box 271
Sacramento, CA 95812-0271
916-445-1490
This guide offers advice on how to write environmental education program grants.

Green Guide
Sierra Club, 1991
730 Polk Street
Berkeley, CA 94109
415-776-2211
Lists approximately 500 resources that cover close to 72 topics. An educator's

guide to free or inexpensive environmental materials.

Green Print for Minnesota: State Plan for Environmental Education
Minnesota Department of Environmental Education, 1993
Capitol Square Building
550 Cedar Street
St. Paul, MN 55155
612-297-2228
Outlines goals for environmental education in Minnesota over the next ten years.

Green Teacher
Green Teacher, 1993
95 Robert Street
Toronto, Ontario, Canada M5S 2K5
416-761-2215
A magazine devoted to environmental education (EE). *Green Teacher* is published 5 times during the school year.

Groundwater Education in America's Schools
American Groundwater Trust, 1991
6375 Riverside Drive
Dublin, OH 43017
614-761-2215
A catalog of 75 resource materials on ground water for elementary and secondary education professionals.

A Guide to Curriculum Planning in Environmental Education
Wisconsin Department of Public Instruction, 1992
Publication Sales, Drawer 179
Milwaukee , WI 53293-0179
800-243-8782
Helps school districts develop a comprehensive K–12 environmental education program.

Guidelines and Features for Outdoor Classrooms
Indiana Division of Forestry, Project Learning Tree, 1992
402 West Washington, Room 296
Indianapolis, IN 46204
317-232-4105
For teachers who are thinking of developing an outdoor classroom.

HBO Environmental Resource Guide for Earth and the American

Dream—Earth Day
Earth Share, 1993
3400 International Drive NW, Suite 2K
Washington, DC 20008
800-875-3863
A resource list that HBO compiled as a supplement to their "Earth and the American Dream, Earth Day 1993" special.

How to Plan a Conservation Education Program
The World Resources Institute, 1987
1709 New York Avenue NW
Washington, DC 20006
202-638-6300
A guide to help natural resource managers and nongovernment organizations in many countries to develop education programs that address local needs.

An Introduction to Project WILD
1983
5430 Grosvenor Lane
Bethesda, MD 20814
301-493-5447
Describes Project WILD, how it should be used, workshops available and how the activity books were developed.

Kimbark's Environmental Education Program, 1990
Zoneth Overbey, MA; Darlene Stoner, PhD and Karen Gilbert, MA
18021 Kenwood Avenue
San Bernardino, CA 92407
714-887-6429
The program is designed to develop a concern for the environment that will be reflected in the student's values, attitudes and behavior.

The Learning Channel (TLC)
TLC Monthly
7700 Wisconsin Avenue NW
Bethesda, MD 20814
301-986-1999
A monthly magazine listing programs that will be on the channel during the month. Programs can easily be used in classrooms to supplement a curriculum.

Life Lab Science Program
1993
156 High Street
Santa Cruz, CA 95064
408-459-2001
Brochures describing the "Growing

Classroom" and "Life Lab" curricula for the California workshops for teachers on using the program.

Marine Debris Curriculum Guide
Center for Marine Conservation, 1989
1725 Desales Street, Suite 500
Washington, DC 20036
202-429-5609
Addresses the importance of the ocean to different cultures, solutions to the marine debris problem and why we should care about the marine environment.

Marine Debris Educational Materials
Center for Marine Conservation, 1992
1725 Desales Street, Suite 500
Washington, DC 20036
202-429-5609
A state-by-state listing of free materials available on water issues.

Marine Education: A Bibliography of Educational Materials Available from the Nation's Sea Grant College Programs
Gulf Coast Research Laboratory, 1991
J.L. Scott Marine Education Center and Aquarium
P.O. Box 7000
Ocean Springs, MS 39564-7000
601-872-4200
Materials outlined in this bibliography are available from the Sea Grant Program or the institution that developed the program.

National Consortium for Environmental Education and Training (NCEET)
1991
430 East University, Room 2544
University of Michigan
School of Natural Resources and Environment
Ann Arbor, MI 48109
313-763-1312
Information on consortium-developed materials and services.

National Science Teacher Association
1742 Connecticut Avenue NW
Washington, DC 20009
202-328-5800

An organization of science education professionals committed to stimulating, improving and coordinating the teaching of science.

Nature Study: Sampler of Tips for Nature and Environment Education

The American Nature Study Society
5881 Cold Brook Road
Homer, NY 13077
607-749-3655
A collection of nature articles and tips that teachers can incorporate into their curricula. Published 2 or 3 times a year.

New England Interstate Environmental 1994 Information Catalog

New England Interstate Environmental Training Center, 1994
2 Fort Road
South Portland, ME 04106
207-767-2539
A catalog of the environmental materials available from the New England Interstate Environmental Training Center.

1993 Teacher Resource Guide

California Foundation for Agriculture in the Classroom, 1993
1601 Exposition Boulevard
Sacramento, CA 95815
916-924-4830
A guide to education materials about agriculture and the projects of the California Foundation for Agriculture in the Classroom.

North American Association for Environmental Education (NAAEE)

P.O. Box 400
Troy , OH 45373
513-339-6835
NAAEE is an integrated network of professionals in the field of environmental education with membership throughout North America and in over 40 additional countries.

The Northeast Field Guide to Environmental Education

Antioch New England Graduate School, 1991
Box C, Roxbury Street
Keene, NH 03431
603-357-3122
A listing of environmental organizations and science associations for educators, state park offices, state science consultants, state agencies and national parks for the 9 northeastern states.

Outdoor Education in Ontario

Council for Outdoor Educators, 1992
34 Blind Lane
Orangeville, Ontario, Canada L9W 3A5
This catalog provides a listing of programs, personnel, sites and services in outdoor education in the province of Ontario.

Outdoor Education Program

Putnam/Northern Westchester BOCES, 1993
Pinesbridge Road
Yorktown Heights, NY 10598
914-245-2700
This catalog is designed to help educators, club sponsors and parents to select and schedule outdoor programs at the Putnam/Northern Westchester BOCES in Yorktown, NY.

Project Learning Tree

1250 Connecticut Avenue NW, Suite 320
Washington, DC 20036
202-463-2462
Basic information about the curriculum with a fact sheet and a sampler of activities.

Renewable Energy Reading List for Young Adults

Conservation and Renewable Energy Inquiry and Referral Service, 1991
P.O. Box 8900
Silver Springs, MD 20907
800-523-2929
A bibliography of books dealing with renewable energy. The appropriate grade level and publication information for each book is provided.

Resource Guide for Teachers, Parents and Youth Leaders

American Horticulture Society—River Farm, 1993
7931 East Boulevard Drive
Alexandria, VA 22308-1300
703-768-5700
This is an introduction to the field of children's gardening. It outlines programs and resources available for adults working with children and wanting to set up gardens.

Resource Guide to Educational Material About Agriculture

U.S. Department of Agriculture, 1986
Technical Information Center
P.O. Box 62
Oak Ridge, TN 37830
615-576-2268
A listing of materials that can help teachers bring agriculture into their classrooms.

School Science Laboratories: A Guide to Some Hazardous Substances

U.S. Consumer Products Safety Commission, 1984
4330 EW Highway
Bethesda, MD 20814
301-504-0785
Identifies potentially hazardous substances that are used in school laboratories so that science instructors can follow safety precautions for their proper storage, handling, use and removal.

Science for Children: Resources for Teachers

National Academy Press, 1988
2101 Constitution Avenue NW
Washington, DC 20418
202-334-3313
Designed to assist teachers working to improve elementary science education.

Science Safety Handbook for California High Schools

California Department of Education, 1987
Bureau of Publications, Sales Unit
P.O. Box 271
Sacramento, CA 95802
916-445-1260
Helps teachers, administrators and other school staff understand and avoid accidents in science labs, on field trips and outdoor education experiences.

Scientists:
Tips for Making
Presentation to Teachers
Sci-Link/Globe-Net, 1993
North Carolina State University
1509 Varsity Drive
Raleigh, NC 27606
919-515-5290
Advice for research scientists who are asked to make presentations to groups of teachers about the nature of their research.

Solid Waste
Educational Curricula
U.S. Environmental Protection Agency, Region 1, 1990
Research Library for Solid Waste
6 John F. Kennedy Federal Building
90 Canal Street
Boston, MA 02272
800-776-0188
Provides samples of the contents of some curricula and refers to the EPA Region 1 (northeastern U.S.) research library of solid waste which can answer many questions teachers might have.

Solid Waste Videos:
A Teacher's Guide to Selected
Videotapes on Solid Waste
Management
Illinois Department of Energy and Natural Resources, 1991
325 West Adams Street, Room 300
Springfield, IL 62704
217-782-6370
Information to assist teachers in choosing videos appropriate for their students and using them effectively in the classroom.

A State-by-State Overview of
Environmental Education
Standards
Environmental Education Associates, Inc., 1993
2000 P Street NW, Suite 515
Washington, DC 20036
202-296-4572
Provides basic information on the status of environmental education for each state and the District of Columbia.

Stepping Stones: A Practical Guide
to Setting Up an Environmental
Education Center
Resource Center for Environmental Education, 1985
P.O. Box 3243
Flagstaff, AZ 86003
602-779-1745
This manual begins with the initial step of inspiration and outlines the process through which time and money create an education center.

TC Tool Kit: A Resource for
Teacher Consultants
National Geographic Society, 1993
17th and M Streets NW
Washington, DC 20036
800-368-2728
Designed to give teacher consultants, who have graduated from the Summer Geographic Institute, the resources and materials necessary to conduct geographic presentations.

Teacher/Student
Water Quality Monitoring
Network
Tennessee Valley Authority, 1992
Environmental Education Section,
Forestry Building, Ridgeway Road
Norris, TN 37828
615-632-1599
This program combines lectures, activities and field work on water chemistry, hydrology, aquatic biology, mapping, study design, data interpretation, field safety and other topics.

Teachers PET (Population
Education Training) Project
Zero Population Growth Annual
1400 16th Street NW, Suite 320
Washington, DC 20036
202-322-2200
A newsletter put out by *Zero Population Growth* that focuses on population activities that teachers can incorporate into their lessons.

Trends and Issues Related to the
Preparation of Teachers for
Environmental Education
ERIC: Clearinghouse for Science, Mathematics and Environmental Education, 1990
Ohio State University
1200 Chambers Road, Room 310
Columbus, OH 43212
614-292-6717
Intended for educators and school

administrators in the training and assessment of teacher competency in areas of environmental education.

Unfinished Agenda:
A New Vision for Child
Development and
Education
Committee for Economic Development, 1991
477 Madison Avenue
New York, NY 10022
212-688-2063
This report urges the development of a comprehensive and coordinated strategy of human investment, one that redefines education as a process that begins at birth.

Volunteers Teaching Children:
A Guide for Establishing
Ecology Education Outreach
Programs
Denver Audubon Society's Urban Education Project, 1991
3000 South Clayton Street, Suite 207
Denver, CO 80210
303-757-8376
This notebook is a guide for establishing ecology education outreach programs. It describes various projects for city children.

Water Quality Educational
Materials Bibliography
Purdue University, Media Publications, 1991
Media Distribution Center
301 South 2nd Street
West Lafayette, IN 47901-1232
317-494-6795
Materials are grouped into 8 categories and arranged by state within each category. Each entry lists all necessary information, title, description, audience, cost and address.

Who's Who in
Environmental
Education
The Pembina Institute for Appropriate Development, 1993
Box 7558
Drayton Valley, Alberta, T0E 0M0
403-542-6272
This directory lists over 350 Canadian environmental education organizations and agencies.

WILD School Sites: A Guide to Preparing Habitat Improvement Projects on School Grounds
Project WILD, 1993
5430 Grosvenor Lane
Bethesda, MD 20814
301-493-5447
A guide to creating a WILD school site. This guide will take educators through a step-by-step plan for their school and implementing it.

Chapter 20

Resources

Supplemental Materials

Chapter 20

CONTENTS

Books

The A to Z Guide to Toxic Foods and How to Avoid Them
Lynn Sonberg
Pocket Books, 1992
1230 Avenue of the Americas
New York, NY 10020

After the Crash: The Emergence of the Rainbow Economy
Guy Dauncey
Green Print, 1988
10 Malden Road
London, England NW5 3HR

The Ages of Gaia
James Lovelock
Bantam Doubleday Dell, 1988
666 Fifth Avenue
New York, NY 10103

Air: The Nature of Atmosphere and the Climate
Michael Allaby
Facts on File, 1992
460 Park Avenue South
New York, NY 10016

All That Dwell Therein: Essays on Animal Rights and Environmental Ethics
Tom Regan
University of California Press, 1982
2120 Berkeley Way
Berkeley, CA 94720-5810

Almanac of the Environment: The Ecology of Everyday Life
Valerie Harms
Putnam and Grosset, 1994
200 Madison Avenue
New York, NY 10016

The American Environment: Interpretations of Past Geographies
Larry Dilsaver
Rowman and Littlefield Publishers, 1992
4720 Boston Way
Lanham, MD 20706

The American Replacement of Nature
William Thompson

Bantam Doubleday Dell, 1993
666 Fifth Avenue
New York, NY 10103

Ancient Voices, Current Affairs: The Legend of the Rainbow Warriors
Steve McFadden
Bear and Company, 1992
P.O. Box 2860
Santa Fe, NM 87504

Animal Factories
Jim Mason and Peter Singer
Crown Publishers, 1990
201 East 50th Street
New York, NY 10022

Animal Liberation
Peter Singer
New York Review of Books, 1990
250 West 57th Street
New York, NY 10107

The Animal Rights Crusade
James M. Jasper and Dorothy Nelkin
Free Press, 1992
866 Third Avenue
New York, NY 10022

The Animal Rights Handbook
Living Planet Press, 1990
2940 Newark NW
Washington, DC 20008

Animals, Nature and Albert Schweitzer
Ann Cotrell Free
Flying Fox Press, 1991
4204 45th Street NW
Washington, DC 20016

The Art of Natural Farming and Gardening
Ralph and Rita Engelken
agAccess, 1985
P.O. Box 2008
Davis, CA 95616

At Odds with Progress
Bret Wallach
University of Arizona Press, 1991
1230 North Park Avenue South, Suite 102
Tucson, AZ 85719

At One with All Life: A Personal Journey in Gaian Communities

Judith L. Boice
Findhorn Press, 1989
The Park
Fiondhorn, Forres, Scotland UK IV36 0TZ

The Atlas of Endangered Species
John Burton
Macmillan, 1991
866 Third Avenue
New York, NY 10022

Atlas of the Environment
Geoffrey Lean, et al.
Prentice Hall, 1990
113 Sylvan Avenue
Englewood Cliffs, NJ 07632

Atlas of United States Environmental Issues
Robert J. Mason and Mark T. Mattson
Macmillan, 1994
866 Third Avenue
New York, NY 10022

The Automobile and the Environment
Maxine Rock
Chelsea Green Publishing, 1992
P.O. Box 130
Post Mills, VT 05058

The Backcountry Classroom: Lesson Plans for Teaching in the Wilderness
Jack Drury
ICS Books, 1992
107 East 89th Avenue
Merrilville, IN 46410

The Backyard Naturalist
Craig Tufts
National Wildlife Federation, 1993
1400 Sixteenth Street NW
Washington, DC 20036-2266

The Beaches Are Moving: The Drowning of America's Shoreline
Wallace Kaufman and Orrin Pilkey
Duke University Press, 1993
P.O. Box 90660
Durham, NC 27708

Bibliography of Environmental Literature
Yale School of Forestry
Island Press, 1993

1718 Connecticut Avenue NW, Suite
300
Washington, DC 20009

Biodiversity
E.O. Wilson, editor
National Academy Press
2101 Constitution Avenue NW
Washington, DC 20418

Bound to the Earth
James A. Swan and Roberta Swan
Avon Books, 1994
1350 Avenue of the Americas
New York, NY 10019

**Boundaries of Home: Mapping for
Local Empowerment**
Doug Aberley
New Society Publishers, 1993
4527 Springfield Avenue
Philadelphia, PA 19143

**Bug Busters: Poison-free Pest
Controls for Your House and
Garden**
Bernice Lifton
Avery Publishing Group, 1991
120 Old Broadway
Garden City Park, NY 11040

The Burning Season
Andrew Revkin
Plume/Penguin Group, 1994
375 Hudson Street
New York, NY 10014

Call to Action
Brad Erickson
Sierra Club, 1990
730 Polk Street
San Francisco, CA 94109

**Campus Ecology: A Guide to
Assessing Environmental Quality
and Creating Strategies for Change**
April Smith
Living Planet Press, 1993
2940 Newark NW
Washington, DC 20008

**The Chemical Connection: How the
Air You Breathe and What You Eat
Affect the Way You Feel and What
You Do...and What You Can Do
About It**
Louise Samways
Greenhouse Publications, 1989

122-126 Ormond Road
Elwood, Victoria, Australia 3184

Chemical Deception
Marc Lappe
Sierra Club, 1991
730 Polk Street
San Francisco, CA 94109

**Chemical Exposure and Human
Health**
Cynthia Wilson
McFarland and Company, 1993
P.O. Box 611
Jefferson, NC 28640

**A Citizen's Guide to Plastics in the
Ocean: More than a Litter Problem**
Kathryn J. O'Hara et al.
Center for Marine Conservation, 1988
1725 Desales Street NW
Washington, DC 20066

**A Citizen's Guide to Promoting
Toxic Waste Reduction**
Lauren Kenworthy
Inform, Inc., 1990
381 Park Avenue South
New York, NY 10016

Clean and Green
Annie Berthold-Bond
Ceres Press, 1990
P.O. Box 87
Woodstock, NY 12498

**Clearer, Cleaner, Safer, Greener: A
Blueprint for Detoxifying Your
Environment**
Gary Null
Random House, 1990
201 East 50th Street
New York, NY 10022

**Climate Change: Environment and
Development**
World Meteorological Organization,
1992
Secretariat of the World Meteorological
Organization
Geneva, Switzerland

Climate: Our Future?
Ulrich Schotterer
University of Minnesota Press, 1990
2037 University Avenue SE
Minneapolis, MN 55455

**Common Groundwork: A Practical
Guide to Protecting Rural and
Urban Land**
Institute for Environmental Education,
1993
18554 Haskins Road
Chagrin Falls, OH 44023-1823

**The Complete Guide to
Environmental Careers**
The CEIP Fund
Island Press, 1989
1718 Connecticut Avenue NW, Suite
300
Washington, DC 20009

**The Concise Oxford Dictionary of
Ecology**
Michael Allaby
Oxford University Press, 1994
200 Madison Avenue
New York, NY 10016

**Confronting Environmental
Racism: Voices from the Grassroots**
Robert Bullard
South End Press, 1993
116 St. Botolph Street
Boston, MA 02115

**Conservation Directory
1994**
Rue E. Gordon
National Wildlife Federation, 1994
1400 Sixteenth Street NW
Washington, DC 20036-2266

**Conserving the World's Biological
Diversity**
Jeffery A. McNeely et al.
WRI Publications, 1990
P.O. Box 4852, Hampden Station
Baltimore, MD 21211

**Consumer Guide to Home Energy
Savings**
Alex Wilson and John Morrill
American Council for an Energy-
Efficient Economy, 1993
1001 Connecticut Avenue NW, Suite
535
Washington, DC 20036

**Consumer Guide to Solar Energy:
Easy and Expensive Applications
for Solar Energy**
Scott Sklar and Kenneth G. Sheinkopf
Bonus Books, Inc., 1991

160 East Illinois Street
Chicago, IL 60611

Consumer's Dictionary of Household, Yard and Office Chemicals
Ruth Winter
Crown Publishers, 1992
201 East 50th Street
New York, NY 10022

Controlling Nonpoint Source Water Pollution: A Citizen's Handbook
Nancy Richardson Hansen et al.
The Conservation Foundation, 1988
1250 24th Street NW
Washington, DC 20037

Corporate Realities and Environmental Truths: Strategies for Leading Your Business in the Environmental Era
Steven J. Bennett, et al.
John Wiley and Sons, 1993
605 Third Avenue
New York, NY 10158-0012

Creative Handmade Paper: How to Make Paper from Recycled and Natural Materials
David Watson
Search Press, 1991
Wellwood, North Farm Road
Tunbridge Wells, Kent, United Kingdom TN2 3DR

Critical Masses
George D. Moffett
Viking/Penguin, 1994
375 Hudson Street
New York, NY 10014

The Culture of Nature
Alexander Wilson
Between the Lines, 1991
394 Euclid Avenue, #203
Toronto, Ontario, Canada M6G1K5

Currents of Death: Power Lines, Computer Terminals and the Attempt to Cover Up Their Threat to Your Health
Paul Brodeur
Simon and Schuster, 1989
1230 Avenue of the Americas
New York, NY 10020

Dead Heat: The Race Against the Greenhouse Effect
Robert Boyle and Michael Oppenheimer
HarperCollins, 1990
10 East 53rd Street
New York, NY 10022

The Decade of Destruction: The Crusade to Save the Amazon Rainforest
Adrian Cowell
Bantam Doubleday Dell, 1990
666 Fifth Avenue
New York, NY 10103

Demanding Clean Food and Water: The Fight for a Basic Human Right
Joan Goldstein
Plenum Publishing, 1990
233 Spring Street
New York, NY 10012

Deserts as Dumps? The Disposal of Hazardous Materials in Arid Eco-Systems
Charles Reith and Bruce Thomson
University of New Mexico Press, 1992
1720 Lomas Boulevard NE
Albuquerque, NM 87131-1591

Design for a Liveable Planet
John Naar
HarperCollins, 1990
10 East 53rd Street
New York, NY 10022

Desperate People
Farley Mowat
Bantam Doubleday Dell, 1980
666 Fifth Avenue
New York, NY 10103

Dictionary of Environmental Quotations
Barbara K. Rodes and Rice Odell
Simon and Schuster, 1992
1230 Avenue of the Americas
New York, NY 10023

Dictionary of Environmental Science
L. Harold Stevenson and Bruce Wyman
Facts on File, 1991
460 Park Avenue South
New York, NY 10016

Dictionary of the Environment, 3rd Edition
Michael Allaby
New York University Press, 1983
State University Plaza
Albany, NY 12246

Diet for the Atomic Age: How to Protect Yourself from Low Level Radiation
Sara Shannon
Avery Publishing Group, 1987
120 Old Broadway
Garden City Park, NY 11040

Diet for a Poisoned Planet
David Steinman
Ballantine Books, 1990
201 East 50th Street
New York, NY 10022

The Diversity of Life
E.O. Wilson
National Academy Press, 1990
2101 Constitution Avenue NW
Washington, DC 20418

The Drinking Water Book
Colin Ingram
Ten Speed Press, 1991
P.O. Box 7123
Berkeley, CA 94707

Dumbing Us Down: The Hidden Curriculum of Compulsory Schooling
John Taylor Gatto
New Society Publishers, 1992
4527 Springfield Avenue
Philadelphia, PA 19143

Dying Forests: A Crisis of Consciousness
Jochen Bockemuhl
Hawthorne Press, 1986
The Mount Main Road
Whiteshill, Stroud, Glouchestershire
UK CL6 6JA

Earl Mindell's Safe Eating
Earl Mindell
Time Warner, 1993
1271 Avenue of the Americas
New York, NY 10020

The Earth Care Annual 1993
National Wildlife Federation
Rodale Press, 1993

33 East Minor Street
Emmaus, PA 18098

Earth Education: A New Beginning
Steve Van Matre
Institute for Earth Education, 1990
Cedar Cove
Greenville, WV 24945

The Earth First Reader: Ten Years of Radical Environmentalism
John Davis, editor
Gibbs Smith Publisher, 1991
P.O. Box 667
Layton, UT 84041

Earth in the Balance
Al Gore
Houghton Mifflin, 1992
222 Berkely Street
Boston, MA 02116

Earth Keeping: Making It a Family Habit
Sydney Donohue
Zondervan Publishing, 1990
1415 Lake Drive SE
Grand Rapids, MI 49506

Earth: Our Planet and Its Resources
Michael Allaby
Facts on File, 1993
460 Park Avenue South
New York, NY 10016

Earth Politics
Ernst Ulrich Von Weizsacker
ZED Books, 1994
165 First Avenue
Atlantic Highlands, NJ 07716

The Earth and You: Eating for Two
April Moore
Potomoc Valley Press, 1993
1424 16th Street NW, Suite 105
Washington, DC 20036

Earthrise: A Personal Responsibility
David Thatcher
Foundation House Publications, 1987
4817 North Country Road, #29
Loveland, CO 80537

EarthScore: Your Personal Environmental Audit and Guide
Donald W. Lotter

Morning Sun Press, 1993
P.O. Box 413
Lafayette, CA 94549

Earthtoons: The First Book of Eco-Humor
Stan Eales
Warner Books, 1992
666 Fifth Avenue
New York, NY 10103

Easy Gardening: No Stress, No Strain
Jack Kramer
Fulcrum Publishing, 1991
350 Indiana Street
Golden, CO 80401

Eco Garden
Nigel Dudley and Sue Stickland
Avon Books, 1991
1350 Avenue of the Americas
New York, NY 10019

Eco-Heroes
Aubrey Wallace
Mercury House, 1993
201 Filbert Street, #400
San Francisco, CA 94133

The Ecological Health Garden: A Book of Survival
Edmond Bordeaux Szekely
International Biogenic Society, 1978
Box 205
Matsqui, B.C., Canada V0X 1S0

Ecological Literacy: Education and the Transition to a Postmodern World
David Orr
State University of New York Press, 1992
State University Plaza
Albany, NY 12246

Ecology for Beginners
Stephen Croall and William Rankin
Random House, 1982
201 East 50th Street
New York, NY 10022

The Ecology of Commerce: A Declaration of Sustainability
Paul Hawkin
HarperCollins, 1993
10 East 53rd Street
New York, NY 10022

Economics as If the Earth Really Mattered: A Catalyst Guide to Socially Conscious Investing
Susan Meeker-Lowry
New Society Publishers, 1988
4527 Springfield Avenue
Philadelphia, PA 19143

Ecopolitics: Building a Green Society
Daniel A. Coleman
Rutgers University Press, 1994
109 Church Street
New Brunswick, NJ 08901

Eco-Renovation
Edward Harland
Chelsea Green Publishing, 1993
P.O. Box 130
Post Mills, VT 05058

Educating for a Change
Rick Arnold et al.
Between the Lines, 1991
394 Euclid Avenue, #203
Toronto, Ontario, Canada M6G1K5

Education, Cultural Myths, and the Ecological Crisis: Toward Deep Changes
C. A. Bowers
State University of New York Press, 1993
State University Plaza
Albany, NY 12246

Education for the Earth: A Guide to Top Environmental Programs
Alliance for Environmental Education
Peterson's, 1993
P.O. Box 2123
Princeton, NJ 08543-2123

Elusive Quest: A Struggle for Equality of Educational Opportunity
Edwin Margolis and Stanley Moses
Apex Press, 1992
P.O. Box 337
Croton, NY 10520

Embracing the Earth
D. Mark Harris
Noble Press, 1990
213 W. Institute Place, Suite 508
Chicago, IL 60610

Encyclopedia of Endangered Species
Mary Emanoil, editor
Gale Research, Inc., 1994
835 Penobscot Building
Detroit, MI 48226-4094

The Encyclopedia of the Environment
Ruth A. Eblen and William R. Eblen, editors
Houghton Mifflin Company, 1994
222 Berkely Street
Boston, MA 02116

Encyclopedia of Environmental Information Sources
Sarojini Balachandran
Gale Research, Inc., 1993
835 Penobscot Bldg.
Detroit, MI 48226-4094

Encyclopedia of Environmental Studies
William Ashworth
Facts on File, 1991
460 Park Avenue South
New York, NY 10016

The End of Nature
Bill McKibben
Random House, 1989
201 East 50th Street
New York, NY 10022

End of the Road
Wolfgang Zuckerman
Chelsea Green Publishing, 1991
P.O. Box 130
Post Mills, VT 05058

The Endangered Kingdom
Roger DiSilvestro
John Wiley and Sons, 1989
605 Third Avenue
New York, NY 10158

Endangered Peoples
Art Davidson
Sierra Club, 1993
730 Polk Street
San Francisco, CA 94101

Endangered Species Handbook
Greta Nilsson
Animal Welfare Institute, 1990
P.O. Box 3650
Washington, DC 20007

Energy and the Environment in the 21st Century
Jefferson W. Tester et al., editors
The MIT Press, 1991
77 Massachusetts Avenue
Cambridge, MA 02139

Energy Efficiency: Perspectives on Individual Behavior
Willet Kempton and Max Neiman
American Council for an Energy-Efficient Economy, 1991
1001 Connecticut Avenue NW, Suite 535
Washington, DC 20036

Energy Management and Conservation
Frank Kreith and George Burmeister
National Conference of State Legislatures, 1993
1560 Broadway, Suite 700
Denver, CO 80202

The Energy-Environment Connection
Jack Hollander
Island Press, 1992
1718 Connecticut Avenue NW, Suite 300
Washington, DC 20009

Environment in Peril
Anthony B. Wolbarst, editor
Smithsonian Press, 1991
470 L'Enfant, Suite 7100
Washington, DC 20560

Environment, Schools and Active Learning
Dathleen Kelley-Lainé and Peter Posch
Organization for Economic Cooperation and Development (OECD), 1991
2, Rue Andre-Pascal
75775 Paris CEDEX 16, France

The Environmental Address Book
Michael Levine
Putnam and Grosset, 1991
200 Madison Avenue
New York, NY 10016

An Environmental Agenda for the Future
Robert Cahn, editor
Island Press, 1985

1718 Connecticut Avenue NW, Suite 300
Washington, DC 20009

Environmental Assessment
R. K. Jain et al.
McGraw-Hill, 1993
1221 Avenue of the Americas
New York, NY 10020

Environmental Career Directory
Brad Morgan, editor
Gale Research, Inc., 1993
835 Penobscot Building
Detroit, MI 48226

The Environmental Career Guide: Job Opportunities with the Earth in Mind
Nicholas Basta
John Wiley and Sons, 1991
605 Third Avenue
New York, NY 10158-0012

Environmental Careers
David Warner
CRC Press, 1992
2000 Corporate Boulevard NW
Boca Raton, FL 33431

Environmental Education: An Approach to Sustainable Development
Hartmut Schneider
Organization for Economic Cooperation and Development (OECD), 1992
2, Rue Andre-Pascal
75775 Paris CEDEX 16, France

Environmental Encyclopedia
William Cunningham et al., editors
Gale Research, Inc.. 1993
835 Penobscot Building
Detroit, MI 48226-4094

Environmental Evolution: The Effects of the Origin and Evolution of Life on Planet Earth
Lynn Margulis and Lorraine Olendzenski, editors
The MIT Press, 1992
77 Massachusetts Avenue
Cambridge, MA 02139

Environmental Jobs for Scientists and Engineers
Nicholas Basta

John Wiley and Sons, 1992
605 Third Avenue
New York, NY 10158-0012

Environmental Journalism: The Best from the Meeman Archive
Paul Nowack, editor
The Meeman Archive, 1987
University of Michigan, School of Natural Resources
Ann Arbor, MI 48109-1115

Environmental Leadership: Developing Effective Skills and Styles
Joyce K. Berry and John C. Gordon
Island Press, 1993
1718 Connecticut Avenue NW, Suite 300
Washington, DC 20009

The Environmental Sourcebook
Edith Stein
Lyons and Burford, 1992
31 West 21st Street
New York, NY 10010

Environmental Strategies Handbook: A Guide to Effective Policies and Practices
Rao V. Kollura
McGraw-Hill, 1994
1221 Avenue of the Americas
New York, NY 10020

Environmental Tips: How You Can Save the Planet
Gordon Johnson
Detselig Enterprises Ltd., 1990
P.O. Box G 399
Calgary, Alberta, Canada T3A 2G3

Environmental Vacations
Stephanie Ocko
John Muir Publications, 1992
P.O. Box 613
Santa Fe, NM 87504

Environmental Viewpoints
Daniel Marowski
Gale Research, Inc., 1992
835 Penobscot Building
Detroit, MI 48226-4094

The Environmentalist's Bookshelf
Robert Meredith
G. K. Hall and Company, 1993

866 Third Avenue
New York, NY 10022

The Environmentalists: A Biographical Dictionary from the 17th Century to the Present
Alan Axelrod and Charles Phillips
Facts on File, 1993
460 Park Avenue South
New York, NY 10016

Ethics and the Environment
Richard Hart
University Press of America, 1992
4720 Boston Way
Lanham, MD 20706

Every Employee's Guide: Save the Earth at Work
Bennett Information Group
Bob Adams, Inc., 1991
260 Center Street
Holbrook, MA 02343

Extinction: The Causes and Consequences of the Disappearing of Species
Paul Ehrlich and Anne Ehrlich
Ballantine Books, 1981
201 East 50th Street
New York, NY 10022

Facing Our Future
Jim Cole
Growing Images, 1992
P.O. Box 2510
Novato, CA 94948

Faith in a Seed
Henry David Thoreau
Island Press, 1993
1718 Connecticut Avenue NW, Suite 300
Washington, DC 20009

Fifty (50) More Things You Can Do to Save the Earth
EarthWorks Group
Earthworks Press, 1991
1400 Shattuck Avenue, #25
Berkeley, CA 94709

Fifty (50) Simple Things You Can Do to Save the Earth
EarthWorks Group
Earthworks Press, 1989
1400 Shattuck Avenue, #25
Berkeley, CA 94709

Fifty (50) Simple Things Your Business Can Do to Save the Earth
EarthWorks Group
Earthworks Press, 1989
1400 Shattuck Avenue, #25
Berkeley, CA 94709

Fight Global Warming: 29 Things You Can Do
Sarah L. Clark
Consumer Reports Books, 1991
101 Truman Avenue
Yonkers, NY 10703

Fire: The Vital Source of Energy
Michael Allaby
Facts on File, 1992
460 Park Avenue South
New York, NY 10016

For the Common Good: Redirecting the Economy Toward Community, the Environment and a Sustainable Future
Herman Daly
Beacon Press, 1989
25 Beacon Street
Boston, MA 02108-2800

For the Conservation of Earth
Vance Martin
Fulcrum Publishing, 1988
350 Indiana Street
Golden, CO 80401

For the Wild Places: Profiles in Conservation
Janet Trowbridge Bohlen
Island Press, 1993
1718 Connecticut Avenue NW, Suite 300
Washington, DC 20009

Forcing the Spring: The Transformation of the American Environmental Movement
Robert Gottlieb
Island Press, 1993
1718 Connecticut Avenue NW, Suite 300
Washington, DC 20009

The Forest for the Trees
Robert Repetto
WRI Publications, 1988
P.O. Box 4852, Hampden Station
Baltimore, MD 21211

The Fragile Environment
Laurie Friday and Ronald Laskey
Cambridge University Press, 1989
32 East 57th Street
New York, NY 10022

The Fragile Species
Lewis Thomas
Charles Scribner's Sons, 1992
866 Third Avenue
New York, NY 10022

G Is for Eco Garden: A Healthy Garden from A to Z
Nigel Dudley
Avon Books, 1991
1350 Avenue of the Americas
New York, NY 10019

From Gaia to Selfish Genes
Connie Barlow
The MIT Press, 1992
77 Massachusetts Avenue
Cambridge, MA 02139

The Gaia Atlas of First Peoples
Julian Burger
Bantam Doubleday Dell, 1990
666 Fifth Avenue
New York, NY 10103

Gaia Atlas of Green Economics
Paul Ekins
Bantam Doubleday Dell, 1992
666 Fifth Avenue
New York, NY 10103

Gaia Connections
Alan S. Miller
Rowman and Littlefield Publishers, 1991
4720 Boston Way
Lanham, MD 20706

Gale Environmental Almanac
Russ Hoyle
Gale Research, Inc., 1993
835 Penobscot Building
Detroit, MI, 48226-4094

Gale Environmental Sourcebooks
Karen Hill and Annette Piccirelli, editors
Gale Research, Inc., 1992
835 Penobscot Building
Detroit, MI 48226-4094

The Garbage Primer
The League of Women Voters, 1993
1730 M Street NW
Washington, DC 20036

Gardening: Plains and Upper Mid-West
Roger Vick
Fulcrum Publishing, 1991
350 Indiana Street
Golden, CO 80401

Getting at the Source: Strategies for Reducing Municipal Solid Waste
World Wildlife Fund
Island Press, 1991
1718 Connecticut Avenue NW, Suite 300
Washington, DC 20009

The Global Brain: Speculations on the Evolutionary Leap to Planetary Consciousness
Peter Russell
J. P. Tarcher, Inc., 1983
11150 Olympic Boulevard, Suite 600
Los Angeles, CA 90069

Global Imperative: Harmonizing Culture and Nature
Chris Maser
Stillpoint Publishing, 1992
P.O. Box 640, Meeting House Road
Walpole, NH 03608

Global Marine Environment: Does the Water Planet Have a Future?
Herman Prager
University Press of America, 1993
4720 Boston Way
Lanham, MD 20706

Global Warming: Understanding the Forecast
Andrew Revkin
Abbeville Press, 1992
488 Madison Avenue
New York, NY 10022

Good Works: A Guide to Careers in Social Change
Jessica Cowan
Barricade Books, 1991
61 Fourth Avenue
New York, NY 10003

The Grafter's Handbook
R. J. Garner
agAccess, 1993
P.O. Box 2008
Davis, CA 95616

The Great Powerline Cover-Up
Paul Brodeur
Little, Brown and Company, 1993
32 Beacon Street
Boston, MA 02108

Green at Work
Susan Cohn
Island Press, 1992
1718 Connecticut Avenue NW, Suite 300
Washington, DC 20009

Green Consumer
John Elkington et al.
Viking/Penguin, 1990
375 Hudson Street
New York, NY 10014

The Green Consumer Supermarket Guide: Brand Name Products that Don't Cost the Earth
Joel Makower et al.
Viking/Penguin, 1991
375 Hudson Street
New York, NY 10014

Green Delusions: An Environmentalist's Critique of Radical Environmentalism
Marin Lewis
Duke University Press, 1992
P.O. Box 90660
Durham, NC 27708-0660

Green Earth Resource Guide
Cheryl Gorder
Blue Bird Publishing, 1991
1713 East Broadway #306
Tempe, AZ 85282

Green Economics
Paul Ekins
Anchor Books, 1992
666 Fifth Avenue
New York, NY 10103

Green Encyclopedia
Irene Franck and David Brownstone
Prentice Hall, 1992
113 Sylvan Avenue
Englewood Cliffs, NJ 07632

Green Groceries: A Mail-Order Guide to Organic Foods
Jeane Heifetz
HarperCollins, 1992
10 East 53rd Street
New York, NY 10022

Green Lifestyle Handbook
Jeremy Rifkin
Henry Holt, 1990
115 West 18th Street
New York, NY 10011

The Green Supermarket Shopping Guide
John Wasik
Time/Warner, 1993
1271 Avenue of the Americas
New York, NY 10020

Greenhouse Gardener's Companion: Growing Food and Flowers in Your Greenhouse or Sunspace
Shane Smith
Fulcrum Publishing, 1992
350 Indiana Street
Golden, CO 80401

Greenhouses
Keith Garzoli, editor
Australian Government Publishing Service, 1988
GPO Box 84
Canberra, Australia ACT2601

The Greenpeace Guide to Anti-environmental Organizations
Greenpeace
Publishers Group West, 1993
P.O. Box 8843
Emeryville, CA 94662

Groundwater Protection: Saving the Unseen Resource
The Conservation Foundation, 1987
1250 24th Street NW
Washington, DC 20007

Growing Greener Cities
Global Releaf
Living Planet Press, 1992
2940 Newark NW
Washington, DC 20008

Growing Organically: A Practical Guide for Commercial and Home

Organic Fruit Growers
Paul Lanphere
Directed Media, Inc., 1989
P.O. Box 3005
Wenatchee, WA 98807

A Growing Problem: Pesticides in the Third World
David Bull
Institute for Food and Development Policy, 1982
145 Ninth Street
San Francisco, CA 94103

Growing Trees on the Great Plains
Margaret Brazell
Fulcrum Publishing, 1992
350 Indiana Street
Golden, CO 80401

Guide to State Environmental Programs
Deborah Hitchcock Jessup
BNA Books, 1990
300 Raritan Center Parkway, P.O. Box 7816
Edison, NJ 08818-7816

Guide to the Management of Hazardous Waste: A Handbook for the Businessman and Concerned Citizen
J. William Haun
Fulcrum Publishing, 1991
350 Indiana Street
Golden, CO 80401

HarperCollins Dictionary of Art Terms and Techniques
Ralph Mayer
HarperCollins, 1969
10 East 53rd Street
New York, NY 10022

Hazardous Waste Management
Benjamin A. Goldman et al.
Island Press, 1986
1718 Connecticut Avenue NW, Suite 300
Washington, DC 20009

Healing Our World: The Other Piece of the Puzzle
Mary Ruwart
Sunstar Press, 1992
P.O. Box 342
Kalamazoo, MI 490005-0342

Healing the Planet: Strategies for Resolving the Environmental Crisis
Paul Ehrlich and Ann Ehrlich
Addison-Wesley, 1991
2725 Sand Hill Road
Menlo Park, CA 94025

Healing with Whole Foods, Oriental Traditions and Modern Nutrition
Paul Pitchford
North Atlantic Books, 1993
2800 Woolsey Street
Berkeley, CA 94705

Health Hazards for Photographers
Siegfried Rempel and Wolfgang Rempel
Lyons and Burford, 1992
31 West 21st Street
New York, NY 10010

Healthful Houses: How to Design and Build Your Own
Clint Good and Debra Lynn Dadd
Guaranty Press, 1988
7315 Wisconsin Avenue, 615 East
Bethesda, MD 20814

The Healthy House
John Bower
Carol Publishing Group, 1993
600 Madison Avenue
New York, NY 10022

Heaven Is Under Our Feet: A Book for Walden Woods
Don Henley and Dave Marsh, editors
Berkeley Books, 1991
200 Madison Avenue
New York, NY 10016

The Heirloom Gardener
Jo Ann Gardner
Storey Communications, 1992
Schoolhouse Road
Pownal, VT 05261

Helping Nature Heal
Richard Nilsen
Ten Speed Press, 1991
P.O. Box 7123
Berkeley, CA 94707

Hidden Dangers
Anne E. Ehrlich and John W. Birks, editors
Sierra Club, 1990

730 Polk Street
San Francisco, CA 94109

The Hole in the Sky: Man's Threat to the Ozone Layer
John Gribbon
Bantam Doubleday Dell, 1988
666 Fifth Avenue
New York, NY 10103

Home Energy Decision Book: Remodeling Your Home for Low-Cost Energy Efficiency
Gigi Coe, et al.
Sierra Club, 1984
730 Polk Street
San Francisco, CA 94109

Home Solar Gardening: Solar Green Houses for Your House, Backyard, or Apartment
John H. Pierce
Key Porter Books, 1992
70 The Esplanade
Toronto, Ontario, Canada M6G1K5

How to Make Your Own Recycled Paper
Malcolm Valentine and Roselind Dace
Search Press, 1990
Wellwood, North Farm Road
Tunbridge Wells, Kent TN2 3DR
United Kingdom

How to Save the Children
Amy Hatkoff and Karen Kelly Klopp
Fireside, 1992
1230 Avenue of the Americas
New York, NY 10020

How to Save Your Neighborhood, City or Town
Maritza Pick
Sierra Club, 1993
730 Polk Street
San Francisco, CA 94109

H₂O
Arthur von Wiesenberger
Woodbridge Press Publishing Company, 1988
P.O. Box 6189
Santa Barbara, CA 93160

If You Love this Planet: A Plan to Heal the Earth
Helen Caldicott
W.W. Norton and Company, 1992

500 Fifth Avenue
New York, NY 10110

Imperiled Planet
Edward Goldsmith et al.
The MIT Press, 1990
77 Massachusetts Avenue
Cambridge, MA 02139

In Defense of Wildlife
Candace Lampe, editor
Defenders of Wildlife, 1989
1244 19th Street
Washington, DC 20036

In Our Backyard: A Guide to Understanding Pollution and Its Effects
Travis Wagner
Van Nostrand Reinhold, 1994
115 Fifth Avenue
New York, NY 10003

The Independent Home: Living Well with Power from the Sun, Wind and Water
Michael Potts
Chelsea Green Publishing, 1993
P.O. Box 130
Post Mills, VT 05058-0130

Indian Water in the New West
Thoma McGuire et al.
University of Arizona Press, 1993
1230 North Park Avenue South, Suite 102
Tucson, AZ 85719

The Indoor Radon Problem
Douglas Brookins
Columbia University Press, 1990
562 West 113th Street
New York, NY 10025

Information Please Almanac 1994
World Resources Institute
Houghton Mifflin, 1994
222 Berkely Street
Boston, MA 02116

Institutions for the Earth
Peter M. Haas et al.
The MIT Press, 1993
77 Massachusetts Avenue
Cambridge, MA 02139

Into the Amazon
Augusta Dwyer

Sierra Club, 1990
730 Polk Street
San Francisco, CA 94109

Introduction to Permaculture
Reny Mia Slay
agAccess, 1991
P.O. Box 2008
Davis, CA 95616

Investing from the Heart
Jack A. Brill and Alan Reder
Crown Publishers, 1992
201 East 50th Street
New York, NY 10022

The Keys to the Car: Electric and Hydrogen Vehicles for the 21st Century
James J. MacKenzie
World Resources Institute, 1994
P.O. Box 4852, Hampden Station
Baltimore, MD 21211

Landscaping with Nature: Using Nature's Designs to Plan Your Yard
Jeff Cox
Rodale Press, 1991
33 East Minor Street
Emmaus, PA 18098

Last Animals at the Zoo
Colin Tudge
Island Press, 1991
1718 Connecticut Avenue NW, Suite 300
Washington, DC 20009

Last Oasis: Facing Water Scarcity
Sandra Postel
Worldwatch Institute, 1992
1776 Massachusetts Avenue NW
Washington, DC 20036

Law of the Mother
Elizabeth Kemf
Sierra Club, 1993
730 Polk Street
San Francisco, CA 94101

Lessons from Nature: Learning to Live Sustainably on Earth
Daniel Chiras
Island Press, 1992
1718 Connecticut Avenue NW, Suite 300
Washington, DC 20009

Living Within Limits
Garrett Hardin
Oxford University Press, 1993
200 Madison Avenue
New York, NY 10016

Living Without Landfills
Marvin Resnikoff
Radioactive Waste Campaign, 1987
625 Broadway, 2nd Floor
New York, NY 10012

The Living Planet
David Attenborough
Little, Brown and Company, 1984
32 Beacon Street
Boston, MA 02108

Looking the Tiger in the Eye
Carl B. Feldbaum and Ronald J. Bee
HarperCollins, 1988
10 East 53rd Street
New York, NY 10022

The Low-Water Flower Gardener
Erica Johnson
Ironwood Press, 1993
2968 West Ina Road, #285
Tucson, AZ 85741

Macrocosm USA
Sandi Brockway
Macrocosm USA, 1992
P.O. Box 969
Cambria, CA 93428

Making Things Happen: How to Be an Effective Volunteer
Joan Wolfe
Island Press, 1991
1718 Connecticut Avenue NW, Suite 300
Washington, DC 20009

The Man Who Planted Trees
Jean Giono
Chelsea Green Publishing, 1985
P.O. Box 130
Post Mills, VT 05058

Market Gardening: Growing and Selling Produce
Ric Staines
Fulcrum Publishing, 1991
350 Indiana Street
Golden, CO 80401

Meals Without Squeals: Childcare Feeding Guide and Cookbook
Christine Berman and Jacki Fromer
Bull Publishing Company, 1991
P.O. Box 208
Palo Alto, CA 94302-0208

Meant to Be Wild: The Struggle to Save Endangered Species Through Captive Breeding
Jan Deblieu
Fulcrum Publishing, 1991
350 Indiana Street
Golden, CO 80401

Mother Nature's Handbook for a Safe Planet
Virginia Sandlin and Anne Von Riegen
Achronova Publishing, 1987
P.O. Box 6014-P
New York, NY 10128-6014

Multiple Exposures: Chronicles of the Radiation Age
Catherine Caufield
University of Chicago Press, 1989
5801 Ellis Avenue
Chicago, IL 60637

National Organic Directory
Candace Lampe
Community Alliance with Family Farmers, 1994
P.O. Box 464
Davis, CA 95617

Native American Stories as Told by Joseph Bruchac
Joseph Bruchac
Fulcrum Publishing, 1991
350 Indiana Street
Golden, CO 80401

The Natural House Book: Creating a Healthy, Harmonious and Ecolgcially Sound Home
David Pearson
Simon and Schuster, 1989
1230 Avenue of the Americas
New York, NY 10020

Natural Insect Repellents
Janette Grainger and Connie Moore
The Herb Bar, 1991
200 East Mary
Austin, TX 78704

Nature and Madness
Paul Shepard
Sierra Club, 1982
730 Polk Street
San Francisco, CA 94109

Nature: The Other Earthlings
James Shreeves
Macmillan, 1987
866 Third Avenue
New York, NY 10022

Nature's Colors: Dyes from Plants
Ida Grae
Robin and Russ Handweavers, 1974
533 North Adams Street
McMinnville, OR 97128

New Complete Guide to Environmental Careers
The Environmental Careers Organization
Island Press, 1993
1718 Connecticut Avenue NW, Suite 300
Washington, DC 20009

The New Organic Grower
Elliot Coleman
Chelsea Green Publishing, 1989
P.O. Box 130
Post Mills, VT 05058

The New Organic Grower: A Master's Manual of Tools and Techniques for the Home and Market Gardener
Elliot Coleman
agAccess, 1993
P.O. Box 2008
Davis, CA 95616

A New Power Base: Renewable Energy Policies for the Nineties and Beyond
Keith L. Kozloff and Roger Dower
World Resources Institute, 1993
P.O. Box 4852, Hampden Station
Washington, DC 20006

The New Seed-Starters Handbook
Nancy Bubel
Rodale Press, 1988
33 East Minor Street
Emmaus, PA 18098

Next One Hundred Years: Shaping the Fate of Our Living Earth
Jonathan Weiner
Bantam Doubleday Dell, 1990
666 Fifth Avenue
New York, NY 10103

1993 Earth Journal: Environmental Almanac and Resource Directory
Editors of Buzzworm
Buzzworm Books, 1993
2305 Canyon Boulevard, #206
Boulder, CO 80302

The Nontoxic Home and Office
Debra Lynn Dadd
J.P. Tarcher, Inc., 1992
11150 Olympic Boulevard, Suite 600
Los Angeles, CA 90064

Nontoxic, Natural and Earthwise
Debra Lynn Dadd
J.P. Tarcher, Inc., 1990
11150 Olympic Boulevard, Suite 600
Los Angeles, CA 90064

The Norton History of the Environmental Sciences
Peter Bowler
W.W. Norton and Company, 1992
500 Fifth Avenue
New York, NY 10110

Not by Timber Alone: Economics and Ecology for Sustaining Tropical Forests
Theodore Panayotou and Peter Ashton
Island Press, 1992
1718 Connecticut Avenue NW, Suite 300
Washington, DC 20009

Not in Our Backyard: The People and Events that Shaped America's Modern Environmental Movement
Mark Mowrey and Tim Redmond
William Morrow, 1993
1350 Avenue of the Americas
New York, NY 10019

Nuclear Madness: What You Can Do!
Dr. Helen Caldicott
Bantam Doubleday Dell, 1980
666 Fifth Avenue
New York, NY 10103

Nuclear Powerplants Worldwide
Peter Dresser
Gale Research, Inc., 1993
835 Penobscot Building
Detroit, MI 48226-4094

Nukespeak
Stephen Hilgartner et al.
Sierra Club, 1992
730 Polk Street
San Francisco, CA 94109

Old MacDonald's Factory Farm
C. David Coats
Continuum Publishing Company, 1989
370 Lexington Avenue
New York, NY 10017

Olympic Battleground: The Power Politics of Timber Preservation
Carsten Lien
Sierra Club, 1991
730 Polk Street
San Francisco, CA 94109

One Earth
Kenneth Brower
HarperCollins, 1990
10 East 53rd Street
New York, NY 10022

101 Ways to Save Money and Save Our Planet
The Green Group
Paper Chase Press, 1992
5721 Magazine Street, Suite 152
New Orleans, LA 70115

1,001 Ways to Save the Planet
Bernadette Vallely
Ballantine Books, 1990
201 East 50th Street
New York, NY 10022

One World, One Earth: Educating Children for Social Responsibility
Merryl Hammond
New Society Publishers, 1993
4527 Springfield Avenue
Philadelphia, PA 19143

The Orchard Almanac: A Spraysaver Guide
Stephen Page
agAccess, 1990
P.O. Box 2008
Davis, CA 95616

Organic Gardener's Handbook of Natural Insect and Disease Control
Barbara Ellis
Rodale Press, 1992
33 East Minor Street
Emmaus, PA 18098

Passive Solar Buildings
J. Douglas Balcomb
The MIT Press, 1992
77 Massachusetts Avenue
Cambridge, MA 02139

The Pesticide Conspiracy
Robert Van Den Bosch
University of California Press, 1978
2120 Berkeley Way
Berkeley, CA 94720-5810

The Pesticide Hazard: A Global Health and Environmental Audit
Barbara Dinham
ZED Books, 1993
165 First Avenue
Atlantic Highlands, NJ 07716

The Pesticide Question: Environment, Economics and Ethics
David Pimentel and Hugh Lehman, editors
Chapman and Hall, 1993
29 West 35th Street
New York, NY 10001-2291

Pesticides in the Diets of Infants and Children
National Research Council
National Science Teachers Association, 1993
1742 Connecticut Avenue NW
Washington, DC 20009

Pests of the West: Prevention and Control for Today's Garden and Small Farm
Whitney Cranshaw
Fulcrum Publishing, 1992
350 Indiana Street
Golden, CO 80401

Pieces of the Puzzle: International Approaches to Environmental Concerns
Anne Blackburn
Fulcrum Publishing, 1986
350 Indiana Street
Golden, CO 80401

Pioneer Ecologist: The Life and Work of Victor Ernest Shelford
Robert Croker
Smithsonian Press, 1991
470 L'Enfant, Suite 7100
Washington, DC 20560

Planetary Overload: Global Environmental Change and the Health of the Human Species
A.J. McMichael
Cambridge University Press, 1993
32 East 57th Street
New York, NY 10022

Plant a Tree: Choosing, Planting and Maintaining This Precious Resource
Michael Weiner
John Wiley and Sons, 1992
605 Third Avenue
New York, NY 10158-0012

Plants for Dry Climates: How to Select, Grow and Enjoy
Mary Rose Duffield and Warren D. Jones
HP Books, 1992
11150 Olympic Boulevard, 6th Floor
Los Angeles, CA 90064

Plantworks
Karen Shanberg and Stan Tekiela
Adventure Publications, 1991
P.O. Box 269
Cambridge, MN 55008

The Plastic Waster Primer
League of Women Voters
Lyons and Burford, 1993
31 West 21st Street
New York, NY 10010

Poisoning Our Children
Nancy Sokol Green
Noble Press, 1991
213 W. Institute Place, Suite 508
Chicago, IL 60610

The Politics of the Solar Age: Alternatives to Economics
Hazel Henderson
Knowledge Systems, Inc., 1978
777 West Morris Street
Indianapolis, IN 46231

The Population Explosion
Paul Ehrlich and Ann Ehrlich

Touchstone, 1990
1230 Avenue of the Americas
New York, NY 10020

The Poverty of Affluence: A Psychological Portrait of the American Way of Life
Paul Wachtel
New Society Publishers, 1989
4527 Springfield Avenue
Philadelphia, PA 19143

The Power of the People: Active Nonviolence in the United States
Robert Cooney
New Society Publishers, 1987
4527 Springfield Avenue
Philadelphia, PA 19143

The Raging Grannies Songbook
Jean Mcleren and Heide Brown, editors
New Society Publishers, 1993
4527 Springfield Avenue
Philadelphia, PA 19143

The Rainforests
D'Arcy Richardson
Smithmark Publishers, 1991
112 Madison Avenue
New York, NY 10016

Rebirth of Nature: New Hope for Endangered Habitats
Roger DiSilvestro
John Wiley and Sons, 1992
605 Third Avenue
New York, NY 10158-0012

Residential Indoor Air Quality and Energy Efficiency
Peter DuPont and John Morrill
American Council for an Energy-Efficient Economy, 1989
1001 Connecticut Avenue NW, Suite 535
Washington, DC 20036

The Rhino Man and Other Uncommon Environmentalists
Winthrop P. Carty and Elizabeth Lee
Seven Locks Press, 1992
3030 Clarendon Boulevard, Suite 202
Arlington, VA 232201

The Rising Tide: Global Warming and World Sea Levels
Lynn Edgerton
Island Press, 1991

1718 Connecticut Avenue NW, Suite 300
Washington, DC 20009

Rodale's All New Encyclopdia of Organic Gardening
Fern Marshall Bradley and Barbara W. Ellis
Rodale Press, 1992
33 East Minor Street
Emmaus, PA 18098

Rodale's Chemical-Free Yard and Garden: The Ultimate Authority on Successful Organic Gardening
Anna Carr et al.
Rodale Press, 1991
33 East Minor Street
Emmaus, PA 18098

Rodale's Illustrated Encyclopedia of Gardening and Landscaping Techniques
Barbara Ellis, editor
Rodale Press, 1990
33 East Minor Street
Emmaus, PA 18098

The Sacred Hoop
Bill Broder
Sierra Club, 1979
730 Polk Street
San Francisco, CA 94109

Safe Food
Michael F. Jacobson et al.
Living Planet Press, 1991
2940 Newark NW
Washington, DC 20008

Safe at School: Awareness and Action for Parents of Kids Grades K–12
Carol Silverman Saunders
Free Spirit Publishing, Inc., 1994
400 First Avenue North, Suite 616
Minneapolis, MN 55401-1730

A Sand County Almanac: And Sketches Here and There
Aldo Leopold
Oxford University Press, 1968
200 Madison Avenue
New York, NY 10016

Save the Earth
Jonathan Porritt and Ellis Nadler
Dorling Kindersley, 1991

232 Madison Avenue
New York, NY 10016

Save Our Planet
Diane MacEachern
Bantam Doubleday Dell, 1990
666 Fifth Avenue
New York, NY 10103

Saving All the Parts: Reconciling Economics and the Endangered Species Act
Rocky Barker
Island Press, 1993
1718 Connecticut Avenue NW, Suite 300
Washington, DC 20009

Saving Seeds: The Gardener's Guide to Growing and Storing Vegetable and Flower Seeds
Marc Rogers
Storey Communications, 1990
Schoolhouse Road
Pownal, VT 05261

Saving Water in the Home and Garden
Jonathan Erickson
Tab Books, 1993
860 Taylor Station Road
Blacklick, OH 43004

Schools that Work: America's Most Innovative Public Education Programs
George H. Wood
Viking/Penguin, 1992
375 Hudson Street
New York, NY 10014

Science for All Americans
F. James Rutherford and Andrew Ahlgren
Oxford University Press, 1990
200 Madison Avenue
New York, NY 10016

Scientists on Gaia
Stephan H. Schneider and Penilope J. Boston
The MIT Press, 1991
77 Massachusetts Avenue
Cambridge, MA 02139

The Second Nature of Things: How and Why Things Work in the Natural World

Will Curtis
Ecco Press, 1992
100 West Broad Street
Hopewill, NJ 08525

Secrets from the Lives of Trees
Jeffrey Goelitz
Planetary Publications, 1991
P.O. Box 66
Boulder Creek, CA 95006

Secrets of the Old Growth Forest
David Kelly and Gary Braasch
Gibbs-Smith Publishing, 1988
P.O. Box 667
Layton, OH 84041

The Self-help Handbook
Jane Schalutz
The Rensselaerville Institute, 1985
Pond Hill Road
Rensselaerville, NY 12147

Shopping for a Better World
The Council on Economic Priorities
Ballantine Books, 1994
201 East 50th Street
New York, NY 10022

Silent Spring
Rachel Carson
Houghton Mifflin, 1962
222 Berkely Street
Boston, MA 02116

The Simple Act of Planting a Tree
Andy and Katie Lipkis
J.P. Tarcher, Inc., 1990
11150 Olympic Boulevard, Suite 600
Los Angeles, CA 90064

Small-Scale Irrigation
Peter Stern
Intermediate Technology Publications Ltd., 1979
103-105 Southampton Row
London, England WC1B 4HH

Smart Start: Elementary Education for the 21st Century
Patte Barth
North American Press, 1992
350 Indiana Street
Golden, CO 80401

Solar Building Architecture
Bruce Anderson
The MIT Press, 1990

77 Massachusetts Avenue
Cambridge, MA 02139

Speaking for Nature
Paul Brooks
Sierra Club, 1980
730 Polk Street
San Francisco, CA 94109

Stand Up and Be Counted: The Volunteer Resource Book
Judy Knipe
Fireside, 1992
1230 Avenue of the Americas
New York, NY 10020

State of the Earth Atlas
Joni Seager
Touchstone, 1990
1230 Avenue of the Americas
New York, NY 10020

**State of the World:
A Worldwatch Institute Report on Progress Toward a Sustainable Society**
Lester R. Brown, Worldwatch Institute
W.W. Norton and Company, 1994
500 Fifth Avenue
New York, NY 10110

Strangers Devour the Land
Boyce Richardson
Chelsea Green Publishing, 1991
P.O. Box 130
Post Mills VT 05058

Suburban Nature Guide
David Mohrhardt and Richard E. Schinkel
Cameron and Kelker Streets, 1991
P.O. Box 1831
Harrisburg, PA 17105

Sustainable Harvest and Marketing of Rain Forest Products
Mark Plotkin and Lisa Famolare
Island Press, 1992
1718 Connecticut Avenue NW, Suite 300
Washington, DC 20009

Sustaining the Earth
Debra Dadd-Redalia
Hearst Books, 1994
1350 Avenue of the Americas
New York, NY 10019

Tackling Toxics in Everyday Products: A Directory of Everyday Products
Nancy Lilienthal et al.
Inform, Inc., 1992
381 Park Avenue South
New York, NY 10016

Taking Population Seriously
Frances Moore Lappe and Rachel Schurman
Institute for Food and Development Policy, 1990
145 Ninth Street
San Francisco, CA 94103

Taking the Environment Seriously
Roger Meiners
Rowman and Littlefield Publishers, 1993
4720 Boston Way
Lanham, MD 20706

Thirty (30) Simple Energy Things You Can Do to Save the Earth
Earthworks Press, 1990
1400 Shattuck Avenue, #25
Berkeley, CA 94709

This Is Your Land: A Guide to North America's Endangered Ecosystems
Jon Naar and Alex Naar
HarperCollins, 1993
10 East 53rd Street
New York, NY 10022

365 Ways for You and Your Children to Save the Earth One Day at a Time
Michael Viner
Warner Books, 1991
666 Fifth Avenue
New York, NY 10103

To Save an Elephant: The Undercover Investigation into the Illegal Ivory Trade
Allan Thornton and Dave Currey
Transworld Publishers, 1991
61-63 Uxbridge Road
London, England W5 5SA

Toxic Struggles:
The Theory and Practice of Environmental Justice
Richard Hofrichter

New Society Publishers, 1993
4527 Springfield Avenue
Philadelphia, PA 19143

Toxic Substances in the Environment
Ronald Kendall
Kendall Hunt Publishing, 1983
4050 Westmark Drive
Dubuque, IA 52002

Transportation and Global Climate Change
David Green and Danilo Santini
American Council for an Energy-Efficient Economy, 1993
1001 Connecticut Avenue NW, Suite 535
Washington, DC 20036

Trees: A Celebration
Jill Fairchild
Weidenfeld and Nicholson, 1989
841 Broadway
New York, NY 10003-4793

Trees: Guardians of the Earth
Donald Nichol
Morningtown Press, 1988
1420 NW Gilman Boulevard
Issaquah, WA 98207

Tropical Forestry
Simon Rietbergen
Earthscan Publications, 1993
3 Endsleigh Street
London, UK N1 9JN

Tropical Rainforest
Arnold Newman
Facts on File, 1990
460 Park Avenue South
New York, NY 10016

Two Minutes a Day for a Greener Planet
Marjorie Lamb
HarperCollins, 1990
10 East 53rd Street
New York, NY 10022

Unwelcome Harvest: Agriculture and Pollution
Gordon Conway
Kogan Page, Ltd., 1991
120 Pentonville Road
London, England N1 9JN

Valuing the Earth: Economics, Ecology, Ethics
Herman E. Daly and Kenneth N. Townshend, editors
The MIT Press, 1993
77 Massachusetts Avenue
Cambridge, MA 02139

Vanishing Amazon
Mirella Ricciardi
Abrams, 1991
100 Fifth Avenue
New York, NY 10011

The Vanishing Manatee
Margaret Goff Clark
Cobblehill Books, 1990
375 Hudson Street
New York, NY 10014

Vegetarian Journal's Guide to Natural Food Restaurants in the U.S. and Canada
Vegetarian Resource Group
Avery Publishing Group, 1993
120 Old Broadway
Garden City Park, NY 11040

Visions of a Rainforest:
A Year in Australia's Tropical Rainforest
Stanley Breeden
Ten Speed Press, 1992
P.O. Box 7123
Berkeley, CA 94707

Vital Signs: Trends that Are Shaping Our Future
Lester R. Brown, editor
W.W. Norton and Company, 1994
500 Fifth Avenue
New York, NY 10110

The Voice of the Earth
Theodore Roszak
Simon and Schuster, 1992
1230 Avenue of the Americas
New York, NY 10020

Voices from the Environmental Movement: Perspectives for a New Era
Donald Snow
Island Press, 1992
1718 Connecticut Avenue NW, Suite 300
Washington, DC 20009

Walden/On the Duty of Civil Disobedience
Henry David Thoreau
Macmillan, 1962
866 Third Avenue
New York, NY 10022

War Resisters League Organizer's Manual
Ed Hedeman
War Resisters League, 1986
339 Lafayette Street
New York, NY 10012

Water: Conserving Plants and Landscapes for the Bay Area
Barrie Coate
East Bay Municipal Utility District, 1990
P.O. Box 24055
Oakland, CA 94623

Water: The Element of Life
Theodor Schwenck and Wolfram Schwenk
Anthroposophic Press, 1989
Bell's Pond, Star Route
Hudson, NY 12534

The Water Encyclopedia
Frits van der Leeden et al.
Lewis Publishers, 1990
121 South Main Street
Chelsea, MI 48118

Water: The International Crisis
Robin Clarke
The MIT Press, 1991
77 Massachusetts Avenue
Cambridge, MA 02139

Water: Its Global Nature
Michael Allaby
Facts on File, 1992
460 Park Avenue South
New York, NY 10016

The Way We Grow
Anne Witte Garland
Berkley Publishing, 1993
200 Madison Avenue
New York, NY 10016

What Can I Do to Make a Difference?
Richard Zimmerman
Plume/Penguin Group, 1991

375 Hudson Street
New York, NY 10014

The Whole Earth Quiz Book: How Well Do You Know Your Planet?
Bill Adler, Jr.
Quill, 1991
105 Madison Avenue
New York, NY 10016

Whose Common Future? Reclaiming the Commons
The Ecologist
New Society Publishers, 1993
4527 Springfield Avenue
Philadelphia, PA 19143

Wild Animals and American Environmental Ethics
Lisa Mighetto
University of Arizona Press, 1991
1230 North Park Avenue South, Suite 102
Tucson, AZ 85719

The Wilderness Condition: Essays on Environment and Civilization
Max Oelschlaeger
Island Press, 1992
1718 Connecticut Avenue NW, Suite 300
Washington, DC 20009

The Wilderness Educator
David Cockrell
ICS Books, 1991
107 East 89th Avenue
Merriville, IN 46410

The Wildflower Handbook
National Wildflower Research Center
Voyageur Press, 1992
P.O. Box 338, 123 North Second Street
Stillwater, MN 55082

Wind Power for Home and Business: Renewable Energy for the 1990's and Beyond
Paul Gipe
Chelsea Green Publishing, 1993
P.O. Box 130
Post Mills, VT 05058-0130

The Wolf
L. David Mech
University of Minnesota Press, 1970
2037 University Avenue, SE
Minneapolis, MN 55455

Women's Encyclopedia of Health and Emotional Healing
Denise Foley et al.
Rodale Press, 1993
33 East Minor Street
Emmaus PA 18098

The Woodland Steward
James R. Fazio
Woodlands Press, 1987
5445 DTC Parkway, Suite 720
Englewood, CO 80111

World on Fire: Saving an Endangered Earth
George Mitchell
Macmillan, 1991
866 Third Avenue
New York, NY 10022

World Resources: A Report by the World Resources Institute in Collaboration with the U.N. Environment Programme and U.N. Development Programme 1994–1995
World Resources Institute, U.N. Environment Programme and U.N. Development Programme
Oxford University Press, 1994
200 Madison Avenue
New York, NY 10016

The Worldwatch Reader on Global Environmental Issues
Lester R. Brown, editor
W.W. Norton and Company, Inc., 1991
500 Fifth Avenue
New York, NY 10110

Xeriscape Gardening: Water Conservation for the American Landscape
Connie Ellefson et al.
Macmillan Publishing, 1992
866 Third Avenue
New York, NY 10022

Your Heart Your Planet
Harvey Diamond
Hay House, 1990
501 Santa Monica Boulevard, P.O. Box 2212
Santa Monica, CA 90406

BOOKS FOR YOUTH

A B Cedar
George Ella Lyon and Tom Parket
Orchard Books, 1989
387 Park Avenue South
New York, NY 10016

A Is for Animals
David Pelham
Simon and Schuster, 1991
1230 Avenue of the Americas
New York, NY 10020

Acid Rain
Peter Tyson
Chelsea Green Publishing, 1992
P.O. Box 130
Post Mills, VT 05058

Air, Light and Water
Mary Jane Wilkins
Random House, 1991
201 East 50th Street
New York, NY 10022

Air Pollution
Gary Lopez
Creative Education, 1992
123 South Broad Street
Mankato, MN 56001

Alejandro's Gift
Richard E. Albert
Chronicle Books, 1994
275 Fifth Street
San Francisco, CA 94103

**The Amateur Naturalist's
Handbook**
Vinson Brown
Fireside, 1992
1230 Avenue of the Americas
New York, NY 10020

Amazing Creatures of the Sea
National Wildlife Federation, 1987
1400 Sixteenth Street NW
Washington, DC 20036-2266

The Amazing Dirt Book
Paulette Bourgeois

Addison-Wesley
1986
2725 Sand Hill Road
Menlo Park, CA 94025

Amazon Boy
Ted Lewin
Macmillan, 1993
866 Third Avenue
New York, NY 10022

Amazon Rainforest
Moira Butterfield
Ideals Publishing, 1992
565 Marriott Drive, #800
Nashville, TN 37210

American Bison
Ruth Berman
Carolrhoda Books, 1992
241 First Avenue
Minneapolis, MN 56401

The American Family Farm
Joan Anderson
Harcourt Brace and Company, 1989
1250 6th Avenue
San Diego, CA 92101

Among the Orangutans
Evelyn Gallardo
Chronicle Books, 1993
275 Fifth Street
San Francisco, CA 94103

An Ancient Forest
Guy J. Spencer
Troll Association, 1988
2 Lethbridge Plaza
Mahwah, NJ 07430

And Still the Turtle Watched
Sheila Magill-Callahan
Dial Books, 1991
375 Hudson Street
New York, NY 10014

And Then There Was One
Margery Facklam
Sierra Club, 1990
730 Polk Street
San Francisco, CA 94109

Animal Homes
World Wildlife Fund
Ladybird, 1988
840 Washington Street
Auburn, ME 04210

Animal Rights: Yes or No?
Marna Owen
Lerner Publications, 1993
241 First Avenue North
Minneapolis, MN 55401

Animalia
Barbara Berger
Celestial Arts, 1982
P.O. Box 707
Berkeley, CA 94707

Animals
World Wildlife Fund
Ladybird, 1986
840 Washington Street
Auburn, ME 04210

Animals in Danger
William McCay and Keith Moseley
Macmillan Publishing, 1990
866 Third Avenue
New York, NY 10022

Antarctica
Helen Cowcher
Farrar, Straus, and Giroux, 1990
19 Union Square West
New York, NY 10003

Antonio's Rainforest
Anna Lewington
Carolrhoda Books, 1992
241 First Avenue
Minneapolis, MN 55401

**The Armadillo from
Amarillo**
Lynne Cherry
Harcourt Brace and Company, 1994
1250 6th Avenue
San Diego, CA 92101

Around Me
Erica Magnus
Lothrop, 1992
1350 Avenue of the Americas
New York, NY 10019

At Home in the Coral Reef
Katy Muzik
Charlesbridge, 1992
85 Main Street
Watertown, MA 02172

At Home in the Rainforest
Diane Willow and LauraJacques
Charlesbridge, 1991

85 Main Street
Watertown, MA 02172

The Atlas of Endangered Animals
Steve Pollock
Facts on File, 1993
460 Park Avenue South
New York, NY 10016

Atlas of Environmental Issues
Nick Middleton
Facts on File, 1989
460 Park Avenue South
New York, NY 10016

Aunt Ippy's Museum of Junk
Rodney A. Greenblat
HarperCollins, 1991
10 East 53rd Street
New York, NY 10022

Baby Animals
Sierra Club, 1989
730 Polk Street
San Francisco, CA 94109

Baby Animals: Five Stories of Endangered Species
Derek Hall
Candlewick Press, 1994
2067 Massachusetts Avenue
Cambridge, MA 02140

The Baby Zoo
Bruce McMillan
Scholastic, 1992
555 Broadway
New York, NY 10012

Backyard Explorer Kit: Leaf and Tree Guide
Rona Beame
Workman Publishing, 1989
708 Broadway
New York, NY 10003

Beachmaster
Tom Shachtman
Henry Holt, 1988
115 West 18th Street
New York, NY 10011

The Bear Family
Dieter Betz
Tambourine, 1991
1350 Avenue of the Americas
New York, NY 10019

Bears
Ian Stirling
Sierra Club, 1992
730 Polk Street
San Francisco, CA 94109

Bears: A Global Look at Bears in the Wild
Joni Phelps Hunt
Blake, 1993
2222 Beebee Street
San Luis Obispo, CA 93401

Berenstain Bears, They Don't Pollute (Anymore)
Stan and Jan Berenstain
Random House, 1991
201 East 50th Street
New York, NY 10022

Big Cats
Seymour Simon
HarperCollins, 1991
10 East 53rd Street
New York, NY 10022

The Big Tree
Bruce Hiscock
Macmillan, 1991
866 Third Avenue
New York, NY 10022

Biology for Every Kid: 101 Easy Experiments that Really Work
Janice Vancleaves
John Wiley and Sons, 1990
605 Third Avenue
New York, NY 10158-0012

Birds
World Wildlife Fund
Ladybird, 1988
840 Washington Street
Auburn, ME 04210

Birdwise
Pamela Hickman
Kids Can Press, Ltd., 1988
585-1/2 Bloor Street West
Toronto, Ontario, Canada M6G1K5

Blue and Beautiful Planet Earth Our Home
Ruth Rocha and Octavio Roth
United Nations Publications, 1990
United Nations Plaza
New York, NY 10158

Blue Planet
Barbara Embury Hehner
Harcourt Brace and Company, 1992
1250 6th Avenue
San Diego, CA 92101

The Blue Whale
Melissa Kim
Ideals Publishing Corporation, 1933
565 Marriott Drive, #800
Nashville, TN 10016

Botany for All Ages: Discovering Nature Through Activities Using Plants
Jorie Hunken
agAccess, 1989
P.O. Box 2008
Davis, CA 95616

Both Sides Now
Joni Mitchell and Alan Baker
Scholastic, 1992
555 Broadway
New York, NY 10012

The Boy Who Found the Light
Dale DeArmond
Sierra Club, 1990
730 Polk Street
San Francisco, CA 94109

Bringing Back the Animals
Teresa Kennedy
Amethyst Books/Talman Company, 1991
P.O. Box 895
Woodstock, NY 12498

Brother Eagle, Sister Sky
Chief Seattle and Susan Jeffers
Dial Books, 1991
375 Hudson Street
New York, NY 10014

Bugs
Nancy Winslow Parker
Mulberry Books, 1987
1350 Avenue of the Americas
New York, NY 10019

Buried in Garbage
Bobbie Kalman and Janine Schaub
Crabtree Publishing company, 1991
350 Fifth Avenue, Suite 3308
New York, NY 10118

Cactus Hotel
Brenda Z. Guiberson
Henry Holt, 1991
115 West 18th Street
New York, NY 10011

Can the Whales Be Saved?
Dr. Philip Whitfield
Viking Krestrel, 1989
40 West 23rd Street
New York, NY 10010

Captain Eco and the Fate of the Earth
Jonathan Porritt
Doring Kindersley, 1991
232 Madison Avenue
New York, NY

Cartons, Cans and Orange Peels: Where Does Your Garbage Go?
Joanna Foster
Clarion Books, 1991
215 Park Avenue South
New York, NY 10003

Cells
Michael George
Creative Education, 1992
123 South Broad Street
Mankato, MN 56001

The Changing Desert
Ada and Frank Graham
Sierra Club, 1981
730 Polk Street
San Francisco, CA 94109

Changing Our World: A Handbook for Young Activists
Paul Fleisher
Zephyr Press, 1993
P.O. Box 13448
Tucson, AZ 85732-3448

Children's Atlas of World Wildlife
Rand McNally, 1991
150 East 52nd Street
New York, NY 10022

Children's Special Places
David Sobel
Zephyr Press, 1993
P.O. Box 13448
Tucson, AZ 85732

A Child's Book of Wildflowers
M.A. Kelly

Four Winds Press/Macmillan, 1992
866 Third Avenue
New York, NY 10022

A Child's Organic Garden: Grow Your Own Delicious Nutritious Foods
Lee Fryer and Leigh Bradford
Acropolis Books, Ltd., 1989
2400 17th Street NW
Washington, DC 20009

The Chimpanzee Family Book
Jane Goodall
Picture Book Studio, 1989
10 Central Street
Saxonville, MA 01701

City Safaris: A Sierra Club Explorer's Guide to Urban Adventures for Grown-ups and Kids
Carolyn Shaffer
Sierra Club, 1987
730 Polk Street
San Francisco, CA 94109

Clouds
Jenny Markert
Creative Education, 1992
123 South Broad Street
Mankato, MN 56001

Coastal Rescue: Preserving Our Seashores
Christina Miller
Macmillan, 1989
866 Third Avenue
New York, NY 10022

Come Back Salmon
Molly Cone
Sierra Club, 1992
730 Polk Street
San Francisco, CA 94109

The Conservationworks Book
Lisa Capone and Cady Goldfield
Appalachian Mountain Club Books, 1992
5 Joy Street
Boston, MA 02108

Contests for Students: All You Need to Know to Enter and Win 600 Contests
Mary Ellen Snodgrass
Gale Research, Inc., 1991

835 Penobscot Boulevard
Detroit, MI 48226

Cora the Crow
Mirabel Cecil
McGraw-Hill, 1980
1221 Avenue of the Americas
New York, NY 10020

Coral Reef
Michael George
Creative Education, 1992
123 South Broad Street
Mankato, MN 56001

Coral Reef
Barbara Taylor
Dorling Kindersley, 1992
232 Madison Avenue
New York, NY 10016

Coral Reefs
Dwight Holing
Blake Publishing, 1990
2222 Beebee Street
San Luis Obispo, CA 93401

Creative Handmade Paper, How to Make Paper from Recycled and Natural Materials
David Watson
Search Press, 1991
North Farm Road
Tunbridge Wells, Kent, United Kingdom TN2 3DR

Creepy Crawlies: In 3-D
Rick and Susan Sammon
The Nature Company, 1993
P.O. Box 188
Florence, KY 41022

Cricket in the Grass
Philip Van Soelen
Sierra Club, 1979
730 Polk Street
San Francisco, CA 94109

Crinkleroot's Guide to Knowing the Trees
Jim Arnosky
Bradbury Press, 1992
866 Third Avenue
New York, NY 10022

Cycles of Nature: An Introduction to Biological Rhythms
Andrew Ahlgren

National Science Teachers Association,
1990
1742 Connecticut Avenue NW
Washington, DC 20009

**Daisy Rothchild: The Giraffe That
Lives with Me**
Betty Leslie-Melville
Bantam Doubleday Dell, 1987
666 Fifth Avenue
New York, NY 10103

**Danger on the African
Grassland**
Elisabeth Sackett
Sierra Club, 1991
730 Polk Street
San Francisco, CA 94109

Danger on the Arctic Ice
Elisabeth Sackett
Sierra Club, 1991
730 Polk Street
San Francisco, CA 94109

**Davy's Dream:
A Young Boy's Adventure with
Wild Orca Whales**
Paul Owen Lewis
Beyond Words Publishing, 1988
Pumpkin Ridge Road, Route 3, Box
492-B
Hillsboro, OR 97123

Dear Mr. President
Marc Davenport
Citadel Press, 1992
600 Madison Avenue
New York, NY 10022

Dear World
Lannis Temple
Random House, 1993
201 East 50th Street
New York, NY 10022

**Desert Giant: The World of the
Saguaro Cactus**
Barbara Bash
Sierra Club, 1989
730 Polk Street
Boston, MA 02108

The Desert
Joni Phelps Hunt
Blake Publishing, 1991
2222 Beebee Street
San Luis Obispo, CA 93401

The Desert Mermaid
Alberto Blanco
Children's Book Press, 1992
6400 Hollis Street, #4
Emeryville, CA 94608

Dinosaurs to the Rescue
Laurie Krasny Brown
Gryphon House, 1992
3706 Otis Street, P.O. Box 275
Mt. Rainier, MD 20712

Discover My World: Forest
Ron Hirsch
Bantam Doubleday Dell, 1991
666 Fifth Avenue
New York, NY 10103

Diving into the Oceans
Ranger Rick
National Wildlife Federation, 1988
1400 Sixteenth Street NW
Washington, DC 20036-2266

Dogsong
Gary Paulsen
Puffin Books, 1987
375 Hudson Street
New York, NY 10014

The Dolphins and Me
Don C. Reed
Sierra Club, 1989
730 Polk Street
San Francisco, CA 94109

Dolphins and Porpoises
Janelle Hatherly
Facts on File, 1990
460 Park Avenue South
New York, NY 10016

**Draw 50 Endangered
Species**
Lee J. James
Bantam Doubleday Dell, 1992
666 Fifth Avenue
New York, NY 10103

Earth Book for Kids
Linda Schwartz
Learning Works, 1990
P.O. Box 6187
Santa Barbara, CA 93160

Earth Facts
Lynn Bresler
Usborne Publishing, 1986

Usborne House, 83-85 Saffron Hill
London, England EC1N8RT

**Earth: The Incredible Recycling
Machine**
Paul Bennet
Thomson Learning, 1993
P.O. Box 6187
New York, NY 10003

Earth Keepers
Joan Anderson
Harcourt Brace and Company, 1993
1250 6th Avenue
San Diego, CA 92101

Earth Kids
Jill Wheeler
Abdo and Daughters, 1993
4940 Viking Drive, Suite 622
Edina, MN 55435

Earth to Matthew
Paula Danziger
Bantam Doubleday Dell, 1991
666 Fifth Avenue
New York, NY 10103

**Earth Science for Every Kid: 101
Easy Experiments that Really
Work**
Janice Vancleaves
John Wiley and Sons, 1991
605 Third Avenue
New York, NY 10158-0012

Earth Songs
Myra Cohn Livingston
Holiday House, 1986
18 East 53rd Street
New York, NY 10022

Earth Words
John Shepard
Abdo & Daughters, 1993
4940 Viking Drive, Suite 622
Edina, MN 55435

**Earth-Friendly Toys: How to Make
Fabulous Toys and Games from
Reusable Objects**
George Pfiffner
John Wiley and Sons, 1994
605 Third Avenue
New York, NY 10158-0012

Earthcycles and Ecosystems
Beth Savan

Addison-Wesley, 1991
2725 Sand Hill Road
Menlo Park, CA 94025

Earthquakes
Franklyn M. Branley
Crowell Junior Books, 1990
10 East 53rd Street
New York, NY 10022

Earthwatch, Earthcycles and Ecosystems
Beth Savan
Addison-Wesley, 1991
2725 Sand Hill Road
Menlo Park, CA 94025

Earthways: Simple Environmental Activities for Young Children
Carol Petrash
Gryphon House, 1992
3706 Otis Street, P.O. Box 275
Mt. Rainier, MD 20712

Earthwise at Home: A Guide to the Care and Feeding of Your Planet
Linda Lowery
Carolrhoda Books, 1993
241 First Avenue
Minneapolis, MN 55401

Easy Green
Marty Westerman
American Camping Association, 1993
5000 State Road 67, North
Martinsville, IN 46151-7902

Eat, Think, and Be Healthy!
Paula Klevan Zeller and Michael F. Jacobson
Center for Science in the Public Interest, 1987
1501 16th Street NW
Washington, DC 20036

Eating the Alphabet: Fruits and Vegetables from A to Z
Lois Ehlert
Harcourt Brace and Company, 1989
1250 6th Avenue
San Diego, CA 92101

Eco-Careers
John Hamilton
Abdo and Daughters, 1993
4940 Viking Drive, Suite 622
Edina, MN 55435

Eco-Disasters
John Hamilton
Abdo and Daughters, 1993
4940 Viking Drive, Suite 622
Edina, MN 55435

Eco-Fairs and Carnivals
Stuart Kallen
Abdo and Daughters, 1993
4940 Viking Drive, Suite 622
Edina, MN 55435

Eco-Groups: Joining Together to Protect the Environment
John Hamilton
Abdo and Daughters, 1993
4940 Viking Drive, Suite 622
Edina, MN 55435

Eco-Solutions: It's in Your Hands
Oliver Owen
Abdo and Daughters, 1993
4940 Viking Drive, Suite 622
Edina, MN55435

EcoArt
Laurie Carlson
Williamson Publishing, 1993
Church Hill Road, P.O. Box 185
Charlotte, VT 05445

Ecology for All Ages: Discovering Nature Through Activities for Children and Adults
Jorie Hunken
The Globe Pequot Press, 1994
P.O. Box 833
Old Saybrook, CT 06475

Ecology: A Practical Introduction with Projects and Activities
Richard Spurgeon
Usborne Publishing, 1988
Usborne House, 83-85 Saffron Hill
London, England EC1N8RT

Ecology Projects for Young Scientists
Martin Gutnik
Franklin Watts, 1984
95 Madison Avenue
New York, NY 10016

The Education of Little Tree
Forrest Carter
University of New Mexico Press, 1976
1720 Lomas Boulevard, NE
Albuquerque, NM 87131-1591

Eevil Weevil
Stephen Cosgrove
Rourke Enterprises, 1984
P.O. Box 3328
Vero Beach, FL 32964

Elephant Bathes
Derek Hall
Sierra Club, 1985
730 Polk Street
San Francisco, CA 94109

Elephant Have the Right of Way
Betty Leslie-Melville
Bantam Doubleday Dell, 1992
666 Fifth Avenue
New York, NY 10103

Elephants
Jean Brody
Blake Books, 1993
2222 Beebee Street
San Luis Obispo, CA 93401

The Empty Lot
Dale Fife
Sierra Club, 1991
730 Polk Street
San Francisco, CA 94109

Endangered Animals
Ranger Rick
National Wildlife Federation, 1989
1400 Sixteenth Street NW
Washington, DC 20036-2266

Endangered Animals of the Rainforest
Sandra Uchitel
Price Stern Sloan, 1992
11835 Olympic Boulevard
Los Angeles, CA 90064

The Endangered Wildlife Shufflebook
Richard Hefter
Museum of Modern Art, 1991
11 West 53rd Street
New York, NY 10102

**Energy and Power:
A Practical Introduction with Projects and Activities**
Usborne Science and Experiments
Usborne Publishing Ltd., 1990
Usborne House, 83-85 Saffron Hill
London, England EC1N8RT

Energy Resources
Robin Kerrod
Thomson Learning, 1993
P.O. Box 6187
New York, NY 10003

The Environment and Health
Brian R. Ward
Franklin Watts, 1989
95 Madison Avenue
New York, NY 10016

Environmental Awareness: Acid Rain
Mary Ellen Snodgrass
Bancroft-Sage Publishing, 1991
601 Elkcam Circle, Suite C-7
P.O. Box 355
Marco, FL 33969-0355

Environmental Awareness: Air Pollution
Mary Ellen Snodgrass
Bancroft-Sage Publishing, 1991
601 Elkcam Circle, Suite C-7
P.O. Box 355
Marco, FL 33969-0355

Environmental Awareness: Land Pollution
Mary Ellen Snodgrass
Bancroft-Sage Publishing, 1991
601 Elkcam Circle, Suite C-7
P.O. Box 355
Marco, FL 33969-0355

Environmental Awareness: Solid Waste
Mary Ellen Snodgrass
Bancroft-Sage Publishing, 1991
601 Elkcam Circle, Suite C-7
P.O. Box 355
Marco, FL 33969-0355

Environmental Awareness: Toxic Waste
Mary Ellen Snodgrass
Bancroft-Sage Publishing, 1991
601 Elkcam Circle, Suite C-7
P.O. Box 355
Marco, FL 33969-0355

Environmental Awareness: Water Pollution
Mary Ellen Snodgrass
Bancroft-Sage Publishing, 1991
601 Elkcam Circle, Suite C-7

P.O. Box 355
Marco, FL 33969-0355

Environmental Science: 49 Science Fair Projects
Robert L. Bonnet
Tab Books, 1990
860 Taylor Station Road
Blacklick, OH 43004

Every Kid's Guide to Saving the Earth
Joy Berry
Ideals Publishing Corp., 1993
565 Marriott Drive, #800
Nashville, TN 37214

Everyone Wins: Cooperative Games and Activities
Sambhava and Josette Luvmour
New Society Publishers, 1990
4527 Springfield Avenue
Philadelphia, PA 19143

The Evolution Book
Sara Stein
Workman Publishing, 1986
708 Broadway
New York, NY 10003

Exploring Nature in Winter
Alan M. Cvancara
Walker and Company, 1992
720 Fifth Avenue
New York, NY 10019

Exploring Sand and the Desert
Gayle Bittinger
Warren Publishing, 1993
P.O. Box 2250
Everett, WA 98203

Exploring Water and the Ocean
Gayle Bittinger
Warren Publishing, 1993
P.O. Box 2250
Everett, WA 98203

Exploring Wood and the Forest
Jean Warren
Warren Publishing, 1993
P.O. Box 2250
Everett, WA 98203

Extremely Weird Endangered Species
Sarah Lovett
John Muir Publications, 1992

P.O. Box 613
Santa Fe, NM 87504

Eyewitness Books: Sharks
Miranda MacQuitty
Knopf, 1992
201 East 50th Street
New York, NY 10022

Eyewitness Books: Volcano and Earthquakes
Susanna Van Rose
Knopf, 1992
201 East 50th Street
New York, NY 10022

Far North: Vanishing Cultures
Jan Reynolds
Harcourt Brace and Company, 1992
1250 6th Avenue
San Diego, CA 92101

Farewell to Shady Glade
Bill Peet
Houghton Mifflin, 1966
222 Berkely Street
Boston, MA 02116

Feed the Birds
Helen Witty and Dick Witty
Workman Publishing, 1991
708 Broadway
New York, NY 10003

Fifty (50) Simple Things Kids Can Do to Recycle
Earthworks Group, 1994
1400 Shattuck Avenue, Box 25
Berkeley, CA 94709

Fifty (50) Simple Things Kids Can Do to Save the Earth
Earth Works Press, 1990
1400 Shattuck Avenue, #25
Berkeley, CA 94709

Finding Out About Our Earth
Jane Chisholm
Usborne Publishing, 1991
Usborne House, 83-85 Saffron Hill
London, England EC1N8RT

Fire Race: A Karuk Coyote Tale
Jonathan London
Chronicle Books, 1993
275 Fifth Street
San Francisco, CA 94103

The First Forest
John Gile
John Gile Communications, 1989
P.O. Box 2321
Rockford, IL 61131-0321

The Fledglings
Sandra Markle
Bantam Doubleday Dell, 1992
666 Fifth Avenue
New York, NY 10103

Flowers
David Birnie
Dorling Kindersley, 1992
232 Madison Avenue
New York, NY 10016

Follow the Water from Brook to Ocean
Arthur Borros
HarperCollins, 1991
10 East 53rd Street
New York, NY 10022

Food Resources
Robin Kerrod
Thomson Learning, 1993
P.O. Box 6187
New York, NY 10003

Footprints and Shadows
Anne Wescott Dodd
Simon and Schuster, 1992
1230 Avenue of the Americas
New York, NY 10020

The Forgotten Forest
Laurence Anholt
Sierra Club, 1992
730 Polk Street
San Francisco, CA 94109

The Four Elements: Air
Maria Ruis and J.M Parramon
Barron's, 1984
250 Wireless Boulevard
Hauppauge, NY 11788

The Four Elements: Fire
Maria Ruis and J.M Parramon
Barron's, 1985
250 Wireless Boulevard
Hauppauge, NY 11788

The Four Elements: Water
Carme Sole Vendrell and J.M. Parramon

Barron's, 1984
250 Wireless Boulevard
Hauppauge, NY 11788

The Fragile Flag
Jane Langton
HarperCollins, 1984
10 East 53rd Street
New York, NY 10022

From Seed to Plant
Gail Gibbons
Holiday House, 1991
18 East 53rd Street
New York, NY 10022

From Trash to Treasure
Liza Alexander
Western Publishing, 1993
1220 Mound Avenue
Racine, WI 53404

Gadabouts and Stick-at-Homes
Lorus and Marjory Milne
Sierra Club, 1980
730 Polk Street
San Francisco, CA 94109

The Galapagos Tortoise
Susan Shafer
Macmillan, 1992
866 Third Avenue
New York, NY 10022

Garbage
Maria Fleming
Scholastic, 1992
555 Broadway
New York, NY 10012

Garbage!
Evan and Janet Hadingham
Simon and Schuster, 1990
1230 Avenue of the Americas
New York, NY 10020

Garbage
Karen O'Connor
Lucent Books, 1991
P.O. Box 289011
San Diego, CA 92198-0011

The Garden Book
Wes Porter
Workman Publishing, 1989
708 Broadway
New York, NY 10003

The Garden in the City
Gerda Muller
Dutton, 1988
375 Hudson Street
New York, NY 10014

The Gift of the Tree
Alvin Tresselt
Tresselt/Sorenson, 1992
1350 Avenue of the Americas
New York, NY 10019

Girls and Young Women Leading the Way: 20 True Stories About Leadership
Karnes and Bean
Free Spirit Publishing, 1993
400 First Avenue North, #616
Minneapolis, MN 55401

The Giving Tree
Shel Silverstein
HarperCollins, 1964
10 East 53rd Street
New York, NY 10022

The Glass Ark: The Story of Biosphere II
Linnea Gentry and Karen Liptak
Viking/Penguin, 1991
375 Hudson Street
New York, NY 10014

Global Warming
Sandy Ransford
Simon and Schuster, 1992
1230 Avenue of the Americas
New York, NY 10020

Global Warming: Assessing the Greenhouse Threat
Laurence Pringle
Arcade Publishing, 1990
32 Beacon Street
Boston, MA 02108

Going Green: A Kid's Handbook to Saving the Planet
Elkington/Hailes/Hill
Puffin Books, 1990
375 Hudson Street
New York, NY 10014

Going on a Whale Watch
Bruce McMillan
Scholastic, 1992
555 Broadway
New York, NY 10012

Golden Sound Story: Rainforest Adventure
Liza Alexander
Western Publishing, 1992
Golden Books
Racine, WI 53404

Good Earth Art
Kohl and Gainer
Ecolokids, 1991
3146 Shadow Lane
Topeka, KS 66601

Good Planets Are Hard to Find
Dehr and Bazar
Earthbeat Press, 1989
P.O. Box 33852, Station D
Vancourer, B.C., Canada V6J 4L6

Gorilla Builds
Derek Hall
Sierra Club, 1985
730 Polk Street
San Francisco, CA 94109

Gray Wolf/Red Wolf
Dorothy Hinshaw Patent
Clarion Books, 1990
215 Park Avenue South
New York, NY 10003

The Great Barrier Reef
Rebecca Johnson
Lerner Publications, 1991
241 First Avenue North
Minneapolis, MN 55401

Great Careers for People Concerned About the Environment
Lesley Grant
Gale Research, Inc., 1993
835 Penobscot Bldg.
Detroit, MI 48226

Great Careers for People Who Like Being Outdoors
Lesley Grant
Gale Research, Inc., 1993
835 Penobscot Bldg.
Detroit, MI 48226

The Great Kapok Tree
Lynne Cherry
Harcourt Brace and Company, 1990
1250 6th Avenue
San Diego, CA 92101

The Great Seed Mystery for Kids
Peggy Henry
BMR, 1992
21 Tamal Vista Boulevard
Corte Madera, CA 94925

The Greenhouse Effect: Life on a Warmer Planet
Rebecca Johnson
Lerner Publications, 1993
241 First Avenue North
Minneapolis, MN 55401

Gregory, the Terrible Eater
Mitchell Sharmat
Scholastic, 1980
555 Broadway
New York, NY 10012

Grizzly Years: In Search of the American Wilderness
Doug Peacock
Kensington Publishing, 1990
475 Park Avenue South
New York, NY 10016

Grover's 10 Terrific Ways to Help Our Wonderful World
Sesame Street
Random House, 1992
201 East 50th Street
New York, NY 10022

Grow It!: An Indoor/Outdoor Gardening Guide for Kids
Erika Markmann
agAccess, 1991
P.O. Box 2008
Davis, CA 95616

Growing Things
Angela Wilkes
EDC Publishing, 1984
10302 East 55th Place
Tulsa, OK 74146

Growing Vegetable Soup
Lois Ehlert
HBJ Books, 1987
1250 Sixth Avenue
San Diego, CA 92101

Grusha
Barbara Bustetter Falk
HarperCollins, 1993
10 East 53rd Street
New York, NY 10022

Habitats
Pamela Hickman
Kids Can Press, 1993
585-1/2 Bloor Street West
Toronto, Ontario, Canada M6G1K5

Habitats: On Land, Under Ground, Sea, Air
Ruis and Parramon
Barron's, 1986
250 Wireless Boulevard
Hauppauge, NY 11788

Hands-on Nature
Jenepher Lingelbach
Vermont Institute of Natural Science, 1986
Church Hill Road
Woodstock, VT05091

Hatchet
Gary Paulsen
Puffin Books, 1987
375 Hudson Street
New York, NY 10014

The Heat Is On: Facing Our Energy Problems
Shelly Tanaka
Firefly Books, 1991
P.O. Box 1325, Elliot Station
Buffalo, NY 14205

The Helping Hands Handbook
Patricia Adams
Random House, 1992
201 East 50th Street
New York, NY 10022

Here Comes the Recycling Truck!
Meyer Seltzer
Albert Whitman, 1992
6340 Oakton Street
Morton Grove, IL 60053

Hey! Get Off Our Train
John Burningham
Crown Publishers, 1989
201 East 50th Street
New York, NY 10022

The Hostage
Theodore Taylor
Bantam Doubleday Dell, 1987
666 Fifth Avenue
New York, NY 10103

How the Earth Works
John Farndon
Reader's Digest, 1992
Customer Service Department
Pleasantville, NY 10570

How Green Are You?
David Bellamy
Potter, 1991
201 East 50th Street
New York, NY 10022

How the Forest Grew
William Jaspersohn
Greenwillow, 1980
1350 Avenue of the Americas
New York, NY 10019

How to Draw Endangered Animals
Georgene Hartophilis
Mallard Press, 1991
666 Fifth Avenue
New York, NY 10103

How to Make Your Own Recycled Paper
Valentine and Dace
Search Press, 1990
Wellwood, North Farm Road
Tunbridge Wells, Kent, United Kingdom TN2 3DR

How Nature Works
Steve Parker
Random House, 1992
201 East 50th Street
New York, NY 10022

How Trees Help Me
Bobbie Kalman and Janinie Schaub
Crabtree Publishing, 1992
350 Fifth Avenue, Suite 3308
New York, NY 10118

I Celebrate Nature
Diane Iverson
Dawn Publications, 1993
14618 Tyler Foote Road
Nevada City, CA 95959

I Helped Save the Earth
Michael O'Brien
Berkley Publishing, 1991
200 Madison Avenue
New York, NY 10016

The Illustrated World of Oceans
Susan Wells

Simon and Schuster, 1991
1230 Avenue of the Americas
New York, NY 10020

I Love Animals
Shelly Neilsen
Abdo and Daughters, 1993
4940 Viking Drive, Suite 622
Edina, MN 55435

I Love Water
Shelly Neilsen
Abdo and Daughters, 1993
4940 Viking Drive, Suite 622
Edina, MN 55435

I Was Good to the Earth Today
Susan Bryer Starr
Starhouse Publishing, 1992
4416 Graywhaler Lane
Rohnert Park, CA 94928

In the Forest
Jim Arnosky
Lothrop, Lee and Shepard, 1989
105 Madison Avenue
New York, NY 10016

In a Pumpkin Shell
Jennifer Storey Gillis
Storey Communications, 1992
Schoolhouse Road
Pownal, VT 05261

In Search of the Last Dodo
Ann and Reg Cartwright
Little, Brown and Company, 1989
32 Beacon Street
Boston, MA 02108

It's My Earth Too: How I Can Help the Earth Stay Alive
Kathleen Krull
Bantam Doubleday Dell, 1992
666 Fifth Avenue
New York, NY 10103

Jack, the Seal and the Sea
Gerald Aschenbrenner
Silver Burdett Press, 1988
Prentice Hall Building, 113 Sylvan Avenue
Englewood Cliffs, NJ 07632

Jitterbug
Stephen Cosgrove
Rourke Enterprises, 1985

P.O. Box 3328
Vero Beach, FL 32964

Joey's Cabbage Patch
Harvey Rosenberg
Go Jolly Publications, 1992
P.O. Box 398
Graton, CA 95444

Journey Through a Tropical Jungle
Adrian Forsyth
Simon and Schuster, 1988
1230 Avenue of the Americas
New York, NY 10020

Journey Through Nature
Jim Flegg
Smithmark Publishers, 1991
112 Madison Avenue
New York, NY 10016

Journey to the Heart of Nature
Joseph Cornell and Michael Deranja
Dawn Publications, 1994
141618 Tyler Foote Road
Nevada City, CA 95959

Julie of the Wolves
Jean Craighead George
HarperCollins, 1972
10 East 53rd Street
New York, NY 10022

June Mountain Secret
Nina Kidd
HarperCollins, 1991
10 East 53rd Street
New York, NY 10022

The Jungle Is My Home
Laura Fischetto
Viking/Penguin, 1991
375 Hudson Street
New York, NY 10014

Jungles
Mark Rauzon
Bantam Doubleday Dell
666 Fifth Avenue
New York, NY 10103

Jungles: A Science Activity Book
Puffin
Viking/Penguin, 1988
375 Hudson Street
New York, NY 10010

Just a Dream
Chris Van Allsberg
Houghton Mifflin, 1990
222 Berkely Street
Boston, MA 02116

Kid Heroes of the Environment
Earthworks Group
Earthworks Press, 1991
1400 Shattuck Avenue, Box 25
Berkely, CA 94709

Kid Vid: Fundamentals of Video Instruction
Kaye Black
Zephyr Press, 1989
P.O. Box 13448
Tucson, AZ 85732-3448

Kid's Environment Book
Anne Pederson
John Muir Publications, 1991
P.O. Box 613
Santa Fe, NM 87504

The Kid's Guide to How to Save the Animals
Billy Goodman
Avon Books, 1991
1350 Avenue of the Americas
New York, NY 10019

The Kid's Guide to How to Save the Planet
Billy Goodman
Avon Books, 1990
1350 Avenue of the Americas
New York, NY 10019

The Kid's Guide to Social Action
Barbara Lewis
Free Spirit, 1991
400 First Avenue North, #616
Minneapolis, MN 55401

The Kid's Nature Book
Susan Milord
Williamson, 1989
Church Hill Road, P.O. Box 185
Charlotte, VT 05445

Kid's Wildlife Book
Warner Shedd
Williamson, 1994
Church Hill Road, P.O. Box 185
Charlotte, VT 05445

Kids Can Save the Animals: 101 Easy Things to Do
Ingrid Newkirk
Warner Books, 1991
666 Fifth Avenue
New York, NY 10103

The Kids Care Book: 50 Class Projects that Help Kids Help Others
Joan Noveli and Beth Chayet
Scholastic, 1991
555 Broadway
New York, NY 10012

The Kids' Earth Handbook
Sandra Markle
Macmillan, 1991
866 Third Avenue
New York, NY 10022

Kids with Courage
Barbara Lewis
Free Spirit Publishing, 1992
400 First Avenue North, #616
Minneapolis, MN 55401

Kids Ending Hunger
Tracy Apple Howard
Andrews and McMee, 1992
4900 Main Street
Kansas City, MO 64112

Kitchen Fun for Kids
Michael Jacobsen
Henry Holt, 1991
115 West 18th Street
New York, NY 10011

Larue and the Brown Sky
David Church
Kresser/Craig, 1992
2425 Colorado Avenue
Santa Monica, CA 90404

Let's Talk Trash: The Kid's Book About Recycling
Kelly McQueen
Waterfront Books, 1991
98 Brookes Avenue
Burlington, VT 05401

Likeable Recyclables
Linda Schwartz
Learning Works, 1992
P.O. Box 6187
Santa Barbara, CA 93160

Linnea's Windowsill Garden
Christina Bjork and Lena Anderson
R and S Books, 1978
19 Union Square West
New York, NY 10003

The Living World: Jungles
Dr. Clive Catchpole
Dial Books, 1985
375 Hudson Street
New York, NY 10016

Long Live Earth
Meighan Morrison
Scholastic, 1993
555 Broadway
New York, NY 10012

Look Inside the Earth
Gina Ingoglia
Grosset and Dunlap, 1989
200 Madison Avenue
New York, NY 10016

Look Inside a Tree
Gina Ingoglia
Grosset and Dunlap, 1987
200 Madison Avenue
New York, NY 10016

Looking at the Environment
David Suzuki
John Wiley and Sons, 1991
605 Third Avenue
New York, NY 10158-0012

The Lorax
Dr. Seuss
Random House, 1971
201 East 50th Street
New York, NY 10022

The Lost Kingdom of Karnica
Richard Kennedy
Sierra Club, 1979
730 Polk Street
San Francisco, CA 94109

The Lost Lake
Allen Say
Houghton Mifflin, 1989
222 Berkely Street
Boston, MA 02116

Love Earth: The Beauty Makeover
Julie Berg

Abdo and Daughters, 1993
4940 Viking Drive, Suite 622
Edina, MN 55435

Loving the Earth
Fredric Lehrman
Celestial Arts, 1990
P.O. Box 707
Berkeley, CA 94707

The Magic Schoolbus on the Ocean Floor
Joanna Cole
Scholastic, 1986
555 Broadway
New York, NY 10012

The Magic Schoolbus at the Waterworks
Joanna Cole
Scholastic, 1986
555 Broadway
New York, NY 10012

Magical Earth Secrets
Della Burford
Western Canada Wilderness
Committee, 1990
20 Water Street
Vancouver, BC, Canada V6J 4L6

Magical Earth Secrets: The Environmental Activity Guide
Della Burford
Western Canada Wilderness
Committee, 1990
20 Water Street
Vancouver, BC, Canada V6J 4L6

Marine Biology
Ellen Doris
Thames and Hudson, 1993
500 Fifth Avenue
New York, NY 10110

Material Resources
Robin Kerrod
Thomson Learning, 1994
115 Fifth Avenue
New York, NY 10003

Matthew's Meadow
Corrinne Demas Bliss
Harcourt Brace and Company, 1992
1250 6th Avenue
San Diego, CA 92101

Maya and the Town that Loved a Tree
Kiki and Kathryn Shaw
Children's Universe, 1992
300 Park Avenue South
New York, NY 10010

Michael Bird-boy
Tomie Depaola
Prentice Hall, 1975
113 Sylvan Avenue
Englewood Cliffs, NJ 07632

Mighty Tree
Dick Gackenbach
Gulliver/HBJ, 1992
1250 6th Avenue
San Diego, CA 92101

Mineral Resources
Robin Kerrod
Thomson Learning, 1994
115 Fifth Avenue
New York, NY 10003

Miss Rumphius
Barbara Cooney
Viking-Penguin, 1982
375 Hudson Street
New York, NY 10014

The Modern Ark
Clair Littlejohn
Dial Books
375 Hudson Street
New York, NY 10014

More Science Activities
Smithsonian Institution
Galison Books, 1988
25 West 43rd Street
New York, NY 10036

Mother Earth
Nancy Luenn
Atheneum, 1992
866 Third Avenue
New York, NY 10022

Mother Nature's Greatest Hits
Bartelby Nash
Living Planet Press, 1991
2940 Newark NW
Washington, DC 20008

The Mountain that Loved a Bird
Alice McLerran
Picture Book Studio, 1985

10 Central Street
Saxonville, MA 01701

Mr. Wizard's Supermarket Science
Don Herbert
Random House, 1980
201 East 50th Street
New York, NY 10022

My Earth Book
Linda Schwartz
Learning Works, 1991
P.O. Box 6187
Santa Barbara, CA 93160

My First Garden Book
Albie Celfe
BMR, 1991
21 Tamal Vista Boulevard
Corte Madera, CA 94925

My First Garden Book: A Life-Size Guide to Growing Things at Home
Angela Wilkes
Knopf, 1992
201 East 50th Street
New York, NY 10022

My First Nature Book
Roger Priddy
Knopf, 1990
201 East 50th Street
New York, NY 10022

My Friend the Manatee
An Ocean Magic Book
Schneider Educational Products, 1991
P.O. Box 472260
San Francisco, CA 94147

My Friend the Penguin
An Ocean Magic Book
Schneider Educational Products, 1991
P.O. Box 472260
San Francisco, CA 94147

My Friend the Polar Bear
An Ocean Magic Book
Schneider Educational Products, 1991
P.O. Box 472260
San Francisco, CA 94147

My Friend the Porpoise
An Ocean Magic Book
Schneider Educational Products, 1991
P.O. Box 472260
San Francisco, CA 94147

My Friend the Sea Otter
An Ocean Magic Book
Schneider Educational Products, 1991
P.O. Box 472260
San Francisco, CA 94147

My Friend the Walrus
An Ocean Magic Book
Schneider Educational Products, 1991
P.O. Box 472260
San Francisco, CA 94147

My Garden Companion
Jaime Jobb
Sierra Club, 1977
730 Polk Street
San Francisco, CA 94109

My Grandma Lived in a Gooligulch
Graeme Base
Harry N. Abrams, 1983
100 Fifth Avenue
New York, NY 10011

My River
Shari Halpern
Macmillan, 1992
866 Third Avenue
New York, NY 10022

Native American Animal Stories
Joseph Bruchac
Fulcrum Publishing, 1992
350 Indiana Street
Golden, CO 80401-5093

Nature with Children of All Ages
Edith Sisson
Prentice Hall, 1982
113 Sylvan Avenue
Englewood Cliffs, NJ 07632

Nature Detective: How to Solve Outdoor Mysteries
Eileen Docedal
Sterling Publishing, 1989
387 Park Avenue South
New York, NY 10016

Nature Hide and Seek: Jungles
John Norris Wood
Knopf, 1987
201 East 50th Street
New York, NY 10022

Nature Hide and Seek: Oceans
John Norris Wood

Knopf, 1985
201 East 50th Street
New York, NY 10022

Nature Scope: Wading into Wetlands
Ranger Rick
National Wildlife Federation, 1989
1400 Sixteenth Street NW
Washington, DC 20036-2266

Nature Search: Rainforest
Paul Sterry
Reader's Digest, 1992
Customer Service Dept.
Pleasantville, NY 10570

Nature's Great Balancing Act: In Our Own Backyard
E. Jaediker Norsgaard
Cobblehill Books, 1990
375 Hudson Street
New York, NY 10014

Naturewatch: Exploring Nature with Your Children
Adrienne Katz
Addison-Wesley, 1986
2725 Sand Hill Road
Menlo Park, CA 94025

Nessa's Fish
Nancy Luenn
Atheneum, 1990
866 Third Avenue
New York, NY 10022

A New True Book: Water Pollution
Darlene Stille
Children's Press, 1990
5440 North Cumberland Avenue
Chicago, IL 60656

No Kidding Around! America's Young Activists Are Changing Our World and You Can Too
Wendy Schaetzel Leski
Information U.S.A., 1992
P.O. Box E
Kensington, MD 20895

Nobody Wants a Nuclear War
Judith Vigna
Albert Whitman and Company, 1986
6340 Oakton Street
Morton Grove, IL 60053

Nuts to You!
Lois Ehlert
Harcourt Brace and Company, 1993
1250 6th Avenue
San Diego, CA 92101

Oceanarium
Joanne Oppenheim
Bantam Doubleday Dell, 1994
666 Fifth Avenue
New York, NY 10036

The Ocean Eco Guide Unfolds
VanDam Publishers, Incorporated
430 West 14th Street
New York, NY 10014

An Ocean World
Peter Sis
Greenwillow Books, 1992
1350 Avenue of the Americas
New York, NY 10019

Of Things Natural, Wild and Free
Marybeth Lorbiecki
Carolrhoda Books, 1993
241 First Avenue
Minneapolis, MN 55401

Oil Spills
Madalyn Klein Anderson
Franklin Watts, 1990
95 Madison Avenue
New York, NY 10016

Old Indian Legends
Zitkala-Sa (Gertrude Bonnin)
University of Nebraska Press
312 North 14th Street
Lincoln, NE 68588-0484

Old Turtle
Douglas Wood
Pfeifer-Hamilton, 1992
1702 East Jefferson Street
Duluth, MN 55812

Oliver and the Oil Spill
Aruna Chandrasekhar
Landmark Editions, 1991
Box 4469, 1402 Kansas Avenue
Kansas City, MO 64127

On the Brink of Extinction: The California Condor
Caroline Arnold

Harcourt Brace and Company, 1993
1250 6th Avenue
San Diego, CA 92101

On the Day You Were Born
Debra Frasier
Harcourt Brace and Company, 1991
1250 6th Avenue
San Diego, CA 92101

Once There Was a Tree
Natalia Romanova
Dial Books, 1985
375 Hudson Street
New York, NY 10014

One Day in the Tropical Rainforest
Gary Allen
HarperCollins, 1990
10 East 53rd Street
New York, NY 10022

One Earth, a Multitude of Creatures
Peter and Connie Roop
Walker and Company, 1992
720 Fifth Avenue
New York, NY 10019

1000 Facts About the Earth
Moira Butterfield
Kingfisher Books, 1992
95 Madison Avenue
New York, NY 10016

1001 Questions and Answers About Planet Earth
Brian and Brenda Williams
Random House, 1993
201 East 50th Street
New York, NY 10022

One World
Michael Foreman
Arcade/Little, Brown, 1990
32 Beacon Street
Boston, MA 02108

Operation Siberian Crane: The Story Behind the International Effort to Save an Amazing Bird
Judi Friedman
Macmillan, 1992
866 Third Avenue
New York, NY 10022

Our Endangered Planet: Antarctica
Suzanne Winckler and Mary M. Rodgers
Lerner Publications, 1992
241 First Avenue North
Minneapolis, MN 55401

Our Endangered Planet: Groundwater
Mary Hoff and Mary M. Rodgers
Lerner Publications, 1991
241 First Avenue North
Minneapolis, MN 55401

Our Endangered Planet: Life on Land
Mary Hoff and Mary M. Rodgers
Lerner Publications, 1992
241 First Avenue North
Minneapolis, MN 55401

Our Endangered Planet: Oceans
Mary Hoff and Mary M. Rodgers
Lerner Publications, 1991
241 First Avenue North
Minneapolis, MN 55401

Our Endangered Planet: Population Growth
Suzanne Winckler and Mary M. Rodgers
Lerner Publications, 1991
241 First Avenue North
Minneapolis, MN 55401

Our Endangered Planet: Rivers and Lakes
Mary Hoff and Mary M. Rodgers
Lerner Publications, 1991
241 First Avenue North
Minneapolis, MN 55401

Our Endangered Planet: Tropical Rainforests
Cornelia F. Muttel and Mary M. Rodgers
Lerner Publications, 1991
241 First Avenue North
Minneapolis, MN 55401

Our Environment
Rebecca Starl
Future Problem Solving Program, 1991
315 West Huron, Suite 140-B
Ann Arbor, MI 48103

Our Future at Stake
Citizen's Policy Center
New Society Publishers, 1985
4527 Springfield Avenue
Philadelphia, PA 19143

Our Planet
Lionel Bender
Simon and Schuster, 1991
1230 Avenue of the Americas
New York, NY 10020

Our World in Danger
World Wildlife Fund
Ladybird, 1989
840 Washington Street
Auburn, ME 04210

Our World (Learning and Caring About)
Gayle Bittinger
Warren Publishing, 1990
P.O. Box 2250
Everett, MA 98203

Outstanding Outsides
Hana Machotska
William Morrow, 1993
1350 Avenue of the Americas
New York, NY 10019

The Paddock: A Story in Praise of the Earth
Lilith Norman
Knopf, 1992
201 East 50th Street
New York, NY 10022

Panda
Jane Goodall
Alladin/Macmillan, 1989
866 Third Avenue
New York, NY 10022

Panther Dream
Bob and Wendy Weir
Hyperion, 1991
114 5th Avenue
New York, NY 10011

Paper by Kids
Arnold Grummer
Dillon Press, 1990
242 Portland Avenue South
Minneapolis, MN 55415

Un Paseo por el Bosque Lluvioso
Kristin Joy Pratt
Dawn Publications, 1993
14618 Tyler Foote Road
Nevada City, CA 95959

The Peach Tree
Norman Pike
Pathway Book Service, 1983
Lower Village
Gilsum, NH 03448

**The People Who Hugged
the Trees**
Deborah Lee Rose
Roberts Rinehart, 1990
P.O. Box 3161
Boulder, CO 80303

The Planet of Trash
George Poppel
Pandamonium Books, 1987
7508 Wisconsin Avenue
Bethesda, MD 20814

Plant Wise
Pamela Hickman
Kids Can Press, 1991
585-1/2 Bloor Street West
Toronto, Ontario, Canada M6G1K5

Planting a Rainbow
Lois Ehlert
Harcourt Brace and Company, 1988
1250 6th Avenue
San Diego, CA 92101

Plants
World Wildlife Fund
Ladybird, 1986
840 Washington Street
Auburn, ME 04210

Plants that Never Bloom
Ruth Heller
Grosset and Dunlap, 1984
200 Madison Avenue
New York, NY 10016

Pond Life
Barbara Taylor
Dorling Kindersley, 1992
232 Madison Avenue
New York, NY 10016

Prince Bear
Helme Heine

McElderry/Macmillan, 1987
866 Third Avenue
New York, NY 10022

Prince William
Gloria and Ted Rand
Henry Holt, 1992
115 West 18th Street
New York, NY 10011

**Projects for a Healthy Planet:
Simple Environmental Experiments
for Kids**
Shar Levine and Allison Grafton
John Wiley and Sons, 1992
605 Third Avenue
New York, NY 10158-0012

Protecting Endangered Species
Felicity Brooks
Usborne, 1990
Usborne House, 83-85 Saffron Hill
London, England EC1N8RT

**Protecting Endangered Species at
the San Diego Zoo**
Georgeanne Irvine
Simon and Schuster, 1990
1230 Avenue of the Americas
New York, NY 10020

**Protecting Our World:
A Beginner's Guide to
Conservation**
David Duthie
Usborne, 1991
Usborne House, 83-85 Saffron Hill
London, England EC1N8RT

Protecting Rivers and Seas
Usborne Conservation Guide
EDC Publishing
10302 East 55th Place
Tulsa, OK 74146

**Protecting Trees and
Forests**
David Duthie
Usborne, 1991
Usborne House, 83-85 Saffron Hill
London, England EC1N8RT

A Pukeko in a Ponga Tree
Kingi M. Ihaka
Little Mammouth, 1991
39 Rawene Road
Birkenhead, Auckland, New Zealand

Pumpkins
Mary Lyn Ray
Harcourt Brace and Company, 1992
1250 6th Avenue
San Diego, CA 92101

**Questions and Answers About
Forest Animals**
Michael Chinery
Kingfisher Books/Grisewood and
Dempsey, Inc., 1994
95 Madison Avenue
New York, NY 10016

**Questions and Answers About
Freshwater Animals**
Michael Chinery
Kingfisher Books/Grisewood and
Dempsey, Inc., 1994
95 Madison Avenue
New York, NY 10016

**Questions and Answers About
Polar Animals**
Michael Chinery
Kingfisher Books/Grisewood and
Dempsey, Inc., 1994
95 Madison Avenue
New York, NY 10016

Rachel Carson
Eve Stwertka
Franklin Watts, 1991
95 Madison Avenue
New York, NY 10016

**Rachel Carson: Pioneer of
Ecology**
Kathleen Kudlinski
Viking/Penguin, 1988
375 Hudson Street
New York, NY 10014

A Raft of Sea Otters
Vicki Leon
Blake Publishing, 1988
2222 Beebee Street
San Luis Obispo, CA 93401

Rain Forest
Helen Cowcher
Farrar, Straus and Giroux, 1988
19 Union Square West
New York, NY 10003

Rain Forest
Barbara Taylor

Dorling Kindersley, 1992
232 Madison Avenue
New York, NY 10016

The Rain Forest Eco Guide Unfolds
VanDam Publishers, Incorporated
430 West 14th Street
New York, NY 10014

Rain Forest Secrets
Arthur Dorros
Scholastic, 1990
555 Broadway
New York, NY 10012

The Rainforests
HRH The Prince of Wales
Chronicle Books, 1989
275 Fifth Street
San Francisco, CA 94103

Raven: A Trickster from the Pacific Northwest
Gerald McDermott
Harcourt Brace and Company, 1993
1250 6th Avenue
San Diego, CA 92101

Recycle!
Gail Gibbons
Little, Brown and Company, 1992
32 Beacon Street
Boston, MA 02108

Recycling
Joan Kalbacken and Emilie U. Lepthien
Children's Press, 1991
5440 North Cumberland Avenue
Chicago, IL 60656

Recyclopedia
Robin Simons
Houghton Mifflin, 1976
222 Berkely Street
Boston, MA 02116

Reducing, Reusing, and Recycling
Bobbie Kalman
Crabtree Publishing Company, 1991
350 Fifth Avenue, Suite 3308
New York, NY 10118

The Ribbon: A Celebration of Life
Lark Books Staff and Marianne Philbin
Lark Books, 1985
50 College Street
Asheville, NC 28801

The River
David Bellamy
Potter, 1988
201 East 50th Street
New York, NY 10022

A River Dream
Allen Say
Houghton Mifflin, 1988
222 Berkely Street
Boston, MA 02116

A River Ran Wild
Lynne Cherry
Gulliver Green/Harcourt, 1992
1250 6th Avenue
San Diego, CA 92101

Salven Mi Selva
Monica Zak
Sistemas Tecnicos de Edicion, 1989
San Marcos, 102
Tlalpan 14000
Mexico, DF

Save the Earth
Linda Longo Hirsch
Troll Associates, 1992
2 Lethbridge Plaza
Mahway, NJ 07430

Save the Earth: An Action Handbook for Kids
Betty Miles
Knopf, 1991
201 East 50th Street
New York, NY 10022

**Save the Earth:
The Big Book of Questions and Answers**
Linda Schwartz
Publications International, 1992
7373 Cicero Avenue
Lincolnwood, IL 60646

Save My Rainforest
Monica Zak
Volcano Press, 1992
P.O. Box 270
Volcano, CA 95689

Save Our Forests
Ron Hirschi
Delacorte/Bantam Doubleday, 1993
666 Fifth Avenue
New York, NY 10036

Save Our Oceans and Coasts
Ron Hirschi
Delacorte/Bantam Doubleday, 1993
666 Fifth Avenue
New York, NY 10036

Scholastic Environmental Atlas of the United States
Mark Mattson
Scholastic, 1993
555 Broadway
New York, NY 10012

Science Activity Book
Smithsonian Institution
Galson Books, 1987
25 West 43rd Street
New York, NY 10036

Science Sampler
Sandra Markle
Learning Works, 1980
P.O. Box 6187
Santa Barbara, CA 93160

Sea Otters
John A. Love
Fulcrum Publishing, 1990
350 Indiana Street
Golden, CO 80401

Seals and Sea Lions
Vicki Leon
Blake Publishing, 1988
2222 Beebee Street
San Luis Obispo, CA 93401

Seashore
Eyewitness Books
Knopf, 1989
201 East 50th Street
New York, NY 10022

Sequoias
Michael George
Creative Education, 1992
123 South Broad Street
Mankato, MN 56001

Sharing the Joy of Nature
Joseph Cornell
Dawn Publications, 1989
14618 Tyler Foote Road
Nevada City, CA 95959

Sharing Nature with Children
Joseph Cornell

Dawn Publications, 1979
14618 Tyler Foote Road
Nevada City, CA 95959

Sierra
Diane Siebert
HarperCollins, 1991
10 East 53rd Street
New York, NY 10022

**The Sign of the Seahorse:
A Tale of Greed and High
Adventure in Two Acts**
Graeme Base
Harry N. Abrams, 1992
100 Fifth Avenue
New York, NY 10011

Silkworms
Sylvia Johnson
Lerner Publications, 1982
241 First Avenue North
Minneapolis, MN 55401

**Snips and Snails and Walnut
Whales**
Phyllis Fiarotta
Workman Publishing Company, Inc.,
1975
708 Broadway
New York, NY 10003

S.O.S.—Elephant
Jill Bailey
Gallery Books, 1991
112 Madison Avenue
New York, NY 10016

S.O.S.—Gorilla
Jill Bailey
Gallery Books, 1991
112 Madison Avenue
New York, NY 10016

S.O.S.—Panda
Jill Bailey
Gallery Books, 1991
112 Madison Avenue
New York, NY 10016

S.O.S.—Rhino
Jill Bailey
Gallery Books, 1991
112 Madison Avenue
New York, NY 10016

S.O.S.—Snow Leopard
Jill Bailey

Gallery Books, 1991
112 Madison Avenue
New York, NY 10016

S.O.S.—Tiger
Jill Bailey
Gallery Books, 1991
112 Madison Avenue
New York, NY 10016

S.O.S.—Whale
Jill Bailey
Gallery Books, 1991
112 Madison Avenue
New York, NY 10016

Somewhere in America
Sara Ball
W.J. Fantasy, 1987
955 Connecticut Avenue
Bridgeport, CT 06607

Song for the Ancient Forests
Nancy Luenn
Macmillan, 1993
866 Third Avenue
New York, NY 10022

Song of the Trees
Mildred Taylor
Dial Books, 1975
375 Hudson Street
New York, NY 10014

**So, You Love Animals: An Action-
Packed, Fun-Filled Book to Help
Kids Help Animals**
Zoe Weil
American Anti-Vivisection Society,
1994
801 Old York Road, Suite 204
Jenkintown, PA 19046-1685

Space Garbage
Isaac Asimov
Bantam Doubleday Dell, 1989
666 Fifth Avenue
New York, NY 10103

The Spider
Luise Woelflein
Stewart, Taboori and Chang, 1992
575 Broadway
New York, NY 10012

**Spill: The Story of the Exxon
Valdez**
Terry Carr

Franklin Watts, 1991
95 Madison Avenue
New York, NY 10016

**Spinning Tales Weaving Hope:
Stories of Peace, Justice and the
Environment**
Ed Brody
New Society Publishers, 1992
4527 Springfield Avenue
Philadelphia, PA 19143

Spring Pool
Ann Downer
Franklin Watts, 1992
95 Madison Avenue
New York, NY 10016

Stop that Noise
Paul Geraghty
Crown Publishers, 1992
201 East 50th Street
New York, NY 10022

**The Story of Rachel Carson and the
Environmental Movement**
Leila M. Foster
Childrens Press, 1990
5440 North Cumberland Avenue
Chicago, IL 60656

Stranded
Ann Coleridge
Bantam Doubleday Dell, 1987
666 Fifth Avenue
New York, NY 10103

**The Student Environmental Action
Guide**
Earthworks Group
Earthworks Press, 1991
1400 Shattuck Avenue, Box 25
Berkeley, CA 94709

**Sumauma, Mae Das Arvores
Uma Historia da Floresta
Amazonica**
Lynne Cherry
Harcourt Brace and Company, 1990
Matriz Rua Rui Barbosa 156 (Bela
Vista)
Sao Paulo, Brazil CEP 01326-010

Survival: Could You Be a Deer
Roger Tabor
Ideals, 1989
565 Marriott Drive, #800
Nashville, TN 37214

Survival: Could You Be a Fox
Roger Tabor
Ideals, 1989
565 Marriott Drive, #800
Nashville, TN 37214

Survival: Could You Be a Frog
Roger Tabor
Ideals, 1990
565 Marriott Drive, #800
Nashville, TN 37214

Survival: Could You Be an Otter
Roger Tabor
Ideals, 1989
565 Marriott Drive, #800
Nashville, TN 37214

A Swim Through the Sea
Kristin Joy Pratt
Dawn Publications, 1994
14618 Tyler Foote Road
Nevada City, CA 95959

Swimming with Sea Lions and Other Adventures in the Galapagos Islands
Ann McGovern
Scholastic, 1992
555 Broadway
New York, NY 10012

Take Action
Ann Love and Jane Drake
Kids Can Press, 1992
585-1/2 Bloor Street West
Toronto, Ontario, Canada M6G1K5

Take 'Em Along: Sharing Wilderness with Your Children
Barbara Euser
Cordillera Press, 1987
P.O. Box 3699
Evergreen, CO 80439

A Tale of Antarctica
Ulco Glimmerveen
Scholastic, 1989
555 Broadway
New York, NY 10012

Talking to Fireflies, Shrinking the Moon
Edward Duensing
Plume/Penguin Group, 1990
375 Hudson Street
New York, NY 10014

Teachables 2
Rhoda Redleaf
Toys-n-Things Press, 1987
906 North Dale Street
St. Paul, MN 55103

Teachables from Trashables: Home-Made Toys that Teach
Rhoda Redleaf
Redleaf Press, 1979
450 North Syndicate, Suite 5
St. Paul, MN 55104

Teaching Children About Food
Christine Berman, M.P.H., R.D. and Jacki Fromer
Bull Publishing Company, 1991
P.O. Box 208
Palo Alto, CA 94302-0208

Teaching Kids to Love the Earth
Marina Lachecki Herman et al.
Pfeifer-Hamilton Press, 1991
1702 East Jefferson Street
Duluth, MN 55812

Tell Me About: Ocean Animals
Michael Chinery
Random House, 1991
201 East 50th Street
New York, NY 10022

Think Like An Eagle: At Work with a Wildlife Photographer
Kathryn Lasky
Little, Brown and Company, 1992
32 Beacon Street
Boston, MA 02108

"Thinking Green" in My Home
Ann Bogart
Smithmark Publishers, 1993
112 Madison Avenue
New York, NY 10016

This Place Is Dry
Cobb and LaVallee
Walker, 1989
720 Fifth Avenue
New York, NY 10019

This Planet Is Mine
Metzger and Whittakerm
Simon and Schuster, 1991
1230 Avenue of the Americas
New York, NY 10020

This Year's Garden
Cynthia Rylant
Macmillan, 1987
866 Third Avenue
New York, NY 10022

Those Amazing Bats
Cheryl Mays Halton
Dillon Press, 1991
242 Portland Avenue South
Minneapolis, MN 55415

Tide Pool
Christiane Gunzi
Dorling Kindersley, 1992
232 Madison Avenue
New York, NY 10016

Tidepools: The Bright World of the Rocky S horeline
Diana Barnhart
Blake Publishing, 1989
2222 Beebee Street
San Luis Obispo, CA 93401

Tiger
Judy Allen
Candlewick Press, 1992
2067 Massachusetts Avenue
Cambridge, MA 02140

Tigress
Helen Cowcher
Farrar, Straus and Giroux, 1991
19 Union Square West
New York, NY 10003

The Tiny Seed
Eric Carle
Gryphon House, 1987
3706 Otis Street, P.O. Box 275
Mt. Rainier, MD 20712

To Save the Planet
Tobin Mueller and Joe Heller
Center Stage Productions, 1991
P.O. Box 51
Nelsonville, WI 54458-0051

Tomorrow's Earth: A Squeaky Green Guide
David Bellamy
Courage Books, 1992
125 South 22nd Street
Philadelphia, PA 19103

Tons of Trash
Joan Rattner Heilman
Avon Books, 1992
1350 Avenue of the Americas
New York, NY 10019

The Tower
Arlette LaVie
Child's Play, 1990
550 Lisbon Street, P.O. Box 821
Lewiston, ME 04240

Trails, Tails and Tidepools in Pails
Docents of Nursery Nature Walks
Nursery Nature Walks, 1992
P.O. Box 844
Pacific Palisades, CA 90272

Trash!
Charlotte Wilcox
Carolrhoda Books, 1988
241 First Avenue
Minneapolis, MN 55401

Trash Bash
Judy Delton
Bantam Doubleday Dell, 1992
666 Fifth Avenue
New York, NY 10103

Tree
Eyewitness Books
Knopf, 1988
201 East 50th Street
New York, NY 10022

Tree Boy
Shirley Nagel
Sierra Club, 1987
730 Polk Street
San Francisco, CA 94109

The Tree Giants: The Story of the Redwoods
Bill Schneider
Falcon Press, 1988
P.O. Box 1718
Helena, MT 59624

A Tree Is Nice
Janice May Udry
Gryphon House, 1956
3706 Otis Street, P.O. Box 275
Mt. Rainier, MD 20712

Trees
Harry Behn
Henry Holt, 1949

115 West 18th Street
New York, NY 10011

Tropical Rainforests
Jean Hamilton
Blake Publishing, 1990
2222 Beebee Street
San Luis Obispo, CA 93401

Trouble at Marsh Harbor
Susan Sharpe
Viking/Penguin, 1990
375 Hudson Street
New York, NY 10014

Under the Sea in 3-D
Rick and Susan Sammon
The Nature Company, 1993
P.O. Box 188
Florence, KY 41022

Underwater Nature Search
Andrew Cleave
Reader's Digest, 1992
Customer Service Dept.
Pleasantville, NY 10570

Urban Roosts
Barbara Bash
Little, Brown and Company, 1990
32 Beacon Street
Boston, MA 02108

Usborne Book of the Earth
Stockley/Watt
EDC Publishing, 1992
10302 East 55th Place
Tulsa, OK 74146

View from the Air
Reeve Lindberg
Viking/Penguin, 1992
375 Hudson Street
New York, NY 10014

The View from the Oak
Judith and Herbert Kohl
Sierra Club, 1977
730 Polk Street
San Francisco, CA 94109

Vivisection and Dissection in the Classroom: A Guide to Conscientious Objection
Francione and Charlton
American Anti-Vivisection Society, 1992
801 Old York Road, #204
Jenkintown, PA 19046-1685

A Vogt for the Environment
John Sailer
Book Publishing Company, 1993
P.O. Box 99
Summertown, TN 38483

The Voice of the Wood
Claude Clement
Viking/Penguin, 1993
375 Hudson Street
New York, NY 10014

Volcanoes
Michael George
Creative Education, 1991
123 South Broad Street
Mankato, MN 56001

Volcanoes
Jenny Wood
Viking/Penguin, 1990
375 Hudson Street
New York, NY 10014

A Walk in the Rainforest
Kristin Joy Pratt
Dawn Publications, 1992
14618 Tyler Foote Road
Nevada City, CA 95959

Walter Warthog
Betty Leslie-Melville
Doubleday, 1989
666 Fifth Avenue
New York, NY 10103

Water
Francois Michel
William Morrow, 1992
1350 Avenue of the Americas
New York, NY 10019

Water Sky
Jean Craighead George
HarperCollins, 1987
10 East 53rd Street
New York, NY 10022

Weather
Eyewitness Books
Knopf, 1991
201 East 50th Street
New York, NY 10022

The Weather Wizard's 5-Year Weather Diary
Robert Rubin
Algonquin Books of Chapel Hill, 1991

P.O. Box 225
Chapel Hill, NC 27515-2225

Weatherwatch
Valarie Wyatt
Kids Can Press, 1990
585-1/2 Bloor Street West
Toronto, Ontario, Canada M6G1K5

Wee Green Witch
Mary Leister
Stemmer House Publishers, 1978
2627 Caves Road
Owings Mills, MD 21117

Welcome to the Greenhouse
Jane Yolan
Putnam and Grosset, 1991
200 Madison Avenue
New York, NY 10016

Wendy Puzzle
Florence Perry Heide
Bantam Doubleday Dell, 1982
666 Fifth Avenue
New York, NY 10103

Whales
Kath Buffington et al.
Scholastic, 1992
555 Broadway
New York, NY 10012

**Whales:
The Gentle Giants**
Joyce Milton
Random House, 1989
201 East 50th Street
New York, NY 10022

Whalesinger
Welwyn Wilton Katz
Bantam Doubleday Dell, 1990
666 Fifth Avenue
New York, NY 10103

Whalesong
Robert Siegel
HarperCollins, 1981
10 East 53rd Street
New York, NY 10022

**What to Do About
Pollution...**
Anne Shelby
Orchard Books, 1993
95 Madison Avenue
New York, NY 10016

What's On My Plate
Ruth Belov Gross
Macmillan, 1990
866 Third Avenue
New York, NY 10022

When the Stars Begin to Fall
James Lincoln Collier
Laurel-Leaf, 1986
666 Fifth Avenue
New York, NY 10103

When the Tide Is Low
Sheila Cole
Lothrop, 1985
105 Madison Avenue
New York, NY 10019

Where Are My Bears
Ron Hirsch
Bantam Doubleday Dell, 1992
666 Fifth Avenue
New York, NY 10103

**Where Are My Prairie Dogs and
Black-Footed Ferrets?**
Ron Hirsch
Bantam Doubleday Dell, 1992
666 Fifth Avenue
New York, NY 10103

**Where Are My Puffins, Whales and
Seals**
Ron Hirsch
Bantam Doubleday Dell, 1992
666 Fifth Avenue
New York, NY 10103

**Where Are My Swans, Whooping
Cranes and Singing Loons**
Ron Hirsch
Bantam Doubleday Dell, 1992
666 Fifth Avenue
New York, NY 10103

**Where Does Our
Garbage Go?**
Joan Bowden
Doubleday, 1992
666 Fifth Avenue
New York, NY, 10103

**Where Does
Rubbish Go?**
Usborne
EDC Publishing, 1991
10302 East 55th Place
Tulsa, OK 74146

**Where the Forest Meets
the Sea**
Jeannie Baker
Greenwillow, 1987
1350 Avenue of the Americas
New York, NY 10019

Whisper from the Woods
Victoria Wirth and Scott Banfill
Green Tiger Press, 1991
1230 Avenue of the Americas
New York, NY 10020

Who Is the Beast?
Keith Baker
Harcourt Brace and Company, 1990
1250 6th Avenue
San Diego, CA 92101

**The Whole Cosmos Catalog of
Science Activities**
Joe Abruscatto
Good Year Books, 1991
1900 East Lake Avenue
Glenview, IL 60025

Why Buffalo Roam
Michael Kershen
Stemmer House, 1993
2627 Caves Road
Owings Mills, MD 21117

**Why Doesn't the Sun
Burn Out? And Other Not
Such Dumb Questions About
Energy**
Vicki Cobb
Lodestar Books, 1990
375 Hudson Street
New York, NY 10014

Wild Animals
Usborne
EDC Publishing
10302 East 55th Place
Tulsa, OK 74146

The Wild Inside
Linda Allison
Sierra Club, 1979
730 Polk Street
San Francisco, CA 94109

Wildlife California
Jill Brubaker
Chronicle Books, 1991
275 Fifth Street
San Francisco, CA 94103

Wildlife Fact File
International Masters Publishers, 1991
4 Gateway Center, 44 Liberty Avenue
Pittsburgh, PA 15222

Wildlife Southwest
Jill Skramstad
Chronicle Books, 1992
275 Fifth Street
San Francisco, CA 94103

Will We Miss Them?
Alexandra Wright
Cambridge University Press, 1992
32 East 57th Street
New York, NY 10022

Wind in the Long Grass
William Higginson
Simon and Schuster, 1991
1230 Avenue of the Americas
New York, NY 10020

Wings Along the Waterway
Mary Barrett Brown
Orchard Books, 1992
387 Park Avenue South
New York, NY 10016

Wolf of Shadows
Whitley Streiber
Sierra Club, 1985
730 Polk Street
San Francisco, CA 94109

The Wonder of Wolves
Sandra Chisholm Robinson
Roberts Rinehart, 1989
P.O. Box 3161
Boulder, CO 80303

Wonderful Worms
Linda Glaser
Millbrook Press, 1992
2 Old New Milford Road
Brookfield, CT 06804

Wonders of the Jungle
Ranger Rick
National Wildlife Federation, 1986
1400 Sixteenth Street NW
Washington, DC 20036-2266

Woodsong
Gary Paulsen
Puffin Books, 1987
375 Hudson Street
New York, NY 10014

World Book Encyclopedia of People and Places, Vol. 1, A–C
World Book, Incorporated, 1992
525 West Monroe Street
Chicago, IL 60661

World Book Encyclopedia of People and Places, Vol. 2, D–H
World Book, Incorporated, 1992
525 West Monroe Street
Chicago, IL 60661

World Book Encyclopedia of People and Places, Vol. 3, I–L
World Book, Incorporated, 1992
525 West Monroe Street
Chicago, IL 60661

World Book Encyclopedia of People and Places, Vol. 4, M–R
World Book, Incorporated, 1992
525 West Monroe Street
Chicago, IL 60661

World Book Encyclopedia of People and Places, Vol. 5, S–T
World Book, Incorporated, 1992
525 West Monroe Street
Chicago, IL 60661

World Book Encyclopedia of People and Places, Vol. 6, U–Z
World Book, Incorporated, 1992
525 West Monroe Street
Chicago, IL 60661

The World of Animals
Tom Stacy
Random House, 1991
201 East 50th Street
New York, NY 10022

The Wump World
Bill Peet
Houghton Mifflin, 1970
222 Berkely Street
Boston, MA 02116

Yellowstone Fires: Flames and Rebirth
Dorothy Hinshaw Patent
Holiday House, 1990
18 East 53rd Street
New York, NY 10022

VIDEOS

Acid Rain: No Simple Solution
Modern Talking Picture Service
5000 Park Street North
St. Petersburg, FL 33709-9989
800-243-MTPS
Category: Atmosphere
Running Time: 29:00

Admiral Splash and His Amazing Submarine
Metropolitan Water District of Southern California
P.O. Box 54153
Los Angeles, CA 90054-9896
213-217-6738
Category: Water
Running Time: 16:00

Alternative Agriculture, Growing Concerns
ERS-NASS
P.O. Box 1608
Rockville, MD 20849-1608
800-999-6779
Category: Soil/Agriculture
Running Time: 19:00

Aluminum Recycling: Your Next Assignment
Modern Talking Picture Service
5000 Park Street North
St. Petersburg, FL 33709-9989
800-243-6777
Category: Recycling
Running Time: 18:00

The American Experience: Rachel Carson's Silent Spring
PBS Video
1320 Braddock Place
Alexandria, VA 22314-1698
800-328-PBS1
Category: Pest Management
Running Time: 60:00

Asbestos: Playing It Safe
The National Audiovisual Center
8700 Edgeworth Drive
Capitol Heights, MD 20743-3701
301-763-1891
Category: Toxics
Running Time: 37:00

Backyard Safari
Jack Schmidling Productions
4501 Moody
Chicago, IL 60630
312-685-1878
Category: Gardening/Landscaping/
Plants
Running Time: 50:00

The Best of Friends
Michael Matlock
117 S. Clark, #105
Los Angeles, CA 90048
310-278-2762
Category: Water
Running Time: 11:20

Bill Nye, the Science Guy: Garbage
Dubs Incorporated, Buena Vista
Production
1220 North Highland Avenue
Hollywood, CA 90038
213-461-3726
Category: Waste
Running Time: 30:00

Biodiversity: The Variety of Life
Bullfrog Films
P.O. Box 149
Oley, PA 19547
800-543-FROG
Category: Biodiversity
Running Time: 42:00

Biological Control: A Natural Alternative
The National Audiovisual Center
8700 Edgeworth Drive
Capitol Heights, MD 20743-3701
301-763-1891
Category: Pest Management
Running Time: 27:00

Blowhard
Carousel Films
260 Fifth Avenue
New York, NY 10001
212-683-1660
Category: Energy
Running Time: 10:00

The Bottom Line: Waste Reduction Case Studies and Strategies in California Business
Keep California Beautiful
1601 Exposition Boulevard, FB15
Sacramento, CA 95815
800-CLEAN-CA

Category: Waste
Running Time: 21:00

California Smith, W.I
Metropolitan Water District of
Southern California
P.O. Box 54153
Los Angeles, CA 90054-9896
213-217-6738
Category: Water
Running Time: 20:00

California Water: What's Next?
University of California
Office of Media Services, Room 9,
Dwinelle Hall
Berkeley, CA 94702
510-643-8637
Category: Water
Running Time: 56:00

Can I Drink the Water?
University of California, Extension
Media Center
2176 Shattuck Avenue
Berkeley, CA 94704
510-642-0460
Category: Water
Running Time: 27:00

Captain Planet and the Planeteers: A Hero for Earth
Turner Multimedia
105 Terry Drive, Suite 120
Newtown, PA 18940
800-742-1096
Category: General/Global
Running Time: 45:00

Captain Planet and the Planeteers: The Power Is Yours
Turner Multimedia
105 Terry Drive, Suite 120
Newtown, PA 18940
800-742-1096
Category: General/Global
Running Time: 45:00

Captain Planet Series
Turner Multimedia
105 Terry Drive, Suite 120
Newtown, PA 18940
800-742-1096
Category: General/Global
Running Time: 45:00

Carnivorous Plants
National Geographic Society

17 and M Street NW
Washington, DC 20036
202-857-7669
Category: Gardening/Landscaping/
Plants
Running Time: 12:00

CBS News: Energy Crunch: The Best Way Out
Carousel Films
260 Fifth Avenue
New York, NY 10001
212-683-1660
Category: Conservation
Running Time: 51:00

CBS Schoolbreak Special: 50 Simple Things Kids Can Do to Save the Earth
Churchill Media
12210 Nebraska Avenue, Dept. 200
Los Angeles, CA 90025-3600
800-334-7830
Category: Action
Running Time: 46:45

Chemical Valley
Appalshop
306 Madison Street
Whitesburg, KY 41858
606-633-0108
Category: Toxics
Running Time: 58:00

Children's Chants and Games
University of California, Extension
Media Center
2176 Shattuck Avenue
Berkeley, CA 94704
510-642-0460
Category: Appreciation
Running Time: 15:00

Choices for the Planet
Idera Films
2678 West Broadway Avenue, Suite
201
Vancouver, BC Canada V6K 2G3
604-738-8815
Category: General/Global
Running Time: 60:00

Clean Air: The Earth at Risk Environmental Video Series
Library Video Company
521 Righters Ferry Road
Bala Cynwyd, PA 19004
800-843-3620

Category: Atmosphere
Running Time: 30:00

Clean Water: Quest for Quality
U.S. Environmental Protection Agency
Multimedia Sevices
401 M Street SW-1705
Washington, DC 20460
202-260-2044
Category: Water
Running Time: 25:00

Cleaning Up Toxics at Home
The Video Project
5332 College Avenue, Suite 101
Oakland, CA 94618
800-4-PLANET
Category: Toxics
Running Time: 24:45

Cleaning Up Toxics in Business
The Video Project
5332 College Avenue, Suite 101
Oakland, CA 94618
800-4-PLANET
Category: Toxics
Running Time: 24:45

Club Connect in Los Angeles
PBS Video
1320 Braddock Place
Alexandria, VA 22314-1698
800-328-PBS1
Category: Water
Running Time: 30:00

CNN Eating Healthy Series: Heart of the World
Turner Multimedia
105 Terry Drive, Suite 120
Newtown, PA 18940
800-742-1096
Category: Food/Nutrition
Running Time: 17:00

CNN Special Report: Not in My Backyard
Turner Multimedia
105 Terry Drive, Suite 120
Newtown, PA 18940
800-742-1096
Category: Waste
Running Time: 30:00

Coastal Ocean in Crisis: Science for Solutions
The National Audiovisual Center
8700 Edgeworth Drive

Capitol Heights, MD 20743-3701
301-763-1891
Category: Water
Running Time: 20:00

Conserving America: The Challenge on the Coast
The Video Project
5332 College Avenue, Suite 101
Oakland, CA 94618
800-4-PLANET
Category: Water
Running Time: 58:00

Conserving America: The Rivers
The Video Project
5332 College Avenue, Suite 101
Oakland, CA 94618
800-4-PLANET
Category: Water
Running Time: 58:00

Crack and Crevice Treatment for Cockroach Management
The National Audiovisual Center
8700 Edgeworth Dr
Capitol Heights, MD 20743-3701
301-763-1891
Category: Pest Management
Running Time: 14:00

Creating a Healthy Home
Midway Productions
2175 Goodyear Avenue, Suite 124
Ventura, CA 93003
800-446-4997
Category: Toxics
Running Time: 23:00

Creativity with Bill Moyers: Garbage, Another Way of Seeing
PBS Video
1320 Braddock Place
Alexandria, VA 22314-1698
800-328-PBS1
Category: Waste
Running Time: 29:00

Curing the Automobile Blues
Union of Concerned Scientists
26 Church Street
Cambridge, MA 02238
617-547-5552
Category: Transportation
Running Time: 13:00

Current Events
Southern California Edison Video

Services
Room 191 GO1, 2244 Walnut Grove Avenue
Rosemead, CA 91770
818-302-1212
Category: Conservation
Running Time: 7:30

Dead Ahead
Videofinders
4401 Sunset Boulevard
Los Angeles, CA 90027
800-343-4727
Category: Water
Running Time: 90:00

Deadly Chemicals: Who's Minding the Store?
Modern Talking Picture Service
5000 Park Street, North
St. Petersburg, FL 33709
800-243-MTPS
Category: Waste
Running Time: 13:00

Death Trap
Time-Life Video
777 Duke Street
Alexandria, VA 22314
800-621-7026
Category: Gardening/Landscaping/ Plants
Running Time: 60:00

Diet for a New America: Your Health, Your Planet
The Video Project
5332 College Avenue, Suite 101
Oakland, CA 94618
800-4-PLANET
Category: Food/Nutrition
Running Time: 60:00

A Diet for All Reasons
Earthsave
706 Frederick Street
Santa Cruz, CA 95062-2205
800-362-3648
Category: Food/Nutrition
Running Time: 110:00

Down in the Dumps
Films for the Humanities
743 Alexander Road
Princeton, NJ 08450
800-257-5126
Category: Waste
Running Time: 26:00

Down the Shore
PBS Video
1320 Braddock Place
Alexandria, VA 22314-1698
800-328-PBS1
Category: Water
Running Time: 60:00

Downwind/Downstream: Threats to the Mountains and Waters of the American West
Bullfrog Films
P.O. Box 149
Oley, PA 19547
800-543-FROG
Category: Water
Running Time: 58:00

Drinking Water: Quality on Tap
The Video Project
5332 College Avenue, Suite 101
Oakland, Ca 94618
800-4-PLANET
Category: Water
Running Time: 27:24

Drive-Thru
Videoware Distributors
7551 Sunset Boulevard
Los Angeles, CA 90046
213-876-1106
Category: Waste
Running Time: 27:00

"E" Think Earth
Education Development Specialists
5505 East Carson Street, Suite 250
Lakewood, CA 90713
310-420-6814
Category: General/Global
Running Time: 27:00

The Earth at Risk Environmental Video Series: Clean Water
Library Video Company
521 Righters Ferry Road
Bala Cynwyd, PA 19004
800-843-3620
Category: Water
Running Time: 30:00

The Earth at Risk Environmental Video Series: Nuclear Energy/Nuclear Waste
Library Video Company
521 Righters Ferry Road
Bala Cynwyd, PA 19004
800-843-3620

Category: Nuclear
Running Time: 30:00

The Earth at Risk Environmental Video Series: Recycling
Library Video Company
521 Righters Ferry Road
Bala Cynwyd, PA 19004
800-843-3620
Category: Recycling
Running Time: 30:00

The Earth Day Special
Warner Home Video
4000 Warner Boulevard
Burbank, CA 91522
818-954-6000
Category: General/Global
Running Time: 99:00

Earth Day: Vision Changes Project
Vision Changers
2 Blair Street West, Suite 100-209
Toronto, Ontario, Canada M4W E32
(416) 924-4449
Category: Action
Running Time: 15:00

The Earth Explored: Geothermal Energy
PBS Video
1320 Braddock Place
Alexandria, VA 22314-1698
800-328-PBS1
Category: Energy
Running Time: 28:00

Earth to Kids
Films Incorporated Video
5547 North Ravenswood Avenue
Chicago, IL 60640-1199
800-323-4222 Ext. 43
Category: Consumerism
Running Time: 28:00

Earthbeat 2: Water
Intellimation
P.O. Box 1922
Santa Barbara, CA 93116-1922
800-346-8355
Category: Water
Running Time: 25:00

Earthbeat 4: Environmental Literacy
Intellimation
P.O. Box 1922
Santa Barbara, CA 93116-1922

800-346-8355
Category: General/Global
Running Time: 25:00

Earthbeat 5: Pure Food
Intellimation
P.O. Box 1922
Santa Barbara, CA 93116-1922
800-346-8355
Category: Food/Nutrition
Running Time: 25:00

Earthbeat 6: Waste
Intellimation
P.O. Box 1922
Santa Barbara, CA 93116-1922
800-346-8355
Category: Waste
Running Time: 25:00

Earthbeat 7: Energy
Intellimation
P.O. Box 1922
Santa Barbara, CA 93116-1922
800-346-8355
Category: Energy
Running Time: 25:00

Earthbeat 8: Clean Air
Intellimation
P.O. Box 1922
Santa Barbara, CA 93116-1922
800-346-8355
Category: Atmosphere
Running Time: 25:00

Earthday Birthday
Home Box Office
2049 Century Park East, #4100
Los Angeles, CA 90067
310-201-9200
Category: Activities
Running Time: 28:15

Earthscope 9: Environmental Animation
Global View Productions, Inc
2901 Connecticut Avenue NW, Suite B-4
Washington, DC 20008
202-667-5968
Category: General/Global
Running Time: 51:00

Eco, You and Simon Too!
Videofinders
4401 Sunset Boulevard
Los Angeles, CA 90027

800-343-4727
Category: General/Global
Running Time: 40:00

Eco-Rap: Voices From the Hood
The Video Project
5332 College Avenue, Suite 101
Oakland, CA 94618
800-4-PLANET
Category: Waste
Running Time: 39:20

Ecological Realities: Natural Laws at Work
University of California, Extension
Media Center
2176 Shattuck Avenue
Berkeley, CA 94704
510-642-0460
Category: General/Global
Running Time: 13:00

Electric Car Video
Solar Electric
116 Fourth Street
Santa Rosa, CA 95401
707-829-4545
Category: Transportation
Running Time: 21:00

The Energetics of Life
Media Guild
11722 Sorrento Valley Road, Suite E
San Diego, CA 92121
619-755-9191
Category: Energy
Running Time: 23:00

Energy Carol
National Film Board of Canada
1251 Avenue of the Americas
New York, NY 10020
212-586-5131
Category: Energy
Running Time: 11:00

The Energy Crisis: Waste, Indecision, Indifference
Modern Talking Picture Service
5000 Park Street North
St. Petersburg, FL 33709-9989
800-243-MTPS
Category: Conservation
Running Time: 16:00

Energy Crunch Series: Bottom of the Oil Barrel
Time-Life Multimedia

777 Duke Street
Alexandria, VA 22314
703-838-7000
Category: Energy
Running Time: 34:00

Energy Efficiency and Renewables: Our Fragile Earth
The Video Project
5332 College Avenue, Suite 101
Oakland, CA 94618
800-4-PLANET
Category: Energy
Running Time: 22:00

Energy: Less is More
Churchill Media
12210 Nebraska Avenue, Dept. 200
Los Angeles, CA 90025-3600
800-334-7830
Category: Conservation
Running Time: 21:00

Energy: New Sources
Churchill Media
12210 Nebraska Avenue, Department 200
Los Angeles, CA 90025-3600
800-334-7830
Category: Energy
Running Time: 24:00

Energy Planning: States Face the Future
National Conference of State
Legislatures
1560 Broadway, Suite 700
Denver, CO 80202
303-830-2054
Category: Conservation
Running Time: 20:00

Energy: The Dilemma
Churchill Media
12210 Nebraska Avenue, Department 200
Los Angeles, CA 90025-3600
800-334-7830
Category: Energy
Running Time: 22:00

Energy Where You Least Expect It
Third Eye Films
12 Arrow Street
Cambridge, MA 02138
617-491-4300
Category: Energy
Running Time: 28:00

Everybody's Talking About the Environment
Scott Worldwide Foodservice
Scott Plaza 2
Philadelphia, PA 19113
800-TEL-SCOT
Category: Waste
Running Time: 15:00

Food for Thought
Bullfrog Films
P.O. Box 149
Oley, PA 19547
800-543-FROG
Category: Food/Nutrition
Running Time: 28:00

Food Without Fear
The Vegetarian Society
P.O. Box 34427
Los Angeles, CA 90034
310-839-6207
Category: Food/Nutrition
Running Time: 20:00

For Export Only: Pesticides
Richter Productions
330 W. 42nd Street, Suite 2410
New York, NY 10036-1395
212-947-1395
Category: Pest Management
Running Time: 57:00

Frontline: Anatomy of an Oil Spill
PBS Video
1320 Braddock Place
Alexandria, VA 22314-1698
800-328-PBS1
Category: Water
Running Time: 60:00

Frontline: In Our Children's Food
PBS Video
1320 Braddock Place
Alexandria, VA 22314-1698
800-328-PBS1
Category: Pest Management
Running Time: 56:00

Frontline Special Report: Global Dumping Ground
The Video Project
5332 College Avenue, Suite 101
Oakland, CA 94618
800-4-PLANET
Category: Waste
Running Time: 60:00

Fueling the Future: No Deposit, No Return
The Video Project
5332 College Avenue, Suite 101
Oakland, CA 94618
800-4-PLANET
Category: Waste
Running Time: 58:00

Fueling the Future: No Place Like Home
The Video Project
5332 College Avenue, Suite 101
Oakland, CA 94618
800-4-PLANET
Category: Conservation
Running Time: 58:00

Fueling the Future: Running on Empty
The Video Project
5332 College Avenue, Suite 101
Oakland, CA 94618
800-4-PLANET
Category: Transportation
Running Time: 58:00

Futures 2: Renewable Energy
PBS Video
1320 Braddock Place
Alexandria, VA 22314-1698
800-328-PBS1
Category: Energy
Running Time: 15:00

Garbage
BFA Educational Media
2349 Chaffee Drive
St. Louis, MO 63146
314-569-0211
Category: Waste
Running Time: 11:00

The Garbage Cantata
John Burt Productions
302 West 79th Street
New York, NY 10024
212-799-8485
Category: Waste
Running Time: 6:45

Garbage Day!
ChildVision Educational Films
P.O. Box 2587
Hollywood, CA 90078-2587
800-488-1913
Category: Waste
Running Time: 30:00

Garbage Tale #93: An Environmental Adventure
Churchill Media
12210 Nebraska Avenue, Department 200
Los Angeles, CA 90025-3600
800-334-7830
Category: Waste
Running Time: 18:30

Gardening Nature's Way: Natural Pest Control, Step 2
Earth to Earth Productions
P.O. Box 1272
Burbank, CA 91507-1272
800-775-4769
Category: Pest Management
Running Time: 39:00

Gardening Nature's Way: Organic Gardening, Step 1
Earth to Earth Productions
P.O. Box 1272
Burbank, CA 91507-1272
800-775-4769
Category: Gardening/Landscaping/Plants
Running Time: 60:00

Get It Together
The Video Project
5332 College Avenue, Suite 101
Oakland, CA 94618
800-4-PLANET
Category: Action
Running Time: 28:00

Get Ready, Get Set, Grow!
Brooklyn Botanic Garden
1000 Washington Avenue
Brooklyn, NY 11225
718-622-4433
Category: Gardening/Landscaping/Plants
Running Time: 15:00

The Giving Tree
Churchill Media
12210 Nebraska Avenue, Department 200
Los Angeles, CA 90025-3600
800-334-7830
Category: Trees/Forests
Running Time: 10:00

Going Green: How to Reduce Your Garbage
Bullfrog Films

P.O. Box 149
Oley, PA 19547
800-543-FROG
Category: Waste
Running Time: 22:00

Ground Water
Encyclopedia Britannica Education Corporation
425 North Michigan Avenue
Chicago, IL 60611
800-554-9862
Category: Water
Running Time: 17:00

Growing Season
Bullfrog Films
P.O. Box 149
Oley, PA 19547
800-543-FROG
Category: Gardening/Landscaping/Plants
Running Time: 25:00

Growlab: A Growing Experience
National Gardening Association
180 Flynn Avenue
Burlington, VT 05401
802-863-1308
Category: Gardening/Landscaping/Plants
Running Time: 15:00

H2O 2010
Water Education Foundation
717 K Street
Sacramento, CA 95814
916-444-6240
Category: Water
Running Time: 25:00

Hazardous Waste: Whose Problem Is It Anyway?
San Diego Regional Household Hazardous Materials Program
450 A Street, Suite 500
San Diego, CA 92101
619-235-2107
Category: Toxics
Running Time: 7:25

The Hazards at Home
KERA/KDTN-TV
3000 Harry Hines Boulevard
Dallas, TX 75201
214-871-1390
Category: Toxics
Running Time: 58:40

Help Save Planet Earth
MCA
70 Universal City Plaza
Universal City, CA 91608
818-777-4315
Category: Action
Running Time: 71:00

Heroes of the Earth
The Video Project
5332 College Avenue, Suite 101
Oakland, CA 94618
800-4-PLANET
Category: People and Places
Running Time: 45:00

Home Composting: Turning Your Spoils to Soil
State of Connecticut, Department of Environmental Protection Recycling Program
165 Capitol Avenue
Hartford, CT 06106
203-722-6240
Category: Composting
Running Time: 17:02

How to Save Water and Save Money
Media International
313 East Broadway, Suite 202
Glendale, CA 91209
818-242-5314
Category: Conservation
Running Time: 35 :00

I Need the Earth and the Earth Needs Me
General Motors Corporation
465 West Milwaukee, Room B901
Detroit, MI 48202
313-556-5000
Category: General/Global
Running Time: 19:42

I'm Saving the Earth. What Are You Doing?
Environmental Video Products
280 Utah Street
San Francisco, CA 94103-4842
415-626-8400
Category: General/Global
Running Time: 12 :00

Indoor Gardening: Advice from Growlab Classrooms
National Gardening Association
180 Flynn Avenue

Burlington, VT 05401
802-863-1308
Category: Gardening/Landscaping/Plants
Running Time: 35:00

Inert Alert: Secret Poisons in Pesticides
The Northwest Coalition for Alternatives to Pesticides (NCAP)
P.O. Box 1393
Eugene, OR 97440
503-344-5044
Category: Pest Management
Running Time: 17:00

Inside the Edwards Aquifer
Zimmerman and Associates, Inc
P.O. Box 6121
San Antonio, TX 78209
210-821-3700
Category: Water
Running Time: 30:00

Integrated Pest Management in Agriculture
San Luis Video Publishing
P.O. Box 6715
Los Osos, CA 93412
805-528-8322
Category: Pest Management
Running Time: 29:00

Integrated Pest Management in the Park
The National Audiovisual Center
8700 Edgeworth Drive
Capitol Heights, MD 20743-3701
301-763-1891
Category: Pest Management
Running Time: 15:00

Integrated Pest Management Series
The National Audiovisual Center
8700 Edgeworth Drive
Capitol Heights, MD 20743-3701
301-763-1891
Category: Pest Management
Running Time: 85:00

Is Your Food Safe?
Ambrose Video Publishing, Inc
1290 Avenue of the Americas, Suite 2245
New York, NY 10104
212-265-7272
Category: Food/Nutrition
Running Time: 45:00

It's Found Underground
Ecology Center of Ann Arbor
417 Detroit St
Ann Arbor, MI 48104
313-761-3186
Category: Water
Running Time: 30:40

A Kid's Eye View of Ecology
The Video Project
5332 College Avenue, Suite 101
Oakland, CA 94618
800-4-PLANET
Category: Activities
Running Time: 28:00

Leaf Composting: "Windrows" of Opportunity
State of Connecticut, Department of Environmental Protection Recycling Program
165 Capitol Avenue
Hartford, CT 06106
203-722-6240
Category: Composting
Running Time: 14:58

Life After the Curb: Recycling Processes
Cornell University Waste Management Institute
7-8 Business and Technology Park
Ithaca, NY 14850
607-255-2091
Category: Recycling
Running Time: 20:00

Living and Non-living Things
Cornet/MTI Film and Video
108 Wilmot Road
Deerfield, IL 60015
800-621-2131
Category: Appreciation
Running Time: 11:00

The Living Planet: Sweet, Fresh Water
Time/Life Video
777 Duke Street
Alexandria, VA 22314
800-621-7026
Category: Water
Running Time: 60:00

Look Again
Bullfrog Films
P.O. Box 149
Oley, PA 19547

800-543-FROG
Category: Appreciation
Running Time: 9:46

The Lorax
Playhouse Video
1211 Avenue of the Americas
New York, NY 10036
212-373-4800
Category: Trees/Forests
Running Time: 30:00

Love, Women and Flowers
Women Make Movies
225 Lafayette Street
New York, NY 10012
212-925-2502
Category: Pest Management
Running Time: 56:00

Mister Rogers' Neighborhood: The Environment and Recycling
Keep America Beautiful, Inc
9 West Broad Street
Stamford, CT 06902
203-323-8987
Category: Recycling
Running Time: 30:00

My First Green Video
Sony Kids' Video
550 Madison Avenue
New York, NY 10022
212-833-8000
Category: Activities
Running Time: 40:00

National Audubon Society Special: Danger at the Beach
PBS Video
1320 Braddock Place
Alexandria, VA 22314-1698
800-328-PBS1
Category: Water
Running Time: 60:00

National Audubon Society Special: Great Lakes, Bitter Legacy
PBS Video
1320 Braddock Place
Alexandria, PA 22314-1698
800-328-PBS1
Category: Water
Running Time: 60:00

The Nature of Things: L.A. Toxic Strike Force
CBC Educational Sales

Box 500 Station A
Toronto, Ontario, Canada M5W-1E6
416-205-6384
Category: Toxics
Running Time: 60:00

Nature's Way: How Wastewater Treatment Works for You
Water Environment Federation
601 Wythe Street
Alexandria, VA 22314-1994
800-666-0206
Category: Water
Running Time: 10:16

Network Earth: Eco-Racism Story: River Rebellion
Turner Broadcasting Service
105 Terry Drive, #120
Newtown, PA 18940-3425
800-742-1096
Category: Waste
Running Time: 8:36

News Addition #707: Not in My Backyard
KERA
3000 Harry Hines Boulevard
Dallas, TX 75201
214-871-1390
Category: Waste
Running Time: 12:00

No Grapes
United Farm Workers of America
P.O. Box 62
Keene, CA 93531
800-835-7671
Category: Pest Management
Running Time: 13:00

No Safe Harbor: A Journey from the Eastern Bays to the Western Sounds
Fishermen Involved in Saving Habitat (F.I.S.H.)
45 SE 82nd Street, Suite 100
Gladstone, OR 97027
503-650-5400
Category: Water
Running Time: 19:03

Nova: Asbestos: A Lethal Legacy
Time-Life Multimedia
777 Duke Street
Alexandria, VA 22314
703-838-7000

Category: Toxics
Running Time: 57:00

Nova: The Green Machine
Time-Life Multimedia
777 Duke Street
Alexandria, VA 22314
703-838-7000
Category: Gardening/Landscaping/Plants
Running Time: 49:00

Nova: Plague on Our Children: Part I, Dioxins
Time-Life Multimedia
777 Duke Street
Alexandria, VA 22314
703-838-7000
Category: Toxics
Running Time: 57:00

Nova: Plague on Our Children: Part II, PCBs
Time-Life Multimedia
777 Duke Street
Alexandria, VA 22314
703-838-7000
Category: Toxics
Running Time: 57:00

101: An Energy-efficient Doghouse
Bullfrog Films
P.O. Box 149
Oley, PA 19547
800-543-Frog
Category: Building
Running Time: 29:00

102: Solar Energy Doghouse: F.R.O.G. Series 1
Bullfrog Films
P.O. Box 149
Oley, PA 19547
800-543-FROG
Category: Energy
Running Time: 29:00

104: City Lights: F.R.O.G. Series 1
Bullfrog Films
P.O. Box 149
Oley, PA 19547
800-543-FROG
Category: Energy
Running Time: 29:00

107: A Wet and Wild Frog Trap
Bullfrog Films
P.O. Box 149

Oley, PA 19547
800-543-FROG
Category: Water
Running Time: 29:00

One Person Can Make a Difference
Earth Communications Office
11466 San Vicente Boulevard
Los Angeles, CA 90049
310-571-3141
Category: Action
Running Time: 14:00

One Second Before Sunrise: A Search for Solutions
Bullfrog Films
P.O. Box 149
Oley, PA 19547
800-543-FROG
Category: General/Global
Running Time: 60:00

Our Fragile Earth: Recycling
The Video Project
5332 College Avenue, Suite 101
Oakland, CA 94618
800-4-PLANET
Category: Recycling
Running Time: 16:00

Pest Control Integrated Pest Management: A Chance for the Future
The National Audiovisual Center
8700 Edgeworth Drive
Capitol Heights, MD 20743-3701
301-763-1891
Category: Pest Management
Running Time: 20:00

Planet Earth: Part 5: Gifts from the Earth
The Annenberg/CPB Project
901 East Street NW
Washington, DC 20004-2037
800-LEARNER
Category: General/Global
Running Time: 60:00

Planet Earth: Part 6: The Solar Sea
The Annenberg/CPB Project
901 East Street NW
Washington, DC 20004-2037
800-LEARNER
Category: Energy
Running Time: 60:00

A Popular Little Planet
WINGS for Learning
1600 Green Hills Road
P.O. Box 660002
Scotts Valley, CA 95067-0002
800-321-7511
Category: Population
Running Time: 30:00

Problems of Conservation: Water
Encyclopedia Britannica Education Corporation
425 North Michigan Avenue
Chicago, IL 60611
800-554-9862
Category: Conservation
Running Time: 16:00

A Question of Risk
Center for Environmental Information
46 Prince Street
Rochester, NY 14607-1016
716-271-3550
Category: Waste
Running Time: 20:00

Race to Save the Planet: Part 6: More for Less
Intellimation
P.O. Box 1922
Santa Barbara, CA 93116-1922
800-346-8355
Category: Energy
Running Time: 60:00

Race to Save the Planet: Part 8: Waste Not Want Not
Intellimation
P.O. Box 1922
Santa Barbara, CA 93116-1922
800-346-8355
Category: Waste
Running Time: 60:00

The Re Team! Reduce, Reuse and Recycle
Hot Pepper Film and Video
700 East 9th Street, #19
New York, NY 10009
N/A
Category: Waste
Running Time: 25:00

Recycle Rex
Coronet/MTI Film and Video
108 Wilmot Road
Deerfield, IL 60015
800-777-8100

Category: Recycling
Running Time: 12:17

Recycle This! Rock 'n' Roll and Recycling
The Dow Chemical Company
P.O. Box 1206
Midland, MI 48641
800-441-4369
Category: Recycling
Running Time: 20:00

Recycling Is Fun
Bullfrog Films
P.O. Box 149
Oley, Pa 19547
800-543-FROG
Category: Recycling
Running Time: 12:00

Recycling Within Reach
Audio-Visual Resource Center
8 Research Park, Cornell University
Ithaca, NY 14850
607-255-2091
Category: Recycling
Running Time: 13:00

Reduce, Reuse, Recycle: It's Elementary
Illinois Department of Energy and Natural Resources
325 West Adams, Room 300
Springfield, IL 62704
217-785-2800
Category: Recycling
Running Time: 19:33

The Resource Revolution
The Council for Solid Waste Solutions
1275 K Street NW, Suite 400
Washington, DC 20005
800-2-HELP-90
Category: Recycling
Running Time: 12 :00

The Rush to Burn
The Video Project
5332 College Avenue, Suite 101
Oakland, CA 94618
800-4-PLANET
Category: Waste
Running Time: 35:00

Ruth Stout's Garden
Arthur Mokin Productions
P.O. Box 1866
Santa Rosa, CA 95402

707-542-4868
Category: Gardening/Landscaping/
Plants
Running Time: 23:00

Save the Earth: A How-to Video
The Video Project
5332 College Avenue, Suite 101
Oakland, CA 94618
800-4-PLANET
Category: Action
Running Time: 60:00

The Saving Water: Conservation Video
Water Environment Federation
601 Wythe Street
Alexandria, VA 22314-1994
800-666-0206
Category: Conservation
Running Time: 54:28 and 8:26

The Science of Biological Decomposition: Effective Composting Methods
San Luis Video Publishing
P.O. Box 6715
Los Osos, CA 93412
805-528-8322
Category: Composting
Running Time: 33:00

Secrets of Science: Planet Earth, Our Home
The Video Project
5332 College Avenue
Oakland, CA 94618
800-4-PLANET
Category: General/Global
Running Time: 24:00

Silent Spring of Rachel Carson
University of California
Extension Media Center
2176 Shattuck Avenue
Berkeley, CA 94704
510-642-0460
Category: Pest Management
Running Time: 54:00

Simple Things You Can Do to Save Energy
The Video Project
5332 College Avenue, Suite 101
Oakland, CA 94618
800-4-PLANET
Category: Conservation
Running Time: 15:00

Sing-Along Earth Songs
Random House
Attn: Order Department
400 Hahn
Westminster, MD 21157
800-875-6217
Category: Appreciation
Running Time: 30:00

60 Minutes: Clean Air, Clean Water, Dirty Fight
CBS Television
51 West 52nd Avenue
New York, NY 10019
800-524-5621
Category: General/Global
Running Time: 15:00

Spaceship Earth: Feast or Famine?
South Carolina ETV Marketing
P.O. Drawer L
Columbia, SC 29250
800-553-7752
Category: Food/Nutrition
Running Time: 30:00

Spaceship Earth: Our Global Environment
The Video Project
5332 College Avenue, Suite 101
Oakland, CA 94618
800-4-PLANET
Category: General/Global
Running Time: 25:00

Spaceship Earth: Running Water
South Carolina ETV Marketing
P.O. Drawer L
Columbia, SC 29250
800-553-7752
Category: Water
Running Time: 30:00

Spaceship Earth: The Swirling Seas
South Carolina ETV Marketing
P.O. Drawer L
Columbia, SC 29250
800-553-7752
Category: Water
Running Time: 30:00

Special Report: You Can Make a Difference
The National Wildlife Federation
1400 16th Street NW
Washington, DC 20036
202-797-6800

Category: General/Global
Running Time: 30:00

Spirit and Nature
The Video Project
5332 College Avenue, Suite 101
Oakland, CA 94618
800-4-PLANET
Category: Ethics/Philosophy Running
Time: 88:00

Strength in Numbers: Recycling in Multi-Family Housing
Association of New Jersey
Environmental Commissions
P.O. Box 157
Mendham, NJ 07945
201-539-7547
Category: Recycling
Running Time: 9:55

The Story of Toxic Waste
Hawkhill Associates, Inc
125 East Gilman Street
Madison, WI 53703
800-422-4295
Category: Toxics
Running Time: 19:00

Structural Inspections: A Way of Managing Wood-inhabiting Insects
The National Audiovisual Center
8700 Edgeworth Drive
Capitol Heights, MD 20743-3701
301-763-1891
Category: Pest Management
Running Time: 23:00

Subterranean Termite Biology
The National Audiovisual Center
8700 Edgeworth Drive
Capitol Heights, MD 20743-3701
301-763-1891
Category: Pest Management
Running Time: 12:00

Surrounded: The Occupational Hazards of Electromagnetic Fields
Labor Institute
853 Broadway, Room 2014
New York, NY 10003
212-674-3322
Category: EMF's
Running Time: 30:00

The Sustainable Landscape: Ecological Design Principles
San Luis Video Publishing

P.O. Box 6715
Los Osos, CA 93412
805-528-8322
Category: Gardening/Landscaping/
Plants
Running Time: 32:00

Take It to the Depot
Association of Vermont Recyclers
(AVR)
P.O. Box 1244
Montpelier, VT 05601
802-229-1833
Category: Recycling
Running Time: 32:00

Tara's Mulch Garden
Wombat Productions
250 West 57th Street, Suite 916
New York, NY 10019
212-315-2502
Category: Gardening/Landscaping/
Plants
Running Time: 21:00

Think Earth
Educational Development Specialists
5505 East Carson Street, Suite 250
Lakewood, CA 90713
310-420-6814
Category: General/Global
Running Time: 7:00

The Three R's
New York State Legislative
Commission on Solid Waste
Management
Agency Building 4, 5th Floor
Empire State Plaza
Albany, NY 12248
518-455-3711
Category: Recycling
Running Time: 20:00

364 Earth Days and 1 Toxic Day
Vermont Toxic Education Project
P.O. Box 120
East Calais, VT 05650
802-472-6996
Category: General/Global
Running Time: 30:00

**3•2•1 Classroom Contact:
Generating Electricity: More Power
to You**
Great Plains National
P.O. Box 80669
Lincoln, NE 68501

800-228-4630
Category: Energy
Running Time: 15:00

3•2•1 Contact: Down the Drain
American Water Works Association
6666 West Quincy Avenue
Denver, CO 80235
303-794-7711
Category: Water
Running Time: 30:00

**3•2•1 Contact Extra: Bottom of the
Barrel**
WINGS for Learning
1600 Green Hills Road
P.O. Box 660002
Scotts Valley, CA 95067-0002
800-321-7511
Category: Energy
Running Time: 30:00

**3•2•1 Contact Extra: Get Busy:
How Kids Can Save the Planet**
WINGS for Learning
1600 Green Hills Road
P.O. Box 660002
Scotts Valley, CA 95067-0002
800-321-7511
Category: Action
Running Time: 30:00

**Time, Space and Spirit, Keys to
Scientific Literacy: Energy and
Society**
Hawkill Associates, Inc
125 East Gilman Street
P.O. Box 1029
Madison, WI 53701-1029
800-422-4295
Category: Energy
Running Time: 35:00

**Tinka's Planet: A 12 Year Old
Launches a Recycling Campaign**
Treepeople
12601 Mulholland Drive
Beverly Hills, CA 90210
818-753-4620
Category: Recycling
Running Time: 12:00

Tomorrow's Energy Today
United States Department of Energy
CAREIRS
P.O. Box 3048
Merrifield, VA 22116
800-523-2929

Category: Energy
Running Time: 23:00

**Tomorrow's Energy Today: The
Energy Efficiency Option**
United States Department of Energy
CAREIRS
P.O. Box 3048
Merrifield, VA 22116
800-523-2929
Category: Conservation
Running Time: 26:00

Trash Thy Neighbor
Educational Video Center
60 East 13th Street, 4th Floor
New York, NY 10003
212-254-2848
Category: Waste
Running Time: 13:00

**Troubled Waters: Plastic in the
Marine Environment**
Bullfrog Films
P.O. Box 149
Oley, PA 19547
800-543-FROG
Category: Water
Running Time: 29:00

**Turning the Tide, #2: Running Out
of Steam**
Bullfrog Films
P.O. Box 149
Oley, PA 19547
800-543-FROG
Category: Conservation
Running Time: 26:19

Underwater Kids
Environmental Media
P.O. Box 1016
Chapel Hill, NC 27514
800-368-3382
Category: Activities
Running Time: 28:00

The Water Cycle
The Video Project
5332 College Avenue, Suite 101
Oakland, CA 94618
800-4-PLANET
Category: Conservation
Running Time: 28:00

Water: More Precious than Oil
PBS Video
1320 Braddock Place

Alexandria, VA 22314-1698
800-328-PBS1
Category: Conservation
Running Time: 58:00

Waterhog Haven
American Water Works Association
6666 West Quincy Avenue
Denver, CO 80235
303-794-7711
Category: Conservation
Running Time: 10:00

Waterquest: Moving from Conflict and Consensus
Water Education Foundation
717 K Street, Suite 517
Sacramento, CA 95814
916-444-6240
Category: Water
Running Time: 28:40

We All Live Downstream
The Video Project
5332 College Avenue, Suite 101
Oakland, CA 94618
800-4-PLANET
Category: Water
Running Time: 30:00

We Can Make a Difference
The Video Project
5332 College Avenue, Suite 101
Oakland, CA 94618
800-4-PLANET
Category: Action
Running Time: 20:00

West Basin Municipal Water Recycling Project
Multimedia Studios
10401 Jefferson Boulevard
Culver City, CA 90232-1928
310-202-0135
Category: Water
Running Time: 9:00

What Do You Know About H$_2$O?
American Water Works Association
6666 West Quincy Avenue
Denver, CO 80235
303-794-7711
Category: Water
Running Time: 22:00

The White Hole
Bullfrog Films
P.O. Box 149

Oley, PA 19547
800-543-FROG
Category: Waste
Running Time: 10:00

Why Waste?
Waste Minimization for Today's Businesses
California Department of Health Services
Toxic Substance Control Program
Sacramento, CA 94234
916-324-1807
Category: Waste
Running Time: 28:00

Why We Conserve Energy: The Witch of the Great Black Pool
Coronet/MTI Film and Video
108 Wilmot Road
Deerfield, IL 60015
800-621-2131
Category: Energy
Running Time: 12:00

A World in Our Backyard: Wetlands Education and Stewardship Program
Environmental Media
P.O. Box 1016
Chapel Hill, NC 27514
800-368-3382
Category: Ecosystems
Running Time: 24:00

W.O.W. 10: Millie Zantow: Recycling Pioneer
Video•Active Productions
Route 2, Box 322
Canton, NY 13617
315-386-8797
Category: Recycling
Running Time: 48:00

W.O.W. 10: The Trashman
Video•Active Productions
Route 2, Box 322
Canton, NY 13617
315-386-8797
Category: Recycling
Running Time: 5:00

W.O.W. 11: Zoo Doo and You Can Too
Video•Active Productions
Route 2, Box 322
Canton, NY 13617
315-386-8797

Category: Composting
Running Time: 59:00

W.O.W. 19: The Difference Between Theory and Practice in Hazardous. Waste Incineration
Video•Active Productions
Route 2, Box 322
Canton, NY 13617
315-386-8797
Category: Waste
Running Time: 53:00

W.O.W. 7: Recycling in the U.S.A.: Don't Take "No" for an Answer
Video•Active Productions
Route 2, Box 322
Canton, NY 13617
315-386-8797
Category: Recycling
Running Time: 60:00

Wrath of Grapes
United Farm Workers of America, AFL-CIO
P.O. Box 62 La Paz
Keene, CA 93531
805-822-5571
Category: Pest Management
Running Time: 15:53

Yakety Yak: Take it Back
A Vision Entertainment
75 Rockefeller Plaza
New York, NY 10019
800-9-YAKETY
Category: Recycling
Running Time: 45:00

The Yes! Tour: Working for Change
Earth Save
706 Frederick Street
Santa Cruz, CA 95062
408-423-4069
Category: Action
Running Time: 28:15

Zort Sorts: A Story About Recycling
Cornet/MTI Film and Video
108 Wilmot Road
Deerfield, IL 60015
800-621-2131
Category: Recycling
Running Time: 15:00

STATE RESOURCE LIST

ALABAMA

State Department of Agriculture and Industry

Office of Plant Protection Pesticide Management
P.O. Box 3336
Montgomery, AL 36109-0336
205-242-2656
8:00 a.m. to 5:00 p.m., Monday through Friday
Services:
• Provides technical assistance through pesticide-enforcement group.
• Speaks to schools or community groups upon request about environmental hazards of pesticides.
Materials offered:
• Pamphlets
• Information on chemicals and standards of practice

State Department of Conservation and Natural Resources

Information and Education Section
64 North Union Street, 4th and 5th Floor
Montgomery, AL 36130
800-262-3151 (park information)
800-252-7275 (brochures)
205-242-3151
8:00 a.m. to 5:00 p.m., Monday through Friday
Services:
• Protects state wildlife, fisheries, park, fresh and saltwater resources and state lands.
• Manages 24 state parks.
Materials offered:
• Brochures on wildlife in the state park
• *Project Wild,* kindergarten through 12th-grade curriculum

State Department of Economic and Community Affairs

Science, Technology and Energy Conservation Office
P.O. Box 5690
Montgomery, AL 36103-5690

205-242-5290
9:00 a.m. to 5:00 p.m., Monday through Friday
Services:
• Administers U.S. Department of Energy Institutional Conservation Program.
Materials offered:
• Educational materials on science and energy

State Department of Education

Science Specialist
Gordon Persons Building
50 North Ripley Street
Montgomery, AL 36130-3901
205-242-8082
7:30 a.m. to 5:30 p.m., Monday through Friday
Services:
• Refers educators to other state programs and agencies.
Materials offered:
• *Science Course Study*, curricula integrating environmental issues throughout the different disciplines
• *Principles of Ecology in the Environment*, 7th-grade curriculum
• Teacher's resource guide

State Department of Environmental Management

Land Division, Office of Public Affairs
P.O. Box 301463
Montgomery, AL 36130-1463
205-271-7726
8:00 a.m. to 5:00 p.m., Monday through Friday
Services:
• Oversees state-mandated recycling, composting and waste reduction programs in local governments, schools and institutions.
• Implements and enforces environmental statutes for toxic substances.
• Lectures on recycling at schools, civic groups and garden clubs.
Materials offered:
• EPA curricula guide
• Posters, coloring books and activity books
• Local government recycling brochures
• Literature on various topics
• *Let's Recycle*, kindergarten through 3rd-grade curriculum
• *Let's Reduce and Recycle*, kindergarten through 12th-grade curriculum

on solid waste management
• *School Recycling Program Handbook*
• *Setting Up a Solid Waste Recycling Center for Schools: Guideline*
• *Procurement Recycling Guide,* list of vendors selling recycled products

State Department of Environmental Management

Environmental Specialist
1751 Congressman W.L. Dickinson Drive
Montgomery, AL 36130
205-271-7938
8:00 a.m. to 5:00 p.m., Monday through Friday
Services:
• Oversees state air, water, land and waste programs.
• Manages coastal protection programs.
• Provides speakers upon request.
Materials offered:
• EPA and general information on all department issues
• Map of water resources
• Kindergarten through 12th-grade interdisciplinary curriculum

State Department of Public Health

Environmental Health Office
434 Monroe Street
Montgomery, AL 36130-1701
800-582-1866 (within state)
205-613-5373
8:00 a.m. to 5:00 p.m., Monday through Friday
Services:
• Oversees state programs on lead contamination, asbestos and radon.
• Implements state Childhood Lead Poisoning Prevention Project.
Materials offered:
• EPA publications on environmental health issues
• Videos for schools
• Homeowners' manual on radon
• Radon coloring books
• Indoor air quality pamphlets
• Lead exposure and abatement pamphlets

State Waterworks

P.O. Box 1631
Montgomery, AL 36102
205-240-1670
8:15 a.m. to 4:45 p.m., Monday

through Friday
Services:
- Inspects sewer systems and other waterworks.
- Offers tours upon request of waterworks facilities.

ALASKA

Alaska Health Project
1818 West Northern Light Boulevard, #103
Anchorage, AK 99517
800-478-2864 (within state)
907-276-2864
8:00 a.m. to 5:00 p.m., Monday through Friday
Services:
- Provides technical assistance, information and advocacy on occupational and environmental health issues.
- Conducts a hazardous waste audit for schools and trains janitorial staff.
- Assists in developing a hazardous materials curriculum and pilot program for Native Americans.
- Conducts school presentation programs.
- Provides community Hazardous Materials Evaluation Program.
Materials offered:
- *Waste Reduction in School Guide*, booklet
- Pollution prevention guides
- *Environmental Health*, curricula
- *Waste Reduction,* 9th-grade through college curricula

State Department of Education
Science Specialist
801 West 10th Avenue, Suite 200
Juneau, AK 99801
907-465-2841
9:00 a.m. to 5:00 p.m., Monday through Friday
Services:
- Oversees environmental education for the state.
Materials offered:
- Variety of materials on environmental issues

State Department of Environmental Conservation
410 Willoughby Avenue
Juneau, AK 99801
800-478-9300 (oil spill hotline)

907-465-5000
8:00 a.m. to 5:00 p.m., Monday through Friday
Services:
- Oversees state air, water and land issues.
Materials offered:
- Brochures
- Departmental handbook/directory

State Department of Environmental Conservation
Office of Pesticide Regulation
500 South Alaska Street
Palmer, AK 99645
907-745-PEST
8:00 a.m. to 5:00 p.m., Monday through Friday
Services:
- Oversees federal EPA laws and implements some state statutes.
- Provides training and certification programs: Pesticides in Schools; Cleansing Agents; Urban Pest Control and Home Pest Control.

State Department of Environmental Conservation
Office of Pollution Prevention
3601 C Street
Anchorage, AK 99503
907-563-6529
8:00 a.m. to 5:00 p.m., Monday through Friday
Services:
- Implements state solid and hazardous waste management.
- Visits schools upon request.
- Assists schools starting recycling programs.
- Awards funds to school projects that meet waste reduction standards.
- Provides contacts and phone numbers of recycling centers.
Materials offered:
- Brochures
- Pollution prevention guide

State Housing Department
Energy Conservation Center
520 East 34th Avenue
Anchorage, AK 99503
907-561-1900
8:30 a.m. to 5:00 p.m., Monday through Friday
Services:
- Administers U.S. Department of Energy ICP Program (907-564-9274).

- Operates state energy conservation programs.
- Operates book and video library.
Materials offered:
- Brochures on energy conservation and alternative energy

State Parks and Natural Resources
P.O. Box 107005
Anchorage, AK 99510
907-762-2261
10:00 a.m. to 5:30 p.m., Monday through Friday
Services:
- Manages state parks and preserves.
- Information on weather conditions, bear sightings and special events.
Materials offered:
- Brochures on various parks and activities

University of Alaska
Cooperative Extensions Services
Fairbanks, AK 99775-6180
907-474-6356
8:00 a.m. to 5:00 p.m., Monday through Friday
Services:
- Administrates *Project Learning Tree,* kindergarten through 12th-grade curriculum.

ARIZONA

Commission on the Environment
1645 West Jefferson, Suite 416
Phoenix, AZ 85007
602-542-2102
8:00 a.m. to 5:00 p.m., Monday through Friday
Services:
- Conducts conferences on various environmental issues.
Materials offered:
- Environmental Directory of Arizona
- Pamphlets on services and issues

Department of State Parks
1300 West Washington
Phoenix, AZ 85007
602-542-4174
Services:
- Manages state parks.
Materials offered:
- Brochures on parks and activities

Department of Water Resources

15 South 15th Avenue
Phoenix, AZ 85007
602-542-1553
8:00 a.m. to 5:00 p.m., Monday
through Friday
Services:
• Responsible for water control, water
management and water quality.
• Provides a training officer and a
hydrologist for presentations.
Materials offered:
• Groundwater floor model for teachers
• Pamphlets and information kits

State Department of Agriculture and Environmental Services

P.O. Box 234
Phoenix, AZ 85001
602-407-2900
8:00 a.m. to 5:00 p.m., Monday
through Friday
Services:
• Responsible for groundwater protection and pesticide safety.
• Provides speakers upon request.
Materials offered:
• EPA coloring books
• EPA brochures
• Information on pesticide safety and
groundwater

State Department of Commerce

Office of Energy
3800 North Central, Suite 1200
Phoenix, AZ 85012
602-280-1430
8:00 a.m. to 5:00 p.m., Monday
through Friday
Services:
• Supervises Arizona Public Service,
Salt River Project and Southwest Gas.
• Holds many school contests on
energy awareness and water conservation.
• Offers teacher workshops on energy
conservation.
• Manages The Energy Patrol
Program.
• Administers U.S. Department of
Energy ICP Program.
Materials offered:
• Audio visuals, videos and classroom activities
• *Bright Ideas*, booklet
• Solar activity package for schools
• *N.E.E.T.*, teacher newsletter

State Department of Education

Environmental Education Specialist
1535 West Jefferson
Phoenix, AZ 85007
800-352-4558 (within state)
602-542-3052
8:00 a.m. to 5:00 p.m., Monday
through Friday
Services:
• Provides environmental education
guidelines for kindergarten through
12th grade.
• Offers a teacher training program.
Materials offered:
• Clearinghouse of information and
materials

State Department of Environmental Quality

Ombudsman
3033 North Central Avenue
Phoenix, AZ 85012
602-207-2214
8:00 a.m. to 5:00 p.m., Monday
through Friday
Services:
• Oversees state air, water, land and
waste programs.
• Offers grants for environmental
education programs.
• Provides funds for a recycling education program where minority college
students teach elementary and junior
high students.
• Works with the Arizona Department of Education and 14 other state
agencies to implement the state
Environmental Education Mandate of
May 1990.
Materials offered:
• Pamphlets on recycling, water conservation, waste reduction and other
topics
• *Environmental Scene,* quarterly
newsletter
• Brochures on Tri-City Landfill and
Overland Trail Subdivision

State Department of Game and Fish

Education Branch
Heritage and Environmental Education
Coordinator
2222 West Greenway
Phoenix, AZ 85023
602-789-3236
8:00 a.m. to 5:00 p.m., Monday
through Friday
Services:
• Is responsible for wildlife habitat
protection and pollution prevention.
• Offers grants for environmental
programs.
• Operates Wildlife Rehabilitation
Centers.
Materials offered:
• *Project Wild*, kindergarten through
12th-grade curriculum
• Regional handbooks and posters
• Teacher handouts and posters
• Videos
• Class on endangered species

State Department of Health

Disease Prevention Services
Office of Risk Assessment and
Investigations
1400 West Washington Avenue
Phoenix, AZ 85007
602-542-7310
8:00 a.m. to 5:00 p.m., Monday
through Friday
Services:
• Responds to public complaints
about lead contamination.
• Investigates contaminated sites.
Materials offered:
• Pamphlets on lead contamination

State Department of Public Works

101 South Central Avenue
Phoenix, AZ 85004
602-262-7251
602-256-3310 (Household Hazardous
Waste Hotline)
8:00 a.m. to 5:00 p.m., Monday
through Friday
Services:
• Provides household hazardous
waste disposal stations.
• Holds household hazardous waste
roundups.
Materials offered:
• Fact sheets covering recycling and
household wastes

State Radiation Regulatory Agency

Radon Division
4814 South 40th Street
Phoenix AZ 85040
602-255-4845
8:00 a.m. to 5:00 p.m., Monday
through Friday
Services:
• Conducts statewide radon survey.
• Offers seminars, lectures and other

presentations upon request.
Materials offered:
- EPA regulations and publications
- Consumer publications

T.R.E.E. Center
200 South 6th Avenue, P.O. Box 2609
Tucson, AZ 85702-2609
520-620-6142
8:00 a.m. to 5:00 p.m., Monday
through Friday
Services:
- Manages environmental education library.
Materials offered:
- Environmental books, magazines and other materials

ARKANSAS

Science and Environmental Education Office
Science and Environmental Education Specialist
#4 State Capitol
Little Rock, AR 72201
501-682-4471
8:00 a.m. to 4:30 p.m., Monday
through Friday
Services:
- Implements state mandate requiring environmental education materials in all public schools.

State Department of Parks and Tourism
One Capitol Mall
Little Rock, AR 72201
501-682-2187
8:00 a.m. to 5:00 p.m., Monday
through Friday
Services:
- Provides interpretative tours and educational programs for all state parks and 3 state museums.
- Develops environmental curriculum.
Materials offered:
- Brochures on state parks and activities
- Educational information available
- *Project Wild,* kindergarten through 12th-grade curriculum
- *Project Learning Tree,* kindergarten through 12th-grade curriculum

State Department of Pollution Control and Ecology
Office of Public Information
P.O. Box 8913
Little Rock, AR 72219-8913
501-562-7444
8:00 a.m. to 5:00 p.m., Monday
through Friday
Services:
- Oversees state air, water, land and waste programs.
- Works with city and county facilities and schools in developing recycling programs.
- Provides reference library.
- Arranges for speakers upon request.
- Disseminates information through University of Arkansas.
Materials offered:
- *Let's Reduce and Reuse,* EPA curricula
- *Keeping the Earth in 4H,* Teacher's Guide and student worksheets developed by the 4H
- Pamphlets on state regulations
- Videos on agency response to environmental crisis

State Health Department
Environmental Health Protection
4815 West Markham Street
Little Rock, AR 72205
800-482-5400 (within state)
501-661-2573
8:00 a.m. to 4:30 p.m., Monday
through Friday
Services:
- Oversees state health programs on radon, lead contamination and asbestos.
- Provides, on request, a proficiency list of contractors for radon testing.
Materials offered:
- EPA publications

State Industrial Development Commission
Arkansas Energy Office
One State Capitol Mall
Little Rock, AR 72201
501-682-1370
8:00 a.m. to 5:00 p.m., Monday
through Friday
Services:
- Promotes energy conservation through TV shows, such as *Home Seasoning* aired on AETN.

- Administers U.S. Department of Energy ICP Program.
Materials offered:
- Over 25 publications available
- Energy conservation books for homes and commercial buildings
- 30-minute video on energy conservation

CALIFORNIA

California Department of Education
Science and Environmental Education Unit
P.O. Box 944272
Sacramento, CA 94244-2720
916-657-4869
916-445-1260 (publications)
916-657-3681 (Art Safe List)
8:00 a.m. to 4:30 p.m., Monday
through Friday
Services:
- Provides publications listing environmental curricula.
- Provides grants for environmental programs.
Materials offered:
- Supplies the following publications: *Science Framework for California Schools, Environmental Education; Compendium for Human Communities, Environmental Education; Compendium for Water Resources, Environmental Education; Compendium for Integrated Waste Management, Environmental Education; Compendium for Energy Resources; California Endangered Species Resource Guide; Science and Environmental Education Resource Guide, California Class Project; Guide for the Self Appraisal and Certification of Resident Outdoor Science School Programs*

California Integrated Waste Management Board
8800 Cal Center Drive
Sacramento, CA 95826
916-255-2296
916-255-2442 (educational resources)
8:00 a.m. to 5:00 p.m., Monday
through Friday
Services:

• Operates recycling hotline (800-553-2962).
• Offers information on where to recycle aluminum, glass, plastic, paper, newspapers, batteries and household hazardous waste in your local community.
Materials offered:
• Various materials on recycling

Coastal Commission
South Coast District Office
245 West Broadway, Suite 380
Long Beach, CA 90802-1450
310-590-5071
8:00 a.m. to 5:00 p.m., Monday through Friday
Services:
• Implements coastal zone management policy.
• Promotes conservation and enforces regulations.
• Organizes Adopt-A-Beach programs and assesses damage caused by trash.
• Sponsors Coast Weeks and Coastal Cleanup Day.
Materials offered:
• Results from coastal clean-ups
• Information about coastal ecosystems

Energy Commission
Energy Efficiency and Local Assistance Division
1516 Ninth Street
Sacramento, CA 95814
800-772-3300 (within state)
916-654-4989
8:00 a.m. to 5:00 p.m., Monday through Friday
Services:
• Promotes energy conservation and efficiency.
• Develops renewable energy resources and alternative energy technology.
• Administers U.S. Department of Energy ICP Program.
Materials offered:
• Conservation, electricity, energy development and fuel reports
• Publications on energy efficiency and alternative energy sources

State Department of Conservation
Division of Recycling Resource Center
801 K Street
Sacramento, CA 95814

916-445-1490
8:00 a.m. to 5:00 p.m., Monday through Friday
Services:
• Offers technical assistance with school recycling programs.
• Operates bilingual recycling hotline (800-732-9253).
Materials offered:
• Education packets for teachers
• Guidebook on how to start recycle programs in the schools
• Over 300 recycle videos available for loan to any California school

State Department of Fish and Game
Education and Public Information Office
1416 Ninth Street
Sacramento, CA 95814
916-653-7664
8:00 a.m. to 5:00 p.m., Monday through Friday
Services:
• Oversees state wildlife conservation programs.
• Promotes public awareness of wildlife conservation.
Materials offered:
• *Project Wild*, kindergarten through 12th-grade curriculum
• Publications on endangered species
• Brochures on state wildlife

State Department of Health Services
Environmental Health Investigations Office
2151 Berkeley Way
Berkeley, CA 94704
510-540-3657
8:00 a.m. to 5:00 p.m., Monday through Friday
Services:
• Researches lead poisoning, radon, asbestos and pesticides.
• Tracks biotoxic levels in coastal shellfish.
Materials offered:
• Published studies on various subjects
• Pamphlets and general information about environmental health issues

State Environmental Protection Agency
Office of External Affairs

555 Capitol Mall, Suite 235
Sacramento, CA 95814
916-324-9670
8:00 a.m. to 5:00 p.m., Monday through Friday
Services:
• Oversees state air, land, water and waste regulations and programs.
• Provides information and services to educators through the Office of Toxic Substance Control.
Materials offered:
• *Recycle Rex,* kindergarten through 6th-grade curriculum
• *Environmentally,* 5th-grade curriculum
• Publications on issues covered by EPA

COLORADO

Colorado Foundation for Agriculture
P.O. Box 28276, WCR-15
Windsor, CO 80216
303-686-7806
8:00 a.m. to 5:00 p.m., Monday through Friday
Services:
• Oversees state industries on food, fiber and natural resources.
• Has resource library.
Materials offered:
• Curricula programs for grades 2 through 7 on recycling and water conservation

Department of Energy
Office of Energy Conservation
1675 Broadway, Suite 1300
Denver, CO 80202-4613
303-620-4292
7:30 a.m. to 5:00 p.m., Monday through Friday
Services:
• Administers U.S. Department of Energy ICP Program.
• Oversees energy conservation and recycling.
Materials offered:
• Energy conservation pamphlets
• Renewable resources guide for recycling

State Department of Education
Environmental Education Office
201 East Colfax Avenue

Denver, CO 80203-1799
303-866-6787
8:00 a.m. to 5:00 p.m., Monday
through Friday
Services:
• Conducts teacher workshops.
• Provides referrals to other resources
and agencies.
Materials offered:
• Newsletter

State Department of Health
4300 Cherry Creek Drive
Denver, CO 80222-1530
800-846-3986 (within state)
303-331-8480
8 a.m. to 5:00 p.m., Monday through
Friday
Services:
• Oversees state radon, lead poison-
ing, asbestos and hazardous waste
programs.
• Coordinates statewide pollution pre-
vention program.
• Offers training seminars on pollu-
tion prevention.
Materials offered:
• EPA guide to radon
• Radon measurement of contract
proficiency list
• *Homeowner Guide to Radon
Reduction,* booklet
• Hazardous waste fact sheets
• Information on various environ-
mental health hazardous

State Department of Natural
Resources
Division of Wildlife
Wildlife Program Specialist
6060 Broadway
Denver, CO 80216
303-291-7300
8:00 a.m. to 5:00 p.m., Monday
through Friday
Services:
• Oversees Rivers of Colorado water
watch network.
• Offers library services.
Materials offered:
• *Project Wild,* kindergarten through
12th-grade curriculum
• National Wildlife Federation infor-
mation packets
• Books for sale on wildlife issues
• *No Time to Waste,* resource guide

for teachers on solid and hazardous
waste
• *A Home for Pearl,* a video with
teacher's guide

State Department of Natural
Resources
State Parks and Recreation Division
1313 Sherman Street, #618
Denver, CO 80203
303-866-3437
8 a.m. to 5:00 p.m., Monday through
Friday
Services:
• Oversees state parks.
• Provides rangers to speak to
schools upon request.
• Conducts interpretative programs at
many of the parks.
• Offers teacher training program.
Materials offered:
• Brochures on parks and activities

State Department of Solid Waste
1390 Decatur Street
Denver, CO 80204
303-640-2512
7:30 a.m. to 4 p.m., Monday through
Friday
Services:
• Coordinates states trash collection
and recycling pick up.
• Offers presentations upon request.
Materials offered:
• Recycling and waste reduction
brochures

State Forest Service
Colorado State University
Fort Collins, CO 80523
303-491-6303
8:00 a.m. to 5:00 p.m., Monday
through Friday
Services:
• Is responsible for forest manage-
ment and wild-fire protection.
• Provides conservation education.
• Offers presentations to schools and
community groups.
• Facilitates workshops for educators
on conservation management.
Materials offered:
• Brochures on forests ecosystems
• *Project Learning Tree,* kindergarten
through 12th-grade curriculum

Bureau of Recreation
State Parks Division
165 Capitol Avenue
Hartford, CT 06106
203-566-2304
8:30 a.m. to 4:30 p.m., Monday
through Friday
Services:
• Supervises state parks.
• Offers speakers to schools on
request.
Materials offered:
• Information on camping, natural
history, dinosaurs, state park historical
sites and other activities

Environmental Epidemiology and
Occupational Health
150 Washington Street
Hartford, CT 06106
203-566-8167
8:30 a.m. to 4:30 p.m., Monday
through Friday
Services:
• Is responsible for lead, asbestos,
radon and pesticide programs along
with other environmental health haz-
ards.
• Conducts lectures upon request.
• Offers on-line computer information
service, with access to the Library of
Congress.
Materials offered:
• Brochures on lead, radon and other
environmental health hazards
• Pamphlets on water conservation
• Videos
• Water supply and conservation
pamphlets

State Department of Education
Division of Curriculum and Instruction
P.O. Box 2219, Room 367
Hartford, CT 06145
203-566-5871
8:00 a.m. to 5:00 p.m., Monday
through Friday
Services:
• Provides for Science Consultant to
speak to schools upon request.
Materials offered:
• Brochures
• Curriculum guides for environmen-
tal studies

State Department of Energy
80 Washington Street
Hartford, CT 06106
203-566-2800
8:30 a.m. to 4:30 p.m., Monday
through Friday
Services:
• Administers Connect Program
(Connecticut Energy Council for
Teachers) for kindergarten through
12th-grade teachers. Offers workshops, conferences, newsletters and
lectures on various environmental subjects.
• Manages small environmental
library that is open to the public.
• Administers U.S. Department of
Energy ICP Program.
Materials offered:
• Connect Program, loans textbooks
to teachers and students
• *New England Education Guide,*
booklet

**State Department of
Environmental Protection**
Office of Environmental Education
165 Capitol Ave, Room 108
Hartford, CT 06106
203-566-8108
8:30 a.m. to 4:30 p.m., Monday
through Friday
Services:
• Oversees state programs on air,
water, land and waste.
• Offers school-assembly programs
for kindergarten through 6th grade on
various subjects.
• Provides speakers upon request.
Materials offered:
• General fact sheets on individual
subjects

Waste Management Bureau
79 Elm Street
Hartford, CT 06106
203-566-2860
8:30 a.m. to 4:30 p.m., Monday
through Friday
Services:
• Oversees state recycling, environmental shopping and waste reduction
programs.
• Offers school-assembly programs
for kindergarten through 6th grade.
• Provides tours of museums and
recycling centers.
Materials offered:

• *Ray Cycle,* activity books plus packet
• Brochures: *Save the Planet in 2
Minutes; Bring Home Less Trash; Get
More Life from Dead Batteries and
Motor Oil; Turn Cans Into Cars*

DELAWARE

Department of Agriculture
2320 South Dupont Highway
Dover, DE 19901
302-739-4811
8:00 a.m. to 4:30 p.m., Monday
through Friday
Services:
• Enforces pesticide regulations and
issues applicator certification.
Materials offered:
• Coppies of pesticide regulations and
laws

**Department of Natural Resources
and Environmental Control**
Division of Parks and Recreation
P.O. Box 1401
Dover, DE 19903
302-739-4401
8:00 a.m. to 4:30 p.m., Monday
through Friday
Services:
• Manages state parks.
• Supervises state lands and wildlife
preserves.
Materials offered:
• Brochures on parks and activities

**Department of Public
Instruction**
Office of Environmental Education
P.O. Box 1402
Dover, DE 19903
302-739-3742
8:00 a.m. to 4:30 p.m., Monday
through Friday
Services:
• Offers teacher workshops.
Materials offered:
• *Project Learning Tree,* kindergarten
through 12th-grade curriculum
• *Project Wild,* kindergarten through
12th-grade curriculum

Division of Facilities Management
P.O. Box 1401
O'Neill Building
Dover, DE 19903

800-282-8616 (within state)
302-739-5644
8:00 a.m. to 4:30 p.m., Monday
through Friday
Services:
• Administers U.S. Department of
Energy ICP Program.
• Coordinates energy conservation
activities.
• Conducts workshops focusing on
different environmental subjects.
Materials offered:
• Brochures, pamphlets and small
booklets on energy conservation

Division of Public Health
Health Systems Protection
P.O. Box 637
Dover, DE 19903
302-739-3787
8:00 a.m. to 4:30 p.m., Monday
through Friday
Services:
• Operates radon hotline (800-554-
4636)
• Oversees state radon programs.
• Provides speakers upon request.
Materials offered:
• Radon measurement of contractor
proficiency lists

**State Department of Natural
Resources and Environmental
Control**
Office of Information and Education
89 Kings Highway, Box 1401
Dover, DE 19903
302-739-4506
7:30 a.m. to 5:00 p.m., Monday
through Friday
Services:
• Oversees air, water, soil, Superfund
sites, recycling programs and waste
management.
Materials offered:
• *Water Quality Education in
Schools,* kindergarten through 12th-
grade curriculum
• Information and educational
resources on environmental issues

State Solid Waste Authority
P.O. Box 455
Dover, DE 19903
302-739-5361
8:00 a.m. to 4:30 p.m., Monday
through Friday
Services:

• Operates Citizens Response Line (800-404-7080).

• Coordinates state recycling programs.

• Offers tours of solid-waste facilities.

Materials offered:

• Coloring books

• Water curricula for kindergarten through 8th grades

DISTRICT OF COLUMBIA (DC)

Department of Energy and Public Works

Education Office
613 G Street NW
Washington, DC 20001
202-727-1800
8:15 a.m. to 4:45 p.m., Monday through Friday
Services:

• Sponsors annual Halloween party to kick off energy-patrol program in schools.

• Provides speakers upon request.

• Offers energy conservation workshops and energy auditing programs in schools.

• Administers U.S. Department of Energy ICP Program.

Materials offered:

• Posters on the environment

• Brochures on energy conservation

• Energy videos and tapes on loan

Department of Health

Environmental Health Office
614 H Street NW
Washington, DC 20001
202-727-7218
8:00 a.m. to 5 p.m., Monday through Friday
Services:

• Is responsible for radon health issues.

• Operates radon hotline (202-727-5728).

Materials offered:

• Free radon test kits

• Radon measurement of contractor proficiency lists for D.C. residents

Department of Public Works

Solid Waste Management Administration

2750 S. Capitol Street SE
Washington, DC 20032
202-767-8512
8:15 a.m. to 4:45 p.m., Monday through Friday
Services:

• Is responsible for recycling, public works, hazardous and solid waste and landfills.

• Assists with the "Make It Green, Keep It Clean" sanitation enforcement program.

• Operates recycling hotline (202-727-5887).

Materials offered:

• Recycling publications

Department of Public Works

Water and Sewer Utility Administration
5000 Overlook Avenue SW
Washington, DC 20032
202-767-7651
8:30 a.m. to 4:30 p.m., Monday through Friday
Services:

• Is responsible for water and sewer services, including storm water management.

Materials offered:

• Pamphlets on water conservation

District Division of Curriculum

Environmental Education Coordinator
Langdon Administrative Unit
20th and Evarts Street NE
Washington, DC 20018
202-576-7817
8:00 a.m. to 5:00 p.m., Monday through Friday
Services:

• Is responsible for D.C. environmental education.

Materials offered:

• Nature camp for 5th- and 6th-grade students, covering geology and ecology

District of Columbia Consumer Regulatory Affairs Agency

Environmental Regulation Administration
2100 Martin Luther King, Jr. Avenue SE, Suite 203
Washington, DC 20020
202-404-1136
8:30 a.m. to 4:30 p.m., Monday through Friday

Services:

• Serves as D.C. environmental regulatory agency, including hazardous and solid waste; water and air quality and storm water management.

• Responsible for D.C. fisheries management.

• Oversees asbestos and lead in drinking water clean-ups.

• Assists with the Chesapeake Bay Clean Up.

Materials offered:

• Pamphlets on environmental improvement in the District of Columbia

FLORIDA

Department of Community Affairs

Florida Energy Office
2740 Centerview Drive
Tallahassee, FL 32399-2100
904-488-6764
8:00 a.m. to 5:00 p.m., Monday through Friday
Services:

• Operates state energy conservation programs.

• Administers U.S. Department of Energy ICP Program.

Materials offered:

• Videos and curriculum on energy efficiency and conservation for grades 1 through 12

Florida Advisory Council on Environmental Education (FACEE)

Room 237, Holland Building
Tallahassee, FL 32399-1400
904-487-0123
9:00 a.m. to 5:00 p.m., Monday through Friday
Services:

• Provides grants for environmental education projects.

• Advises government representatives and agencies on environmental education.

Florida Solar Energy Center

300 State Road 401
Cape Canaveral, FL 32920
407-783-0300
9:00 a.m. to 5:00 p.m., Monday through Friday

Services:
- Provides mobile service delivery system for educators distributing environmental education materials.
- Offers workshops and courses on various energy topics.
- Sponsors regional resource fairs.

Materials offered:
- Information on solar energy

State Department of Education
Office of Environmental Education
325 West Gaines Street, Room 224C
Tallahassee, FL 32399
904-487-7900
8:00 a.m. to 5:00 p.m., Monday through Friday
Services:
- Integrates environmental education into schools and colleges.
- Provides speakers upon request.
- Serves as on-line clearinghouse of resources for teachers.
- Offers teachers in service.
- Oversees regional environmental education centers.

Materials offered:
- Pamphlets
- Newsletter
- *Four R's*, curriculum
- *Solid Wastes*, curriculum
- *Biodiversity: The Florida Story*, curriculum
- Directory of State Agency Environmental Educator Resources

State Department of Environmental Protection
Division of Education, Environmental Education Specialist
2600 Blair Stone Road
Tallahassee, FL 32399-2400
904-488-9334
8:00 a.m. to 5:00 p.m., Monday through Friday
Services:
- Oversees state air, water, land and waste programs.
- Manages state parks, as well as any environmental centers within the parks.
- Retains Environmental Education Specialist on staff.
- Sponsors annual Enviro-Thon that focuses on a broad environmental issue, with high school students participating in workshops and outdoor activities.

- Operates Partners of Excellence program.

Materials offered:
- *State of the Environment*, booklet
- *Your Environment for Schools*
- *Guide to Parks and Trails*
- *Environmental Field and Classroom Experiment Book*
- Booklets on Florida ecosystems and habitats

South Florida Water Management District
P.O. Box 24680
West Palm Beach, FL 33416
407-686-8800
8:00 a.m. to 5:00 p.m., Monday through Friday
Services:
- Is responsible for water quality and resources in southern Florida.
- Hosts annual 3-day teacher training on everglades and water management.

Materials offered:
- Annually distributes primary and secondary curricula to public schools in the 16 south Florida counties. Curricula focuses on water resource management and the everglades and comes with audiovisual supplements.
- Brochures and pamphlets on various water issues
- Co-produces other environmental publications and programs

State Division of Health and Rehabilitative Services
Environmental Health Office
1317 Winewood Boulevard
Tallahassee, FL 32399-0700
904-488-6811
8:00 a.m. to 5:00 p.m., Monday through Friday
Services:
- Studies indoor air quality, lead poisoning and radon contamination.

Materials offered:
- Pamphlets on all three subjects

GEORGIA

Environmental Health
445 Winn Way, Suite 320
Decatur, GA 30030
404-508-7900
8:00 a.m. to 5:00 p.m., Monday

through Friday
Services:
- Tests well water.
- Conducts OSHA training; inspects food service facilities and personal care homes for contamination; ensures proper sewage disposal and vector control.

Materials offered:
- General information on environmental health issues

State Department of Agriculture
Entomology and Pesticides
Capitol Square
Atlanta, GA 30334
404-656-3600
8:00 a.m. to 4:30 p.m., Monday through Friday
Services:
- Registers pesticides and certifies applicators.
- Inspects and issues licenses for nurseries and irrigation systems.
- Offers training for certification exams.

Materials offered:
- Training manuals for certified applicators
- Brochures on pesticides
- Enforcement reports and actions
- Information packet on Georgian agricultural history

State Department of Community Affairs
Recycling and Solid Waste Management
100 Peachtree Street, Suite 1200
Atlanta, GA 30303
404-656-3851
8: a.m. to 5:00 p.m., Monday through Friday
Services:
- Operates city and county district recycling programs, drop-offs and curbside collection.
- Conducts recycling workshops and teacher training.

Materials offered:
- *Clean and Beautiful Program*, curriculum
- *Waste and Place*, curriculum
- *Waste: The Hidden Resource*, curriculum

State Department of Education
Science Consultant

1766 Twin Towers East
Atlanta, GA 30334
404-656-4028
8:00 a.m. to 5:00 p.m., Monday
through Friday
Materials offered:
 • *Quality Core*, kindergarten through
12th-grade curriculum

State Department of Natural Resources

Environmental Protection Division
205 Butler Street SE
Suite 1152, East Tower
Atlanta, GA 30334
404-656-4713
8:00 a.m. to 4:30 p.m., Monday
through Friday
Services:
 • Oversees state air, water, land and
waste programs.
 • Offers lectures upon request.
 • Sponsors geologic survey.
Materials offered:
 • Brochures available on all subjects

State Department of Natural Resources

Forestry Commission
200 Piedmont Avenue, Floyd Building
West Tower, Suite 810
Atlanta, GA 30334
404-656-3204
8:00 a.m. to 4:30 p.m., Monday
through Friday
Services:
 • Protects natural resources.
 • Manages landowner's timber.
 • Coordinates an urban forestry pro-
gram.
 • Sponsors a tree-education planting
program.
Materials offered:
 • Pamphlets and booklets on forestry
and state natural resources
 • *Project Learning Tree,* kindergarten
through 12th-grade curriculum

State Department of Natural Resources

Parks, Recreation and Historic Site
Division
205 Butler, Suite 1352
Atlanta, GA 30334
404-656-2770
8:00 a.m. to 5:00 p.m., Monday
through Friday
Services:

 • Manages state parks and historical
sites.
 • Visits schools, churches, etc. with a
slide show and lecture.
Materials offered:
 • Brochures on parks and activities
 • Teacher packet
 • Videos

State Office of Energy Resources

100 Peachtree Street, Suite 2080
Atlanta, GA 30334
404-656-5176
8:00 a.m. to 4:45 p.m., Monday
through Friday
Services:
 • Supervises state energy conserva-
tion programs.
 • Administers U.S. Department of
Energy ICP Program.
Materials offered:
 • Pamphlet on construction/building
of low-energy buildings
 • Curriculum supplement
 • Books on renewable energy
resources
 • High school science energy projects
 • *Adventures in Energy,* curriculum
and teacher's guide for grades 4
through 7
 • Various publications on energy

State Wildlife Resources Division

Fishery Management
Education Coordinators
2123 Highway 278
Social Circle, GA 30279
404-918-6418
8:00 a.m. to 5:00 p.m., Monday
through Friday
Services:
 • Coordinates *Project Wild.*
 • Provides aquatic supplement for
Project Wild.
Materials offered:
 • Posters
 • Brochures
 • Videos
 • *Project Wild*, kindergarten through
12th-grade curriculum

HAWAII

Environmental Health Administration

Environmental Management Division

2828 Paa Street, Suite 3080
Honolulu, HI 96819
808-831-6600
8:00 a.m. to 5:00 p.m., Monday
through Friday
Services:
 • Oversees hazardous waste evaluation, emergency response, environmental planning and resources.
 • Is responsible for air, water, safe
drinking water, waste and waste
water.

State Department of Agriculture

Pesticides Division
711 Keeaumoku Street
Honolulu, HI 96814
808-973-9401
8:00 a.m. to 5:00 p.m., Monday
through Friday
Services:
 • Regulates use of pesticides.
 • Licenses pesticide applicators.
Materials offered:
 • Coppies of aws and regulations of
pesticides

State Department of Education

Environmental Education Specialist
189 Lunalilo Home Road, 2nd Floor
Honolulu, HI 96825
808-396-2572
8:00 a.m. to 5:00 p.m., Monday
through Friday
Services:
 • Oversees environmental education
for public schools.
 • Coordinates teacher workshops.

State Department of Health

Office of Environmental Quality
Environmental Planning Office
Five Waterfront Plaza, 500 Ala Moana
Boulevard, Suite 250
Honolulu, HI 96813
808-586-4337
8:00 a.m. to 5:00 p.m., Monday
through Friday
Services:
 • Works with state department of
education to disseminate environmen-
tal materials.
Materials offered:
 • Curriculum materials
 • Informational brochures on clean
water, litter control and pollution man-
agement

State Department of Land and Natural Resources

P.O. Box 621
Honolulu, HI 96809
808-587-0300
9:00 a.m. to 5:00 p.m., Monday
through Friday
Services:
• Manages states parks.
Materials offered:
• Information of parks and activities

State Energy Office

Energy Information Specialist
335 Merchant Street, Room 110
Honolulu, HI 96813
808-587-3800
8:00 a.m. to 5:00 p.m., Monday
through Friday
Services:
• Makes classroom presentations.
• Coordinates Energy Awareness
Month exhibit.
• Holds 6-day energy conferences for
junior high students and teachers
focusing on "How to teach others
about energy."
• Implements Institutional
Conservation Program from the U.S.
Department of Energy.
• Administers U.S. Department of
Energy ICP Program.
Materials offered:
• Videos
• General information
• In state publication: kindergarten
through 3rd grade coloring book
• Information booklet for grades 4
through 6
• Energy resource fact sheets
• Annual report reviewing the year's
events

IDAHO

Community Programs

1410 North Hilton
Boise, ID 83720
208-334-5800
9:00 a.m. to 5:00 p.m., Monday
through Friday
Services:
• Responds to state water problems
including underground storage tanks
and drinking water.
• Studies the different life cycles of

trout in a stream for the Department of
Fish and Game.
Materials offered:
• Safe drinking water brochures
• Environmental regulation for the
State
• Air, water and toxic waste
brochures

Department of Agriculture

Division of Agriculture Technology
P.O. Box 2270,
Old Peneten Canyon Road
Boise, ID 83701
208-334-3240
8:00 a.m. to 5:00 p.m., Monday
through Friday
Services:
• Enforces pesticide laws and regulations and issues applicator and dealer
permits.
• Conducts seminar on pesticide
application.

Department of Parks and Recreation

Public Information Office
P.O. Box 83720
Boise, ID 83720-0065
208-34-4199
8:00 a.m. to 5:00 p.m., Monday
through Friday
Services:
• Supervises state parks.
Materials offered:
• *Idaho State Parks Guide,* booklet
• *Idaho Recreation Review
Quarterly,* magazine
• Traveling Trunks program with
videos for teachers

Department of Water Resources

Energy Division
1301 North Orchard, State House
Boise, ID 83720
208-327-7910
8:00 a.m. to 5:00 p.m., Monday
through Friday
Services:
• Promotes energy conservation.
• Provides lectures upon request.
• Administers U.S. Department of
Energy ICP Program.
• Library of materials on energy con-
servation and alternative resources.
Materials offered:
• 100 publications including videos,
magazines and brochures

State Department of Education

Science and Environmental Education
Consultant
P.O. Box 83720
Boise, ID 83720-0027
208-334-2281
9:00 a.m. to 5:00 p.m., Monday
through Friday
Services:
• Oversees state environmental edu-
cation programs.
• Refers teachers to appropriate
resources and services.

State Division of Environmental Quality

Environmental Education Specialist
1410 North Hilton
Boise, ID 83706
208-334-5879
9:00 a.m. to 5:00 p.m., Monday
through Friday
Services:
• Oversees state water, land, waste
and air management issues.
• Arranges for regional staff members
to work with local teachers on special
projects.
Materials offered:
• Curricula on specific environmental
topics

ILLINOIS

Department of Agriculture

Bureau of Environmental Programs
State Fairgrounds, P.O. Box 19281
Springfield, IL 62794-9281
217-782-6297
8:00 a.m. to 4:30 p.m. Monday
through Friday
Services:
• Works with Illinois Soil and Water
Districts to protect the state's natural
resources.
• Certifies and licenses all pesticide
dealers and applicators.
• Conducts tours on protecting soil
and water at all facilities.
• Provides some teacher training.
Materials offered:
• Brochures on soil and water
• Information on pesticide laws and
regulations
• Videos and slides

Department of Conservation
524 South Second Street, Lincoln Tower Plaza
Springfield, IL 62701
217-524-4126
8:00 a.m. to 5:00 p.m., Monday through Friday
Services:
• Provides educational programs such as Kids for Conservation.
• Oversees state parks, fisheries, wildlife, forests and natural heritage.
Materials offered:
• Brochures on hiking, biking, canoeing, animals, plants and forestry
• *Kids for Conservation,* youth magazine for Illinois residents
• Education kits, videos, posters

Department of Energy and Natural Resources
Office of Energy and Environmental Education Network
325 West Adams, Room 300
Springfield, IL 62704-1892
217-785-3412
7:30 a.m. to 5:00 p.m., Monday through Friday
Services:
• Is an information clearinghouse for the state (800-252-8955).
• Promotes energy conservation and use of alternative energy resources.
• Administers U.S. Department of Energy ICP Program.
• Provides tours of solar-powered building.
Materials offered:
• Newsletters to teachers and students
• Curricular materials on waste reduction and recycling for kindergarten through 8th grade
• Games related to energy

Department of Energy and Natural Resources
Office of Recycling and Waste Reduction
325 West Adams, Room 300
Springfield, IL 62704
217-524-5454
9:00 a.m. to 5:00 p.m., Monday through Friday
Services:
• Promotes recycling and waste reduction.
• Helps start school recycling programs.

• Hosts workshops for teachers and college students on recycling and waste reduction.
Materials offered:
• Recycling and waste reduction materials

Department of Nuclear Safety
1301 Knotts Street
Springfield, IL 62703
800-325-1245 (within state)
217-786-7127
9:00 a.m. to 5:00 p.m., Monday through Friday
Services:
• Manages state radon program.
• Provides radon measurement of contract proficiency test.
Materials offered:
• *Citizen's Guide to Radon,* booklet
• Radon Reduction Methods

State Department of Education
Science Coordinator
100 North First Street
Springfield, IL 62777
217-782-2826
8:00 a.m. to 5:00 p.m., Monday through Friday
Services:
• Provides Illinois educators with video library, service center and resources.
• Provides competitive grants for scientific literacy programs.
• Offers technical assistance for developing and implementing environmental education programs by providing a science supervisor and advisors.
Materials offered:
• List of funded programs
• *Solid Waste: From Problems to Solutions,* teacher's handbook on waste reduction
• Legislative requirements by the state

State Department of Health
Environmental Health Office
525 West Jefferson Street
Springfield, IL 62761
217-782-4674
8:00 a.m. to 5:00 p.m., Monday through Friday
Services:
• Oversees state radon, pesticides, lead and asbestos programs.
Materials offered:

• Pamphlets on various environmental health issues

State Environmental Protection Agency
Office of Public Information
2200 Churchill Road
Springfield, IL 62794
217-782-5562
8:00 a.m. to 5:30 p.m., Monday through Friday
Services:
• Supervises state environmental laws concerning air, water, land and waste.
• Provides speakers upon request.
Materials offered:
• Brochure on water tanks, tires and hazardous waste
• Teaching aides for air, water and recycling issues

INDIANA

Department of Natural Resources
Division of Nature Preserves
402 West Washington, Room W267
Indianapolis, IN 46204
317-232-4052
8:00 a.m. to 4:30 p.m., Monday through Friday
Services:
• Protects nature areas, endangered species of plants and animals.
Materials offered:
• *Directory of Indiana Nature Preserves,* book
• Brochure about nature preserves
• Brochure on Indiana's natural heritage

Office of Pollution Prevention and Technical Assistance
100 North Senate Avenue, P.O. Box 6015
Indianapolis, IN 46206-6015
317-232-5964
8:15 a.m. to 4:45 p.m., Monday through Friday
Services:
• Oversees state composting and recycling education programs.
• Provides speakers upon request.
Materials offered:
• Brochures on composting and recycling

State Department of Education
Environmental Science Consultant
229 State House
Indianapolis, IN 46204
317-232-9141
8:00 a.m. to 4:30 p.m., Monday
through Friday
Services:
• Offers workshops on Native
Americans and environmental issues.
• Promotes international agricultural
awareness.
Materials offered:
• *Waste Reduction Guide for Indiana
Schools,* booklet
• *Save Our Streams/Water Ways,* an
interdisciplinary module
• *Unifying Energy; Expanding
Indian's Energy Resources,* booklet
• *Take Pride in America,* booklet
• *Energy, Economics and the
Environment,* booklet
• *My Culture, Your Culture, Our
Culture,* booklet
• *Completing the Cycle—It's Up to
You,* curriculum
• *Triple E—Energy, Economics and
Environment*, curriculum
• *Wet and Wild Water,* curriculum
• *Project Wild,* curriculum
• *Project Learning Tree,* curriculum
• *Outdoor Classroom,* curriculum

State Department of Environmental Management
Department of Air
Department of Water
100 North Senate Avenue, P.O. Box
6015
Indianapolis, IN 46206
317-232-5586 (air)
317-232-8476 (water)
Services:
• Operates environmental health hotline (800-451-6027).
• Enforces air pollution laws through
the Department of Air.
• Issues permits for waste water and
water quality standards, checks for
violations, handles public water and
groundwater, as well as lead in water,
through the Department of Water.

State Department of Health
Industrial Hygiene Radiological Health
1330 West Michigan Avenue
Indianapolis, IN 46206
317-633-0100

8:00 a.m. to 5:00 p.m., Monday
through Friday
Services:
• Is responsible for radon, lead and
asbestos programs.
Materials offered:
• Brochures on radon, lead and
asbestos

State Department of Natural Resources
Division of Forestry
402 West Washington Street, Room
W-296
Indianapolis, IN 46204
317-232-4105
8:15 a.m. to 4:45 p.m., Monday
through Friday
Services:
• Manages state owned forests and
nurseries.
• Assists with reforestation.
• Educates farmers and land owners
about land management.
• Offers a conservative education res-
ident camp for teachers.
Materials offered:
• Brochures on state wildlife, tree
planting and instructions on foresting
land
• *Project Learning Tree*, kindergarten
through 12th-grade curriculum

State Department of Natural Resources
Division of Parks
402 West Washington Street Room,
W-298
Indianapolis, IN 46204
317-232-4124
8:00 a.m. to 5:00 p.m., Monday
through Friday
Services:
• Supervises state parks.
Materials offered:
• Brochures on parks and activities
• Recreation guide

State Office of Energy Policy
One North Capitol, Suite 700
Indianapolis, IN 46204-2288
317-232-8940
8:00 a.m. to 4:30 p.m., Monday
through Friday
Services:
• Operates energy hotline for Indiana
(800-382-4631).

• Oversees state energy efficiency
and recycling programs.
• Administers U.S. Department of
Energy ICP Program.
Materials offered:
• *In Energy*, quarterly newsletter

IOWA

Department of Agriculture
Pesticide Division
Wallace Building, 1st Floor
Des Moines, IA 50319-0051
515-281-8591
8:00 a.m. to 4:30 p.m., Monday
through Friday
Services:
• Regulates pesticides use, certifica-
tion, product requirements and applica-
tor licenses.
• Conducts tours of the laboratory.
Materials offered:
• Regulation and laws

Springbrook Education Center
Education Specialist
2473 160th Road
Guthrie Center, IA 50115
515-747-8383
8:30 a.m. through 5:30 p.m., Monday
through Friday
Services:
• Works with the State Department of
Education.
• Serves as an environmental
resource center for educators and students.

State Department of Education
Environmental Education Consultant
Bureau of Instructional Services
Grimes State Office Building
Des Moines, IA 50319-0146
515-281-3146
8:00 a.m. to 4:30 p.m., Monday
through Friday
Services:
• Oversees environmental education
for the state.
• Provides regular teacher workshops
and training.
• Offers grants for curricula and pro-
gram development.
Materials offered:
• *Clean Sweep*, curriculum
• *Project Wild,* kindergarten through
12th-grade curriculum

625

- *Project Aquatic Wild,* kindergarten through 12th-grade curriculum
- *Outlook: Environmental Education Enrichment*, curriculum
- *Nature Scope,* curriculum
- *Project Learning Tree,* kindergarten through 12th-grade curriculum

State Department of Health
Public Health Division
321 East 12th Street
Des Moines, IA 50319
515-281-3478
8:00 a.m. to 4:30 p.m., Monday through Friday
Services:
- Administers health regulations on radon, lead and asbestos.
- Conducts public awareness programs on radon, provides speakers upon request.
- Conducts radon tests.
Materials offered:
- Brochures on radon, ionizing and nonionizing radiation and water treatment devices

State Department of Natural Resources
Division of State Parks
Wallace State Office Building
Des Moines, IA 50319-0034
515-281-6158
8:00 a.m. to 4:30 p.m., Monday through Friday
Services:
- Manages state parks and preserves.
- Offers interpreters for guided tours of some parks upon request.
Materials offered:
- Brochures on parks, preserves and activities

State Department of Natural Resources
Wallace Building
900 East Grand
Des Moines, IA 50319-0034
515-281-8693
7:30 a.m. to 4:00 p.m., Monday through Friday
Services:
- Oversees state air, water, soil, energy and waste issues.
Materials offered:
- Brochures on all environmental topics
- Newsletters

- Waste reduction information packets
- Videos, slides and teaching aides

State Division of Energy and Geological Resources
Wallace State Office Building
Des Moines, IA 50319-0034
515-281-5145
9:00 a.m. to 5:00 p.m., Monday through Friday
Services:
- Administers U.S. Department of Energy ICP Program.

KANSAS

Board of Agriculture
901 South Kansas Avenue
Topeka, KS 66612-1281
913-296-2263
8:00 a.m. to 5:00 p.m., Monday through Friday
Services:
- Enforces pesticide laws and procedures.
Materials offered:
- Environmental chart
- Pesticide brochure

Board of Radiation Control
Forbes Field, Building 283
Topeka, KS 66620
913-296-1561
8:00 a.m. to 5:00 p.m., Monday through Friday
Services:
- Conducts radiation control program.
- Provides presentations and information booths at public events and school functions.
Materials offered:
- Brochure on radon and radiation
- Slide program
- Video library for all radiation and radon information

Bureau of Environmental Remediation
Forbes Field, Building 740
Topeka, KS 66620-0001
913-296-1660
8:00 a.m. to 4:30 p.m., Monday through Friday
Services:
- Conducts toxic spill clean-ups, pol-

lution investigations, pesticides and underground-tank pollution prevention programs.
Materials offered:
- List of chemically contaminated sites in the state

Kansas Corporation Commission
Energy Program Section
1500 Arrowhead Road
Topeka, KS 66604-4027
913-271-3349
8:00 a.m. to 5:00 p.m., Monday through Friday
Services:
- Promotes energy conservation.
- Administers U.S. Department of Energy ICP Program.

Kansas Department of Health and Environment
Health and Environmental Education
900 SW Jackson, Room 1051
Topeka, KS 66612
913-296-1529
8:00 a.m. to 5:00 p.m., Monday through Friday
Services:
- Conducts air, waste, water and environmental quality clean-ups.
- Provides management of land, air and water to protect public health.
- Oversees state environmental health issues, such as asbestos, pesticides, lead poisoning and radon contamination.
- Offers lectures by staff to schools upon request.
Materials offered:
- Pamphlets on air, land, water, radon, asbestos, recycling and waste
- Some books available for reference
- *Earth Day Environmental Awareness Activity Guide,* booklet

State Department of Education
Education Specialist
120 East Tenth Street
Topeka, KS 66612
913-296-3201
9:00 a.m. to 5:30 p.m., Monday through Friday
Services:
- Advises state agencies on environmental education within the state through the Kansas Advisory Council for Environmental Education.
Materials offered:

- Educational materials that cover a variety of topics

State Department of Wildlife and Parks

900 Jackson, Suite 502
Topeka, KS 6612
913-296-2281
8:00 a.m. to 5:00 p.m., Monday through Friday
Services:
- Manages state parks.
- Offers boating classes.
Materials offered:
- Brochures on activities, camps and state parks

KENTUCKY

Department of State Parks

Capitol Plaza Towers, 10th Floor
Frankford, KY 40601
502-564-2172
8:00 a.m. to 5:00 p.m., Monday through Friday
Services:
- Manages state parks.
- Runs recreation programs at many of the parks.
Materials offered:
- Brochures on parks and activities

Division of Air Quality

803 Schenkel Lane
Frankfort, KY 40601
502-573-3382
8:00 a.m. to 4:30 p.m., Monday through Friday
Services:
- Serves as regulatory agency for air pollution, asbestos removal, school asbestos management and inspections.
- Coordinates clean air for Kentucky educational program.
Materials offered:
- Public awareness brochures
- Air pollution teaching-aides packet

Division of Waste Management

14 Reilly Road
Frankfort, KY 40601
502-654-6716
8:00 a.m. to 4:30 p.m., Monday through Friday
Services:
- Regulates solid and hazardous

wastes (landfills, land farming).
- Educates citizens on proper disposal, conservation and recovery of waste.
- Oversees Clean Community Program.
- Monitors Abandoned Vehicle Program.
- Oversees Environmental Watch Program.
Materials offered:
- Information about various programs

Environmental Quality Commission

14 Reilly Road
Frankfort, KY 40601
502-564-2150
8:00 a.m. to 4:30 p.m., Monday through Friday
Services:
- Integrates environmental education in schools.
- Offers workshops.
Materials offered:
- Teacher guides on environment
- State environmental trends report

State Department of Agriculture

Division of Pesticides
100 Fairoaks Lane
Frankfort, KY 40601
502-564-7274
8:00 a.m. to 4:00 p.m., Monday through Friday
Services:
- The state regulatory and licensing agency for pesticide application.
Materials offered:
- Brochures on pesticide control in schools
- Pesticide laws and regulations

State Department of Education

Environmental Education Contact
Capitol Plaza Tower, 18th Floor
Frankford, KY 40601
502-564-2106
8:00 a.m. to 5:00 p.m., Monday through Friday
Services:
- Responsible for implementing state declared environmental education policy of 1990 through Contact for Kentucky Environmental Council.
Materials offered:
- *Project Wild*, curriculum
- Other informational materials being developed

State Division of Energy

691 Teton Trail
Frankfort, KY 40601
502-564-7192
8:00 a.m. to 4:30 p.m., Monday through Friday
Services:
- Oversees state programs on energy efficiency and alternative energy sources.
- Administers U.S. Department of Energy ICP Program.
Materials offered:
- Brochures on energy efficiency and alternative energy sources
- Science activities
- Coloring book

State Division of Water

14 Reilly Road
Frankfort, KY 40601
502-564-3410
8:00 a.m. to 4:30 p.m., Monday through Friday
Services:
- Oversees public awareness and education concerning water resource management.
- Coordinates environmental review of water quality.
- Conducts lead contamination prohibition program.
- Provides basic training programs on biological monitoring, visual assessment and reporting procedures.
Materials offered:
- Various environmental education materials
- *Wild River,* curriculum and activities
- *Adopt-A-Stream*, curriculum and activities
- Water Watch program supplemented with *Ollie Otter* curriculum

State Natural Resources and Environmental Protection Cabinet

Coordinator of Environmental Education
Capital Plaza Tower, 4th Floor
Frankfort, KY 40601
502-0564-5525
8:30 a.m. to 5:30 p.m., Monday through Friday
Services:
- Oversees the protection and management of the state natural resources and environment.

Materials offered:
• Educational materials on air quality, conservation, endangered species, energy, forestry and waste management

LOUISIANA

Department of Culture, Recreation and Tourism
Office State Parks
Chief of Interpretive Services
P.O. Box 44426, 1051 North Third Street
Baton Rouge, LA 70804-4426
504-342-8111
8:00 a.m. to 4:00 p.m., Monday through Friday
Services:
• Manages 14 parks and one preservation area.
• Offers 176 interpretive programs in parks or schools.
Materials offered:
• Guide to state parks and recreational areas
• Calendar of interpretive programs
• Guides to birds and trails of each park

Office of Forestry
P.O. Box 631
Baton Rouge, LA 70821-0631
504-925-4500
8:00 a.m. to 4:00 p.m., Monday through Friday
Services:
• Manages state forests and lands.
• Conducts *Project Learning Tree* workshops.
• Disseminates public information on forests and wildfire prevention.
• Produces 50 million seedlings annually (pine and hardwood) for landowners.
• Operates a 400-acre genetically improved seed orchard that produces improved slash and loblolly pine.
• Promotes and directs urban forestry projects.
Materials offered:
• Various pamphlets on forests, timber harvests, state lands and trees

Office of the Secretary
Program Manager, Technical Support Program

P.O. Box 82263
Baton Rouge, LA 70884
504-765-0720
8:30 a.m. to 5:00 p.m., Monday through Friday
Services:
• Works with State Department of Education to develop materials.
Materials offered:
• Three-volume environmental education series on a variety of issues

State Department of Agriculture
Pesticides Division
P.O. Box 631
Baton Rouge, LA 70821-0631
504-925-3763
8:00 a.m. to 4:00 p.m., Monday through Friday
Services:
• Regulates pesticides.
Materials offered:
• Coppies of pesticide regulations and laws

State Department of Education
Program Manager, Science and Environmental Education
P.O. Box 94064
Baton Rouge, LA 70804
504-342-1136
8:30 a.m. to 5:00 p.m., Monday through Friday
Services:
• Oversees environmental education in the state as outlined in the guideline.
Materials offered:
• Environmental Science Bulletin #1792
• Litter Control, Waste Management and Recycling Resource Unit Bulletin #1722
• Other curricular materials

State Department of Energy
625 North Fourth Street
Baton Rouge, LA 70802
504-342-1399
8:00 a.m. to 5:00 p.m., Monday through Friday
Services:
• Promotes and manages energy conservation programs.
Materials offered:
• General publications on energy conservation and alternative energy sources

State Department of Environmental Quality
P.O. Box 82263
Baton Rouge, LA 70884-2263
504-765-0645
8:00 a.m. to 4:00 p.m., Monday through Friday
Services:
• Oversees air, water, land and waste issues.
Materials offered:
• Each division provides information in its particular field.

State Department of Health
Safe Drinking Water Program
325 Loyola Avenue, Room 403
New Orleans, LA 70112
504-568-5101
8:00 a.m. to 5:00 p.m., Monday through Friday
Services:
• Manages safe drinking water program.
Materials offered:
• General publications on safe drinking water

State Department of Wildlife and Fisheries
P.O. Box 98000
Baton Rouge, LA 70898-9000
504-765-2800
8:00 a.m. to 5:00 p.m., Monday through Friday
Services:
• Protects, conserves and replenishes state natural resources and wildlife.
• Provides library facilities.
Materials offered:
• *Louisiana Conservationist,* magazine
• *Project Wild,* kindergarten through 12th-grade curriculum

MAINE

Department of Environmental Protection
Public Information Education Unit
Station House 17
Augusta, ME 04333
207-287-2812
8:00 a.m. to 5:00 p.m., Monday through Friday
Services:
• Oversees land, air, water and waste issues.

• Gives presentations to schools using outreach staff.

• Member of Earthminders: Partners in Environmental Education.

Materials offered:

• Publications on land, air, water and waste issues

• Catalog of resources on water quality

• Coloring book

Division of Health Engineering

Health and Environmental Testing Lab
Station House 12
Augusta, ME 04333
207-287-2727
8:00 a.m. to 5:00 p.m., Monday through Friday

Services:

• Conducts environmental contamination assessments of air, water and soil.

• Conducts tests for lead poisoning.

• Gives presentations to schools.

Materials offered:

• Information on all subjects covered by the department

State Department of Agriculture

Board of Pesticide Control
State House, Station 28
Augusta, ME 04333
207-287-2731
8:00 a.m. to 5:00 p.m., Monday through Friday

Services:

• Oversees all aspects of sale, distribution, use and storage of pesticides including registration and license certification.

• Regulates the use of pesticides for groundwater protection.

• Offers a speaker's bureau with a toxicologist and public information officer that go to schools.

• Trains pesticide users.

Materials offered:

• *BPC Communicator,* quarterly newsletter for pesticide users and general public

• *Before You Use Pesticides,* booklet

• *Licensing Requirements for Pesticide Applicators in the State of Maine,* brochure

• *Pesticide Use and Personal Protective Equipment,* brochure

• Federal worker protection standards

• Community right to know agricultural operation

State Department of Education

Public Information and Education
Station House 17
Augusta, ME 04333
207-287-2811
8:00 a.m. to 5:00 p.m., Monday through Friday

Services:

• Develops curricula with FFA focusing on agricultural training.

Materials offered:

• *Project Wet,* kindergarten through 12th-grade curriculum

State Department of Energy Conservation

Station House 130
Agusta, ME 04333
207-624-6842
8:00 a.m. to 5:00 p.m., Monday through Friday

Services:

• Responsible for state energy conservation programs.

• Administers U.S. Department of Energy ICP Program.

Materials offered:

• Brochures on energy conservation

Waste Management Agency

Office of Waste Reduction and Recycling
Station House 154
Augusta, ME 04333
207-287-5300
8:00 a.m. to 5:00 p.m., Monday through Friday

Services:

• Oversees mandatory recycling of paper and corrugated cardboard for offices and businesses with 15 or more employees.

• Offers lectures to schools and organizations.

Materials offered:

• Various pamphlets on waste reduction and recycling

• Guide for towns to start recycling programs

MARYLAND

State Department of Agriculture

50 Harry Street Truman Parkway
Annapolis, MD 21401
410-841-5700

8:00 a.m. to 5:00 p.m., Monday through Friday

Services:

• Regulates application and licensing of pesticide users.

• Assists soil conservation districts with protecting state waters from agricultural nonpoint source pollution.

Materials offered:

• Coppies of regulations and laws on pesticides

State Department of Education

Gary Heath
Environmental Education Specialist
200 West Baltimore Street
Baltimore, MD 21201
410-333-2318
8:00 a.m. to 5:00 p.m., Monday through Friday

Services:

• Oversees state environmental education programs.

State Department of the Environment

Department of Parks
Tawes State Office Building
Annapolis, MD 21401
410-974-3771
8:00 a.m. to 5:00 p.m., Monday through Friday

Services:

• Manages state parks.

Materials offered:

• Brochures on parks and activities

State Department of the Environment

Office of Community Assistance and Public Affairs
2500 Broening Highway
Baltimore, MD 21224
410-631-3000
8:00 a.m. to 5:00 p.m., Monday through Friday

Services:

• Protects state air, water and land resources to ensure the long-term protection of public health and quality of life.

• Oversees state waste management and recycling programs.

• Handles radon, lead and asbestos through the Environmental Health Coordination Office.

• Provides library services.

Materials offered:

• Regulatory calendar

- Annual air quality data report
- Biennial water quality report
- List of potential hazardous waste sites

State Department of Natural Resources
Aquatic Resources Education Coordinator
Tidewater Administration B-2
Tawes State Office Building
580 Taylor Avenue
Annapolis, MD 21401
410-974-3765
8:30 a.m. to 5:30 p.m., Monday through Friday
Services:
- Co-sponsors Maryland's Aquatic Resources Education Grants Program with the Maryland Department of Education.
- Conducts four mini-conferences during the school year.
Materials offered:
- Brochures on a variety of topics
- *Kids Fishing for a Clean Environment*

State Department of Natural Resources
Public Communications Office
580 Taylor Street, Tawes State Office Building
Annapolis, MD 21401
410-974-3987
8:00 a.m. to 5:00 p.m., Monday through Friday
Services:
- Manages state wildlife, natural resources and Chesapeake Bay Program.
- Enforces state regulations on fisheries, forests and parks.
Materials offered:
- *Maryland Outdoors Begins with Me*, a curriculum that gives a general overview of state environmental education opportunities
- Information on many other programs and resources

State Department of Wildlife
Tawes State Office Building
580 Taylor Avenue
Annapolis, MD 21401
410-974-3195
Services:
- Manages state wildlife and natural resources.

Materials offered:
- *Project Wild*, kindergarten through 12th-grade curriculum

State Energy Administration
45 Calvert Street
Annapolis, MD 21401
800-72-ENERGY
410-974-2511
8:00 a.m. to 5:00 p.m., Monday through Friday
Services:
- Promotes alternative energy and conservation programs.
- Administers U.S. Department of Energy institutional conservation programs.
Materials offered:
- *Scouting for Energy,* one-week curriculum with teacher's guide
- Publications on alternative energy resources and energy conservation

MASSACHUSETTS

Department of Environmental Protection
Office of Public Affairs
One Winter Street, 4th Floor
Boston, MA 02018
617-292-5500
617-727-2834 (state house bookstore)
8:00 a.m. to 5:00 p.m., Monday through Friday
Services:
- Oversees air, water, land and waste protection programs.
Materials offered:
- General information on lead in drinking water, compost, recycling, and household hazardous waste
- *The Solid Waste Management Resource Guide for Massachusetts Schools,* an interdisciplinary, activity-oriented school resource guide for kindergarten through 12th grade

Department of Food and Agriculture
Bureau of Pesticides
100 Cambridge Street
Boston, MA 02202
617-727-3020
8:30 a.m. to 4:30 p.m., Monday through Friday

Services:
- Registers pesticides and pesticide applicators.
- Regulates and controls pesticide use.
Materials offered:
- Brochures on pesticides

Division of Energy Resources
100 Cambridge Street, Room 1500
Boston, MA 02202
617-727-4732
9:00 a.m. to 5:00 p.m., Monday through Friday
Services:
- Implements state energy plan.
- Administers U.S. Department of Energy ICP Program.
- Promotes alternative transportation and energy.
- Offers lectures to schools.
Materials offered:
- Brochures concerning home energy
- Teaching aides

Division of Solid Waste Management
Office of Public Affairs
One Winter Street
Boston, MA 02108
617-292-5988
8:00 a.m. to 5:00 p.m., Monday through Friday
Services:
- Promotes recycling programs throughout the state.
- Trains educators and helps to set up recycling programs in schools.
- Offers tours at the Springfield recycling plant.
Materials offered:
- Brochures on recycling and waste reduction
- Solid Waste Management Resources Guide

Massachusetts Executive Office of Environmental Affairs
100 Cambridge Street
Boston, MA 02202
617-727-9800
8:30 a.m. to 5:30 p.m., Monday through Friday
Services:
- Advises the State Department of Education.
Materials offered:
- *Environmental Education in Massachusetts: A Resource Guide*

Metropolitan District Commissions
20 Somerset Street
Boston, MA 02108
617-727-5250
9:00 a.m. to 5:00 p.m., Monday
through Friday
Services:
• Maintains parks and public lands.
• Provides professional management
for natural and cultural resources.
• Offers lectures to schools upon
request.
Materials offered:
• Brochures on parks and activities

State Department of Public Health
150 Treemont Street, 10th Floor
Boston, MA 02111
617-727-0651
8:00 a.m. to 5:00 p.m., Monday
through Friday
Services:
• Oversees state environmental
health issues, such as radon, safe
drinking water and asbestos.
Materials offered:
• General information about environmental health issues

MICHIGAN

Department of Agriculture
Pesticide and Plant Pest Management
Division
P.O. Box 30017
Lansing, MI 48909
800-292-3939 (within state)
517-373-1087
8:00 a.m. to 5:00 p.m., Monday
through Friday
Services:
• Regulates pesticide licensing and
applicators.
• Investigates misuse or complaints
of pesticides.
Materials offered:
• List of state regulations regarding
different pesticides

Department of Natural Resources
Press Office
517-373-2199
300 South Washington Square
Lansing, MI 48909
517-373-9542
8:00 a.m. to 5:00 p.m., Monday

through Friday
Services:
• Oversees state programs and pro-
tection of air, water, land and waste.
Materials offered:
• General information on various
environmental issues
• List of companies which provide
alternatives to landfills

Department of Public Health
Environmental and Occupational
Health
P.O. Box 30195
Lansing, MI 48909
517-335-9218
8:00 a.m. to 5:00 p.m., Monday
through Friday
Services:
• Addresses problems and questions
on radon, asbestos, formaldehyde,
lead, indoor air quality and electro-
magnetic fields in schools.
Materials offered:
• General information on environ-
mental and occupational health issues

State Department of Education
Science Specialist
P.O. Box 30008
Lansing, MI 48909
517-373-4223
8:30 a.m. to 5:00 p.m., Monday
through Friday
Services:
• Provides consultant to work with
school to develop math, science and
environmental programs.
• Incorporates environmental issues
into three science disciplines based on
state guidelines.
Materials offered:
• Curricula materials for kindergarten
through 12th grade.

**State Department of Natural
Resources**
Parks and Recreation Division
Box 30257
Lansing, MI 48909
517-373-9900
8:00 a.m. to 5:00 p.m., Monday
through Friday
Services:
• Supervises 86 state parks.
Materials offered:
• Brochures on parks and activities

**State Public Service
Commission**
Energy Resource Division
P.O. Box 30221
Lansing, MI 48909
517-334-6261
8:00 a.m. to 5:00 p.m., Monday
through Friday
Services:
• Oversees Institutional Conservation
Program (517-334-6270).
• Promotes and implements state
energy programs.
• Monitors eight major utility compa-
nies and develops conservation plans.
• Administers U.S. Department of
Energy ICP Program.
Materials offered:
• General information about energy
conservation and alternatives

MINNESOTA

**Department of
Education**
Environmental Education Office
550 Cedar Street, 543 Capitol Square
Building
St. Paul, MN 55101
612-297-2723
8:00 a.m. to 4:30 p.m., Monday
through Friday
Services:
• Emphasizes relationship between
human race and its environment and
offers suggestions on what people can
do to help.
• Integrates environmental education
into all subjects.
Materials offered:
• *Greenprint,* state plan to incorporate environmental education

Department of Health
Division of Environmental Health
925 SE Delaware Street
P.O. Box 59040
Minneapolis, MN 55459-0040
612-627-5100
8:00 a.m. to 4:30 p.m., Monday
through Friday
Services:
• Oversees state environmental
health issues, such as safe drinking
water, lead poisoning, radon, asbestos
and indoor air quality.

Materials offered:
* Brochures about all environmental health issues
* Radon test kits

Department of Natural Resources
Division of Forestry
500 Lafayette Road
St. Paul, MN 55155-4044
612-296-4491
8:00 a.m. to 5:00 p.m., Monday through Friday
Services:
* Manages state forests and campgrounds.
Materials offered:
* Provides information on construction, state forests and timber harvesting

Energy Information Center
Department of Public Services
121 7th Place East, Suite 200
St. Paul, MN 55101-2145
612-296-5175
8:30 a.m. to 5:00 p.m., Monday through Friday
Services:
* Provides energy specialists to answer questions and offer advice on energy conservation and fuel alternatives.
* Administers U.S. Department of Energy ICP Program.
Materials offered:
* Residential and commercial energy use information
* General information

Minnesota Environmental Quality Board
Centennial Building, Room 300
658 Cedar Street
St. Paul, MN 55155
612-296-9027
8:30 a.m. to 5:30 p.m., Monday through Friday
Services:
* Serves on state environmental education advisory board.
Materials offered:
* Information on forestry, genetic engineering and water quality

Office of Waste Management
1350 Energy, Suite 201
St. Paul, MN 55108
612-649-5750

8:00 a.m. to 5:00 p.m., Monday through Friday
Services:
* Organizes recycling programs.
* Conducts tours of landfills and recycling centers upon request.
Materials offered:
* Information clearinghouse for waste and recycling

Pollution Control Agency
520 Lafayette Road
St. Paul, MN 55155
612-296-7777
8:00 a.m. to 4:30 p.m., Monday through Friday
Services:
* Responsible for identifying and overseeing clean-up of state Superfund sites.
* Makes recommendations on how to clean up hazardous waste sites.
Materials offered:
* Pamphlets on hazardous waste and Superfund clean-ups

State Department of Agriculture
Information Services
90 West Plato Boulevard
St. Paul, MN 55107
612-296-4659
8:00 a.m. to 5:00 p.m., Monday through Friday
Services:
* Enforces laws to protect public health, promote family farming, implement pesticide regulations and conserve soil and water.
Materials offered:
* Pesticide laws and regulations

State Department of Natural Resources
500 Lafayette Road
St. Paul, MN 55155-4001
612-296-6157
8:00 a.m. to 5:00 p.m., Monday through Friday
Services:
* Protects and conserves state natural water, land and wildlife resources.
* Provides library services.
Materials offered:
* *The Minnesota Volunteer,* magazine
* Information on state natural resources

MISSISSIPPI

State Department of Agriculture and Commerce
P.O. Box 1609
Jackson, MS 39215-1609
601-354-7050
8:00 a.m. to 5:00 p.m., Monday through Friday
Services:
* Regulates pesticides and issues applicator permits.
Materials offered:
* Pesticide laws and regulations

State Department of Economics and Community Development
Energy Division
Programs Department
P.O. Box 850
Jackson, MS 39205-0850
601-359-6600
8:00 a.m. to 5:00 p.m., Monday through Friday
Services:
* Promotes states energy conservation programs.
* Administers U.S. Department of Energy ICP Program.
Materials offered:
* Pamphlets on alternative energy resources and energy conservation programs

State Department of Education
Science Coordinator
P.O. Box 771, Suite 806
Jackson, MS 39205
601-359-3778
8:00 a.m. to 5:00 p.m., Monday through Friday
Services:
* Revised science structure for kindergarten through 12th-grade to incorporate environmental issues across the board.
* Developed ecology course that high school students may take as an elective.
* Developed competency standards in earth, physical and life science covering the lithosphere, hydrosphere and atmosphere for kindergarten through 8th-grade students.
* Provides resource list of programs and environmental education agencies in the state.

Materials offered:
- *Project Learning Tree,* kindergarten through 12th-grade curriculum
- *Project Wild,* kindergarten through 12th-grade curriculum
- *A-Way with Waste,* curriculum

State Department of Environmental Quality
Office of Public Relations
P.O. Box 10385
Jackson, MS 39289-0385
601-961-5015
8:00 a.m. to 5:00 p.m., Monday through Friday
Services:
- Oversees state air, land, water and waste programs.
Materials offered:
- General information on all subjects

State Department of Health
Environmental Health Division
P.O. Box 1700
Jackson, MS 39215-1700
601-960-7518
8:00 a.m. to 5:00 p.m., Monday through Friday
Services:
- Oversees state programs on environmental health issues, such as radon, safe drinking water and asbestos.
Materials offered:
- General information on all subjects

State Department of Wildlife, Fisheries and Parks
Public Information Office
2906 Building, P.O. Box 451
Jackson, MS 39205
601-364-2124
8:00 a.m. to 5:00 p.m., Monday through Friday
Services:
- Manages, conserves and develops state parks, wildlife and marine resources.
- Provides continuing recreational, educational and ecological benefits for present and future generations.
- Offers grants for outdoor recreation programs.
- Provides library services at the Museum of Natural Science.
Materials offered:
- *Mississippi Outdoors* and *Mississippi Sounding,* two magazines

- Publications about zoology, botany and wildlife and fisheries management

MISSOURI

Department of Agriculture
Plant Division
P.O. Box 630
Jefferson City, MO 65102
314-751-2462
8:00 a.m. to 5:00 p.m., Monday through Friday
Services:
- Oversees all pesticide use and regulation enforcement in the state.
- Licenses pesticide applicators.
Materials offered:
- Brochures on different brands of pesticides

Department of Energy
Remediation Project at Wellington Springs
7295 Highway 94
South St. Charles, MO 63304
314-441-8978
8:00 a.m. to 5:00 p.m., Monday through Friday
Services:
- Responsible for clean-up of old chemical plants in St. Charles.
- Offers tours of old chemical plants.
- Visits schools to discuss their work as well as other environmental issues.
Materials offered:
- Brochures about the remediation project

State Department of Conservation
P.O. Box 180
Jefferson City, MO 65102
314-751-4115
8:00 a.m. to 5:00 p.m., Monday through Friday
Services:
- Manages state forests, fish and wildlife resources.
- Provides state-owned land where hunting and fishing are sanctioned.
- Operates nature centers at parks that provide information.
Materials offered:
- Brochures and pamphlets on fishing, hunting and natural areas
- *Learning with Otis,* curricula and activities program

State Department of Education
Science Consultant
P.O. Box 480
Jefferson City, MO 65102
314-751-4445
9:00 a.m. to 5:00 p.m., Monday through Friday
Services:
- Oversees state environmental education that is incorporated into existing science curricula.

State Department of Health
Bureau of Radiological Health
P.O. Box 570
Jefferson City, MO 65102
800-669-7237 (hotline)
314-751-6083
8:00 a.m. to 5:00 p.m., Monday through Friday
Services:
- Oversees radon control.
Materials offered:
- List of providers for radon test kits

State Department of Natural Resources
Division of State Parks
P.O. Box 176
Jefferson City, MO 65102
314-751-2479
8:00 a.m. to 5:00 p.m., Monday through Friday
Services:
- Manages state parks and historic sites.
- Offers an outside recreation assistant program.
Materials offered:
- Brochures of parks, historical sites and preservation programs

State Department of Natural Resources
P.O. Box 176
Jefferson City, MO 65102
314-751-3443
8:00 a.m. to 5:00 p.m., Monday through Friday
Services:
- Supervises separate divisions that handle air, water, land, waste and hazardous waste issues.
Materials offered:
- Information available through each division
- *How to Maintain and Manage It,* brochure with information on house-

hold hazardous waste
• Information on how to obtain permits for hazardous waste

State Department of Natural Resources
Solid Waste Education Program
P.O. Box 176
Jefferson City, MO 65102
314-526-6627
8:00 a.m. to 5:00 p.m., Monday through Friday
Services:
• Oversees landfills, transfer stations and demolition sites.
• Offers tours of landfills and incinerators.
Materials offered:
• Brochure on recycling, household hazardous waste and yard waste
• Provides a list of Solid Waste Management Districts to find out more about local services
• Occasional workshops on solid waste management and recycling

State Department of Natural Resources
Technical Assistance Program
Environmental Education Office
P.O. Box 176
Jefferson City, MO 65102
314-751-2452
8:00 a.m. to 5:00 p.m., Monday through Friday
Services:
• Teacher in-service training workshops offered for college credit, includes publications and activities.
Materials offered:
• *Project Learning Tree*, kindergarten through 12th-grade curriculum

MONTANA

Department of Health and Environmental Services
Publication Office
Cogswell Building
Helena, MT 59620
406-444-2929
8:00 a.m. to 5:00 p.m., Monday through Friday
Services:
• Oversees state programs on air, land, water and waste.

• Supervises state Superfund sites.
• Manages occupational health programs.
• Manages state environmental health programs pertaining to radon and lead contamination.
Materials offered:
• Information on all subjects from individual divisions

Office of Public Instruction
Science Consultant
P.O. Box 202501
Helena, MT 59620
406-444-4439
8:00 a.m. to 5:00 p.m., Monday through Friday
Services:
• Oversees state mandate requiring environmental education to be incorporated into all subject areas.
• Offers in-service training facilitators for curricula.
Materials offered:
• List of resources and references of environmental education programs
• Curricula from WREEC
• *Project Wet*, kindergarten through 12th-grade curriculum
• *Project Wild*, kindergarten through 12th-grade curriculum
• *Project Learning Tree*, kindergarten through 12th-grade curriculum

State Department of Agriculture
P.O. Box 200201
Helena, MT 59620-0201
406-444-2944
8:00 a.m. to 5:00 p.m., Monday through Friday
Services:
• Licenses and registers all pesticides and applicators.
• Provides programs to prevent pesticide abuse.
• Provides speakers to schools upon request.
Materials offered:
• Copies of pesticide laws and regulations

State Department of Natural Resources
Resource Specialist
1520 East Sixth Avenue
Helena, MT 59620-2301
406-444-6667
8:30 a.m. to 5:00 p.m., Monday

through Friday
Services:
• Collaborates with the state Department of Education on various efforts.
• Administers grant programs and issues money to use towards the development or purchase of environmental education curricula materials.
Materials offered:
• *Conservation Education Directory*
• Brochures, video and display for the state's wetlands project

State Department of Natural Resources and Conservation
Energy Division
1520 East Sixth Avenue
Helena, MT 59620
406-444-6697
8:00 a.m. to 5:00 p.m., Monday through Friday
Services:
• Oversees state energy facilities.
• Provides emergency preparedness plans and promotes energy efficiency programs.
• Administers U.S. Department of Energy ICP Program.
Materials offered:
• Various publications on energy conservation and alternative fuel sources

State Environmental Education Association
P.O. Box 928
Dillon, MT 59725-0928
Unlisted
Services:
• Promotes environmental education in Montana.
Materials offered:
• *Bug Net,* an environmental education newsletter, published three times a year

State Parks
1420 East Sixth Avenue
Helena, MT 59620
406-444-3750
8:00 a.m. to 5:00 p.m., Monday through Friday
Services:
• Manages state parks, historical sites and recreation areas.
Materials offered:
• Brochures on parks and activities

NEBRASKA

Game and Parks Commission
Division of State Parks
2200 North 33rd Street
Lincoln, NE 68503
402-471-5497
8:00 a.m. to 5:00 p.m., Monday
through Friday
Services:
• Manages 8 state parks.
Materials offered:
• Brochures about parks and activities

Games and Parks Commission
Outdoor Education
220 North 33rd Street
Lincoln, NE 68503
402-471-5479
8:00 a.m. to 5:00 p.m., Monday
through Friday
Services:
• Conducts hunting and boating education programs.
Materials offered:
• Videos on fishing and hunting
• Coloring books
• *Project Wild*, kindergarten through 12th-grade curriculum

State Department of Health
Bureau of Environmental Health
301 Centennial Mall South
P.O. Box 95007
Lincoln, NE 68509-5007
402-471-2541
8:00 a.m. to 5:00 p.m., Monday
through Friday
Services:
• Conducts environmental surveillance of nuclear power plants.
• Provides speakers to schools upon request.
• Implements state radon, lead and asbestos health programs.
Materials offered:
• Brochures on all subjects
• Radon test kits
• Lists of companies who can do testing and remediational work

State Division of Environmental Quality
Public Information Officer
P.O. Box 98922
Lincoln, NE 68509-8922

402-471-2186
8:00 a.m. to 5:00 p.m., Monday
through Friday
Services:
• Implements state programs and regulations on air, water, land and waste.
• Oversees hazardous waste cleanup sites.
• Provides lectures for schools on occasion.
Materials offered:
• Brochures on all subjects

State Energy Office
Policy Research Office
1200 North Street, Suite 110
P.O. Box 95085
Lincoln, NE 68509-5085
402-471-2867
9:00 a.m. to 5:00 p.m., Monday
through Friday
Services:
• Administers U.S. Department of Energy ICP Program.

NEVADA

Department of Natural Resources
Division of Environmental Protection
333 West Nye Lane
Carson City, NV 89710
702-687-4360
8:00 a.m. to 5:00 p.m., Monday
through Friday
Services:
• Oversees state programs on air, water, waste, land and mining.

Division of Forestry
123 West Nye Lane
Carson City, NV 82710
702-687-4350
8:00 a.m. to 5:00 p.m., Monday
through Friday
Services:
• Manages and protects state forests.
• Supervises timber harvests.
• Conducts fire prevention program.
Materials offered:
• *Project Learning Tree*, kindergarten through 12th-grade curriculum
• *Project Nature*, curriculum
• Videos
• Coloring books
• Brochures on trees, forests and fire safety

Division of Health
Bureau of Health Protection Services
505 East King Street, Room 103
Carson City, NV 89710
702-687-4670
8:00 a.m. to 5:00 p.m., Monday
through Friday
Services:
• Implements environmental health-protection programs, such as lead and radon.
• Enforces the Safe Drinking Water Act and Lead Contamination Control Act.
• Certifies and licenses waste haulers.
• Provides speakers upon request.

State Department of Agriculture
P.O. Box 11100
Reno, NV 89510-1100
702-688-1180
8:00 a.m. to 5:00 p.m., Monday
through Friday
Services:
• Regulates and licenses pesticide use.
• Protects groundwater and wildlife against pesticide contamination.
Materials offered:
• Copies of regulations and laws

State Department of Education
Director of Elementary and Secondary Education
400 West King Street, Capitol Complex
Carson City, NV 89710
702-687-3136
8:30 a.m. to 5:00 p.m., Monday
through Friday
Services:
• Ensures that all state educators take necessary courses in environmental education to receive certificates.

State Energy Office
Department of Business and Industry
1050 East William Street, Suite 401
Carson City, NV 89710
702-687-4990
9:00 a.m. to 5:00 p.m., Monday
through Friday
Services:
• Administers U.S. Department of Energy ICP Program.
Materials offered:
• Various publications on energy conservation and alternative energy sources

NEW HAMPSHIRE

Department of Agriculture
Division of Pesticide Control
P.O. Box 2042
Concord, NH 03302-2042
603-271-3551
8:00 a.m. to 4:00 p.m., Monday
through Friday
Services:
• Regulates pesticides, including registration and licensing of applicators
and enforces rules and regulations
regarding pesticide use.
• Protects against endangered species
and groundwater contamination.
Materials offered:
• Regulatory rules and classification
lists
• Reports on amounts of pesticide use
• List of licensed applicators
• Educational materials through corporate extension service

Department of Environmental Services
Public Information Coordinator
6 Hazen Drive
Concord, NH 03301
603-271-2900
8:00 a.m. to 4:00 p.m., Monday
through Friday
Services:
• Operates hotline to report illegal
dumping (800-346-4009).
• Implements state programs on air,
land, water, waste and recycling.
• Provides tours of the water treatment facilities.
• Offers educational courses on
water.
Materials offered:
• Publication list available
• Over 100 fact sheets on a variety of
topics

Department of Health and Welfare
Office of Waste Management
Division of Public Health Services
6 Hazen Drive
Concord, NH 03301-6527
603-271-4674
8:00 a.m. to 4:00 p.m., Monday
through Friday
Services:
• Oversees state environmental
health programs, such as radon, lead

and asbestos.
• Licenses users of radioactive materials.
• Provides speakers upon request.
Materials offered:
• EPA and state publications

Department of Resources and Economic Development
Division of Forest and Lands
P.O. Box 1856
Concord, NH 03302-1856
603-271-2214
8:00 a.m. to 4:00 p.m., Monday
through Friday
Services:
• Protects state forests by issuing
burn permits, managing logging and
timber harvesting and fighting the
spread of diseases.
• Develops and promotes urban
forests.
Materials offered:
• Brochures on state forests
• Smokey the Bear materials
• *Project Learning Tree*, kindergarten
through 12th-grade curriculum

Governor's Energy Office
57 Regional Drive
Concord, NH 03301
603-271-2711
8:00 a.m. to 4:30 p.m., Monday
through Friday
Services:
• Operates energy conservation hotline (800-852-3466).
• Regulates energy use in the building sector, industrial sector, solar technologies, private industry and residential.
• Administers U.S. Department of
Energy ICP Program.
• Promotes energy conservation
through educational outreach program.
• Opens library to public by appointment.
Materials offered:
• Pamphlets, booklets and fact sheets

Governors Recycling Program
Office of State Planning
2 1/2 Beacon Street
Concord, NH 03301
603-271-1098
8:00 a.m. to 5:00 p.m., Monday
through Friday
Services:

• Promotes and develops state recycling programs.
Materials offered:
• Video on source reduction, recycling
and shopping for the environment
• Teacher activity packets for kindergarten through 6th grade

State Department of Education
Curriculum Supervisor for Science
101 Pleasant Street
Concord, NH 03301
603-271-2632
8:00 a.m. to 5:00 p.m., Monday
through Friday
Services:
• Develops state curricula that incorporates environmental issues into science and social studies.
• Coordinates programs with other
state agencies.
• Provides Eisenhower Fund grants
for environmental projects.
Materials offered:
• *Project Learning Tree*, kindergarten
through 12th-grade curriculum
• *Project Wild*, kindergarten through
12th-grade curriculum
• *Project Wet*, kindergarten through
12th-grade curriculum

State Parks
Education Officer
P.O. Box 1856
Concord, NH 03302
603-271-3556
8:00 a.m. to 5:00 p.m., Monday
through Friday
Services:
• Offers interpretive tours of many of
the state parks with a naturalist.
• Manages and promotes all 55 state
parks.
• Houses lending library of materials
on state historical and natural sites.
• Sponsors annual Robert Frost
Poetry Contest.
• Promotes "Share with Care" campaign at major events through
Chumley the Chipmunk.
Materials offered:
• Brochures on state parks and activities
• *Along the Way*, 4th grade teachers
packet on NH seacoast historic sites
• Coloring books

NEW JERSEY

Department of Community Affairs
Energy Conservation
101 South Broad Street
Trenton, NJ 08625-0814
609-292-9847
8:00 a.m. to 5:00 p.m., Monday
through Friday
Services:
• Promotes and implements state
energy conservation programs.
• Manages community based organi-
zations in low-income housing areas.
Materials offered:
• Brochures on energy conservation

Department of Environmental Protection
Pesticide Control Program
CN 411
Trenton, NJ 08625
609-530-4011
8:00 a.m. to 5:00 p.m., Monday
through Friday
Services:
• Enforces pesticide laws and regula-
tions.
• Issues applicator licenses.
• Researches health effects of pesti-
cides.
Materials offered:
• Pamphlets on pesticides
• Coppies of regulations and laws of
pesticide use

State Department of Environmental Protection and Energy
Environmental Education Unit
CN 402
Trenton, NJ 08625
609-777-4322
8:00 a.m. to 5:00 p.m., Monday
through Friday
Services:
• Administers U.S. Department of
Energy ICP Program (609-292-5383).
• Implements state programs and reg-
ulations on air, water, soil, waste and
energy.
• Provides funding for environmental
education projects, training and materi-
als.
• Promotes *Project Learning Tree* and
Project Wild through speaker's bureau.
Materials offered:

• *Project Wild*, kindergarten through
12th-grade curriculum
• *Project Learning Tree,* kindergarten
through 12th-grade curriculum
• *The Literature Guide*, a compilation
of department resources
• *Environmental Education in New
Jersey: A Proposed Plan of Action*

State Parks and Forestry
501 East State Street
Trenton, NJ 08625
609-292-2797
8:00 a.m. to 5:00 p.m., Monday
through Friday
Services:
• Manages state parks, natural areas,
forests, marinas and recreational areas.
• Offers tours and naturalist programs
at some locations.
Materials offered:
• Brochures about facilities and activities

NEW MEXICO

Forestry and Resources Conservation Division
P.O. Box 1948
Sante Fe, NM 87504-1948
505-827-5830
8:00 a.m. to 5:00 p.m., Monday
through Friday
Services:
• Responsible for timber sales,
forestry management and protection of
endangered plants.
• Studies impact of private forestry on
surrounding ecosystems.
• Provides speakers for classroom or
outdoor settings.
Materials offered:
• Guidebooks on state forests
• Pamphlets on state ecosystems,
species and forest habitats
• *Project Learning Tree*, kindergarten
through 12th-grade curriculum

Hazardous and Radioactive Materials Bureau
525 Camino De Los Marquez
Sante Fe, NM 87503
505-827-4308
8:00 a.m. to 5:00 p.m., Monday
through Friday
Services:

• Enforces state and federal hazardous waste regulations and laws.
• Tests homes and schools for radon
contamination. (Since 1988, the
bureau has tested over 5,000 homes
and schools.)
• Provides speakers to schools upon
request.
Materials offered:
• Pamphlets for small businesses who
work with hazardous waste
• EPA materials on hazardous and
radioactive materials
• Videos, slides and curricula about
radon—how it gets into your home,
it's health effects and how to get rid of
it.

State Department of Education
Science Coordinator
300 Donjaspir, Education Building
Sante Fe, NM 87501-2786
505-827-6579
8:00 a.m. to 5:00 p.m., Monday
through Friday
Services:
• Oversees state environmental education.

State Department of Energy Conservation and Management
2040 South Pacheco Street
Sante Fe, NM 87505
505-827-5900
8:00 a.m. to 5:00 p.m., Monday
through Friday
Services:
• Operates energy conservation pro-
grams in schools and hospitals.
• Administers U.S. Department of
Energy ICP Program.
• Provides speakers upon request.
• Supervises the state ride-share pro-
gram.
Materials offered:
• Publications on various energy and
transportation issues
• Coloring books
• Teacher's aids

State Environment Department
P.O. Box 26110
1190 St. Francis Drive
Harold Renold Building
Sante Fe, NM 87502
505-827-2844
7:00 a.m. to 4:00 p.m., Monday
through Friday

Services:
- Responsible for air, water and soil quality, hazardous waste regulation and recycling programs.
- Provides speakers upon request.
- Helps schools and institutions set up recycling programs.

Materials offered:
- Brochures on all environmental issues
- Videos about source reduction, composting and recycling

State Parks and Recreation
408 Galisteo
Sante Fe, NM 87501
505-827-7465
8:00 a.m. to 5:00 p.m., Monday through Friday
Services:
- Supervises all state parks.
- Provides boating officer to teach water safety to elementary schools.

Materials offered:
- Trailhead guide listing all state parks

NEW YORK

Bureau of Environmental Radiation Protection
Two University Place
Albany, NY 12203
800-458-1158 (within state)
518-458-6461
8:30 a.m. to 4:30 p.m., Monday through Friday
Services:
- Is responsible for state radon and radiation protection programs.

Materials offered:
- General information about radon and low level radiation
- Videos

State Department of Education
Coordinator of Environmental Education
Room 212 EB
Albany, NY 12234
518-474-5890
9:00 a.m. to 5:00 p.m., Monday through Friday
Services:
- Oversees state environmental edu-

cation and the assimilation into existing curriculum at the local level.
Materials offered:
- Distributes various resources to each school district

State Department of Environmental Conservation
Office of Public Affairs
50 Wolf Road, Room 505
Albany, NY 12233-4000
800-462-6553 (within state)
518-457-0840
8:30 a.m. to 4:30 p.m., Monday through Friday
Services:
- Oversees air, water, land and environmental habitat issues.
- Offers How-to-Recycle and Reduce Waste education programs.
- Provides speakers and makes school presentations.
- Conducts workshops for small businesses on waste reduction through Office of Pollution Prevention.
- Provides several environmental education centers and camps that are open to the public that cover a wide range of issues.
- Administers Governor's Environmental Education Task Force.

Materials offered:
- Curriculum listings for state
- Videos on various subjects
- *25 Things You Can Do to Prevent Water Waste,* pamphlet
- Pamphlets and guidebooks for school waste reduction and recycling programs
- Guidelines for how to prepare hazardous waste reduction plans.

State Department of Health
Bureau of Child and Adolescent Health
ESP Tower Building, Room 208
Albany, NY 12237
518-473-4602
8:00 a.m. to 5:00 p.m., Monday through Friday
Services:
- Operates the Childhood Lead Poisoning Prevention Program.
- Investigates buildings for lead paint poisoning.

Materials offered:
- Pamphlets on lead poisoning

State Energy Office
Two Rockefeller Plaza
Albany, NY 12223
800-423-7283 (within state)
518-474-2161
8:00 a.m. to 5:00 p.m., Monday through Friday
Services:
- Administers energy-efficiency programs.
- Provides grants and technical assistance to energy conservation programs within the state.
- Offers workshops and seminars on a variety of energy related topics.
- Administers U.S. Department of Energy ICP Program.

Materials offered:
- *Energy Mobile*, kindergarten through 6th-grade curriculum with teacher's guide
- Videos on energy (for NY residents only)
- Brochures and publications on various energy issues

State Parks
Agency Building #1 ESP
Albany, NY 12238
518-474-0456
8:00 a.m. to 5:00 p.m., Monday through Friday
Services:
- Supervises all the state parks.
- Operates several nature centers at various parks.
- Operates summer camp programs with the public schools.
- Takes New York City students to regional parks on day and overnight trips through program called Operation Explore.

Materials offered:
- Information on state park sites, activities and trails.

NORTH CAROLINA

North Carolina Division of Parks and Recreation
P.O. Box 27687
Raleigh, NC 27611
919-733-4181
8:00 a.m. to 5:00 p.m., Monday through Friday
Services:
- Manages state parks.

Materials offered:
• Brochures about individual state parks and recreational activities

State Department of Agriculture
Division of Pesticides
P.O. Box 27647
Raleigh, NC 27611
919-733-3556
8:00 a.m. to 5:00 p.m., Monday through Friday
Services:
• Oversees state pesticides application and regulation enforcement.
Materials offered:
• Booklet on programs and services
• Copies of pesticide laws and regulations

State Department of Economic and Community Development
Energy Division
P.O. Box 25249
Raleigh, NC 27611
919-733-2230
8:00 a.m. to 5:00 p.m., Monday through Friday
Services:
• Manages state energy conservation program.
• Sponsors the Solar Center, a home and resource center run completely on solar energy.
• Administers U.S. Department of Energy ICP Program.
Materials offered:
• Various materials on alternative energy sources and energy conservation

State Department of Environment, Health and Natural Resources
Office of Environmental Education
P.O. Box 27687
Raleigh, NC 27611-7687
919-733-0711
7:30 a.m. to 5:00 p.m., Monday through Friday
Services:
• Oversees state environmental education.
• Manages state natural resources, forests, zoos, parks and recreation areas.
• Provides speakers and classroom field trips to various sites upon request.
• Oversees Environmental Education Learning Experience Workshop.

• Manages Summer Zoo Adventures program for teachers.
• Oversees Project Estuary—Sound Ideas Workshop.
Materials offered:
• Teacher's Guide to Environmental Education Programs and Resources
• *Project Learning Tree*, kindergarten through 12th-grade curriculum
• Videos on forestry, waste reduction and recycling
• *Investigate Your Environment*, science curriculum
• *Using the Outdoors to Teach Experiential Science*, booklet
• *Wildlife of North Carolina*, magazine
• North Carolina Wildstore Catalog

NORTH DAKOTA

Office of Intergovernmental Assistance
State Capitol Building, 14th Floor
600 East Boulevard
Bismarck, ND 58505
701-224-2094
8:00 a.m. to 5:00 p.m., Monday through Friday
Services:
• Supports community development programs to promote energy conservation and alternative resources.
• Operates federal program to weatherize low-income housing.
• Administers U.S. Department of Energy ICP Program.
Materials offered:
• Over 40 publications on energy
• *Energy Source*, curriculum kits

State Department of Agriculture
Pesticide Division
600 East Boulevard
Bismarck, ND 58505-0020
701-224-4756
8:00 a.m. to 5:00 p.m., Monday through Friday
Services:
• Works in conjunction with the EPA to enforce all pesticide regulations and licensing laws.
Materials offered:
• List of commercially certified applicators and distributors
• *Signs and Symptoms of Pesticide*

Poisoning, pamphlet
• List of canceled pesticides

State Department of Public Instruction
Social Studies Coordinator
600 East Boulevard Avenue
Bismarck, ND 58505-0440
701-224-2260
8:00 a.m. to 5:00 p.m., Monday through Friday
Services:
• Oversees state environmental education.

State Division of Water Quality
1200 Missouri Avenue
Bismarck, ND 58501
701-221-5210
8:00 a.m. to 5:00 p.m., Monday through Friday
Services:
• Oversees all state water resources, including ground, surface and lake restoration and monitors industry and coal mine discharge.
• Provides speakers upon request.
Materials offered:
• Copies of water laws
• Brochures on groundwater protection

State Health Department
Environmental Health Section
P.O. Box 5520
Bismarck, ND 58502
701-221-5150
8:00 a.m. to 5:00 p.m., Monday through Friday
Services:
• Implements state environmental health programs on radon, safe drinking water, sewage water, indoor air quality and hazardous and solid waste.
• Operates a water and waste training facility.
• Operates radon control and testing for low-income housing, schools and daycare.
• Enforces the Lead Control Act.
Materials offered:
• EPA publications
• Some teaching aids
• List of sources for radon test kits or contractors

State Parks and Tourism
604 East Boulevard Avenue
Bismarck, ND 58505

701-221-5357
8:00 a.m. to 5:00 p.m., Monday through Friday
Services:
• Supervises 11 parks.
• Provides speakers to schools or for guided tours of parks.
Materials offered:
• Videos and pamphlets on parks and resources

State Water Commission
900 East Boulevard #1
Bismarck, ND 58505
701-224-4833
8:00 a.m. to 5:00 p.m., Monday through Friday
Services:
• Develops and implements water resource planning.
Materials offered:
• *Project Wet*, kindergarten through 12th-grade curriculum

OHIO

Office of Energy Efficiency
77 South High Street, 26th Floor
Columbus, OH 43266-0413
614-466-6797
7:30 a.m. to 5:00 p.m., Monday through Friday
Services:
• Implements federal and state energy efficiency programs.
• Coordinates Governor's Energy Science Day Award, recognizing students that excel in energy conservation.
• Administers U.S. Department of Energy ICP Program.
Materials offered:
• Information on award program and energy conservation and alternative energy sources

State Department of Agriculture
Pesticides Regulation
8995 East Main Street
Reynoldsburg, OH 43068
618-866-6361
8:00 a.m. to 5:00 p.m., Monday through Friday
Services:
• Enforces pesticide regulations and licensing laws.

Materials offered:
• EPA Brochures
• Copies of pesticide laws and regulations

State Department of Education
Environmental Education Consultant
65 South Front Street, Room 1005
Columbus, OH 43266-0308
614-466-5795
9:00 a.m. to 5:00 p.m., Monday through Friday
Services:
• Oversees environmental education for elementary, secondary and teacher education.
Materials offered:
• *Super Saver Investigators,* kindergarten through 6th-grade recycling and waste management interdisciplinary curriculum and in-service program
• *Project Learning Tree*, kindergarten through 12th-grade curriculum
• *Project Wild*, kindergarten through 12th-grade curriculum

State Department of Health
410 South High Street, 4th Floor
Columbus, OH 43215-4562
614-462-3160
8:00 a.m. to 5:00 p.m., Monday through Friday
Services:
• Oversees state environmental health issues, such as radon.
• Provides speakers upon request.
Materials offered:
• Radon test kits
• Pamphlets on radon health effects
• Quarterly newsletter

State Department of Natural Resources
Office of Public Information and Education
1889 Fountain Square
Columbus, OH 43224
614-265-6789 (information/education)
614-265-6561 (parks)
8:00 a.m. to 5:00 p.m., Monday through Friday
Services:
• Manages state parks and natural resources.
Materials offered:

• Information about state's natural resources, parks and activities

State Environmental Protection Agency
Environmental Conservation/Education Office
1800 Watermark Drive
Columbus, OH 43266-0149
614-644-2873
9:00 a.m. to 5:00 p.m., Monday through Friday
Services:
• Is responsible for state air, waste water, drinking water, hazardous waste and land pollution control.
• Provides speakers upon request.
• Offers tours of the labs.
• Oversees Keep America Beautiful campaign.
• Promotes recycling programs.
• Administers grants to develop environmental education materials and programs.
Materials offered:
• Brochures on household hazardous waste, composting, community right-to-know laws and pollution prevention

OKLAHOMA

Alternative Fuels Program
3301 North Sante Fe
Oklahoma City, OK 73118
405-521-4687
8:00 a.m. to 5:00 p.m., Monday through Friday
Services:
• Administers U.S. Department of Energy ICP Program (405-843-9770).
• Promotes state alternative fuel programs.
Materials offered:
• Brochures on alternative fuels

Division of Community Affairs and Development
P.O. Box 26980
Oklahoma City, OK 73126-0980
405-841-9329
8:00 a.m. to 5:00 p.m., Monday through Friday
Services
• Conducts environmental reviews.
• Enforces water and sewer regulations.

Materials offered:
• Kindergarten through 6th-grade teacher packets

State Board of Agriculture

Plant Industry Division
2800 North Lincoln Boulevard
Oklahoma City, OK 73105
405-521-3864
8:00 a.m. to 5:00 p.m., Monday through Friday
Services:
• Implements state laws and licensing regulations for pesticides.
Materials offered:
• Copies of pesticide laws and regulations

State Department of Education

Instructional Programs Office
2500 North Lincoln Boulevard
Oklahoma City, OK 73105-4599
405-521-3361
8:00 a.m. to 5:00 p.m., Monday through Friday
Services:
• Oversees environmental education as outlined in the state guidelines.
• Handles referrals to environmental education programs.
Materials offered:
• Various resources and information
• *Oklahoma Natural Resources Directory*

State Department of Environmental Quality

Public Information Office
1000 NE Tenth Street, Room 1213
Oklahoma City, OK 73117
405-271-7353
8:00 a.m. to 5:00 p.m., Monday through Friday
Services:
• Oversees state environmental health and welfare programs involving radon, hazardous waste and lead contamination.
• Supervises recycling program and workshop.
Materials offered:
• *A Way with Waste*, curriculum
• Catalog of recycled products
• Recycling directory
• EPA brochures

State Department of Wildlife Conservation

P.O. Box 53465
Oklahoma City, OK 73152
405-521-3855
8:00 a.m. to 5:00 p.m., Monday through Friday
Services:
• Protects and preserves the state natural resources.
• Oversees Critters in Concepts program.
• Offers giant inflatable whale that students can walk into on loan to schools with large auditoriums.
Materials offered:
• Videos and brochures on environmental issues
• Resource Trunk of activities
• *Project Wild,* curriculum
• *Blue Bird,* curriculum and teacher's packet
• *Playa Lake*, curriculum and teacher's packet
• *Deer Habitat*, curriculum and teacher's packet
• *Winter Bird*, curriculum and teacher's packet

State Parks Division

500 Will Rogers Building
Oklahoma City, OK 73105
405-521-3411
8:00 a.m. to 5:00 p.m., Monday through Friday
Services:
• Manages 55 state parks.
Materials offered:
• Parks and resort guide

OREGON

Department of Environmental Quality

Environmental Education Office
811 West Sixth Avenue
Portland, OR 97204
800-452-4011 (within state)
503-229-6823
8:00 a.m. to 5:00 p.m., Monday through Friday
Services:
• Offers information about agency programs on air, land, water and waste.
• Collaborates with Project Resource

Clearinghouse.
Materials offered:
• *Rethinking Recycling*, curriculum, teacher's activities and resource guide
• Video on waste reduction
• *Oregon Environmental Atlas*
• *Oregon Skies,* teacher's guide to air pollution
• *Environmental Clean-up Game*, board game on Oregon's environmental clean-up program
• Informational brochures on various topics

Department of Fish and Wildlife

Division of Wildlife Information and Education
2501 SW First Street
Portland, OR 97207
503-229-5454, ext. 432
8:00 a.m. to 5:00 p.m., Monday through Friday
Services:
• Manages state wildlife areas, enforcing hunting and fishing laws.
• Provides tours of hatcheries.
Materials offered:
• *Stream Scene*, curriculum
• Hunting and fishing rule and season booklet

Environmental Education Association of Oregon

P.O. Box 40047
Portland, OR 97240
503-656-0155
Services:
• Promotes environmental education and serves as a networking organization.
Materials offered:
• *Clearing*, quarterly journal listing environmental education opportunities for teachers

Oregon State University Extension Program

Batcheller Hall 344
Corvallis, OR 97331
503-737-3004
8:00 a.m. to 5:00 p.m., Monday through Friday
Services:
• Provides education resources and training to teachers on environmental issues.
Materials offered:
• Teacher's guide to energy conser-

vation for grades 3 through 8
• *Energy and the Environment,* resource guide

State Department of Education
Science Education Specialist
700 Pringle Parkway SE
Salem, OR 97310-0290
503-378-3602
9:00 a.m. to 5:00 p.m., Monday through Friday
Services:
• Oversees environmental education as it is recommended in the state core science curriculum.
• Offers *Project Learning Tree* and *Project Wild* teacher training workshops.

State Department of Energy
625 Marion Street, NE
Salem, OR 97310
503-378-4040
8:00 a.m. to 5:00 p.m., Monday through Friday
Services:
• Operates Oregon's energy hotline (800-457-9394).
• Promotes and manages state's alternative energy and energy conservation programs.
• Offers a modified version of the U.S. Department of Energy's institutional conservation program.
• Administers U.S. Department of Energy ICP Program.
Materials offered:
• Pamphlets on alternative energy and energy conservation
• Catalog of educator resources and videos developed with Bonneville Power and Oregon State University Extension Service

State Department of Forestry
2600 State Street
Salem, OR 97310
503-945-7200
8:00 a.m. to 5:00 p.m., Monday through Friday
Services:
• Manages state forests, protects them against wildfires and supervises timber sales.
• Provides speakers upon request.
Materials offered:
• Publications on state forests
• Educational videos and slides

State Department of Parks and Recreation
Natural Resources Program
1120 SW 5th Street, Suite 1320
Portland, OR 97204
503-378-5006
8:00 a.m. to 5:00 p.m., Monday through Friday
Services:
• Manages state parks, natural areas and historical preservations.
Materials offered:
• Curriculum about state parks
• Pamphlets on parks and activities

State Health Division
Department of Environmental Health
800 NE Oregon Street
Portland, OR 97232
503-731-4012
8:00 a.m. to 5:00 p.m., Monday through Friday
Services:
• Oversees state environmental health issues.
Materials offered:
• Rules and regulations for handling substances that impact on environment and/or public health

PENNSYLVANIA

State Department of Education
Office of Environmental Education
333 Market Street, 8th Floor
Harrisburg, PA 17126-0333
717-787-9845
8:30 a.m. to 5:00 p.m., Monday through Friday
Services:
• Oversees environmental education as outlined in the state's Quality Goal for Environment and Ecology.
Materials offered:
• Some curricular materials available, though it is primarily the responsibility of the local districts.

State Department of Energy
116 Pine Street
Harrisburg, PA 17101
717-783-9981
8:00 a.m. to 4:00 p.m., Monday through Friday
Services:
• Oversees all state energy programs

and enforces laws and regulations.
• Administers U.S. Department of Energy ICP Program.
Materials offered:
• Information on energy conservation, solar and other alternative energy sources

State Department of Environmental Resources
Office of Parks and Forestry
P.O. Box 2063
Harrisburg, PA 17105-2063
717-787-2869
9:00 a.m. to 5:00 p.m., Monday through Friday
Services:
• Manages state forests and parks.
• Offers interpretive programming at various parks year round.
• Sponsors environmental forum.
• Engages in environmental problem-solving.
• Oversees water quality monitoring program.
• Offers in-service and pre-service teacher workshops.
• Oversees youth environmental learning program.
• Provides field learning experiences for school groups at environmental education centers, supplemented by *Activities for Environmental Learning* curriculum.
Materials offered:
• Pamphlets and information about activities and parks
• *Project Learning Tree,* kindergarten through 12th-grade curriculum
• *Project Wild,* kindergarten through 12th-grade curriculum
• *Activities for Environmental Learning,* kindergarten through 12th-grade curriculum
• *Keystone Aquatic Resources Education,* kindergarten through 12th-grade curriculum
• Various materials concerning earth day, recycling, water resources and Chesapeake Bay protection

State Department of Environmental Resources
Office of Public Affairs
P.O. Box 2063
Harrisburg, PA 17105-2063
717-787-9580
8:00 a.m. to 4:30 p.m., Monday

through Friday
Services:
• Oversees all environmental issues on air, water, land and waste.
• Responsible for radon protection and nuclear safety.
• Regulates drinking-water standards to protect against lead poisoning.
Materials offered:
• Pamphlets and brochures on various topics
• Information on Pennsylvania Earth Week classroom program

RHODE ISLAND

Governor's Office of Housing, Energy and Intergovernmental Affairs
275 Westminster Street
Providence, RI 02903
401-277-3370
8:30 a.m. to 4:30 p.m., Monday through Friday
Services:
• Promotes energy conservation.
• Oversees state energy programs.
• Offers teacher training workshops on energy conservation.
• Administers U.S. Department of Energy ICP Program.
Materials offered:
• N.E.E.D. program focuses on energy awareness
• Various publications on alternative energy and conservation

State Department of Education
Science Supervisor
22 Hayes Street, Room 201
Providence, RI 02908
401-277-2821
9:00 a.m. to 5:00 p.m., Monday through Friday
Services:
• Works in conjunction with state Environmental Education Association to oversee environmental education programs.
Materials offered:
• None. Local districts have developed their own materials.

State Department of Environmental Management
83 Park Street

Providence, RI 02903
401-277-3434
8:30 a.m. to 4:00 p.m., Monday through Friday
Services:
• Oversees air, land and waste issues.
• Oversees state recycling programs.
• Serves as regulatory agency for pesticides.
Materials offered:
• Information on all issues, laws and regulations
• *Oscar's Options*, curriculum focusing on recycling available through workshop participation

State Department of Environmental Management
Division of Fish and Wildlife
Field Headquarters, P.O. Box 218
West Kingston, RI 02892
401-789-0281
8:00 a.m. to 4:30 p.m., Monday through Friday
Services:
• Conducts tours of fish hatcheries.
• Organizes beach clean-ups.
Materials offered:
• *Project Wild*, kindergarten through 12th-grade curriculum
• Information on marine animal entrapment by plastics and human waste

State Department of Environmental Management
Division of Parks and Recreation
2321 South Hartford
Johnston, RI 02919
401-277-2632
8:00 a.m. to 5:00 p.m., Monday through Friday
Services:
• Supervises 8 parks.
Materials offered:
• Brochures on parks and activities

State Department of Health
206 Cannon Building, 3 Capitol Hill
Providence, RI 02908
401-277-2438
8:00 a.m. to 4:30 p.m., Monday through Friday
Services:
• Provides informational assistance to property owners on radon and lead contamination.
• Tests schools for radon.

Materials offered:
• Radon test kits
• Community action kits (slides, video and radon information)
• Reports on lead-contaminated water
• Brochures

State Department of Water Resources
291 Promenade Street
Providence, RI 02908
401-277-3961
8:30 a.m. to 4:00 p.m., Monday through Friday
Services:
• Enforces surface, well and ground-water quality regulation.
Materials offered:
• Science kits to check chlorine levels in water

SOUTH CAROLINA

Governor's Office of Energy Programs
1205 Pendleton Street
Columbia, SC 29201
803-734-1740
8:30 a.m. to 5:00 p.m., Monday through Friday
Services:
• Administers U.S. Department of Energy ICP Program (803-734-0329).
• Manages state energy conservation program.
Materials offered:
• Guidelines for energy conservation
• Supplemental energy conservation curricula for kindergarten through 12th grade
• Information about alternative energy sources

Pesticide and Fertilizer Control Department
257 Polle Street, Agricultural Center
Clempson, SC 29634-0394
803-656-3171
8:00 a.m. to 4:00 p.m., Monday through Friday
Services:
• Oversees the state pesticide applications, licensing and public awareness program.

- Enforces proper pesticide use at schools.
Materials offered:
- Information on pesticides

State Department of Education
Science Coordinator
801 Ruthledge Boulevard
Columbia, SC 29201
803-734-8368
8:00 a.m. to 5:00 p.m., Monday through Friday
Services
- Refers teachers and students to other agencies with environmental programs.
- Works closely with state Environmental Education Association which conducts teacher workshops and publishes a newsletter.
- Works with Sea Grant Consortium.

State Department of Forestry Commission
P.O. Box 21707
Columbia, SC 29221
803-737-8800
8:30 a.m. to 5:00 p.m., Monday through Friday
Services:
- Manages and protects state forests.
- Educates public on soil erosion and fire prevention.
- Educates private landowners on maintaining forests and how to plant and raise trees.
- Educates the public on maintaining wetlands and wildlife habitats.
- Provides speakers to schools about forest and wildlife.
Materials offered:
- *Project Learning Tree*, kindergarten through 12th-grade curriculum
- Resources on fire control, raising trees and protecting the forests
- Teacher's aids and videos for kindergarten through 6th grade

State Department of Health and Environmental Control
Public Information Office
Office of Solid Waste Reduction and Recycling
2600 Bull Street
Columbia, SC 29201
803-734-4957
8:30 a.m. to 5:00 p.m., Monday through Friday

Services:
- In-state recycling information (800-76-USE-IT).
- Oversees state programs and enforces laws regarding air, land, water and waste issues.
- Conducts annual Champions of the Environment contest.
- Promotes public awareness of safe drinking water and lead poisoning issues. Provides list of labs that can test water.
- Provides lists of companies that do radon testing.
- Regulates toxic and hazardous waste disposal and management.
- Provides speakers upon request.
Materials offered:
- Curriculum and video on recycling for kindergarten through 8th grade
- Environmental newsletter featuring student involvement
- General information on radon and list of companies who do testing
- Brochures on recycling, household hazardous waste, air and water pollution

State Department of Parks, Recreation and Tourism
State Parks Division
1205 Pendleton Street
Columbia, SC 29201
803-734-0101
8:30 a.m. to 5:00 p.m., Monday through Friday
Services:
- Manages 50 parks and Welcome Interpretive Centers.
Materials offered:
- Brochures on parks and activities

University of Clemson
Teaching K.A.T.E.
272 Lehotsky Hall
Clemson, SC 29634-1003
803-656-4836
8:00 a.m. to 4:30 p.m., Monday through Friday
Services:
- Operates two 4H Club Centers.
- Operates *Teaching Kids About the Environment* program.
Materials offered:
- Newsletter
- Brochures about programs

Game, Fish and Parks Department
Information and Education Office
523 East Capitol, Joe Foss Building
Pierre, SD 57501-3182
605-773-3485
8:00 a.m. to 5:00 p.m., Monday through Friday
Services:
- Focuses on wildlife education.
- Oversees aquatic education program that includes school presentations, fishing clinics with tackle loans and interpretive tours of hatcheries.
Materials offered:
- Identification books, activity posters, fact sheets and brochures on state's wildlife
- *Project Wild*, kindergarten through 12th-grade curriculum

State Department of Agriculture
523 East Capitol, Joe Foss Building
Pierre, SD 57501-3185
605-773-3375
8:00 a.m. to 5:00 p.m., Monday through Friday
Services:
- Enforces pesticide regulations and laws.
Materials offered:
- Brochures on pesticides

State Department of Environment and Natural Resources
Division of Technical and Support Services
523 East Capitol, Joe Foss Building
Pierre, SD 57501
605-773-3151
8:00 a.m. to 5:00 p.m., Monday through Friday
Services:
- Enforces state laws on air, water, land and waste.
- Provides speakers upon request.
Materials offered:
- *Water and Environment Today,* magazine
- Various publications and brochures

State Department of Health
Regulation and Quality Assurance
445 East Capitol Avenue
Pierre, SD 57501-3185
605-773-3364

8:0 a.m. to 5:00 p.m., Monday through Friday
Services:
• Oversees state programs involving radon, lead contamination and asbestos.
Materials offered:
• General information on environmental health issues

State Division of Education
Secondary Curriculum Specialist
700 Governors Drive
Pierre, SD 57501-2291
605-773-4670
8:30 a.m. to 5:00 p.m., Monday through Friday
Services:
• Oversees environmental education in conjunction with other state agencies.
Materials offered:
• *Project S.A.V.E.,* studies public awareness and value of the environment
• Various other materials

TENNESSEE

Energy, Environment and Resources Center
University of Tennessee
327 South Stadium Hall
Knoxville, TN 37996-0710
615-974-4251
8:00 a.m. to 5:00 p.m., Monday through Friday
Services:
• Administers U.S. Department of Energy ICP Program (615-741-2994).
• Explores and researches energy issues.
• Provides grants for local projects with international impact.
Materials offered:
• Information about the program and general energy issues

State Department of Agriculture
Ellington Agriculture Center
P.O. Box 40627, Melrose Station
Nashville, TN 37204
615-360-0117
8:00 a.m. to 4:30 p.m., Monday through Friday

Services:
• Enforces pesticide laws and regulation.

State Department of Education
Office of Conservation Education
8 Gateway Plaza, 8th Floor
710 James Robertson Pkwy.
Nashville, TN 37243
615-532-6280
8:00 a.m. to 4:30 p.m., Monday through Friday
Services:
• Has partnerships with 5 other agencies to provide services and resources to educators.
• Promotes integration of environmental education in all curricula areas.
• Provides in-service training, workshops and resources to state teachers.
• Conducts a solid-waste workshop for art classes.
Materials offered:
• *Project Wild*, kindergarten through 12th-grade curriculum
• *Project Aquatic,* kindergarten through 12th-grade curriculum
• *Project Learning Tree,* kindergarten through 12th-grade curriculum
• *Cents,* quarterly newsletter

State Department of Environment and Conservation
Commissioners Office
401 Church Street
Nashville, TN 37243
615-532-0109
8:00 a.m. to 5:00 p.m., Monday through Friday
Services:
• Promotes, protects and preserves state natural resources: air, water and land.
• Manages solid and hazardous waste, recycling and Superfund sites.
Materials offered:
• *Tennessee Conservationist,* magazine

State Department of Environment and Conservation
Office of Pollution Prevention
401 Church Street
Nashville, TN 37243
615-532-0760
8:00 a.m. to 5:00 p.m., Monday through Friday
Services:

• Oversees state research and protection programs involving radon and lead poisoning.
Materials offered:
• Brochures on radon, lead contamination and health effects

State Department of Environment and Conservation
Parks Department
401 Church Street
Nashville, TN 37243
615-532-0025
8:00 a.m. to 5:00 p.m., Monday through Friday
Services:
• Manages state parks.
Materials offered:
• Brochures on parks and activities

Tennessee Environmental Education Association
Lowell Thomas State Office Building, Suite 302A
255 Dr. Martin Luther King, Jr. Drive
Jackson, TN 38301
901-426-0536
9:00 a.m. to 5:00 p.m., Monday through Friday
Services:
• Sponsors annual educators' conference.
• Facilitates environmental education network.
• Conducts workshops.
• Awards mini-grants and scholarships annually.
Materials offered:
• Newsletter

TEXAS

Department of Health
Bureau of Environmental Health
1100 West 49th Street
Austin, TX 78756
512-834-6640
8:00 a.m. to 5:00 p.m., Monday through Friday
Services:
• Oversees state radon, asbestos and lead contamination programs.
Materials offered:
• Information differs depending on the particular office

Natural Resources Conservation Commission

Division of Public Information and Education
P.O. Box 13087
Austin, TX 78711-3087
512-239-0010
8:00 a.m. to 5:00 p.m., Monday through Friday
Services:
• Oversees *Texas Tree Challenge*, activity and curricula for 4th grade.
• Sponsors annual art and poetry contest connected with Texas Tree Challenge.
• Focuses on elementary education.
Materials offered:
• *Recycling Is Elementary; Texas Watch and Texas Recycler,* newsletters
• *Visit the Triple R Ranch*, notebook of resources for Texas educators
• General information on air and water pollution and recycling
• *Wet Instruction Handbook*
• *Water Education Teams*, 4th through 6th-grade curriculum

Parks and Wildlife Department

4200 Smith School Road
Austin, TX 78744
52-389-4800
8:00 a.m. to 5:00 p.m., Monday through Friday
Services:
• Manages state parks, public lands, fisheries and wildlife protection programs.
Materials offered:
• *Texas Parks and Wildlife*, magazine.

State Department of Agriculture

Pesticide Division
P.O. Box 12847
Austin, TX 78711
512-463-1093
8:00 a.m. to 5:00 p.m., Monday through Friday
Services:
• Oversees pesticide regulation and law enforcement.
Materials offered:
• Pesticide regulations and laws

State Department of Education

Environmental Education Consultant
1701 North Congress Avenue
Austin, TX 78701-1494
512-475-3667
8:00 a.m. to 5:00 p.m., Monday through Friday
Services:
• Certifies over 70 training facilities for educators to earn contact hours in environmental education.
• Organizes workshops on various environmental education issues.
• Works with a consortium of state agencies to develop a document listing all environmental education resources in the state.
Materials offered:
• Various resources and information
• List of reviewed materials and curricula available to teachers

State Energy Conservation Office

P.O. Box 13047
Austin, TX 78711
512-475-2553
8:00 a.m. to 5:00 p.m., Monday through Friday
Services:
• Administers U.S. Department of Energy ICP Program (512-463-1931).
• Promotes alternative energy resources and energy conservation programs.
• Oversees U.S. Department of Energy institutional conservation program.
Materials offered:
• Brochures

Texas Association for Environmental Education

RR 2 Box 25-H
Trinity, TX 75862-9470
Unlisted
Services:
• Facilitates networking between agencies and educators for environmental education.
Materials offered:
• Newsletter

UTAH

State Department of Agriculture

Information Office
350 North Redwood Road
Salt Lake, UT 84116
801-538-7100
8:00 a.m. to 5:00 p.m., Monday through Friday
Services:
• Enforces state rules and regulations of pesticides.
Materials offered:
• Copies of pesticides rules and regulations

State Department of Natural Resources

Division of Parks and Recreation
1636 West North Temple
Salt Lake City, UT 84116-3156
801-538-7220
8:00 a.m. to 5:00 p.m., Monday through Friday
Services:
• Manages state parks.
Materials offered:
• Brochures on parks and activities

State Department of Natural Resources

Division of Wildlife Resources
1596 West North Temple
Salt Lake City, UT 84116-3156
801-538-4700
8:00 a.m. to 5:00 p.m., Monday through Friday
Services:
• Protects and develops state wildlife and natural resources.
Materials offered:
• *Project Wild*, kindergarten through 12th-grade curriculum

State Department of Natural Resources

Office of Energy Services
324 South State, Suite 230
Salt Lake City, UT 84111
801-538-8690
8:00 a.m. to 5:00 p.m., Monday through Friday
Services:
• Promotes energy conservation and alternative energy sources.
• Sponsors Annual Energy Debate to discuss state energy policy for 4th to 8th grade.
• Promotes Energy Patrol program for elementary students to monitor efficiency and conservation efforts in their own schools.
• Offers "In Concert with the Environment," a program about natural gas.

- Provides speakers to schools.
- Administers U.S. Department of Energy ICP Program.
Materials offered:
- Information about energy and the programs offered

State Department of Natural Resources
Public Affairs Office
1636 West North Temple, Suite 316
Salt Lake City, UT 84116
801-538-7306
8:00 a.m. to 5:00 p.m., Monday through Friday
Services:
- Oversees Take Pride in Utah program.
Materials offered:
- *Project Wet*, kindergarten through 12th-grade curriculum
- List of publications on a variety of topics

Utah Society for Environmental Education
500 East 230 South, Suite 280
Salt Lake City, UT 84102
801-328-1549
8:00 a.m. to 5:00 p.m., Monday through Friday
Services:
- Serves as a link between state environmental agencies and educational institutes.
- Sponsors summer workshops to bring state agencies and educators together.
Materials offered:
- *Project Learning Tree*, kindergarten through 12th-grade curriculum
- 1,500-piece library includes videos, curricula, books and pamphlets

VERMONT

Agency of Natural Resources
Department of Environmental Conservation
103 South Main Street
Waterbury, VT 05671-0407
802-244-7831
7:45 a.m. to 4:30 p.m., Monday through Friday
Services:
- Implements state programs on recy-

cling, waste, composting, air and water quality and natural resource conservation issues.
Materials offered:
- Educator's guide
- Pamphlets and brochures
- Curriculum information
- *Be an Environmental Shopper,* pamphlet

Agency of Natural Resources
Department of Forests, Parks and Recreation
103 South Main Street
Waterbury, VT 05671-0407
802-244-7831
8:00 a.m. to 5:00 p.m., Monday through Friday
Services:
- Manages state parks and forests.
Materials offered:
- *Project Wild*, kindergarten through 12th-grade curriculum
- *Project Learning Tree*, kindergarten through 12th-grade curriculum
- Brochures on parks and forests

Department of Education
120 State Street
Montpellier, VT 05620
802-828-3111
7:45 a.m. to 4:30 p.m., Monday through Friday
Services:
- Assists school districts in generating their own materials based on simple guidelines set at state level.
- Refers schools and teachers to programs, organizations and other state agencies.

Department of Health
Agency of Human Services
Division of Environmental Health
108 Cherry Street, P.O. Box 70
Burlington, VT 05402
802-863-7223
7:45 a.m. to 4:30 p.m., Monday through Friday
Services:
- Conducts asbestos control and certifies contractors.
- Handles toxic risk assessment of earth, water and air.
- Operates lead detection programs.
Materials offered:
- Fact sheets and pamphlets
- Free lead detection kits

State Department of Agriculture
116 State Street, Drawer 20
Montpellier, VT 05620-2901
802-828-2500
8:00 a.m. to 5:00 p.m., Monday through Friday
Services:
- Enforces pesticide laws and regulations.
- Issues applicator licenses.
Materials offered:
- Copies of laws and regulations on pesticides

State Department of Public Service
120 State Street
Montpellier, VT 05620-2601
800-642-3281 (within state)
802-828-2393
8:00 a.m. to 5:00 p.m., Monday through Friday
Services:
- Administers U.S. Department of Energy ICP Program (802-828-2811).
- Acts as resource center and information clearinghouse for state agencies.
- Operates a lending library.
Materials offered:
- Information on energy conservation and alternative fuel sources

VIRGINIA

Department of Education
Science, Early Childhood Division
P.O. Box 2120
Richmond, VA 23216
804-225-2651
9:00 a.m. to 5:00 p.m., Monday through Friday
Services:
- Oversees environmental education for the state as outlined in the Environmental Stewardship Dimension in the Virginia Common Core of Learning.
- Provides recommendations for recycling and energy conservation.
Materials offered:
- Lists of resources, including waste management, wildlife, the Chesapeake Bay, forest resources and safe art products

State Department of Conservation and Recreation
State Parks and Preservation Center
203 Governor Street, Suite 302
Richmond, VA 23219
804-786-2132
8:30 a.m. to 4:00 p.m., Monday through Friday
Services:
• Supervises 25 state parks.
• Is responsible for educational programs and centers within each park.
Materials offered:
• Brochures on parks and activities

State Department of Environmental Quality
Environmental Education Coordinator
629 East Main Street, P.O. Box 10009
Richmond, VA 23240-0009
804-786-4500
8:30 a.m. to 5:00 p.m., Monday through Friday
Services:
• Oversees state air, water, land and waste programs.
• Oversees state Chesapeake Bay program.
• Co-hosts annual Environmental Literacy Conference.
Materials offered:
• List of local curbside collection and drop-off centers
• *Environmental Education Resource Directory*
• General information on environmental subjects

State Department of Health
Main Street Station
1500 East Main Street
Richmond, VA 23219
804-7863561
8:00 a.m. to 5:00 p.m., Monday through Friday
Services:
• Protects the public from environmental health risks, such as radon, lead and asbestos.
Materials offered:
• General information brochures

State Department of Mines, Minerals and Energy
Division of Energy
202 North Ninth Street, 8th Floor
Richmond, VA 23219
804-692-3200

8:30 a.m. to 4:00 p.m., Monday through Friday
Services:
• Oversees state energy programs.
• Admnisters U.S. Department of Energy ICP Program.
Materials offered:
• Brochures on alternative energy sources and conservation

State Department of Agriculture
Pesticide Management Division
1111 Washington Street SE
NRB Building, 2nd Floor
Olympia, WA 98504
206-902-2010
8:00 a.m. to 5:0 p.m., Monday through Friday
Services:
• Regulates pesticides.
Materials offered:
• Copies of regulation and laws

State Department of Ecology
P.O. Box 47600
Olympia, WA 98504-7600
206-407-7472
8:00 a.m. to 5:00 p.m., Monday through Friday
Services:
• Implements state programs and regulations for air, water, land and waste.
• Oversees radon, lead and asbestos protection programs.
• Promotes and develops local recycling programs.
Materials offered:
• *Discover the Wetlands,* curriculum and video
• *How to Start Recycling Programs,* guidelines
• Brochures on issues

State Department of Energy
925 Plum Street, Building 4
Olympia, WA 98504
206-956-2076 (library)
9:00 a.m. to 5:00 p.m., Monday through Friday
Services:
• Oversees Education and Training Unit (800-962-9731).
• Offers library of energy information.
• Provides referral service to agencies

with programs or information.
• Is responsible for U.S. Department of Energy institutional conservation program.
• Conducts teacher workshops and school presentations through Education and Training Unit.
Materials offered:
• *Energy Matters,* sourcebook for in-state teachers

State Department of Natural Resources
Office of Public Affairs
P.O. Box 47001
Olympia, WA 98504-7001
206-902-1023
8:00 a.m. to 5:00 p.m., Monday through Friday
Services:
• Manages state lands, forests, minerals and aquatic areas.
Materials offered:
• Information on all state natural resources

State Office of Environmental Education
Superintendent of Public Instruction
2800 NE 200th Street
Seattle, WA 98155
206-365-3893
8:00 a.m. to 5:00 p.m., Monday through Friday
Services:
• Is responsible for environmental education in public schools for grades K–12.
• Provides curriculum resources and training to teachers in environmental education.
• Evaluates curriculum and programs for effectiveness.
Materials offered:
• *Clean Waters,* curriculum
• *Streams and Fish: A Holistic View of Watersheds,* curriculum
• *Energy Food and You,* curriculum
• *Coastal Zone Studies,* curriculum
• Population Task Cards

State Parks and Recreation Commission
7150 Cleanwater Lane, KY-11
Olympia, WA 98504-5711
206-902-8563
Services:
• Acquires, develops and maintains

state parks.
Materials offered:
• Brochures on parks and recreation areas

WEST VIRGINIA

Environmental Health Services
Asbestos, Lead and Radon
815 Quarrier Street, Suite 418
Charleston, WV 25301
304-558-2981
8:00 a.m. to 4:30 p.m., Monday through Friday
Services:
• Conducts asbestos inspections in schools.
• Conducts lead testing in school drinking water.
• Answers questions about radon.
Materials offered:
• Provides list of companies that do radon testing
• Information about asbestos, lead and radon contamination

State Department of Education
State Science Coordinator
1900 Kanawha Boulevard East
Capitol Complex, Building 6, Room 330
Charleston, WV 25305-0330
304-558-7805
9:00 a.m. to 5:00 p.m., Monday through Friday
Services:
• Oversees environmental education programs for the state as incorporated into the kindergarten through 10th-grade science curriculum.
• Provides referral service for resources, programs or materials.
Materials offered:
• *Mountaineer Pride*, solid waste and litter control curriculum

State Department of Natural Resources
Division of Environmental Protection
Public Information Office
10 McJunkin Road
Nitro, WV 25143
304-759-0515
8:00 a.m. to 4:30 p.m., Monday through Friday
Services:

• Oversees all environmental issues concerning air, water, land, waste, mining, oil and gas.
Materials offered:
• Provides information on all subjects

State Department of Natural Resources
Education/Litter Control
1900 Kanawan Boulevard, Building 3, Room 732
Charleston, WV, 25305
304-558-3370
9:00 to 5:00 p.m., Monday through Friday
Services:
• Conducts litter control education programs.
• Promotes environmental awareness and education.
Materials offered:
• Brochures promoting environmental education
• *Mountaineer Pride*, kindergarten through 12th-grade curriculum

State Parks and Recreation
Division of State Parks
Building 6, Room B-451, Capitol Complex
Charleston, WV 25305
304-558-2764
8:30 a.m. to 4:00 p.m., Monday through Friday
Services:
• Supervises 36 state parks, 8 forests and 7 wildlife areas.
• Conducts naturalist programs and other activities.
• Provides field interpreters at some parks to give guided tours.
• Sends park interpreters and superintendents to schools to give presentations upon request.
Materials offered:
• Brochures on parks, forests and preserves
• Information on activities and naturalist programs

WISCONSIN

Department of Natural Resources
Bureau of Information and Education
101 South Webster
Madison, WI 53707

608-266-2747
7:30 a.m. to 4:30 p.m., Monday through Friday
Services:
• Operates publications-order line (800-243-8782).
• Is responsible for state natural resources, including fisheries, wildlife, forests, parks and protection of endangered resources.
• Is responsible for state environmental quality, including air, water, land and waste.
• Operates nature centers and environmental centers that are open to the public.
• Provides speakers upon request.
• Conducts workshops for educators.
Materials offered:
• List of publications, curricula and programs
• *EE News,* quarterly newsletter

Department of Natural Resources
Bureau of Parks and Recreation
101 South Webster
Madison, WI 53707
608-266-2185
7:30 p.m. to 4:30 a.m., Monday through Friday
Services:
• Manages state parks.
• Provides park interpreters to give tours of parks.
• Oversees Junior Ranger Program that teaches basic environmental appreciation.
Materials offered:
• Brochures on parks and activities

Department of Public Instruction
Environmental Education Consultant
P.O. Box 7841, 3rd Floor
Madison, WI 53707-7841
608-267-9279
8:00 a.m. to 5:00 p.m., Monday through Friday
Services:
• Promotes environmental education throughout the state schools.
• Conducts workshops for teachers.
Materials offered:
• *A Guide to Curriculum Planning in Environmental Education*
• *Groundwater Study Guide*
• *Recycling Study Guide*

- *Recycling Study Guide and K-3 Supplement*
  - List of other publications

State Bureau of Health
Radiation Control
1414 East Washington Avenue
Madison, WI 53703-3044
608-267-4796
8:00 a.m. to 5:00 p.m., Monday through Friday
Services:
- Keeps records of radon contaminated sites in the state and companies that conduct radon tests.
- Provides speakers upon request.
Materials offered:
- Brochures about radon measurement

State Center for Environmental Education
4th Floor, Learning Resource Center, UW-SP
Stevens Point, WI 54481
715-346-4943
9:00 a.m. to 5:00 p.m., Monday through Friday
Services:
- Offers library of environmental education materials.
- Coordinates EE Network.
- Provides outreach courses and workshops for in-service teachers.
- Supervises a Masters Degree Program through the University of Wisconsin—-Stevens Point.
- Facilitates development, dissemination, implementation and evaluation of environmental education programs.
Materials offered:
- *Guide to Curriculum Planning*

State Department of Agriculture
Wisconsin Trade and Consumer Protection
P.O. Box 8911
Madison, WI 53708
608-266-7129
7:45 a.m. to 4:30 p.m., Monday through Friday
Services:
- Regulates pesticides.
Materials offered:
- Brochures on various pesticides
- Regulation and laws on pesticides

State Department of Energy
P.O. Box 7868
Madison, WI 53703
608-266-8234
7:00 a.m. to 5:00 p.m., Monday through Friday
Services:
- Administers U.S. Department of Energy ICP Program (608-266-8234).
- Implements state programs on energy conservation and alternative energy resources.
Materials offered:
- *Wisconsin Energy,* bimonthly newsletter
- Videos and publications list

Wisconsin Association for Environmental Education
7290 County MM
Amherst Junction, WI 54407
715-824-2428
7:30 a.m. to 4:00 p.m., Monday through Friday
Services:
- Is the professional organization for environmental education in the state.
- Sponsors annual event.
- Holds workshops.
- Sponsors Spring Adventure in Outdoor Education.
- Gives awards to schools and youth groups for outstanding environmental projects.
Materials offered:
- *WAEE Bulletin,* quarterly newsletter
- Earth Day information

WYOMING

State Department of Agriculture
2219 Carey Avenue
Cheyenne, WY 82002-0100
307-777-7321
8:00 a.m. to 5:00 p.m., Monday through Friday
Services:
- Handles various aspects of agriculture and the environment through six departments.
- Enforces laws for agricultural pesticides pertaining to wetlands and water and air quality.
- Provides speakers upon request.
Materials offered:

- Pamphlets and brochures on agriculture and pesticides

State Department of Education
Science, Mathematics and Environmental Education Coordinator
Hathaway Building, 2nd Floor
2300 Capitol Avenue
Cheyenne, WY 82002-0050
307-777-6247
8:00 a.m. to 5:00 p.m., Monday through Friday
Services:
- Oversees environmental education programs for the state.
Materials offered:
- *Project Wild*, kindergarten through 12th-grade curriculum
- *Project Learning Tree,* kindergarten through 12th-grade curriculum

State Department of Environmental Quality
Solid Waste Program
Herschler Building, 4W
122 West 25th Street
Cheyenne, WY 82002
307-777-7752
8:00 a.m. to 5:00 p.m., Monday through Friday
Services:
- Provides tours of recycling centers to junior high and high school students.
Materials offered:
- Recycling directories
- Rule and regulations for solid and hazardous waste handling
- Videos and teacher's aids on recycling

State Department of Game and Fish
Education Section
5400 Bishop Boulevard
Cheyenne, WY 82006
307-777-4538
8:00 a.m. to 5:00 p.m., Monday through Friday
Services:
- Protects, conserves and develops state natural wildlife resources.
- Provides services at several visitor centers.
- Enforces state hunting and fishing laws.

Materials offered:
  • Brochures on state fish and game laws
  • Brochures on state wildlife.

State Department of Health and Social Services

Environmental Health
Hathawa Building, Suite 487
Cheyenne, WY 82002
307-777-7957
8:00 a.m. to 5:00 p.m., Monday through Friday
Services:
  • Tests all schools for radon.
  • Speaks to schools about food, health and radon.
Materials offered:
  • Pamphlets on radon and food sanitation

State Department of Natural Resources

2219 Carey Avenue
Cheyenne, WY 82002-0100
307-777-7321
8:00 a.m. to 5:00 p.m., Monday through Friday
Services:
  • Administers U.S. Department of Energy ICP Program (307-777-7131).
  • Oversees state air, water, land and waste programs.
Materials offered:
  • Videos on managing range land

SCHOOL WALK ABOUT

The following is a list of questions to determine what your school may want to address concerning environmental health, environmental lessons and environmental modeling. Each of the areas noted below lists possible environmental problems as well as the chapters you can turn to for explanations and useful resources.

THE CLASSROOM

• Are environmental issues integrated into activities?
Chapter 19

• Are there plants in classrooms to reduce indoor air pollution?
Chapter 1

• Are nontoxic cleaning products used?
Chapter 14

• Are cleaners stored correctly?
Chapters 1 and 14

• Has your school been tested for radon?
Chapter 1

• Has an accredited inspector identified location(s) and the condition of asbestos at your school?
Chapter 1

• How are pest infestations handled?
Chapter 3

• Do you know why you have pest problems?
Chapter 3

• What kind of construction materials have been used in the past and/or will be used in the future? (For instance, have wood products been treated with chemicals?)
Chapter 1

• Are the filters for heating and air conditioning units on a regular maintenance schedule?
Chapters 1 and 7

• When was the ventilation system last serviced?
Chapters 1 and 7

• Is cigarette smoking permitted anywhere on campus?
Chapter 1

• Do buses and cars park by classroom windows and doors?
Chapter 1

• Do you know how exposure to lead affects children?
Chapters 1 and 6

• Have you wondered about the dangers of personal care products?
Chapter 15

• Looking for ideas for preschool age children?
Chapter 16

THE SCIENCE ROOM

• Want to audit the level of safety in your science room?
Chapter 9

• Are lab chemicals labeled and stored safely?
Chapter 9

• Do you question the necessity of removing frogs (or other animals for dissection purposes) from their habitat in order to learn about their internal structures?
Chapter 9

THE ART ROOM

• Are the art supplies used on campus safe for children?
Chapters 10 and 16

• Are the art supplies nontoxic and chemical free?
Chapter 10

- Looking for safe ways to explore art?
Chapter 10

- Confused by all those words on art supply packages?
Chapter 10

THE SCHOOL LIBRARY

- What sort of environmental books does the school library have? Consider resource books as well as appreciation and empowerment books.
Chapter 19

THE CAFETERIA

- Do students bring their lunches to school?
Chapter 11

- Do school-prepared lunches consider student health?
Chapter 4

- Do the food choices offered take environmental impact into consideration?
Chapter 4

- Are reusable trays, plates and utensils used or one-time disposable items?
Chapter 11

- Does the school promote recycling in the cafeteria?
Chapter 11

SOLID WASTE AND RECYCLING

- Are vegetable wastes being composted for school ground fertilizer?
Chapter 5

- Next to every waste bin on campus (inside and outside) are there bins for recyclable wastes such as aluminum, glass, plastics, white paper, mixed paper and cardboard?
Chapter 12

- Curious about the many routinely wasteful habits we all have?
Chapter 11

- What exactly is recyclable?
Chapter 12

- Do you know how to set up a school recycling program?
Chapter 12

- Have the school administration, faculty and students been educated about the school recycling program?
Chapter 12

THE SCHOOL GROUNDS AND GARDEN

- Are students taking part in tree and plant choices, plantings, garden design and maintenance?
Chapter 5

- Are homes for wildlife (bird feeders, flowers, shrubs, trees) being created?
Chapter 5

- Is your school producing its own compost?
Chapter 5

- Take a look at the vegetation on campus; if it is not adapted to your region, it is not going to be tolerant to pests.
Chapters 3 and 5

- Want some school grown, pesticide free, fruits and veggies?
Chapter 5

- Does your school have a garden for students?
Chapter 5

- Interested in turning school food waste into black gold?
Chapter 5

- Are you interested in preserving biodiversity?
Chapter 5

- Does the school practice Integrated Pest Management?
Chapter 5

- Do you know what bioregion you live in?
Chapter 5

- Are the plants on campus native to your region?
Chapter 5

ENERGY

- Are you taking advantage of natural sunlight (light and warmth), or are the walls and open spaces insulated?
Chapter 7

- Check for leaks around windows, doors, corners of the building, chimneys and where pipes, wires and vents enter the building.
Chapter 7

- Has your administration hired an energy auditor to assess energy consumption on your campus?
Chapter 7

- Are broken windows being repaired?
Chapter 7

- Who is controlling the thermostat? During cold weather, is it kept low and is everyone encouraged to wear sweaters?
Chapter 7

- Is energy-consuming office equipment turned off when not in use?
Chapter 7

- Is there an enforced school policy to turn off energy-consuming appliances during school breaks?
Chapter 7

- What would it take to replace lights with newer, more efficient bulbs and ballasts?
Chapter 7

- Is concrete and asphalt really necessary? Could some native trees be planted to provide shade on hot days and shelter from cold winds?
Chapter 7

- Remodeling? The sun's energy is free. Anyone, anywhere can install solar panels (for hot water and lighting) and photovoltaic cells.
Chapter 7

- Want to update those school buses?
Chapter 7

EMFs AND YOUR SCHOOL

- Concerned about high tension wires crossing the school yard?
Chapter 8

- Do you know what EMF stands for?
Chapter 8

- Are computer stations setup so that they are the proper distance apart?
Chapter 8

- Does your school have an EMF meter?
Chapter 8

WATER

- Are your toilets all ultra-low flush? If not, have water dams been added to reduce water flow?
Chapter 6

- Do water faucets all have aerators to reduce water flow?
Chapter 6

- Do locker-room showers have low flow shower heads?
Chapter 6

- Are the school water fountains leaking?
Chapter 6

- What are your city ordinances regarding gray water systems? Would this diversion system work for your school and provide a bonus source of irrigation?
Chapters 5 and 6

- Is the vegetation on your campus native to the area and therefore compatible with the climate?
Chapters 5 and 6

• Is the lawn being overwatered?
Chapters 6

• Will the school cut down on meat consumption? Livestock production is very water consumptive.
Chapters 4 and 6

SCHOOL CONSCIOUSNESS

• Has your school investigated a project or an issue that helps your local community enviromentally?
Chapter 18

• Is there school encouragement and support for writing campaigns, planting and clean-up events and fundraising to promote an empowered citizenry?
Chapter 13

• Is your school conducting assemblies, bringing in guest speakers, participating in projects that celebrate Earth Day and other environmental celebrations?
Chapters 12 and 18

• Does the school dedicate space for student posters, projects and displays that promote the environment, health issues or responsible citizen behavior?
Chapter 18

• Are used books, clothes or materials exchanged or donated to places in the community in need?
Chapters 12 and 18

TAKING ACTION

• Do you want your ideas and opinions heard by school administrators, government officials and businesses?
Chapter 13

• Tired of getting lots of junk mail?
Chapter 13

• Need some activity ideas for your school environmental group?
Chapter 18

• Are you an educator in search of money for a project?
Chapter 18

• What kind of materials are available for integrating environmental education into the learning environment?
Chapter 19

• Wondering about the books and videos that are available?
Chapter 20

• Need resources for where to get information on what your state is doing to address all the issues mentioned in this book?
Chapter 20

Endnotes

Chapter 1

1. Ethel Romm, "All About Radon: A Compendium of Information," Niton Corporation, Bedford, MA.
2. U.S. Enviornmental Protection Agency, *The ABCs of Asbestos in Schools,* Pesticides and Toxic Substances (TS-799), Washington, DC, June 1989.
3. U.S. Enviornmental Protection Agency, *The ABCs of Asbestos in Schools,* Pesticides and Toxic Substances (TS-799), Washington, DC, June 1989.
4. U.S. Environmental Protection Agency, Air and Radiation, *Sick Building Syndrome* Indoor Air Facts No. 4 (revised), Washington, DC, 1991.
5. Nancy Sokol Green, *Poisoning Our Children* (Chicago, IL: Noble Press, 1991), p. 81.
6. Linda Mason Hunter, *The Healthy Home: An Attic-to-Basement Guide to Toxin Free Living* (Emmaus, PA: Rodale Press. 1989).

Chapter 3

1. U.S. EPA, Office of Prevention, Pesticides and Toxic Substances, *Pesticides Industry Sales and Usage: 1992 and 1993 Market Estimates*, Washington, DC, 1994.
2. Phillip Howard, *Handbook of Environmental Fate and Exposure Data for Organic Chemicals*, Vol. III Pesticides (Chelsea MI, Lewis Publishers). U.S. Department of Health and Human Services, Public Health Searvice, Agency for Toxic Substances and Disease Registry, *Toxicological Profile for Toxaphene* (Washington, DC: 1990). M. Brown, "Toxic Wind," *Discover* (November 1987), pp. 42-49.
3. U.S. Department of the Interiors, U.S. Geological Survey, *Herbicides in Atmospheric Wet Deposition in the Upper Midwest and Northeast United States* (Reston, VA: April 19, 1991).
4. D.A. Glotfelty, "Pesticides in Fog" (letter), *Nature* (February 1987).
5. U.S. EPA, Office of Water, Office of Pesticide and Toxic Substances, *Another Look: National Survey of Pesticides in Drinking Water Wells: Phase II Report* (Washington, DC: January 1992).
6. J. Blondell, "Human Exposures Reported to Poison Control Centers in 1992," U.S. EPA Office of Pesticide Programs, Washington, DC, September 1993.
7. U.S. EPA Office of Prevention, Pesticides and Toxic Substances, Health Effects Division, "List of Chemicals Evaluated for Carcinogenic Potential," memo from Reto Engler, August 31, 1993.
8. U.S. EPA, Office of Prevention, Pesticides and Toxic Substances, *Pesticide Reregistration Progress Report*, Washington, DC, April 1994.
9. Concern, Inc., *Pesticides in Our Communities: Choices for Change*, Washington, DC, 1992, pp. 3-4.
10. James R. Davis, et al., "Family Pesticide Use and Childhood Brain Cancer," *Arch. of Environmental Contaminants Toxicol.* (1993), pp. 87-92.
11. U.S. EPA Office of Pesticides and Toxic Substances, *Guidance for the Reregistration of Pesticide Products Containing Diazinon as the Active Ingredient*, Washington, DC, 1988.
12. U.S. EPA, Office of Pesticide Programs, *Tolerance Assessment System Routine Chronic Analysis for Chlorpyrifos,* Washington, DC, 1994.
13. R.A. Fenske et al., "Potential Exposure and Health Risks of Infants Following Indoor Residential Pesticide Applications," *American Journal of Public Health,* vol. 80, no. 6 (1990), pp. 689-693.
14. California Department of Food and Agriculture, Division of Pest Management, Environmental Protection and Worker Safety, Health and Safety Unit, *Summary of Illnesses and Injuries Reported by California Physicians as Potentially Related to Pesticides*, Sacramento, CA, 1982-1988.
15. Letter from Jon H. Arvik, Environmental Affairs Manager, Monsanto Agricultural Company, to Kay Rumsey, Landscape Management Advisory Committee, School District 4J, Eugene, OR, February 26, 1991 (Roundup contains POEA). Y. Sawada et al., "Probable Toxicity of Surface-active Agent in Commerical Herbicide Containing Glyphosate," *Lancet* (1988), p. 299 (POEA is 3 times more toxic than glyphosate). U.S. EPA Office of Pesticide Programs, *Guidance for the Reregistration of Pesticide Products Containing Glyphosate*, Washington, DC, 1986 (Chronic toxicity studies are done on glyphosate alone).
16. Concern, Inc., *Pesticides in Our Communities, Choices for Change*, Washington, DC, 1992.
17. Northwest Coalition for Alternatives to Pesticides, *Steps Parents and Teachers Can Take to Reduce School Pesticide Use*, Eugene, OR, 1994.
18. U.S. EPA, Office of Prevention, Pesticides and Toxic Substances, *Pesticide Fact Sheet*, Washington, DC, 1994.

Chapter 4

1. Alan B. Durning and Holly B. Brough, "Taking Stock: Animal Farming and the Environment," Worldwatch Paper 103, Worldwatch Institute, Washington, DC, 1991.
2. Frances Moore Lappe, *Diet for a Small Planet* (New York: Ballantine Books, 1991), pp. 67-70.
3. Sonja Williams, *Exploding the Hunger Myths* Institute for Food and Development Policy (San Francisco: 1978).
4. *What's the Beef and Who Pays?* EarthSave Foundation (San Francisco: 1993).
5. John Robbins, "Can Earth Survive the Big Mac Attack?" *Garbage* (January/February 1992), p. 42.
6. John Robbins, "Can Earth Survive the Big Mac Attack?" *Garbage* (January/February 1992), p. 42.
7. John Robbins, "Can Earth Survive the Big Mac Attack?" *Garbage* (January/February 1992), p. 42.
8. Alan Durning, "Poverty and the Environment: Reversing the Downward Spiral," Worldwatch

Paper 92, Worldwatch, Washington, DC, 1989.

9. Anne Witte Garland, "For Our Kids' Sake," Natural Resources Defense Council, New York, 1989.

10. *Rodale's All-New Encyclopedia of Organic Gardening* (Emmaus, PA: Rodale Press, 1992).

11. "A Vicious 'Circle of Poison,'" *U.S. News & World Report*, June 10, 1991. Catherine Broihier, M.A., R.D., "How Safe Are Imported Foods? 'Circle of Poison' Sounds a Warning," *Environmental Nutrition* (February 1991), p.7.

12. Jodi Godfrey, "The Hidden Cost of Convienience," *Environmental Nutrition* (April 1993).

13. *Diet and Nutrition Letter*, Tufts University, Boston, MA, September 1992, vol 10, no. 7.

14. David Steinmen, *Diet for a Poisoned Planet* (New York: Ballantine Books, 1990), p. 84.

15. David Steinmen, *Diet for a Poisoned Planet* (New York: Ballantine Books, 1990), p.79.

16. David Steinmen, *Diet for a Poisoned Planet* (New York: Ballantine Books, 1990), pp. 43-44.

17. Geofrey S. Becker, Congressional Research Service, The Library of Congress, *CRS Report for Congress: Provisions of the 1990 Farm Bill*, Washington, DC, November 16, 1990.

18. *The New Four Food Groups: The First Major Change in Nutrition Policy Since 1956*, PCRM Update, Washington, DC, May/June 1991.

Chapter 6

1. William P. Cunningham, Terence Ball et al., *Environmental Encyclopedia* (Detroit, MI: Gale Research Inc., 1994), p. 883.

2. Environmental Defense Fund, *Facts at Your Fingertips on the World's Water,* Oakland, CA, 1994.

3. Geoffrey Lean, Don Hinrichsen, and Adam Markham, *WWf Atlas of the Environment* (Engelwood Cliffs, NJ: Prentice Hall, 1990), p. 59.

4. The World Resources Institute, World Resources 1994-95 (New York, Oxford University Press, 1994), p. 346.

5. *Water Conservation at Home,*

American Water Works Association, Denver, CO, 1989.

6. *The ABC's of Water Conservation,* Channing L. Bete, South Deerfield, MA, 1991.

7. John Cary Stewart, *Drinking Water Hazards* (Hiram, OH: Envirographics, 1990), p. 1.

8. City of Los Angeles, Department of Public Works Clean Water Program, *Facts: Water Reuse*, Los Angeles, CA, 1990.

9. Lester R. Brown et al., *State of the World 1993* (New York: W. W. Norton & Company, 1993), p. 31.

10. Environmental Defense Fund, *Facts at Your Fingertips on the World's Water,* Oakland, CA, 1994.

11. *Water: The Source of Life*, America's Clean Water Foundation, Washington, DC, 1992.

12. *Water: The Source of Life*, America's Clean Water Foundation, Washington, DC, 1992.

13. Joel Haveman, *Why Oil Spills are Increasing, Los Angeles Times*, March 26, 1993, p. 1.

14. Travis Wagner, *In Our Backyard* (New York: Van Nostrand Reinhold, 1994), p. 63.

15. Travis Wagner, *In Our Backyard* (New York: Van Nostrand Reinhold, 1994), p. 283.

16. William P. Cunningham et al, *Environmental Encyclopedia* (Detroit, MI: Gale Research, Inc., 1994), p. 876.

17. Buzz Buzzelli et al., *How to Get Water Smart* (Santa Barbara, CA: Terra Firma Publishing, 1991), p. 13.

18. Sandra Postel, *Last Oasis: Facing Water Scarcity* (New York: W. W. Norton & Company, 1992), p. 61.

19. William P. Cunningham et al., *Environmental Encyclopedia* (Detroit, MI: Gale Research, Inc., 1994), p. 586.

20. Gordon Meeks, Jr. and L. Cheryl Runyon, "Wetlands Protection and the States," National Conference of State Legislatures, April 1990.

21. John Cary Stewart, *Drinking Water Hazards* (Hiram, OH: Envirographics, 1990), p. 63.

22. *Water: The Source of Life,* America's Clean Water Foundation, Washington, DC, 1992.

23. *Water: The Source of Life,* America's Clean Water Foundation, Washington, DC, 1992.

24. John Javna, Seth Zuckerman and Chris Calwell, 30 *Simple Energy Things You Can Do to Save the Earth* (Berkeley, CA: EarthWorks, 1990), p. 24.

25. Sandra Postel, *Last Oasi* (New York: W.W. Norton & Company, 1992), p. 104.

26. Jonathan Erickson, *Saving Water in the Home and Garden* (Blue Ridge Summit, PA: TAB Books, 1993), p.132.

27. Jeremy Rifkin, *Beyond Beef* (New York: Dutton, 1992), p. 219.

28. *Water: The Source of Life,* Clean Water Foundation, Washington, DC, 1992.

29. John Robbins, *Diet for a New America* (Walpole, NH: Stillpoint Publishing, 1987), p. 367.

Chapter 7

1. Environment Canada, *Fact Sheet: Atmospheric Environment Service,* Downsview, Ontario, 1991.

2. Raw data from *Annual Energy Review, 1992*, Energy Information Administration, Office of Energy Markets and End Use, Department of Energy, Washington, DC, June 1993.

3. Raw data from *Annual Energy Review, 1992*, Energy Information Administration, Office of Energy Markets and End Use, Department of Energy, Washington, DC, June 1993.

4. Stacy Davis and Sonja Strang, *Transportation Energy Data Book: Edition 13,* Oak Ridge National Laboratory, Department of Energy, Washington, DC, 1993.

5. Bonnie J. Cornwall, Senior Manager, California Energy Extension Service (CEES), personal correspondence, August 1994.

6. Bonnie J. Cornwall et al., "Maintaining in the Nineties: Energy Management for Maintenance and Custodial Staff", California Energy Extension Service, 1991.

7. Michael Brower, "Cool Energy: The Renewable Solution to Global Warming," Union of Concerned Scientists, 1990.

Chapter 8

1. "Electromagnetic Fields (EMFs) in the Modern Office: A Training Workbook for Working People," The Labor Institute, New York, April, 1993. (See the box How EMFs May Cause Cancer.)
2. Robert Becker, M.D., *Cross Currents* (Los Angeles, Jeremy P. Tarcher, 1990), pp. 206-207.
3. Robert O. Becker, M.D. and Gary Selden, *The Body Electric* (New York: Quill, 1985), pp. 247-249.
4. Robert O. Becker, M.D. and Gary Selden, *The Body Electric* (New York: Quill, 1985), pp. 249-250.
5. Matthew Connelly and Louis Slesin, "EMFs: The Darker Side of Electricity," *Mothering* (Fall 1991), pp. 48-52.
6. Paul Brodeur, *The Great Power-Line Cover-Up* (New York: Little Brown and Company, 1993), p. 11.
7. Paul Brodeur, *The Great Power-Line Cover-Up* (New York: Little Brown and Company, 1993), p. 151.
8. Cynthia Hacinli, "Unplugging Electromagnetic Pollution," *Garbage* (January/February 1992), pp. 38-43.
9. Suzanne Stefanac, "At Arm's Length," *MacWorld* (July 1990), p. 145.
10. "Electromagnetic Fields (EMFs) in the Modern Office: A Training Workbook for Working People," The Labor Institute, New York, April, 1993. The following drawing illustrates this.
11. Cynthia Hacinli, "Unplugging Electromagnetic Pollution," *Garbage* (January/February 1992), pp. 38-43.
12. Cynthia Hacinli, "Unplugging Electromagnetic Pollution," *Garbage* (January/February 1992), pp. 38-43.
13. Cynthia Hacinli, "Unplugging Electromagnetic Pollution," *Garbage* (January/February 1992), pp. 38-43.
14. Cynthia Hacinli, "Unplugging Electromagnetic Pollution," *Garbage* (January/February 1992), pp. 38-43.
15. Cynthia Hacinli, "Unplugging Electromagnetic Pollution," *Garbage* (January/February 1992), pp. 38-43.

Chapter 9

1. California Department of Education, *Science Framework for California Public Schools: Kindergarten Through Grade Twelve,* Sacramento, CA, 1990.

Chapter 10

1. U.S. Department of Health and Human Services, Public Health Service, Centers for Disease Control, *Preventing Lead Poisoning in Young Children,* Atlanta, GA, 1991.
2. U.S. Department of Health and Human Services, Public Health Service, Centers for Disease Control, *Preventing Lead Poisoning in Young Children,* Atlanta, GA, 1991.
3. Lucinda Sikes, "Art and the Craft of Avoidance," U.S. PIRG, Washington, DC, 1991.
4. Lucinda Sikes, "Art and the Craft of Avoidance," U.S. PIRG, Washington, DC, 1991.
5. Annie Berthold-Bond, "Back to Basics," *Greenkeeping* (September/October 1991), p. 16.
6. Angela Babin, Perri A. Pelts, and Monona Rossol, "Children's Art Supplies Can Be Toxic," Center for Safety in the Arts, New York, 1989.

Chapter 11

1. The Buy Recycled Campaign, "An Ounce of Prevention: Strategies for Cutting Packaging Waste," Californians Against Waste Foundation, 1994.
2. Debi Kimball, *Recycling in America,* Santa Barbara, ABC-CLIO, 1992, pp. 35-42.
3. Richard A. Denison and John Ruston, *Recycling and Incineration: Evaluating the Choices,* Washington, DC, Island Press, 1990, p. 44.
4. Rennie Harris, "Environmental Costs and Benefits of Switching from Polystyrene Disposable Ware to Polycarbonate Permanent Ware," prepared for Portland, Oregon, Board of Education, Portland, OR, April 1991.
5. Nutrition Services Department, "Economic Impacts on Specific Options for Cafeteria Service Ware," a report prepared for the Portland, Oregon, Board of Education, Portland, OR, April 1991.
6. Polystyrene Packaging Council, "Polystyrene: Recycle It," Washington, DC, 1990.
7. Californians Against Waste Foundation, *Polystyrene Overview,* Sacramento, CA, 1989.
8. *Californians Against Waste Foundation Issue Paper on Packaging: Why Pick on Plastics?* Sacramento, CA, Californians Against Waste Foundation, 1989.
9. *The Problem with Polystyrene,* National Institute of Government Purchasing, Falls Church, VA, 1992.
10. *The Problem with Polystyrene,* National Institute of Government Purchasing, Falls Church, VA, 1992.
11. George Baggett, "Styrene Migration into Human Adipose Tissue," Kansas City, KS, August 14, 1990.
12. Martin B. Hocking, "Paper Versus Polystyrene: A Complex Choice," *Science* (February 1991), pp. 504-505.
13. Martin B. Hocking, "Paper Versus Polystyrene: A Complex Choice," *Science* (February 1991), pp. 504-505.
14. Martin B. Hocking, "Paper Versus Polystyrene: A Complex Choice," *Science* (February 1991), pp. 504-505.
15. Martin B. Hocking, "Paper Versus Polystyrene: A Complex Choice," *Science* (February 1991), pp. 504-505.

Chapter 12

1. Debi Kimball, *Recycling in America,* Santa Barbara, ABC-CLIO, Inc., 1992, p. 49.
2. "Garbage at the Grocery: Life Cycle of an Aseptic Juice Box," *Garbage,* The Practical Journal for the Environment, 1990.
3. Debi Kimball, *Recycling in America,* Santa Barbara, CA, ABC-CLIO, Inc., 1992, p. 36.
4. Jennifer Carless, *Taking Out the Trash,* Washington, DC, Island Press, 1992, p. 64.

5. Jennifer Carless, *Taking Out the Trash* (Washington, DC: Island Press, 1992), p. 61-64.
6. Debi Kimball, *Recycling in America,* Santa Barbara, CA, ABC-CLIO, Inc., 1992, p. 38.
7. *If You're Not Recycling You're Throwing It All Away,* Environmental Defense Fund, New York, 1988.
8. EarthWorks Group, *50 Simple Things You Can Do to Save the Earth* (Berkeley, CA: Earthworks Press, 1989), p. 64.
9. Jennifer Carless, *Taking Out the Trash* (Washington, DC: Island Press, 1992), pp. 58-59.
10. Jennifer Carless, *Taking Out the Trash* (Washington, DC: Island Press, 1992), p. 58.
11. Earth Works Group, *The Recycler's Handbook* (Berkeley, CA: EarthWorks Press, 1990), p.66.
12. Earth Works Group, *The Recycler's Handbook* (Berkeley, CA: EarthWorks Press, 1990), p.68.

Chapter 14

1. Phillip Dickey, "A Database for Safer Substitutes for Hazardous Household Products (Phase II), Washington Toxics Coalition, 1991.

Chapter 15

1. Steve Coffel, "The Great Fluoride Fight," *Garbage* (May/June 1992), p. 34.
2. Steve Coffel, "The Great Fluoride Fight," *Garbage* (May/June 1992), p. 34.
3. Steve Coffel, "The Great Fluoride Fight," *Garbage* (May/June 1992), p. 34.
4. Steve Coffel, "The Great Fluoride Fight," *Garbage* (May/June 1992), p. 34.
5. Steve Coffel, "The Great Fluoride Fight," *Garbage* (May/June 1992), p. 34.
6. Steve Coffel, "The Great Fluoride Fight," *Garbage* (May/June 1992), p. 37.
7. "A Guide to Avoiding Cosmetics," *Greenkeeping* (March/April 1992), p.13.
8. Irene Wilkenfeld, "Perfume or Pollutant?" *Green Alternatives* (November/December 1992), p. 32.
9. Irene Wilkenfeld, "Perfume or Pollutant?" *Green Alternatives* (November/December 1992), pp. 32-34.
10. Irene Wilkenfeld, "Perfume or Pollutant?" *Green Alternatives* (November/December 1992), pp. 32-34.
11. David Steinman, " Sunscreen Alone Is Not Enough," *Natural Health* (May/June 1994), p. 56.
12. David Steinman, " Sunscreen Alone Is Not Enough," *Natural Health* (May/June 1994), p. 56.
13. Seventh Generation Catalog, Colchester, VT (Summer 1992), p. 17.
14. Seventh Generation Catalog, Colchester, VT (Summer 1992), p. 20.
15. Population Education Committee, "The Real Fire," Santa Monica, CA, 1992.
16. "How-to-Guides: Cosmetics," *Green Alternatives*, 1993, p. 5.
17. "How-to-Guides: Cosmetics," *Green Alternatives*, 1993, p. 5.
18. "Hair Dyes from Vegetables and Herbs," *Green Alternatives* (December/January 1993-94), p. 39.
19. Hannah Holmes, "The Truth About Tampons," *Garbage* (November/December 1990), pp. 50-55.
20. Hannah Holmes, "The Truth About Tampons," *Garbage* (November/December 1990), pp. 50-55.
21. Hannah Holmes, "The Truth About Tampons," *Garbage* (November/December 1990), pp. 50-55.
22. Hannah Holmes, "The Truth About Tampons," *Garbage* (November/December 1990), pp. 50-55.
23. Hannah Holmes, "The Truth About Tampons," *Garbage* (November/December 1990), p. 53.
24. Hannah Holmes, "The Truth About Tampons," *Garbage* (November/December 1990), pp. 50-55.
25. U.S. Department of State, *U.S. National Report on Population,* Washington, DC, 1994.
26. Zero Population Growth, *Teens: A Generation of Difference,* Washington, DC, 1990.
27. Zero Population Growth, "Demographic Facts of Life in the U.S.A.," Washington, DC, 1990.

Index